MX

Macromedia
Dreamweaver
Comprehensive Concepts and Techniques

Gary B. Shelly
Thomas J. Cashman
Dolores J. Wells

THOMSON™
COURSE TECHNOLOGY

COURSE TECHNOLOGY
25 THOMSON PLACE
BOSTON MA 02210

SHELLY
CASHMAN
SERIES®

Australia • Canada • Denmark • Japan • Mexico • New Zealand • Philippines • Puerto Rico • Singapore
South Africa • Spain • United Kingdom • United States

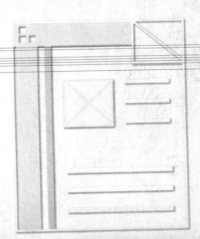

THOMSON

COURSE TECHNOLOGY

Macromedia Dreamweaver MX
Complete Concepts and Techniques

Gary B. Shelly
Thomas J. Cashman
Dolores J. Wells

Executive Editor:
Cheryl Costantini

Developmental Editor:
Ginny Harvey

Senior Product Manager:
Alexandra Arnold

Product Manager:
Erin Runyon

Associate Product Manager:
Reed Cotter

Editorial Assistant:
Emilie Perreault

Print Buyer:
Laura Burns

Director of Production:
Becky Herrington

Production Editors:
Kristen Guevara
Debbie Masi

Production Assistant:
Jennifer Quiambao

Proofreader:
Lori Silfen

Illustrator:
Michelle French

Cover Design:
Kenny Tran

Signing Representative:
Cheryl Costantini

Compositor:
Michelle French
GEX Publishing Services

Printer:
Banta Company

Dreamweaver MX

Comprehensive Concepts and Techniques

Contents

Preface

The Shelly Cashman Series® offers the finest textbooks in computer education. We are proud of the fact that our textbook series has been the most widely used series in educational instruction. We are pleased to announce the addition of the Macromedia® Dreamweaver® MX textbooks to the series with *Macromedia Dreamweaver MX: Comprehensive Concepts and Techniques*. This book continues with the innovation, quality, and reliability that you have come to expect from the Shelly Cashman Series.

Macromedia Dreamweaver is known as the standard in visual authoring. Macromedia Dreamweaver MX enhances the work experience for users in the following ways: (1) an intuitive new workspace that uses panels and views; (2) templates designed for customized layout control; (3) prebuilt code libraries; (4) increased server support for ASP, JSP, and ColdFusion® applications; (5) XML and Web Standards support; (6) improved cascading style sheet support; and (7) new coding and accessibility features.

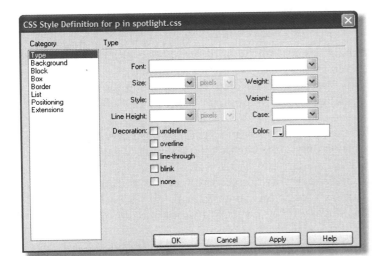
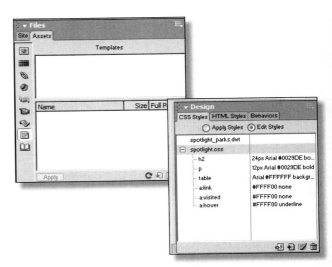

In this *Macromedia Dreamweaver MX* book, you will find an educationally sound and easy-to-follow pedagogy that combines a step-by-step approach with corresponding screens. All projects and exercises in this book are designed to take full advantage of the Dreamweaver MX enhancements. The popular Other Ways and More About features offer in-depth knowledge of Dreamweaver MX. The project material is developed carefully to ensure that students will see the importance of learning Dreamweaver for future coursework.

1 **Click Insert on the Scroll to the top of the Document window.**

The layer-code marker is selected because the layer is selected (Figure 7-13).

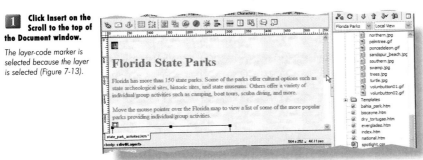

FIGURE 7-13

Objectives of This Textbook

Macromedia Dreamweaver MX: Comprehensive Concepts and Techniques is intended for a 12- to15-week course that teaches Dreamweaver MX and creation of Web sites. No experience with a computer is assumed, and no mathematics beyond the high school freshman level is required. The objectives of this book are:

- To teach students how to use Dreamweaver MX
- To expose students to proper Web site design and management techniques
- To acquaint students with the proper procedures to create Web sites suitable for coursework, professional purposes, and personal use
- To develop an exercise-oriented approach that allows learning by doing
- To encourage independent study, and help those who are working alone

The Shelly Cashman Approach

Features of the Shelly Cashman Series *Macromedia Dreamweaver MX* books include:

- **Project Orientation:** Each project in the book presents a practical problem and complete solution in an easy-to-understand approach.
- **Step-by-Step, Screen-by-Screen Instructions:** Each of the tasks required to complete a project is identified throughout the project. Full-color screens accompany the steps.
- **Thoroughly Tested Projects:** Every screen in the book is correct because it is produced by the author only after performing a step, resulting in unprecedented quality.
- **Other Ways Boxes:** The Other Ways boxes displayed at the end of many of the step-by-step sequences specify the other ways to do the task completed in the steps. Thus, the steps and the Other Ways box make a comprehensive reference unit.
- **More About Feature:** These marginal annotations provide background information and tips that complement the topics covered, adding depth and perspective.
- **Integration of the World Wide Web:** The World Wide Web is integrated into the Dreamweaver MX learning experience by (1) More About annotations that send students to Web sites for up-to-date information and alternative approaches to tasks; and (2) the Dreamweaver companion Web site, scsite.com/dreamweavermx.

Organization of This Textbook

Macromedia Dreamweaver MX: Comprehensive Concepts and Techniques provides detailed instruction on how to use Dreamweaver MX. The material is divided into an introduction chapter, nine projects, four appendices, and a quick reference summary.

Other Ways

1. On Window menu point to Others, click Timelines on Others submenu to display Timelines panel

More *About*

Removing a Frameset

You can remove a frame by dragging its borders. You cannot, however, remove a frameset entirely by dragging borders. To remove a frameset, close the Document window in which it is displayed. If the frameset file has been saved, delete the file.

Introduction – Introduction to Web Development and Macromedia Dreamweaver
In the Introduction, students are presented with the basics of the Internet and World Wide Web and their associated terms. Topics include differentiating between Web pages and Web sites and types of Web pages; identifying Web browser features; an overview of planning, designing, developing, testing, publishing, and maintaining a Web site; a discussion of HTML; various methods and tools used in Web site creation; and a brief description of the new features in Dreamweaver MX.

Project 1 – Creating a Dreamweaver Web Page and Local Site In Project 1, students are introduced to the Dreamweaver environment. Students create a local site and the home page for the Web site that they develop throughout the projects in the book. Topics include starting and quitting Dreamweaver; an introduction to the Dreamweaver workspace; creating a local site; creating a Web page and applying a color scheme and formatting properties of the Web page; inserting line breaks and special characters; inserting a horizontal rule and an absolute link; using the Check Spelling feature; previewing and printing a page in a Web browser; and an overview of Dreamweaver Help.

Project 2 – Adding Web Pages, Links, and Images In Project 2, students learn how to add new pages to an existing Web site and then how to add links and images. Topics include using Dreamweaver's integrated file browser feature; understanding and modifying image file formats; adding background and page images to a Web page; creating relative, absolute, and e-mail links; changing the color of links and editing and deleting links; using the site map and Link Checker; showing the page in Code view; and using Code view to modify HTML code.

Project 3 – Tables and Page Layout In Project 3, students are introduced to techniques for using tables in Web site design. Topics include an introduction to page layout using Standard view and Layout view to design a Web page; modifying a table structure; understanding HTML table tags; adding content to a table and formatting the content; formatting the table; and creating head content.

Project 4 – Page Layout with Frames In Project 4, students learn how to use frames to design the presentation of a Web page. Topics include understanding and creating a frameset and frames; setting and modifying the properties for a frame and a frameset; adding static content to a frame; and adding Flash buttons as navigation elements.

Project 5 – Forms In Project 5, students are introduced to the concept of forms and form processing. Topics include client-side versus server-side processing; designing and creating a form; the different form objects; adding text fields and text areas to a form; using a table to help with form layout; form accessibility options; and how to add behaviors to a form.

Project 6 – Templates and Style Sheets In Project 6, students learn how to use templates and style sheets. Topics include describing and creating a template; the difference between HTML styles and cascading style sheets; creating a cascading style sheet and applying CSS attributes to a template; creating a Web page from a template; and using the Assets panel.

Project 7 – Layers, Image Maps, and Navigation Bars In Project 7, students learn how to add layers and create image maps and navigation bars. Topics include understanding the concept of a layer and how to resize, name, and align layers; how an image map works; how to create an image map and how to assign behaviors to manipulate layers within the map; how to create a navigation bar with Flash buttons; and how to insert the Date object.

Project 8 – Animation and Behaviors In Project 8, students learn the concept of animation using the timeline and how to create linear and nonlinear timelines. Topics include understanding the concept of a timeline and using the Timelines panel, adding a layer to a timeline, adding the Play and Stop Timeline, Show and Hide Layers behaviors to layers within the Timeline, and adding a Play button to play the animations.

Project 9 – Media Objects In Project 9, students learn about different media objects and how to add media objects to a Web site. Topics include inserting Flash text and Flash movies into a Web page; adding linked sound and embedded sound to a Web page and adding the necessary parameters; inserting a video into a Web page and adding the necessary parameters; checking for plug-ins; and inserting Shockwave movies and Java Applets into a Web page.

Appendices The book includes four appendices. Appendix A presents an introduction to the Macromedia Dreamweaver Help system. Appendix B describes Dreamweaver Authoring for Accessibility features; Appendix C explains how to use Fireworks for image modification within Dreamweaver; and Appendix D illustrates how to define and publish a Web site to a remote server.

Quick Reference Summary In Dreamweaver, you can accomplish a task in a number of ways, such as using the mouse, menu, context menu, and keyboard. The Macromedia MX Quick Reference for Windows at the back of this book provides a quick reference to common keyboard shortcuts.

End-of-Project Student Activities

A notable strength of the Shelly Cashman Series *Macromedia Dreamweaver MX* books is the extensive student activities at the end of each project. Well-structured student activities can make the difference between students merely participating in a class and students retaining the information they learn. The activities in the Shelly Cashman Series *Macromedia Dreamweaver MX* books include the following:

- **What You Should Know** A listing of the tasks completed within a project together with the pages on which the step-by-step, screen-by-screen explanations appear.

- **Apply Your Knowledge** This exercise usually requires students to open and manipulate a file on the Data Disk. To obtain a copy of the Data Disk, follow the instructions on the inside back cover of this textbook.

- **In the Lab** Three in-depth assignments per project require students to apply the knowledge gained in the project to solve problems on a computer.
- **Cases and Places** Five unique real-world case-study situations.

Shelly Cashman Series Instructor Resources

The ancillaries that accompany this textbook are Instructor Resources (ISBN 0-7895-6677-X) and Online Content. These ancillaries are available to adopters through your Course Technology representative or by calling one of the following telephone numbers: Colleges and Universities, 1-800-648-7450; High Schools, 1-800-824-5179; Private Career Colleges, 1-800-347-7707; Canada, 1-800-268-2222; Corporations with IT Training Centers, 1-800-648-7450; and Government Agencies, Health-Care Organizations, and Correctional Facilities, 1-800-477-3692.

Instructor Resources CD-ROM

The contents of the Instructor Resources CD-ROM are listed below.

- **Instructor's Manual (Lesson Plan and Teaching Tips)** The Instructor's Manual includes the following for each project: project objectives; a file listing table with all files from the Data Disk and created from scratch; and detailed lecture notes that include teacher notes with page number and figure references, classroom activities, and projects to assign.

- **Syllabus** Any instructor who has been assigned a course at the last minute knows how difficult it is to come up with a course syllabus. For this reason, sample syllabi are included that can be customized easily to a course.

- **PowerPoint Presentation** This lecture ancillary contains a PowerPoint presentation for each project in the textbook. You also may make these PowerPoint presentations available to students on a network for project review, or to be printed for distribution.

- **Figures Files (Illustrations from the Text)** Illustrations for every screen and table in the textbook are available in electronic form.

- **Solutions to Exercises** Solutions to the end-of-project exercises including required files for all the In the Lab assignments and sample answers for any Cases and Places assignment that supplies data at the end of each project are available.

- **Test Bank & Test Engine** ExamView is a state-of-the-art test builder that is easy to use. With ExamView, you quickly can create printed tests, Internet tests, and computer (LAN-based) tests. You can enter your own test questions or use the test bank that accompanies ExamView. A Word document version of the test bank containing 110 questions for every project (25 multiple-choice, 50 true/false, and 35 fill-in-the-blank) with page number references and transparency references also is available.

- **Data Files for Students** All files required by students to complete the Apply Your Knowledge and In the Lab exercises are included.

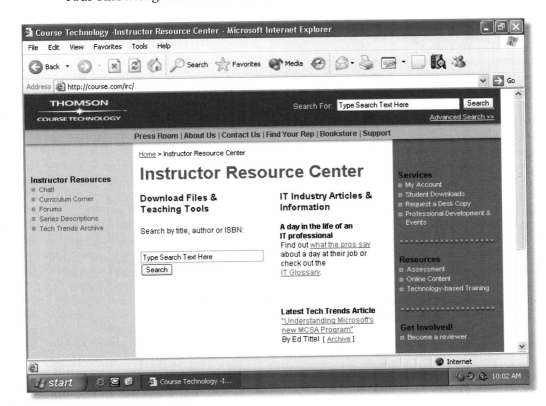

Online Content

If you use Blackboard or WebCT, a free test bank for this textbook is available in a simple, ready-to-use format. Visit the Instructor Resource Center for this textbook at course.com to download the test bank, or contact your local sales representative for details.

Acknowledgments

The Shelly Cashman Series would not be the leading computer education series without the contributions of outstanding publishing professionals. First, and foremost, among them is Becky Herrington, director of production and designer. She is the heart and soul of the Shelly Cashman Series, and it is only through her leadership, dedication, and tireless efforts that superior products are made possible.

Under Becky's direction, the following individuals made significant contributions to these books: Ken Russo, senior Web and graphic designer; Michelle French, graphic artist and cover designer; Jennifer Quiambao, production assistant; Andrew Bartel, graphic artist; Jeanne Black, Betty Hopkins, and Kellee LaVars, QuarkXPress compositors; Ginny Harvey, developmental/copy editor; Lori Silfen, proofreader; and Cristina Haley, indexer. We also would like to thank Alex White for his attention to detail in validating this text.

Finally, we would like to thank Kristen Duerr, executive vice president and publisher; Cheryl Costantini, executive editor; Jim Quasney, series consulting editor; Alexandra Arnold, senior product manager; Erin Runyon, product manager; Reed Cotter, associate product manager; and Emilie Perreault, editorial assistant.

We were fortunate to have a truly dedicated person whose critical technical evaluations of the initial manuscript were of great value during the preparation of this book. Special thanks go to Julie Hallstrom from Macromedia.

Gary B. Shelly
Thomas J. Cashman
Dolores J. Wells

Macromedia Dreamweaver MX 30-Day Trial Edition

A copy of the Dreamweaver MX 30-Day trial edition can be found on the Macromedia Web site (www.macromedia.com). Click DOWNLOADS in the left pane and follow the on-screen instructions. When you activate the software, you will receive a license that allows you to use the software for 30 days. Course Technology and Macromedia provide no product support for this trial edition. When the trial period ends, you can purchase a copy of Macromedia Dreamweaver MX, or uninstall the trial edition and reinstall your previous version.

The minimum system requirements for the 30-day trial edition is a Pentium II-class processor, 300+ MHz; Windows XP, 2000, NT, ME, or 98 (160 MB RAM); Netscape Navigator or Internet Explorer 4.0 or higher; 96 MB of available RAM (128 MB recommended); 275 MB available disk space; and a 256-color monitor capable of 800 × 600 resolution (1024 × 768, millions of colors recommended).

Shelly Cashman Series — Traditionally Bound Textbooks

The Shelly Cashman Series presents the following computer subjects in a variety of traditionally bound textbooks. For more information, see your Course Technology representative or call 1-800-648-7450. For Shelly Cashman Series information, visit Shelly Cashman Series at course.com/shellycashman.

COMPUTERS	
Computers	Discovering Computers 2004: A Gateway to Information, Web Enhanced, Complete Edition
	Discovering Computers 2004: A Gateway to Information, Web Enhanced, Introductory Edition
	Discovering Computers 2004: A Gateway to Information, Web Enhanced, Brief Edition
	Teachers Discovering Computers: Integrating Technology in the Classroom 3e
	Exploring Computers: A Record of Discovery 4e
	Study Guide for Discovering Computers 2004: A Gateway to Information, Web Enhanced
	Essential Introduction to Computers 5e (40-page)

WINDOWS APPLICATIONS	
Microsoft Office	Microsoft Office XP: Essential Concepts and Techniques (5 projects)[1]
	Microsoft Office XP: Brief Concepts and Techniques (9 projects)[1]
	Microsoft Office XP: Introductory Concepts and Techniques, Windows XP Edition, Course One (15 projects)
	Microsoft Office XP: Introductory Concepts and Techniques, Enhanced Edition, Course One (15 projects)[1]
	Microsoft Office XP: Advanced Concepts and Techniques, Course Two (11 projects)
	Microsoft Office XP: Post Advanced Concepts and Techniques, Course Three (11 projects)
	Microsoft Office 2000: Essential Concepts and Techniques (5 projects)
	Microsoft Office 2000: Brief Concepts and Techniques (9 projects)
	Microsoft Office 2000: Introductory Concepts and Techniques, Enhanced Edition (15 projects)
	Microsoft Office 2000: Advanced Concepts and Techniques (11 projects)
	Microsoft Office 2000: Post Advanced Concepts and Techniques (11 projects)
Integration	Integrating Microsoft Office XP Applications and the World Wide Web: Essential Concepts and Techniques
PIM	Microsoft Outlook 2002: Essential Concepts and Techniques
Microsoft Works	Microsoft Works 6: Complete Concepts and Techniques[2] • Microsoft Works 2000: Complete Concepts and Techniques[2]
Microsoft Windows	Microsoft Windows XP: Complete Concepts and Techniques[3]
	Microsoft Windows XP: Brief Concepts and Techniques
	Microsoft Windows 2000: Complete Concepts and Techniques (6 projects)[3]
	Microsoft Windows 2000: Brief Concepts and Techniques (2 projects)
	Microsoft Windows 98: Essential Concepts and Techniques (2 projects)
	Microsoft Windows 98: Complete Concepts and Techniques (6 projects)[3]
	Introduction to Microsoft Windows NT Workstation 4
Word Processing	Microsoft Word 2002[3] • Microsoft Word 2000[3]
Spreadsheets	Microsoft Excel 2002[3] • Microsoft Excel 2000[3]
Database	Microsoft Access 2002[3] • Microsoft Access 2000[3]
Presentation Graphics	Microsoft PowerPoint 2002[3] • Microsoft PowerPoint 2000[3]
Desktop Publishing	Microsoft Publisher 2002[2] • Microsoft Publisher 2000[2]

PROGRAMMING	
Programming	Microsoft Visual Basic .NET: Complete Concepts and Techniques[3] • Microsoft Visual Basic 6: Complete Concepts and Techniques[2] • Programming in QBasic • Java Programming 2e: Complete Concepts and Techniques[2] • Structured COBOL Programming 2e

INTERNET	
Browser	Microsoft Internet Explorer 6: Introductory Concepts and Techniques • Microsoft Internet Explorer 5: An Introduction • Netscape Navigator 6: An Introduction
Web Page Creation and Design	Web Design: Introductory Concepts and Techniques • HTML: Complete Concepts and Techniques 2e[3] Microsoft FrontPage 2002: Essential Concepts and Techniques • Microsoft FrontPage 2002[3] Microsoft FrontPage 2000[2] • JavaScript: Complete Concepts and Techniques 2e[2] • Macromedia Dreamweaver MX: Complete Concepts and Techniques[3]

SYSTEMS ANALYSIS	
Systems Analysis	Systems Analysis and Design 5e

DATA COMMUNICATIONS	
Data Communications	Business Data Communications: Introductory Concepts and Techniques 4e

[1] Available running under Windows XP or running under Windows 2000
[2] Also available as an Introductory Edition, which is a shortened version of the complete book
[3] Also available as an Introductory Edition, which is a shortened version of the complete book and as a Comprehensive Edition, which is an extended version of the complete book

Macromedia Dreamweaver MX

INTRODUCTION

Introduction to Web Development and Macromedia Dreamweaver

You will have mastered the material in this project when you can:

O B J E C T I V E S

- Describe the significance of the Internet and its associated terms
- Describe the World Wide Web and its associated terms
- Identify the difference between the Internet and the World Wide Web
- Specify the difference between a Web page and a Web site
- Define Web browsers and identify their main features
- Identify the six types of Web pages
- Discuss how to plan, design, develop, test, publish, and maintain a Web site
- Identify the various methods and tools used to create a Web page and Web site
- Recognize the basic tags within HTML
- Discuss the advantages of using Web page authoring programs such as Dreamweaver
- Describe the new features of Dreamweaver MX

Macromedia Dreamweaver MX

Introduction to Web Development and Macromedia Dreamweaver

The Internet

The **Internet**, sometimes simply called the **Net**, is a global network, connecting millions of computers. Within this global network, a user who has permission at any one computer can access and obtain information from any other computer within the network. A **network** is a group of computers and associated devices that are connected by communications facilities. A network can span a global area and involve permanent connections, such as cables, or temporary connections made through telephone or other communications links. Within this global network are local, regional, national, and international networks. Each of these networks provides communications, services, and access to information.

The Internet has had a relatively brief, but explosive history. This network grew out of an experiment begun in the 1960s by the U.S. Department of Defense (DOD). Today, the Internet is a public, cooperative, and self-sustaining facility that is accessible to hundreds of millions of people worldwide.

The World Wide Web and Web Browsers

The **World Wide Web** (**WWW**), also called the **Web**, is the most popular service on the Internet. The Web consists of a system of global **network servers** that supports specially formatted documents and provides a means for sharing these resources with many people at the same time. A network server is known as the **host computer**, and your computer, from which you access the information, is called the **client**. The protocol that enables the transfer of data from the host computer to the client is the **Hypertext Transfer Protocol** (**HTTP**).

Accessing the Web

Users access Web resources, such as text, graphics, sound, video, and multimedia, through a **Web page**. Every Web page is identified by a unique address, or Uniform Resource Locator (URL). The URL provides the global address of the location of the Web page. URLs are discussed later in this Introduction. To view data contained on a Web page requires a Web browser. A **Web browser** is a software program that requests a Web page, interprets the code contained within the page, and then displays the contents of the Web page on your computer display device.

Web Browsers

Web browsers contain special buttons and other features to help you navigate through Web sites. The more popular Web browser software programs are **Microsoft Internet Explorer** and **Netscape Navigator**. This book uses Internet Explorer. When you start Internet Explorer, it opens to a Web page that has been set as the start, or home, page (Figure I-1). The home page can be any page on the Web and can be designated by the user through the browser Tools menu. Important features of Internet Explorer are summarized in Table I-1 on the next page.

More *About*

Protocols

Another widely used protocol is File Transfer Protocol (FTP), which is a protocol used on the Internet for uploading files. To learn more about protocols, visit the Dreamweaver MX More About Web page (scsite.com/ dreamweavermx/ more.htm) and then click Protocols.

FIGURE I-1

Table I-1 Internet Explorer Features	
FEATURE	**DEFINITION**
Title bar	Displays the name of the program and the name of the Web page you are viewing
Menu bar	Displays the name of the menus; each menu contains a list of commands you can use to perform tasks such as printing, saving, editing, and so on
Standard Buttons toolbar	Contains buttons, boxes, and menus that allow you to perform tasks more quickly than using the menu bar and related menus
Address bar	Displays the Web site address, or URL, of the Web page you are viewing
Document window	Contains the Web page content

Nearly all Web pages have unique characteristics, but almost every Web page contains the same basic elements. Common elements you find on most Web pages are headings or titles, text, pictures or images, background enhancements, and hyperlinks. A **hyperlink**, or **link**, can link to another place in the same Web page or to an entirely different Web page. Normally, you click the hyperlink to follow the link pathway. Figure I-2 illustrates navigating a Web site using different types of links.

Most Web pages are part of a Web site. A **Web site** contains a home page, which generally is the first Web page visitors see when they enter the site. A **home page** provides information about the Web site's purpose and content. Most Web sites also contain additional content and pages. Each Web site is owned and managed by an individual, company, or organization.

NAVIGATING USING A VARIETY OF LINKS

FIGURE 1-2a Link Displays in Different Color

FIGURE 1-2b Link Underlined

FIGURE 1-2c Graphical Image Used as Link

More About

Wireless Service Providers

Wireless service providers (WSPs) offer a broad range of plans and may include features such as no roaming charges or unlimited minutes. To learn more about WSPs, visit the Dreamweaver MX More About Web page (scsite.com/ dreamweavermx/ more.htm) and then click Service Providers.

Accessing the Web requires a connection through a regional or national Internet service provider (ISP), an online service provider (OSP), or a wireless service provider (WSP). An **Internet service provider** (**ISP**) is a business that has a permanent Internet connection and provides temporary connections to individuals, companies, or other organizations. An **online service provider** (**OSP**) is similar to an ISP, but provides additional member-only services, such as financial data, travel information, and so on. America Online is an example of an OSP. A **wireless service provider** (**WSP**) provides Internet access to users with Web-enabled devices or wireless modems. Generally, all of these services charge a fee.

Figure I-3 below illustrates ways to access the Internet using these service providers. **Point of presence** (**POP**) is a telephone number that gives you dial up access.

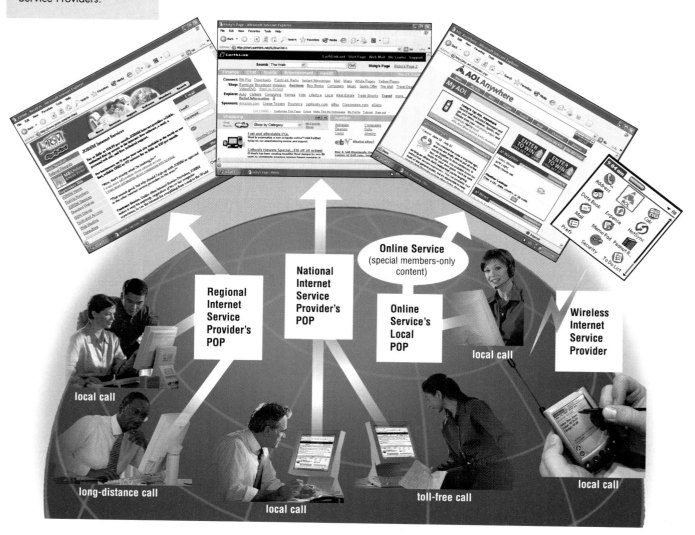

FIGURE I-3

Types of Web Pages

The six basic types of Web pages are portal, news, business/marketing, advocacy, informational, and personal. A **portal Web page** (Figure I-4a) provides a variety of Internet services from a single, convenient location. Most portals offer free services such as search engines, local, national, and worldwide news, sports and weather, reference tools, maps, stock quotes, newsgroups, chat rooms, calendars, and so on. A **news Web page** (Figure I-4b) contains news articles relating to current events. A **business/marketing Web page** (Figure I-4c) contains content that promotes or sells products or services. Within an **advocacy Web page** (Figure I-4d), you will find content that describes a cause, question, or idea. An **informational Web page** (Figure I-4e on the next page) contains factual information, such as research, statistics, sports scores, and so on. Governmental agencies and nonprofit organizations are the primary providers of informational Web pages. A **personal Web page** (Figure I-4f on the next page) is published by an individual. As you progress through this book, you will have an opportunity to develop these types of Web pages.

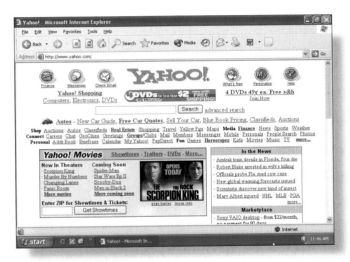

(a) Portal Web Page

(b) News Web Page

(c) Business/Marketing Web Page

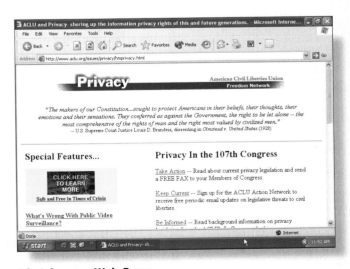

(d) Advocacy Web Page

FIGURE I-4

(e) Informational Web Page

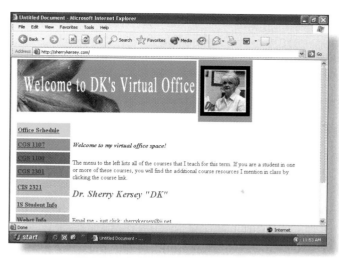

(f) Personal Web Page

FIGURE I-4 (continued)

Planning a Web site

Although it is easy to publish a Web page, advanced planning is paramount in ensuring a successful Web site. Publishing a Web site, which makes it available on the Internet, is discussed later in this Introduction. Thousands of individuals create and publish Web pages every day, some using word processing software or markup languages to create their pages. Others use professional HTML editors such as Dreamweaver.

Planning Basics - Purpose

Those who rush into the publishing process without the proper planning tend to design Web sites that are unorganized and difficult to navigate. Visitors to this type of Web site will lose interest quickly and will not return. As you begin planning your Web site, consider the following guidelines to ensure you set realistic goals and attain them.

PURPOSE AND GOAL Determine the purpose and goal of your Web site. Create a focus by developing a **purpose statement**, which communicates the intention of the Web site. Consider the six basic types of Web pages previously mentioned. Will your Web site consist of just one basic type or a combination of two or more types?

TARGET AUDIENCE Identify your audience. The people who visit your Web site will determine whether your Web site is a success. Although you welcome all visitors, you need to know as much as possible about your target audience. To learn more about the visitors to your Web site, determine whether you want to attract people with similar interests, and consider gender, education, age range, income, profession/job field, and computer proficiency.

NEW WEB TECHNOLOGIES Evaluate whether your potential visitors have access to high-speed broadband media or baseband media, and use this information to determine what elements to include within your Web site. **Broadband** transmits multiple signals simultaneously and includes media and hardware such as **T1 lines, DSL**

Web Site Planning

The first step in creating your Web site is to define the purpose. Consider what you want to accomplish and then list your objectives. To learn more about Web site planning, visit the Dreamweaver MX More About Web page (scsite.com/dreamweavermx/more.htm) and then click Web Site Planning.

(digital subscriber lines), or cable modems. Baseband transmits one signal at a time and includes media and hardware such as 28K to 56K modems. Baseband works well with a Web site composed mostly of text and small images. Web sites that contain many images or multimedia, such as video and animations, generally require that the visitor has a broadband connection.

WEB SITE COMPARISON   Visit other Web sites that are similar to your proposed site. What do you like about these sites? What do you dislike? Look for inspirational ideas. How can you make your Web site better?

Planning Basics – Content

An informative, well-planned Web site is not difficult to create. To ensure a successful Web experience for your visitors, consider the following guidelines to provide appropriate content and other valuable Web page elements.

VALUE-ADDED CONTENT   Consider the different types of content to include within your Web site. Use the following as guidelines:

▶ What topics do you want to cover?
▶ How much information will you present about each topic?
▶ What will attract your target audience to your Web site?
▶ What methods will you use to keep your audience returning to your site?
▶ What changes will you have to make to keep your site updated?

TEXT   Because text is the primary component of most Web pages, be brief and incorporate lists whenever possible. Use common words and simple language, and check your spelling and grammar. Create your textual content to accomplish your goals effectively.

IMAGES   After text, images are the most commonly included content. Ask yourself these questions with respect to your use of images:

▶ Will you have a common logo and/or theme on all Web pages?
▶ Are these images readily available?
▶ What will you have to locate?
▶ What will you have to create?
▶ How many images per page?

MULTIMEDIA   Multimedia adds interactivity and action to your Web pages. Animation, audio, and video are types of multimedia. If you plan to add multimedia, determine whether the visitor will require plug-ins. A plug-in extends the capability of a Web browser. Some of the more commonly used plug-ins are Shockwave™ Player, Macromedia Flash™, and RealNetworks® RealPlayer®. Most plug-ins are free and can be downloaded from the Web.

COLOR PALETTE   The color palette you select for your Web site can enhance or detract from your message or goal. Do not think in terms of your favorite colors, but consider how color can support your goal. Ask yourself the following questions:

▶ Do your selected colors work well with your goal?
▶ Are the colors part of the universal 216 browser-safe color palette?
▶ Did you limit the number of colors to a selected few?

More About

DSL

DSL technology uses existing 2-wire copper telephone wiring to deliver high-speed data services to homes and businesses. DSL provides almost instant access to bandwidth-intensive applications such as streaming audio/video, online games, application programs, video conferencing, and other high-bandwidth services. To learn more about DSL, visit the Dreamweaver MX More About Web page (scsite.com/dreamweavermx/more.htm) and then click DSL.

Designing a Web Site

It is not possible to predict how a visitor will access a Web site or at what point the visitor will enter within the Web site structure. Visitors can arrive at any page within a Web site by a variety of ways: a hyperlink, a search engine, a directory, typing a Web address directly, and so on. On every page of your Web site, you must provide clear answers to the two basic questions your visitors will ask, Where am I? and Where do I go from here? A well-organized Web site provides the answers to these questions. Once the visitor is at a Web site, **navigation**, which is the pathway through your site, must be obvious and intuitive. Individual Web pages cannot be isolated from the rest of the site if the site is to be successful. Most Web designers use a navigation map to visualize the navigation pathway.

Design Basics – Navigation Map

A **navigation map** outlines the structure of the entire Web project, showing all of the pages within the site and the connections from one page to others. The navigation map provides the structure, or road map, through the Web site, but does not provide detail as to the content of the individual pages. Consider the following for site navigation.

STRUCTURE The goal and the type of a Web site is a major determinant in the type of structure selected for a specific Web site. The navigation map serves as a blueprint for your navigational structure. Consider the following navigational structure types and determine which one best meets your needs:

- In a **linear structure**, (Figure I-5a) the user navigates sequentially, moving from one page to the next. This is the simplest way to organize a Web site. Information that flows as a narrative, timeline, or in logical order is ideal for sequential treatment. Simple sequential organization, however, usually works only for smaller sites. Many online tutorials use a linear structure.
- A **hierarchical structure** (Figure I-5b) is one of the better ways to organize complex bodies of information. This type of structure is well-suited for Web sites because most visitors are familiar with hierarchical charts. For a hierarchical structure to be effective requires thorough organization of content.
- A **web structure** (Figure I-5c), which also is called a **random structure**, poses few restrictions on organizational patterns. This type of structure is associated with the free flow of ideas and can be confusing to a user. Random structure is better suited for experienced users looking for further education or enrichment and is not recommended if your goal is a basic understanding of a particular topic. If a Web site is relatively small, however, a random structure could work well.
- If a Web site consists of a number of topics of equal importance, a **grid structure** (Figure I-5d) could be the best navigational choice. Procedural manuals, events, and item lists are examples of content suited for this type of structure.
- Large Web sites frequently use a **hybrid structure**, which is a combination of the above listed structures, to organize information (Figure I-6).

More About

Design

Poor site design will discourage Web site visitors. To learn more about good Web site design, visit the Dreamweaver MX More About Web page (scsite.com/ dreamweavermx/ more.htm) and then click Web Site Design.

(a) Linear Structure

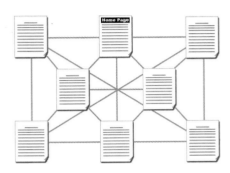

(b) Hierarchical Structure

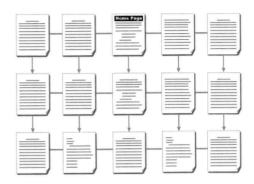

(c) Web Structure

(d) Grid Structure

FIGURE I-5

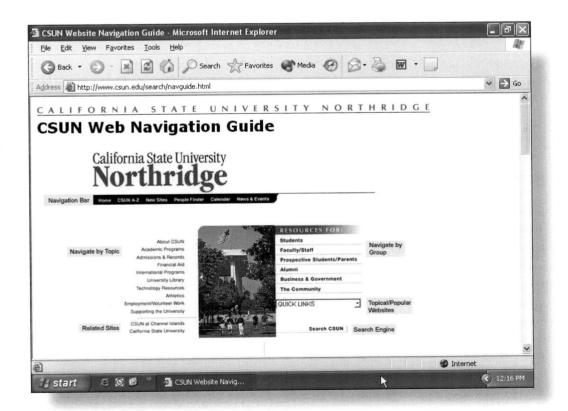

FIGURE I-6

TOOLS Determine the tool to be used to create the navigation map. If your Web site is small, the organizational chart included in the Microsoft Office applications, shown in Figure I-7 using PowerPoint, is an easy-to-use tool. For larger, more diverse Web sites, Visio Professional, Flow Charting PDQ, FlowCharter Professional, and OrgPlus are programs you can use to chart and organize your Web site.

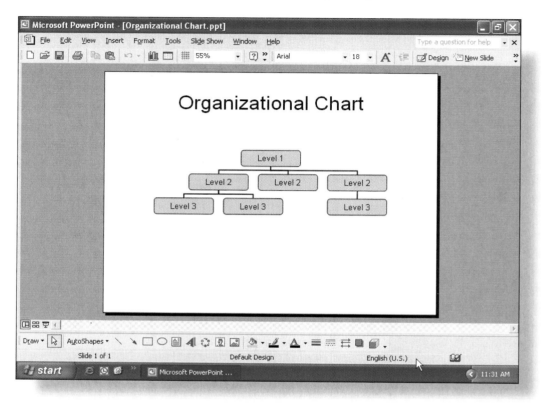

FIGURE I-7

NAVIGATION ELEMENTS The more common types of navigation elements include text, buttons, other images, image maps, a site index, menu, search feature, and frames. Depending on the complexity of your Web site, you may want to include some or all of these elements.

Developing a Web Site

Once the structure is complete, the next step is to develop the Web site. Because text and images are a Web site's more common elements, make them your main focus. Then consider page layout and color.

Development Basics – Typography, Images, Page Layout, and Color

The combination of typography, images, page layout, and color comprise the elements of your finished Web page. Correct use of these elements plays an important part in the development process. Consider the following guidelines.

TYPOGRAPHY Good **typography**, which is the appearance and arrangement of characters that make up your text, is just as important for a Web page as it is in any other medium. A **font** consists of all the characters available in a particular style and weight for a specific design. Selecting fonts for display on a computer screen, however, is different from selecting fonts for a magazine, a book, or other printed medium. Although the text displays on a computer screen and not on a piece of paper, it still should be easy to read. As a viewer of a Web page, you may consciously never notice the **typeface**, which is the design of the text characters, but the typeface subconsciously affects your reaction to the page.

When selecting the font, determine its purpose. Is it to be used for a title? For onscreen reading? Is it likely to be printed? Will the font fit in with the theme of the Web site? Is it a Web-safe font, such as Times New Roman, Courier, or Arial? **Web-safe fonts** are the more popular fonts and ones that most visitors are likely to have installed on their computers.

IMAGES Using images can enhance almost any Web page if used appropriately. Without the visual impact of shape, color, and contrast, Web pages can be uninteresting graphically and will not motivate the visitor to investigate their contents. Images and page performance are issues for many visitors. When adding images, consider your potential audience and the technology they have available. Also remember that a background image or a graphical menu increases visitor download time. You may lose visitors who do not have broadband access if your Web page contains an excessive number of graphical items.

PAGE LAYOUT The importance of proper page layout cannot be overemphasized. A suitable design draws visitors to your Web site. Although no single design is appropriate for all Web pages, a consistent, logical layout allows you easily to add text and images. The Web page layouts shown in Figure I-8 illustrate two different layouts. The layout on the left (Figure I-8a) illustrates a plain page without text or images. The page layout on the right (Figure I-8b) presents strong visual contrast by using a variety of layout elements. In laying out your Web pages, consider the following guidelines to ensure visitors have the best viewing experience.

- ◗ Include only one topic per page
- ◗ Control the vertical and horizontal size of the page
- ◗ Start text on the left to accommodate the majority of individuals who read from left to right
- ◗ Use concise statements to get your point across; studies indicate most people scan the text

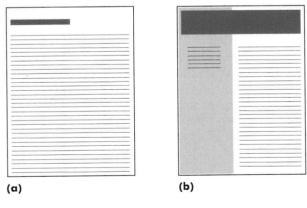

(a)   (b)

FIGURE I-8

COLOR When creating a Web page, use color to add interest and vitality to your site. Color can be used in tables, as backgrounds, and with fonts. Use the right combination of colors to decorate the layout and to tie the Web site pages together.

Reviewing and Testing a Web Site

More About

Reviewing and Testing Your Web Site

A Web site should be tested at various stages of the development process. A compatibility test verifies that the Web site works with a variety of browser versions. To learn more about Web site testing, visit the Dreamweaver MX More About Web page (scsite.com/ dreamweavermx/ more.htm) and then click Testing Your Web Site.

Some Web site developers argue that reviewing and testing should take place throughout the developmental process. While this may be true, it also is important to review and test the final product. This ongoing process ensures that you identify and correct any problems before publishing to the Web. When reviewing and testing your Web site, ask the following questions.

- Is the Web site free of spelling and/or grammatical errors?
- Is the page layout consistent and does it generate a sense of balance and order?
- Are any links broken?
- Do multimedia interactivity and forms function correctly?
- Does the Web site display properly in the most widely used browsers?
- Does the Web site function in different browsers, including older browser versions?
- Have you initiated a **group test** in which you have asked other individuals to test your Web site and provide feedback?

Publishing a Web Site

After thoroughly testing your Web site, it can be published. **Publishing** a Web site is the process of making it available to your visitors. This step involves the actual uploading of the Web site to a server. After the uploading process is completed, all pages within the Web site should be tested again.

Publishing Basics — Domain Name, Server Space, and Uploading

With a Web site thoroughly tested and problems corrected, you must make the site available to your audience by obtaining a domain name, acquiring server space, and uploading your Web site. Consider the following to ensure site availability.

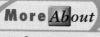

More About

Domain Names

It is not unusual to read news articles describing where domain name owners fail to pay their registration fees and then lose their domain names. To learn more about domain name registration, visit the Dreamweaver MX More About Web page (scsite.com/ dreamweavermx/ more.htm) and then click Domain Names.

OBTAIN A DOMAIN NAME So visitors can access your Web site, you must obtain a domain name. Web sites are accessed by an IP address or a domain name. An **IP address (Internet Protocol address)** is a number that uniquely identifies each computer or device connected to the Internet. A **domain name** is the text version of an IP address (Figure I-9). The **Domain Name System (DNS)** is an Internet service that translates domain names into IP addresses. The **Uniform Resource Locator (URL)**, also called a **Web address,** tells the browser on which server to locate the Web page. A URL consists of a communications standard, such as **HTTP (Hypertext Transfer Protocol)**, the domain name, and sometimes the path to a specific Web page.

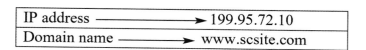

FIGURE I-9

Domain names are unique and must be registered. The **Accredited Registrar Directory** provides a listing of **Internet Corporation for Assigned Names and Numbers** (**ICANN**) accredited domain name registrars. Your most difficult task likely will be to find a name that is not already registered. Use a specialized search engine at one of the many accredited domain name registrars you will find listed on the ICANN Web site (icann.org) to locate a name. In addition to registering your business name as a domain name, you may want to register the names of your products, services, and/or other related names. Expect to pay approximately $20 to $35 per year for a domain name.

Consider the following guidelines when selecting a domain name.

- Select a name that is easy to pronounce, spell, and remember.
- Select a name that relates to the Web site content and suggests the nature of your product or service.
- If the Web site is a business, use the business name.
- Select a name that is free and clear of trademark issues.

Some ISPs will obtain a domain name for you if you use their service to host your Web site.

ACQUIRE SERVER SPACE Locate an ISP that will host your Web site. Recall that an ISP is a business that has a permanent Internet connection. These providers offer temporary connections to individuals and companies free or for a fee.

If you select an ISP that provides free server space, most likely your visitors will be subjected to advertisements and pop-up windows. Other options to explore for free server space include the provider from which you obtain your Internet connection; **online communities,** such as Yahoo! GeoCities (geocities.yahoo.com), Tripod (tripod.com), and MSN Web Communities (communities.msn.com); and your educational institution's Web server.

If the purpose of your Web site is to sell a product or service or to promote a professional organization, you should consider a fee-based ISP. Use a search engine such as Google (google.com) and search for Website hosting, or visit Hosting Repository (hostingrepository.com) where you will find thousands of Web hosting plans and reviews and ratings of Web hosting providers. Selecting a reliable provider requires investigation on your part. Many providers provide multiple hosting plans. Consider the following questions and how they apply to your particular situation and Web site when selecting an ISP:

1. What is the monthly fee? Is a discount available if you sign up for a year? Are setup fees charged?
2. How much server space is provided for the monthly fee? Can you purchase additional space? If so, how much does it cost?
3. What is the average uptime on a monthly basis? What is the average downtime?
4. What are the server specifications? Can they handle many users? Do they have battery backup power?
5. Are **server logs,** which keep track of the number of accesses, available?
6. What is their connectivity – how do they connect to the Internet: OC3, T1, T3, or other?
7. Is a money-back guarantee offered?
8. What technical support do they provide and when is it available? Do they have an online knowledge base?
9. Does the server on which the Web site will reside have CGI capabilities and Active Server Page (ASP) support?
10. Does the server on which the Web site will reside support e-commerce, multimedia, and **Secure Sockets Layer** (**SSL**) for encrypting confidential data such as credit card numbers? Are additional fees required for these capabilities?

More About

Selecting a Domain Name

When selecting a domain name, keep it simple. If possible, it is best to avoid hyphens. To learn more about domain name selection, visit the Dreamweaver MX More About Web page (scsite.com/dreamweavermx/more.htm) and then click Domain Name Selection.

INTRODUCTION

UPLOAD THE WEB SITE Copy, or upload, the files from your computer to the server where your Web site will be accessible to anyone on the Internet. **Uploading** is the process of transmitting from your computer all the files that comprise your Web site to the selected server or host computer. Files that make up your Web site can include Web pages, images, audio, video, and animation.

A variety of tools and methods exist to manage the upload task. Some of the more popular of these are FTP applications, Windows Web Publishing Wizard, Web Folders, and Web authoring programs such as Dreamweaver. These tools allow you to link to a remote server, enter a password, and then upload your files. An FTP program, such as WS_FTP, is the most widely used method to upload files. Dreamweaver contains a built-in function similar to independent FTP programs. The Dreamweaver FTP function to upload your Web site is covered in Project 3.

Maintaining a Web Site

Most Web sites require maintenance and updating. Some types of ongoing Web maintenance include the following:

- Changing content, either adding new or deleting obsolete text and images
- Checking for broken links and adding new links
- Documenting the last change date (even when no revisions have been made)

Use the information from the server logs provided by your ISP to determine what needs to be updated or changed. Statistics contained within these logs generally include the number of visitors trying to access your site at one time, what resources they request, how long they stay on the site, at what point they enter the site, pages they view, and what errors they encounter. Learning to use and apply the information contained within the server log will help you to make your Web site successful.

After updates and/or changes are made to the site, notify your viewers with a What's New announcement.

Methods and Tools Used to Create Web Pages

Web developers have several options for creating Web pages: a text editor, an HTML editor, software applications, or a WYSIWYG editor. Microsoft Notepad and WordPad are examples of a **text editor**. These simple, easy-to-use programs allow the user to enter, edit, save, and print text. An **HTML editor** is a more sophisticated version of a text editor. In addition to basic text-editing functions, more advanced features, such as syntax highlighting, color-coding, and spell checking are available. **Software applications**, such as Microsoft Word, Excel, and Publisher, provide a Save as Web Page command on the File menu. This feature converts the application document into an HTML file. Examples of a **WYSIWYG editor** are programs such as Microsoft FrontPage and Macromedia Dreamweaver. These programs provide an integrated text editor with a graphical user interface that allows the user to view both the code and the document as it is being created.

A Web developer can use any of these options to create Web pages. Regardless of the option selected, however, it still is important to understand the specifics of HTML.

HTML

Web pages are written in plain text and saved in the American Standard Code for Information Interchange format. The **American Standard Code for Information Interchange**, or **ASCII** (pronounced ASK-ee), is the most widely used coding system to represent data. Using the ASCII format makes Web pages universally readable by different Web browsers regardless of the computer platform on which they reside.

Hypertext Markup Language (**HTML**) is an authoring language that defines the structure and layout of a document so that it displays as a Web page in a Web browser, such as Microsoft Internet Explorer or Netscape Navigator. A Web page has two components: source code and document content. The **source code**, which contains tags, is program instructions. The **tags** within the source code control the appearance of the document content. **Document content** is the text and images that the browser displays. The browser interprets the tags contained within the code. The code instructs the browser how to display the Web page. For instance, if you define a line of text on your Web page as a heading, the browser knows to display this line as a heading.

All HTML tag formats are the same. They start with a left angle bracket (< or less than symbol) followed by the name of the tag and end with a right angle bracket (> or greater than symbol). Most tags have a start and an end tag and are called **two-sided tags**. The end tags are the same as the start tags except they are preceded by a forward slash (/). Some HTML tags, such as the one used to indicate a line break <BR>, do not have an end tag. These are known as **one-sided tags**. Other tags, such as the one to indicate a new paragraph <P>, have an end tag, but the end tag can be omitted. For consistency with this type of tag, it is better to include both the start and end tags.

Some tags can contain an **attribute**, or **property**, which is additional information placed within the angle brackets. Attributes are not repeated or contained in the end tag. Some attributes are used individually and other attributes can include a value modifier. A **value modifier** specifies conditions within the tag. For example, you can use a value modifier to specify the font type or size or the placement of text on the page. To create and display a centered heading, for instance, you would use the following code:

```
<H1 ALIGN="CENTER">This is the largest header tag and the text will be centered</H1>
```

In this example, H1 is the HTML tag, ALIGN is the attribute, and CENTER is the value modifier. Notice that the attribute does not appear as part of the end tag.

You can use Microsoft Notepad or WordPad (which are text editors) to create HTML documents. You place each tag in a pair around the text or section that you want to define (**mark up**) with that tag. HTML tags are not case sensitive; therefore, you can enter HTML tags in uppercase or lowercase or a combination of both. To be consistent, however, you should adopt a standard practice when typing tags. Examples in this book use uppercase.

HTML tags also are used to format the hyperlinks that connect information on the World Wide Web. HTML tags number in the hundreds, but some are used more than others. All documents, however, require four basic tags. Figure I-10 on the next page illustrates the basic tags required for all HTML documents. Table I-2 on the next page summarizes the most commonly used HTML tags.

More *About*

HTML

The World Wide Web Consortium (W3C) develops and updates Web protocols. To learn more about the most recent changes to HTML, visit the Dreamweaver MX More About Web page (scsite.com/ dreamweavermx/ more.htm) and then click W3C.

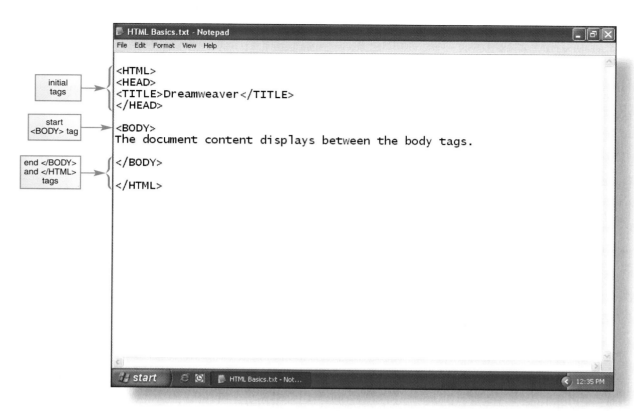

FIGURE I-10

Table I-2	Commonly Used HTML Tags
TAG	**STRUCTURE**
<HTML>...</HTML>	Encloses the entire HTML document
<HEAD>...</HEAD>	Encloses the head of the HTML document
<BODY>...</BODY>	Encloses the body of the HTML document
TAG	**TITLE AND HEADINGS**
<TITLE>...</TITLE>	Indicates the title of the document
<H1>...</H1>	Heading level 1
<H2>...</H2>	Heading level 2
<H3>...</H3>	Heading level 3
<H4>...</H4>	Heading level 4
<H5>...</H5>	Heading level 5
<H6>...</H6>	Heading level 6
TAG	**PARAGRAPHS, BREAKS, AND SEPARATORS**
<P>...</P>	Plain paragraph; end tag optional
 	Line break
<HR>	Horizontal rule line

TAG	**LISTS**
<OL>...</OL>	Ordered, numbered list
<UL>...</UL>	Unordered, bulleted list
<MENU>...</MENU>	Menu list of items
<DIR>...</DIR>	Directory listing
<LI>...</LI>	List item, used with <OL>,<UL>,<MENU>,<DIR>
<DL>...</DL>	Definition of glossary list
<DT>...</DT>	Definition term; part of a definition list
<DD>...</DD>	Corresponding definition to a definition term
TAG	**CHARACTER FORMATTING**
<B>...</B>	Bold text
<U>...</U>	Underline text
<I>...</I>	Italic text
TAG	**LINKS**
<A>...</A>	Combined with the HREF attribute, creates a link to another document or anchor
<A>...</A>	Combined with the NAME attribute, creates an anchor which can be linked to
TAG	**IMAGE**
<IMG>...</IMG>	Inserts an image into the document

Web Page Authoring Programs

Many of today's Web page authoring programs, including Dreamweaver, are a What You See Is What You Get (WYSIWYG) HTML text editor. A **WYSIWYG text editor** allows a user to view a document as it will appear in the final product and to edit the text, images, or other elements directly within that view. Before programs such as Dreamweaver existed, Web page designers were required to type, or hand-code, Web pages. Educators and Web designers still debate the issue surrounding the necessity of knowing HTML. You do not need to know HTML to create Web pages in Dreamweaver, but an understanding of HTML will help you if you need to alter Dreamweaver-generated code. If you know HTML, then you can make changes to code and Dreamweaver will accept the changes.

Macromedia Dreamweaver® MX

Dreamweaver is the standard in visual authoring. Macromedia Dreamweaver MX is part of the new MX product family that includes Macromedia Flash™ MX, ColdFusion® MX and Fireworks® MX. Dreamweaver includes features that access these separate products. Some of the new features of Dreamweaver MX include the following:

- An intuitive new workspace
- Templates designed for customized layout control
- Prebuilt code libraries
- Server technology to support ColdFusion MX, ASP.NET, and PHP websites
- Increased server support for ASP, JSP and ColdFusion applications
- XML and Web Standards Support
- Improved cascading style sheet support
- New coding features
- New accessibility features

Dreamweaver makes it easy to get started and provides you with helpful tools to enhance your Web design experience. Working in a single environment, you create, build, and manage Web sites and Internet applications. The workspace environment is customizable to fit your particular needs.

Coding tools and features included within Dreamweaver are references for HTML, cascading style sheets (CSS), and JavaScript and code editors that allow you to edit the code directly. **Macromedia Roundtrip® HTML technology** imports HTML documents without reformatting the code. Downloadable extensions from the Macromedia Web site make it easy to add functionality to any Web site. Examples of some of these extensions include shopping carts and online payment features.

Instead of writing individual HTML files for every page, use a database to store content and then retrieve the content dynamically in response to a user's request. Implementing and using this feature, you can update the information one time instead of manually editing many pages.

Dreamweaver allows you to publish Web sites with relative ease to a local area network that connects computers in a limited geographical area or on the Web for anyone with Internet access. The concepts and techniques presented in this book provide the tools you need to plan, develop, and publish professional Web sites, such as Web sites shown in Figures I-11 and I-12 on the next page.

More About

Macromedia

Evaluation copies of Dreamweaver MX and other Macromedia products are available on the Macromedia Web site. To learn more about Macromedia products, visit the Dreamweaver MX More About Web page (scsite.com/dreamweavermx/more.htm) and then click Macromedia.

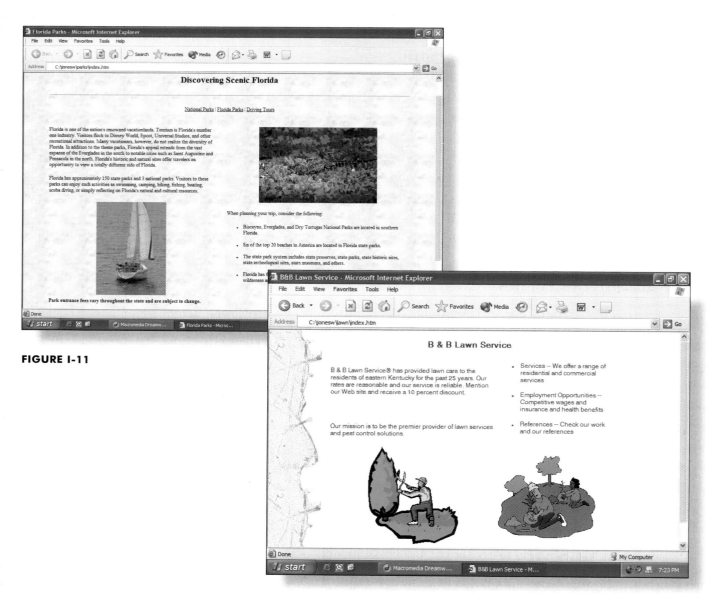

FIGURE I-11

FIGURE I-12

Summary

The Introduction to Web Development and Macromedia Dreamweaver provided an overview of the Internet and the World Wide Web and the key terms associated with those technologies. An overview of the six basic types of Web pages was presented. The Introduction presented information on developing a Web site, including planning basics. Designing a Web site and each phase within this process was discussed. Testing, publishing, and maintaining a Web site was also presented, including an overview of obtaining a domain name, acquiring server space, and uploading a Web site. Methods and tools used to create Web pages were introduced. A short overview of HTML and some of the more commonly used HTML tags were presented. Finally, the advantages of using Dreamweaver in Web development were discussed. These advantages include a WYSIWYG editor; a visual, customizable development environment; accessibility compliance; downloadable extensions; database access capabilities; and in-product reference sources.

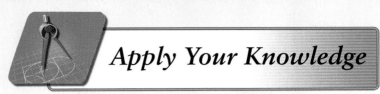

Apply Your Knowledge

1 Web Page Creation

Instructions: As discussed in this chapter, creating a Web site involves planning, designing, developing, reviewing and testing, publishing, and maintaining. Open the applyI.doc file on the Dreamweaver Data Disk. See the inside back cover of this book for instructions for downloading the Data Disk or see your instructor for information on accessing the files required for this book. As shown in Table I-3, the applyI.doc file contains information about the Web site creation process. Enter your answer to the questions in this table to develop a plan for creating a Web site.

Table I-3 Creating a Web Site		
PLANNING		
Web site name:	What is your Web site name?	
Web site type:	What is the Web site type: portal, news, business/ marketing, advocacy, informational, personal?	
Web site purpose:	What is the purpose of your Web site?	
Target Audience:	How can you identify your target audience?	
Web Technologies to be used:	Will you design for broadband or baseband? Explain your selection.	
Content:	What topics will you cover? How much information will you present on each topic? How will you attract your audience? What will you do to entice your audience to return to your Web site? How will you keep the Web site updated?	
Text, images, and multimedia:	Will your site contain text only? What type of images will you include? Where will you obtain your images? Will you have a common logo? Will plug-ins be required?	
DESIGNING		
Navigation map:	What type of structure will you use? What tools will you use to design your navigation map?	
Navigational elements:	What navigational elements will you include?	
DEVELOPING		
Typography:	What font will you use? How many different fonts will you use on your site?	
Images:	How will you use images to enhance your site? Will you use a background image?	

(continued)

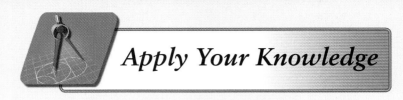

Apply Your Knowledge

Web Page Creation *(continued)*

Table I-3 Creating a Web Site		
DEVELOPING (continued)		
Page Layout:	What type of layout will you use? How many topics per page? How will text be presented: bulleted or paragraph style? Will the audience need to scroll the page?	
Color:	What color combinations will you use for your site? To what elements will you apply the color(s) — fonts, background, tables, other elements?	
REVIEWING AND TESTING		
Review:	What elements will you review? Will you use a group review?	
Testing:	What elements will you test? Will you use self-testing? Will you use group testing?	
PUBLISHING		
Domain name:	What is your domain name? Have you registered your domain name? What ISP will host your Web site? What criteria did you use to select the ISP?	
MAINTAINING		
Ongoing maintenance:	How often will you update your Web site? What elements will you update? Will you add additional features? Does your ISP provide server logs? Will you use the server logs for maintenance purposes?	

Perform the following steps using your word processing program and browser.

1. With the file applyI.doc open in your word processing program, select a name for your Web site.
2. Use a specialized search engine at one of the many accredited domain name registrars to verify that your selected Web site name is available.
3. Answer each question in the table. Type your answers in column 3.
4. Save the document with the file name, knowI-1.doc. Print a copy of the document and hand it in or e-mail it to your instructor.

In the Lab

1 Using Internet Explorer

Problem: Internet Explorer (IE) 6 is Microsoft's latest Web browser. IE has many new features that can make your work on the Internet more efficient. Using the Media bar, for example, you can play music, video, or multimedia files, listen to your favorite Internet radio station, and enhance your browsing experience. You can customize the image toolbar that displays when you point to an image on a Web page. IE also includes other enhancements. Visit the Microsoft Internet Explorer How-to Articles Web page (Figure I-13) and select three articles containing topics with which you are not familiar. Read the articles and then create a word processing document detailing what you learned.

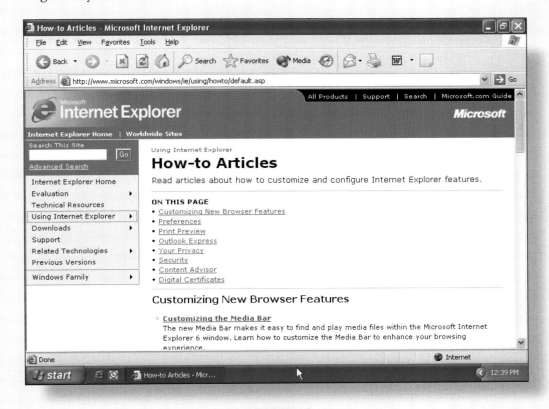

FIGURE I-13

Instructions: Perform the following tasks.

1. Start your browser. Open the Microsoft Internet Explorer How-to Articles Web page (microsoft.com/windows/ie/using/howto/default.asp).
2. Select three articles that contain information with which you are not familiar.
3. Click the link for each article and read the article.
4. Start your word processing program.
5. List three important points that you learned from this Web site.
6. Write a summary of what you learned from each article. Include within your summary your opinion of the article and if you will apply what you learned or use it with your Web browser.
7. Save the document with the file name, labI-1.doc. Print a copy of the document and hand it in or e-mail it to your instructor.

In the Lab

2 Types of Web Pages

Problem: A Web designer is familiar with different types of Web pages and the type of information displayed on these types of Web pages. The Introduction describes six types of Web pages. Search the Internet and locate at least one example of each type of Web page.

Instructions: Perform the following tasks.

1. Start your browser. Open the Google (google.com) search engine Web page (Figure I-14) and search for an example of the following types of Web pages: portal, news, business/marketing, advocacy, informational, and personal.

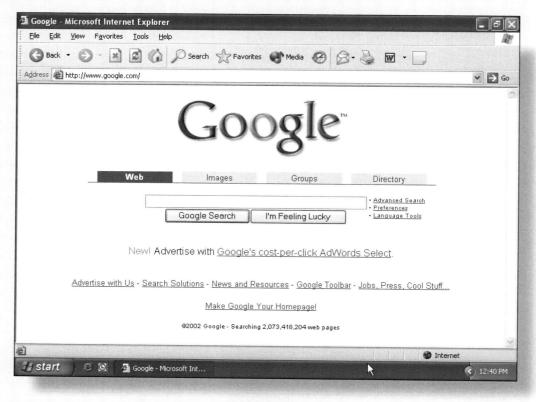

FIGURE I-14

2. Start your word processing program.
3. Copy and paste the link from each of these Web page types into your word processing document.
4. Identify the type of Web page for each link.
5. Explain why you selected this Web page and how it fits the definition of the specific type.
6. Save the document with the file name, labI-2.doc. Print a copy of the document and hand it in or e-mail it to your instructor.

In the Lab

3 Web Site Hosting

Problem: Selecting the correct host or ISP for your Web site can be a confusing process. Many Web sites offer this service, but determining which one is best for your particular needs can be somewhat complicated. Assume your Web site will sell a product. Compare several ISPs and select one that will best meet your needs.

Instructions: Perform the following tasks.

1. Review the information and questions on page DW I.15 discussing guidelines for acquiring active service space to host your Web site.
2. Start your browser. Open the Hosting Repository Web page shown in Figure I-15.

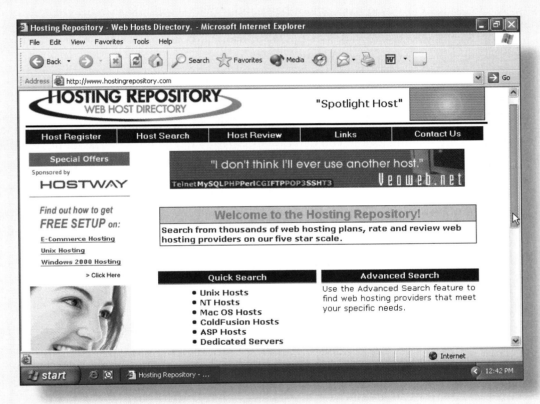

FIGURE I-15

3. Click the Dedicated Servers link.
4. Click one of the host server links and review the information relating to the services offered by your selected ISP.
5. Start your word processing program.
6. Read and answer the ten questions on page DW I.15. Use the information provided in the services offered by your selected ISP.
7. Write a short summary explaining why you would or would not select this ISP to host your Web site.
8. Save the document with the file name, labI-3.doc. Print a copy of the document and hand it in or e-mail it to your instructor.

Cases and Places

The difficulty of these case studies varies:
▶ are the least difficult; ▶▶ are more difficult; and ▶▶▶ are the most difficult.

1 ▶ Use a search engine such as Google (google.com) and research information about planning a Web site. Use your word processing program and write a two-page summary of what you learned. Save the document as caseI-1.doc. Print a copy and hand it in or e-mail a copy to your instructor.

2 ▶ Your goal is to create a personal Web site navigation map that contains three pages – the home page, a page about your favorite hobbies, and a page about places you like to visit. On a piece of paper, draw a navigation map for your proposed Web site. Write a sentence or two describing the type of structure you used and why you selected that structure. Save the document as caseI-2.doc. Print a copy of the document and hand it in or e-mail it to your instructor.

3 ▶▶ Plug-ins are used on many Web sites. Start your browser and search for plug-ins. Prepare a list of the plug-ins you found. Create a summary statement describing how and why you could use each plug-in in a Web site. Include the link where you can download each of the plug-ins. Save the document as caseI-3.doc. Print a copy of the document and hand it in or e-mail it to your instructor.

4 ▶▶ Typography within a Web page is one of its more important elements. Start your browser and search for examples of Web sites that include what you consider appropriate typography and Web sites with inappropriate typography. Write a short summary of why you consider these appropriate and inappropriate. Copy and paste the Web site addresses into your document. Save the document as caseI-4.doc. Print a copy of the document and hand it in or e-mail it to your instructor.

5 ▶▶▶ Web site structures are of four types: linear, hierarchical, grid, and random. Search the Internet for Web sites illustrating each of these structures. Describe the Web site and explain why you think this is an appropriate or inappropriate structure for that particular Web site. Include the Web site addresses for each site. Save the document as caseI-5.doc. Print a copy of the document and hand it in or e-mail it to your instructor

Macromedia Dreamweaver MX

Creating a Dreamweaver Web Page and Local Site

You will have mastered the material in this project when you can:

O B J E C T I V E S

- Describe Dreamweaver and identify its key features
- Start Dreamweaver
- Describe the Dreamweaver window and workspace
- Open and close panels
- Create a local site using the Site Definition Wizard
- Create a Web page
- Apply a color scheme
- Display and describe the Property inspector
- Format and modify text elements on a Web page
- Insert a horizontal rule
- Define and display the Insert bar
- Define and insert a line break and special characters
- Change a Web page title
- Check spelling
- Insert an absolute link
- Save a Web page
- Preview a Web page in a Web browser
- Print a Web page
- Define Dreamweaver Help
- Quit Dreamweaver
- Open a Web page

Macromedia Dreamweaver MX

Creating a Dreamweaver Web Page and Local Site

CASE PERSPECTIVE

Florida native Will Jones worked with you last summer at a state environmental agency. Your job at the agency included Internet communications. Because you both love the outdoors, particularly Florida's state and national parks, you became good friends. Will visits several parks every year. During each visit, he discovers something new and exciting. Will wants to share his knowledge and provide a way to make Florida residents and visitors aware of the uniqueness, beauty, and wildlife of the parks.

Will knows the far-reaching capabilities of the Internet. He wants to use the Web to communicate to the public about Florida's parks, but he has limited knowledge about Web design and development. Will knows that your interest and experience with the Internet could assist him in this endeavor, and he asks for your help. You like the idea and tell him that you can create a Web site using Dreamweaver. You get together to plan the index page. When you are finished creating the Discovering Scenic Florida Web page, you will show it to Will for his feedback.

What Is Macromedia Dreamweaver® MX?

Macromedia Dreamweaver® MX is a powerful Web page authoring and Web site management software program and HTML editor used to design, code, and create professional-looking Web pages. The visual editing features of Dreamweaver allow you to create pages without writing a line of code. Dreamweaver provides many tools and features, including the following:

- **Automatic Web Page Creation** – Dreamweaver provides the tools you can use to develop your Web pages without having to spend hours writing HTML code. Dreamweaver automatically generates the HTML code necessary to publish your Web pages.
- **Web Site Management** – Dreamweaver enables you to view a site, including all local and remote files associated with the selected site. Using Dreamweaver, you can perform standard maintenance operations such as viewing, opening, and moving files; transferring files between local and remote sites; designing your site navigation with the Site Map; and more.
- **Standard Macromedia Web Authoring Tools** – Dreamweaver includes a user interface that is consistent across all Macromedia authoring tools. This consistency enables easy integration with other Macromedia Web-related programs, such as Macromedia Flash™, Director® Shockwave® Studio, ColdFusion®, and others.

Other key features include the integrated user interface, the integrated file explorer, panel management, database integration, and standards and accessibility support. Dreamweaver MX is customizable and can run in operating systems such as Windows XP, Windows 2000, Windows NT, and Mac OS X.

Project One — Florida Parks

To create documents similar to those you will encounter on the Web and in academic, business, and personal environments, you can use Dreamweaver to produce Web pages such as the Discovering Scenic Florida Web page shown in Figure 1-1. The Web page shown in Figure 1-1 is the index page for the Florida Parks Web site. This informational page provides interesting facts about Florida's state and national parks. The page begins with a centered main heading, followed by a horizontal rule. Following the rule are two short informational paragraphs. The first paragraph contains two occurrences of the registered trademark symbol. Following the second paragraph is an introductory sentence for a bulleted list. The list contains four bulleted items. A concluding sentence, the author's name, and current date end the page. A Dreamweaver color scheme is applied to the page.

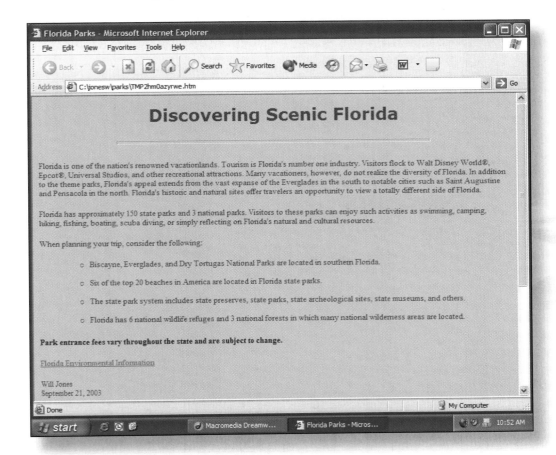

FIGURE 1-1

Starting Dreamweaver

Getting started in Dreamweaver is as easy as opening an existing HTML document or creating a new document. The Dreamweaver environment consists of toolbars, windows, objects, panels, inspectors, and tools you use to create your Web pages and to manage your Web site, which is a collection of Web pages. It is important to understand the basic concepts behind the Dreamweaver workspace and how to choose options, use inspectors and panels, and set preferences that best fit your work style.

The first time Dreamweaver is launched after the initial installation, a Workspace Setup dialog box is displayed with two options: Dreamweaver MX Workspace or Dreamweaver 4 Workspace. If you are installing the program on your own computer, select Dreamweaver MX Workspace. The Dreamweaver program starts and the Welcome window is displayed. If you choose to do so, select a tutorial category or categories to review and then close the Welcome window. This startup screen is a one-time event. The tutorials, however, are still accessible through Dreamweaver Help. If you are opening Dreamweaver from a computer at your school, most likely the program is set up and ready to use.

To start Dreamweaver, Windows must be running. Perform the following steps or ask your instructor how to start Dreamweaver.

Steps To Start Dreamweaver

1 **Click the Start button on the Windows taskbar, point to All Programs on the Start menu, point to Macromedia on the All Programs submenu, and then point to Macromedia Dreamweaver MX on the Macromedia submenu.**

The Start menu, All Programs submenu, and Macromedia submenu are displayed (Figure 1-2).

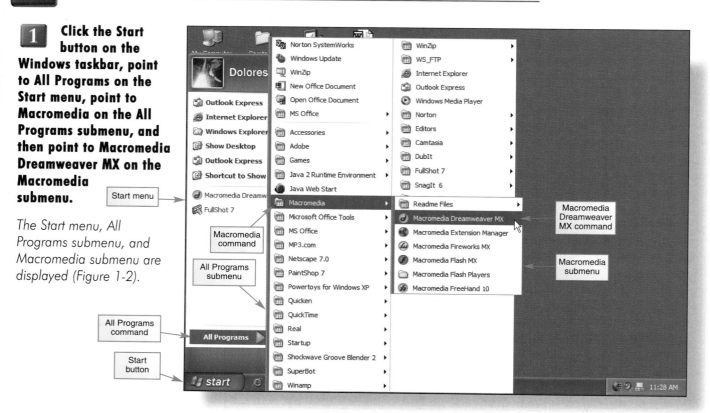

FIGURE 1-2

2 **Click Macromedia Dreamweaver MX. If necessary, maximize the Dreamweaver window and the Document window by clicking the Maximize button in the upper-right corner of the windows.**

The Macromedia splash screen is displayed instantaneously and then Dreamweaver displays an untitled Document window (Figure 1-3). The Dreamweaver window contains menu names, tool-bars, and panel groups. The Windows taskbar displays the Macromedia Dreamweaver MX button, indicating Dreamweaver is running. Dreamweaver retains the settings last used when the program was closed, so your window may look different.

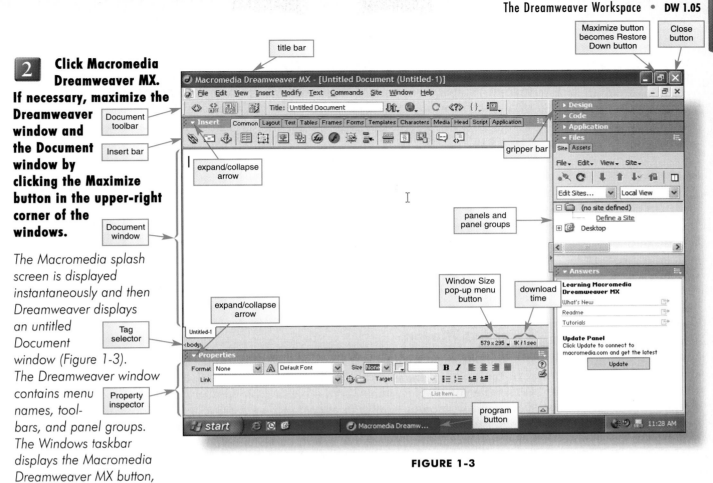

FIGURE 1-3

Other Ways

1. Double-click Dreamweaver icon on desktop

The screen in Figure 1-3 shows how the Dreamweaver window looks the first time you start Dreamweaver after installation on most computers. The **workspace** is an integrated environment in which the Document window and panels are incorporated into one larger application window. The panel groups are docked, or attached, on the right. The Insert bar is located at the top of the Document window and the Property inspector is located at the bottom of the Document window. Panels can be moved, resized, and/or collapsed to accommodate individual preferences.

The Dreamweaver Workspace

The **Dreamweaver workspace** consists of a variety of components to make your work more efficient and Web pages appear more professional. This section discusses the following components of the Dreamweaver window: title bar, Document window, panels and panel groups, status bar, menu bar, and toolbars.

As you learn to use each of these tools, you will discover some redundancy among these elements. To apply a Font tag, for instance, you can access the command through the Property inspector or on the Text menu. The different options are available for various user preferences. The projects in this book present the more commonly used methods. The Other Ways boxes at the end of many of the step-by-step sequences give other ways to accomplish a task when they are available. As you become proficient working in the Dreamweaver environment, you will develop a technique for using the tools that best suits your personal preferences.

Title Bar

The **title bar** (Figure 1-3 on page DW 1.05) displays the application name, Macromedia Dreamweaver MX; in brackets, the Web page title; and, in parentheses, the file path and file name of the displayed Web page. In Figure 1-3, the title bar displays [Untitled Document (Untitled-1)]. Untitled Document represents the Web page title and Untitled-1 represents the file path and file name. Following the file name, Dreamweaver displays an asterisk (shown in Figure 1-4) if you have made changes that have not yet been saved. After you give a Web page a title and save the document, the title bar reflects these changes by displaying the title and path and removing the asterisk.

Document Window

The **Document window** displays the current document, or Web page, including text, tables, graphics, and other items. In Figure 1-3, the Document window is blank. Each time you start Dreamweaver, a blank untitled document is created. The Document window is similar in appearance to the Internet Explorer or Netscape browser window. You work in the Document window in one of three views: **Design view**, the design environment where you assemble your Web page elements and design your page (Figure 1-3 displays Design view); **Code view**, which is a hand-coding environment for writing and editing code; or **Code view and Design view**, which allows you to see both Code view and Design view for the same document in a single window. When you start Dreamweaver, the default is Design view. These views are discussed in Project 2.

Panels and Panel Groups

Panel groups are sets of related panels docked together below one heading. Panels provide control over a wide range of Dreamweaver commands and functions. Each panel group can be expanded or collapsed, and can be docked or undocked with other panel groups. Panel groups also can be docked to the integrated application window. This makes it easy to access the panels you need without cluttering your workspace. Panels within a panel group appear as tabs.

To expand a panel group, click the expand/collapse arrow to the left of the group's name; to undock and move a panel group, drag the gripper bar at the left edge of the group's title bar (Figure 1-3). To open panels, use the Window menu. Each panel is explained in detail as it is used in the projects throughout the book.

Some panels, such as the Property inspector and the Insert bar, are stand-alone panels. The **Insert bar** allows quick access to objects and behaviors. It contains buttons for creating various types of objects, such as images, tables, layers, frames, and tags, and inserting them into a document. The buttons are organized into tabs. Each object on a tab is a piece of HTML code that allows you to set various attributes as you insert it. For example, you can insert an image by clicking the Image button on the Insert bar and then set the alignment attribute through the Property inspector. The default position for the Insert bar is at the top of the Document window.

The **Property inspector** displays settings for the selected element's properties, or attributes. This panel is **context sensitive** because it changes based on the selected element, which can include text, tables, images, and other elements. When Dreamweaver starts, the Property inspector is positioned at the bottom of the Document window and displays text properties. Clicking the expand/collapse arrow of the Insert bar or Property inspector expands or collapses these panels (Figure 1-3 on page DW 1.05). To move the Insert bar or Property inspector, drag the gripper at the left edge of the title bar (Figure 1-4).

Status Bar

The **status bar** at the bottom of the Document window (Figure 1-3) provides additional information about the document you are creating. The status bar presents the following information.

▶ **Tag selector:** Displays the hierarchy of tags surrounding the current selection. Click any tag in the hierarchy to select that tag and all its contents.

▶ **Window Size pop-up menu button:** Displays the Window Size pop-up menu, which includes the window's current dimensions (in pixels).

▶ **Estimated document size and download time:** Displays the size and estimated download time of the current page. Dreamweaver MX calculates size based on the entire contents of the page, including all linked objects such as images and plug-ins.

Menu Bar

The **menu bar** displays the Dreamweaver menu names (Figure 1-4). Each menu contains a list of commands you can use to perform tasks such as retrieving, storing, printing, previewing, and exporting data in your Web page. When you point to a menu name on the menu bar, the area of the menu bar containing the name is highlighted.

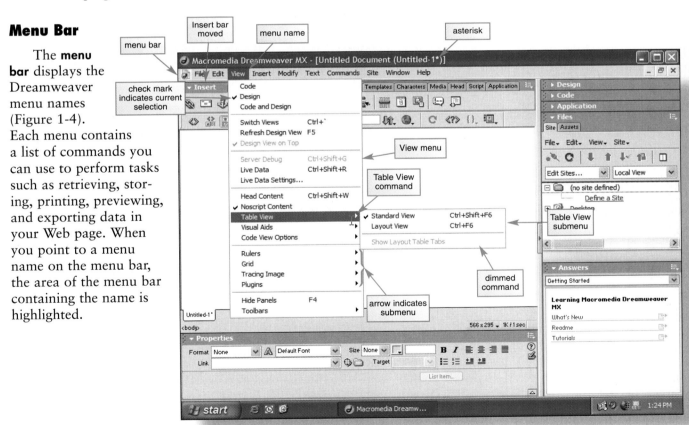

FIGURE 1-4

To display a menu, such as the View menu (Figure 1-4 on page DW 1.07), click the View menu name on the menu bar. If you point to a command on a menu that has an arrow to its right edge, a submenu displays another list of commands. Most menus display some commands that appear gray, or dimmed, instead of black, which indicates they are not available for the current selection.

Toolbars

Dreamweaver contains two toolbars: the Document toolbar and the Standard toolbar. You can choose to display or hide the toolbars by clicking View on the menu bar and then clicking Toolbars. If a toolbar name has a check mark next to it, it is displayed in the window. To hide the toolbar, you click the name of the toolbar with the check mark, and it no longer is displayed.

The **Document toolbar** (Figure 1-5) is the default toolbar that displays in the Document window. It contains buttons that provide different views of the Document window (e.g., Show Code View, Show Code and Design Views, Show Design View, and Live Data View); access to the Reference panel; and some common operations such as file management, browser preview, Code Navigation, and the Title text box through which you name your Web page. All View option commands also are available through the View menu.

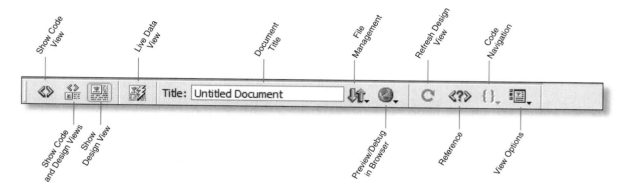

FIGURE 1-5

The Standard toolbar (Figure 1-6) contains buttons for common operations from the File and Edit menus: New, Open, Save, Save All, Cut, Copy, Paste, Undo, and Redo. The Standard toolbar does not display by default in the Dreamweaver Document window when you first start Dreamweaver. You can display the Standard toolbar through the Toolbars command on the View menu, or by right-clicking a toolbar anywhere but on a button and then clicking Standard on the shortcut menu.

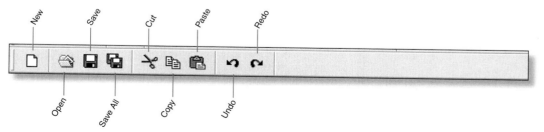

FIGURE 1-6

Opening and Closing Panels in the Workspace

The Dreamweaver workspace accommodates different styles of working and levels of expertise. Through the workspace, you can open and close the panel groups and other Dreamweaver features as needed. To open a panel group, select and then click the name of a panel on the Window menu. Closing unused panels provides uncluttered workspace in the Document window. To close an individual panel group, click Close Panel Group on the Options menu accessed through the panel group's title bar (Figure 1-7). To expand/collapse a panel, click the panel's expand/collapse arrow.

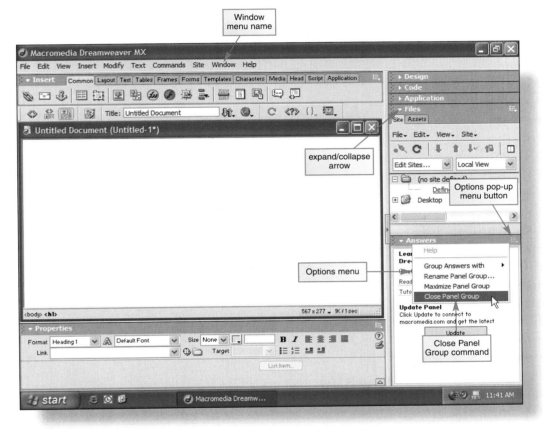

FIGURE 1-7

Opening and closing each panel individually is a time-consuming task. Dreamweaver provides a shortcut to accomplish this job quickly. The F4 **key** is a toggle key that opens and/or closes all panels and toolbars, except the Document toolbar and menu bar, at one time. The following step closes all open panels.

To Close All Open Panels

1 **Press the F4 key.**

All the open panels and inspectors close and maximum workspace is available within the Document window (Figure 1-8).

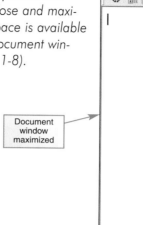

Document window maximized

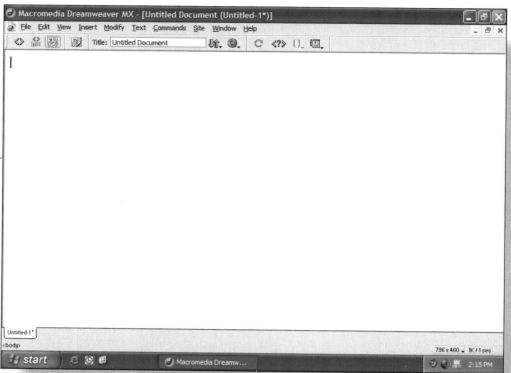

FIGURE 1-8

Creating a Local Site

Web design and Web site management are two important skills that a builder of Web sites must understand and apply. Dreamweaver MX is a site creation and management tool. To use Dreamweaver efficiently, you first must develop the local site. After defining the local site, you then publish to a remote site. Publishing to a remote site is covered in Project 3.

The general definition of a **site**, or Web site, is a set of linked documents with shared attributes, such as related topics, a similar design, or a shared purpose. In Dreamweaver, however, site can refer to any of the following:

- A **Web site**, which is a set of pages on a server that are viewed through a Web browser by a visitor to the site.

- A **remote site**, which are files on the server that make up a Web site, from the author's point of view rather than a visitor's point of view.

- A **local site**, which are files on your local disk that correspond to the files on the remote site. You edit the files on your local disk, and then upload them to the remote site.

- A Dreamweaver **site definition**, which is a set of defining characteristics for a local site, plus information on how the local site corresponds to a remote site.

As a builder and designer of Web sites, you will find that the site structure feature provides a way to maintain and organize your files.

All Dreamweaver Web sites begin with a local root folder. As you become familiar with Dreamweaver and complete the projects in this book, you will find references to a **local root folder**, a **root folder**, and **root**. These terms are interchangeable. This folder is no different from any other folder on your hard drive, except for the way in which Dreamweaver views it. When Dreamweaver looks for Web pages, links, images, and other media, the program defaults to the designated root folder. Any media within the Web site that are outside of the root folder will not display when the Web site is previewed in a Web browser. Within the root folder, you can create additional folders or subfolders to organize graphics and other elements. A **subfolder** (also called a **nested folder**) is a folder inside another folder.

Dreamweaver provides two options to create a site: create the root folder and any subfolders; or, create the pages and then create the folders when saving the files. In this project, you create the root folder and then create the Web page.

One of Dreamweaver's more prominent organizational tools is its Site panel. Use the **Site panel** for standard file maintenance operations, such as the following:

- Creating files
- Viewing, opening, and moving files
- Creating folders
- Deleting items

The Site panel enables you to view a site, including all local, remote, and testing server files associated with a selected site. In this project you view only the local site.

Using Site Definition to Create a Local Site

Because many files are required for a Dreamweaver Web site, it is advisable to create the projects using another location rather than the floppy disk drive (A:). Steps in this project instruct you to create the local site at the C:\ on the computer's hard drive. It is suggested, however, that you check with your instructor to verify the location and path you will use to create and save your local Web site. Other options may include a Zip® drive or a network drive. You first will create a folder using your last name and first initial. Examples in this book use Will Jones as the Web site author. Thus, the Will Jones folder is jonesw. Next, you will create a subfolder and name it parks. All Florida Parks-related files and subfolders are stored within the parks folder. When you navigate through this folder hierarchy, you are navigating along the path.

When creating a Web site, it is important to understand paths. The term, path, is sometimes confusing for new users of the Web. It is, however, a simple concept: A **path** is the succession of folders that must be navigated to get from one folder to another. In the DOS world, folders are referred to as **directories**. These two terms often are used interchangeably. To organize a Web site and understand how Web documents are accessed, it is important to understand paths and folders.

A typical path structure has a **master folder**, usually called the root and designated by the backslash (\) symbol. This folder contains within it all other nested folders or subfolders. Further, each folder may contain additional nested folders or subfolders. The Web site files are contained in these folders. The path and folder within the Florida Parks Web site are C:\jonesw\parks\. In Project 2, you will add an images folder to the site, and the path to that folder will be C:\jonesw\parks\Images\. When you create the site, you will use your last name and first initial for the root folder (the your name folder). In all references to jonesw, substitute your last name and first initial.

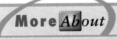

More About

Site Definition

For more advanced users, the Site Definition dialog box includes an Advanced tab based on the Dreamweaver 4 interface.

You create a site using the Site Definition dialog box. Two approaches are available: Basic or Advanced. The Basic approach, or **Site Definition Wizard**, guides you through site setup step by step. As you become more proficient in Dreamweaver, you can switch to the Advanced method.

Use the Site Definition Wizard and perform the following steps to create a local Web site.

Steps **To Use the Site Definition Wizard to Create a Local Web Site**

1 **Click Site on the menu bar and then point to New Site (Figure 1-9).**

Dreamweaver displays the Site menu and the New Site command is highlighted (Figure 1-9).

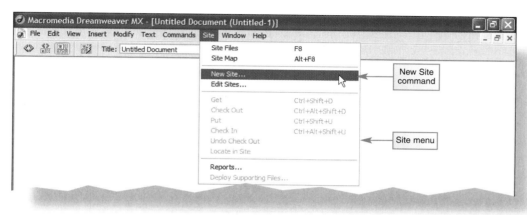

FIGURE 1-9

2 **Click New Site. If necessary, click the Basic tab.**

Dreamweaver displays the Site Definition dialog box with the Editing Files options (Figure 1-10)

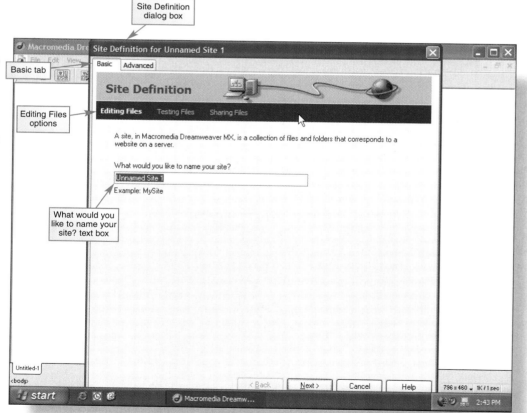

FIGURE 1-10

3 **Type** Florida Parks **in the What would you like to name your site? text box. Point to the Next button.**

Florida Parks is displayed in the What would you like to name your site? text box (Figure 1-11). This name is for reference only. It is not part of the path.

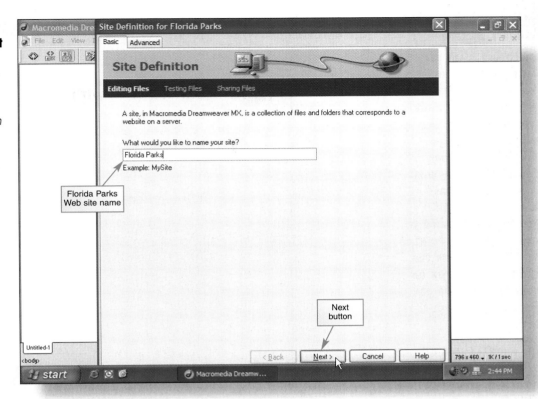

FIGURE 1-11

4 **Click the Next button. If necessary, click No, I do not want to use a server technology. Point to the Next button.**

The Site Definition dialog box displays the Editing Files, Part 2 options (Figure 1-12).

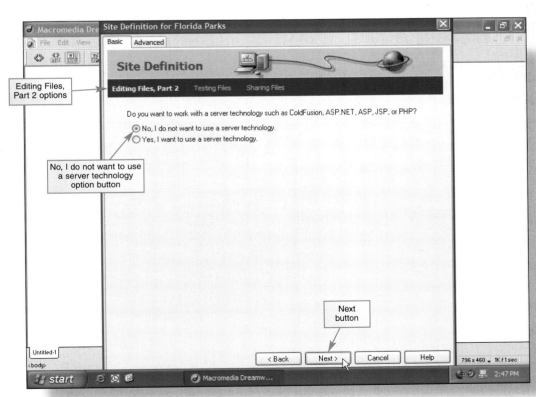

FIGURE 1-12

5 Click the Next button. If necessary, click Edit local copies on my machine, then upload to server when ready (recommended). If necessary, change the Where on your computer do you want to store your files? path to C:\ or the location designated by your instructor. Point to the Folder icon to the right of the Where on your computer do you want to store your files? text box.

The Site Definition dialog box displays the Editing Files, Part 3 options (Figure 1-13). The path in the Where on your computer do you want to store your files? text box is C:\.

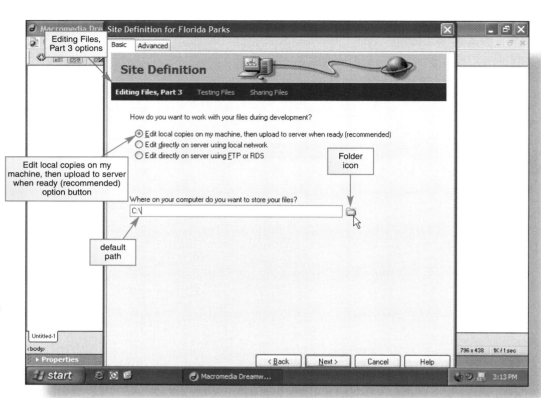

FIGURE 1-13

6 Click the folder icon. Point to the Create New Folder button.

The Choose Local Root Folder for Site Florida Parks dialog box is displayed (Figure 1-14). Settings on your computer will determine what displays in the Select box. Folders on your computer will be different. In Figure 1-14, Local Disk (C:) is the default.

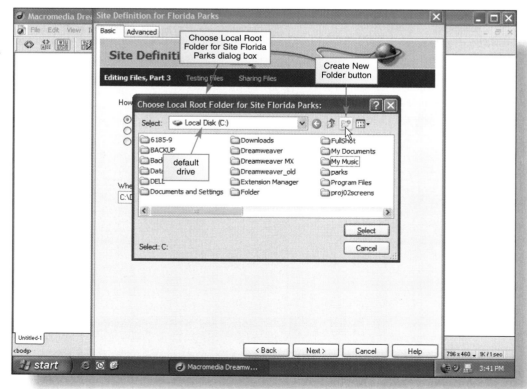

FIGURE 1-14

7 **Click the Create New Folder button.**

The New Folder text box is displayed (Figure 1-15). New Folder is highlighted.

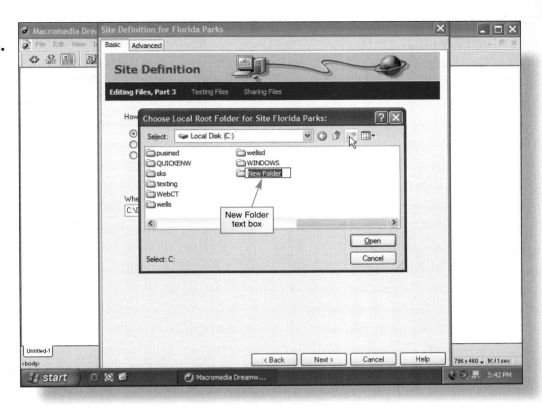

FIGURE 1-15

8 **Type your last name and first initial as the folder name and then press the ENTER key to select the folder. Point to the Open button.**

The last name and first initial of the Web page author are displayed (Figure 1-16). As shown in Figure 1-16, jonesw is the author in this project. Within the your name folder, you create a subfolder for each Web site you define. All of your projects, including end-of-project exercises, will be saved in subfolders under the your name folder.

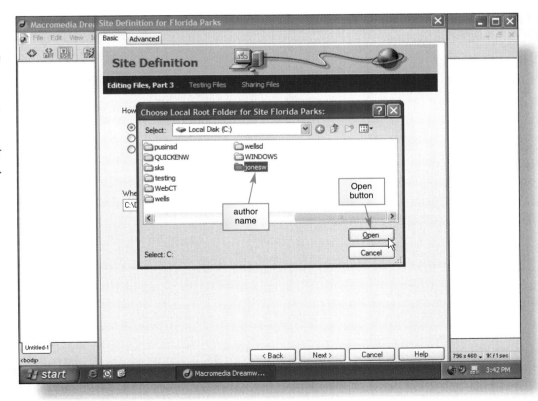

FIGURE 1-16

9   **Click the Open button and then point to the Create New Folder button (Figure 1-17).**

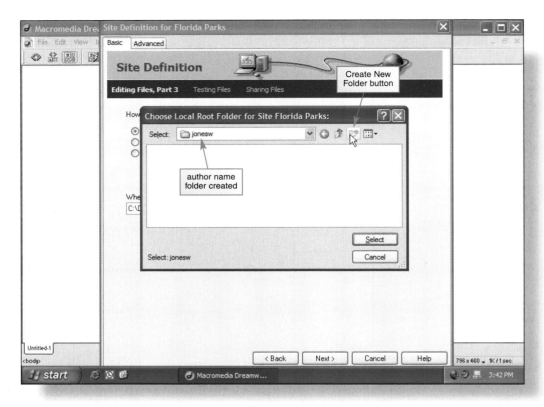

FIGURE 1-17

10   **Click the Create New Folder button.**

The New Folder text box is displayed (Figure 1-18).

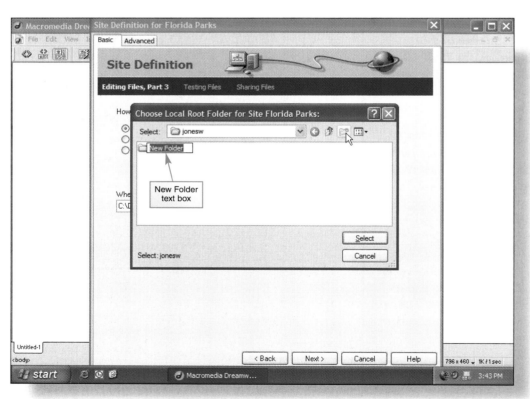

FIGURE 1-18

11 **Type** parks **in the New Folder text box and then press the** ENTER **key to select the folder. Point to the Open button.**

The parks subfolder is created (Figure 1-19).

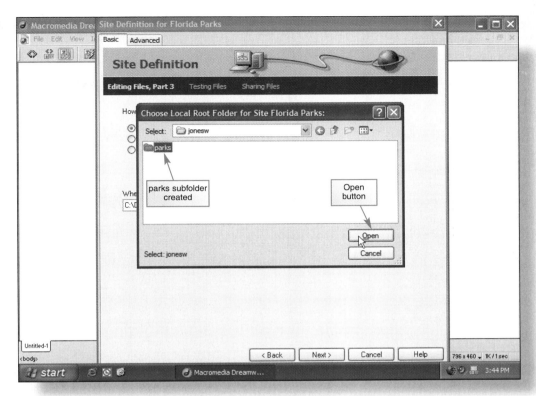

FIGURE 1-19

12 **Click the Open button and then point to the Select button.**

The parks subfolder name displays in the Select box (Figure 1-20). You have created a local root folder for the Florida Parks Web site. All subfolders and files pertaining to the parks site will be saved in this local root folder.

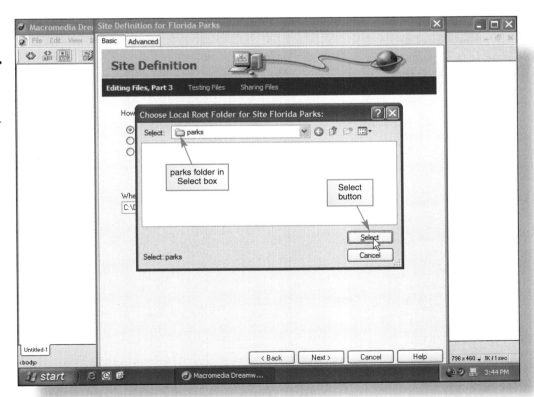

FIGURE 1-20

13 **Click the Select button and then point to the Next button.**

The Site Definition dialog box displays the Editing Files, Part 3 options with C:\jonesw\parks\ displayed in the Where on your computer do you want to store your files? text box (Figure 1-21). Your name and initial will display instead of jonesw. The path C:\jonesw\parks is the name of the local root folder. The folder jonesw is an organizational folder for this Web site and any additional Web sites you create.

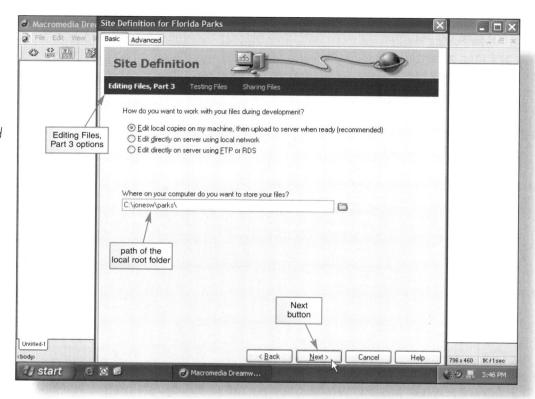

FIGURE 1-21

14 **Click the Next button. Point to the How do you connect to your remote server? box arrow.**

The Site Definition dialog box displays the Sharing Files options (Figure 1-22).

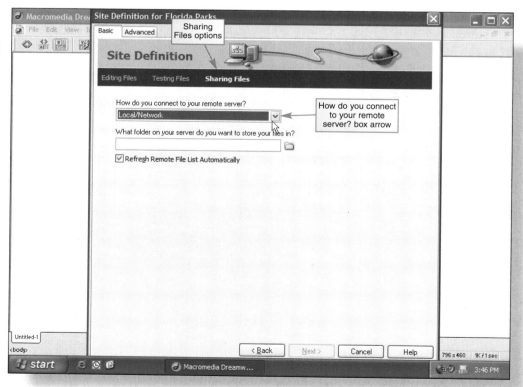

FIGURE 1-22

15 Click the How do you connect to your remote server? box arrow and then point to None in the list.

None is highlighted in the list (Figure 1-23).

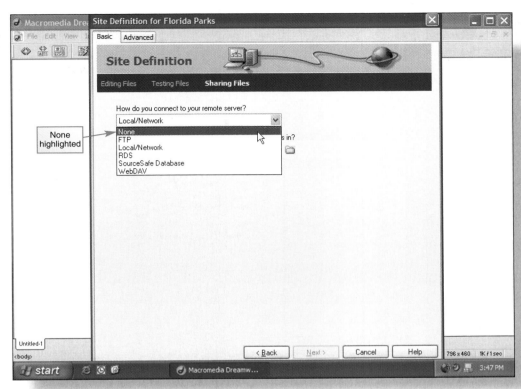

FIGURE 1-23

16 Click None and then point to the Next button.

Selecting None means that you are not connecting to a server at this time (Figure 1-24).

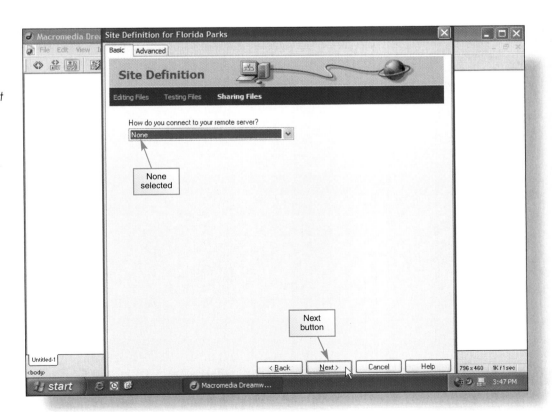

FIGURE 1-24

17 **Click the Next button and then point to the Done button.**

The Site Definition dialog box displays the Summary options (Figure 1-25). A summary of your selected settings is shown.

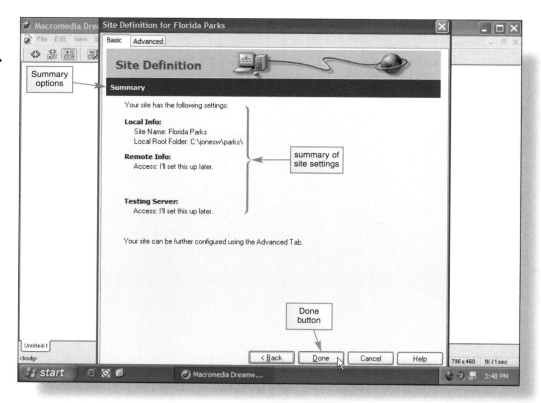

FIGURE 1-25

18 **Click the Done button.**

Dreamweaver displays the Document window and the Site panel in the Files panel group (Figure 1-26). The path to the Florida Parks site is displayed in the Site panel.

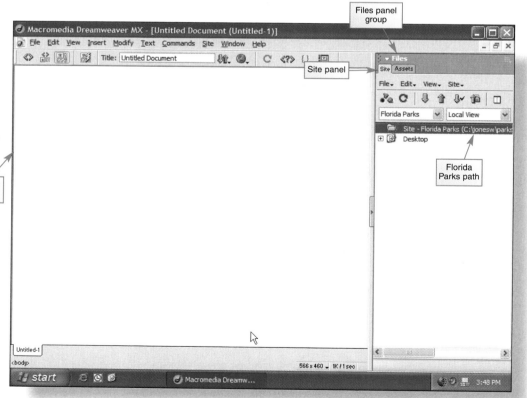

FIGURE 1-26

Other Ways

1. On Site menu click New Site, click Advanced tab

Deleting or Editing a Web Site

For various reasons, such as simply starting over, you may need to delete or edit a Web site. To delete or edit a Web site, click Site on the menu bar and then click Edit Sites. Invoking the **Edit Sites command** displays the Edit Sites dialog box (Figure 1-27). Select the site name and then click the Remove button to delete the site. Dreamweaver displays a Macromedia Dreamweaver MX caution dialog box providing you with an opportunity to cancel. Click the No button to cancel. Otherwise, click the Yes button and Dreamweaver deletes the site. To edit a site, click the site name and then click the Edit button. Dreamweaver displays the Site Definition dialog box, and from there, you can change any of the options you selected when you first created the site (Figure 1-27). Deleting a site in Dreamweaver removes the settings for the site. The files and folders remain and must be deleted separately.

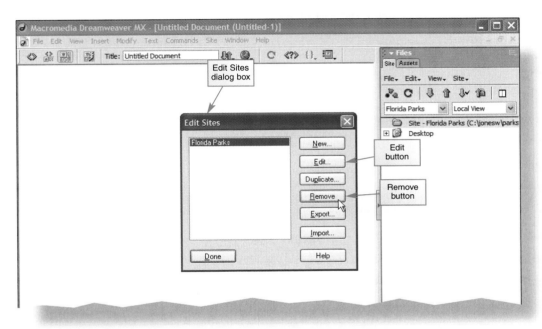

FIGURE 1-27

Color Schemes

Most Web pages display with a default white or gray background. Generally, the browser used to display the Web page determines the default background. You can enhance your Web page by adding a background image and/or background color. You add a background color by applying a color scheme in this project and add a background image in Project 2.

When you use a background color, you want to use Web-safe colors. **Web-safe colors** are colors that will display correctly on the computer screen when someone is viewing your Web page in a browser.

Adding a Color Scheme

Dreamweaver provides a series of Web-safe preset color schemes. Each scheme includes a background, text, active links, and visited links colors. Complete the steps on the next two pages to add a color scheme to the Florida Parks Web page.

To Add a Color Scheme

1 **Click Commands on the menu bar and then point to Set Color Scheme.**

The Commands menu is displayed (Figure 1-28).

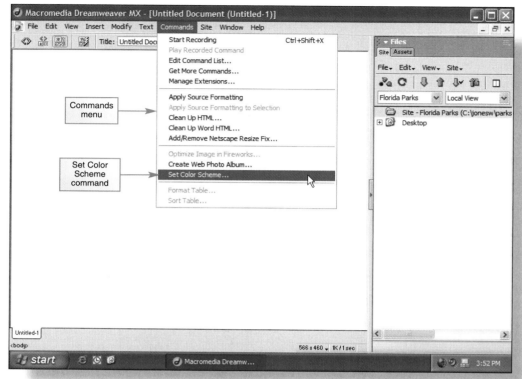

FIGURE 1-28

2 **Click Set Color Scheme and then point to Green in the Background list.**

The Set Color Scheme Command dialog box is displayed (Figure 1-29).

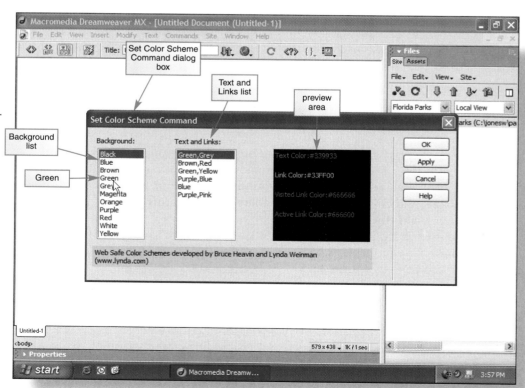

FIGURE 1-29

3 **Click Green in the Background list** and then click Blue, Brown,Green in the Text and Links list. Point to the OK button.

The Green background and the Blue,Brown,Green Text and Links are selected (Figure 1-30).

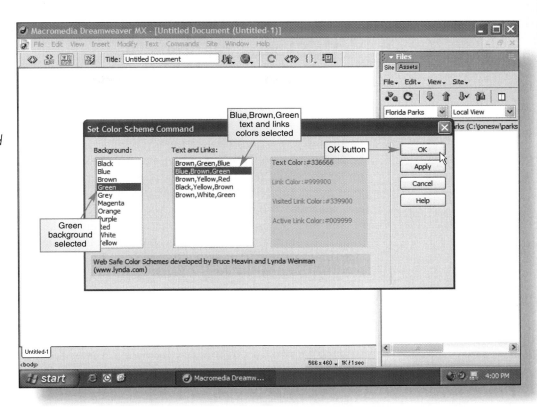

FIGURE 1-30

4 **Click the OK button.**

The background color is applied to the Document window (Figure 1-31). As you type text and insert links, the selected colors will be applied.

FIGURE 1-31

Web Page Creation

In Dreamweaver, you can create a Web page in several ways: (1) you can type a new document; (2) you can open an existing HTML document, even if it was not created in Dreamweaver; (3) you can copy and paste text; and (4) you can import a Word document.

In this project, you create the index page for Florida Parks Web page by typing the text in the Document window. Entering text into a Dreamweaver document is similar to typing text in a word processing document. You can position the insertion point at the top left of the Document window or within another element containing text, such as a table cell. Pressing the ENTER key creates a new paragraph and inserts a blank line. Web browsers automatically insert a blank line of space between paragraphs. To start a new single line without a blank line between lines of text requires a **line break**. You can insert a line break by holding down the SHIFT key and then pressing the ENTER key or by clicking the Line Break button on the Insert bar.

If you type a wrong letter and notice the error before pressing the ENTER key, press the BACKSPACE key to erase all the characters back to and including the one that is incorrect. If you mistakenly press the ENTER key and then discover the error, simply press the BACKSPACE key to return the insertion point to the previous line. Clicking the **Undo** button on the Standard toolbar reverses the most recent steps. The **Redo** button reverses the last undo action. The Undo and Redo commands also are accessible through the Edit menu.

Organizing Your Workspace

To organize your workspace, you close the Site panel and display the Standard toolbar. This gives you the maximum window space in the Dreamweaver Document window and gives you access to Standard toolbar buttons.

Complete the following steps to organize your workspace.

 To Close the Site Panel and Display the Standard Toolbar

1 **Right-click the Files panel title bar. Point to Close Panel Group.**

Dreamweaver displays the Files panel context menu. The Close Panel Groups command is highlighted (Figure 1-32).

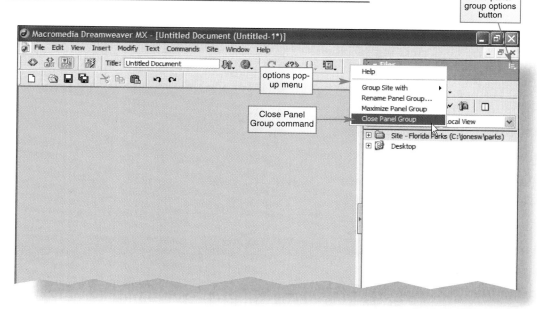

FIGURE 1-32

2 **Click Close Panel Group.**

The Files panel closes (Figure 1-33).

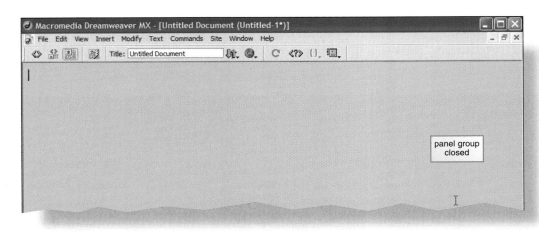

panel group closed

FIGURE 1-33

3 **Click View on the menu bar, point to Toolbars, and then point to Standard on the Toolbars submenu.**

Dreamweaver displays the View menu and the Toolbars submenu (Figure 1-34).

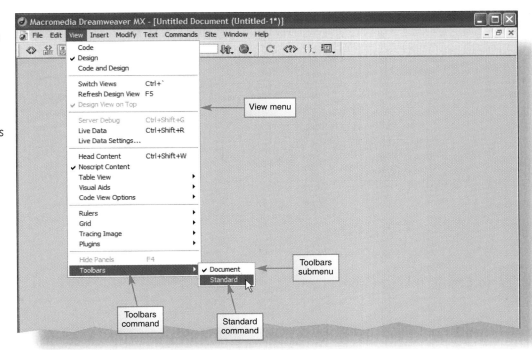

View menu

Toolbars submenu

Toolbars command

Standard command

FIGURE 1-34

4 **Click Standard.**

The Standard toolbar is displayed in the Document window (Figure 1-35).

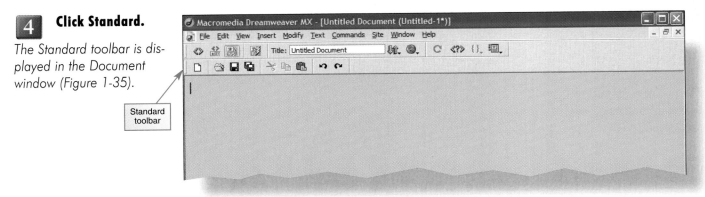

Standard toolbar

FIGURE 1-35

Adding Text

Table 1-1 includes the text for the Florida Parks Web page. After typing the sections of the document, you will press the ENTER key to insert a blank line.

Table 1-1	Discovering Scenic Florida Web Page Text		
SECTION	**HEADING, PART 1 AND PART 2**	**SECTION**	**PART 3, ITEMS FOR BULLETED LIST, AND CLOSING**
Heading	Discovering Scenic Florida	Part 3	When planning your trip, consider the following:
Part 1	Florida is one of the nation's renowned vacationlands. Tourism is Florida's number one industry. Visitors flock to Walt Disney World, Epcot, Universal Studios, and other recreational attractions. Many vacationers, however, do not realize the diversity of Florida. In addition to the theme parks, Florida's appeal extends from the vast expanse of the Everglades in the south to notable cities such as Saint Augustine and Pensacola in the north. Florida's historic and natural sites offer travelers an opportunity to view a totally different side of Florida.	Items list	Biscayne, Everglades, and Dry Tortugas National Parks are located in southern Florida. Six of the top 20 beaches in America are located in Florida state parks. The state park system includes state preserves, state parks, state archeological sites, state museums, and others. Florida has 6 national wildlife refuges and 3 national forests in which many national wilderness areas are located.
Part 2	Florida has approximately 150 state parks and 3 national parks. Visitors to these parks can enjoy such activities as swimming, camping, hiking, fishing, boating, scuba diving, or simply reflecting on Florida's natural and cultural resources.	Closing	Park entrance fees vary throughout the state and are subject to change.

The following steps create the Web page and insert blank lines between sections of text.

Steps To Create a Web Page

1 Type the heading Discovering Scenic Florida **as shown in Table 1-1, and then press the ENTER key.**

The heading is entered in the Document window (Figure 1-36). The text color is blue. Pressing the ENTER key creates a new paragraph.

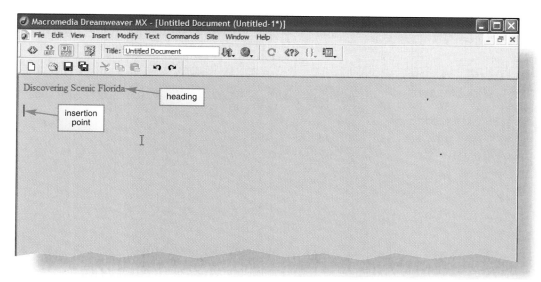

FIGURE 1-36

2 **Type the text of Part 1 shown in Table 1-1 and then press the ENTER key.**

The introductory paragraph is entered (Figure 1-37). Pressing the ENTER key creates a new paragraph.

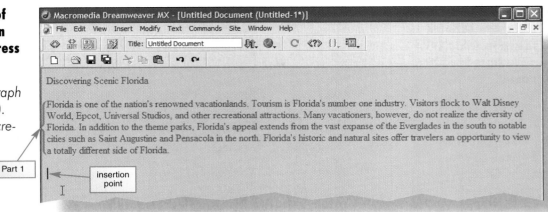

FIGURE 1-37

3 **Type the text of Part 2 shown in Table 1-1 and then press the ENTER key.**

The second paragraph is entered (Figure 1-38).

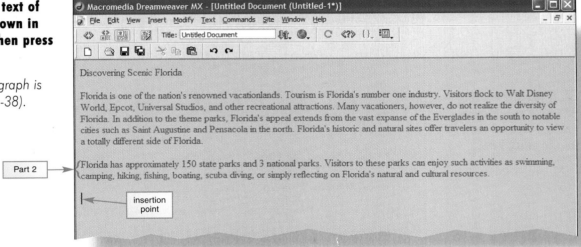

FIGURE 1-38

4 **Type the text of Part 3 shown in Table 1-1 and then press the ENTER key.**

The third paragraph is entered (Figure 1-39).

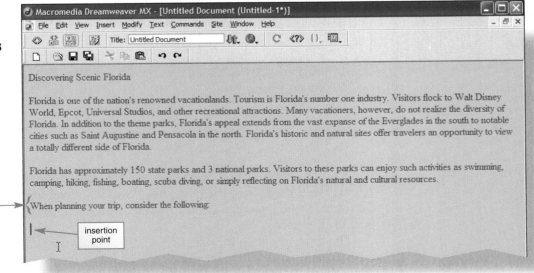

FIGURE 1-39

5 **Type the four items for the bulleted list shown in Table 1-1. Press the ENTER key after each entry.**

The items for the bulleted list are entered (Figure 1-40). Later in this project, you will format the list so that it becomes a bulleted list.

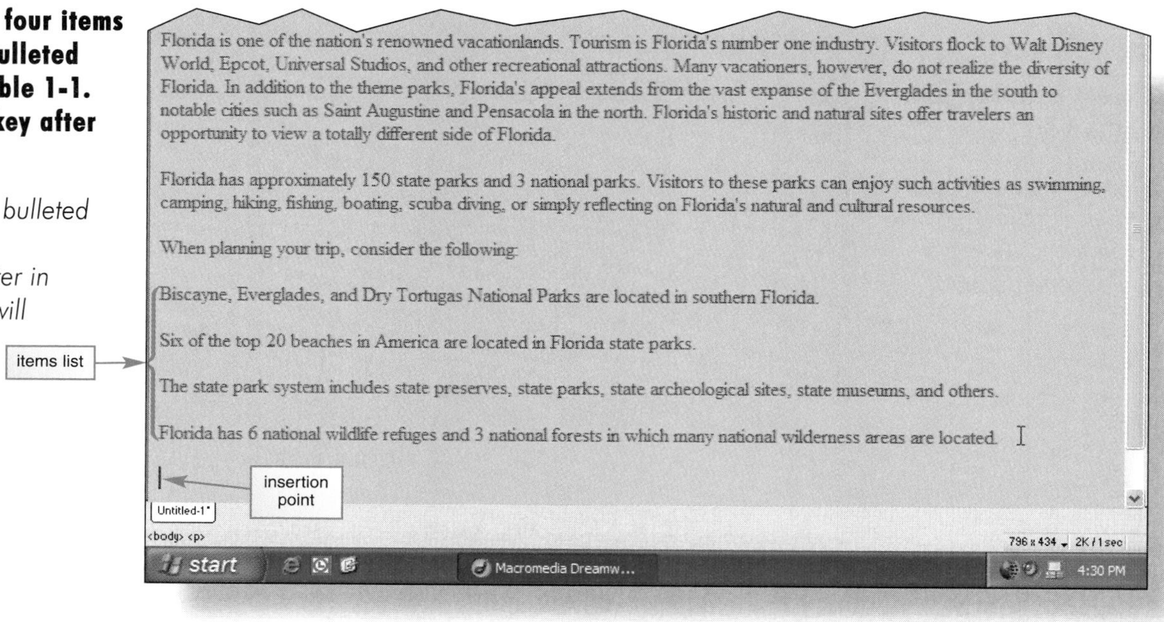

Florida is one of the nation's renowned vacationlands. Tourism is Florida's number one industry. Visitors flock to Walt Disney World, Epcot, Universal Studios, and other recreational attractions. Many vacationers, however, do not realize the diversity of Florida. In addition to the theme parks, Florida's appeal extends from the vast expanse of the Everglades in the south to notable cities such as Saint Augustine and Pensacola in the north. Florida's historic and natural sites offer travelers an opportunity to view a totally different side of Florida.

Florida has approximately 150 state parks and 3 national parks. Visitors to these parks can enjoy such activities as swimming, camping, hiking, fishing, boating, scuba diving, or simply reflecting on Florida's natural and cultural resources.

When planning your trip, consider the following:

Biscayne, Everglades, and Dry Tortugas National Parks are located in southern Florida.

Six of the top 20 beaches in America are located in Florida state parks.

The state park system includes state preserves, state parks, state archeological sites, state museums, and others.

Florida has 6 national wildlife refuges and 3 national forests in which many national wilderness areas are located.

items list → *insertion point*

Untitled-1*
<body> <p>
796 x 434 — 2K / 1 sec

FIGURE 1-40

6 **Type the closing paragraph shown in Table 1-1, and then press the ENTER key.**

The paragraph is entered (Figure 1-41).

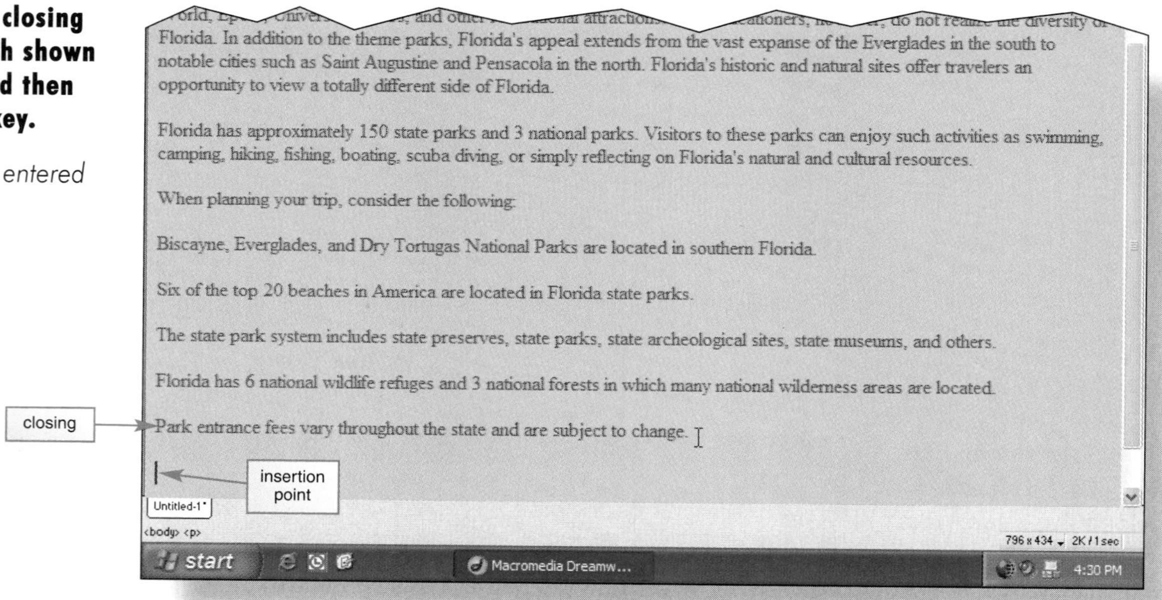

...orld, Ep... Univer... ...s, and other ...nal attractions... ...ationers, h...r, do not reali... the diversity of Florida. In addition to the theme parks, Florida's appeal extends from the vast expanse of the Everglades in the south to notable cities such as Saint Augustine and Pensacola in the north. Florida's historic and natural sites offer travelers an opportunity to view a totally different side of Florida.

Florida has approximately 150 state parks and 3 national parks. Visitors to these parks can enjoy such activities as swimming, camping, hiking, fishing, boating, scuba diving, or simply reflecting on Florida's natural and cultural resources.

When planning your trip, consider the following:

Biscayne, Everglades, and Dry Tortugas National Parks are located in southern Florida.

Six of the top 20 beaches in America are located in Florida state parks.

The state park system includes state preserves, state parks, state archeological sites, state museums, and others.

Florida has 6 national wildlife refuges and 3 national forests in which many national wilderness areas are located.

closing → Park entrance fees vary throughout the state and are subject to change.

insertion point

Untitled-1*
<body> <p>
796 x 434 — 2K / 1 sec

FIGURE 1-41

If you feel you need to start over for any reason, Dreamweaver makes it easy to delete a Web page. Save the page, display the Site panel by pressing the F8 key, click the name of the page you want to delete, right-click to display the context menu, and then click Delete.

The next step is to format the text. Dreamweaver provides two options for formatting text: the Text menu and the Property inspector. To format the Discovering Scenic Florida Web page, you will use the Property inspector.

The Property Inspector

The Property inspector is one of the panels you will use most often when creating Web pages. The **Property inspector** initially displays the more commonly used attributes, or properties, of the selected object. The object can be text, graphics, layers, frames, or hotspots. A **layer** is a container you create on your Web page to hold text, images, or other content. Dreamweaver enables you to stack layers on top of other layers. A **hotspot** is a clickable area on an image map. Options within the Property inspector change relative to the selected object. Perform the following steps to open the Property inspector.

More About

The Property Inspector

The Property inspector initially displays the most commonly used properties of the selected object. Click the expander arrow in the lower-right corner of the Property inspector to see more of the element's properties.

 To Open the Property Inspector

1 **Click Window on the menu bar and then point to Properties.**

The Window menu is displayed (Figure 1-42).

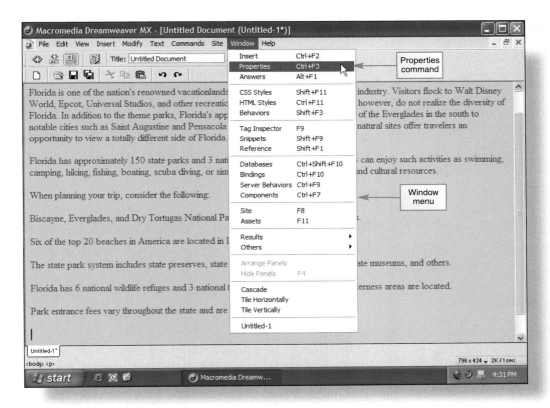

FIGURE 1-42

2 **Click Properties. If necessary, click the expander arrow to collapse the Property inspector.**

Dreamweaver opens the Property inspector below the Document window (Figure 1-43).

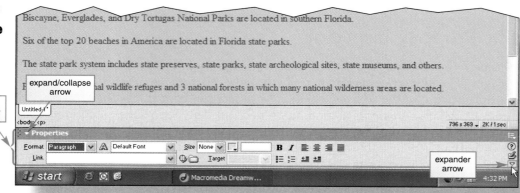

FIGURE 1-43

Other **Ways**

1. Press CTRL+F3

Property Inspector Features

The Property inspector lets you see the current properties of an element and allows you to alter or edit them. The Property inspector is divided into two sections. Clicking the expander arrow in the lower-right corner of the Property inspector collapses the Property inspector to show only the more commonly used properties for the selected element or expands the Property inspector to show more options. Some objects, such as text, do not contain additional properties within the expanded panel (Figure 1-44). The question mark icon opens the Help window.

FIGURE 1-44

By default, the Property inspector displays the properties for text on a blank document. Most changes you make to properties are applied immediately in the Document window. For some properties, however, changes are not applied until you click outside the property-editing text fields, press the ENTER key, or press the TAB key to switch to another property. The following section describes the text-related features of the Property inspector (Figure 1-45).

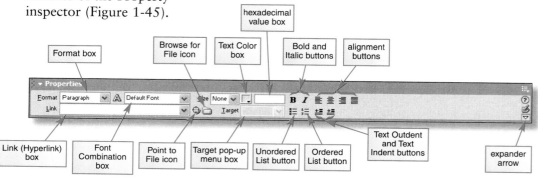

FIGURE 1-45

FORMAT   The **Format box** allows you to apply a Paragraph, Heading, or Preformatted style to the text. Clicking the Format box displays a pop-up menu from which you can select a style.

The **Paragraph style** is the normal default style for text on a Web page. **Paragraph formatting** is the process of changing the appearance of a paragraph. **Heading styles** are used to create divisions and separate one segment of text from another. The Heading numbers range from 1 through 6 and correspond to the HTML elements H1, H2, and so on. The smaller the number of the heading, the bigger the text displayed when viewed in a Web browser. These formats are displayed based on how different browsers interpret the tags, offering little consistency and control over layout and appearance. When you apply a heading tag to a paragraph, Dreamweaver automatically adds the next line of text as a standard paragraph. Use the **Preformatted style** when you do not want a Web browser to change the line of text in any way.

Font combination applies the selected font combination to the text and determines how a browser displays text on your Web page. The browser uses the first font in the combination that is installed on the user's system. If none of the fonts in the combination are installed, the browser displays the text as specified by the user's browser preferences. Most font faces in common usage on the Web are serif, sans-serif, or monospace fonts. The default font used on most Web pages is Times (also called Times New Roman or New Times), which is a serif font. The most commonly used sans-serif fonts are Arial, Helvetica, Geneva, and Verdana, while the most commonly used monospace font is Courier (also called Courier New). Use the Font Combination pop-up menu to apply a font combination.

SIZE   The **Text Size box** provides options that allow you to apply a font size to a single character or to an entire page of text. Font sizes in HTML range from 1 through 7, with size 7 being the largest. The default HTML font size, or **BASEFONT**, is 3, which equates to 12 points in a word processing document. A way to specify a particular point size for fonts in an HTML tag is not available. One method, however, that you can use is to set approximate sizes. Using the **relative size method**, the FONT tag can be used with the SIZE attribute to define text sizes in terms relative to the base font. Relative sizes can range from +1 through +7 or from -1 through -7. For example, the tag <FONT SIZE=+3> tells the browser to use a font size that is three times higher than the base font. The tag <FONT SIZE = -1> tells the browser to use a font size that is one time less than the base font.

TEXT COLOR   When you create a new document in Dreamweaver, the default text color is black. The **Text Color** box contains palettes of colors you can apply to emphasize, differentiate, and highlight topics. To display the text in a selected Web-safe color, click the Text Color box to access the different methods of selecting preset colors or creating custom ones. Colors also are represented by a hexadecimal value (for example, #FF0000) in the adjacent text field.

BOLD AND ITALIC   The **Bold button** and the **Italic button** allow you to format text using these two font styles in the Property inspector. These are the two more commonly used styles. Dreamweaver also supports a variety of other font styles available through the Text menu. To view these other styles, click Text on the menu bar and then point to Style.

LEFT, CENTER, RIGHT ALIGN, AND JUSTIFY In Dreamweaver, the default alignment for text is left alignment. To change the default alignment, select the text you want to align or simply position the mouse pointer at the beginning of the text. Click an alignment button: Align Center, Align Right, or Justify. You can align and center complete blocks of text, but you cannot align or center part of a heading or part of a paragraph.

LINK The **Link (Hyperlink) box** allows you to make selected text or other objects a hyperlink to a specified URL or Web page. To select the URL or Web page, you can click the Point to File or Browse for File icon to the right of the Link box to browse to a page in your Web site and then type the URL, or drag a file from the site window into the Link box. Links are covered in detail in Project 2.

TARGET In the **Target pop-up menu box**, you specify the frame or window in which the linked page should load. If you are using frames, the names of all of the frames in the current document are displayed in the list. If the specified frame does not exist when the current document is opened in a browser, the linked page loads in a new window with the name you specified. Once this window exists, other files can be targeted to it.

UNORDERED LIST Web developers often use a list to structure a page. An unordered list turns the selected paragraph or heading into an item in a bulleted list. If no text is selected before clicking the **Unordered List button**, a new bulleted list is started.

ORDERED LIST An ordered list is similar to an unordered list. This type of list, however, turns the selected paragraph or heading into an item in a numbered list. If no text is selected before clicking the **Ordered List button**, a new numbered list is started.

INDENT AND OUTDENT To set off a block quote, you can use the Indent feature. The **Text Indent button** will indent a line or a paragraph from both margins. In HTML, this is the BLOCKQUOTE tag. The **Text Outdent button** removes the indentation from the selected text by removing the BLOCKQUOTE tag. In a list, indenting creates a nested list and removing the indentation unnests the list. A **nested list** is one list inside another list.

Formatting Text

The text for your Web page is displayed in the Document window. The next step in creating your Web page is to format this text. **Formatting** means to apply different fonts, change heading styles, insert special characters, and insert other such elements that enhance the appearance of the Web page. You use commands from the Property inspector to format the text.

Within Dreamweaver, you can format text before you type, or you can apply new formats after you type. If you have used word processing software, you will find many of the Dreamweaver formatting commands similar to the commands within a word processing program. Your Web page contains only text, so the Property inspector displays attributes related to text.

To set block formatting, such as formatting a heading or an unordered list, position the insertion point in the line or paragraph and then format the text. To set character formatting, such as choosing a font or font size, however, you first must select the character, word, or words.

More About

Web Page Design

Web pages reach a global audience. Therefore, to limit access to certain kinds of information, avoid including any confidential data. In particular, do not include your home address, telephone number, or other personal information.

Formatting Text Headings

Just as in a word processing document, the heading structure in a Web page is used to set apart document or section titles. The six levels of headings in this structure are Heading 1 through Heading 6. **Heading 1** (**H1**) produces the largest text and **Heading 6** (**H6**) the smallest. By default, browsers will display the six heading levels in the same font, with the point size decreasing as the importance of the heading decreases. Complete the following steps to format the heading.

 To Format Text with Heading 1

1 If necessary, scroll up and then position the insertion point anywhere in the heading text, Discovering Scenic Florida (Figure 1-46). Point to the Format box arrow in the Property inspector.

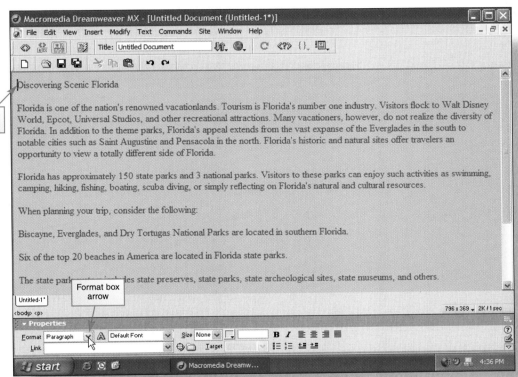

FIGURE 1-46

More About

Text Size

You can set the size of the text in your Web page, but viewers of your Web page also can change the size through their browser. When creating a page, use the font size that looks right for the page you are creating.

| **2** | **Click the Format box arrow in the Property inspector and then point to Heading 1.** |

The Format pop-up menu displays a list of formatting styles. Heading 1 is high-lighted in the list (Figure 1-47).

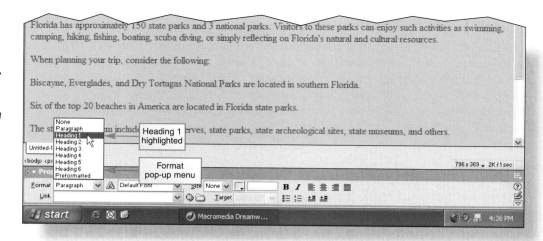

FIGURE 1-47

| **3** | **Click Heading 1.** |

The Heading 1 style is applied to the Discovering Scenic Florida heading (Figure 1-48).

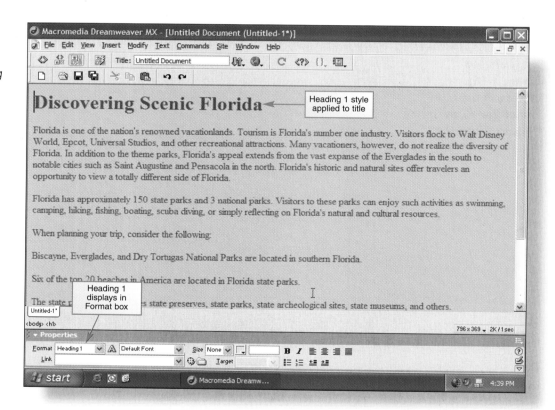

FIGURE 1-48

Centering Text

Using the **Align Center button** in the Property inspector allows you to center text. This button is very similar to the Center button in a word processing program. To center a single line or a paragraph, position the mouse pointer in the line or para-graph, and then click the button to center the text. You do not need to select a single line or single paragraph to center it. To center more than one paragraph at a time, however, you must select all paragraphs. The following step illustrates centering the heading.

Steps **To Center the Web Page Heading**

1 **If necessary, click somewhere in the heading, Discovering Scenic Florida. Click the Align Center button in the Property inspector.**

The heading, Discovering Scenic Florida, is centered (Figure 1-49).

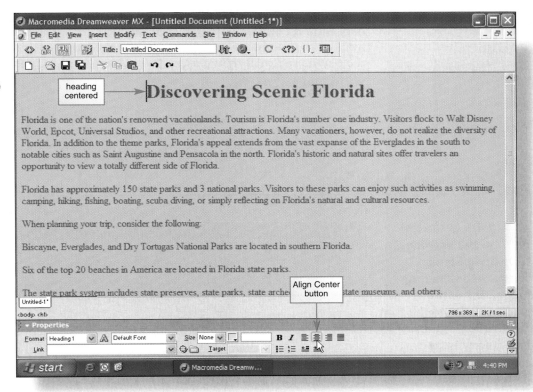

FIGURE 1-49

Text is one of the more important elements of most any Web page. How the text displays on a Web page can attract or detract from the overall appearance. Using the appropriate font type can enhance and entice viewers to browse your Web site.

Specifying the Font Type

Type is important because it attracts attention, sets the style and tone of a Web page, influences how readers interpret the words, and defines the feeling of the page. The **font type** refers to the basic design of the lettering. Several methods are used to classify fonts. The most common way is to place them in different families based on shared characteristics. The five basic font type families are:

1. Serif, such as Times or Times New Roman
2. Sans-serif, such as Helvetica and Arial
3. Monospace, such as Courier
4. Cursive, such as Brush Script
5. Decorative and fantasy

Two general categories of typefaces are serif and sans-serif. **Sans-serif** typefaces are composed of simple lines, whereas **serif** typefaces use small decorative marks to embellish characters and make them easier to read. Helvetica and Arial are sans-serif types and Times New Roman is a serif type. A **monospace** font, such as Courier, is one in which every character takes up the same amount of horizontal space. **Cursive** font styles emulate handwritten letterforms. **Decorative and fantasy** is a family for fonts that do not fit any of the other families.

Other Ways

1. On Text menu click Align, click Center on Align submenu
2. Right-click selected text, point to Align on context menu, click Center on Align submenu
3. Press CTRL+ALT+SHIFT+C

Formatting Text

Research shows that people read text on-screen differently than they read the printed word. They are more apt to scan and look for the important concepts. Many changes in formatting could make the site confusing.

Most Web pages use only the first three families. Dreamweaver provides a font combination feature available in the Property inspector. **Font combinations** determine how a browser displays your Web page's text. In the Property inspector, you can select one of six font combinations. A browser looks for the first font in the combination on the user's computer, then the second, and then the third. If none of the fonts in the combination are installed on the user's computer, the browser displays the text as specified by the user's browser preferences. Perform the following steps to change the font type.

 To Change the Font Type

1 **Click to the left of the heading, Discovering Scenic Florida, and then drag through the entire heading. Point to the Font Combination box arrow in the Property inspector.**

The heading is selected (Figure 1-50).

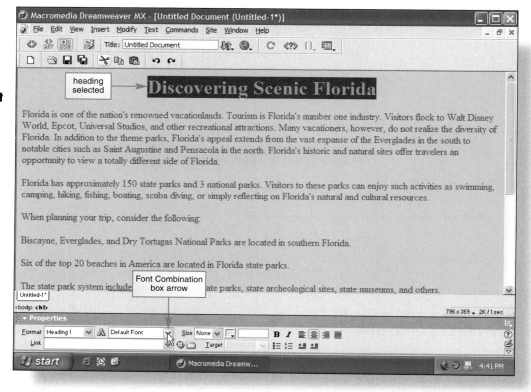

FIGURE 1-50

2 **Click the font combination box arrow and then point to Verdana, Arial, Helvetica.**

The Font Combination pop-up menu is displayed and the Verdana, Arial, Helvetica combination is highlighted (Figure 1-51). The menu includes six different font combinations and the default font.

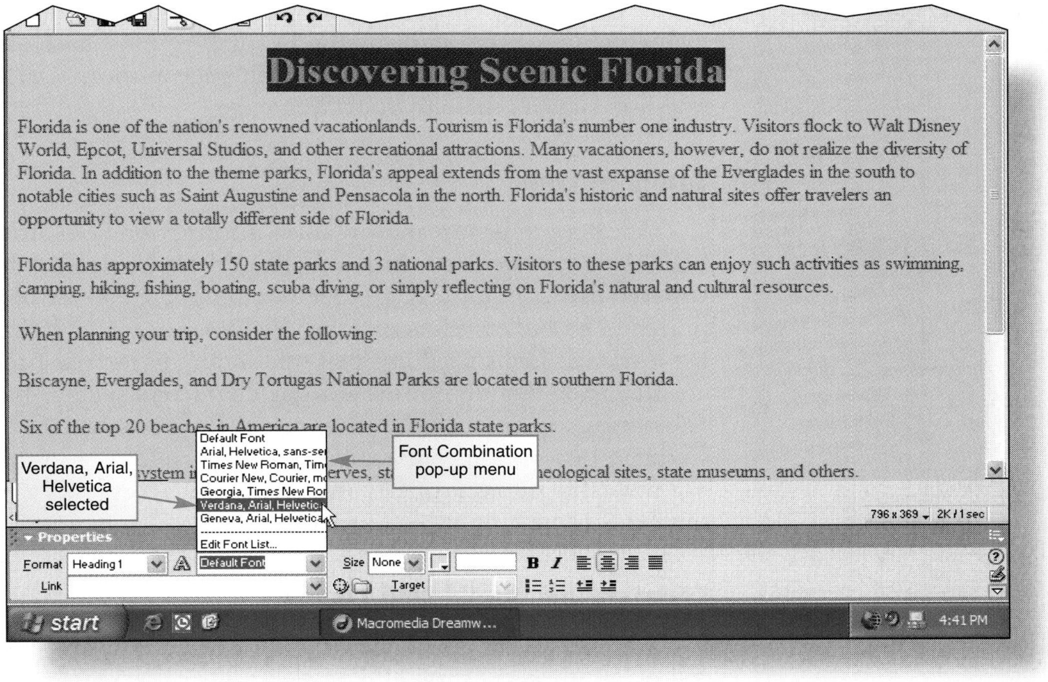

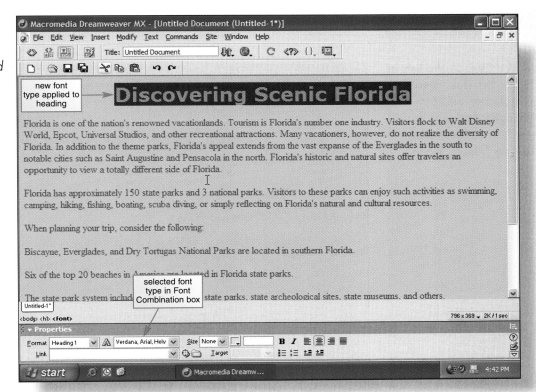

FIGURE 1-51

3 **Click Verdana, Arial, Helvetica.**

The new font type is applied to the selected heading (Figure 1-52).

FIGURE 1-52

In addition to headings and font type attributes, other text design options are available. Presenting information in small chunks, such as bulleted or numbered lists, is a design element used by many Web page authors. Dreamweaver makes it easy to add lists such as these to your Web page.

Types of Lists

One way to group and organize information is by using lists. Web pages can have three types of lists: ordered or numbered, unordered or bulleted, and definition. **Ordered lists** contain text preceded by numbered steps. **Unordered lists** contain text preceded by bullets (dots or other symbols) or image bullets. You use an unordered list if the list items need not be listed in any particular order.

Definition lists do not use leading characters such as bullet points or numbers. Glossaries and descriptions often use this type of list. The Unordered List and Ordered List buttons are available in the Property inspector. The Definition List is not available in the Property inspector. You access this type of list command through the Text menu.

Creating an Unordered List

You can create a new list or you can create a list using existing text. Perform the following steps to create an unordered list using existing text.

More About

Lists

You can remove the bullets or numbers from a formatted list just as easily as you added them. Select the formatted list. Click the button in the Properties inspector that you used originally to apply the formatting.

Steps **To Create an Unordered List**

---

1 **Click to the left of the line, Biscayne, Everglades, and Dry Tortugas National Parks are located in southern Florida (Figure 1-53).**

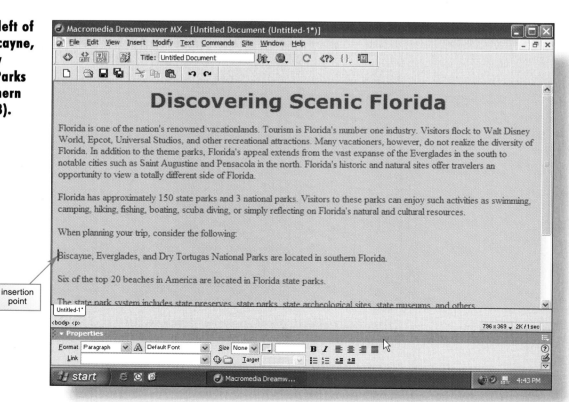

FIGURE 1-53

2 **Drag to select the text, Biscayne, Everglades, and Dry Tortugas National Parks are located in southern Florida, and the next three lines. Point to the Unordered List button in the Property inspector.**

The text is selected (Figure 1-54).

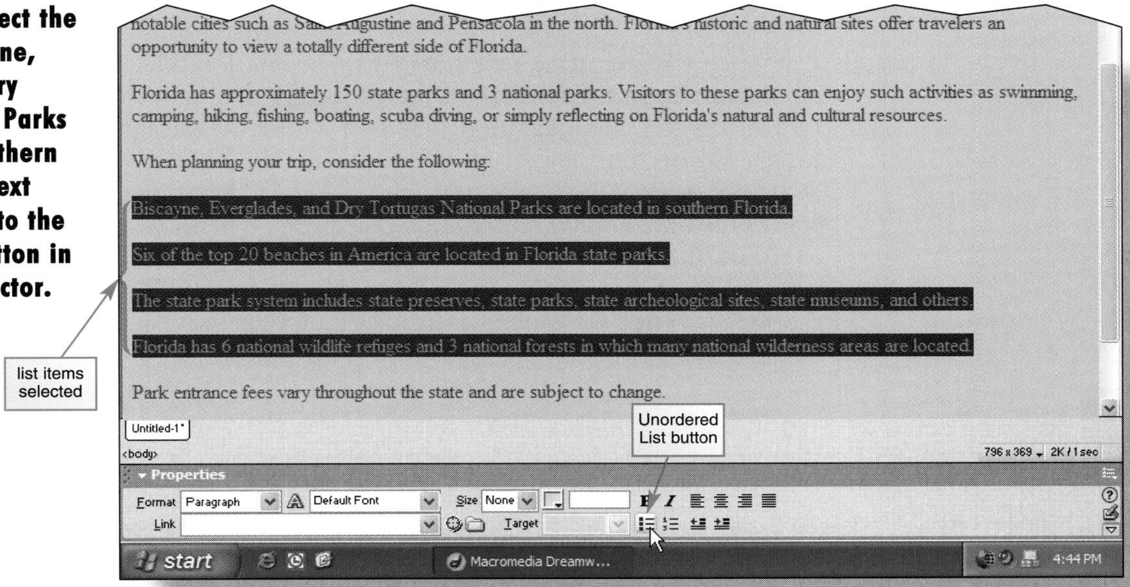

list items selected

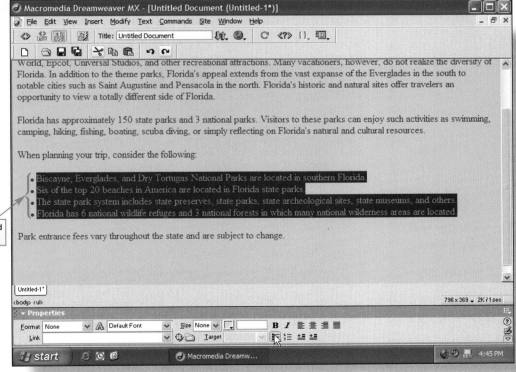

FIGURE 1-54

3 **Click the Unordered List button.**

A bullet is added to each line, the four lines are indented, and the space between each item is deleted (Figure 1-55). Later in this project, you will insert a blank line between each of the bulleted items.

bullets applied to list items

FIGURE 1-55

Other Ways

1. On Text menu point to List, click Unordered List on List submenu

To emphasize the bulleted items further, you can use Text Indent. Text Indent will indent a line or a paragraph from both margins.

Using Text Indent

When you are using **Text Indent**, the indentation takes place from both the left and right margins. Each side of the paragraph will move in by the same amount — two spaces for each indention. The text within the paragraph will rewrap to account for the shorter line length. In HTML, this is the BLOCKQUOTE tag. Text Outdent is the opposite of Text Indent. Clicking **Text Outdent** moves the paragraph back two spaces toward the margin for each indention. When you use Text Indent with a bulleted list, the shape of the bullet changes. Clicking the Text Indent button within a bulleted list, however, does not create a BLOCKQUOTE tag. Instead, a nested list is created. A **nested list** is one list inside of another.

Steps **To Use Text Indent to Indent a Bulleted List**

1 **If necessary, select the bulleted list. Point to the Text Indent button in the Property inspector (Figure 1-56).**

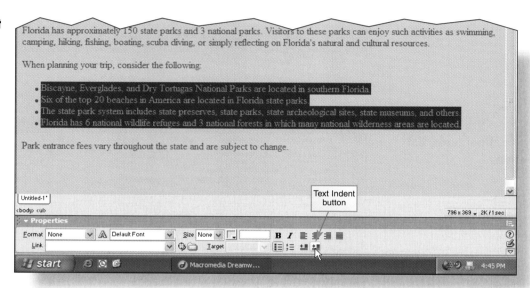

FIGURE 1-56

2 **Click the Text Indent button.**

The bulleted list indents and the shape of the bullet changes from a filled circle to a hollow circle (Figure 1-57).

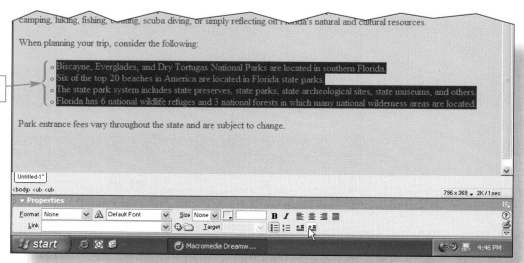

FIGURE 1-57

Other text formatting options are applying bold or italic styles to text. **Bold** characters display somewhat thicker and darker than those that are not bold. *Italic* characters slant to the right. The Property inspector contains buttons for both bold and italic font styles.

Applying Bold Formatting

To bold text within Dreamweaver is a simple procedure. If you have used word processing software, you are familiar with this process. The next step is to emphasize a sentence by applying bold formatting.

Steps **To Bold Text**

1 **If necessary, scroll down to display the closing paragraph. Drag through the text to select the entire paragraph (Figure 1-58). Point to the Bold button in the Property inspector.**

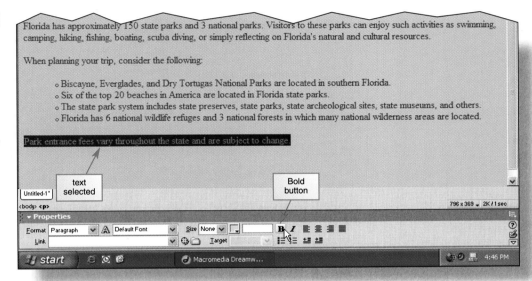

FIGURE 1-58

2 **Click the Bold button and then click anywhere in the Document window to deselect the text.**

Bold formatting is applied to the paragraph (Figure 1-59).

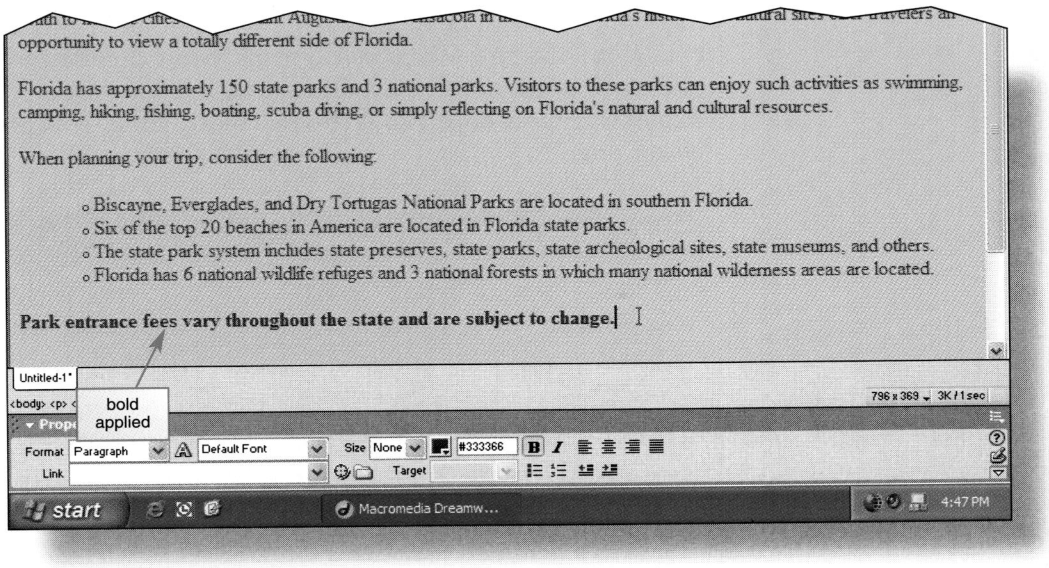

FIGURE 1-59

You also can use color for emphasis. Adding color to text can attract attention to important information.

Web-Safe Colors

It is easy to change the color of an individual character, a word, a line, a paragraph, or the text of an entire document. In HTML, colors are expressed either as hexadecimal values (for example, #FF0000) or as color names (red).

Use the **color picker** to select the colors for your page or text. Through the Property inspector, Dreamweaver provides access to five different color palettes: Color Cubes, Continuous Tone, Windows OS, Mac OS, and Grayscale. Color Cubes is the default color palette. Figure 1-60 shows the Color Cubes color palette available on the color palette pop-up menu.

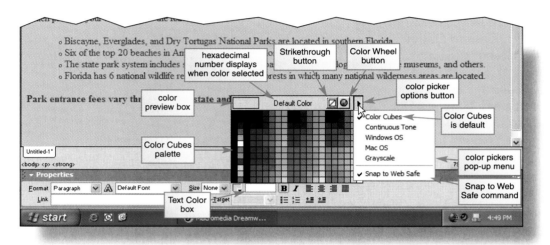

FIGURE 1-60

Two of the color palettes, Color Cubes and Continuous Tone, display Web-safe colors. Recall that Web-safe colors are colors that display correctly on the screen when someone is viewing your Web page through a browser. A Web-safe color is one that appears the same in Netscape Navigator and Microsoft Internet Explorer on both Windows and Macintosh systems. Most experts agree that approximately 212 to 216 Web-safe colors exist. Testing by experts, however, suggests that Internet Explorer renders only 212 Web-safe colors. Table 1-2 contains a list of the color picker options.

Table 1-2 Color Picker Options	
OPTION	**FUNCTION**
Color preview box	Provides a preview of the currently selected color or the color picked up by the eyedropper
Hex value area	Displays the hexadecimal value of the current color or the color picked up by the eyedropper
Strikethrough button	Clears current color and retains default color
Color Wheel button	Opens the system color pickers via the operating system Color dialog box
Option button	Displays a pop-up menu from which you can select five color pickers and Snap to Web Safe command
Snap to Web Safe command	Automatically changes non-Web-safe colors to the nearest Web-safe values

Dreamweaver has an **eyedropper** feature that lets you select colors and make perfect color matches. When you are working with color palettes, you can use the eyedropper to choose a color from anywhere on the screen, including outside of Dreamweaver, and apply the color to a selected object in the Document window. You place the eyedropper over the color you want to select and then click the mouse button. As soon as you click the mouse button, the color automatically is applied to the selected object. If you move the eyedropper to an object outside of Dreamweaver, the eyedropper changes to the block arrow mouse pointer shape until you move it back into the Dreamweaver window. Clicking the color picker options button and then selecting the Snap to Web Safe command will ensure the selected color is a Web-safe color.

Changing Text Color

The default color for Dreamweaver text is black. Adding a color scheme, however, changed the default text color to the color specified in the color scheme. The color scheme applied to the Web page changed the text color to a shade of blue. The colors for the supplied color schemes come from the Continuous Tone color picker. Perform the following steps to change the text color of the last sentence to dark blue. This color is a darker shade of the current text color.

 To Change the Text Color

1 **Select the closing paragraph and then click the Text Color box in the Property inspector.**

The Continuous Tone color palette is displayed (Figure 1-61). The color palette includes Web-safe colors, the color preview box, and the six-digit hexadecimal number that represents the selected color. In Figure 1-61, the hexadecimal number is #336666. This is the color of the text within this selected color scheme.

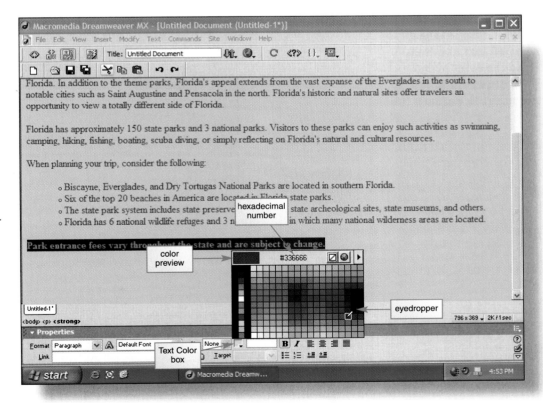

FIGURE 1-61

2 **Position the eyedropper on the shade of blue represented by hexadecimal number #333366 (row 5 from the bottom and column 3 from the right).**

The selected color appears in the color preview box, and the hexadecimal value area displays the number for the color (Figure 1-62).

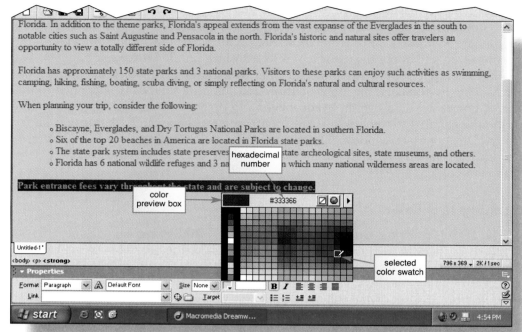

FIGURE 1-62

3 **Click the eyedropper to apply the color to the selected text and then close the color picker. Click anywhere in the document to deselect the text.**

The color is applied to the text. The paragraph is displayed in the dark blue color (Figure 1-63). Occasionally you may have to press the ESC key to close the picker.

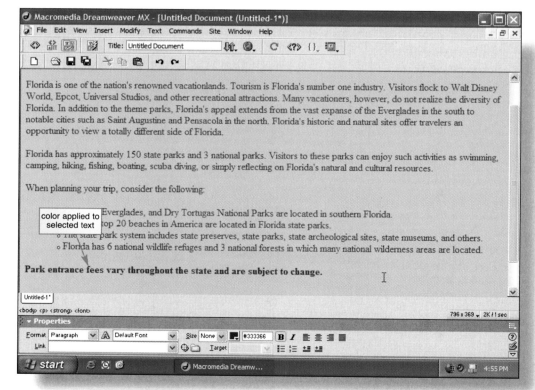

FIGURE 1-63

To add additional details to the Florida Parks Web page, a horizontal rule is inserted. Many Web designers use a horizontal rule to divide a Web page into sections and as a style element.

Horizontal Rules

A **horizontal rule** (or line) is useful for organizing information and visually separating text and objects. You can specify the width and height of the rule in pixels or as a percentage of the page size. The rule can be aligned to the left, center, or right, and you can add shading or draw the line in a solid color. These attributes are available in the Property inspector. The HTML tag for a horizontal rule is <HR>.

Inserting a Horizontal Rule

On the Discovering Scenic Florida Web page, you will insert a horizontal rule between the document heading and text. You will use the default shaded line, but change the width and the height of the rule and then center the rule.

 To Insert a Horizontal Rule

1 **If necessary, scroll to the top of the page. Click to the right of the heading, Discovering Scenic Florida, and then press the END key.**

Pressing the END key moves the insertion point outside the HTML tags surrounding the heading (Figure 1-64).

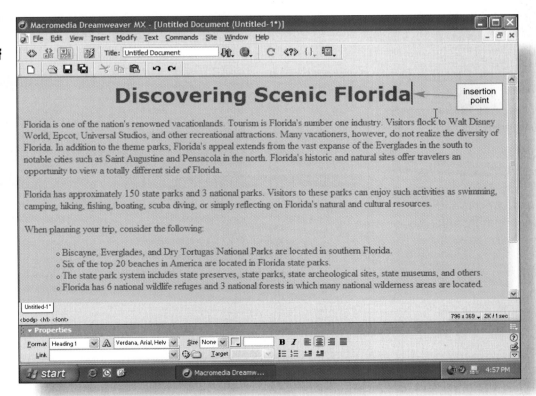

FIGURE 1-64

2 **Click Insert on the menu bar and point to Horizontal Rule (Figure 1-65).**

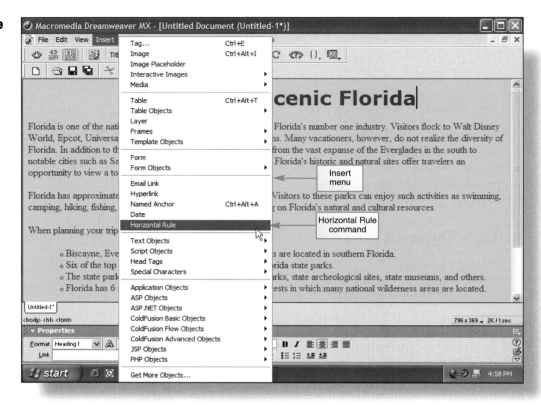

FIGURE 1-65

3 **Click Horizontal Rule. Click the Width box in the Property inspector.**

The horizontal rule is inserted below the heading (Figure 1-66). The attributes in the Property inspector change to those for the horizontal rule.

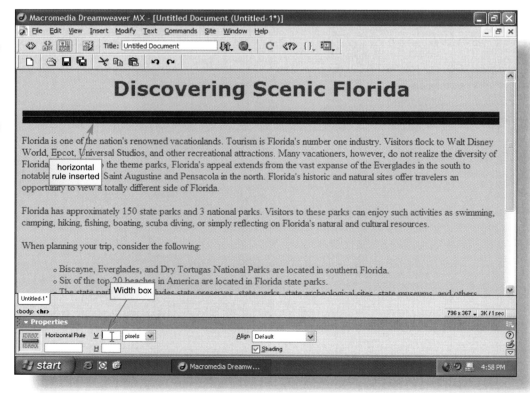

FIGURE 1-66

<table>
<tr>
<td>

4 **Type** 500 **and then press the ENTER key. Click the Height box.**

The width of the line decreases (Figure 1-67).

</td>
<td>

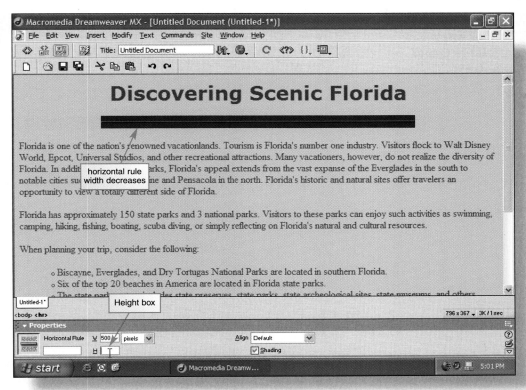

</td>
</tr>
</table>

FIGURE 1-67

<table>
<tr>
<td>

5 **Type** 6 **and then press the ENTER key. Point to the Align box arrow.**

The height of the line increases (Figure 1-68).

</td>
<td>

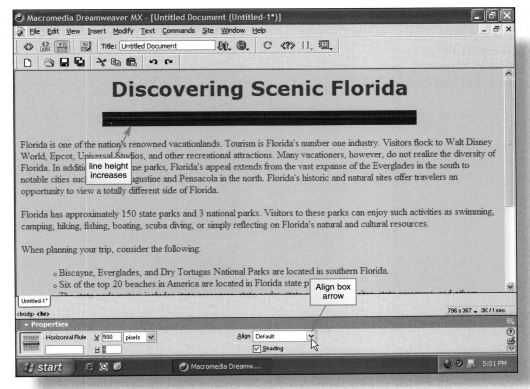

</td>
</tr>
</table>

FIGURE 1-68

6 Click the Align box arrow and then point to Center (Figure 1-69).

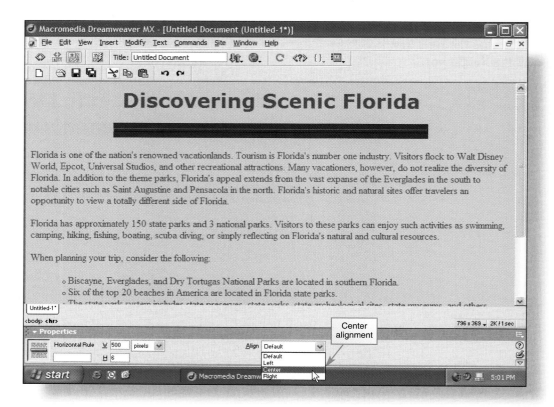

FIGURE 1-69

7 Click Center and then click anywhere in the Document window to deselect the horizontal rule.

The rule is centered (Figure 1-70). Even though the rule appeared centered before applying the Center attribute, it would not necessarily appear centered when viewed in all browsers. Adding the Center attribute assures that it always will be centered below the heading.

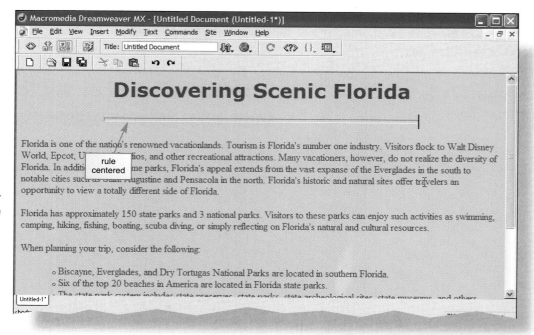

FIGURE 1-70

The next step illustrates using the Insert bar to insert a line break between the bulleted items.

The Insert Bar

The **Insert bar** is a panel consisting of 12 categories organized into tabs. Within each category are buttons for inserting common page elements. Clicking a tab accesses the buttons for that category. The **Characters category** includes the Line Break button and other buttons that allow you to insert a variety of symbols into your Web pages. A **line break** starts a new line of text at the exact point at which the LINE BREAK tag is encountered. The HTML tag for a line break is <BR>.

Perform the following steps to display the Insert bar.

Steps | **To Display the Insert Bar**

1 **Click Window on the menu bar and then point to Insert.**

The Window menu is displayed and the Insert command is highlighted (Figure 1-71).

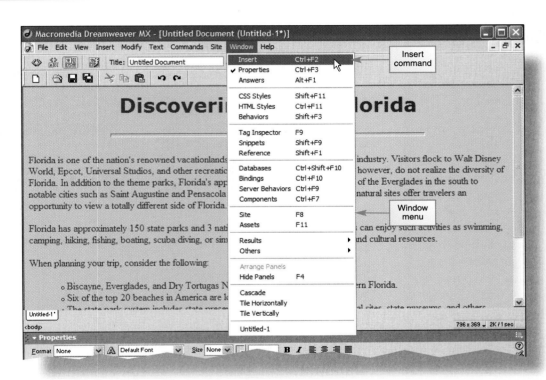

FIGURE 1-71

2 **Click Insert.**

Dreamweaver displays the Insert bar in the Document window (Figure 1-72). The Insert bar can display to the right of the Standard toolbar or above or below the Standard toolbar. Monitor resolution and the settings within the Dreamweaver window determine where the Insert bar is displayed.

FIGURE 1-72

HTML

For more information about HTML, visit the Dreamweaver MX More About Web page (scsite.com/dreamweavermx/more.htm) and then click HTML.

Inserting a Line Break

When you added bullets to the items list earlier in this project, the blank line between each item was removed. Removing the blank line between items is a result of how Dreamweaver interprets the HTML code. A blank line between the bulleted items, however, will provide better spacing and readability when the Web page is viewed through a browser. You can add blank lines in several ways. You might assume that pressing the ENTER key at the end of each line would be the quickest way to accomplish this. Pressing the ENTER key, however, adds another bullet. The easiest way to accomplish the task of adding blank lines is to insert line breaks. Recall that the line break starts a new single line without inserting a blank line between lines of text. Inserting two line breaks, however, adds a single blank line. Perform the following steps to add a blank line between each of the bulleted items.

 To Add a Line Break

1 **Click the Characters tab in the Insert bar.**

The Characters tab displays buttons with special characters (Figure 1-73). The Line Break button inserts a line break rather than a blank line. As soon as the browser encounters a <BR> tag, it starts a new line with the text that follows the tag. Adding two consecutive <BR> tags will create a blank line.

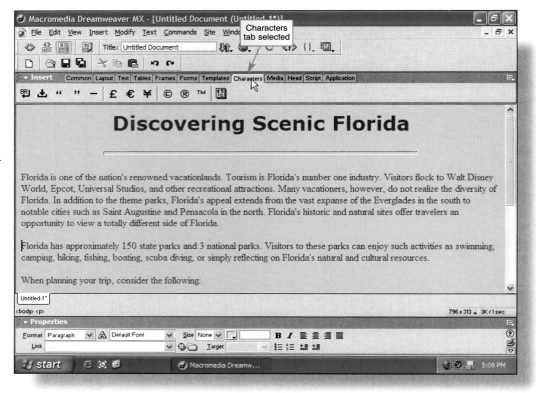

FIGURE 1-73

2 If necessary, scroll down and then click at the end of the first bulleted item. Point to the Line Break button on the Characters tab in the Insert bar (Figure 1-74).

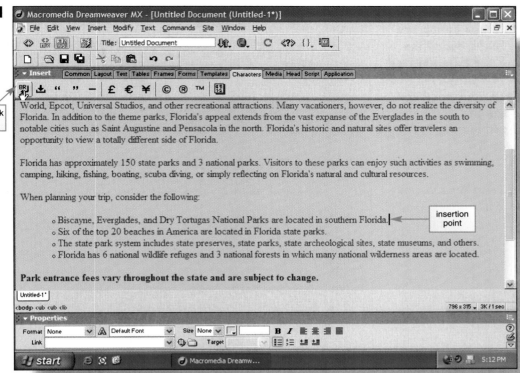

FIGURE 1-74

3 Click the Line Break button two times.

Two line breaks are inserted (Figure 1-75). When the Web page is viewed in Dreamweaver, it appears that two blank lines are inserted. When viewed in a browser, however, only one blank line will be displayed between each item. You will view your Web page in a browser later in this project.

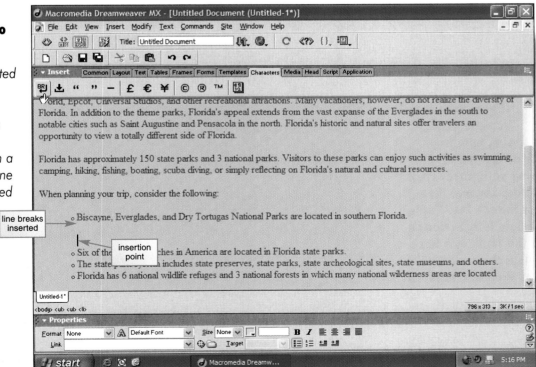

FIGURE 1-75

4 **Click the Line Break button two times at the end of the second and third bulleted items to insert blank lines between the second and third and the third and fourth bulleted list items.**

The bulleted items display with two blank lines between them in the Document window (Figure 1-76).

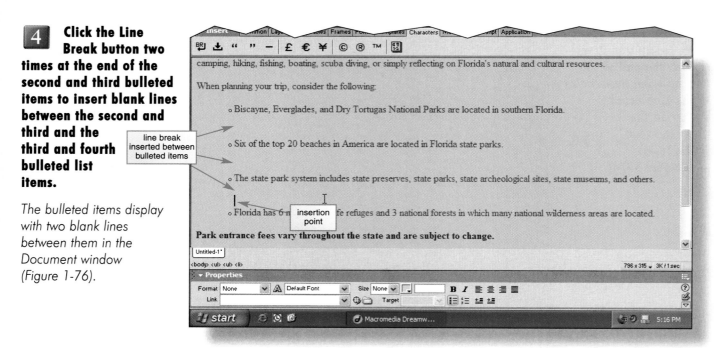

FIGURE 1-76

When creating a Web document, it is a good idea to add your name and current date to the document. Insert a single line break between your name and the date. Complete the following steps to add this information.

 To Add Your Name and Current Date

1 **If necessary, scroll down to display the closing paragraph. Click at the end of the closing paragraph. Press the ENTER key and then press the END key. Verify that Bold is not selected and the Text Color box displays the correct color in the Property inspector.**

The insertion point moves to the next paragraph (Figure 1-77). Pressing the END key insures that you are not within the HTML code used to bold and add color to the closing line.

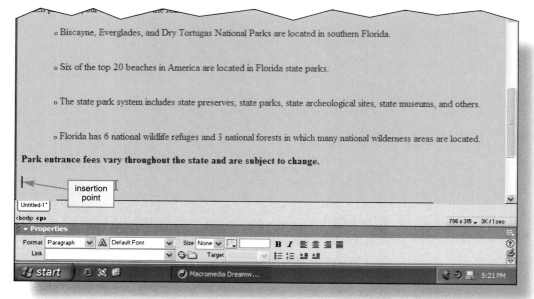

FIGURE 1-77

2 Type your name. Do not press the ENTER key. Point to the Line Break button (Figure 1-78).

Line Break button

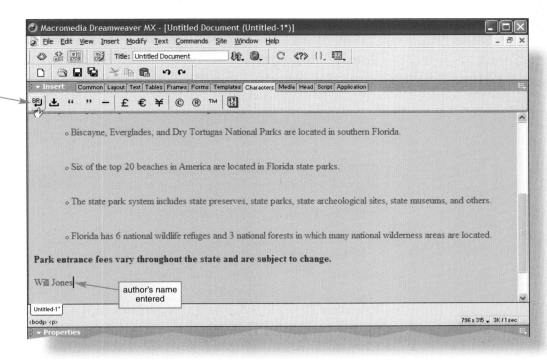

FIGURE 1-78

3 Click the Line Break button. Type the current date and then press the ENTER key.

The insertion point moves to the next line (Figure 1-79). No line space displays between the name and the date.

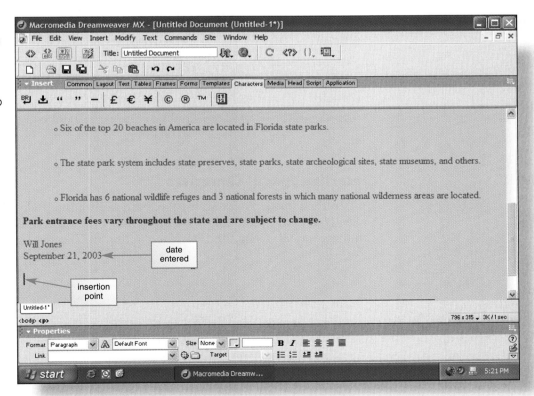

FIGURE 1-79

Other Ways

1. Press CTRL+ENTER

You now will use the Insert bar to add special characters to your Web page.

Special Characters

In addition to the line break character you used earlier, the Characters tab in the Insert bar also contains buttons that allow you to enter special characters, including the copyright, registered trademark, and trademark symbols. Table 1-3 lists all the button names and descriptions available on the Characters tab.

Table 1-3	Buttons on the Characters Tab	
BUTTON NAME	**DESCRIPTION**	**HTML TAGS AND CHARACTER ENTITIES**
Line Break	Places a line break at the insertion point	
Non-Breaking Space	Places a non-breaking space at the insertion point	
Left Quote	Places opening, curved double quotation marks at the insertion point	&#147;
Right Quote	Places closing, curved double quotation marks at the insertion point	&#148;
Em Dash	Places an em dash at the insertion point	&#151;
Pound	Places a pound (currency) symbol at the insertion point	&pound;
Euro	Places a euro (currency) symbol at the insertion point	&euro;
Yen	Places a yen (currency) symbol at the insertion point	&yen;
Copyright	Places a copyright symbol at the insertion point	&copy;
Registered Trademark	Places a registered trademark symbol at the insertion point	&reg;
Trademark	Places a trademark symbol at the insertion point	&#153;
Other Characters	Provides a set of special characters from which to select	Other ASCII characters

Inserting Special Characters

In the Florida Parks Web page, both Walt Disney World® and Epcot® are registered names. The following steps insert the registered trademark symbol next to these names, using the Characters tab in the Insert bar.

Steps | To Insert a Registered Trademark Character

1 **Scroll up to display the first paragraph in the Web page. Click to the right of World (in Walt Disney World) and before the comma and then point to the Registered Trademark button on the Characters tab (Figure 1-80).**

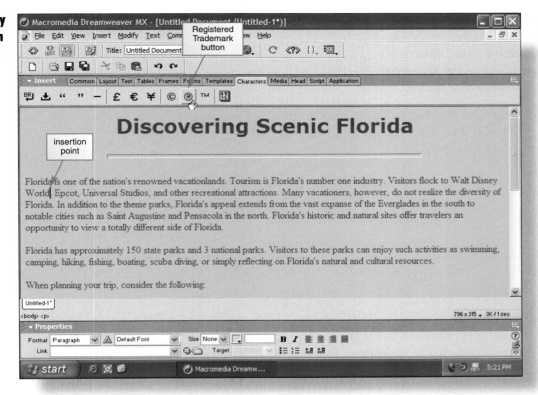

FIGURE 1-80

2 **Click the Registered Trademark button.**

The registered trademark symbol is inserted into the document (Figure 1-81).

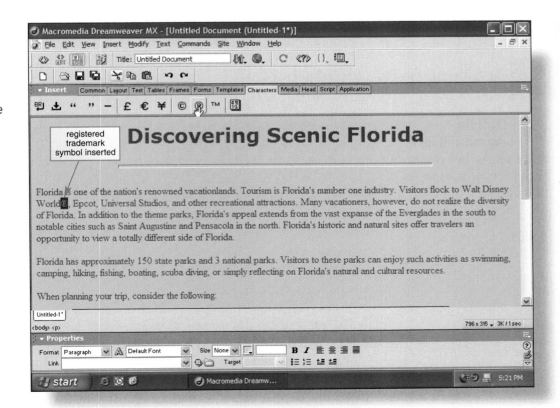

FIGURE 1-81

3 **Click to the right of Epcot and before the comma and then click the Registered Trademark button on the Characters tab. Click anywhere in the document to deselect the symbol.**

The registered trademark symbol is inserted into the document (Figure 1-82).

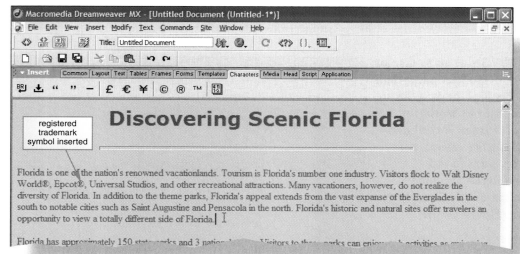

FIGURE 1-82

With the formatting complete, the next step is to collapse the Property inspector.

Collapsing the Property Inspector

Panels such as the Property inspector displaying in the Dreamweaver window require considerable space. If you are finished working with a panel, generally it is better to collapse or close it. **Collapsing** it leaves the title bar in the window, which allows you to expand it easily by clicking the expand/collapse arrow instead of using the Properties command on the Window menu. **Closing** it removes it completely from the Document window. The following step collapses the Property inspector.

 To Collapse the Property Inspector

1 **Click the expand/collapse arrow on the left corner of the Property inspector title bar.**

The Property inspector collapses (minimizes) (Figure 1-83).

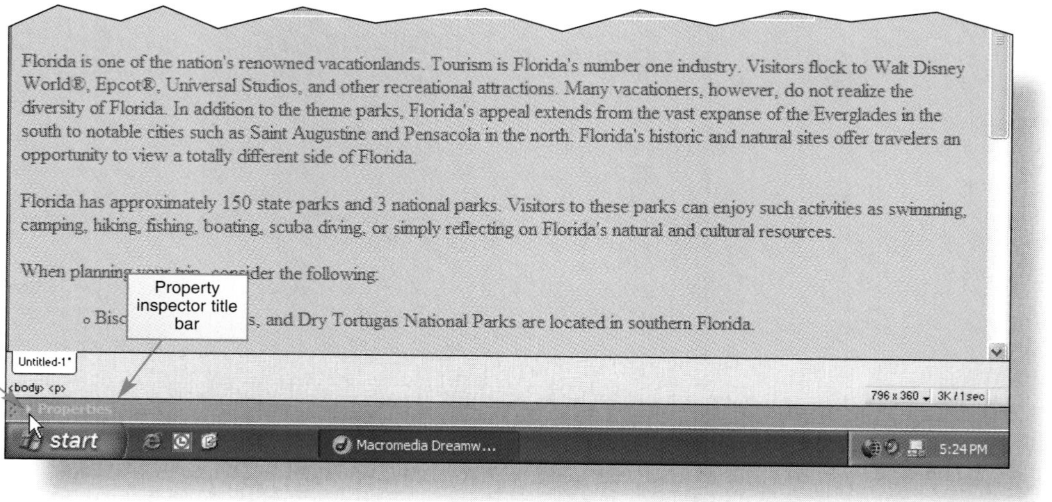

FIGURE 1-83

One of the more important elements of your Web page is the title. An appropriate and meaningful title adds value to a Web page.

Web Page Titles

A **Web page title** helps Web site visitors keep track of what they are viewing as they browse. It is important to give your Web page an appropriate title. When visitors to your Web page create bookmarks or add the Web page to their Favorites lists, the title is used for the reference. If you do not title a page, the page will appear in the browser window, Favorites lists, and history lists as Untitled Document. Because many search engines use the Web page title, it is important to use a creative and meaningful name. (Giving the document a file name by saving it is not the same as giving the page a title.)

Changing a Web Page Title

The current title of your Web page is Untitled Document. Unless you change the title of the Web page, this name will be displayed on the browser title bar when the page is opened in a browser window. Perform the following steps to change the name of the Web page to Florida Parks.

 To Change the Web Page Title

1 **Drag through the text, Untitled Document, in the Title text box on the Document toolbar.**

The text is highlighted to indicate that it is selected (Figure 1-84).

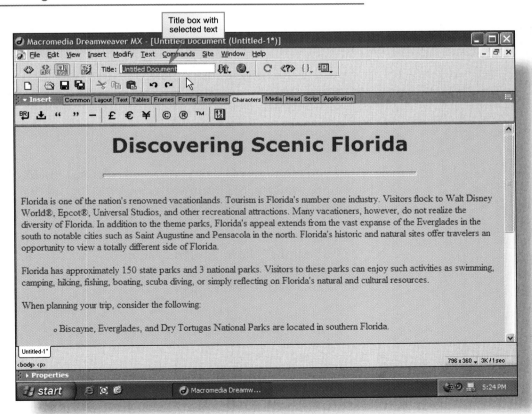

FIGURE 1-84

2 **Type** Florida Parks **in the Title text box and then press the ENTER key.**

The new name, Florida Parks, is displayed in the Title text box and on the Dreamweaver title bar (Figure 1-85).

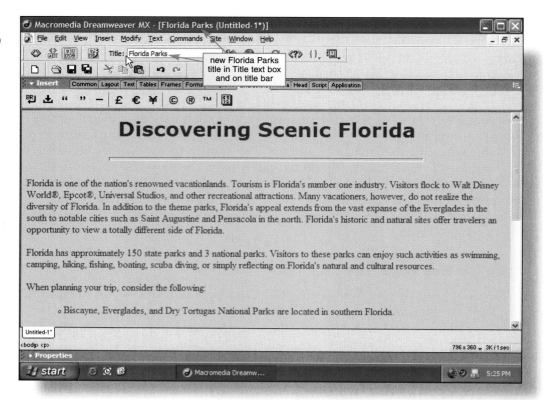

FIGURE 1-85

With all the text of the document entered, you can check the spelling of the document.

Checking Spelling

After you create a Web page, you should check it visually for spelling errors. In addition, you can use Dreamweaver's Check Spelling command to identify possible misspellings. The Check Spelling command ignores HTML tags and attributes. Recall from the Introduction that attributes are additional information contained within an HTML tag.

Perform the following steps to start the Check Spelling command and check your entire document. Your Web page may contain different misspelled words depending on the accuracy of your typing.

Steps | **To Check Spelling**

1 **Click Text on the menu bar and then point to Check Spelling.**

Dreamweaver displays the Text menu (Figure 1-86).

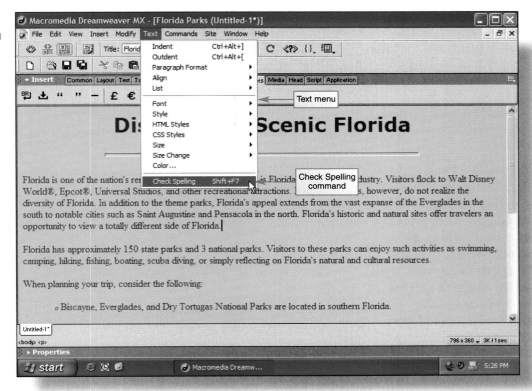

FIGURE 1-86

2 **Click Check Spelling. Point to the Ignore button.**

The Check Spelling dialog box is displayed (Figure 1-87). The Dreamweaver spelling checker displays the word, Epcot, in the Word not found in dictionary box. Suggestions for the correct spelling are displayed in the Suggestions list.

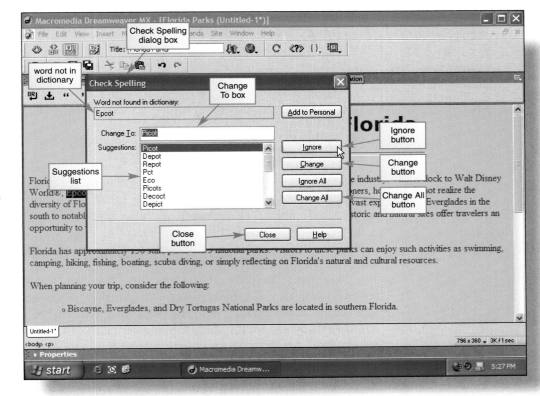

FIGURE 1-87

Dreamweaver MX

3 **Click the Ignore button.**

The spelling checker ignores the word, Epcot, and continues searching for additional misspelled words. If the spelling checker identifies a word that is spelled correctly, clicking the Ignore button skips the word.

4 **Correct any misspelled word by accepting the suggested replacement or by typing the correct word in the Change To box. Click the Change or Change All button, and then point to the OK button in the Macromedia Dreamweaver MX dialog box.**

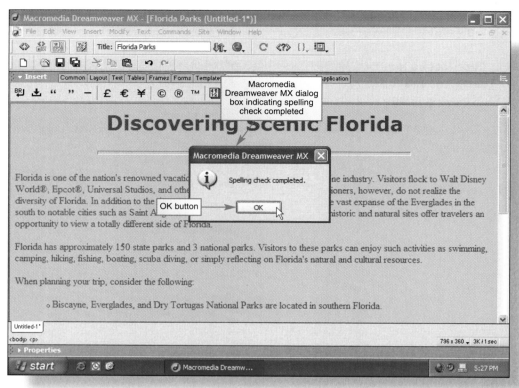

FIGURE 1-88

When Dreamweaver has checked all text for misspellings, it displays the Macromedia Dreamweaver MX dialog box informing you that the spelling check is complete (Figure 1-88).

5 **Click the OK button.**

Dreamweaver closes the Check Spelling dialog box and displays the Document window.

Other Ways

1. Press SHIFT+F7

Types of Links

Links are a distinguishing feature of the World Wide Web. A **link**, also referred to as a **hyperlink**, is the path to another document, to another part of the same document, or to other media such as an image or a movie. Most links are displayed as colored and/or underlined text, although you also can link from an image or other object. Clicking a link accesses the corresponding document, other media, or another place within the same document. If you place the mouse pointer over the link, the link address or path usually appears at the bottom of the window on the status bar.

Three types of link paths are available: absolute, relative, and root-relative. An **absolute link** provides the complete URL of the document. This type of link also is referred to as an **external link**. Absolute links contain the protocol (such as http://) and primarily are used to link to documents on other servers. Project 2 contains detailed information on the other types of links. In the following steps, you enter text and create an absolute link to a Florida environmental Web site. The link will be between the closing paragraph and your name. You will create the link using the Property inspector Link box.

To Create an Absolute Link

1 **Click the expand/collapse arrow in the Property inspector. Position the insertion point at the end of the closing paragraph, press the ENTER key, and then press the END key.**

The Property inspector is displayed and the insertion point is between the closing line and your name (Figure 1-89).

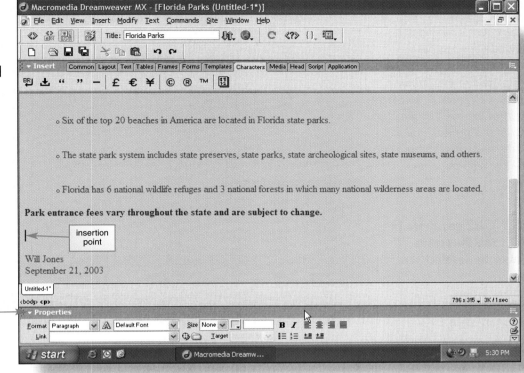

FIGURE 1-89

2 **Type** Florida Environmental Information **and then drag to select the text you typed. Click the Link box in the Property inspector.**

The text for the link is selected (Figure 1-90).

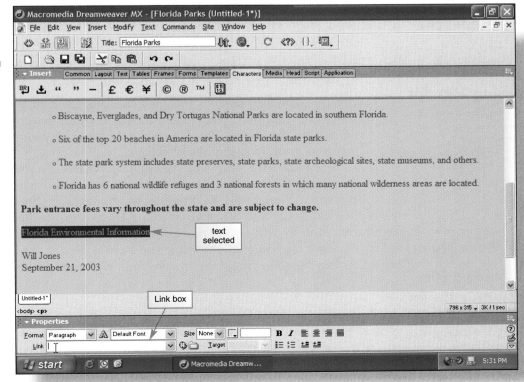

FIGURE 1-90

3 **Type**
http://www.dep
.state.fl.us **and then
press the ENTER key.**

*The link text is highlighted
and underlined in the
Document window. The link
is displayed in the Link box
(Figure 1-91). The link color
is part of the color scheme.
Later in this project, you will
test the link when you preview the Web page in a
browser.*

4 **Click anywhere in
the Document
window to deselect the
link.**

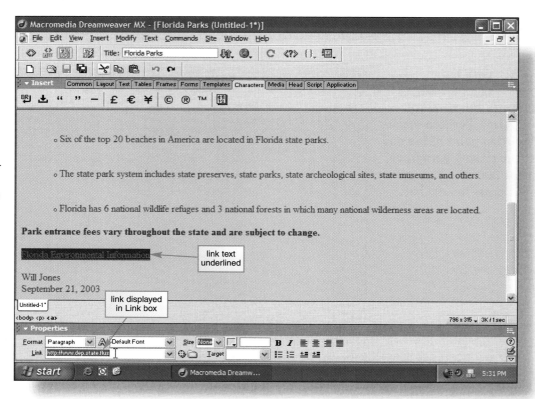

FIGURE 1-91

As you create a Web page in Dreamweaver, the computer stores it in memory.
If you turn off the computer or if you lose electrical power, the document in memory
is lost. Hence, it is necessary to save any document that you will use later.

Saving Your File

It is a good idea to save
your file as soon as you
have created it. Continue
to save the file as you add
more content.

Saving the Web Page

With the document entered and spell checked, the next step is to save the Web page.
Earlier in this project, you created the parks subfolder on the Local Disk (C:) when
you defined the Florida Parks Web site. Verify with your instructor that this is the
correct location to save your Web page.

When you save your Web page, Dreamweaver automatically appends the
extension .htm to the file name. Documents with the **.htm** extension display in Web
browsers. Although the Web page is saved, the Web page also remains in your computer's memory and is displayed in the Document window. It is a good practice to
save regularly while you are working in Dreamweaver. By doing so, you protect
yourself from losing all the work you have done since the last time you saved.
Perform the following steps to save your Web page within the parks subfolder.

Naming a File

When saving a file, use a
meaningful file name. Do
not put spaces in the file
name. To prevent problems
with any server, use no
more than eight lowercase
letters in the file name.

Steps **To Save a Web Page**

1 **Click the Save button on the Standard toolbar (Figure 1-92).**

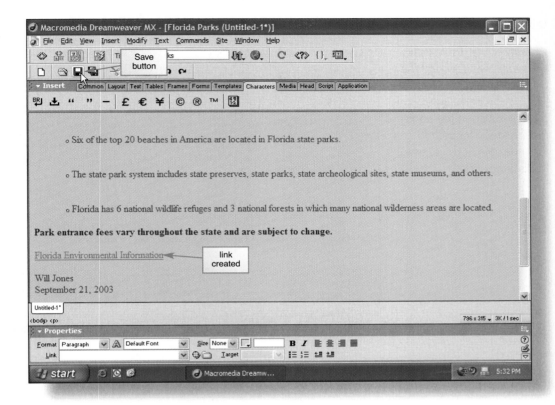

FIGURE 1-92

2 **Type** index **in the File name text box and then point to the Save button in the Save As dialog box.**

The Save As dialog is displayed (Figure 1-93). The parks folder name is displayed in the Save in box. The index file name is displayed in the File name box.

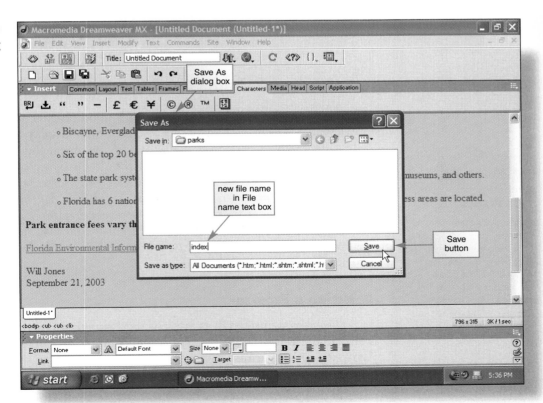

FIGURE 1-93

3 **Click the Save button and then press the F8 key to display the Site panel.**

Dreamweaver displays the Document window and the Site panel (Figure 1-94). The Florida Parks index.htm page is saved in the parks local folder. The path to the index file is C:\jonesw\ parks\index.htm.

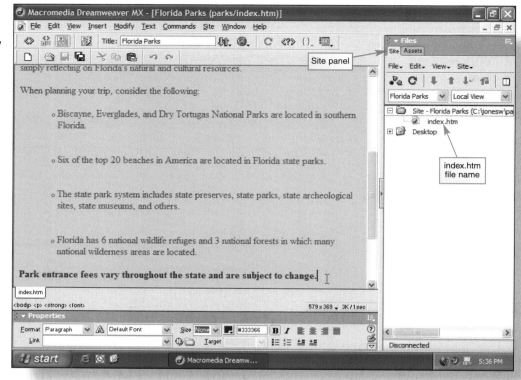

FIGURE 1-94

Other Ways

1. Press CTRL+S

With your Web page ready to share with the world, you next must select browsers to ensure your visitors can view the page properly. The two more popular browsers are Internet Explorer and Netscape.

Selecting Primary and Secondary Target Browsers

After you have created a Web page, it is a good practice to test your Web pages by previewing them in Web browsers to ensure they display correctly. Using this strategy helps you catch errors so you will not copy or repeat them.

As you create your Web page, you should be aware of the variety of available Web browsers. More than 24 different Web browsers are in use, most of which have been released in more than one version. Most Web developers target recent versions of Netscape Navigator and Microsoft Internet Explorer, which are used by the majority of Web users. You also should know that visitors viewing your Web page might have earlier versions of these browsers. You can define up to 20 browsers for previewing.

Selecting a Browser

The browser preferences are selected through the Preferences dialog box. Perform the following steps to select your target browsers: Microsoft Internet Explorer and Netscape Navigator. To complete these steps requires that you have both Internet Explorer and Netscape installed on your computer.

Browsers

Just as you determined a primary and secondary browser, you also can remove a browser from your list. Click Edit on the menu bar and then click Preferences. Select the name of the browser you want to remove and then click the minus (–) button.

Steps **To Select Primary and Secondary Target Browsers**

1 **Right-click the Files panel menu bar and close the panel group. Click File on the menu bar, point to Preview in Browser, and then point to Edit Browser List on the Preview in Browser submenu.**

Dreamweaver displays the File menu and Preview in Browser submenu (Figure 1-95).

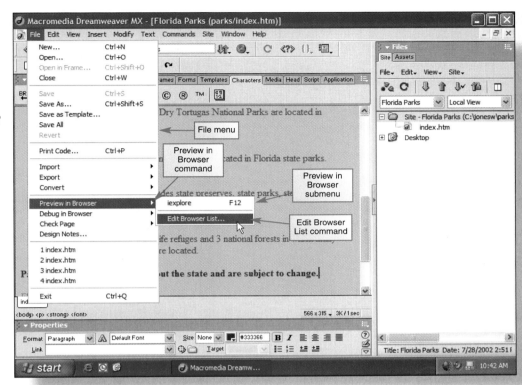

FIGURE 1-95

2 **Click Edit Browser List and point to the plus (+) button.**

The Preferences dialog box is displayed and the Preview in Browser category is selected (Figure 1-96). The primary browser was selected when Dreamweaver was installed on your computer. In this book, the primary browser is Internet Explorer. The browser name, iexplore, was selected automatically during the Dreamweaver installation.

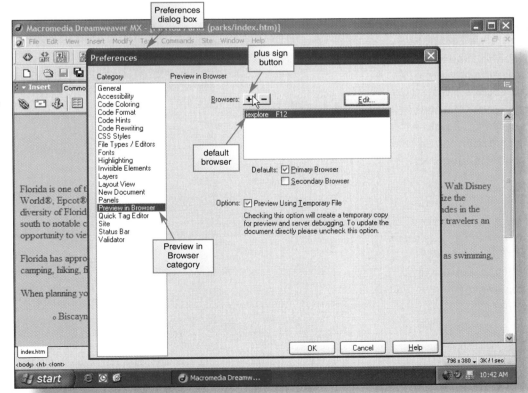

FIGURE 1-96

3 Click the plus (+) button in the Preview in Browser area. Point to the Browse button.

Dreamweaver displays the Add Browser dialog box (Figure 1-97).

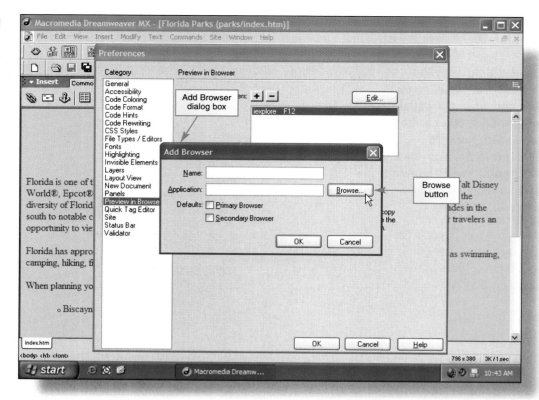

FIGURE 1-97

4 Click the Browse button and then locate the Netscp.exe file. Most likely this file is located on Local Drive (C:). Use the following path to locate the file: C:\Program Files\ Netscape\Netscape\ Netscp.exe. Point to the Open button in the Select Browser dialog box.

The Select Browser dialog box is displayed (Figure 1-98). The Netscp.exe file is selected. Different versions of Netscape may display a different file name or a different path.

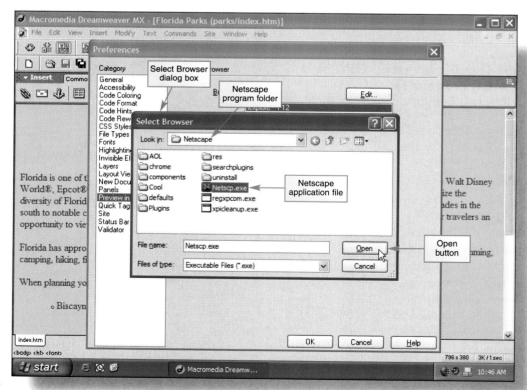

FIGURE 1-98

Click the Open button. Click Secondary Browser and then point to the OK button in the Add Browser dialog box.

The Name box displays Netscp.exe. The Application box displays the path and file name (Figure 1-99). The path and spelling of Netscape on your computer may be different from those shown.

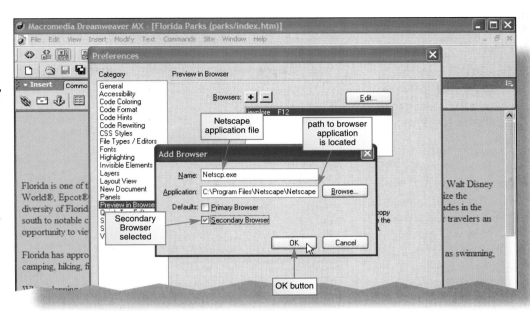

FIGURE 1-99

 Click the OK button. If necessary, click Preview Using Temporary File to select it. Point to the OK button in the Preferences dialog box.

Netscape is added as the secondary browser (Figure 1-100).

 Click the OK button.

The target browsers are selected, and Dreamweaver displays the Document window.

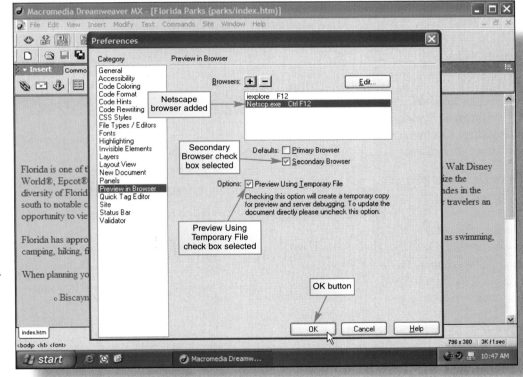

FIGURE 1-100

Previewing a Web Page in a Browser

With the target browsers set up, you can preview your Web pages in the browsers at any time. You do not have to save the document first. The steps on the next two pages illustrate how to preview a Web page.

Steps **To Preview the Web Page**

1 Click File on the menu bar, point to Preview in Browser, and then point to iexplore.

The File menu and Preview in Browser submenu are displayed (Figure 1-101). The Preview in Browser submenu includes the names of both your primary and secondary browsers and the Edit Browser List command. Clicking the Edit Browser List command displays the Preferences dialog box.

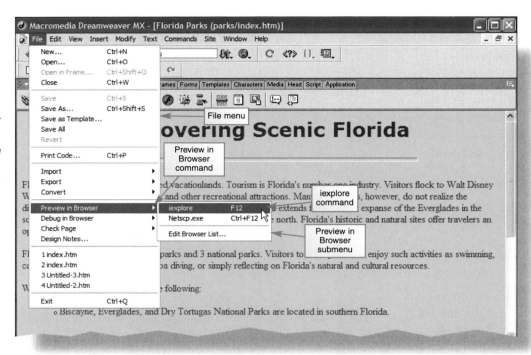

FIGURE 1-101

2 Click iexplore (Internet Explorer). If necessary, maximize your browser window.

Internet Explorer starts and displays the Web page in a browser window (Figure 1-102). Your browser name may be different. The file name displayed in the Address bar is a temporary name.

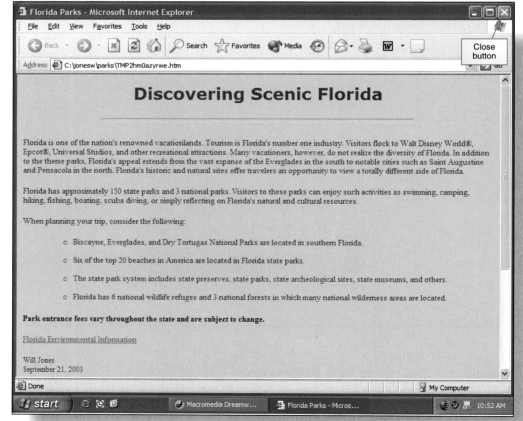

FIGURE 1-102

3 **Click Internet Explorer's Close button. Click File on the menu bar, point to Preview in Browser, and then click Netscp.exe on the Preview in Browser submenu.**

Netscape opens and displays the Web page in a browser window (Figure 1-103). Your browser name may be different. Compare how the files display in the two browsers.

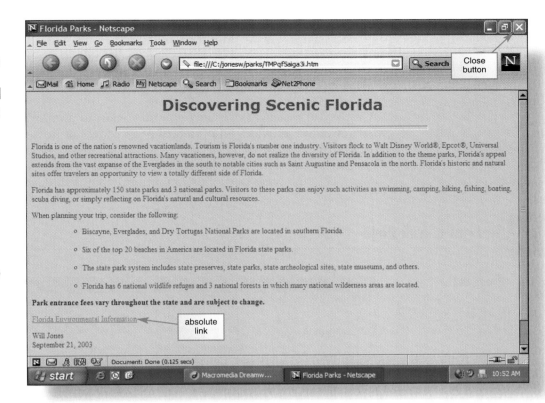

FIGURE 1-103

4 **If necessary, scroll down the page and click the absolute link to the Florida Environmental Information Web site.**

The Florida Department of Environmental Protection Web site is displayed (Figure 1-104). You must be online to complete this step.

5 **Click Netscape's Close button. If necessary, click the Dreamweaver button on the taskbar.**

The Dreamweaver Document window is displayed.

Other Ways

1. Press F12
2. Press CTRL+F12

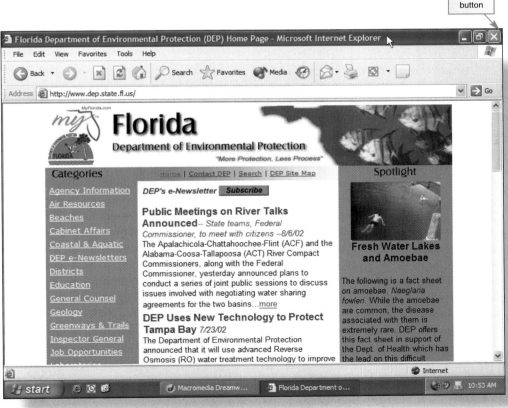

FIGURE 1-104

Your instructor may require that you print a copy of your Web page. The next step illustrates how to print a page.

Printing a Web Page

A variety of reasons exists why you may want to print a Web page. Interestingly, Dreamweaver provides an option to print code, but does not provide a print option to print the Design view. To print a Web page, first you must preview it in a browser. Printing a page from your browser is similar to printing a word processing document. The following steps illustrate printing the Web page in the browser.

To Print a Web Page

 Press F12.

The Web page is displayed in Internet Explorer.

2 **Click File on the menu bar and then point to Print (Figure 1-105).**

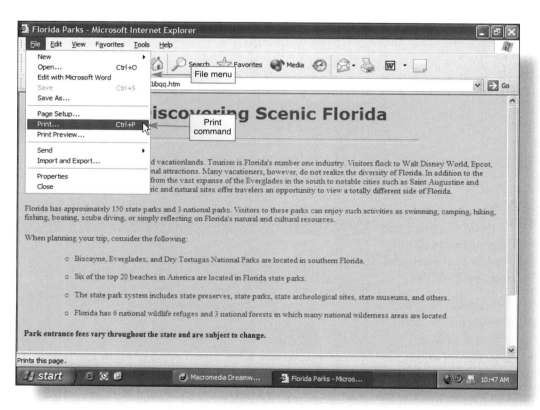

FIGURE 1-105

3 **Click Print. If necessary, select an appropriate printer. Point to the Print button.**

Internet Explorer displays the Print dialog box (Figure 1-106). Your selected printer is likely to be different from the one shown in Figure 1-106.

4 **Click the Print button.**

The Print dialog box closes and your Web page is sent to the printer.

5 **Retrieve the printout and then click Internet Explorer's Close button.**

The browser closes and Dreamweaver displays the Document window.

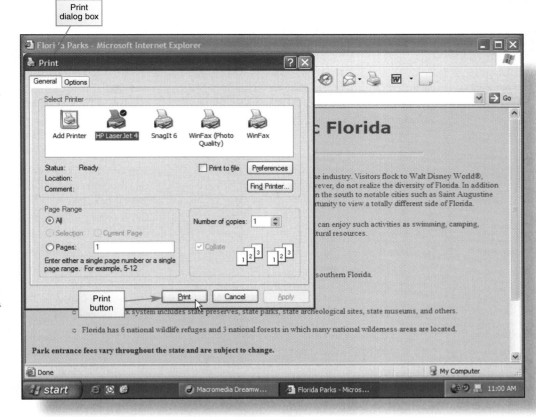

FIGURE 1-106

Dreamweaver Help System

Reference materials and other forms of assistance are available using the Dreamweaver Help system. You can display these materials, print them, or copy them to a word processing document. Table 1-4 on the next page summarizes the categories of online Help available. Several methods are available to activate the first four types listed in the table. Appendix A provides detailed instructions on using Dreamweaver Help.

Table 1-4 Dreamweaver Help System

TYPE	DESCRIPTION	HOW TO ACTIVATE
Contents sheet	Use the Contents sheet to view information organized by topic and then by subtopic, as you would in the table of contents of a book.	• Press the F1 key. Click the Contents tab. • Click Help on the menu bar and then click Using Dreamweaver. Click the Contents tab. • Click the options button on the title bar of a panel group and then click Help on the options pop-up menu. Click the Contents tab.
Index sheet	Use the Index sheet to look up specific terms or concepts, as you would in the index of a book.	• Press the F1 key. Click the Index tab. • Click Help on the menu bar and then click Using Dreamweaver. Click the Index tab. • Click the options button on the title bar of a panel group and then click Help on the options pop-up menu. Click the Index tab.
Search sheet	Use the Search sheet to find any character string, anywhere in the text of the Help system.	• Press the F1 key. Click the Search tab. • Click Help on the menu bar and then click Using Dreamweaver. Click the Search tab. • Click the options button on the title bar of a panel group and then click Help on the options pop-up menu. Click the Search tab.
Question Mark button or Help icon	Clicking the Question Mark button provides context-sensitive help in dialog boxes and inspectors.	• Click a Help button or Question Mark button in a dialog box. • Click the Help icon in an inspector or other kind of window.
Tutorials	Step-by-step lessons that focus on a specific Web design feature or topic.	• Click Help on the menu bar and then click Tutorials.
Dreamweaver online tutorials	Step-by-step online tutorials	• Access the Dreamweaver tutorial Web site at macromedia.com/desdev/mx/dreamweaver/index.html

Quitting Dreamweaver

After you create, save, preview, and print the Florida Parks Web page and review how to use Help, Project 1 is complete. To close the Web page, quit Dreamweaver MX, and return control to Windows, perform the following step.

Other Ways

1. On File menu click Exit
2. Press CTRL+W

TO CLOSE THE WEB SITE AND QUIT DREAMWEAVER

1 Click the Close button on the right corner of the Dreamweaver title bar.

The Dreamweaver window, the Document window, and Florida Parks Web site all close. If you have unsaved changes, Dreamweaver will prompt you to save the changes. Clicking the Yes button in the Dreamweaver MX dialog box saves the changes.

CASE PERSPECTIVE SUMMARY

The local Web site and Web page are complete. Will is pleased that he now can share his affection for Florida's Parks with others on the Internet. During the process, Will learned a lot about using Dreamweaver to define a Web site and to create simple, yet informative Web pages. He was amazed at how easy it was to add a color scheme, format and add color to text, create a bulleted list, and insert a rule to add variety to the elements of the page. He was happy to learn about absolute links and that visitors using virtually any Web browser would be able to view his Web page once it was uploaded to a server. He is looking forward to doing more with this Web site using these and other Dreamweaver tools.

Opening a Web Page

Opening a Web page in Dreamweaver is much the same as opening an existing document in most other software applications: that is, you use the File menu and Open command. If, however, the page is part of a Dreamweaver Web site, you also can open the file from the Site panel.

To open a Web page from the Site panel, you must select the appropriate Web site. The site pop-up menu in the Site panel lists sites you have defined. When you open the site, a list of pages and subfolders within the site displays. To open the page, double-click the file name. After opening the page, you can modify text, images, tables, and any other elements.

Project Summary

Project 1 introduced you to starting Dreamweaver, defining a Web site, and creating a Web page. You added a color scheme and used Dreamweaver's Property inspector to format text, change font color, and center text. You also learned how to apply color to text, add a horizontal rule, and use an unordered list to organize information. You used the Insert bar to add line breaks and special characters. Using the Property inspector, you added an absolute link. Once your Web page was completed, you learned to save the Web page, preview it in a browser, and test your absolute link. You learned how to print using the browser. To enhance your knowledge of Dreamweaver further, you learned basics about the Dreamweaver Help system.

What You Should Know

Having completed this project, you now should be able to perform the tasks shown in Table 1-5.

Table 1-5	Project 1 What You Should Know		
TASK NUMBER	*TASK*	*PAGE NUMBER*	
1	Start Dreamweaver	DW 1.04	
2	Close All Open Panels	DW 1.10	
3	Use the Site Definition Wizard to Create a Local Web Site	DW 1.12	
4	Add a Color Scheme	DW 1.22	
5	Close the Site Panel and Display the Standard Toolbar	DW 1.24	
6	Create a Web Page	DW 1.26	
7	Open the Property Inspector	DW 1.29	
8	Format Text with Heading 1	DW 1.33	
9	Center the Web Page Heading	DW 1.35	
10	Change the Font Type	DW 1.36	
11	Create an Unordered List	DW 1.38	
12	Use Text Indent to Indent a Bulleted List	DW 1.40	
13	Bold Text	DW 1.41	
14	Change the Text Color	DW 1.43	

TASK NUMBER	*TASK*	*PAGE NUMBER*
15	Insert a Horizontal Rule	DW 1.45
16	Display the Insert Bar	DW 1.49
17	Add a Line Break	DW 1.50
18	Add Your Name and Current Date	DW 1.52
19	Insert a Registered Trademark Character	DW 1.55
20	Collapse the Property Inspector	DW 1.56
21	Change the Web Page Title	DW 1.57
22	Check Spelling	DW 1.59
23	Create an Absolute Link	DW 1.61
24	Save a Web Page	DW 1.63
25	Select Primary and Secondary Target Browsers	DW 1.65
26	Preview the Web Page	DW 1.68
27	Print a Web Page	DW 1.70
28	Close the Web Site and Quit Dreamweaver	DW 1.72

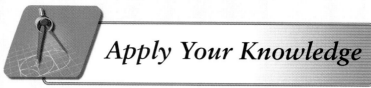

Apply Your Knowledge

1 Defining a Web Site and Creating a Web Page

Instructions: Start Dreamweaver. Perform the following tasks to define a Web site and create and format a Web page for B & B Lawn Service. The Web page as it displays in a browser is shown in Figure 1-107. The text for the Web site is shown in Table 1-6.

Software and hardware settings determine how a Web page is displayed in the browser. Your Web pages may display differently in your browser than those in the figures. For an updated list of links, visit the Dreamweaver MX Links Web page (scsite.com/dreamweavermx/links) and then click Project 1 Links.

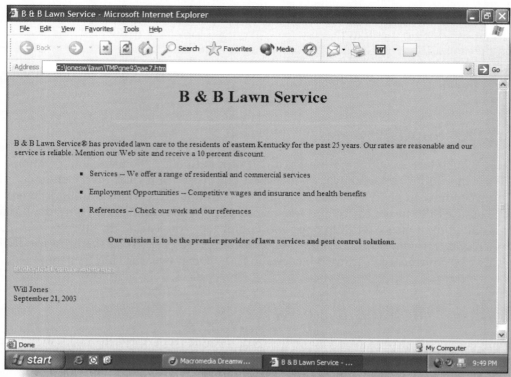

FIGURE 1-107

Table 1-6 B & B Lawn Service Web Page	
SECTION	**WEB PAGE TEXT**
Heading	B & B Lawn Service
Introductory Paragraph	B & B Lawn Service has provided lawn care to the residents of eastern Kentucky for the past 25 years. Our rates are reasonable and our service is reliable. Mention our Web site and receive a 10 percent discount.
List Item 1	Services -- We offer a range of residential and commercial services
List Item 2	Employment Opportunities -- Competitive wages and insurance and health benefits
List Item 3	References -- Check our work and our references
Closing	Our mission is to be the premier provider of lawn services and pest control solutions.
Link Text	Ecological Lawn Maintenance

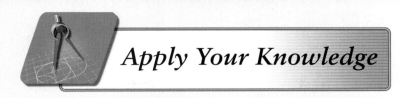

Apply Your Knowledge

1. Press F4 to close all open panels. Click Site on the menu bar and then click New Site. Use the Site Definition Wizard to create a local Web site under the your name folder. In Site Definition Editing Files options, name the site Lawn Service. Click the Next button. In the Site Definition Editing Files, Part 2 options, click No, I do not want to use a server technology. Click the Next button. In the Site Definition Editing Files, Part 3 options, create a new subfolder under jonesw (your name), and name the new subfolder lawn. The path will be C:\jonesw\lawn. Click the Next button. In the Site Definition Sharing options, select None in the How do you connect to your remote server? list. Click the Next button. In the Site Definition Summary options, click the Done button.

2. Click Commands on the menu bar and then click Set Color Scheme. Select the Green background and Brown, Yellow, Red for text and links.

3. Click in the Document window. Type the Web page text in Table 1-6. Press the ENTER key after typing the text in each section and after each one of the list items in the table.

4. Click Window on the menu bar and then click Properties to display the Property inspector. Select the heading text and then apply Heading 1. Click the Align Center button in the Property inspector to center the heading.

5. Select the three list items. Click the Unordered List button in the Property inspector to create a bulleted list with these three items. Click the Text Indent button in the Property inspector two times.

6. Select the closing paragraph. Click the Align Center button and then click the Bold button in the Property inspector. Do not deselect the sentence.

7. Click the Text Color box and select hexadecimal color #993333. This color swatch is located in the 5th column from the right and 5th row from the bottom.

8. Click at the end of the heading and then press the END key. Click Insert on the menu bar and then click Horizontal Rule. Specify a width of 450 pixels, a height of 4, center alignment, and no shading.

9. Click Window on the menu bar and then click Insert to display the Insert bar. Click the Characters tab. Click to the right of B & B Lawn Service in the first paragraph. Insert a registered trademark symbol.

10. Click at the end of the first bulleted item. Insert two line breaks between the first and second bulleted items and then insert two line breaks between the second and third bulleted items.

11. Title the Web page, B & B Lawn Service, using the Title text box on the Document toolbar.

12. Select the link text. Create an absolute link. Type http://www.eap.mcgill.ca/Publications/EAP68.htm in the Link box.

13. Click to the right of the inserted link, press the END key, and then press the ENTER key to insert a blank line after the linked text.

14. Type your name. Insert a line break and then type the current date.

15. Click Text on the menu bar and then click Check Spelling. Spell check your document and correct any errors.

16. Click File on the menu bar and then click Save to save the Web page in the C:\jonesw\lawn folder (use the your name folder). Type index in the File name text box and then click the Save button in the Save As dialog box.

17. Click Site on the menu bar and then click Site Files to verify that you saved the file correctly.

18. Press the F12 key to view the Web page in the browser. Test the link. Print a copy if required and hand it in to your instructor. Click the browser's Close button.

19. Click the Dreamweaver Close button to quit Dreamweaver.

In the Lab

1 Creating a Business Web Site

Problem: A friend of yours, Mary Stewart, is starting her own business selling candles. She has asked you to assist her in preparing a Web page to help her advertise her candles (Figure 1-108).

Software and hardware settings determine how a Web page is displayed in the browser. Your Web pages may display differently in your browser than those in the figures. For an updated list of links, visit the Dreamweaver MX Links Web page (scsite.com/ dreamweavermx/ links) and then click Project 1 Links.

Instructions: Start Dreamweaver. Perform the following tasks to define a Web site and

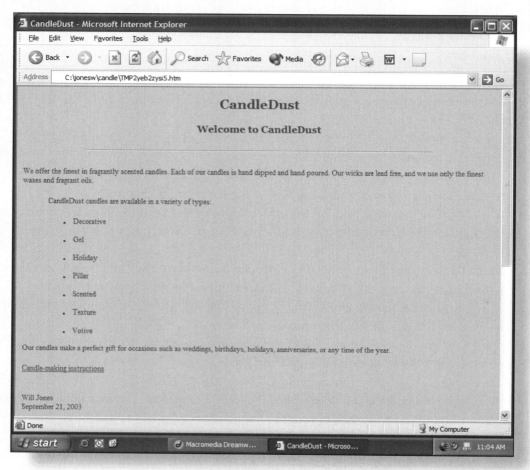

FIGURE 1-108

create and format a Web page for CandleDust. The text for the Web page is shown in Table 1-7.

1. Press F4 to close all open panels. Click Site on the menu bar and then click New Site. Use the Site Definition Wizard to create a local Web site under the your name folder. In Site Definition Wizard Editing Files options, name the site CandleDust. In the Editing Files, Part 3 options, create a new subfolder under the your name folder and name the new subfolder candle. All other selections in the Site Definition Wizard are the same as those for the parks Web site.

2. Set the Color Scheme to a Purple background and Blue,Purple,Green for text and links.

3. Click in the Document window and then type the Web page text in Table 1-7. Press the ENTER key after typing each section and after each list item in the table.

In the Lab

Table 1-7 CandleDust Web Page	
SECTION	**WEB PAGE TEXT**
Heading	CandleDust
Subheading	Welcome to CandleDust
Introductory Paragraph	We offer the finest in fragrantly scented candles. Each of our candles is hand dipped and hand poured. Our wicks are lead free, and we use only the finest waxes and fragrant oils.
Second Paragraph	CandleDust candles are available in a variety of types:
List Item 1	Decorative
List Item 2	Gel
List Item 3	Holiday
List Item 4	Pillar
List Item 5	Scented
List Item 6	Texture
List Item 7	Votive
Closing	Our candles make a perfect gift for occasions such as weddings, birthdays, holidays, anniversaries, or any time of the year.

4. Display the Property inspector. Select the heading text and apply Heading 1. Select the subheading text and apply Heading 2. Select both headings and then click the Align Center button in the Property inspector to center the titles. Change the font type to Georgia, Times New Roman.

5. Select the introductory paragraph text. Click the Text Indent button in the Property inspector to indent the paragraph. Select the list items. Click the Unordered List button in the Property inspector and then click the Text Indent button in the Property inspector two times.

6. Click at the end of CandleDust and then press the END key. Click Insert on the menu bar and then click Horizontal Rule. Change the width to 550 pixels, and align center.

7. Click Window on the menu bar and then click Insert to display the Insert bar. Click the Characters tab. Click at the end of the first bulleted item. Click the Line Break button on the Characters tab two times to insert two line breaks between the first and second bulleted list items. Insert two line breaks between the other bulleted list items.

8. Select the text in the Title text box on the Document toolbar. Type CandleDust as the title.

9. Click at the end of the closing paragraph and then press the ENTER key. Type Candle-making instructions as the link text.

10. Select the link text and create an absolute link using the Link box in the Property inspector. Type http://candleandsoap.about.com/cs/candlemaking1/ for the URL.

11. Click to the right of the link, press the END key, and then press the ENTER key to insert a blank line after the last line.

12. Type your name. Insert a line break and then type the current date.

13. Spell check your document and correct any errors.

(continued)

In the Lab

Creating a Business Web Site *(continued)*

14. Click File on the menu bar and then click Save to save the Web page in the C:\jonesw\candle folder (use the your name folder). Type index in the File name text box and then click the Save button in the Save As dialog box.
15. Click Site on the menu bar and then click Site Files to verify that you saved the file correctly.
16. View the Web page in the browser. Test the link. Print a copy if required and hand it in to your instructor. Close the browser.
17. Quit Dreamweaver.

2 Credit Protection Web Page

Problem: Marcy Cantu is an intern in a small law practice. She recently lost her wallet, which contained all of her credit cards. She called the credit card companies and canceled her credit cards. One of the attorneys suggested she also call the three credit bureaus to make them aware of this problem. Because searching for the names, telephone numbers, and addresses of the three credit bureaus was quite time consuming, Marcy decided she wants to have this information readily available in the event she needs it again and for others who might find themselves in a similar situation. She has asked you to prepare the Web page shown in Figure 1-109.

Software and hardware settings determine how a Web page is displayed in the browser. Your Web pages may display differently in your browser than those in the figures. For an updated list of links, visit the Dreamweaver MX Links Web page (scsite.com/dreamweavermx/links) and then click Project 1 Links.

Instructions: Start Dreamweaver. Perform the following tasks to define a Web site and create and format an informational Web page on credit protection. The text for the Web page is shown in Table 1-8.

Table 1-8 Credit Protection Web Page	
SECTION	*WEB PAGE TEXT*
Heading	Credit Protection
Introductory Paragraph	A credit card can be a great financial tool, but it also is a big responsibility. Applying for and receiving a credit card generally is an easy procedure. Offers from credit card companies arrive frequently in the regular mail.
Second Paragraph	Many people, particularly first-time users, do not fully understand the implications of a credit card. They may charge more than they can repay. This can damage a credit rating and create credit problems that can be difficult to fix.
Third Paragraph	Before you submit a credit application, obtain a copy of your credit report from one of the three major credit reporting agencies to make sure it is accurate.
List Item 1	Equifax Information Services, LLC P.O. Box 740241 Atlanta, GA 30374
List Item 2	Experian Consumer Opt-Out 701 Experian Parkway Allen, TX 75013
List Item 3	TransUnion LLC's Name Removal Option P.O. Box 97328 Jackson, MS 39288-7328

In the Lab

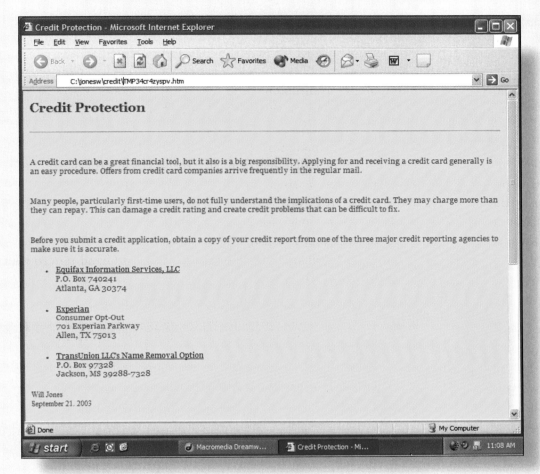

FIGURE 1-109

1. Close all open panels. Use the Site Definition Wizard to create a local Web site under the your name folder. Name the site Credit Protection. Create a new subfolder under your name and name the new subfolder credit. All other selections in the Site Definition Wizard are the same as those for the parks Web site.

2. Set the Color Scheme to a Yellow background and Green,Blue,Purple for text and links.

3. Type the heading and first three paragraphs of the Web page text in Table 1-8. Press the ENTER key after typing each section of the text in the table.

4. Type list item 1. Insert a line break after the company name and after the address. Press the ENTER key after the city and state. Type list items 2 and 3. Insert a line break after the company name and address and press the ENTER key after the city and state.

5. Display the Property inspector. Select the heading text and apply Heading 1. Align to the left (to ensure the heading is displayed properly in the browser). Insert a horizontal rule following the heading.

6. Click Edit on the menu bar and then click Select All. Change the font type to Georgia, Times New Roman for all the text on the Web page.

7. Select the three list items (companies and addresses) and create an unordered (bulleted) list. If necessary, use the Line Break button to add a blank line between the bulleted items.

(continued)

In the Lab

Credit Protection Web Page *(continued)*

8. Select the name of company in the first bulleted list item (Equifax Information Services, LLC) and create an absolute link using http://www.equifax.com. Create a link from the other two company names, using http://www.experian.com and http://www.transunion.com.

9. Select Untitled Document in the Title text box on the Document toolbar and type Credit Protection as the title of the Web page.

10. Click at the end of the last line of text and then press the ENTER key. If a bullet displays, click the Bullet button in the Property inspector to remove the bullet and then click the Text Outdent button in the Property inspector. Type your name and then type the current date.

11. Spell check your document and correct any errors.

12. Save the Web page in the credit folder. Type index for the file name.

13. On the Site menu, click Site Files to verify that you saved the file correctly.

14. View the Web page in the browser. Test the links. Print a copy if required and hand it in to your instructor. Close the browser and then quit Dreamweaver.

3 Plant City Web Page

Problem: Juan Benito recently moved to Plant City, Florida. He has discovered that Plant City has a colorful history and that many consider the city to be the Strawberry Capital of the United States. He has asked you to help prepare a Web page (Figure 1-110) so he can share information with friends, relatives, and visitors to Florida about the city's historical facts.

Software and hardware settings determine how a Web page is displayed in the browser. Your Web pages may display differently in your browser than those in the figures. For an updated list of links, visit the Dreamweaver MX Links Web page (scsite.com/dreamweavermx/links) and then click Project 1 Links.

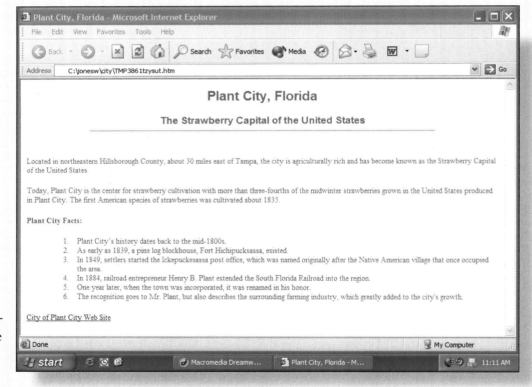

FIGURE 1-110

In the Lab

Instructions: Start Dreamweaver. Perform the following tasks to define a Web site and create and format an informational Web page on Plant City, Florida. The text of the Web page is shown in Table 1-9.

Table 1-9	Plant City, Florida Web Site
SECTION	*WEB PAGE TEXT*
Heading	Plant City, Florida
Subheading	The Strawberry Capital of the United States
Introductory Paragraph	Located in northeastern Hillsborough County, about 30 miles east of Tampa, the city is agriculturally rich and has become known as the Strawberry Capital of the United States.
Second Paragraph	Today, Plant City is the center for strawberry cultivation with more than three-fourths of the midwinter strawberries grown in the United States produced in Plant City. The first American species of strawberries was cultivated about 1835.
Third Paragraph	Plant City Facts:
List Item 1	Plant City's history dates back to the mid-1800s.
List Item 2	As early as 1839, a pine log blockhouse, Fort Hichipucksassa, existed.
List Item 3	In 1849, settlers started the Ickepuckesassa post office, which was named originally after the Native American village that once occupied the area.
List Item 4	In 1884, railroad entrepreneur Henry B. Plant extended the South Florida Railroad into the region.
List Item 5	One year later, when the town was incorporated, it was renamed in his honor.
List Item 6	The recognition goes to Mr. Plant, but also describes the surrounding farming industry, which greatly added to the city's growth.
Link Text	City of Plant City Web Site

1. Close all open panels. Use the Site Definition Wizard to create a local Web site under the your name folder. Name the site Plant City. Create a subfolder and name it city. All other selections in the Site Definition Wizard are the same as those for the parks Web site.
2. Set the Color Scheme to a White background and Brown,Red,Orange for text and links.
3. Click in the Document window and then type the Web page text in Table 1-9. Press the ENTER key after typing the text in each section in the table.
4. Display the Property inspector. Select the heading text and apply Heading 1. Select the subheading text and apply Heading 2. Center both headings. Change the heading font type to Arial, Helvetica, sans-serif.
5. Insert a centered horizontal line, 550 pixels in width, below the subtitle.
6. Select the third paragraph, Plant City Facts, and then apply bold formatting to the text.
7. Select the list items 1 through 6 and apply an ordered list. Text Indent one time.
8. Change the Web page title to Plant City, Florida.
9. Select the link text and then create an absolute link using http://www.ci.plant-city.fl.us/ as the URL.
10. Insert your name and the current date on the Web page.
11. Spell check your document and correct any errors. Save the Web page in the C:\jonesw\city folder. Type index for the file name.
12. Check the Site Files to verify that you saved the file correctly.
13. View the Web page in the browser. Test the link. Print a copy if required and hand it in to your instructor. Close the browser. Quit Dreamweaver.

Cases and Places

The difficulty of these case studies varies:
▶ are the least difficult; ▶▶ are more difficult; and ▶▶▶ are the most difficult.

1 ▶ Define a Web site named Favorite Sports with a subfolder named sports. Prepare a Web page listing your favorite sports and favorite teams. Include a title for your Web page. Bold and center the title, and then apply the Heading 1 style. Include a sentence or two explaining why you like the sport and why you like the teams. Bold and italicize the names of the teams and the sports. Give the Web page a meaningful title. Apply a color scheme to your Web page. Spell check the document. Use the concepts and techniques presented in the project to format the text. Save the file in the sports folder.

2 ▶ Your instructor has asked you to create a Web page about one of your hobbies. Define the Web site using Hobbies for the site name and hobby for the subfolder name. Italicize and center the title, and then apply the Heading 2 style. Type a paragraph of three or four sentences explaining why you selected the subject. Select and center the paragraph. Add a list of three items and create an ordered list from the three items. Include line breaks between each numbered item. Title the Web page the name of the hobby you selected. Spell check your document. Use the concepts and techniques presented in the project to format the text.

3 ▶▶ Define a Web site and create a Web page that gives a description and information about your favorite type of music. Name the Web site Favorite Music and the subfolder music. Apply a color scheme to the Web page. Include a left-aligned heading formatted with the Heading 1 style. Include a subheading formatted with Heading 2. Insert a horizontal rule following the subheading. List four facts about why you selected this type of music. Include the names of three of your favorite songs and the names of the artists. Bold and italicize the name of the songs and artists and apply a font color of your choice. Create an ordered list from the four facts. Text Indent your list. Title the Web page Favorite Music. Save the file as index in the music folder. Use the concepts and techniques presented in the project to format the text.

4 ▶▶ Assume you are running for office in your city's local government. Define a Web site using the name of the city in which you live and a subfolder named office. Include the following information in your Web page: Your name, centered, with Heading 1 and a font color of your choice; the name of the office for which you are running, bold and italicized; and a paragraph about the duties of the office in Courier font. Create a bulleted list within your Web page. Change the title of the Web page from Untitled Document to your name. Locate a related site online and create an absolute link to the site. Use the concepts and techniques presented in the project to format the text.

5 ▶▶ Your school has a budget for student trips. Your assignment is to put together a Web site and Web page, listing locations and trips from which the student body can select. Apply a color scheme. Include a title, formatted with Heading 1, and a subtitle, formatted with Heading 2. Insert a shaded horizontal line following the subtitle. List three locations. Bold and apply a font color to each location name and use Text Indent on the three items. Add a bullet to each location name. Include information about each location. Title the page Student Government. Add an absolute link to a related Web site. Use the concepts and techniques presented in the project to format the text.

Macromedia Dreamweaver MX

Adding Web Pages, Links, and Images

You will have mastered the material in this project when you can:

O B J E C T I V E S

- Copy files and folders using the integrated file browser
- Set a home page
- Add pages to a Web site
- Describe image file formats
- Add a background image to a Web page
- Insert, resize, and align images within a Web page
- Describe the different types of links
- Create a relative, absolute, and e-mail link
- Change the color of links
- Edit and delete links
- Describe and display the Site Map
- Use the Link Checker
- Describe Code View and Design View
- Use Code View to modify HTML code

Macromedia Dreamweaver MX

Adding Web Pages, Links, and Images

PROJECT

CASE PERSPECTIVE

A coworker at the state environmental agency, Joan Komisky, who also is interested in Florida's parks, viewed the Web page that you and Will created. She has offered some suggestions and asked to help with the design. Both you and Will agreed, and the three of you have become a team.

Joan suggests adding images to the home page. Will proposes that the Web site should include a page for Florida's three national parks and another page with information about his three favorite state parks located in northwest Florida. You explain to Will and Joan that the addition of each new page will require hyperlinks from the home page and links from each page back to the home page. You assure them that Dreamweaver includes all the tools they need to add many types of links to other related Web sites as well as e-mail links. You create a navigation map to illustrate how the links will work among the three pages. All team members agree that these two new pages should be added and will include images and links. With the addition of these two pages, the Web page will become a Web site.

Introduction

Project 2 introduces the addition of Web pages to the local site created in Project 1 and the integration of links and graphics into the Web pages that make up the site. Recall from Project 1 that a site or a Web site is a set of linked documents with shared attributes, such as related topics, a similar design, or a shared purpose.

The site structure feature provides a way to maintain and organize your files. A Web page essentially is a text document and a collection of HTML code. The HTML (HyperText Markup Language) defines the structure and layout of a Web document and is generated automatically by Dreamweaver. Images and other media content are separate files. For example, a page that displays text and three images consists of four separate files — one for the text document and one for each of the three images.

Most Web site builders include images on their Web pages. It is important that you take the time to learn about images, image properties, and the types of images best suited for a particular situation. Image properties, such as alternative text for accessibility issues, alignment, and changing the size, help you to understand the effects of using images on Web pages.

When a file or image is referenced within the HTML document, a link (or hyperlink) exists within the HTML code to the external file or image. Recall from Project 1 that a link (hyperlink) is a Web page element that, when clicked, accesses another Web page, or a different place within the existing Web page. A Web page can contain different types of links: internal or relative, absolute (the type you created in Project 1), e-mail, and links to a specific place within a document. This project discusses how to create these links.

DW 2.02

Project Two — Adding Links and Images to the Florida Parks Web Site

In this project, you continue with the creation of the Florida Parks Web site. You add two additional Web pages and add an image background, page images, and links to the index page (Figure 2-1a) and the two new pages (Figure 2-1b on the next page) and (Figure 2-1c on the next page).

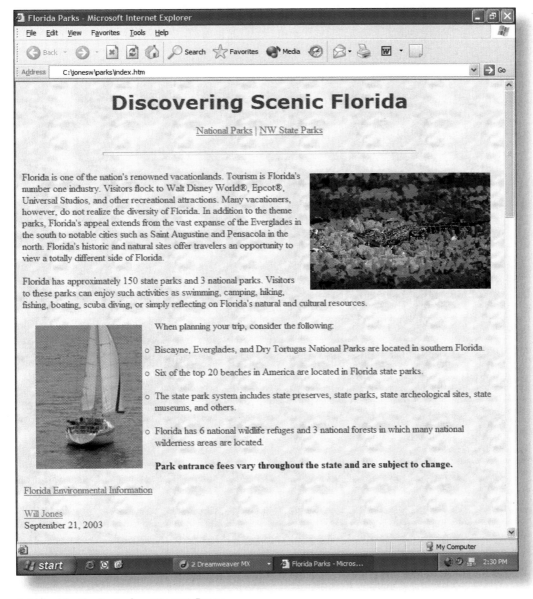

(a) Florida Parks Index (Home) Page

FIGURE 2-1

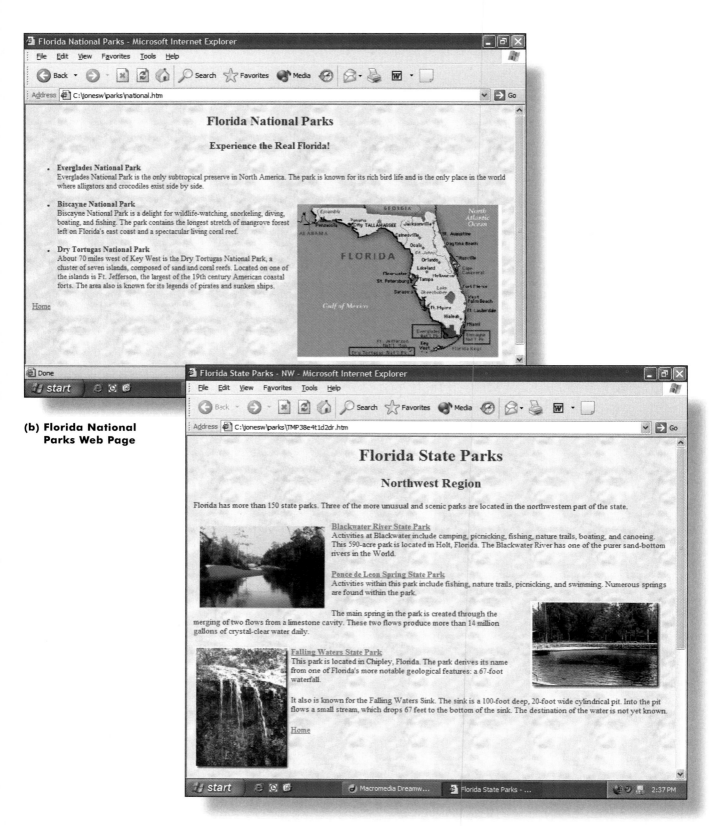

(b) Florida National Parks Web Page

(c) Florida State Parks Web Page

FIGURE 2-1 (continued)

In the Introduction (page I-13), four types of Web structures were illustrated: linear, hierarchical, web or random, and grid. This project uses a hierarchical structure (Figure 2-2). The index page is the home page, or entrance to the Web site. From this page, the visitor to this site can link to a page about Florida national parks or to a page about state parks in northwest Florida.

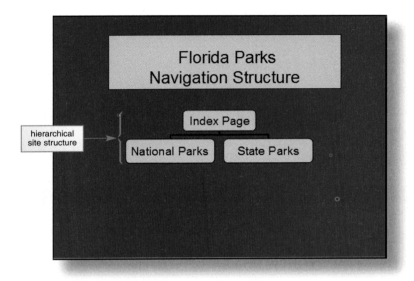

FIGURE 2-2

Managing a Web Site

Organization is a key element of Web design. Dreamweaver works best with entire sites rather than individual Web pages and has many built-in tools to make site creation easy, such as checking links and organizing files. You defined the parks Web site in Project 1 and created the index page. You can add pages to your site by creating a new page and saving it as part of the site or by opening an existing page from another source and saving it as part of the site. In this project, you will create two new pages.

Almost all Web sites have a home page. Compare the home page to your front door. Generally, the front door is the first thing guests see when they visit you. The same applies to a Web site's home page. When someone visits a Web site, he or she usually enters through the home page.

The home page is named **index.htm** or **index.html**. This file name has special significance. Most Web servers recognize index.htm (or index.html) as the default home page and automatically display this page without requiring that the user type the full Uniform Resource Locator (URL), or Web address. For example, if you type http://www.scseries.com into a Web browser address box and access the Web site, what you see is http://www.scseries.com/index.htm, even though you did not type it as such.

Organizing and using Dreamweaver's site management features can assure you that the media within your Web page will display correctly. Bringing all of these elements together will start you on your way to becoming a successful Web site developer.

Starting Dreamweaver and Closing Open Panels

When you start Dreamweaver, generally most or all of the panels are displayed by default. Closing unused panels provides uncluttered workspace in the Document window. To organize your workspace, you close or collapse the open panels. This gives you the maximum window space in the Dreamweaver Document window.

TO START DREAMWEAVER AND CLOSE OPEN PANELS

1 Click the Start button on the Windows taskbar. Point to All Programs on the Start menu, point to Macromedia on the All Programs submenu, and then click Macromedia Dreamweaver MX on the Macromedia submenu.

2 If necessary, maximize the Document window and then press the F4 key.

Dreamweaver displays the maximized Document window and closes all the open panels (Figure 2-3).

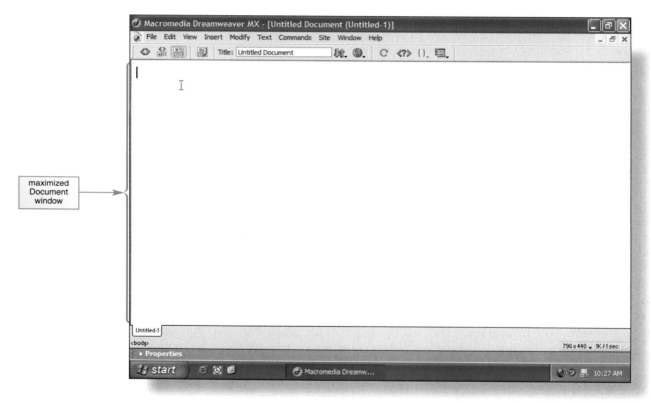

FIGURE 2-3

Accessing a Web Site and Opening a Web Page

Once you have created and saved a Web page or copied a Web page to a Web site, you often will have reason to retrieve it from disk. Opening an existing Web page in Dreamweaver is much the same as opening an existing document in most other software applications; that is, you use the File menu and Open command. If, however, the page is part of a Dreamweaver Web site, you also can open the file from the Site panel.

To open a Web page from the Site panel, you must switch to the appropriate Web site. The **site pop-up menu** in the Site panel lists sites you have defined. When you open the site, a list of pages and subfolders within the site displays. After opening the page, you can modify text, images, tables, and any other elements.

The following steps illustrate how to access a Web site and open a Web page from a local site in the Site panel.

To Access a Web Site and Open a Web Page from a Local Web Site

1 Press the F8 key to display the Site panel. If necessary, click the Site box arrow and then point to Florida Parks on the site pop-up menu (Figure 2-4).

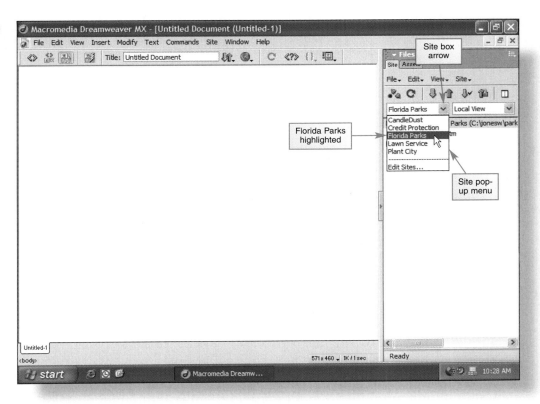

FIGURE 2-4

2 **Click Florida Parks. Double-click index.htm in the Site panel.**

The Florida Parks index page is displayed in the Document window and the name of the page is displayed on the tab at the bottom of the window (Figure 2-5). The tab for the initial Document window, (Untitled-1), displays to the left of the index.htm tab.

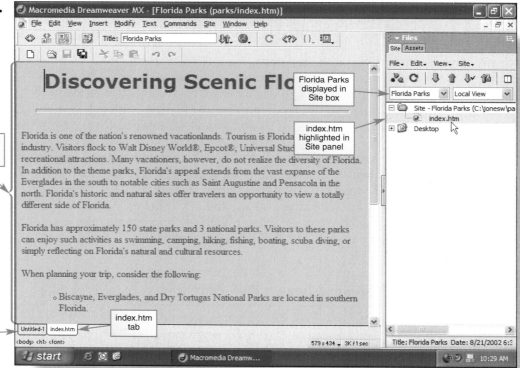

FIGURE 2-5

Other Ways

1. Click file name on Site panel
2. On File menu, click Open

he Integrated File Browser

Organization is one of the keys to a successful Web site. Creating documents without considering where in the folder hierarchy they should go generally creates a difficult-to-manage Web site. The Dreamweaver integrated file browser provides a view of the devices and folders on your computer and shows how these devices and folders are organized. You can create new folders and files for your site through the integrated file browser, which is similar to the Windows XP file organization. You also can use the **integrated file browser** to drag or copy and paste files to your Web site.

The main directory of a disk is called the **root directory** or the **top-level directory**. A small device icon or folder icon is displayed next to each object in the list. The **device icon** represents a device such as the Desktop or a disk drive, and the **folder icon** represents a folder. Many of these icons have a plus or minus sign next to them, which indicates whether the device or folder contains additional folders. Windows XP arranges all of these objects — root directory, folders, subfolders, and files — in a hierarchy. The plus and minus signs are controls that you can click to expand or collapse the view of the file hierarchy. In the integrated file browser, Dreamweaver uses the same hierarchy arrangement, but site folders appear in a different color than non-site folders so that you easily can distinguish between the two.

Copying Data Files to the Local Web Site

Your Data Disk contains images for Project 2. These images are in an Images folder. You use the integrated file browser to copy the Project 2 Images folder to your parks local root folder. The Images folder will become a subfolder within the parks Web site. See the inside back cover for instructions for downloading the Data Disk or see your instructor for information about accessing the files required for this book.

The Data Files folder for this project is stored at Local Disk (C:). The location on your computer may be different. If necessary, verify with your instructor the location of the Data Files folder. Complete the following steps to copy the files to the parks local root folder.

More About

Refreshing the Site Panel

To refresh the Site panel, click the Refresh button on the Site panel toolbar, click View on the menu bar and then click the Refresh command, or press the F5 key.

 To Copy Data Files to the Parks Web Site

1 **Point to the plus sign (+) located to the left of the Desktop icon in the Site panel (Figure 2-6).**

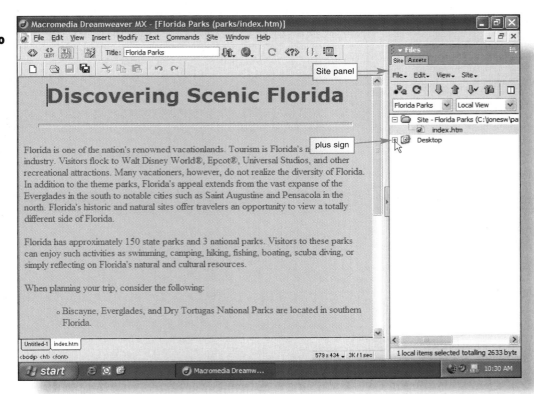

FIGURE 2-6

Dreamweaver MX

2 Click the plus sign (+) to the left of the Desktop icon in the Site panel. Click the plus sign to the left of the My Computer icon and then point to the plus sign to the left of Local Disk (C:).

A list of devices on your computer is displayed (Figure 2-7). The list on your computer will be different.

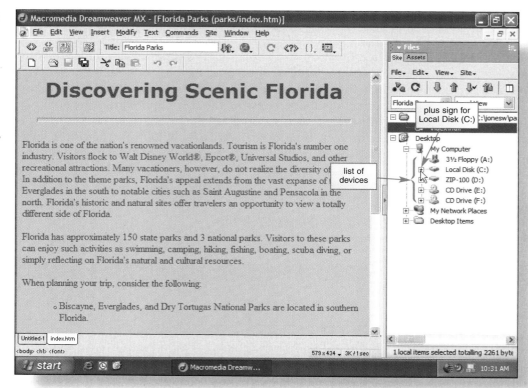

FIGURE 2-7

3 Click the plus sign to the left of Local Disk (C:) and then point to the plus sign to the left of Data Files.

The view of the file hierarchy is expanded and the list of folders is displayed (Figure 2-8). The list on your computer will be different.

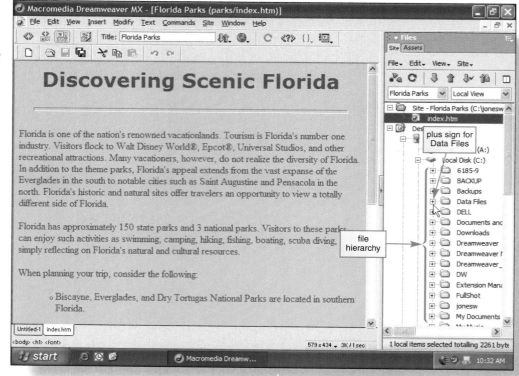

FIGURE 2-8

4 **Click the plus sign to the left of the Data Files folder. Point to the plus sign to the left of the Proj02 folder.**

The file hierarchy expands to display two subfolders: Proj02, and Proj03 (Figure 2-9).

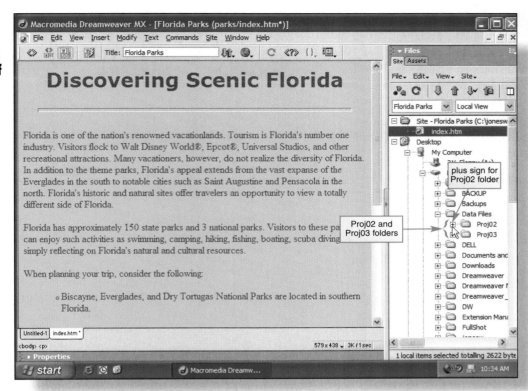

FIGURE 2-9

5 **Click the Proj02 plus sign.**

The Proj02 folder is expanded and contains the Images folders for the parks Web site and the four end-of-project exercises (Figure 2-10).

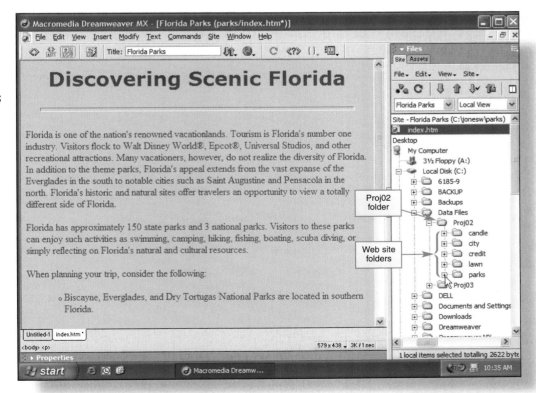

FIGURE 2-10

6   If necessary, use the Site panel horizontal and vertical scroll bars to display the folder list, so you can see it better. Click the plus sign to the left of the parks folder. Point to the Images folder.

The file hierarchy of the parks folder expands to display the Images folder (Figure 2-11).

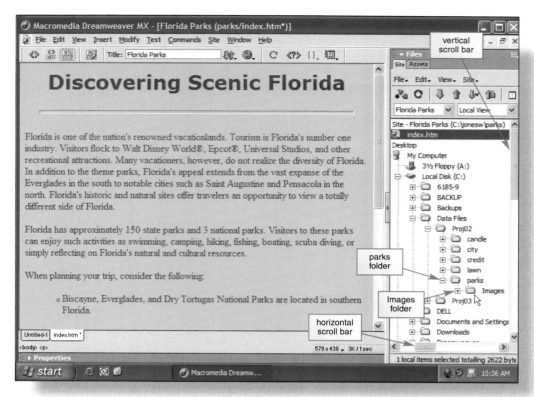

FIGURE 2-11

7   Right-click the Images folder and then point to Copy on the context menu.

The context menu is displayed (Figure 2-12). The files in the Images folder will be copied to the Florida Parks Web site.

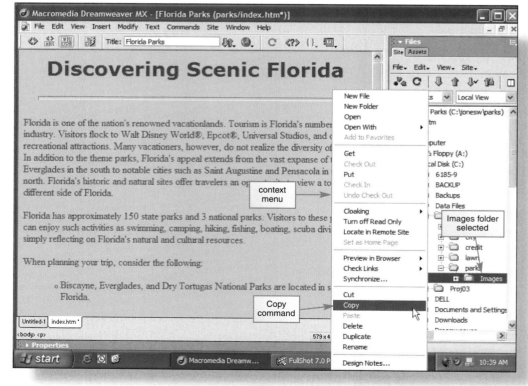

FIGURE 2-12

8 **Click Copy. If necessary, scroll to the top of the Site panel. Right-click Site - Florida Parks and then use the scroll bars to display the parks Web site hierarchy. Point to Paste on the context menu.**

The context menu is displayed (Figure 2-13).

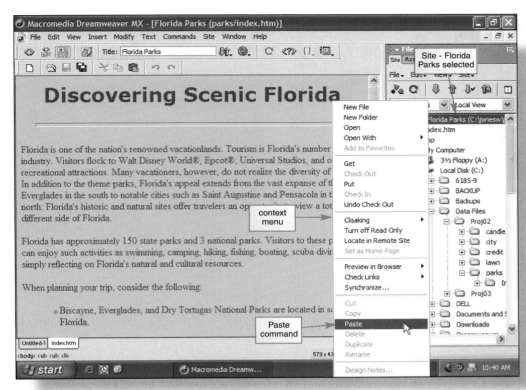

FIGURE 2-13

9 **Click Paste. Point to the minus sign to the left of the Desktop icon.**

The Images folder is copied to the Florida Parks site (Figure 2-14) and becomes a subfolder within the site.

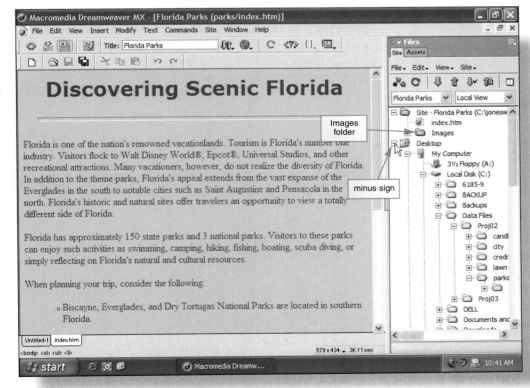

FIGURE 2-14

10 **Click the minus sign to collapse the file list.**

The list of files displaying below Desktop is closed (Figure 2-15).

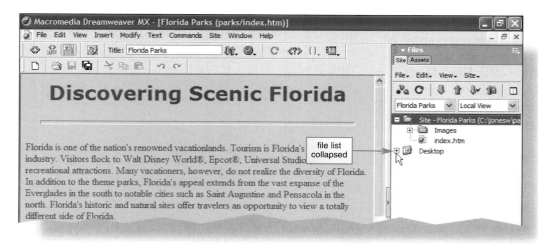

FIGURE 2-15

Most Web sites have a starting point, called a home page. In a personal home page within a Web site, for example, you would probably list your name, your e-mail address, some personal information, and links to other information on your Web site. The index page you created in Project 1 is the home page for the parks Web site. The next section sets the home page.

Setting a Home Page

Each Web site you create within Dreamweaver should have a home page. A **home page** is similar to a table of contents or an index in a book. The home page generally contains links to all pages within the Web site. Most home pages are named index.htm or index.html. Complete the following steps to define the home page through the Site panel.

Steps **To Set a Home Page**

1 **Click the index.htm file name in the Site panel. Point to Site on the Site panel menu bar.**

The index.htm file name is highlighted (Figure 2-16).

FIGURE 2-16

2   **Click Site on the Site panel menu bar and then point to Set as Home Page.**

The Site menu is displayed (Figure 2-17).

3   **Click Set as Home Page.**

The index.htm file is set as the home page for the parks Web site. In the files list, however, no changes are evident.

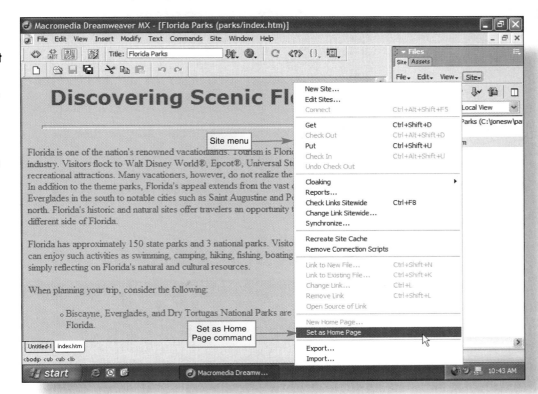

FIGURE 2-17

Although you cannot tell which page in a Web site is the home page by viewing the site files, Dreamweaver provides a graphical option to view the home page — the Site Map. You access the Site Map through the Site panel. You will use the Site Map to view the Web site later in this project.

Dreamweaver can have any number of open Document windows. When you started Dreamweaver, a blank untitled Document window opened. You will use this Document window to create a new Web page.

Adding Pages to a Web Site

You copied the images necessary to begin creating your Web site to the parks local root folder in the Site panel. It is time to start building and enhancing your site. You will add two additional pages to the Web site: Florida National Parks and Florida State Parks. You will add links, a background image, and page images to the index page and to the two new pages.

Dreamweaver offers many tools, such as the Standard toolbar, Property inspector, and Insert bar, to help you create a Web page. The tools you display in one Document window display in all other open Document windows. Complete the steps on the next page to prepare the workspace and to select the Untitled-1 Document window.

Other Ways

1. Right click file name, click Set as Home Page on shortcut menu

More About

Site Organization

Critical to Web development is the hierarchy of folders and files in a Web site. Even for the very simplest of sites, you should create a separate folder for the images. The folder name can be any name you choose, but it is best to use a descriptive, meaningful name.

TO PREPARE THE WORKSPACE

1 If necessary, click View on the menu bar, point to Toolbars, and then click Standard on the View submenu to display the Standard toolbar.

2 Click Window on the menu bar and then click Properties.

3 Click Window on the menu bar and then click Insert to display the Insert bar.

4 Right-click the Files title bar and then click the Close Panel Group command.

5 Click the Untitled-1 tab.

The Untitled-1 Document window, toolbar, and panels are displayed and the Files Panel group is closed (Figure 2-18).

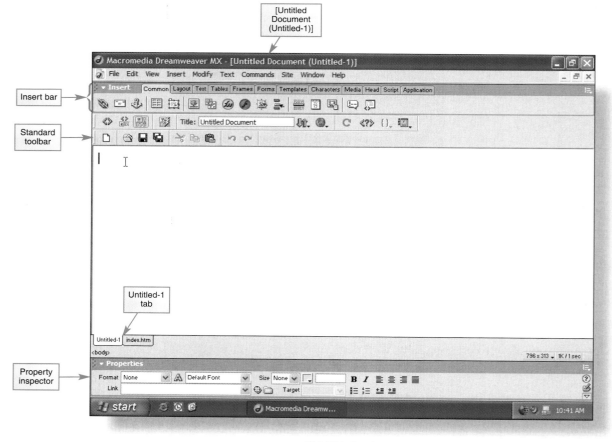

FIGURE 2-18

With the workspace prepared and the Document window displayed, you can begin creating the Web page for Florida National Parks.

Creating the National Parks Web Page

To create the page for Florida National Parks, you type the text in the untitled Document window. Table 2-1 includes the text for the Florida National Parks Web page. Press the ENTER key or insert a line break <BR> as indicated in the instructions in Table 2-1.

Table 2-1	Florida National Parks Web Page Text
SECTION	**WEB PAGE TEXT**
Heading	Florida National Parks <ENTER>
Subheading	Experience the Real Florida! <ENTER>
Part 1	Everglades National Park \nEverglades National Park is the only subtropical preserve in North America. The park is known for its rich bird life and is the only place in the world where alligators and crocodiles exist side by side. <ENTER>
Part 2	Biscayne National Park \nBiscayne National Park is a delight for wildlife-watching, snorkeling, diving, boating, and fishing. The park contains the longest stretch of mangrove forest left on Florida's east coast and a spectacular living coral reef. <ENTER>
Part 3	Dry Tortugas National Park \nAbout 70 miles west of Key West is the Dry Tortugas National Park, a cluster of seven islands, composed of sand and coral reefs. Located on one of the islands is Ft. Jefferson, the largest of the 19th century American coastal forts. The area also is known for its legends of pirates and sunken ships. <ENTER>
Closing	Home <ENTER>

The following steps create the Web page and insert blank lines and line breaks between sections of text.

More About

Using the Keyboard Shortcut Editor

For more information about using the Keyboard Shortcut Editor to create your own shortcut keys, edit existing shortcuts, or use a predetermined set of shortcuts, visit the Dreamweaver MX More About Web page (scsite.com/ dreamweavermx/more) and then click Dreamweaver MX Shortcut Editor.

Steps To Create the National Parks Web Page

1 **Type the heading** Florida National Parks **as shown in Table 2-1. Press the ENTER key.**

The heading is entered in the Document window (Figure 2-19). Pressing the ENTER key creates a new paragraph.

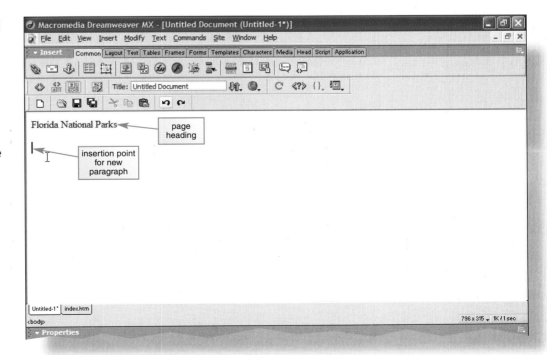

FIGURE 2-19

2 **Type the subheading**

Experience the Real Florida! **as shown in Table 2-1, and then press the ENTER key.**

The subheading is entered in the Document window (Figure 2-20).

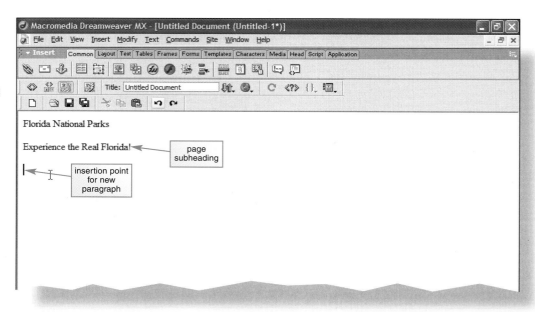

FIGURE 2-20

3 **Type the rest of the text in Table 2-1. Press the ENTER key or insert a line break as indicated in the instructions.**

The text for the Florida National Parks is entered (Figure 2-21).

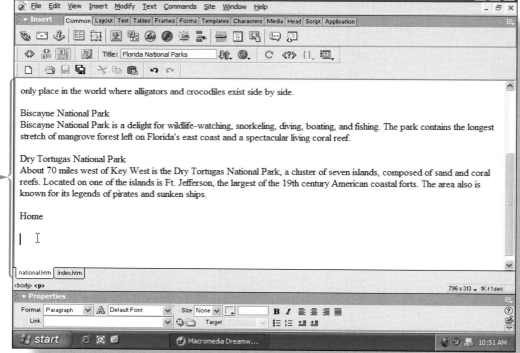

FIGURE 2-21

In Project 1, you formatted the index page by adding headings and bullets, centering, using text indent, and bolding text. The following steps apply similar formatting to the national parks page.

TO FORMAT THE FLORIDA NATIONAL PARKS PAGE

1 If necessary, scroll up to the top of the Web page and then apply Heading 1 to the heading text.

2 Apply Heading 2 to the subheading text.

3 Center the heading and subheading.

4 Add bullets to the following three lines: Everglades National Park, Biscayne National Park, and Dry Tortugas National Park.

5 Bold each of these three lines: Everglades National Park, Biscayne National Park, and Dry Tortugas National Park.

6 Add two line breaks after the text describing the Everglades National Park and the Biscayne National Park.

7 Type Florida National Parks for the title.

8 Press F12 to view the page in the browser and to verify the line spacing is correct as shown in Figure 2-22. Close the browser.

9 Save the Web page as national in the parks folder.

The Florida National Parks Web page text is entered, formatted, and saved.

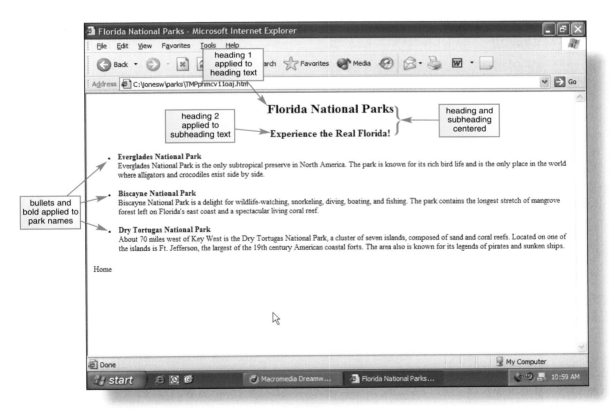

FIGURE 2-22

When you created the Florida National Parks Web page, you used the Untitled-1 page that displayed when you opened Dreamweaver. For the Florida States Park Web page, you need to open a new Document window. Complete the steps on the next two pages to open a new blank Document window.

To Open a New Document Window

1 **Click File on the menu bar and then point to New.**

The File menu is displayed (Figure 2-23).

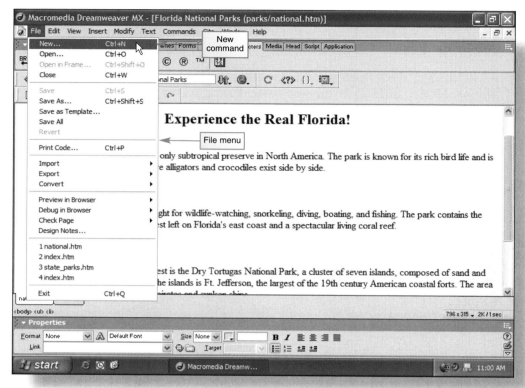

FIGURE 2-23

2 **Click New. If necessary, click the General tab and then click Basic Page in the Category list. Point to the Create button.**

The New Document dialog box is displayed (Figure 2-24). Basic Page is highlighted in the Category list. HTML is the default in the Basic Page list.

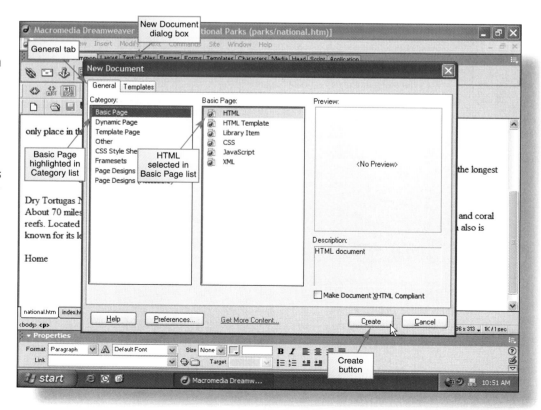

FIGURE 2-24

3 **Click the Create button.**

A new Untitled-2 Document window displays (Figure 2-25).

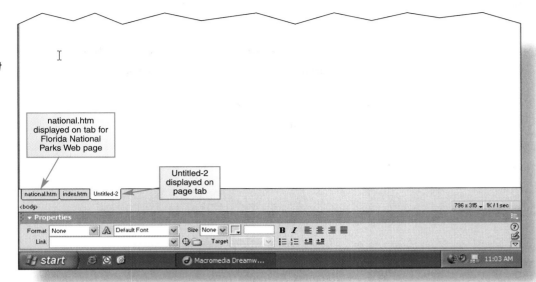

national.htm displayed on tab for Florida National Parks Web page

Untitled-2 displayed on page tab

national.htm index.htm Untitled-2

<body>

796 x 315 ▾ 1K / 1 sec

▾ Properties

Format None   A Default Font   Size None   **B** *I* ≡ ≡ ≡ ≡
Link   Target   ⊞ ⊟ ⋮⋮ ⋮⋮

start Macromedia Dreamw... 11:03 AM

FIGURE 2-25

Creating the State Parks Web Page

You created the page for Florida National Parks by typing the text in the untitled Document window that displayed when you started Dreamweaver. You will enter the text for the Florida State Page the same way you entered text for the Florida National Parks page. Table 2-2 includes all the text for the Florida State Web page.

Table 2-2	Florida State Parks Web Page Text
SECTION	**WEB PAGE TEXT**
Heading	Florida State Parks <ENTER>
Subheading	Northwest Region <ENTER>
Part 1	Florida has more than 150 state parks. Three of the more unusual and scenic parks are located in the northwestern part of the state. <ENTER>
Part 2	Blackwater River State Park Activities at Blackwater include camping, picnicking, fishing, nature trails, boating, and canoeing. This 590-acre park is located in Holt, Florida. The Blackwater River has one of the purer sand-bottom rivers in the world. <ENTER>
Part 3	Ponce de Leon Spring State Park Activities within this park include fishing, nature trails, picnicking, and swimming. Numerous springs are found within the park.<ENTER> The main spring in the park is created through the merging of two flows from a limestone cavity. These two flows produce more than 14 million gallons of crystal-clear water daily. <ENTER>
Part 4	Falling Waters State Park This park is located in Chipley, Florida. The park derives its name from one of Florida's more notable geological features: a 67-foot waterfall. <ENTER> It also is known for the Falling Waters Sink. The sink is a 100-foot deep, 20-foot wide cylindrical pit. Into the pit flows a small stream, which drops 67 feet to the bottom of the sink. The destination of the water is not yet known. <ENTER>
Closing	Home <ENTER>

More About

Accessibility Issues

For more information about authoring for accessibility, visit the Dreamweaver MX More About Web page (scsite.com/ dreamweavermx/more) and then click Dreamweaver MX Accessibility Issues.

Type the text for the State Parks Web page using Table 2-2 and the following step. Press the ENTER key or insert a line break <BR> as indicated in the table.

TO CREATE THE STATE PARKS WEB PAGE

1 Type the text of the Web page shown in Table 2-2.

The text for Florida State Parks is entered (Figure 2-26).

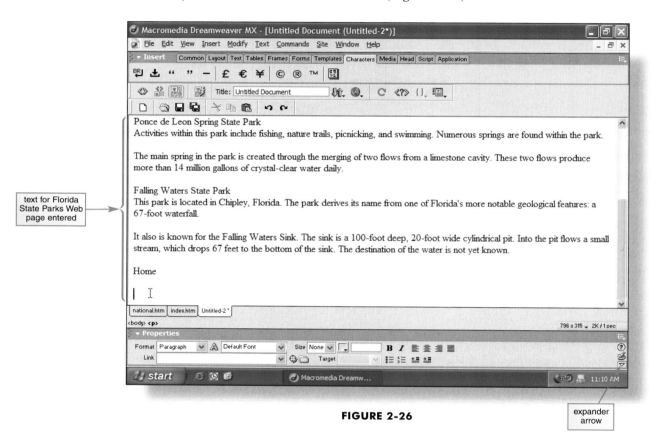

text for Florida State Parks Web page entered

FIGURE 2-26

expander arrow

TO FORMAT THE FLORIDA STATE PARKS PAGE

1 If necessary, scroll to the top of the Web page and then apply Heading 1 to the heading.

2 Apply Heading 2 to the subheading.

3 Center the heading and subheading.

4 Bold the names of each of the three parks where they are used as subtitles.

5 Type Florida State Parks - NW for the title.

6 Press F12 to view the page in the browser and to verify the line spacing is correct as shown in Figure 2-27. Close the browser.

7 Save the Web page as state_parks in the parks folder.

The text for the Florida State Parks page is entered, formatted, and saved.

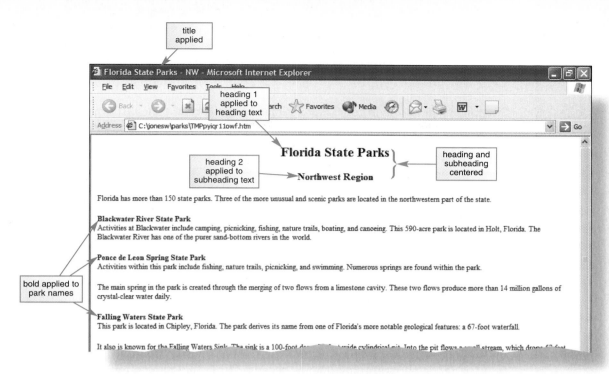

FIGURE 2-27

You have completed entering and formatting the text for the two new pages and copied the images to the parks local root folder in the Site panel. It is time to start enhancing your site. You will add a background image, page images, and links to the Web pages. You begin by adding images.

Images

If used correctly and with an understanding of the Web site audience, images add excitement and interest to a Web page. When selecting images for a Web site, it is important to understand that the size and type of image or images used within a Web page affect how fast the Web page downloads and displays in the viewer's Web browser. A Web page that downloads too slowly will turn away visitors.

Image File Formats

Graphical images used on the Web are in one of two broad categories: vector and bitmap. **Vector** images are composed of key points and paths, which define shapes and coloring instructions, such as line and fill colors. The vector file contains a description of the image expressed mathematically. The file describes the image to the computer and the computer draws it. This type of image generally is associated with Macromedia's Flash or Adobe's LiveMotion animation programs. One of the benefits of vector images is file size, particularly relative to the file size of bitmap images. Dreamweaver contains a feature that allows the user to modify the properties and content of Flash objects.

Bitmap images are the more common type of image file. Bitmap files map out or plot the image on a pixel-by-pixel basis. A **pixel**, or **picture element**, is the smallest point in a graphical image. Graphic monitors display images by dividing the display screen into thousands (or millions) of pixels, arranged in a **grid** of rows and columns. The pixels appear connected because they are so close together. This grid of pixels is a **bitmap**. The **bit-resolution** of an image is described by the number of bits used to represent each pixel. An 8-bit image supports up to 256 colors, and a 24- or 32-bit image supports up to 16.7 million colors.

Web browsers currently support three bitmap image file types: GIF, JPEG, and PNG.

GIF GIF (.gif) is an acronym for **Graphics Interchange Format**. The GIF format uses 8-bit resolution, supports up to a maximum of 256 colors, and uses combinations of these 256 colors to simulate colors beyond that range. The GIF format is best for displaying images such as logos, icons, buttons and other images with even colors and tones. GIF images come in two different versions: GIF87 and GIF89a format. The GIF89a format contains three features not available in the GIF87 or JPEG formats: transparency, interlacing, and animation. The **transparency** feature allows the user to specify a transparency color, which allows the background color or image to display. The **interlacing** feature lets the browser begin to build a low-resolution version of the full-sized GIF picture on the screen while the file is still downloading. Using an animated GIF editor, GIF89a images can be **animated**. Animated GIF images are simply a number of GIF images saved into a single file and looped, or repeated over and over. A number of shareware GIF editors are available to create animated GIFs. If you do not want to create your own animations, you can find thousands of free animated GIFs on the Internet available for downloading.

JPEG JPEG (.jpg) is an acronym for **Joint Photographic Experts Group**. JPEG files are the best format for photographic images because JPEG files can contain up to 16.7 million colors. **Progressive JPEG** is a new variation of the JPEG image format. This image format supports a gradually built display such as the interlaced GIFs. Older browsers do not support progressive JPEG files.

PNG PNG stands for **Portable Network Graphics**. PNG is the native file format of Macromedia Fireworks. PNG files retain all the original layer, vector, color, and effect information (such as a drop shadow), and all elements are fully editable at all times. This format is not supported by many browsers without a special plug-in. Generally, it is better to use GIF or JPEG images in your Web pages.

When developing a Web site that consists of many pages, you should maintain a consistent, professional layout and design throughout all of the pages. The pages in a site, for example, should use similar features such as background colors or images, margins, and headings.

Background Images

If you add a background image to your Web page, select an image that does not clash with the text and other content. The background image should not overwhelm the Web page.

Adding a Background Color and Background Image

Most Web pages display with a default white or gray background. Generally, the browser used to display the Web page determines the default background. You can enhance your Web page by adding a background image and/or background color. In Project 1, you added a color scheme and part of the scheme included the background color.

You can add a background color, however, without applying a color scheme. If you use a background color, the same cautions apply to background color as they do to text color. You want to use Web-safe colors, such as those in the Dreamweaver color schemes. This means the colors will display correctly on the computer screen when someone is viewing your Web page. To define an image or color for the page background, you use the Page Properties dialog box. When you display the Page Properties dialog box, you will see the color scheme selections you made in Project 1.

Background images are used to add texture and interesting color to a Web page. If you use both a background image and a background color, the color appears while the image downloads, and then the image covers up the color. Use background images cautiously. Web page images displayed on top of a busy background image may not mix well, and text may be difficult to read. Complete the following steps to add a background image to the index page. You will begin by closing the Insert bar and collapsing the Property inspector to provide additional workspace.

Steps To Add a Background Image to the Index Page

1 Click Window on the menu bar, click insert, and then click the Property inspector expander arrow.

Dreamweaver closes the Insert bar and collapses the Property inspector.

2 Click the index.htm tab to select the home page in the Document window. Click Modify on the menu bar and then point to Page Properties.

Dreamweaver displays the index.htm page and the Modify menu (Figure 2-28).

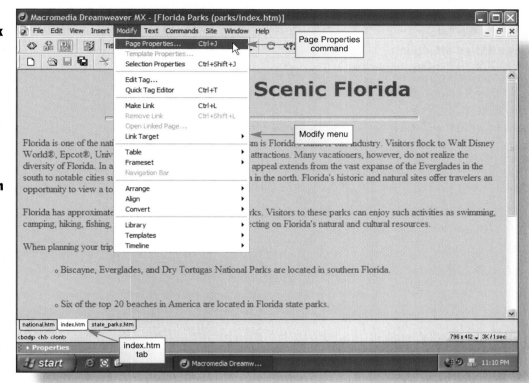

FIGURE 2-28

3 Click Page Properties. Point to the Browse button in the Page Properties dialog box.

The Page Properties dialog box displays (Figure 2-29). The colors and hexadecimal numbers are displayed for the Background, Text, Links, Visited Links, and Active Links. This is the result of the color scheme applied in Project 1.

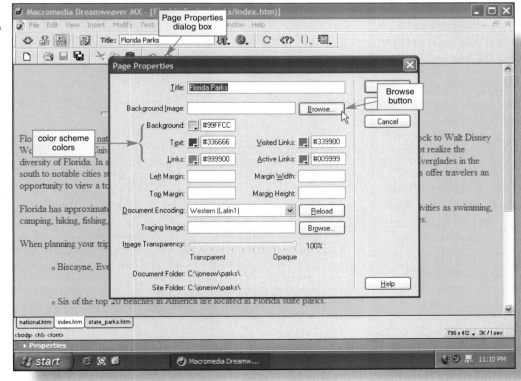

FIGURE 2-29

4 Click the Browse button and then click the Images folder name. Point to the OK button in the Select Image Source dialog box.

Dreamweaver displays the Select Image Source dialog box (Figure 2-30). The parks folder name is displayed in the Look in box and the Images folder is highlighted.

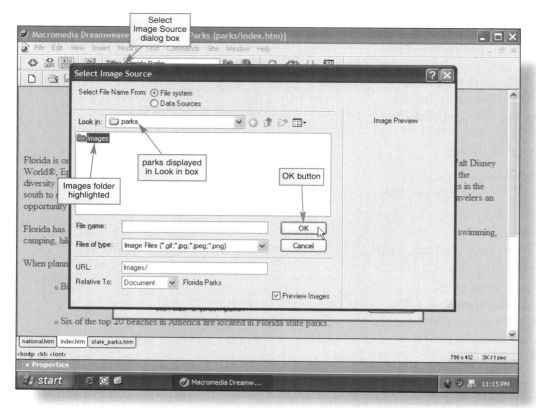

FIGURE 2-30

5 Click the OK button. Click background.jpg. If necessary, click the Preview Images box to select it and then point to the OK button.

The Images folder is opened and a list of file images is displayed (Figure 2-31). The file name, background.jpg, is displayed in the File name text box. A preview of the image is displayed in the Image Preview area. The dimensions of the image, type of image, file size, and download time are listed below the image.

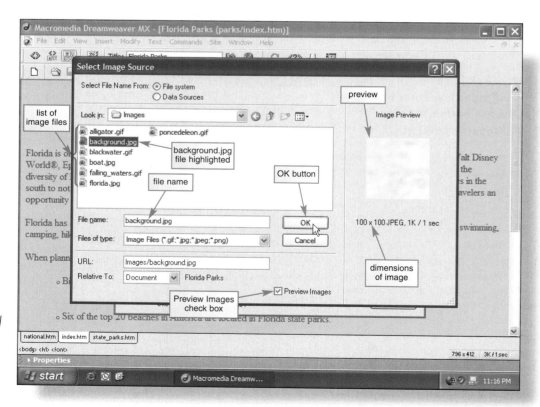

FIGURE 2-31

6 Click the OK button in the Select Image Source dialog box and then point to the OK button in the Page Properties dialog box.

The Page Properties dialog box displays the folder and file name in the Background Image box (Figure 2-32).

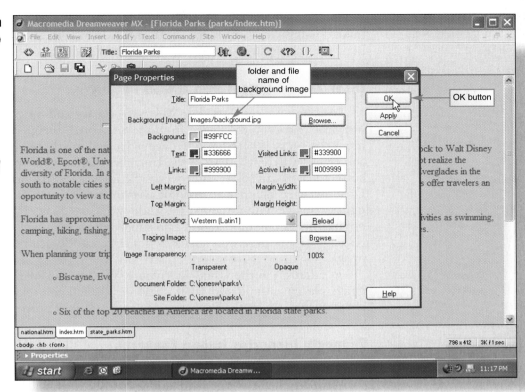

FIGURE 2-32

7 Click the OK button.

The background image is applied to the Florida Parks index page (Figure 2-33). The background color displays only during the down-loading process when viewed through a browser.

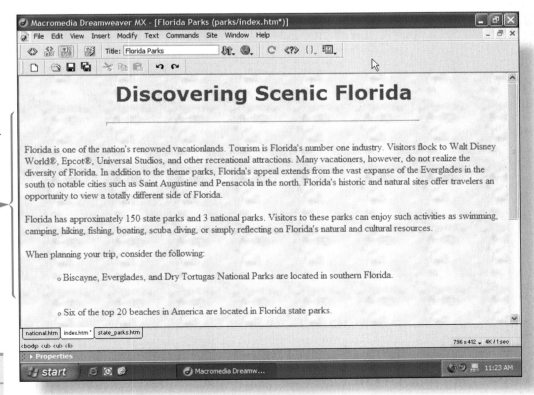

FIGURE 2-33

Other Ways

1 Right-click Document window, click Page Properties on context menu

To enhance your index Web page further, you will add two images. One of the images will display at the top right of the document and the second image will display at the bottom to the left of the bulleted list.

Inserting an Image into a Web Page

Inserting images into your Web page is easy and quick with Dreamweaver — just drag and drop the image from the Site panel. Image placement, however, can be more complex. When the Web page is viewed in a browser, the image may display somewhat differently than in the Document window. If the images do not display correctly, you can select and modify the images directly in the Document window. Dreamweaver includes an **invisible element marker** that shows the location of the inserted image within the HTML code when the image is moved from the insertion point. This visual aid displays as a small yellow icon when the image is selected and displays as blue when the image is not selected. You can drag the icon to move the image.

In addition to the visual aid feature, you use the Property inspector to help with image placement and add other attributes. When you select an image within the Document window, the Property inspector displays properties specific to the image.

Property Inspector Image Features

The Property inspector lets you see the current properties of the selected element. The Property inspector is divided into two sections. Clicking the expand/collapse arrow in the lower-right corner of the Property inspector collapses the Property inspector to show only the most commonly used properties for the selected element or expands the Property inspector to show more options.

The following section describes the image-related features of the Property inspector (Figure 2-34).

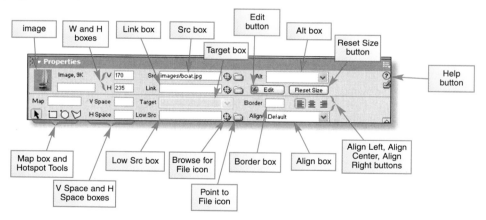

FIGURE 2-34

W AND H The **W** and **H** boxes indicate the width and height of the image, in pixels. Dreamweaver automatically displays the dimensions when a image is inserted into the page. You can specify the image size in the following units: pc (picas), pt (points), in (inches), mm (millimeters), cm (centimeters), and combinations, such as 2in+5mm. Dreamweaver converts the values to pixels in the HTML source code.

LINK   The **Link** box allows you to make a selected image a hyperlink to a specified URL or Web page. To create a link, you can click the Point to File or Browse for File icon to the right of the Link box to browse to a page in your Web site, or drag a file from the site window into the Link box. For an external link, you can type the URL directly into the Link box or use copy and paste.

ALIGN   **Align** sets the alignment of an image in relation to other elements in the same paragraph, table, or line. Align is discussed in more detail later in this project.

ALT   **Alt** specifies alternative text that appears in place of the image for text-only browsers or for browsers that have been set to download images manually. For visually impaired users who use speech synthesizers with text-only browsers, the text is spoken out loud. In some browsers, this text also appears when the pointer is over the image.

MAP NAME AND HOTSPOT TOOLS   Use **Map Name** and the **Hotspot tools** to label and create a client-side image map.

V SPACE AND H SPACE   V Space and H Space add space, in pixels, along the sides of the image. **V Space** adds space along the top and bottom of an image. **H Space** adds space along the left and right of an image.

TARGET   **Target** specifies the frame or window in which the linked page should load. This option is not available when the image is linked to another file.

LOW SRC   **Low Src** specifies the image that should load before the main image. Many designers use a small black and white version of the main image because it loads quickly and gives visitors an idea of what they will see.

BORDER   **Border** is the width, in pixels, of the image's border. The default is no border.

EDIT   **Edit** launches an external image editor, such as Macromedia Fireworks.

RESET SIZE   If an image size is changed, **Reset Size** resets the W and H values to the original size of the image.

LEFT, CENTER, AND RIGHT ALIGN   In Dreamweaver, the default alignment for an image is left alignment. To change the default alignment, select the image you want to align. Click an alignment button: Align Center, Align Right, or Justify.

SRC   **Src** specifies the source file for the image.

To insert images in the home page, complete the steps on the next two pages.

Steps | **To Insert an Image into the Index Page**

1 **Click the expander arrow in the Properties inspector.**

The Property inspector expands and displays a lower panel (Figure 2-35). The Document window contains text only; therefore, no additional attributes display in the expanded Property inspector at this time.

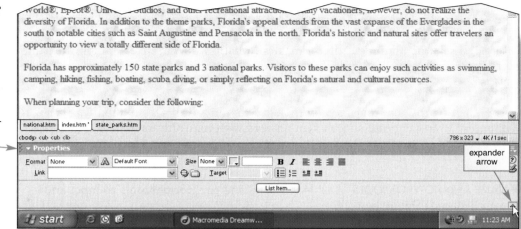

FIGURE 2-35

2 **Press F8. Point to the plus (+) sign to the left of the Images folder in the Site panel.**

The Site panel is displayed (Figure 2-36).

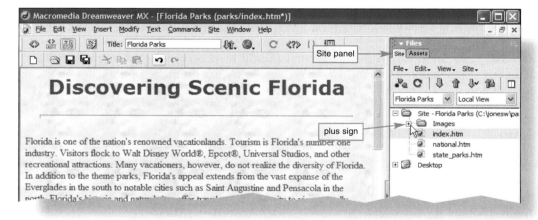

FIGURE 2-36

3 **Click the plus (+) sign to open the Images folder.**

The Images folder is opened and displays a list of seven images (Figure 2-37). Some of the images are gif files and others are jpg files. One of the files is the background image. All other images will be inserted into the three Web site pages.

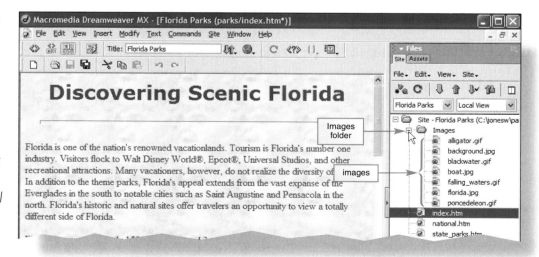

FIGURE 2-37

4 If necessary, scroll to the top of the page in the Document window and position the insertion point so that it is to the left of the first line of the first paragraph (Figure 2-38). Drag alligator.gif from the Site panel file list to the insertion point. Do not release the mouse button.

When you start to drag, a page icon displays next to the mouse pointer (Figure 2-38), indicating the image is being dragged.

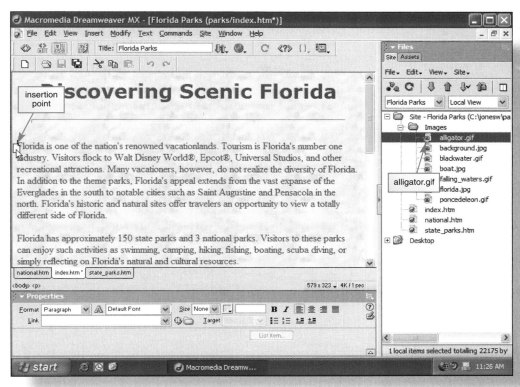

FIGURE 2-38

5 Release the mouse button and then click the alligator image to select it.

The border and handles around the image indicate it is selected. The attributes change in the Property inspector to reflect the selected object (Figure 2-39).

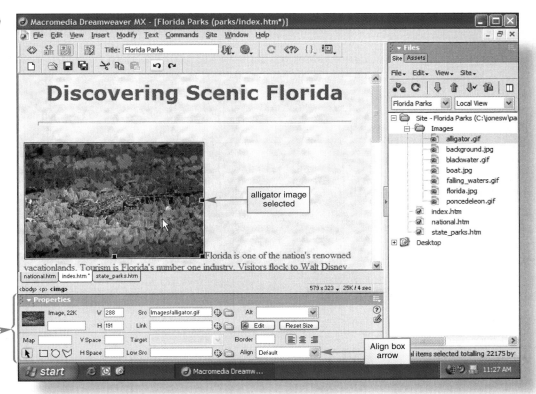

FIGURE 2-39

Aligning an Image

When you insert an image into a Web page, by default, the text around the image aligns to the bottom of the image. The image alignment options on the Align pop-up menu in the Property inspector let you set the alignment for the image in relation to other page content. Dreamweaver provides ten alignment options for images. Table 2-3 describes these image alignment options.

Table 2-3	Image Alignment Options
ALIGNMENT OPTION	**DESCRIPTION**
Default	Aligns the image with the baseline of the text in most browser default settings
Baseline	Aligns the image with the baseline of the text regardless of the browser setting
Top	Aligns the image with the top of the item; item can be text or another object
Middle	Aligns the image with the baseline of the text or object at the vertical middle of the image
Bottom	Aligns the image with the baseline of the text or the bottom of another image regardless of the browser setting
Text Top	Aligns the image with the top of the tallest character in a line of text
Absolute Middle	Aligns the image with the middle of the current line of text
Absolute Bottom	Aligns the image with the bottom of the current line of text or another object
Left	Aligns the image at the left margin
Right	Aligns the image at the right margin

As indicated in Table 2-3, the Align pop-up menu contains ten alignment options. The more widely used options are left, right, and center. Complete the following steps to align the alligator image to the right and create text wrapping to the left of the image.

 To Align an Image

1 **If necessary, click the alligator image to select it and then click the Align box arrow in the Property inspector. Point to Right on the pop-up menu.**

The Align pop-up menu is displayed and Right is highlighted (Figure 2-40).

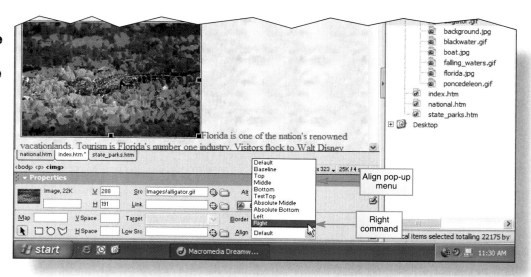

FIGURE 2-40

2 Click Right.

The image moves to the right side of the window (Figure 2-41). A visual aid displays to indicate the location of the insertion point.

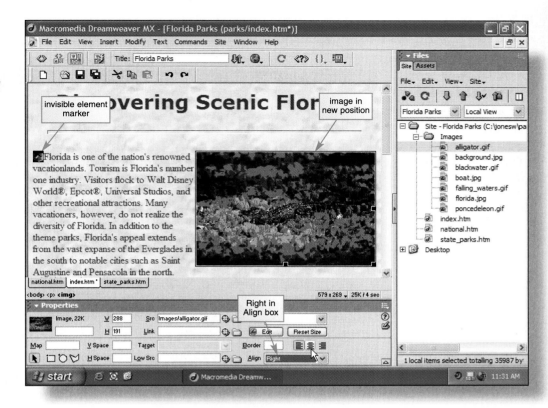

FIGURE 2-41

The spacing between the text and the image is very small. You can add vertical and horizontal spacing between the image and text, however, to display the Web page proportionally. In the next steps, you adjust the horizontal and vertical spacing around the image.

Adjusting Space Around Images

When aligning an image, by default, only about three pixels of space are inserted between the image and adjacent text. You can adjust the amount of vertical and horizontal space between the image and text through the V Space and H Space settings. The V Space setting controls the vertical space above or below an image. The H Space setting controls horizontal space to the left or right side of the image. You add vertical and horizontal spacing in the step on the next page.

Steps ## To Adjust the Horizontal and Vertical Space

1 **Click the V Space text box and then type 6 as the vertical space. Click the H Space box and then type 12 as the horizontal space. Press the ENTER key.**

Dreamweaver adds additional horizontal and vertical space between the image and the text (Figure 2-42).

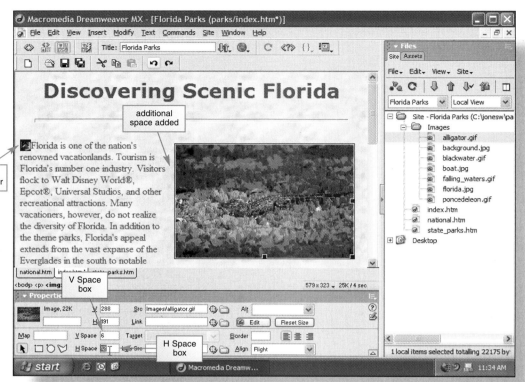

FIGURE 2-42

Another feature within the Property inspector is Alt text. For individuals who are visually impaired, the Alt text can be interpreted by their screen readers. Dreamweaver supports two screen readers — JAWS and Window-Eyes.

Specifying the Alt Text

The **Alt** text is short for **Alternative Text** and provides an alterative source of information about the image. The text typed in the Alt box displays as the image is downloading. This text also appears as a ScreenTip as the mouse pointer is moved over the image when it is displayed in some browsers. Complete the following step to add Alt text to the alligator image.

Steps | To Add Alt Text

1 **If necessary, click the alligator image to select it. Click the Alt box and then type** Florida alligator **as the alternate text. Press the ENTER key.**

The Alt text is entered in the Alt text box (Figure 2-43).

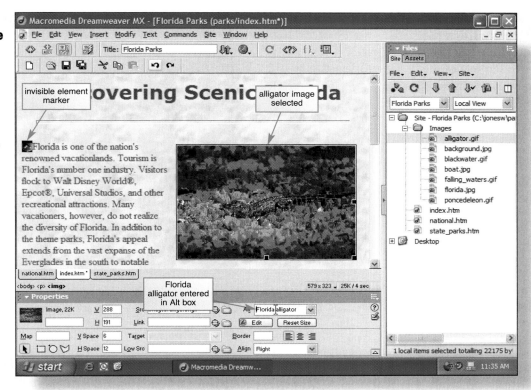

FIGURE 2-43

To enhance your Web page further, you will add a second image of a sailboat. This image is displayed on the left side of the page, to the left of the bulleted items. Perform the steps on the next four pages to insert an image of a sailboat in the Web page.

Steps **To Insert a Second Image**

1 **Scroll down and position the insertion point so that it is to the left of the sentence introducing the bulleted list (Figure 2-44).**

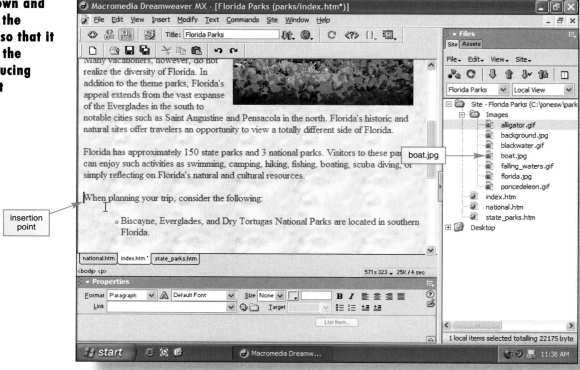

FIGURE 2-44

2 **Drag the boat.jpg image from the Site panel to the insertion point and then click the image to select it. Point to the Align box arrow in the Property inspector.**

The image is displayed (Figure 2-45). The border and handles around the image indicate it is selected.

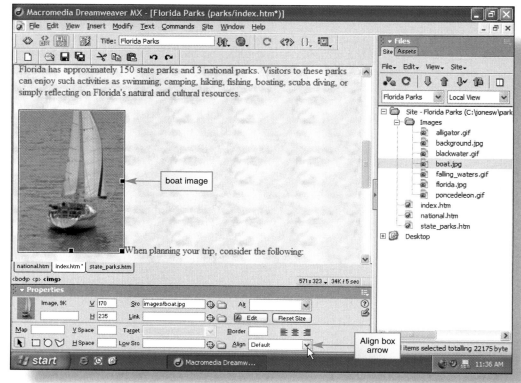

FIGURE 2-45

3 Click the Align box arrow and then click Left in the Align pop-up menu.

The image moves to the left side of the window and the text adjusts to the right side (Figure 2-46). The bullets do not display and some of the text is hidden by the image. Adjusting the spacing will display the bullets and text.

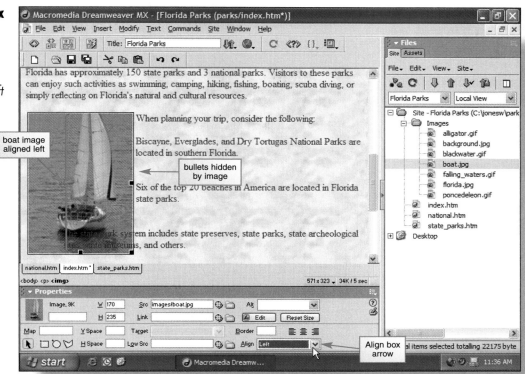

FIGURE 2-46

4 Click the V Space box and then type 6 as the vertical space. Click the H Space box and then type 20 as the horizontal space. Press the ENTER key. Click anywhere in the Document window.

Additional horizontal and vertical space is added between the image and the text, and the bullets are displayed (Figure 2-47).

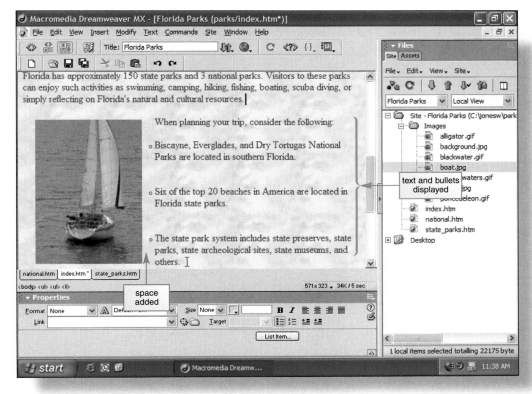

FIGURE 2-47

5 Click the image to select it. Click the **Alt box and then type** Sailboat **as the alternate text. Press the ENTER key.**

The Alt text is applied (Figure 2-48).

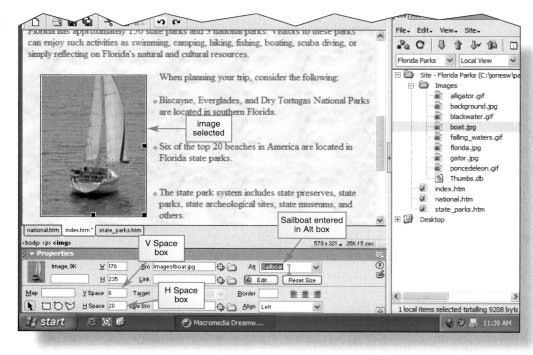

FIGURE 2-48

6 Press the **F12 key.**

The index page displays in your browser (Figure 2-49). Web pages may display differently in your browser. The browser and selected text size affect how a Web page displays.

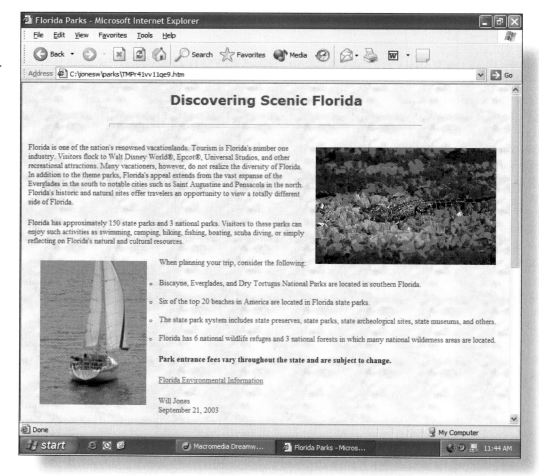

FIGURE 2-49

7 **Close the browser to return to Dreamweaver. Click the Save button on the Standard toolbar.**

All changes to the index page are saved (Figure 2-50). The asterisk no longer displays to the right of the file name in the index.htm tab or on the title bar.

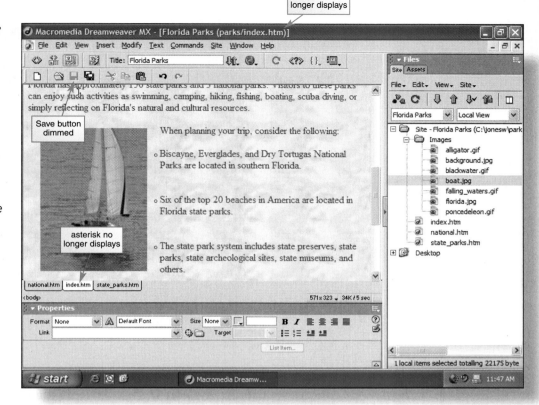

FIGURE 2-50

Consistency in Web pages ties the Web site together. Using the same color scheme and background image on all pages within the site is one way to achieve consistency. Next, you will add the same color scheme and background images to the national parks Web page that you applied to the index page. Complete the following steps to add the color scheme and background image to the Web page.

TO ADD A COLOR SCHEME AND BACKGROUND IMAGE TO THE NATIONAL PARKS WEB PAGE

1 Click the national.htm tab. Click Commands on the menu bar and then click Set Color Scheme.

2 Select Green in the Background list and Blue,Brown,Green in the Text and Links list. Click the OK button.

3 Click Modify on the menu bar and then click Page Properties. Click the Browse button to the right of the Background Image box.

4 Click background.jpg and then click the OK button in the Select Image Source dialog box.

5 Click the OK button in the Page Properties dialog box.

The background image and color scheme are applied to the National Parks page (Figure 2-51 on the next page).

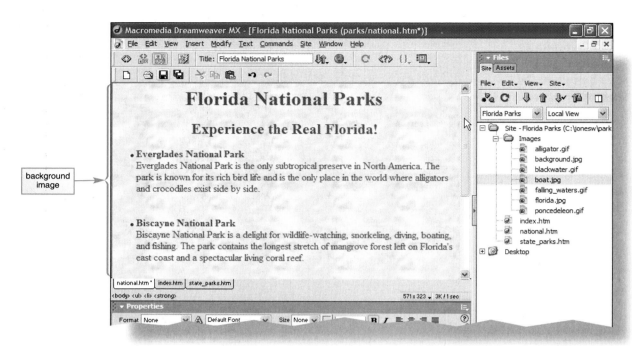

FIGURE 2-51

To develop the national parks page further and add information showing the location of the three Florida national parks, you will add a Florida map. References to each park are contained on the map. Complete the following steps to add the Florida map image to the national parks Web page.

 To Insert an Image in the National Parks Web Page

1 **If necessary, scroll to the top of the page. Position the insertion point between the bullet and the text heading of the second bulleted item (Biscayne National Park).**

The insertion point is positioned to the left of Biscayne National Park and to the right of the bullet (Figure 2-52).

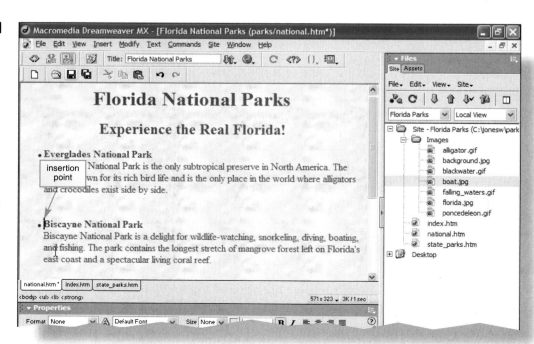

FIGURE 2-52

2 **Drag the florida.jpg file from the Site panel to the insertion point and then click the image to select it. Point to the Align box arrow in the Property inspector.**

The border and handles around the image indicate it is selected (Figure 2-53). The attributes change in the Property inspector to reflect the selected object.

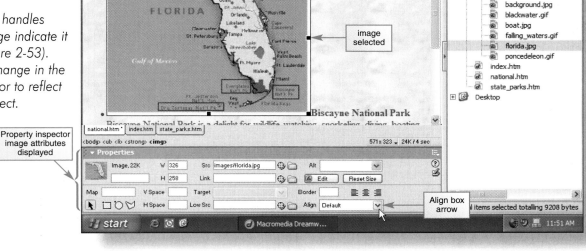

FIGURE 2-53

3 **Click the Align box arrow and then click Right.**

The image is aligned to the right in the Document window (Figure 2-54).

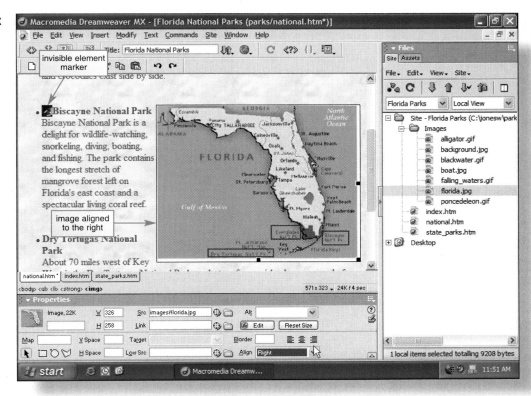

FIGURE 2-54

4 Click the Alt box and then type Florida Map as the alternate text. Click the V Space box and then type 8 as the vertical space. Click the H Space box and then type 10 as the horizontal space. Press the ENTER key (Figure 2-55).

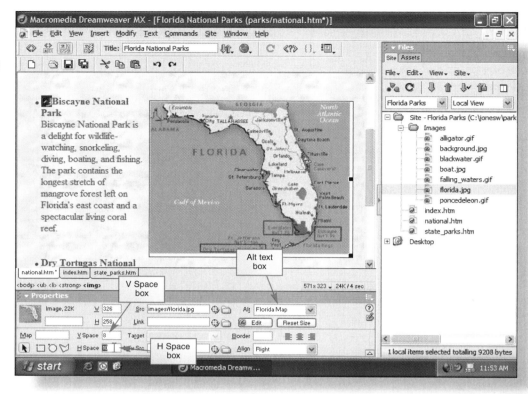

FIGURE 2-55

5 Press the F12 key.

The Florida National Parks Web page is displayed in the browser (Figure 2-56).

6 Close the browser to return to Dreamweaver. Click the Save button on the Standard toolbar.

The Florida National Parks Web page is saved.

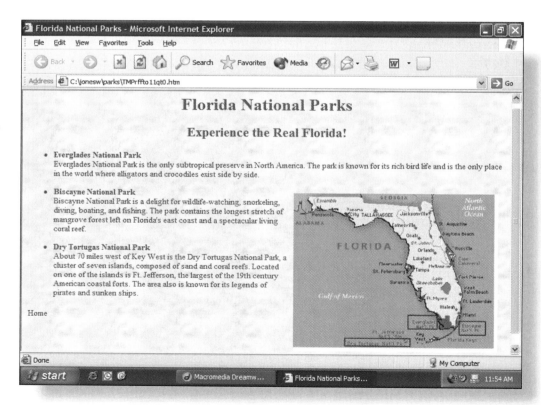

FIGURE 2-56

The third page in your Web site is northwest Florida state parks. Again, you need to add the color scheme and background image to this page. To add interest to the page, you will add three images. You will align two of the images to the left and one to the right. Complete the following steps to add the color scheme and background image to the northwest state parks Web page.

TO ADD A COLOR SCHEME AND BACKGROUND IMAGE TO THE STATE PARKS WEB PAGE

1 Click the state_parks.htm tab. Click Commands on the menu bar and then click Set Color Scheme.

2 Select Green in the Background list and Blue,Brown,Green in the Text and Links list. Click the OK button.

3 Click Modify on the menu bar and then click Page Properties. Click the Browse button to the right of the Background Image box.

4 Click background.jpg and then click the OK button in the Select Image Source dialog box.

5 Click the OK button in the Page Properties dialog box.

The color scheme and background image are applied to the northwest state parks page (Figure 2-57).

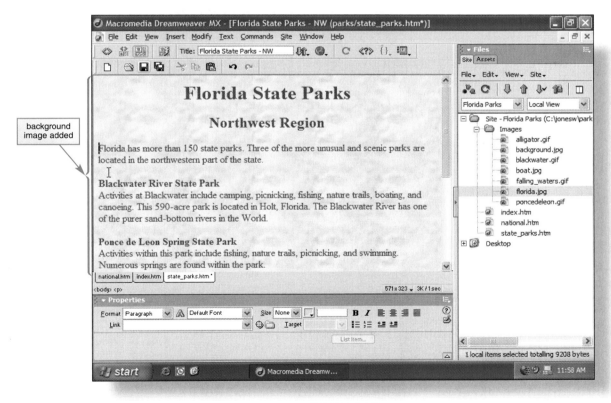

FIGURE 2-57

Next, you will add the three images to the state parks page. Complete the steps on the next five pages to insert and align the images.

To Insert and Align Images in the State Parks Web Page

1 If necessary, scroll to the top of the document. Position the insertion point to the left of Blackwater River State Park (Figure 2-58).

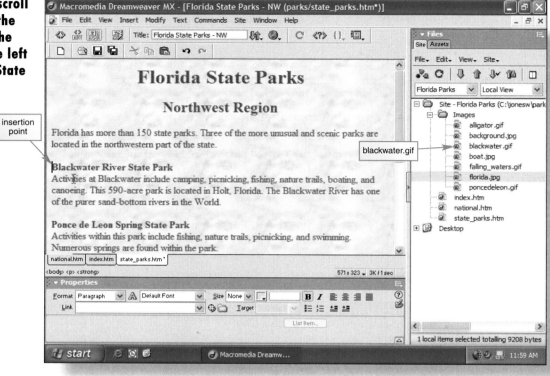

FIGURE 2-58

2 Drag the blackwater.gif file from the Site panel to the insertion point. Click the image to select it and then click the Align box arrow in the Property inspector. Click Left on the Align pop-up menu.

The image aligns to the left (Figure 2-59).

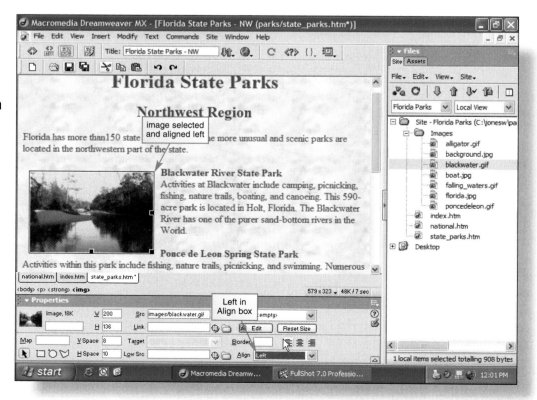

FIGURE 2-59

3 **Click the V Space box and then type** 8 **as the vertical space. Click the H Space box and then type** 10 **as the horizontal space. Press the ENTER key. Click the Alt box, type** Blackwater River State Park **as the alternate text, and then press the ENTER key.**

The image is selected. The Alt text, V Space, and H Space attributes are added to the state parks Web page (Figure 2-60).

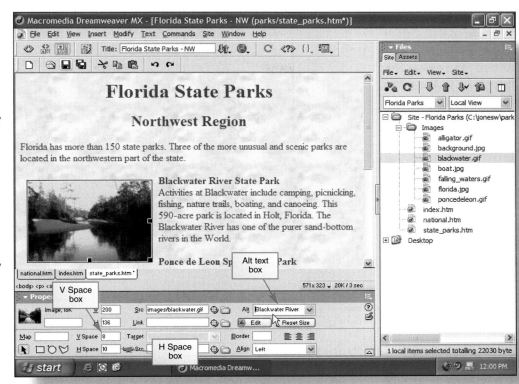

FIGURE 2-60

4 **If necessary, scroll down and then position the insertion point to the right of the word, park, in the last line in the Ponce de Leon Spring State Park paragraph.**

The insertion point is to the right of the last sentence in the third paragraph (Figure 2-61).

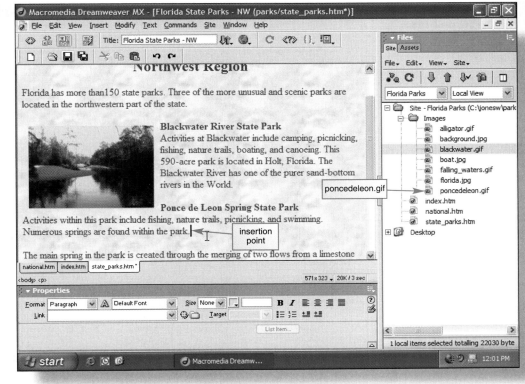

FIGURE 2-61

5 Drag the poncedeleon.gif image to the insertion point and then select the image. Point to the Align box arrow.

The image is selected (Figure 2-62).

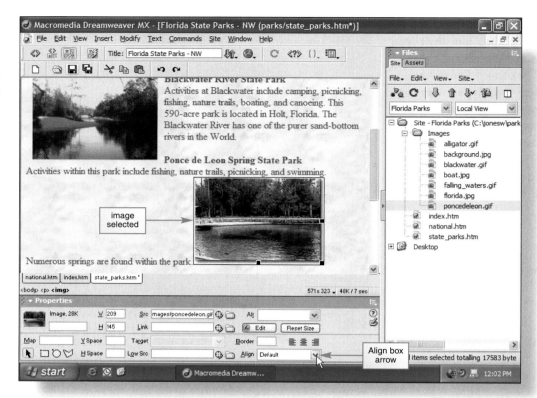

FIGURE 2-62

6 Click the Align box arrow and then click Right on the Align pop-up menu.

The poncedeleon.gif image moves to the right side of the window (Figure 2-63). The visual aid displays because the image is aligned to the right.

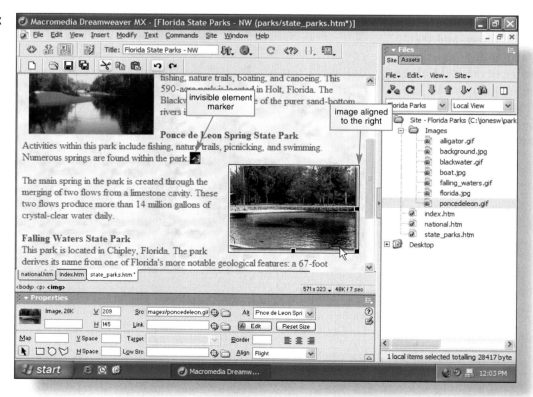

FIGURE 2-63

7 Click the V Space box and then type 6 as the vertical space. Click the H Space box and then type 12 as the horizontal space. Click the Alt box, type Ponce de Leon Spring State Park as the alternate text, and then press the ENTER key. Position the insertion point to the left of Falling Waters State Park.

The image is positioned on the page (Figure 2-64).

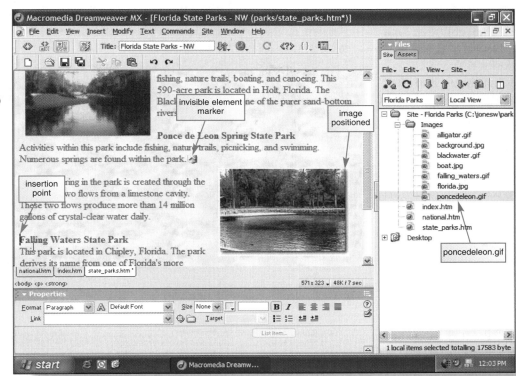

FIGURE 2-64

8 Drag the falling_waters.gif from the Site panel to the insertion point and then select the image. Click the Align box arrow and then click Left on the Align pop-up menu.

The Falling Waters image is aligned to the left (Figure 2-65).

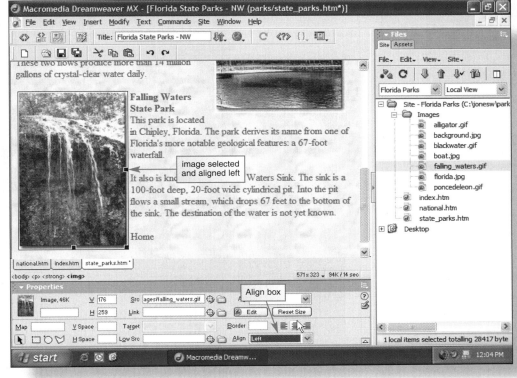

FIGURE 2-65

9 **Click the V Space box and then type 8 as the vertical space. Click the H Space box and then type 12 as the horizontal space. Click the Alt box, type** Falling Waters State Park **as the alternate text, and then press the ENTER key.**

The image is positioned on the page (Figure 2-66).

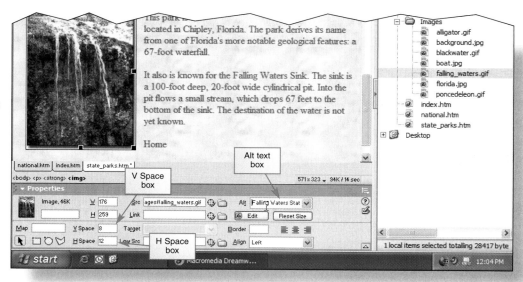

FIGURE 2-66

10 **Press the F12 key.**

The state parks page is displayed in the browser (Figure 2-67).

11 **Close the browser.**

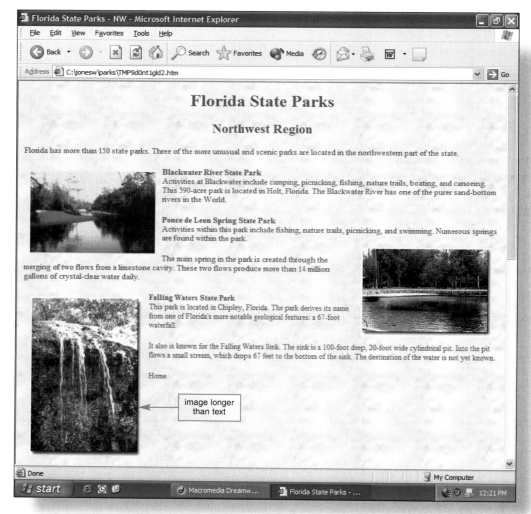

FIGURE 2-67

In Figure 2-67, the height of the Falling Waters image makes the Web page appear out of balance. The image needs to be resized. Resizing images, in this case, the Falling Waters image, will balance the image and the text so they are displayed attractively spaced in the browser.

Resizing Images

Dreamweaver provides two methods to resize an image: visual and numeric. When a file is resized, the image displays at a different size, but the size of the image does not change. If you have several images to resize, it is best to do this in a graphics and photo editor program such as Macromedia Fireworks, Adobe® Photoshop®, or Jasc® PaintShop Pro®.

When an image is selected, resize handles appear at the bottom and right sides of the image and in the bottom-right corner. To resize the image visually, do one of the following:

▶ To adjust the width of the image, drag the selection handle on the right side.
▶ To adjust the height of the image, drag the bottom selection handle.
▶ To adjust the width and the height of the image at the same time, drag the corner selection handle.
▶ To preserve the image's proportions (its width-to-height ratio) as you adjust its dimensions, hold down the SHIFT key and drag the corner selection handle.

To resize an image numerically, change the W and H fields in the Property inspector. To return an image to its original size, click the Property inspector Reset Size button.

After you insert the image into the Web page and then select it, the Property inspector displays features specific to images. As discussed earlier, alignment is one of these features. **Alignment** determines where on the page the image displays and if and how text wraps around the image. The following steps resize an image.

Steps To Resize an Image

1 If necessary, select the Falling Waters image. Double-click the W box and then type 150 as the new value. Double-click the H box and then type 200 as the new value. Press the ENTER key.

The image size is reduced on the screen (Figure 2-68). The values in the W box and H box are displayed bold to indicate that the image size was changed.

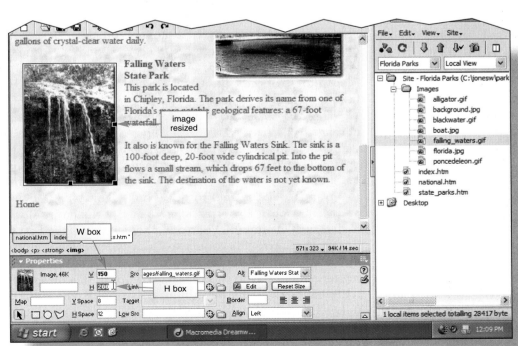

FIGURE 2-68

2 Press the F12 key to view the resized image (Figure 2-69).

3 Close the browser to return to the Dreamweaver window. Click the Save button on the Standard toolbar.

The state parks page is saved.

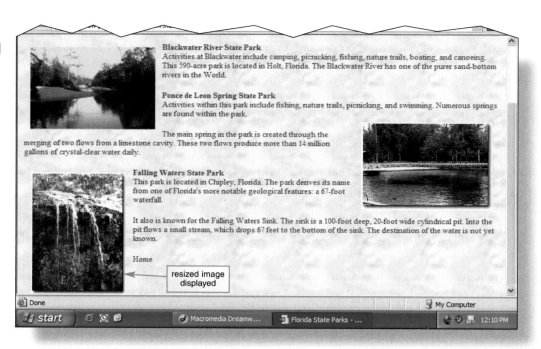

FIGURE 2-69

To connect the pages within the Web site and to display the navigation structure of the pages in the Site Map, they must be linked. In the next section, the different types of links are discussed.

Understanding Different Types of Links

Links are the distinguishing feature of the World Wide Web. A link, also referred to as a hyperlink, is the path to another document, to another part of the same document, or to other media such as an image or a movie. Most links display as colored and/or underlined text, although you also can link from an image or other object. Clicking a link accesses the corresponding document, other media, or another place within the same document. If you place the mouse pointer over the link, the Web address of the link, or path, usually appears at the bottom of the window on the status bar.

Three types of link paths are available: absolute, relative, and root-relative. An **absolute link** (created in Project 1) provides the complete URL of the document. This type of link also is referred to as an **external link**. Absolute links generally contain the protocol (such as http://) and primarily are used to link to documents on other servers.

You use **relative links** for local links. This type of link also is referred to as a **document-relative link** or an **internal link**. If the linked documents are in the same folder, such as those in your parks folder, this is the best type of link to use. You also can use a relative link to link to a document in another folder, such as the images folder. All the files you see in the Site panel Local View are internal files and are referenced as relative links. You accomplish this by specifying the path through the folder hierarchy from the current document to the linked document. Consider the following examples.

- To link to another file in the same folder, specify the file name. Example: everglades.htm
- To link to a file in a subfolder of the current Web site folder (such as the Images folder), the link path would consist of the name of the subfolder, a forward slash (/), and then the file name. Example: Images/gator.jpg.

You use the **root-relative link** primarily when working with a large Web site that requires several servers. Web developers generally use this type of link when they must move HTML files from one folder or server to another folder or server. Root-relative links are beyond the scope of this book.

Two other types of links are named anchor and e-mail. A **named anchor** lets the user link to a specific location within a document. An **e-mail link** creates a blank e-mail message containing the recipient's address. A third type of link is a **null**, or **script, link**. This type of link provides for attaching behaviors to an object or executes JavaScript code.

Relative Links

Another Dreamweaver feature is the variety of ways in which to create a relative link. Two of the more commonly used methods are drag-and-drop and browse for file. The **drag-and-drop method** requires that the Property inspector be open and that the site files display in the Site panel. The **browse for file method** is accomplished through a dialog box. The next step is to add the text to create the relative links between the home page and the national and state park pages. You will then use drag and drop to create a relative link from the text to a specific Web page.

Adding Text for the Relative Links

To create relative links from the index page, you add text to the index page and use the text to create the links to the other two Web pages in your Web site. You will center the text directly below the Discovering Scenic Florida heading. You add the text for the links in the following steps.

Steps **To Add Text for Relative Links**

 Click the index.htm tab. If necessary, scroll to the top of the page and then position the insertion point at the end of the title, Discovering Scenic Florida. Press the ENTER key and then press the END key.

The insertion point is centered below the title (Figure 2-70). Pressing the END key positions the insertion point outside of the heading </H1> tag.

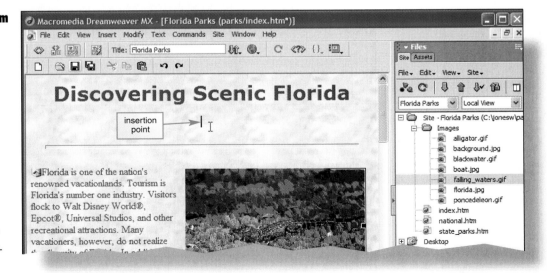

FIGURE 2-70

2 Type National
Parks **and then
press the** SPACEBAR.

*The text for the first link,
National Parks, is displayed
in the Document window
(Figure 2-71).*

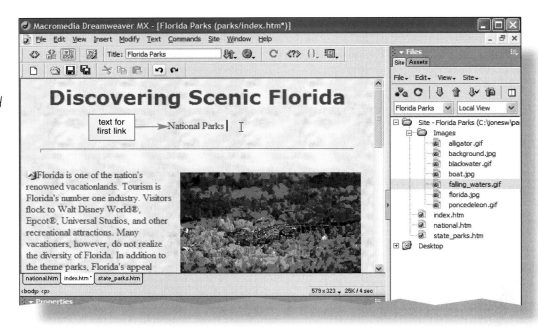

FIGURE 2-71

3 **Hold down the**
SHIFT **key and then
press the** VERTICAL LINE KEY
(|). **Press the** SPACEBAR **and
then type** NW State
Parks **for the second
link.**

*Text for both links is dis-
played in the Document
window (Figure 2-72).*

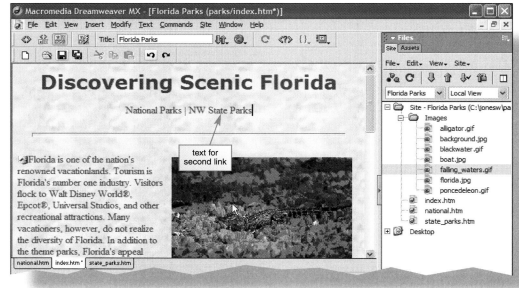

FIGURE 2-72

You will use the text, National Parks, to create a link to the national parks Web
page and the text, NW State Parks, to create a link to the northwest state parks
page.

Creating a Relative Link Using Drag and Drop

A relative link is used to create links between local files or files within one Web
site. The drag-and-drop method requires that the Property inspector be displayed.
Complete the following steps to use the drag-and-drop method to create a relative
link from the Florida Parks home page to the national parks Web page.

Steps **To Create a Relative Link Using Drag and Drop**

1 **Click the expander arrow in the lower-left corner of the Property inspector to collapse it. Drag to select the text National Parks.**

The National Parks text is highlighted (Figure 2-73).

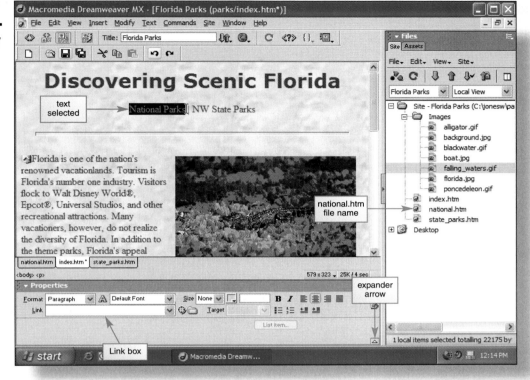

FIGURE 2-73

2 **Drag the national.htm file to the Link box in the Property inspector.**

When you start to drag, a page icon displays next to the mouse pointer, indicating the link is being copied. When the mouse pointer is over the Link box, it changes to a circle with a centered line (Figure 2-74). This circle indicates the link is established.

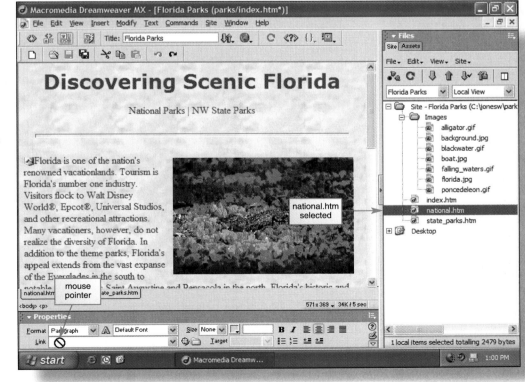

FIGURE 2-74

Dreamweaver MX

3 **Release the mouse button. Click National Parks to display the linked text.**

The linked text displays underlined and in a different color in the Document window, and the link text displays in the Link box (Figure 2-75). If you click anywhere else in the document, the linked document name does not display in the Link box.

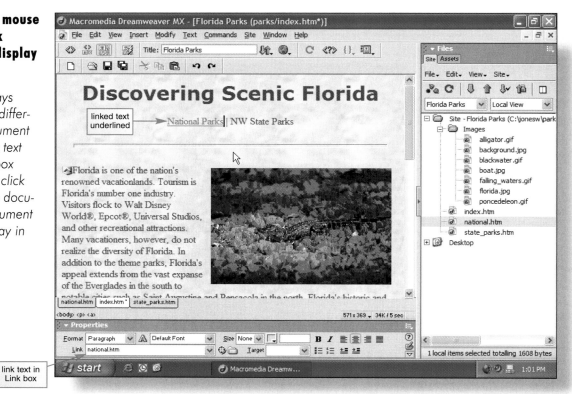

FIGURE 2-75

Creating a Relative Link Using Browse for File

The **Browse for File method** is a second way to create a link. Using this method, you select the file name from the Select File dialog box. In the following steps, you use the Browse for File method to create a link to the state parks page.

Steps To Create a Relative Link Using Browse for File

1 Drag to select NW State Parks and then point to the Browse for File icon in the Property inspector.

The text NW State Parks is highlighted (Figure 2-76).

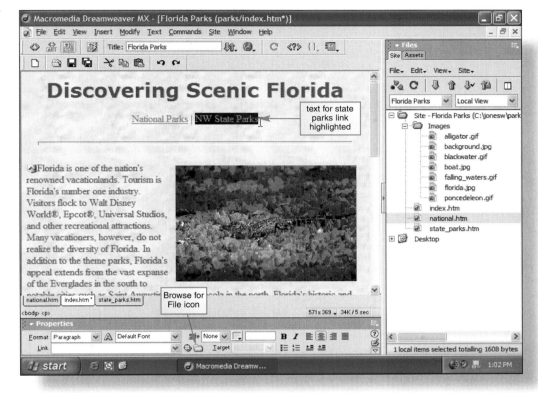

FIGURE 2-76

2 Click the Browse for File icon and then click state_parks.htm. Point to the OK button.

The Select File dialog box is displayed (Figure 2-77).

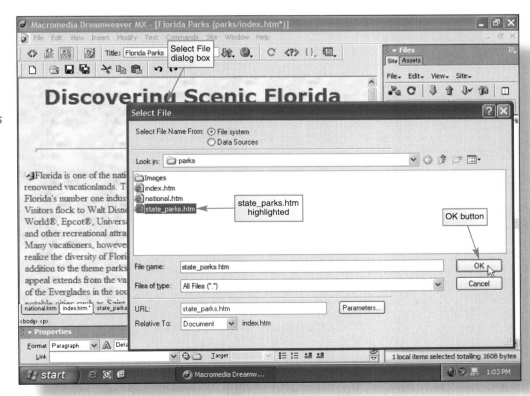

FIGURE 2-77

3 Click the OK button and then click the selected text, NW State Parks, to display the link.

The linked text displays underlined and in a different color in the Document window and the link text displays in the Link box (Figure 2-78). If you click anywhere else in the document, the linked document name does not display in the Link box.

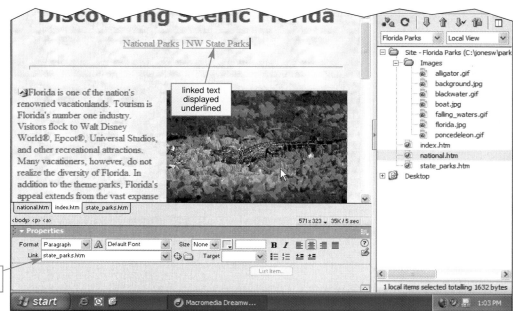

FIGURE 2-78

Creating Relative Links to the Home Page and the Three National Parks Pages

You created a relative link from the home page to each of the other two pages within the Web site. Visitors can enter a Web site at any point, however, so it is important always to include a link from each page within the site back to the home page. Complete the following steps to create a link from the national parks page and a link from the state parks page to the home page.

Then, on the national parks page, create links from the three park names to the respective park pages. These links will be activated in Project 3 when you create the three pages for the three national parks.

Steps To Create a Relative Link to the Home Page

1 Click the national.htm tab and then scroll to the bottom of the page. Drag to select Home.

The text, Home, is highlighted (Figure 2-79). This text will become a link.

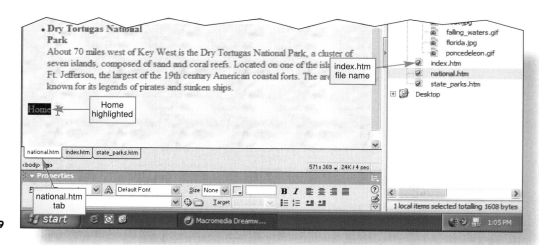

FIGURE 2-79

2 **Drag the index.htm file name from the Site panel to the Link box. Click the text, Home, to display the link. Click the Save button on the Standard toolbar. Point to the state_parks.htm tab.**

The link is created and index.htm displays in the Link box (Figure 2-80). The national parks page is saved and the asterisk no longer displays on the tab or title bar.

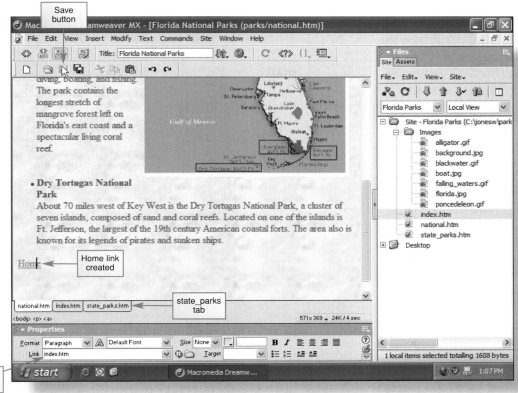

FIGURE 2-80

3 **Click the state_parks.htm tab. If necessary, scroll to the end of the document and then drag to select the text, Home (Figure 2-81).**

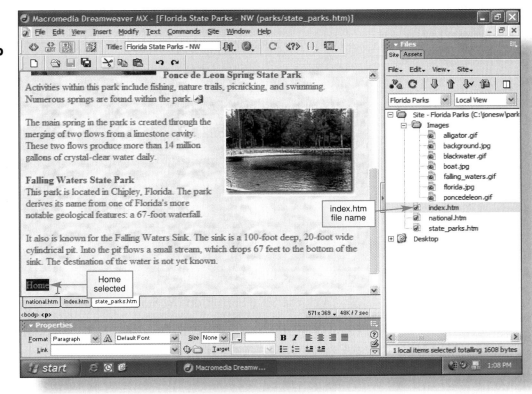

FIGURE 2-81

Dreamweaver MX

4 **Drag the index.htm file name from the Site panel to the Link box. Click the Save button on the Standard toolbar.**

The link is created and index.htm displays in the Link box (Figure 2-82). The state parks page is saved.

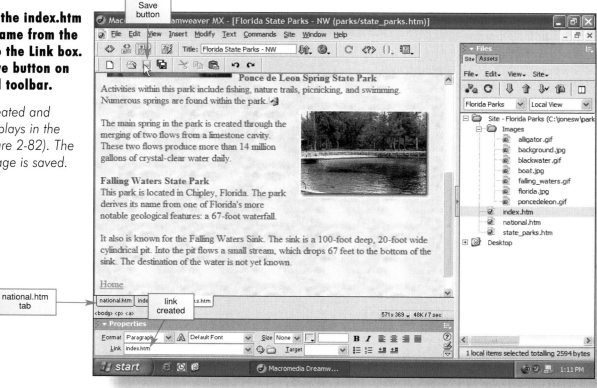

FIGURE 2-82

Other Ways

1 Click Link box, type file name

The following steps create relative links to the national parks pages.

TO CREATE RELATIVE LINKS TO THE THREE NATIONAL PARKS PAGES

1 Click the national.htm tab.

2 Drag to select the bulleted text, Everglades National Park.

3 Click the Link box and then type `everglades.htm` for the link text.

4 Drag to select the bulleted text, Biscayne National Park.

5 Click the Link box and then type `biscayne.htm` for the link text.

6 If necessary, scroll down. Drag to select the bulleted text, Dry Tortugas National Park.

7 Click the Link box and then type `dry_tortugas.htm` for the link text.

8 Click the Save button on the Standard toolbar.

The three relative links are added to the Florida National Parks page and the Web page is saved. You create the pages for these links in Project 3.

Absolute Links

In Project 1, you created an absolute link from the index page to the Florida Environmental Department. To create an absolute link, you must know the URL or the path of the external site to which you want to link. You can type the link in the Link box or copy and paste the link.

Creating an Absolute Link

You now will create three absolute (external) links in the NW State Parks page. These links are from the name of each of the three parks to a Web page about the selected park. Perform the following steps to create the three absolute links.

TO CREATE AN ABSOLUTE LINK

1. If necessary, scroll to the top of the page. Drag to select the text, Blackwater River State Park.

2. Click the Link box and then type http://www.dep.state.fl.us/parks/ district1/blackwater/index.asp.

3. Drag to select the text, Ponce de Leon Spring State Park. Click the Link box and then type http://www.dep.state.fl.us/parks/district1/ poncedeleon/index.asp.

4. If necessary, scroll down and then drag to select the text, Falling Waters State park. Click the Link box and then type http://www.dep.state.fl.us/parks/ district1/fallingwaters/index.asp.

5. Click the Save button on the Standard toolbar.

The three absolute links are added to the respective state parks page (Figure 2-83) and the Web page is saved.

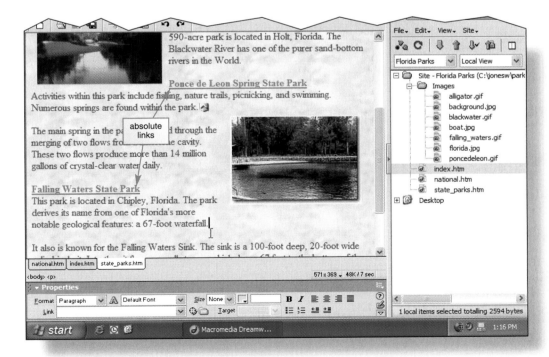

FIGURE 2-83

E-mail Links

An **e-mail link** is one of the foundation elements of any successful Web site. It is important for visitors to be able to contact you for additional information or to comment on the Web page or Web site. When visitors click an e-mail link, their default e-mail program opens to a new e-mail message. The e-mail address you specify is inserted automatically in the To box.

Creating an E-mail Link

The next steps create an e-mail link for your home page using your name as the linked text. You do this through the Insert menu.

Steps **To Add an E-mail Link**

1 Click the index.htm tab, scroll down, and then drag to select your name. Click Insert on the menu bar and then point to Email Link.

Your name is highlighted and the Insert menu is displayed (Figure 2-84).

FIGURE 2-84

2 Click Email Link.

The Email link dialog box is displayed. Will Jones is highlighted in the Text text box (Figure 2-85). On your computer, your name is displayed in the Text box.

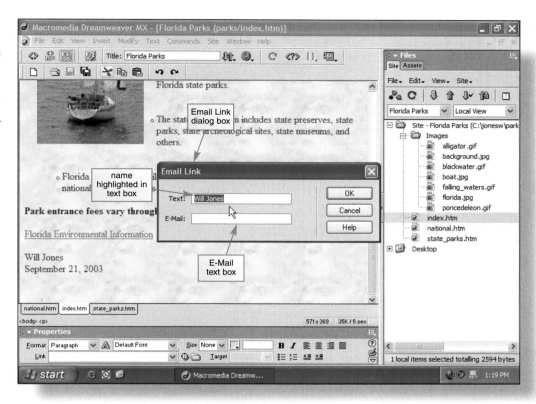

FIGURE 2-85

3 Click the E-Mail text box and then type your e-mail address. Point to the OK button.

The e-mail address for Will Jones is displayed in the E-Mail text box. On your computer, Dreamweaver displays your e-mail address (Figure 2-86).

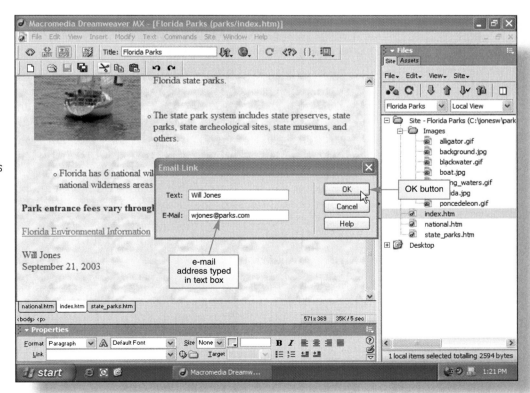

FIGURE 2-86

4 **Click the OK button. Click the Save button on the Standard toolbar and then click the highlighted text (your name).**

The selected text for the e-mail link, Will Jones, is displayed as linked text. The Link box displays the e-mail address (Figure 2-87). On your computer, Dreamweaver displays your name as the linked text.

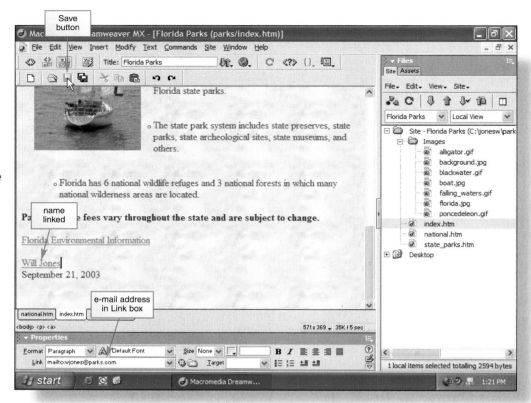

FIGURE 2-87

Changing the Color of Links

Web page links can have three colors: Link (the link has not been clicked), Active Link (the link changes color when the user clicks it), and Visited Link (the link has been visited). By default, linked text follows the color scheme established in your default Web browser. In Internet Explorer, linked text is blue and visited links are dark red. It is easy to make changes to these default settings and select colors that complement the background and other colors you are using on your Web pages. This is accomplished through the Page Properties dialog box. You display the Page Properties dialog box by clicking Modify on the menu bar. You then can click the box that corresponds to one of the three types of links and select a color to match your color scheme.

Editing and Deleting Links

Web development is a never-ending process. At some point, it will be necessary to edit or delete a link. For instance, an e-mail address may change, a URL to an external link may change, or an existing link may contain an error.

Dreamweaver makes it easy to edit or delete a link. First, select the link or click within the link you want to change. The linked document name displays in the Link box in the Property inspector. To delete the link without deleting the text, delete the text from the Link box. To edit the link, make the change in the Link box.

A second method to edit or delete a link is to use the context menu. Right-click within the link you want to change and then click Remove Link on the context menu to eliminate the link; click Change Link on the context menu to edit the link.

The Site Map

Dreamweaver provides a visual site map for viewing the relationships among files. The **site map** is a graphical representation of the structure of a Web site. You visually can design and modify the Web site structure through the site map. The home page displays at the top level of the map, and linked pages display at the lower levels. The site map view allows you to create, change, display, save, and print a Web site's structure and navigation. As previously discussed, a Web site structure is the relationships among the pages in a Web site.

Viewing the Site Map

The home page now contains links to other pages in the site and each page in the site contains links back to the home page. The state parks page contains a link to three external Web sites outside of the local site and located on a different server. The index page also contains a link to an external Web site.

You created links from the home page to the two other pages in the Web site (national parks and state parks) and links from these two pages back to the home page. You can use the site map to view a graphical image of these links. In addition to viewing the site map, Dreamweaver also has an option that lets you view your file list and site map simultaneously.

Displaying the Site Map and Local Files

The site map shows the pages as icons and displays links in the order in which they are encountered in the HTML source code. Starting from the home page, the site map default displays the site structure two levels deep. The relative links have a plus sign to their left. If you click the plus (+) sign, pages below the second level display. Some pages have a minus sign to their left. If you click the minus (–) sign, pages linked below the second level are hidden. Text displayed in blue and marked with a globe icon indicates a file on another site or a special link such as an e-mail link. Text displayed in red indicates a broken link. You access the site map through the Site panel. Complete the following steps to display the newly created links among the pages in the Florida Parks Web site.

 To Display the Site Map and Local Files List

1 **Click the View box arrow and then point to Map View in the View pop-up menu (Figure 2-88).**

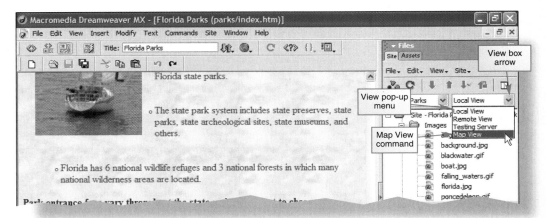

FIGURE 2-88

2 **Click Map View and then point to the Expand/Collapse button on the Site panel toolbar.**

Dreamweaver displays a graphical view of the Web site in the Site panel (Figure 2-89).

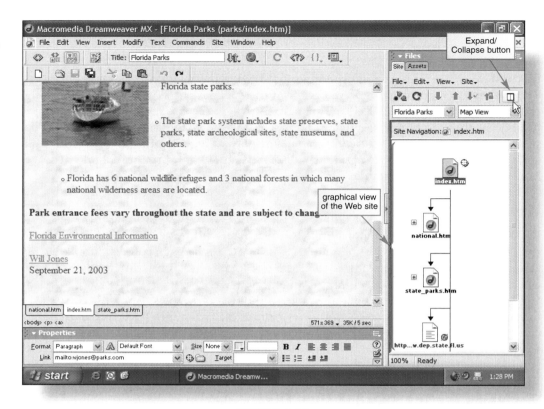

FIGURE 2-89

3 **Click the Expand/ Collapse button. Point to the plus sign to the left of the national.htm icon.**

The site map expands and displays a graphical structure of the links between the index page and the other two pages and external links (Figure 2-90). The plus signs to the left of the national.htm and state_parks.htm pages indicate that additional files or links are below those pages. The files list is displayed on the right in the Local Files panel.

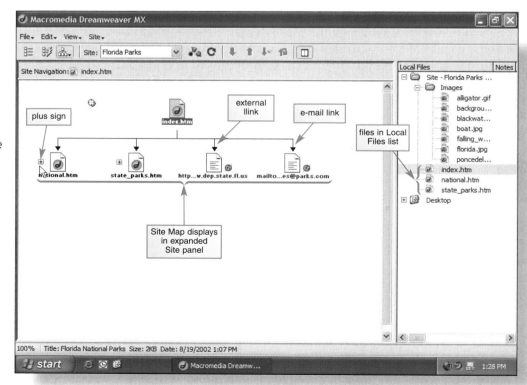

FIGURE 2-90

4 **Click the plus sign to the left of the national.htm icon and then point to the plus sign to the left of the state_parks.htm icon.**

The structure further expands and displays the relative link to the index page from the national.htm page (Figure 2-91).

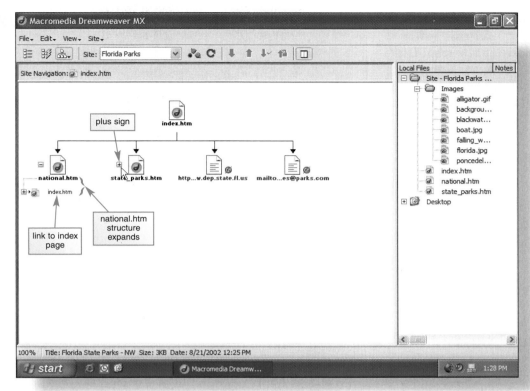

FIGURE 2-91

5 **Click the plus sign to the left of the state_parks.htm icon and then point to the Expand/Collapse button on the expanded Site map toolbar.**

The structure further expands and displays the relative link to the index page from the state parks page and the external links (Figure 2-92).

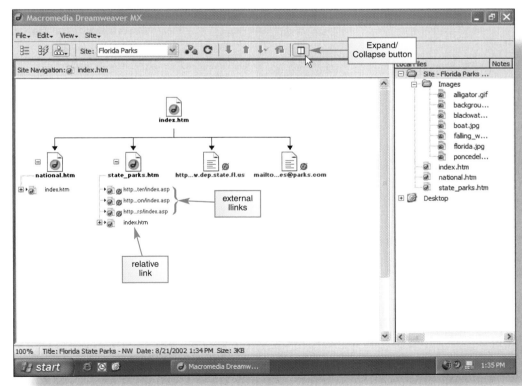

FIGURE 2-92

6 **Click the Expand/Collapse button to close the site map. Click the View box arrow and then point to Local View in the View pop-up menu (Figure 2-93).**

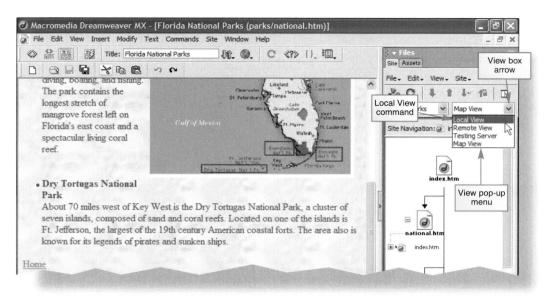

FIGURE 2-93

7 **Click Local View.**

The Site - Florida Parks file hierarchy displays (Figure 2-94).

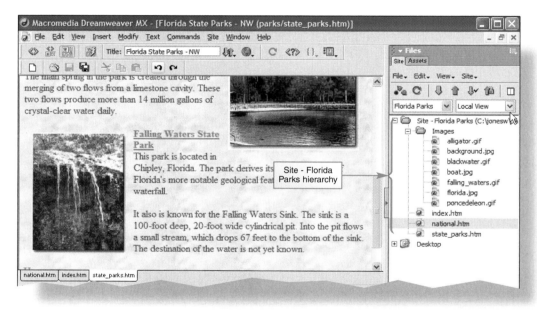

FIGURE 2-94

Verifying Links

It is important that you check and verify that your links work. Links are not active within Dreamweaver; that is, you cannot open the linked document by clicking the link in the Document window. You can check any type of link by displaying the page in a browser. Using a browser is the only available option for absolute or external and e-mail links. For relative or internal links, Dreamweaver provides the Link Checker feature. Use the Link Checker to check internal links in a document, folder, or entire site.

Using the Link Checker

A large Web site can contain hundreds of links that can change over time. Dreamweaver's **Link Checker** searches for broken links and unreferenced files in a portion of a local site or throughout an entire local site. This feature is limited, however, because it verifies internal links only. A list of external links is compiled, but not verified. External links are checked through a browser.

The Link Checker does have advantages, however. When you use this feature, the Link Checker displays a statistical report that includes broken links, orphaned files, and external links. An **orphaned file** is a file that is not connected to any page within the Web site. The orphaned file option is for informational purposes only. The orphaned file report, however, is particularly valuable for a large site since it displays a list of all files not part of the Web site. Deleting unused files from a Web site increases disk space and streamlines your site. You can use the Link Checker to check links throughout your entire site from any Web page within your site. The following steps verify internal links using the Link Checker.

Steps **To Verify Internal Links with the Link Checker**

1 Click the Site menu in the Site panel and then point to Check Links Sitewide (Figure 2-95).

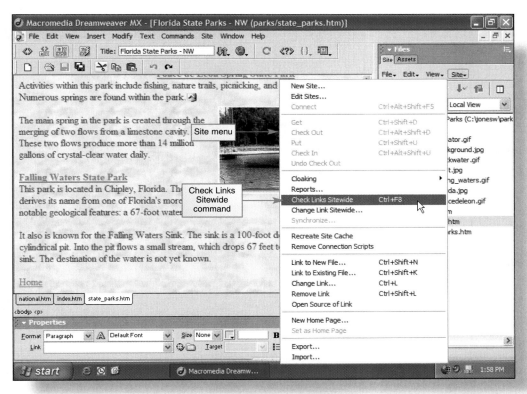

FIGURE 2-95

2 **Click Check Links Sitewide.**

The Results panel is displayed. The report shows a total of 10 files within the site, including 10 Total, 3 HTML, 8 Orphaned, 15 All Links, 0 Broken, and 5 External links (Figure 2-96). External links are not verified. Your report may include different results.

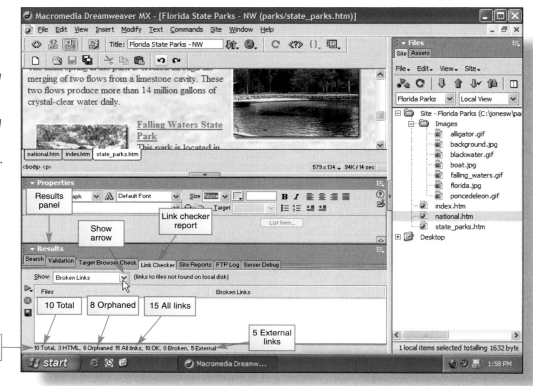

FIGURE 2-96

3 **Click the Show box arrow and then click External Links in the Show pop-up menu.**

The five external links are displayed (Figure 2-97). These are links to absolute Web site and e-mail links. External links are not verified through the Link Checker.

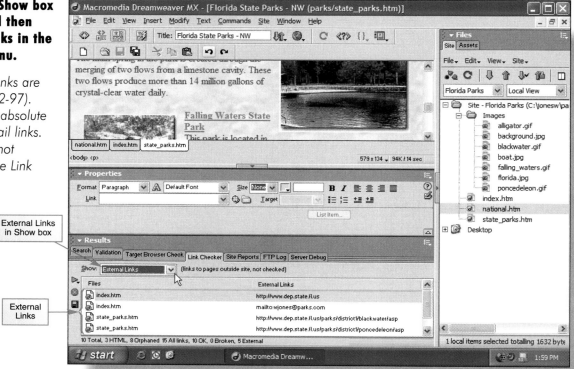

FIGURE 2-97

4 **Click the Show down arrow and then point to and click Orphaned Files. Point to the Options button on the Results panel.**

The list of orphaned files is displayed (Figure 2-98). Orphaned files are files that are not linked to any file in the site or links to external sites.

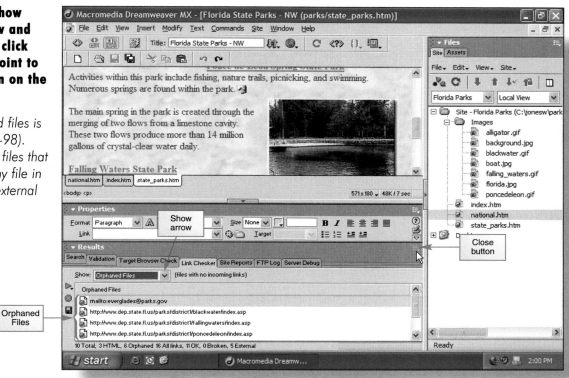

FIGURE 2-98

5 **Click the Options button and then click the Close Panel Group to close the Results window (Figure 2-99).**

The Results panel closes.

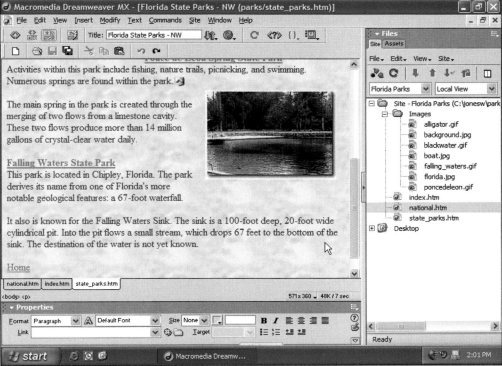

FIGURE 2-99

Viewing Your Site in a Browser

Now that you have completed adding images and verifying links in your Web pages, you will view them through a browser. Complete the following steps to view your Web pages and test your external links.

Steps **To View Your Web Site in a Browser**

1 **Click the index.htm tab and then press the F12 key. Point to the National Parks link.**

The browser displays your index page (Figure 2-100). When you point to a link, the mouse changes to a pointing hand.

Florida Parks Web page displayed in browser

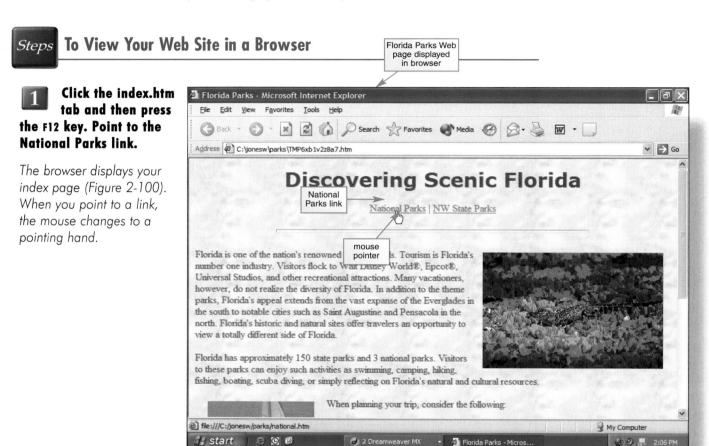

National Parks link

mouse pointer

FIGURE 2-100

2 Click the National Parks link.

The Florida National Parks page is displayed in the browser (Figure 2-101).

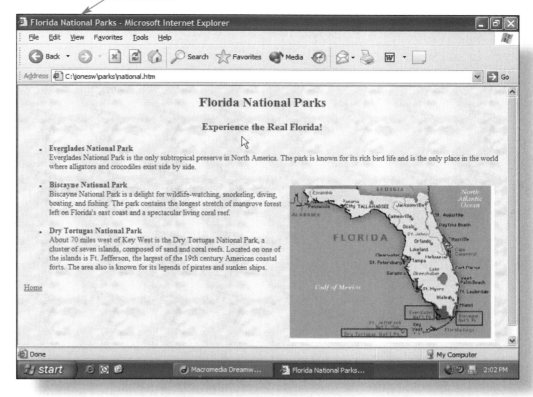

FIGURE 2-101

3 Scroll down and click the Home link to return to the index page. Click the NW State Parks link.

The state parks Web page displays (Figure 2-102).

4 Click each of the three absolute (external) links to view the state park Web sites. Click the browser Back button after you view each page.

5 Click Home to return to the index page. Click the browser Close button to close the browser.

FIGURE 2-102

HTML Code View

Dreamweaver provides two views, or *ways*, to look at a document: **Design view** and **Code view**. Thus far, you have been working in Design view. As you create and work with documents, Dreamweaver automatically generates the underlying HTML code. Recall that the HTML code defines the structure and layout of a Web document by using a variety of tags and attributes. Even though Dreamweaver generates the code, occasions occur that necessitate the tweaking or modifying of code.

Dreamweaver provides several options for viewing and working with HTML code. You can split the Document window so that it displays both the Code view and the Design view. You can display only the Code view in the Document window, or you can open the Code inspector. The **Code inspector** opens in a separate window, so you can keep the whole Document window reserved for Design view.

Using Code View and Design View

In Code view and Design view, you work in a split-screen environment. You can see the design and the code at the same time. Splitting the Document window to view the code makes it easier to view the visual design while you make changes in the HTML code. When you make a change in Design view, the HTML code also is changed. Viewing the code at this early stage may not seem important, but the more code you learn, the more productive you will become.

Within the HTML code, tags can be entered in uppercase, lowercase, or a combination of upper- and lowercase. The letter combination has no effect on how the browser displays the output. When you view the code in Code view in Dreamweaver, some HTML tags display in lowercase letters and some attributes in uppercase letters. This is the Dreamweaver default.

In this book when describing HTML tags, we use uppercase letters for tags and attributes to make it easier to differentiate from the other text. Entering tags as uppercase also is the standard used by many Web page authors who write their own HTML code. Within the steps, however, we use lowercase letters to match the displayed code.

In the following steps, you use the Code View and Design View option to look at the code for the
 (line break) and <P> (paragraph) tags. The paragraph tag has an opening tag <P> and a closing tag </P>. The
 (line break) tag does not have a closing tag.

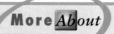

More About

Using the Quick Tag Editor

For more information about using the Quick Tag Editor to review and edit HTML tags, visit the Dreamweaver MX More About Web page (scsite.com/ dreamweavermx/more) and then click Dreamweaver MX Quick Tag Editor.

To View Design View and Code View Simultaneously

1 Collapse the Property inspector and close the Site panel. Position the insertion point to the left of the heading, Florida State Parks. Point to the Show Code and Design Views button on the Document toolbar (Figure 2-103).

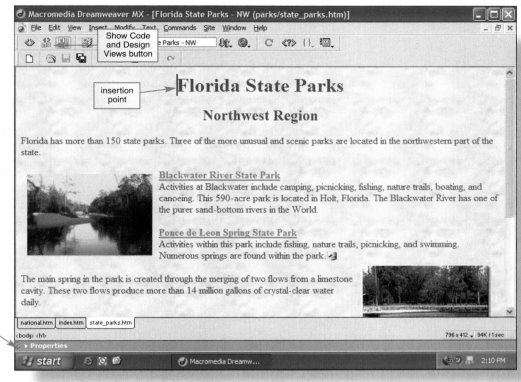

FIGURE 2-103

2 Click the Show Code and Design Views button. If necessary, click the View menu, point to Code View Options, and then click Line Numbers.

The window splits. The upper window displays Code view and the lower window displays Design view (Figure 2-104). The insertion point is displayed in Code view in the same location as in Design view (to the left of the heading). The lines are numbered in Code view. The HTML code is displayed in color and in lowercase surrounded by < (less than) and > (greater than) symbols. Your window may display Design view in the upper window and Code view in the lower window.

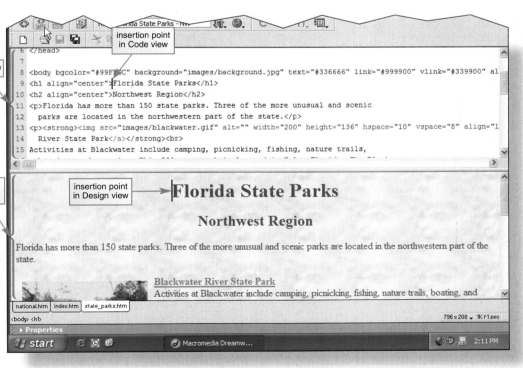

FIGURE 2-104

Modifying HTML Code

One of the more common problems within Dreamweaver and the HTML code is related to line breaks and paragraphs. Occasionally, you inadvertently press the ENTER key or insert a line break and need to remove the tag. Or, you may copy and paste or open a text file that contains unneeded paragraphs or line breaks.

Pressing the BACKSPACE key or DELETE key may return you to the previous line, but does not always delete the line break or paragraph tag within the HTML code. The deletion of these tags is determined by the position of the insertion point when you press the BACKSPACE or DELETE keys. If the insertion point is still inside the HTML code, pressing the BACKSPACE key will not delete these tags and your page will not display correctly.

In the following steps, you practice deleting a line break and a paragraph tag. Then you use Undo to restore them to their original position.

Steps To Delete and Restore the Line Break Tag and the Paragraph Tag

1 In Code view, position the insertion point to the right of the `<br>` tag in line 14 as shown in Figure 2-105.

The insertion point is to the right of the `<br>` tag in Code view in Line 14 (Figure 2-105). This is the line break tag between the paragraph heading, Blackwater River State Park, and the paragraph describing the park. The line number may be different on your screen.

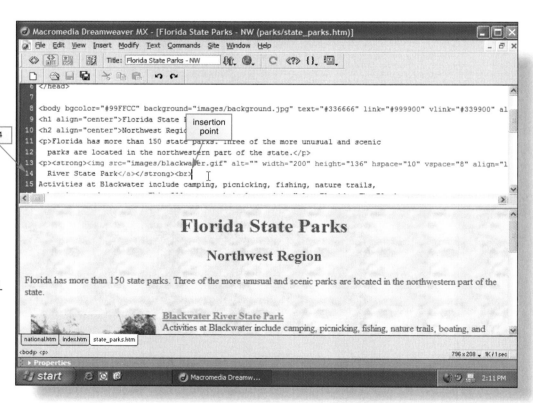

FIGURE 2-105

2 **Press the BACKSPACE key four times or the number of times necessary to delete the <br> tag.**

The <br> tag is deleted and the insertion point is to the left of the </strong> tag (Figure 2-106). Dreamweaver uses the <strong> tag to indicate bold.

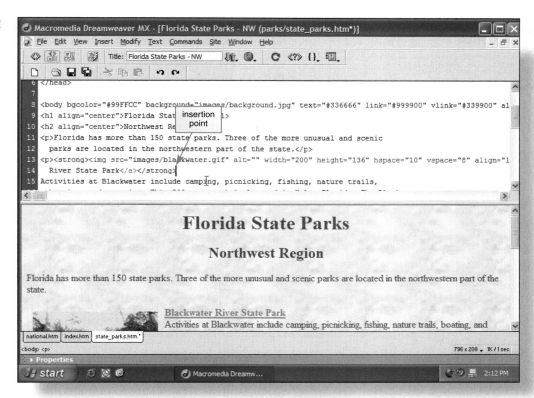

FIGURE 2-106

3 **Click anywhere in Design view. Point to the Undo button on the Standard toolbar.**

The line break between the paragraph heading and the paragraph is deleted and the paragraph heading is displayed on the same line with the paragraph. The insertion point displays at the same location in both Design view and Code view (Figure 2-107).

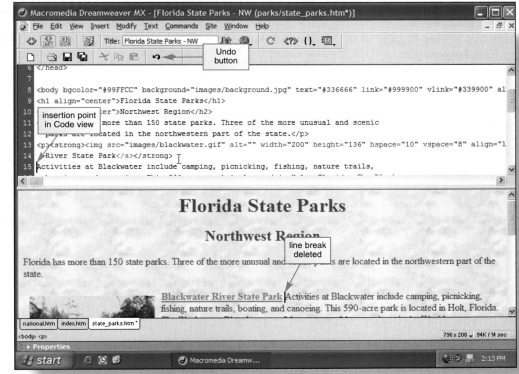

FIGURE 2-107

Dreamweaver MX

4 **Click the Undo button.**

The Web page returns to its original format (Figure 2-108).

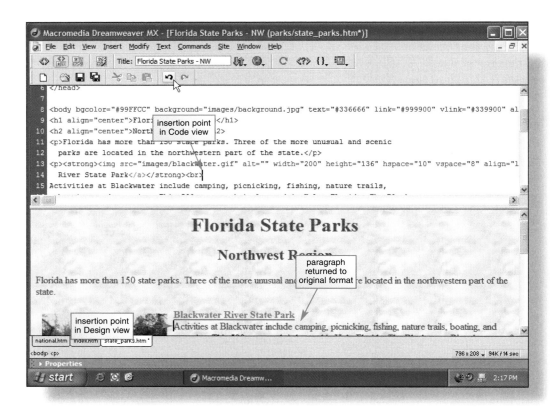

FIGURE 2-108

5 **In Code view, scroll down to display the Falling Waters State Park information (line 29). Position the insertion point to the right of the <p> tag as shown in Figure 2-109.**

The insertion point is positioned to the right of the <p> tag (Figure 2-109).

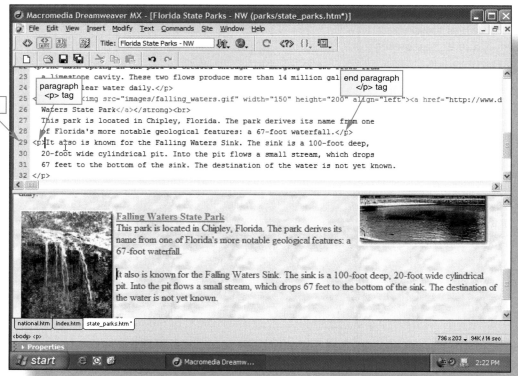

FIGURE 2-109

6 **Press the BACKSPACE key until you have deleted both the `<p>` and `</p>` tags. Click anywhere in Design view. Point to the Undo button on the Standard toolbar.**

The line between the two paragraphs is deleted (Figure 2-110).

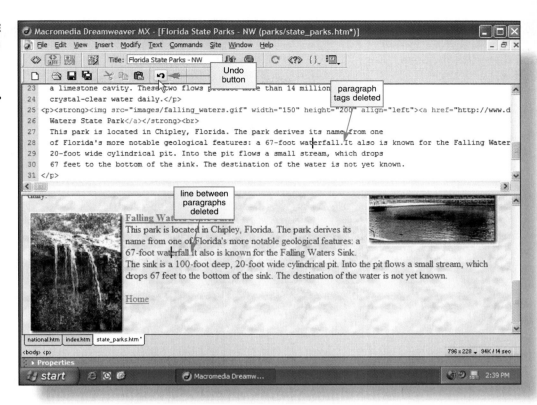

FIGURE 2-110

7 **Click the Undo button and then click anywhere in Design view. Point to the Show Design View button on the Document toolbar.**

The page is restored to its original format (Figure 2-111).

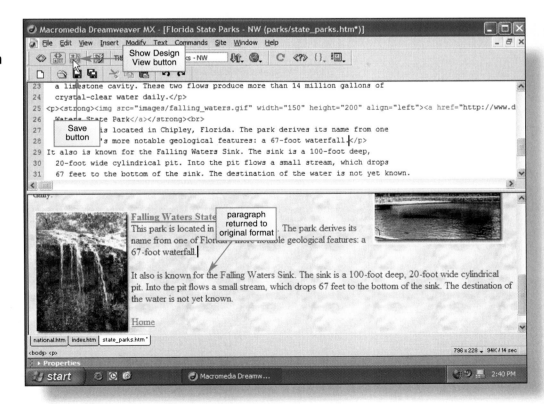

FIGURE 2-111

8 **Click the Show Design View button and then click the Save button.**

The split window is removed and the page is displayed in Design view (Figure 2-112). The Web page is saved.

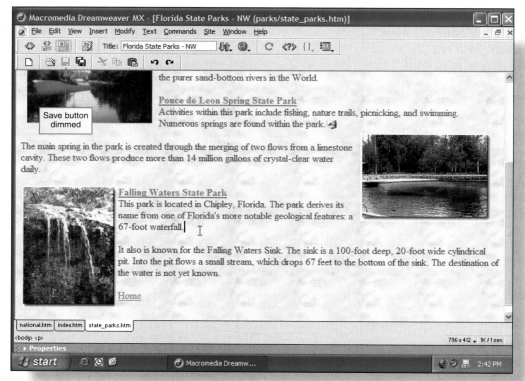

FIGURE 2-112

Quitting Dreamweaver

After you add pages to your Web site, including images and links, and then verify links using the site map and Link Checker, Project 2 is complete. To close the Web site, quit Dreamweaver MX, and return control to Windows, perform the following step.

TO CLOSE THE WEB SITE AND QUIT DREAMWEAVER

1 Click the Close button on the right corner of the Dreamweaver title bar.

The Dreamweaver window, the Document window, and the Florida Parks Web site all close. If you have unsaved changes, Dreamweaver will prompt you to save the changes. Clicking the Yes button in the Dreamweaver MX dialog box saves the changes.

CASE PERSPECTIVE SUMMARY

Will and Joan work well together and are a good team. They are pleased with the new pages on Florida's national and state parks. Both expressed great enthusiasm about learning how to add images and links to a Web page. Joan was particularly impressed with the site map and Link Checker features. Will was surprised at how easy it was to modify the HTML code and is looking forward to learning more about other HTML code revision. Will and Joan are anxious to get started on the next project.

Project Summary

Project 2 introduced you to images, links, the site map, and how to view and modify HTML code. You began the project by using Dreamweaver's integrated file browser to copy data files to the local site. You added two new pages — one for Florida national parks and one for Florida state parks — to the Web site you created in Project 1. Next, you added a background image and page images to the index page. Following that, you applied a color scheme, a background image, and page images to the national and state parks pages. Then, you added relative links to all three pages. You added an e-mail link to the home page and three absolute links to the state parks page. You learned to use the site map and the Link Checker. Finally, you learned how to view and modify HTML code.

What You Should Know

Having completed this project, you now should be able to perform the tasks shown in Table 2-4.

Table 2-4 • Project 2 What You Should Know

TASK NUMBER	TASK	PAGE NUMBER	TASK NUMBER	TASK	PAGE NUMBER
1	Start Dreamweaver and Close Open Panels	DW 2.06	19	Add a Color Scheme and Background Image to the State Parks Web Page	DW 2.43
2	Access a Web Site and Open a Web Site from a Local Web Site	DW 2.07	20	Insert and Align Images in the State Parks Web Page	DW 2.44
3	Copy Data Files to the Parks Web Site	DW 2.09	21	Resize an Image	DW 2.49
4	Set a Home Page	DW 2.14	22	Add Text for Relative Links	DW 2.51
5	Prepare the Workspace	DW 2.16	23	Create a Relative Link Using Drag and Drop	DW 2.53
6	Create the National Parks Web Page	DW 2.17	24	Create a Relative Link Using Browse for File	DW 2.55
7	Format the Florida National Parks Page	DW 2.19	25	Create a Relative Link to the Home Page	DW 2.57
8	Open a New Document Window	DW 2.20	26	Create an Absolute Link	DW 2.59
9	Create the State Parks Web Page	DW 2.22	27	Add an E-mail Link	DW 2.60
10	Format the Florida State Parks Page	DW 2.22	28	Display the Site Map and Local Files List	DW 2.63
11	Add a Background Image to the Index Page	DW 2.25	29	Verify Internal Links with the Link Checker	DW 2.67
12	Insert an Image into the Index Page	DW 2.30	30	View Your Web Site in a Browser	DW 2.70
13	Align an Image	DW 2.32	31	View Design View and Code View Simultaneously	DW 2.73
14	Adjust the Horizontal and Vertical Space	DW 2.34	32	Delete and Restore the Line Break Tag and the Paragraph Tag	DW 2.74
15	Add Alt Text	DW 2.35	33	Close the Web Site and Quit Dreamweaver	DW 2.78
16	Insert a Second Image	DW 2.36			
17	Add a Color Scheme and Background Image to the National Parks Web Page	DW 2.39			
18	Insert an Image in the National Parks Web Page	DW 2.40			

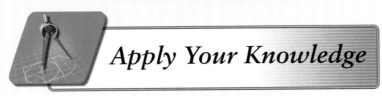

1 Modifying the B & B Lawn Service Web Site

Instructions: Start Dreamweaver. If the panels display, press the F4 key to close all panels. Data and image files for the B & B Lawn Service Web site are included on the Data Disk. See the inside back cover of this book for instructions for downloading the Data Disk or see your instructor for information on accessing the files in this book.

You add three new pages to the B & B Lawn Service Web site: a services page, an employment page, and a references page. In this exercise, you add relative and absolute links to each page. You apply a color scheme to each new page and then add a background image to all pages. Next, you insert images on all pages and use the settings in Table 2-5 to align the images and enter the Alt text. You then add an e-mail link to the home page and relative links from the three new pages to the home page. The pages for the Web site are shown in Figures 2-113a through 2-113d.

Software and hardware settings determine how a Web page is displayed in the browser. Your Web pages may display differently in your browser than those in the figures. For an updated list of links, visit the Dreamweaver MX Links Web page (scsite.com/dreamweavermx/links) and then click Project 2 Links.

Table 2-5 Image Property Settings for the B & B Lawn Service Web Site						
IMAGE NAME	*W*	*H*	*PROPERTY/ALT TEXT* *V SPACE*	*H SPACE*	*ALIGN*	*ALT*
trimming2.gif	174	193	6	6	Right	Tree trimming
shovel.gif	124	166	6	8	Left	Shovel
mowing.gif	120	135	None	20	Left	Grass mowing
shakehands.gif	200	170	None	150	Right	Shaking hands
planting.gif	186	165	6	None	Right	Tree planting
planting2.gif	122	125	8	8	Left	Tree planting

Perform the following tasks:

1. Display the Site panel. Select Lawn Service on the Site pop-up menu in the Site panel. Double-click the index.htm file in the Site panel. Display the Property inspector. Click the expander arrow to expand the Property inspector. If necessary, display the Standard toolbar.

2. Use Dreamweaver's integrated file browser to copy the Images folder and data files to your Proj02 lawn folder. Click the plus sign to the left of the Desktop icon and then navigate through the file hierarchy to the Data Files folder as you did for Florida Parks. Click the Images folder. Hold down the SHIFT key and then click services.htm. Copy the Images folder and the three htm files to the jonesw/lawn folder using Copy and Paste on the context menu.

3. Click Modify on the menu bar and then click Page Properties. Click the Links box arrow and change the color to hexadecimal #CC3333 (row 5 from the bottom, column 11 from the left). Click the Browse button in the Page Properties dialog box, double-click the Images folder, and then select the background.gif image. Click the OK button in the Select Image Source dialog box and in the Page Properties dialog box. Click index.htm in the Site panel to select it. Use the Site panel Site menu to set the index.htm page as the home page.

Apply Your Knowledge

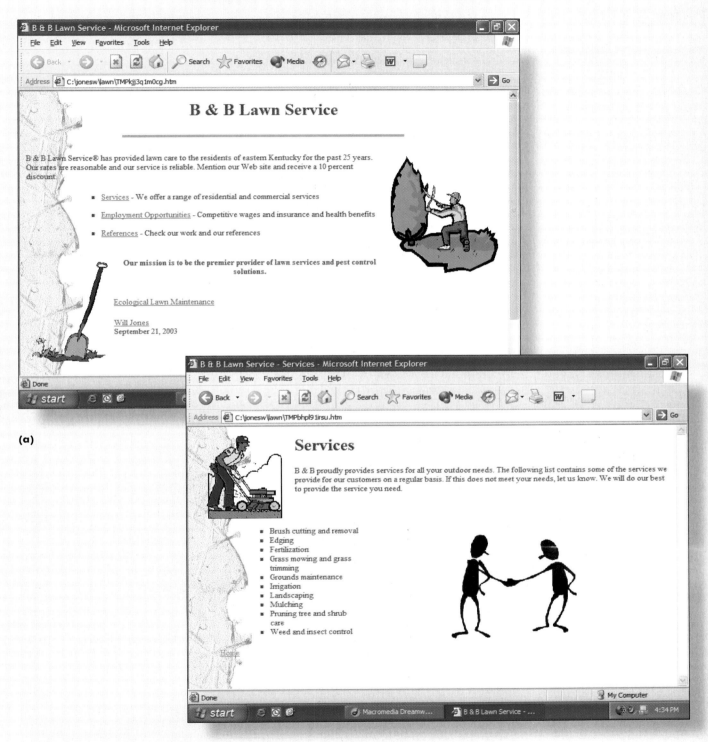

(a)

(b)

FIGURE 2-113

(continued)

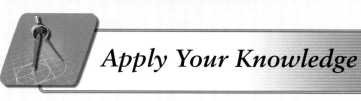

Apply Your Knowledge

Modifying the B & B Lawn Service Web Site *(continued)*

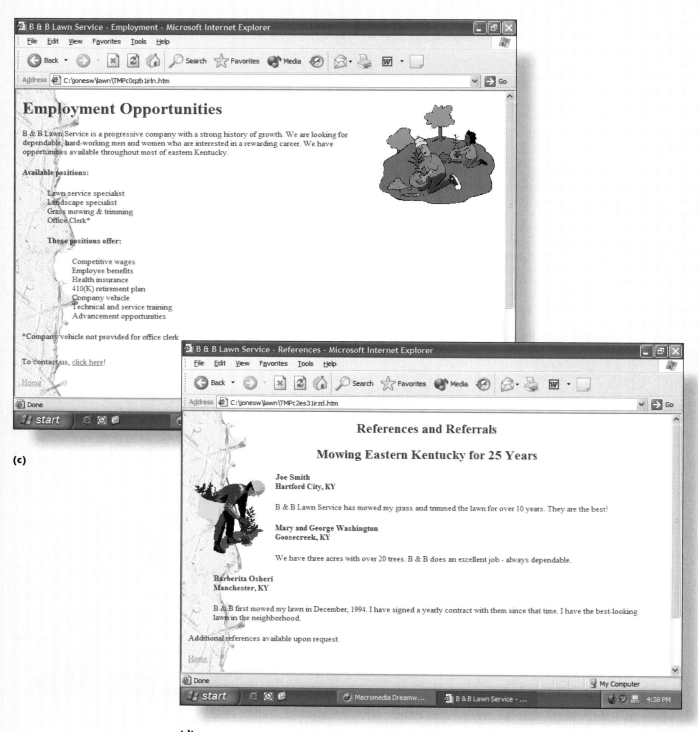

(c)

(d)

FIGURE 2-113 *(continued)*

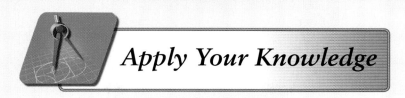

Apply Your Knowledge

4. Position the insertion point to the left of the first line of the first paragraph. Drag the trimming2.gif image to the insertion point and then select the image. Apply the settings in Table 2-5 on page DW 2.80 to align the image and enter the Alt text. If necessary, scroll down. Position the insertion point to the left of the last sentence on the Web page. Drag the shovel.gif image to the insertion point and then select the image. Apply the settings in Table 2-5.

5. If necessary, scroll up. Select Services (the first bulleted item heading). Use either the drag-and-drop or Browse for File method to create a link to the services page. Repeat this process to add links from Employment Opportunities and References (the second and third bulleted item headings) to the respective Web pages. Select your name. Use the Insert menu to create an e-mail link using your name. Save the index page (Figure 2-113a).

6. Open services.htm. Use the Commands menu to apply the color scheme (Green background and Brown,Yellow,Red text and links) you added in Project 1 to the index page. Display the Page Properties dialog box. Change the Links color to hexadecimal #CC3333 and add the background image to the services.htm page as you did in step 3 to the index.htm page.

7. Position the insertion point to the left of the page heading, drag the mowing.gif image to the insertion point, and then select the image. Apply the settings in Table 2-5. Position the insertion point to the right of the first bulleted item and then drag the shakehands.gif to the insertion point. Select the image. Apply the settings in Table 2-5.

8. If necessary, scroll down. Select Home and then create a relative link to the index page. Title the page B & B Lawn Service - Services. Save the services page (Figure 2-113b).

9. Open employment.htm. Apply the same color scheme you applied to services.htm in step 6. Change the links color and add the background image to the employment page as you did in step 3 to the index.htm page.

10. Position the insertion point to the left of the heading and then drag the planting.gif image to the insertion point. Select the image. Apply the settings in Table 2-5.

11. Scroll to the bottom of the page. Select the words, click here, in the last sentence on the page, To contact us, click here! Use the Insert menu to create an e-mail link using your e-mail address. Select Home at the bottom of the page and then drag index.htm to the Link box in the Property inspector to create a relative link to the index.htm file. Title the page B & B Lawn Service - Employment. Save the employment page (Figure 2-113c).

12. Open references.htm. Apply the same color scheme and background image you applied to the other pages in this Web site. Change the links color as you did in step 3 to the index.htm page.

13. Create a link from Home to the index page.

14. Position the insertion point to the left of the text, Joe Smith. Drag the planting2.gif image to the insertion point. Select the image. Apply the settings in Table 2-5. Title the page B & B Lawn Service - References. Save the references page (Figure 2-113d).

15. View the Web site in your browser. Check each link to verify that it works. Print a copy of each page if required and hand the copies in to your instructor. Close the browser. Quit Dreamweaver.

In the Lab

1 Modifying the CandleDust Web Site

Problem: Mary Stewart, for whom you created the CandleDust Web site and Web page, is very pleased with the response she has received. She has asked you to create a second page with links and images added to the index page. Mary wants the new page to include information about her company's history. The revised Web site is shown in Figures 2-114a and 2-114b. Table 2-6 includes the settings and Alt text for the images. Software and hardware settings determine how a Web page displays in the browser. Your Web pages may display differently in your browser than those in the figures. For an updated list of links, visit the Dreamweaver MX Links Web page (scsite.com/dreamweavermx/links) and then click Project 2 Links.

IMAGE NAME	W	H	PROPERTY/ALT TEXT		ALIGN	ALT
			V SPACE	H SPACE		
candle1.gif	126	192	6	15	Left	Logo
candle2.gif	192	178	None	75	Right	Candles
candle_dip.gif	164	191	10	50	Left	Candle dipping

Table 2-6   Image Property Settings for the CandleDust Web Site

Instructions: Perform the following tasks:

1. Start Dreamweaver. Display the Site panel. Select CandleDust on the Site pop-up menu in the Site panel. Double-click the index.htm file in the Site panel. Display the Property inspector. Click the expander arrow to expand the Property inspector. If necessary, display the Standard toolbar.

2. Use Dreamweaver's integrated file browser to copy the Images folder and data file to your candle folder. Click the plus sign to the left of the Desktop icon and then navigate through the file hierarchy to the candle folder in Proj02. Click the plus sign to the left of candle and then select and copy the Images folder and data file to the jonesw/candle folder using Copy and Paste on the context menu.

3. Click Modify on the menu bar and then click Page Properties. Click the Browse button in the Page Properties dialog box, click the Images folder, and then select the background.gif image. Click the OK button in the Select Image Source dialog box and in the Page Properties dialog box. Click index.htm in the Site panel to select it. Click Site on the Site panel menu bar and then set the index.htm page as the home page.

4. Position the insertion point to the left of the heading and then drag the candle1.gif to the insertion point. Select the image. Apply the settings in Table 2-6 to align the image and enter the Alt text.

5. Position the insertion point to the right of CandleDust candles are available in a variety of types: and then drag the candle2.gif to the insertion point. Select the image and then apply the settings in Table 2-6.

6. Scroll to the bottom of the page and then drag through the text, company history. Use the drag-and-drop method to create a link to the history.htm page. Use the Insert menu to create an e-mail link using your e-mail address. Save the index page (Figure 2-114a).

7. Open history.htm. Use the Command menu to apply the color scheme, Purple background and Blue,Purple,Green for text and links (the same color scheme you applied to the index page in Project 1). Apply the background image to the history page as you did in step 3 to the index page.

In the Lab

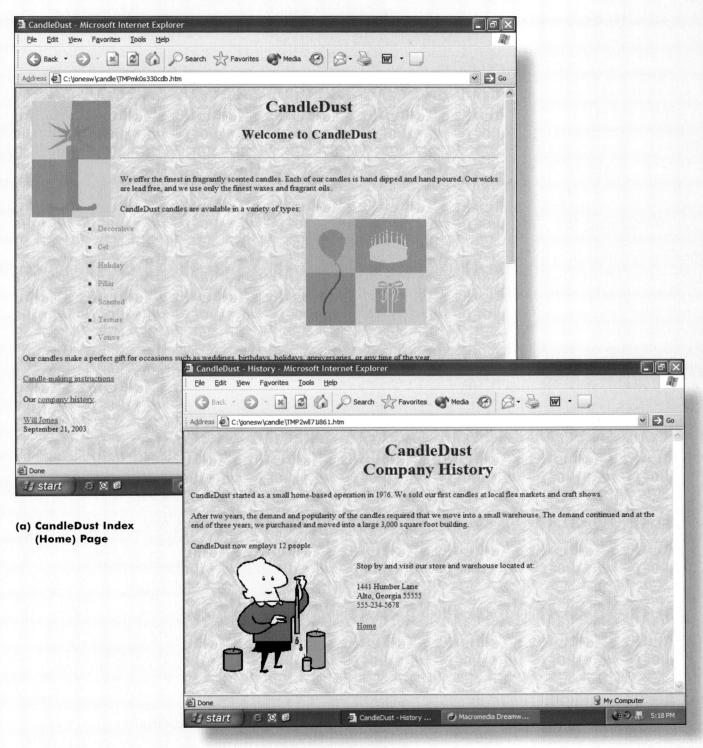

**(a) CandleDust Index
(Home) Page**

(b) CandleDust - History Web Page

FIGURE 2-114

(continued)

In the Lab

Modifying the CandleDust Web Site (continued)

8. Position the insertion point at the end of the third paragraph and then drag the candle_dip.gif to the insertion point. Select the image and then apply the settings in Table 2-6 on page DW 2.84. Title the page CandleDust - History.

9. Select Home and then create a relative link to the index page. Save the history page (Figure 2-114b on the previous page).

10. View your pages in your browser and verify that your links work. Print a copy of each page if required and hand the copies in to your instructor. Close your browser. Quit Dreamweaver.

2 Modifying the Credit Protection Web Site

Problem: Marcy Cantu has received favorable comments about the Web page and site you created about credit information. Her law firm wants to utilize the Web site to provide additional information to its clients. Marcy has asked you if you would be willing to work with her and another intern at the firm to create two more Web pages in the site. They want one of the pages to discuss credit protection and the other page to contain information about identity theft. The revised Web site is shown in Figures 2-115a, 2-115b, and 2-115c. Table 2-7 includes the settings and Alt text for the images. Software and hardware settings determine how a Web page displays in the browser. Your Web pages may display differently in your browser than those in the figures. For an updated list of links, visit the Dreamweaver MX Links Web page (scsite.com/dreamweavermx/links) and then click Project 2 Links.

Table 2-7	Image Property Settings for the Credit Protection Web Site						
IMAGE NAME	W	H	PROPERTY/ALT TEXT V SPACE	H SPACE	ALIGN	ALT
money1.gif	174	110	None	20	Absolute Middle	Money
answer.gif	202	176	None	200	Right	Reporting options
protection.gif	240	170	14	20	Left	Identity theft
theft.gif	172	169	20	75	Right	Protect personal information
question.gif	148	366	None	15	Right	Questions?

Instructions: Perform the following tasks:

1. Start Dreamweaver. Display the Site panel. Select Credit Protection on the Site pop-up menu in the Site panel. Open index.htm.

2. Use Dreamweaver's integrated file browser to copy the Images folder and data files to your credit folder. The data files consist of the Images folder and two data files — questions.htm and theft.htm.

3. If necessary, display the Property inspector and the Standard toolbar. Expand the Property inspector.

4. Click the index.htm file and set the page as the home page. Apply the background.jpg image (located in the Images folder) to the index page.

In the Lab

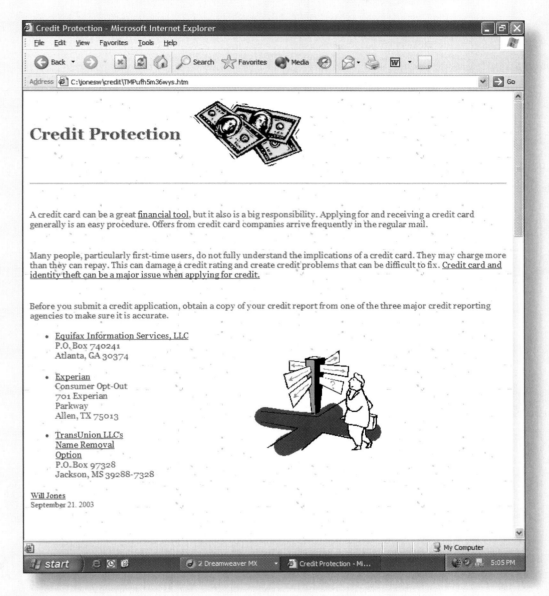

(a) Credit Protection Index (Home) Page

FIGURE 2-115

5. Position the insertion point to the right of the heading and then drag the money1.gif image to the insertion point. Select the image and then apply the settings in Table 2-7. Position the insertion point to the right of the text, Equifax Information Services, LLC. Drag the answer.gif image to the insertion point and then select the image. Apply the settings in Table 2-7.

6. Select the text, financial tool, located in the first sentence of the first paragraph. Create a relative link from the selected text to questions.htm.

(continued)

In the Lab

Modifying the Credit Protection Web Site *(continued)*

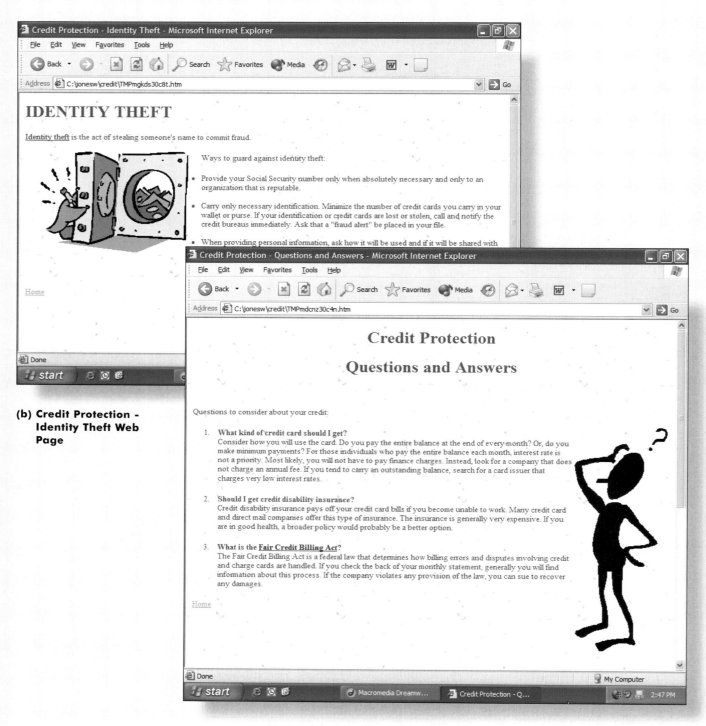

(b) Credit Protection – Identity Theft Web Page

(c) Credit Protection – Questions and Answers Web Page

FIGURE 2-115 *(continued)*

In the Lab

7. Position the insertion point at the end of the second paragraph. Press the SPACEBAR. Type Credit card and identity theft can be a major issue when applying for credit. Select the text you just typed and then create a relative link to the theft.htm file. Save the index page (Figure 2-115a on page DW 2.87).

8. Open theft.htm and then apply the same color scheme (Yellow background and Green,Blue,Purple for text and links) you applied to the index.htm page in Project 1. Apply the background image to the theft.htm page as you did in step 4 to the index.htm page.

9. Position the insertion point to the left of the second line and then drag the protection.gif to the insertion point. Select the image. Apply the settings in Table 2-7 on page DW 2.86. Position the insertion point to the right of the third bulleted item and then drag the theft.gif to the insertion point. Select the image. Apply the settings in Table 2-7.

10. Drag to select the text, Identity theft, at the beginning of the first sentence and then create an absolute link using http://www.consumer.gov/idtheft/ for the URL. Create an absolute link from the protection.gif image using the same URL. Select the image and then type the URL in the Link box. Select Home and then create a relative link to the index.htm page. Title the page Credit Protection - Identity Theft. Save the theft page (Figure 2-115b).

11. Open questions.htm. Apply the same color scheme and background image that you added to the theft.htm page in step 8.

12. Position the insertion point to the right of the first line of text and then drag the question.gif image to the insertion point. Select the image. Apply the settings in Table 2-7.

13. Create an absolute link from the Fair Credit Billing Act text in question 3. Use http://www.ftc.gov/bcp/conline/pubs/credit/fcb.htm for the URL. Select Home and then create a relative link to the index page. Title the page Credit Protection - Questions and Answers. Save the questions page (Figure 2-115c).

14. Click Site on the Site panel menu bar and then click Check Links Sitewide. Use the Link Checker in the Results panel to check the relative links in your Web site. View the site in the site map. Modify the URLs to correct any link problems.

15. View the Web site in your browser and verify that your external links work. Hint: Click the image on the theft.htm page. Print a copy of each page if required and hand the copies in to your instructor. Close your browser and quit Dreamweaver.

3 Modifying the Plant City Web Page

Problem: Juan Benito recently became a member of a marketing group promoting Plant City's strawberry history. He wants to expand the Web site you created for him by adding two new Web pages that will highlight other features of Plant City, Florida. Juan explains that some members of the committee are not fond of the text color within the original color scheme, so they want you to change it. You inform Juan that you can create the new pages and make the changes to the color scheme. The revised Web site is displayed in Figures 2-116a, 2-116b, and 2-116c (on pages DW 2.91 and DW 2.92). Table 2-8 on the next page includes the settings and Alt text for the images. Software and hardware settings determine how a Web page displays in the browser. Your Web pages may display differently in your browser than those in the figures. For an updated list of links, visit the Dreamweaver MX Links Web page (scsite.com/dreamweavermx/links) and then click Project 2 Links.

(continued)

In the Lab

Modifying the Plant City Web Page *(continued)*

Table 2-8 Image Property Settings for the Plant City Web Site						
IMAGE NAME	*W*	*H*	*PROPERTY/ALT TEXT* *V SPACE*	*H SPACE*	*ALIGN*	*ALT*
strawberry01.gif	77	75	None	80	Right	Strawberry
train.gif	225	140	6	8	Right	Train
strawberry02.gif	200	145	None	25	Right	Strawberry

Instructions: Perform the following tasks:

1. Start Dreamweaver. Display the Site panel. Select Plant City on the Site pop-up menu.
2. Use Dreamweaver's integrated file browser to copy the data files to the city folder. The data files consist of an Images folder and two Web pages — facts.htm and recipes.htm.
3. Open index.htm. If necessary, display the Property inspector and the Standard toolbar. Expand the Property inspector.
4. Select the index.htm file and set the index.htm page as the home page. Open the Page Properties dialog box and then click the Text box arrow. Change the text color to black. Apply the border.gif image as the background image. Click Edit on menu bar and then click Select All. Click the Text Indent button in the Property inspector two times.
5. Position the insertion point after the last numbered item (6) on the page and then press the ENTER key. Click the Ordered List button to deselect the numbered list and then click the Text Outdent button two times. Type Facts | Recipes as the link text.
6. Create a relative link from Facts to the facts.htm page and then create a relative link from Recipes to the recipes.htm page.
7. Position the insertion point to the right of the first line of the first paragraph and then drag the strawberry01.gif image to the insertion point. Select the image. Apply the settings in Table 2-8.
8. Insert the train.gif image to the right of the first numbered item. Apply the settings in Table 2-8. Use the Border box to add a 3-pixel border to the image. Save the index page (Figure 2-116a).
9. Open facts.htm and then select all of the text except for the heading. Click the Text Indent button in the Property inspector two times. Apply the border.gif image to the background. Display the Page Properties dialog box and change the Links color to hexadecimal #FF0000 (row 7, column 2 from the left).
10. Position the insertion point to the left of the heading and then drag the strawberry02.gif image to the insertion point. Select the image. Apply the settings in Table 2-8.
11. Scroll to the bottom of the page and then select Home. Create a relative link to the index.htm page. Click to the right of Home. Press the ENTER key and then type Strawberry Varieties. Select the text and create an absolute link to http://www.extension.umn.edu/extensionnews/2002/New StrawberryVarieties.html. Title the page Plant City, Florida - Strawberry Facts. Save the facts page (Figure 2-116b).

In the Lab

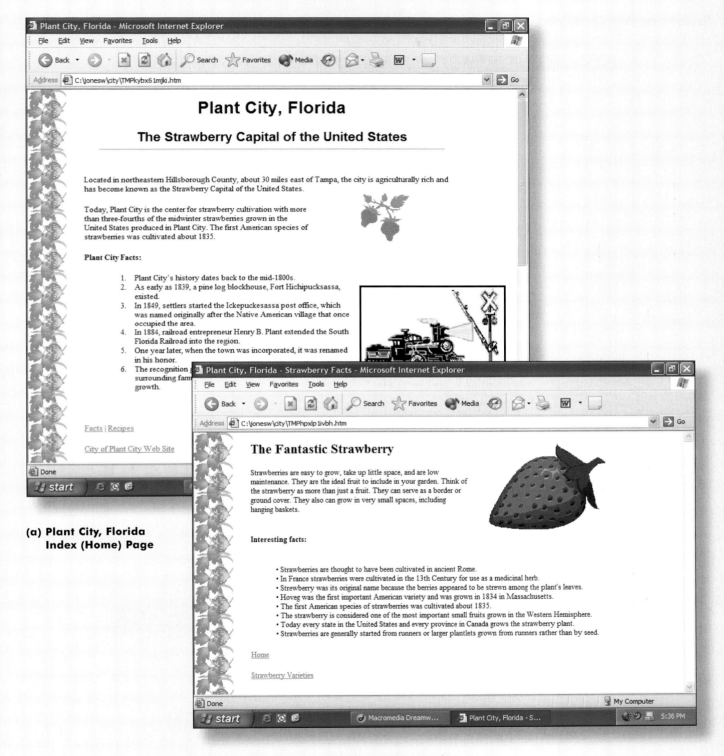

(a) Plant City, Florida Index (Home) Page

(b) Plant City, Florida - Strawberry Facts Web Page

FIGURE 2-116

(continued)

In the Lab

Modifying the Plant City Web Page *(continued)*

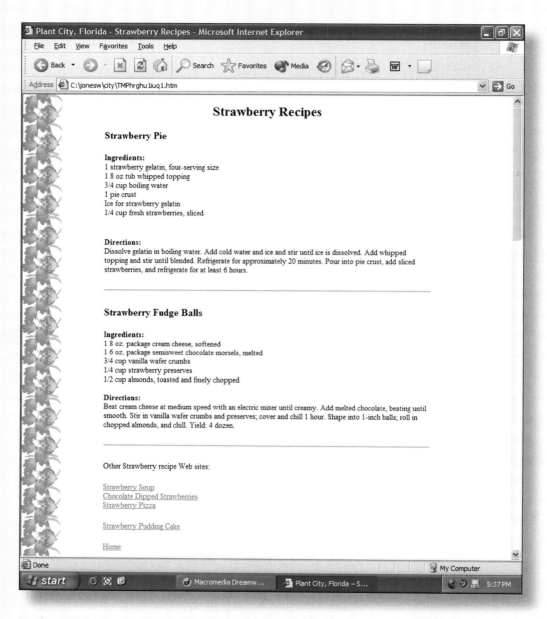

(c) Plant City, Florida - Strawberry Recipes Web Page

FIGURE 2-116 *(continued)*

In the Lab

12. Open recipes.htm. Select all the text except the heading and then click the Text Indent button in the Property inspector two times. Apply the border.gif image to the background. Display the Page Properties dialog box and change the Links color to hexadecimal #FF0000 (row 7, column 9 from the left).

13. Position the insertion point at the end of the second horizontal rule and then press the ENTER key. Type the following text. Press the ENTER key after typing each line of text:

    ```
    Strawberry Soup
    Chocolate Dipped Strawberries
    Strawberry Pizza
    ```

    Add absolute links to these three items as follows:
    For Strawberry Soup, type `http://www.sweettechnology.com/straw1.htm` as the URL; for Chocolate Dipped Strawberries, type `http://momo.essortment.com/recipestrawberr_pwh.htm` as the URL; and for Strawberry Pizza, type `http://www.pallensmith.com/features/recipes/strawpizza.htm` as the URL.

14. Use a search engine and find another Web site with strawberry recipes. Select a recipe you like and make a note of the URL. Position the insertion point at the end of the Web page. Type the name of the recipe you selected and then create an absolute link to the Web site.

15. Title the page Plant City, Florida - Strawberry Recipes. Save the recipes page (Figure 2-116c).

17. Use the Link Checker to verify the internal links. View the Web site in your browser and verify the external links. Close your browser and quit Dreamweaver.

Cases and Places

The difficulty of these case studies varies:
▶ are the least difficult; ▶▶ are more difficult; and ▶▶▶ are the most difficult.

1   ▶   In Project 1, you created a Web site and a Web page listing your favorite sport. Now, you want to add another page to the site. Create and format the page. The page should include general information about your selected sport. Create a relative link from the home page to the new page and from the new page to the home page. Add a background image to both pages and insert an image on one of the pages. Include an appropriate title for the page. Save the page in the sports subfolder. For a selection of images and backgrounds, visit the Dreamweaver MX Media Web page (scsite.com/dreamweavermx/media) and then click Media below Project 2.

Cases and Places

2 ▶ Several friends of yours were impressed with the Web page and Web site you created about your favorite hobby in Project 1. They have given you some topics they think you should include on the site. You decide to create an additional page that will consist of details about your hobby and the topics. Format the page. Add an absolute link to a related Web site and a relative link from the home page to the new page and from the new page to the home page. Add a background image to the index page and to the new page. Create an e-mail link on the index page. Title the page the name of the selected hobby. Save the page in the hobby subfolder. For a selection of images and backgrounds, visit the Dreamweaver MX Media Web page (scsite.com/dreamweavermx/media) and then click Media below Project 2.

3 ▶▶ Modify the favorite type of music Web site you created in Project 1 by creating a new page. Format the page. Discuss your favorite artist or band on the new page. Apply a color scheme to the new page and add an image to both pages. On the index page, align the image right, and on the new page, align the image left. Position each image appropriately on the page by adding H Space and V Space. Add appropriate Alt text for each image. Add an e-mail link on the index page and add text and a relative link from the new page to the index page. View your Web pages in your browser. Give the page a meaningful title and then save the page in your music subfolder. For a selection of images and backgrounds, visit the Dreamweaver MX Media Web page (scsite.com/dreamweavermx/media) and then click Media below Project 2.

4 ▶▶ In Project 1, you created a Web site and a Web page to publicize your running for office campaign. Develop two additional pages to add to the site. Apply a color scheme, and include a background image on all three pages. Apply appropriate formatting to the two new pages. Scan a picture of yourself or make a picture with a digital camera and include the picture on the index page. Add a second image illustrating one of your campaign promises. Include at least two images on one of the new pages and one image on the other new page. Add appropriate H Space and V Space to position the images and add Alt text for all images. Add a border to one of the images. Create e-mail links on all three pages, and create relative links from the home page to both pages and from each of the pages to the home page. Create an absolute link to a related site on one of the pages. Use the site map to verify your links. Give each page a meaningful title and then save the pages in the office subfolder. For a selection of images and backgrounds, visit the Dreamweaver MX Media Web page (scsite.com/dreamweavermx/media) and then click Media below Project 2.

5 ▶▶▶ The student trips Web site you created in Project 1 is a success. Students love it. The dean is so impressed that she asks if you will continue with the project. You create and format three additional Web pages — one for each of three possible locations for the trip. Add a background image to all pages. Add two images to each of the pages, including the index page. Resize one of the images. Add appropriate H Space and V Space to position each image and then add Alt text for each image. Create a link from the index page to each of the three new pages and a link from each page to the index page. Create an absolute link to a related informational Web site on each of the three new pages. Add an appropriate title to each page. Preview in a browser to verify the links. Save the pages in your trips subfolder. For a selection of images and backgrounds, visit the Dreamweaver MX Media Web page (scsite.com/dreamweavermx/media) and then click Media below Project 2.

Macromedia Dreamweaver MX

Tables and
Page Layout

You will have mastered the material in this project when you can:

O B J E C T I V E S

- Understand and plan page layout
- Describe Standard view and Layout view
- Design a Web page using tables in Standard view
- Design a Web page using tables in Layout view
- Describe visual guides
- Modify a table structure
- Describe HTML table tags
- Add content to a table
- Format table content
- Format a table
- Create head content

Macromedia Dreamweaver MX

Tables and Page Layout

CASE PERSPECTIVE

The Florida Parks Web site has been very successful thus far. Will has received several e-mail messages asking for additional information about the three national parks. Joan suggests that a separate page on each park would be a good addition to the Web site. Both Will and you agree this is a good idea. The two of you volunteer to research various sources and to create the content for the three new pages.

Joan further suggests that, in addition to adding the same color scheme and background as the rest of the site, the three new pages also should have some consistency in the displayed information. The team decides that each page should include a header with the name of the park, that the information contained in the body content should describe the location and contain some interesting facts, and that each page should list the park's address, including an e-mail link. The footer will contain links to the home page and to the other two national parks pages. You all are eager to get started on this new addition to the Florida Parks Web site.

Introduction

Project 3 introduces the use of tables for page layout and the addition of head content elements. Page layout is an important part of Web design. Page layout refers to the way your page will display in the browser, which is one of the major challenges for any Web designer. Dreamweaver's table feature is a great tool for designing a Web page. The table feature is very similar to the table feature in word processing programs, such as Microsoft Word. A table allows you to add vertical and horizontal structure to a Web page. Using a table, you can put just about anything on your page and have it display in a specific location. You can lay out tabular data. You can create columns of text or navigation bars. You can delete, split, and merge rows and columns; modify table, row, or cell properties to add color and alignment; and copy and paste cells.

Dreamweaver provides two views, or ways, to use the table feature: Standard view and Layout view. Standard view uses the Insert Table dialog box, and Layout view is a free-form process in which you draw the table and the individual cells. This project discusses both views and the advantages and disadvantages of each. The second part of the project discusses the addition and value of head content.

When you create a Web page, the underlying HTML code is made up of two main sections: the head section and the body section. The body section contains the page content that displays in the browser. In Project 1 and Project 2, you created your Web pages in the body section. The head section contains a variety of information. With the exception of the page title, all head content is invisible when viewed in the Dreamweaver Document window or in a browser. Some head content is accessed by other programs, such as search engines, and some content is accessed by the browser. This project discusses the head content options and the importance of this content.

Project Three — Florida Parks Page Layout

In this project, you continue with the creation of the Florida Parks Web site. You use tables to create three new Web pages focusing on Florida's three national parks. You will add these new pages to the parks Web site and link to them from the national.htm Web page (Figure 3-1a, Figure 3-1b on the next page, and Figure 3-1c on page DW 3.05). When you complete your Web page additions, you will add keywords and a description as the head content.

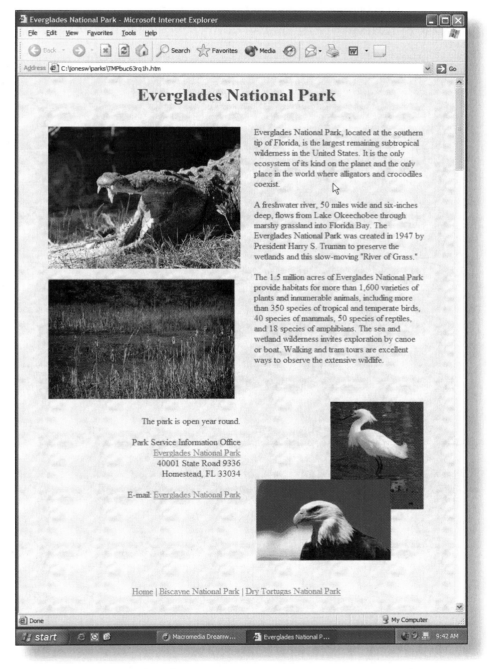

(a) Everglades National Park Page

FIGURE 3-1

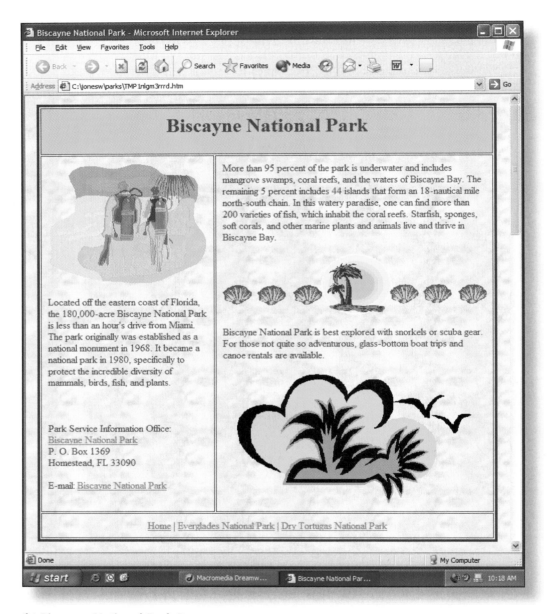

(b) Biscayne National Park Page

FIGURE 3-1 *(continued)*

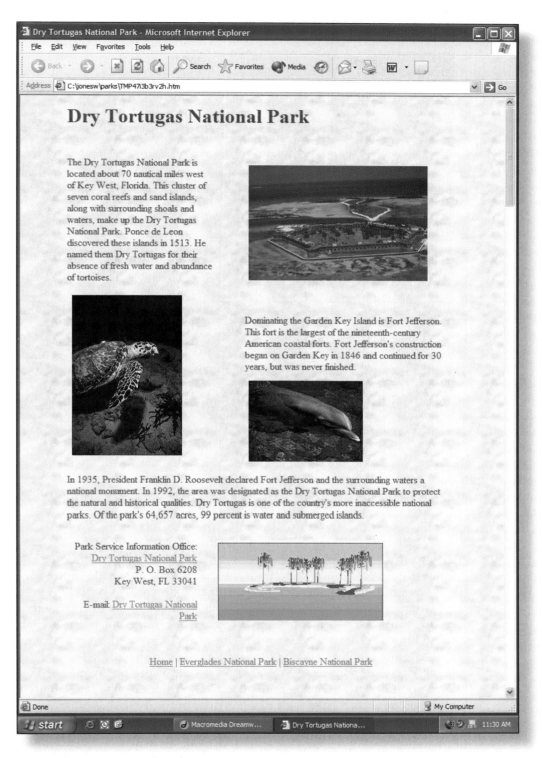

(c) Dry Tortugas National Park Page

FIGURE 3-1 (continued)

This project uses a hierarchical structure. The structure is now expanded to include the three new pages (Figure 3-2).

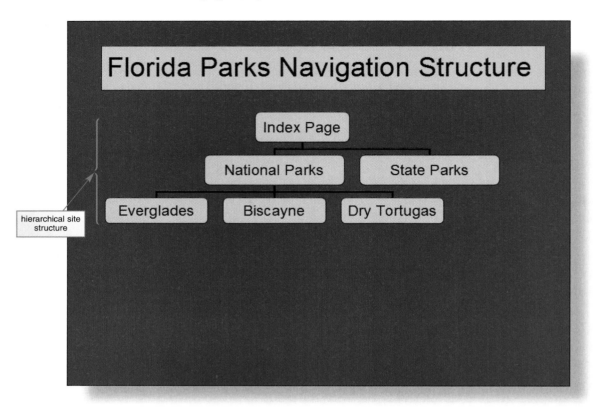

FIGURE 3-2

Understanding and Planning Page Layout

Page layout is the process of arranging the text, images, and other elements on the page. The basic rules of page layout are that your site should be easy to navigate, easy to read, and quick to download. Studies have indicated that visitors will lose interest quickly in your Web site if the majority of a page does not download within 15 seconds. One popular design element that downloads quickly is tables.

Tables download very fast because they are created with HTML code. They can be used anywhere — for the home page, menus, images, navigation bars, frames, and so on. Tables originally were intended for use in presenting data arranged by rows and columns, such as tabular data within a spreadsheet. Web designers, however, quickly seized upon the use of tables to produce specific layout effects. You can produce good designs by using tables creatively. Tables provide the ability to position elements on a Web page with much greater accuracy. Using tables for layout provides the Web page author with endless design possibilities.

A typical Web page is composed of three sections: the header, the body, and the footer (Figure 3-3). The **header**, generally located at the top of the page, can contain logos, images, or text that identifies the Web site. The header also may contain hyperlinks to other pages within the Web site.

The **body** of the Web page contains informational content about your site. This content may be in the form of text, graphics, animation, video, and audio.

The **footer** provides hyperlinks for contact information. Many Web designers also include navigational controls in the footer. This may be in addition to the navigation controls in the header. Other common items contained within a footer are the name and e-mail address of the author or of the webmaster. Sometimes, hyperlinks to other resources or to Help information are part of the footer. A typical Web page structure is displayed in Figure 3-3.

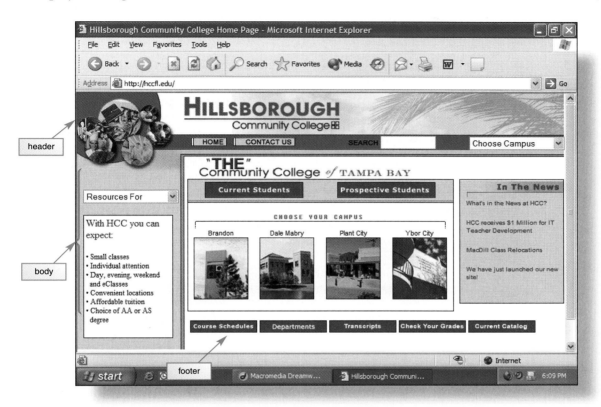

FIGURE 3-3

It is easy to create this header/body/footer structure with tables or to create any other layout structure applicable for your specific Web page needs. The entire structure can be contained within one table or a combination of multiple and nested tables. You will use a structure similar to Figure 3-3 to create the three new pages for the Florida Parks Web site.

Standard View and Layout View

Dreamweaver provides two options for creating tables: Standard view and Layout view. In **Standard view,** tables are presented as a grid of rows and columns. This view is similar to a Microsoft Excel spreadsheet or a table created in a word processing program such as Microsoft Word. In **Layout view,** you can draw, resize, and move boxes on the page while Dreamweaver still uses tables for the underlying structure. If you have used a desktop publishing program such as Microsoft Publisher or QuarkXPress, then you are familiar with the format in which layout tables are created. Using Layout view, you can place content at any location in the Document window.

Starting Dreamweaver and Closing Open Panels

When you start Dreamweaver, generally most of or all of the panels are displayed. Closing unused panels provides uncluttered workspace in the Document window. To organize your workspace, you close the open panels and then display the panels and toolbars you will use. This project includes using the Site panel, the Standard toolbar, the Insert bar, and the Property inspector.

TO START DREAMWEAVER AND CLOSE OPEN PANELS

1 Start Dreamweaver. If necessary, maximize the Document window. Press the F4 key to close all open panels.

2 Press the F8 key to display the Site panel. If necessary, select the Florida Parks site.

3 If necessary, use the View menu to display the Standard toolbar.

4 Use the Window menu to display the Property inspector, and then, if necessary, click the expander arrow to collapse the Property inspector.

Dreamweaver displays the maximized Document window, the Site panel, the Standard toolbar, and the Property inspector (Figure 3-4). Your toolbar may display above or below the Document toolbar or may be docked somewhere in another location.

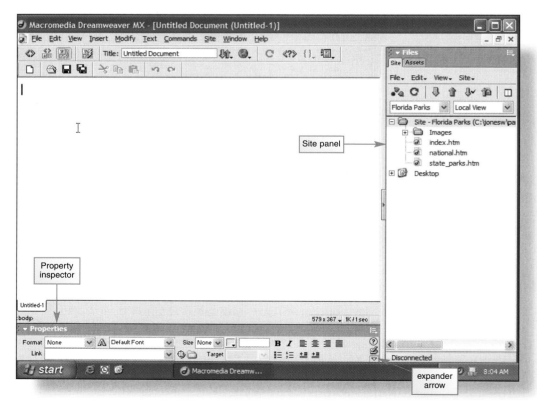

FIGURE 3-4

The Web pages you create in this project require additional images. These images need to be copied from the Data Files to the parks Web site.

Copying Data Files to the Local Web Site

Your Data Disk contains images for Project 3. These images are located in the Proj03 folder. You use Dreamweaver's integrated file browser to copy the Project 3 images to the parks Images folder you created in Project 2. The Images folder is a subfolder within the parks Web site.

The Data Files folder for this project is stored on Local Disk (C:). The location on your computer may be different. If necessary, verify with your instructor the location of the Data Files folder. Complete the following steps to copy the files to the parks local root folder.

TO COPY DATA FILES TO THE PARKS WEB SITE

1 Click the plus sign (+) to the left of the Desktop icon in the Site panel. Click the plus sign to the left of the My Computer icon and then navigate through the file hierarchy to the Data Files folder as you did in Project 2.

2 Click the plus sign to the left of the Proj03 folder and then click the plus sign to the left of the parks folder.

3 Click the plus sign to the left of the Images folder.

4 Click birds.gif. Hold down the SHIFT key and then click the turtle.jpg image.

5 Copy the ten images to the jonesw/parks/Images folder (your name folder) using Copy and Paste on the context menu (Figure 3-5).

6 Click the minus sign to the left of the Desktop icon to collapse the file list.

7 Click the minus sign to the left of the Images icon to collapse the Images folder.

The Project 3 images are pasted into the parks Images subfolder (Figure 3-5).

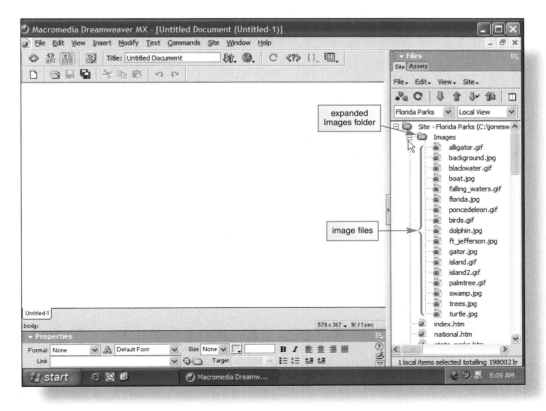

FIGURE 3-5

Adding Pages to a Web Site

You copied the images necessary to begin creating your new Web pages to the parks local root folder in the Site panel. You will add three additional pages to the Web site — Everglades, Biscayne, and Dry Tortugas national parks. You first create the Everglades National Park Web page. You will add a color scheme, the background image, and a heading to the new page. Then you will use Dreamweaver's Standard view to insert tables and add text, images, and links to the cells within the table. Table 3-1 lists the color scheme and image information to be used for all three Web pages.

Table 3-1	Color Scheme and Background Image for Florida Parks Web Pages	
COLOR SCHEME	**IMAGE**
Commands menu, Set Color Scheme command	Modify menu, Page Properties command
Green background	Browse button/Images folder
Blue, Brown, Green text and links	background.jpg

Creating the Everglades National Park Web Page

You use the Untitled-1 default page that displayed when you started Dreamweaver to begin creating the Everglades page. You start by applying a color scheme and background image. This is the same color scheme and background image you used for the Florida Parks Web site pages in Projects 1 and 2.

TO ADD A COLOR SCHEME AND BACKGROUND IMAGE TO THE EVERGLADES NATIONAL PARK WEB PAGE

1. Apply the settings in Table 3-1 to add the color scheme and then click the OK button in the Set Color Scheme Command dialog box.

2. Apply the settings in Table 3-1 to add the background image. Click the OK button in the Page Properties dialog box.

The background image is applied to the Everglades National Park page (Figure 3-6).

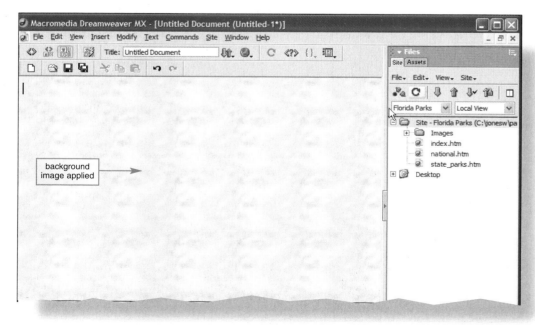

FIGURE 3-6

Next, you will insert, center, and format a page heading. Then, you will add a page title and save the Web page. You close the Site panel to provide additional workspace and a better view of the Document window. Perform the following steps to insert and format the heading and close the Site panel.

TO INSERT AND FORMAT THE HEADING

1 Click the Document window. Type `Everglades National Park`.

2 Apply Heading 1, click the Align Center button in the Property inspector, and then press the ENTER key.

3 Click the Align Left button.

4 Title the page Everglades National Park.

5 Right-click the Files panel group title bar and then click Close Panel Group on the context menu.

6 Click the Save button on the Standard toolbar. Type `everglades` for the file name and then click the Save button in the Save As dialog box. The file is saved in the parks folder.

The heading is centered and formatted and the title is added (Figure 3-7). The Web page is saved in the parks folder.

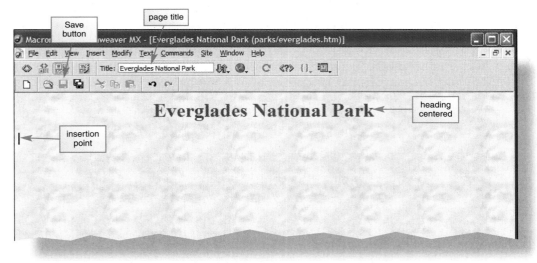

FIGURE 3-7

Understanding Tables

Tables have many uses in HTML design. The most obvious is a table of data, but tables also are used for page layout, such as placing text and graphics on a page at just the right location. Tables provide Web designers a method to add vertical and horizontal structure to a page. A **table** consists of three basic components: rows, columns, and cells. A **row** is a horizontal collection of cells, and a **column** is a vertical collection of cells. A **cell** is the container created when the row and column intersect. Each cell within the table can contain any standard element you use on a Web page. This includes text, images, and other objects.

Inserting a Table into the Everglades National Park Page

You will add two tables to the Everglades National Park page and then add text and images to the cells within the tables. The first table will consist of three rows and two columns with cell padding of 2 and cell spacing of 20. The border is set to 0. When the table displays in Dreamweaver, a border outline is displayed around the table. This outline, however, does not display when viewed in a browser when the border is set to 0.

The table width is 90 percent. When specifying the width, you can select percent or pixels. A table with width specified as a **percent** expands with the width of the window and monitor size in which it is being viewed. A table with width specified as **pixels** will remain the same size regardless of the window and monitor size. If you select percent and an image is larger than the selected percent, the cell and table will expand to accommodate the image. Likewise, if the **No Wrap** property is enabled and the text will not fit within the cell, the cell and table will expand to accommodate the text. It is not necessary to declare a table width. When no value is specified, the table is displayed as small as possible and then expands as content is added. If modifications are necessary to the original specified table values, these values can be changed in the Property inspector.

The second table is a one-cell table, consisting of one row and one column. This table will contain links to the Home page and to the other two national parks. You use the Insert bar with the Layout category and the Property inspector to control and format the tables. Complete the following step to display the Insert bar and select the Layout category.

TO DISPLAY THE INSERT BAR AND SELECT THE LAYOUT CATEGORY

1 Click Window on the menu bar and then click Insert. Click the Layout tab. The Insert bar may display in a different location on your screen.

The Insert bar is displayed. The Layout tab is selected (Figure 3-8).

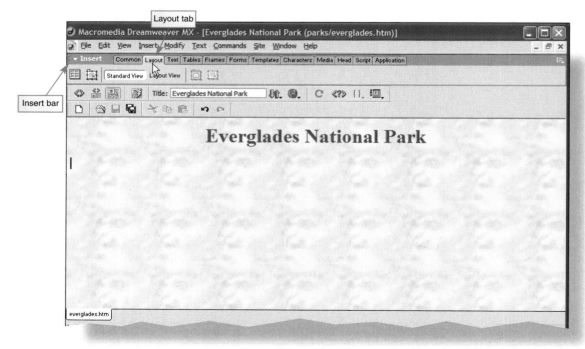

FIGURE 3-8

Table Views

The Layout category (Figure 3-9) enables you to work with tables and layers. Dreamweaver provides two ways to create tables — Standard view and Layout view. In Standard view, a table displays as a grid and expands as you add text and images. You define the structure of the table using the Insert Table dialog box. In Layout view, you create tables and cells by drawing them. You will work with Layout view later in this project. Table 3-2 lists the button names and descriptions available on the Layout tab.

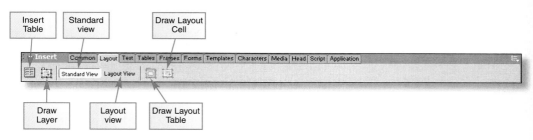

FIGURE 3-9

Table 3-2 Buttons on the Layout Tab	
BUTTON NAME	**DESCRIPTION**
Insert Table	Places a table at the insertion point
Draw Layer	Creates a layer
Standard View	Displays a table as a grid of lines
Layout View	Displays a table as boxes that can be drawn, dragged, and resized
Draw Layout Cell	Used to draw individual table cells in the Design view of the Document window
Draw Layout Table	Used to draw a table in the Design view of the Document window

Dreamweaver Features

For more information about Dreamweaver MX table views, visit the Dreamweaver MX More About Web page (scsite.com/ dreamweavermx/ more.htm) and then click Dreamweaver MX Tables.

Perform the following steps to insert a table with 3 rows and 2 columns into the Everglades National Park Web page.

 To Insert a Table Using Standard View

1 Point to the Insert Table button on the Insert bar (Figure 3-10).

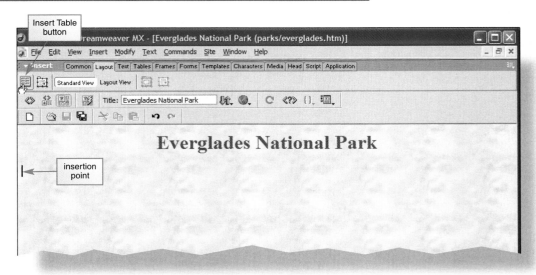

FIGURE 3-10

2 **Click the Insert Table button.**

The Insert Table dialog box is displayed (Figure 3-11). The settings displayed are the default settings from the last table created.

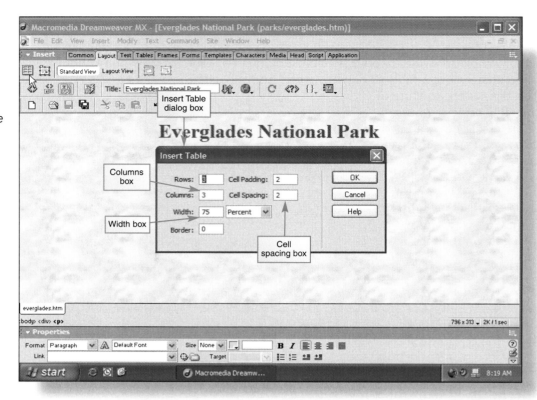

FIGURE 3-11

3 **Double-click the Columns box and then type 2 as the new value. Double-click the Cell Spacing box and then type 20 as the new value. Double-click the Width box and then type 90 as the new value. Point to the OK button.**

The Insert Table dialog box is displayed with the new settings as shown in Figure 3-12.

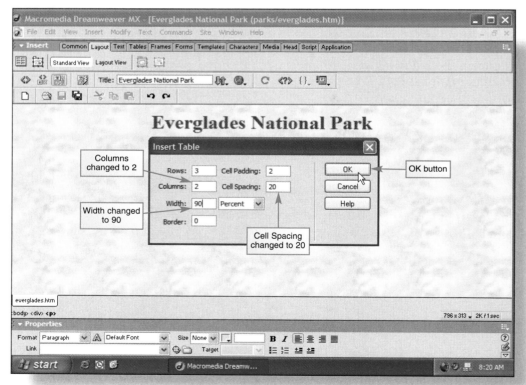

FIGURE 3-12

4 **Click the OK button. Point to the Property inspector expander arrow.**

The table is inserted into the Document window (Figure 3-13). The dark border around the table and the three handles on the lower and right borders indicate the table is selected. The <table> tag displays as bold in the tag selector, also indicating the table is selected. Cell spacing between each cell is 20 pixels. The default alignment for the table is left. The border is set to 0 and displays as an outline when viewed in Dreamweaver. When viewed in a browser, however, no border is displayed.

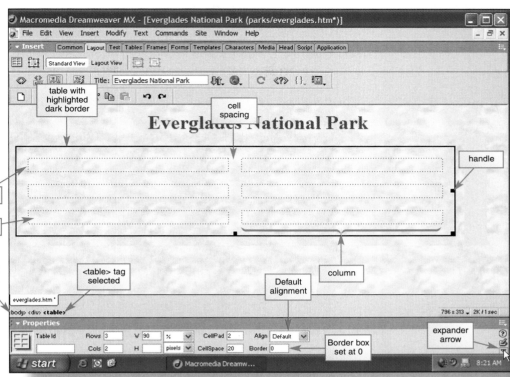

FIGURE 3-13

5 **Click the Property inspector expander arrow.**

The Property inspector expands to display additional table properties (Figure 3-14). The property settings you selected in the Insert Table dialog box display in the top half of the Property inspector.

Other **Ways**

1. On Insert menu click Table, select table properties, click OK button

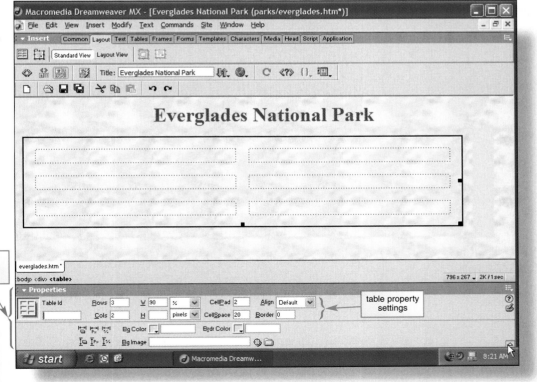

FIGURE 3-14

Property Inspector Table Features

As you have seen, the Property inspector options change depending on the selected object. You use the Property inspector to modify and add table attributes. When a table is selected, the Property inspector displays table properties. Properties are contained in both panels within the Property inspector when a table is selected. When another table element is selected — row, column, and cell — the displayed properties change and are determined by the selected element. The following section describes the table-related features of the Property inspector shown in Figure 3-15.

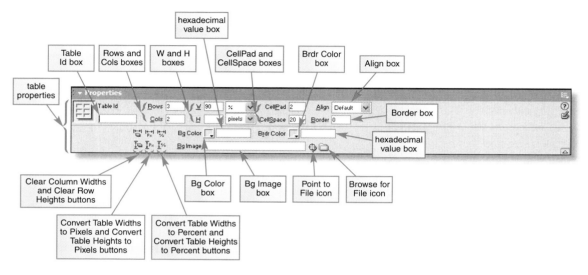

FIGURE 3-15

TABLE ID   An identifier used for cascading style sheets or for scripting; it is not required to assign a name.

ROWS AND COLS   The number of rows and columns in the table.

W   Used to specify the minimum width of the table in either pixels or percentage. If a size is not specified, the size can vary depending on the monitor and browser settings. A table width specified in pixels is displayed at the same size in all browsers. A table width specified in percentage is altered in appearance based on the user's monitor resolution and browser window size.

H   Used to specify the height of the table in either pixels or percentage. Generally, the height of a table consists of the height of the collective rows and is not specified.

CELLPAD   The number of pixels between the cell border and the cell content.

CELLSPACE   The number of pixels between adjacent table cells.

ALIGN   Determines where the table appears, relative to other elements in the same paragraph such as text or images. The default alignment is to the left.

BORDER   Specifies the border width in pixels.

CLEAR COLUMN WIDTHS AND CLEAR ROW HEIGHTS   Deletes all specified row height or column width values from the table.

CONVERT TABLE WIDTHS TO PIXELS AND CONVERT TABLE HEIGHTS TO PIXELS Sets the width or height of each column in the table to its current width in pixels and also sets the width of the whole table to its current width in pixels.

CONVERT TABLE WIDTHS TO PERCENT AND CONVERT TABLE HEIGHTS TO PERCENT Sets the width or height of each column in the table to its current width expressed as a percentage of the Document window's width and also sets the width of the whole table to its current width as a percentage of the Document window's width.

BG COLOR The table background color.

BRDR COLOR The table border color.

BG IMAGE The table background image.

Row, Column, and Cell Properties

When a row, column, or cell is selected, the properties in the upper pane of the Property inspector are the same as the standard ones for text. You can use these properties to incorporate standard HTML formatting tags within a cell, row, or column. The part of the table selected determines which properties display in the lower pane of the Property inspector. The properties for all three features (row, column, and cell) are the same, except for one element — the icon displayed in the lower-left pane of the Property inspector. The following section describes the row-related features (Figure 3-16), column-related features (Figure 3-17), and cell-related features (Figure 3-18 on the next page) of the Property inspector.

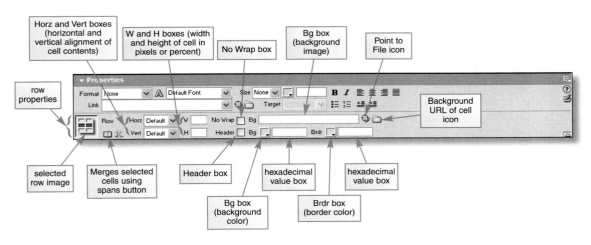

FIGURE 3-16

FIGURE 3-17

cell image

Splits cell into rows or columns button

FIGURE 3-18

HORZ   Specifies the horizontal alignment of the contents of a cell, row, or column — contents can be aligned to the left, right, or center of the cells.

VERT   Specifies the vertical alignment of the contents of a cell, row, or column — contents can be aligned to the top, middle, bottom, or baseline of the cells.

W AND H   Specifies the width and height of selected cells in pixels or as a percentage of the entire table's width or height.

BG (UPPER TEXT FIELD)   The file name of the background image for a cell, column, or row.

BG (LOWER COLOR BOX AND TEXT FIELD)   The background color of a cell, column, or row, using the color picker.

BRDR   The border color for the cells.

NO WRAP   Prevents line wrapping, keeping all text in a given cell on a single line. If No Wrap is enabled, cells widen to accommodate all data as it is typed or pasted into a cell.

HEADER   Formats the selected cells as table header cells. The contents of table header cells are bold and centered by default.

MERGE CELLS   Combines selected cells, rows, or columns into one cell (available when rows or columns are selected).

SPLIT CELLS   Divides a cell, creating two or more cells (available when a single cell is selected).

Table Formatting Conflicts

When formatting tables in Standard view, you can set properties for the entire table or for selected rows, columns, or cells in the table. When applying these properties, however, a potential for conflict exists. To resolve this potential conflict, HTML assigns levels of precedence. The order of precedence for table formatting is cells, rows, and table. When a property, such as background color or alignment, is set to one value for the whole table and another value for individual cells, cell formatting takes precedence over row formatting, which in turn takes precedence over table formatting.

Table Formatting Conflicts

For more information about Dreamweaver MX table formatting conflicts, visit the Dreamweaver MX More About Web page (scsite.com/ dreamweavermx/ more.htm) and then click Dreamweaver MX Tables.

If you set the background color for a single cell to green, and then set the background color of the entire table to red, for example, the green cell does not change to red, because cell formatting takes precedence over table formatting. Dreamweaver, however, does not always follow the precedence. The program will override the settings for a cell if you change the settings for the row that contains the cell. To eliminate this problem, you should change the cell settings last.

Understanding HTML Structure within a Table

As you work with and become more familiar with tables, it is helpful to have an understanding of the HTML structure within a table. Suppose, for example, you have a table with two rows and two columns, displaying a total of four cells, such as the following:

First cell	Second cell
Third cell	Fourth cell

The general syntax of the table is:

```
<TABLE>
<TR>
     <TD> First cell </TD>
     <TD> Second cell </TD>
</TR>
<TR>
     <TD> Third cell </TD>
     <TD> Fourth cell </TD>
</TR>
</TABLE>
```

When viewing your table in Dreamweaver, the tag selector displays the <table>, <td>, and <tr> tags. The <table> tag indicates the whole table. Clicking the <table> tag in the tag selector selects the whole table. The <td> indicates table data. Clicking the <td> tag in the tag selector selects the cell containing the insertion point. The <tr> tag indicates table row. Clicking the <tr> tag in the tag selector selects the row containing the insertion point.

Selecting the Table and Selecting Cells

The Property inspector displays table attributes only if the entire table is selected. You can select the table from within the Document window by clicking the upper-left corner of the table or by clicking anywhere on the right or lower edge. As discussed previously, another method for selecting a table is to click anywhere in the table and then click the <table> tag in the tag selector. When selected, the table will display with a dark border and selection handles on the table's lower and right edges (Figure 3-19 on the next page).

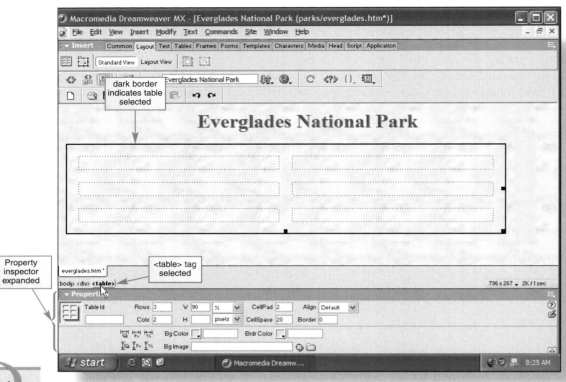

FIGURE 3-19

Selecting a row, column, or cell is easier than selecting the entire table. When a cell, row, or column is selected, the selected item has a dark border. To select a cell, click inside the cell. To select a row or column, click inside one of the cells in the row or column and drag to select the other cells. A second method for selecting a row or column is to point to the left edge of a row or the top edge of a column. When the pointer changes to a selection arrow, click to select the row or column. In Figure 3-20, the selection arrow is pointing to a row and the row is selected.

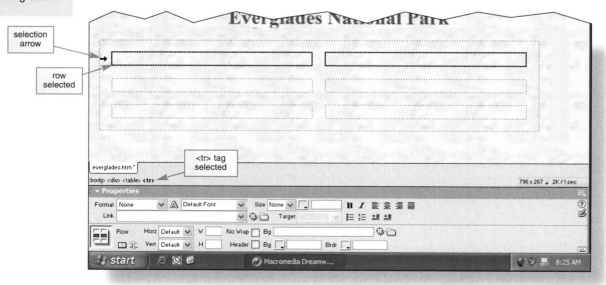

FIGURE 3-20

To select nonadjacent cells, click one cell, hold down the CTRL key and then click the other cells you want to select.

Centering a Table

When a table is inserted into the Document window with a specified width, it defaults to the left. Using the Property inspector, you can center the table by selecting it and then applying the Center command. Perform the following steps to select and center the table.

 | **To Select and Center a Table**

1 **Click row 1, column 1. Point to <table> in the tag selector.**

The insertion point is in the first cell of the first row and the first column (Figure 3-21).

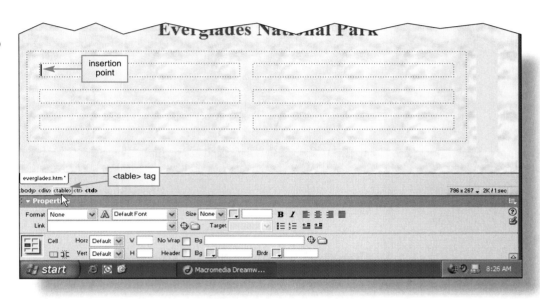

FIGURE 3-21

2 **Click <table>. Click the Align box arrow in the Property inspector and then point to Center on the pop-up menu.**

The table is selected and handles are displayed on the lower and right border of the table. The <table> tag is bold, indicating it is selected. Center is highlighted in the Align pop-up menu (Figure 3-22).

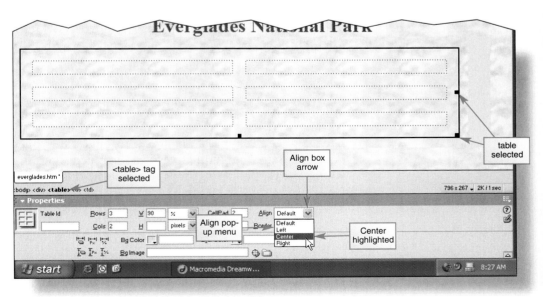

FIGURE 3-22

3 **Click Center.**

The table is centered in the Document window (Figure 3-23).

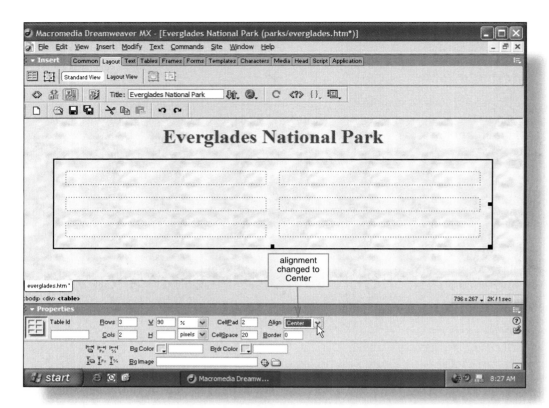

FIGURE 3-23

Changing the Default Cell Alignment

The default horizontal cell alignment is left. When you enter text or add an image to a cell, it defaults to the left margin of the cell. You can change the left alignment through the Property inspector by clicking the cell and then changing the default to center or right. The default vertical cell alignment is middle, which aligns the cell content in the middle of the cell. Other vertical alignment options include the following:

 ▶ Top — aligns the cell content at the top of the cell.
 ▶ Bottom — aligns the cell content at the bottom of the cell.
 ▶ Baseline — aligns the cell content at the bottom of the cell (same as Bottom).

You can change the vertical alignment through the Property inspector by clicking the cell and then selecting another vertical alignment option.

Complete the following steps to select the cells and change the default vertical alignment from middle to top.

To Change Vertical Alignment from Middle to Top

1 **Click row 1, column 1. Drag to select the three rows in the table. Click the Vert box arrow and then point to Top in the Vert pop-up menu.**

The three rows in the table are selected. The Property inspector changes to reflect the properties for a row. The Vert pop-up menu is displayed and Top is highlighted (Figure 3-24).

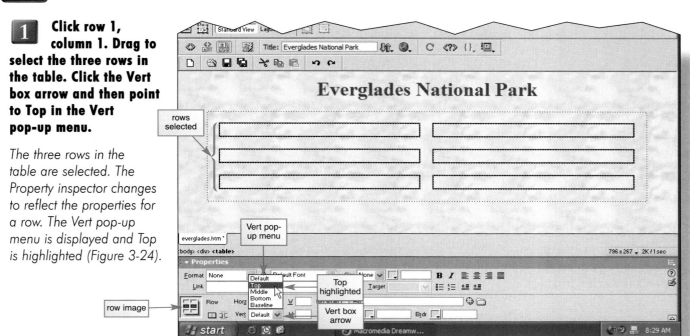

FIGURE 3-24

2 **Click Top.**

The vertical alignment is changed to Top (Figure 3-25). This change does not display in the Document window.

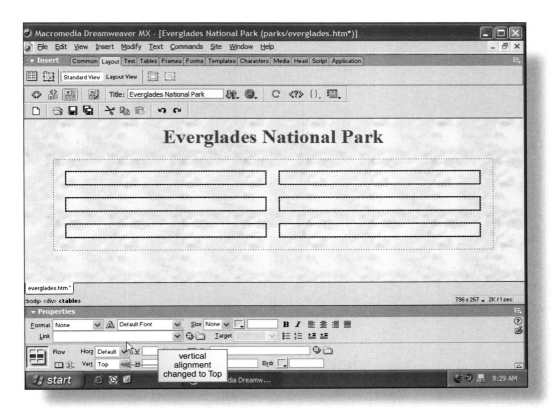

FIGURE 3-25

Specifying Column Width

When a table width is specified as a percentage, column width expands to accommodate the text or image. When adding content to the table, this expansion can distort the table appearance and make it difficult to visualize how the final page will display. You can control this expansion by setting the column width. The objective for the Everglades National Park page is to display the page in two columns of equal width or 50 percent.

Steps **To Specify Column Width**

1 **Click the cell in row 1, column 1 and then drag to select all cells in column 1. Click the W box in the Property inspector. Type** 50% **and then press the ENTER key.**

2 **Click the cell in row 1, column 2 and then drag to select all cells in column 2. Click the W box in the Property inspector. Type** 50% **and then press the ENTER key.**

The width for column 1 and column 2 is specified as 50% (Figure 3-26). This change does not display in the Document window.

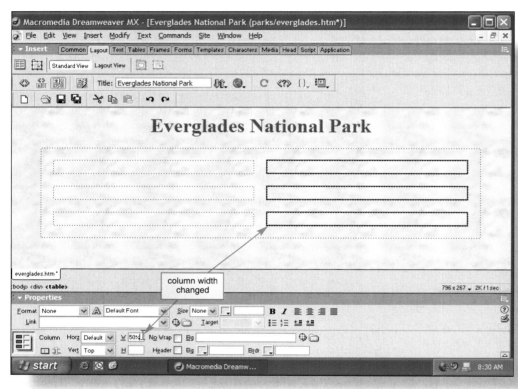

FIGURE 3-26

Adding Text to the Everglades National Park Web Page

Next, you will enter and format the text for the Everglades National Park Web page. Table 3-3 includes the text for the first table. The text is entered into the table cells. If you have not set the width and height of a cell, when you begin to enter text into a table cell, the cell expands to accommodate the text. The other cells may appear to shrink, but they also will expand when you type in the cells, or add an image to the cells.

Complete the following steps to add text to the Everglades National Park page. Press the ENTER key or insert a line break <BR> as indicated in the table. Press SHIFT+ENTER to insert a line break. Press the TAB key to move from cell to cell.

Table 3-3	Everglades National Park Web Page Text
SECTION	TEXT FOR EVERGLADES NATIONAL PARK WEB PAGE
Part 1	Everglades National Park, located at the southern tip of Florida, is the largest remaining subtropical wilderness in the United States. It is the only ecosystem of its kind on the planet and the only place in the world where alligators and crocodiles coexist.<ENTER>
A freshwater river, 50 miles wide and six-inches deep, flows from Lake Okeechobee through marshy grassland into Florida Bay. The Everglades National Park was created in 1947 by President Harry S. Truman to preserve the wetlands and this slow-moving "River of Grass." <ENTER>
The 1.5 million acres of Everglades National Park provide habitats for more than 1,600 varieties of plants and innumerable animals, including more than 350 species of tropical and temperate birds, 40 species of mammals, 50 species of reptiles, and 18 species of amphibians. The sea and wetland wilderness invites exploration by canoe or boat. Walking and tram tours are excellent ways to observe the extensive wildlife.
Part 2	The park is open year round. <ENTER>
Park Service Information Office
Everglades National Park
40001 State Road 9336
Homestead, FL 33034 <ENTER>
E-mail: Everglades National Park

Table Data

If you have a table that contains data that requires sorting, you can perform a simple table sort based on the contents of a single column, or you can perform a more complicated sort based on the contents of two columns. Click Commands on the menu bar and then click Sort Table.

Steps | To Add Everglades National Park Text

1 Click the Insert bar expand/collapse arrow to collapse the Insert bar. Click the Property inspector expand/collapse arrow to collapse the Property inspector.

The Insert bar and Property inspector panels are collapsed (Figure 3-27). Additional workspace is provided in the Document window.

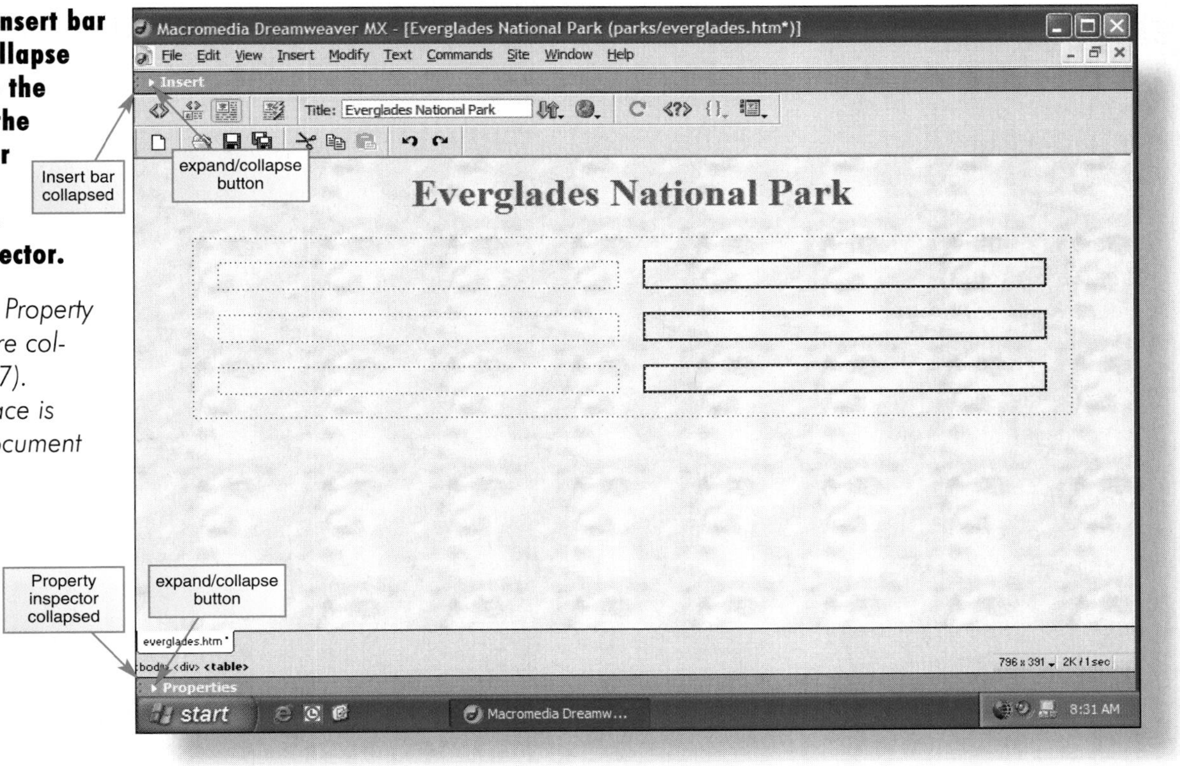

FIGURE 3-27

2 **Type the three paragraphs of Part 1 in Table 3-3 on the previous page in row 1, column 2 of the table in the Document window.**

The three paragraphs are entered into row 1, column 2 (Figure 3-28).

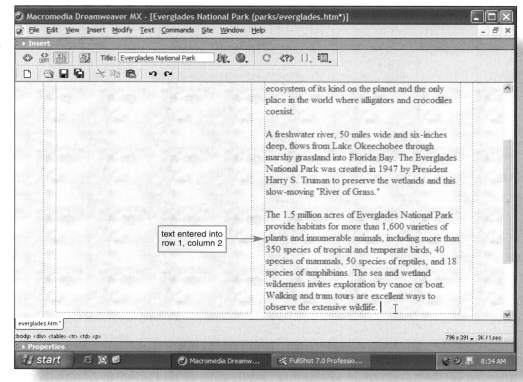

FIGURE 3-28

3 **If necessary, scroll down to display the rest of the table. Type the text of Part 2 in Table 3-3 in row 3, column 1 of the Document window. Use SHIFT+ENTER to insert the line breaks. Point to the Property inspector expand/collapse button.**

The text is entered (Figure 3-29). The insertion point is still within the cell and does not display because a line break was added. A line break moves the insertion point to the next line, but does not create a blank space such as when the ENTER key is pressed.

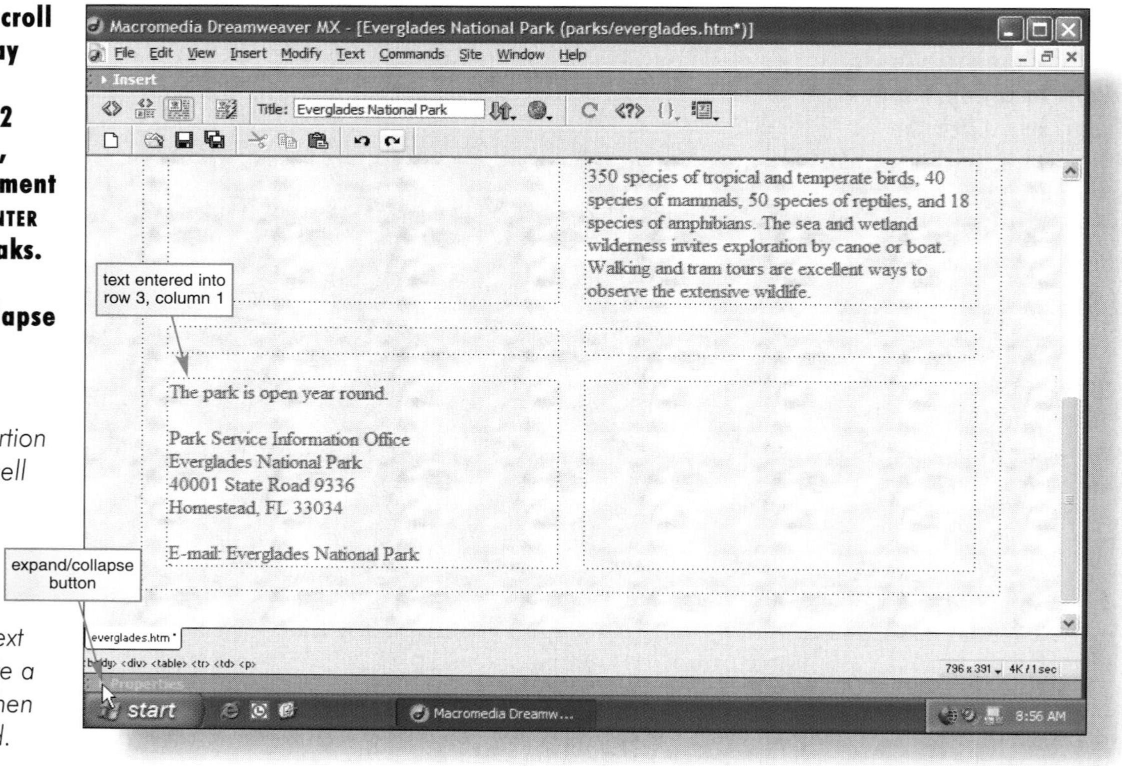

FIGURE 3-29

4 Click the expand/collapse button to display the Property inspector. Select the text in row 3, column 1. Click the Align Right button in the Property inspector.

The Property inspector is displayed and the text is aligned to the right in the cell (Figure 3-30).

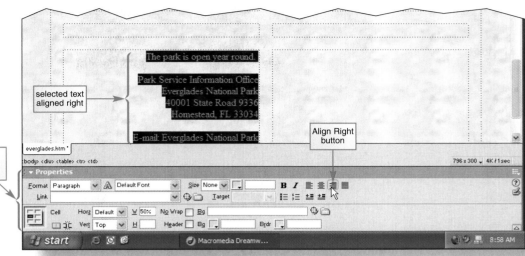

FIGURE 3-30

Other Ways

1. Right-click selected text, point to Align on context menu, click Right on Align submenu

Adding a Second Table to the Everglades National Park Web Page

Next, you will add a second table to the Everglades National Park Web page. This table will contain one row and one column and will serve as the footer for your Web page. The text is centered in the cell and will contain links to the home page and to the other two national parks Web pages. Complete the following steps to add the second table and text.

Steps **To Add a Second Table to the Everglades National Park Web Page**

1 Click outside the right border of the existing table to position the insertion point outside the table.

The insertion point is located and blinking to the right of the table border (Figure 3-31).

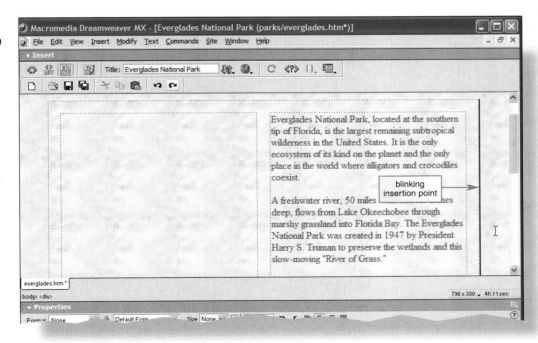

FIGURE 3-31

2 **Press the ENTER key. Point to the Insert bar expand/collapse arrow.**

The insertion point is centered below the first table (Figure 3-32). The insertion point is still within the centered HTML table tags. Otherwise, it would default to the left.

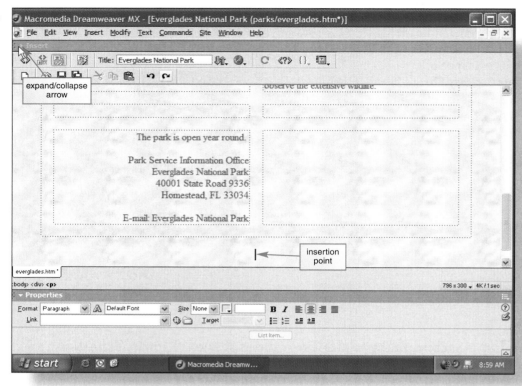

FIGURE 3-32

3 **Click the Insert bar expand/collapse button. If necessary, click the Layout tab and then click the Insert Table button.**

The Insert Table dialog box is displayed (Figure 3-33). The dialog box retains the settings from the first table. The dialog box on your computer may show different settings.

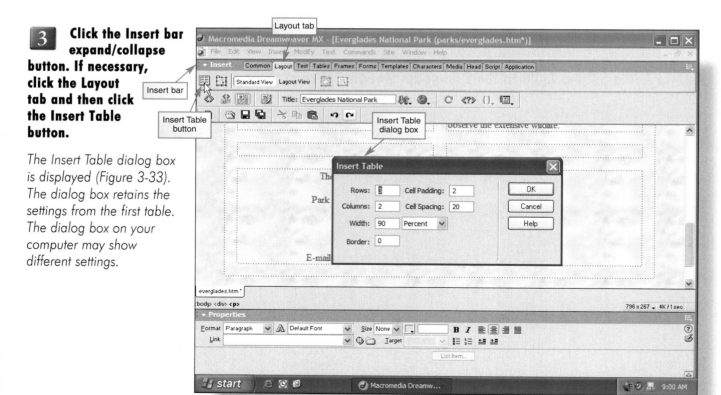

FIGURE 3-33

4 **Change the number of rows to 1, the number of columns to 1, cell spacing to 10, and width to 75. If necessary, change other settings to match the settings shown in Figure 3-34. Point to the OK button.**

The Insert Table dialog box displays the new table settings as shown in Figure 3-34.

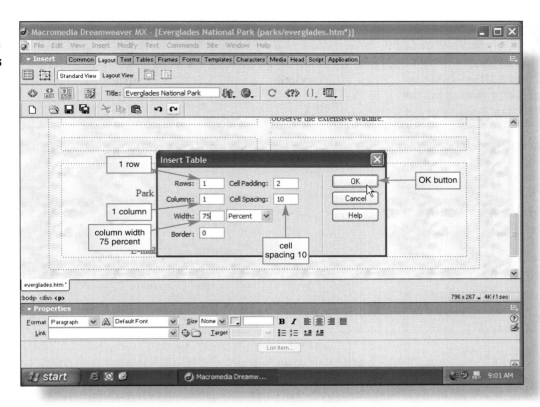

FIGURE 3-34

5 **Click the OK button.**

The table is inserted into the Document window (Figure 3-35). The dark border and handles indicate the table is selected.

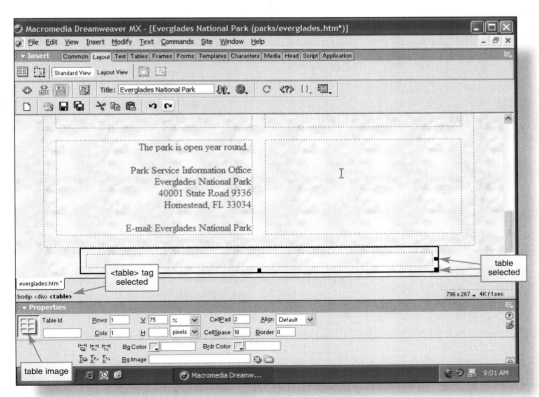

FIGURE 3-35

6 **Click the table. Type** Home **and then press the SPACEBAR. Press SHIFT + | (VERTICAL BAR) and then press the SPACEBAR. Type** Biscayne National Park **and then press the SPACEBAR. Press SHIFT + | and then press the SPACEBAR. Type** Dry Tortugas National Park **as the last link text.**

The text is entered into the table (Figure 3-36).

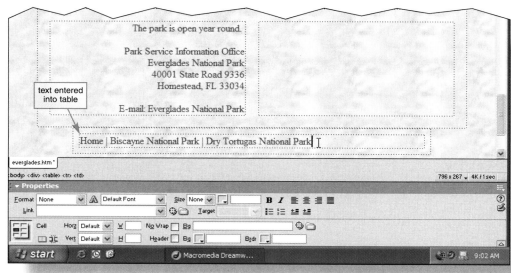

FIGURE 3-36

Adjusting the Table Width

Determining table width sometimes is a matter of judgment. You may overestimate or underestimate the table width when first inserting it into the Document window. When this happens, it is easy to make adjustments to the table width through the Property inspector. The table with the names that will contain links is too wide for the text it contains and needs to be adjusted. You adjust the table width by selecting the table and then changing the width in the Property inspector.

 To Adjust the Table Width

1 **If necessary, click the cell in table 2. Click <table> in the tag selector to select the table. Double-click the W box in the Property inspector. Type** 60 **and then press the ENTER key.**

The dark border around the table indicates the table is selected. The Property inspector displays table properties. The table width is decreased (Figure 3-37).

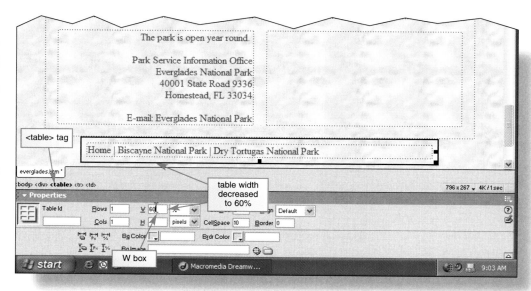

FIGURE 3-37

2   **Click the cell and then drag to select the text. Click the Align Center button in the Property inspector.**

The text is centered in the cell (Figure 3-38). This is a one-cell table, so the text also is centered in the table.

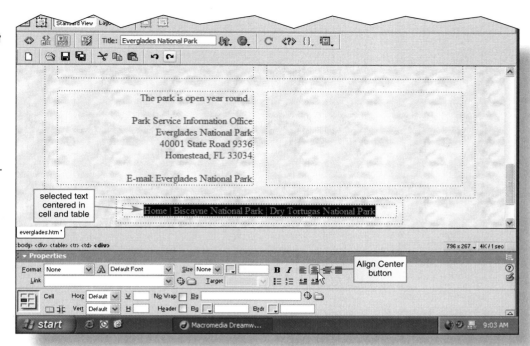

FIGURE 3-38

Next, you will add relative, absolute, and e-mail links to the Everglades National Park page. Perform the following steps to add the links.

TO ADD LINKS TO THE EVERGLADES NATIONAL PARK PAGE

1 Select the first instance of Everglades National Park located in the first table in row 3, column 1. Type http://www.nps.gov/ever/ in the Link box to create an absolute link.

2 Select the second instance of Everglades National Park located in the first table, row 3, column 1. Click Insert on the menu bar and then click Email Link. When the Email Link dialog box is displayed, type everglades@parks.gov for the e-mail address. Click the OK button.

3 Select Home in the second table. Type index.htm in the Link box to create the relative link.

4 Select Biscayne National Park in the second table. Type biscayne.htm in the Link box to create the relative link.

5 Select Dry Tortugas National Park in the second table. Type dry_tortugas.htm in the Link box to create the relative link.

6 Click the Save button on the Standard toolbar.

7 Press the F12 key to view the Web page. Scroll down to view the links as shown in Figure 3-39 on the next page.

8 Close the browser and return to the Dreamweaver window.

The links are added to the Web page (Figure 3-39). The links for Biscayne National Park and Dry Tortugas National Park are not active at this point. You will add these two pages later in this project.

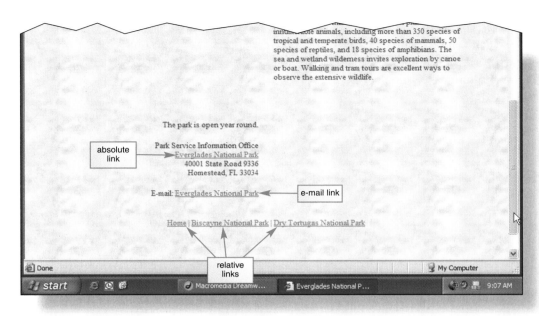

FIGURE 3-39

Editing and Modifying Table Structure

Thus far, you have created two tables and made adjustments in Dreamweaver for the Everglades National Park Web page. For various reasons, as you create and develop Web sites, you will need to edit and modify a table, change the dimensions of a table, add rows and columns, or delete the table and start over. The following section describes how to accomplish editing, modifying, and deleting table elements within the structure.

DELETE A ROW OR COLUMN Select a row or column and then press the DELETE key. You also can delete a row or column by clicking a cell within the row or column, right-clicking to display the context menu, pointing to Table, and then clicking Delete Row or Delete Column on the Table submenu.

INSERT A ROW OR COLUMN To insert a row or column, click in a cell. Right-click to display the context menu, point to Table, and then click Insert Row or Insert Column on the Table submenu. To insert more than one row or column and to control the row or column insertion point, click in a cell, right-click to display the context menu, point to Table, and then click Insert Rows or Columns on the Table submenu to display the Insert Rows or Columns dialog box (Figure 3-40). Make your selections and then click the OK button. To add a row automatically, press the TAB key in the last cell of a table.

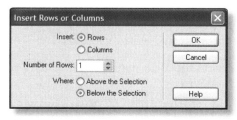

FIGURE 3-40

MERGE AND SPLIT CELLS By merging and splitting cells, you can set alignments more complex than straight rows and columns. To merge two or more cells, select the cells and then click Merge Cells in the Property inspector. The selected cells must be contiguous and in the shape of a rectangle. You can merge any number of adjacent cells as long as the entire selection is a line or a rectangle. To split a cell, click the cell and then click Split Cells in the Property inspector to display the Split Cell dialog box (Figure 3-41). In the Split Cell dialog box, specify how to split the cell and then click the OK button. You can split a cell into any number of rows or columns, regardless of whether it was previously merged. When you split a cell into two rows, the other cells in the same row as the split cell are not split. The same is true if a cell is split into two or more columns: the other cells in the same column are not split. To select a cell quickly, click the cell and then click the <td> tag on the tag selector.

FIGURE 3-41

RESIZING A TABLE, COLUMNS, AND ROWS You can resize an entire table or resize individual rows and columns. To resize the table, select the table and change the W (width) in the Property inspector. A second method is to select the table and then drag one of the table selection handles. When you resize an entire table, all of the cells in the table change size proportionately. If you have assigned explicit widths or heights to a cell or cells within the table, resizing the table changes the visual size of the cells in the Document window but does not change the specified widths and heights of the cells. To resize a column or row, select the column or row and change the properties in the Property inspector. A second method to resize a column is to select the column and then drag the right border of the column. To resize a row, select the row and then drag the lower border of the row.

DELETE A TABLE You easily can delete a table. Select the table tag in the tag selector and then press the DELETE key. All table content is deleted along with the table.

Merging Cells and Adding Images

The concept of merging cells probably is familiar to you if you have worked with spreadsheets or word processing tables. In HTML, however, this is a complicated process. Dreamweaver makes this easy by hiding some complex HTML table restructuring code behind an easy-to-use interface in the Property inspector. Dreamweaver also makes it easy to add images to a table. When you add and then select an image in a table cell, the Property inspector displays the same properties as were displayed when you added and selected an image in the Document window in Project 2. When the image in the cell is not selected, the Property inspector displays the same properties as it does for any cell. These properties were described earlier in this project.

You will merge two cells (row 1, columns 1 and 2) and add three images to the Everglades National Park page. The first and second images go into the merged cells and the third image goes in row 3, column 2. Perform the steps on the next page to merge two cells.

More *About*

Splitting and Merging Cells

An alternative approach to merging and splitting cells is to increase or decrease the number of rows or columns spanned by a cell.

Steps | **To Merge Two Cells**

1 **Click the expand/collapse arrow to collapse the Insert bar. Press F8 to display the Site panel. If necessary, scroll up and then click row 1, column 1. Drag to select the cells in rows 1 and 2 in column 1. Point to the Merge Cells button in the Property inspector.**

The two cells are selected (Figure 3-42). The Site panel is displayed.

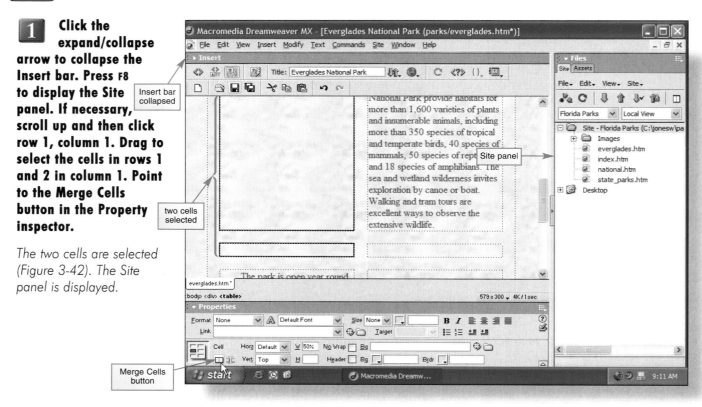

FIGURE 3-42

2 **Click the Merge Cells button.**

The two cells are merged (Figure 3-43).

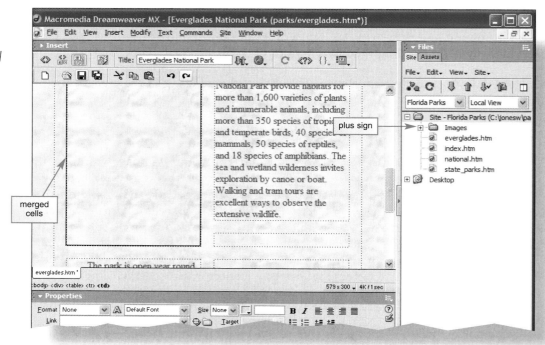

FIGURE 3-43

Next, you will add three images to the table. You align and modify the size of the images. Complete the following steps to display the image file names in the Site panel and then add, align, and modify images in a Standard view table.

Steps **To Add Images to a Standard View Table**

1 **Click the plus sign (+) to the left of Images in the Site panel. Scroll to the top of the table and then click the cell in row 1, column 1.**

The Images folder is expanded and the insertion point is positioned in the merged cell (Figure 3-44). The gator.jpg image will be inserted at the location of the insertion point.

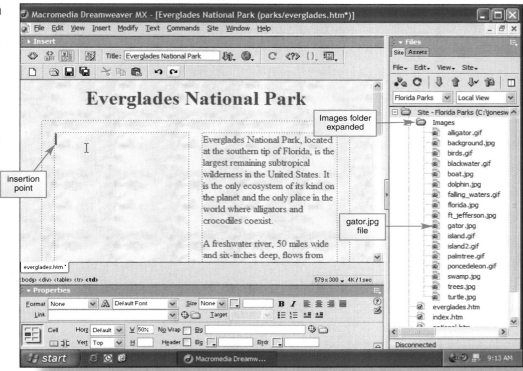

FIGURE 3-44

2 **Drag the gator.jpg image to the insertion point in the merged cell.**

The gator.jpg image is inserted in the cell (Figure 3-45). The insertion point is blinking to the right of the image.

FIGURE 3-45

3 **Press the ENTER key.**

The insertion point is displayed below the gator.jpg image (Figure 3-46). The swamp.jpg image will be inserted at the location of the insertion point.

FIGURE 3-46

4 **Drag the swamp.jpg image to the insertion point.**

The swamp.jpg image is displayed below the gator.jpg image and the insertion point is blinking to the right of the swamp.jpg image (Figure 3-47). The image is larger than the cell, and the cell expands to accommodate the image. The horizontal scroll bar may display because the full table width is no longer visible.

FIGURE 3-47

5 Click the gator.jpg image to select it.

The gator.jpg image is selected (Figure 3-48). The Property inspector displays image properties.

FIGURE 3-48

6 Double-click the W box in the Property inspector. Type 340 and then press the TAB key to move to the H box. Type 260 as the new value. Click the Alt box, type Florida alligator and then press the ENTER key.

The properties are applied to the gator.jpg image (Figure 3-49).

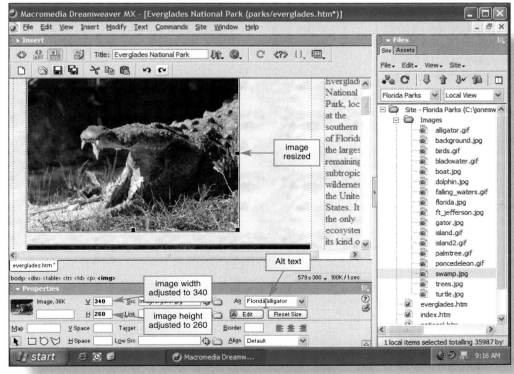

FIGURE 3-49

7 **Scroll down and then click the swamp.jpg image to select it.**

The swamp.jpg image is selected (Figure 3-50).

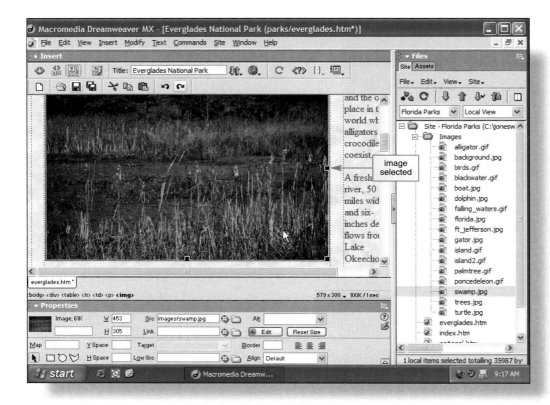

FIGURE 3-50

8 **Double-click the W box in the Property inspector. Type** 330 **and then press the TAB key to move to the H box. Type** 220 **as the new value. Click the Alt box. Type** Florida swamp **and then press the ENTER key.**

The properties are applied to the swamp.jpg image (Figure 3-51).

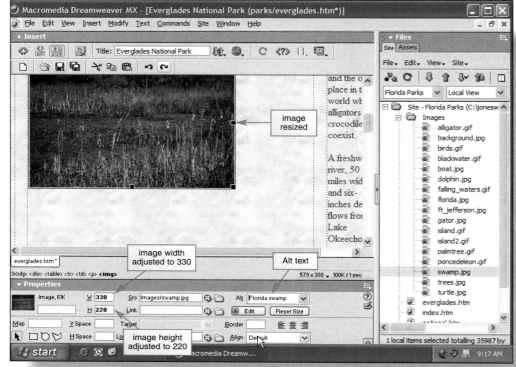

FIGURE 3-51

9 | **Scroll down. Click row 3, column 2.**

The insertion point is displayed in the cell (Figure 3-52). The birds.gif image will be inserted at the location of the insertion point.

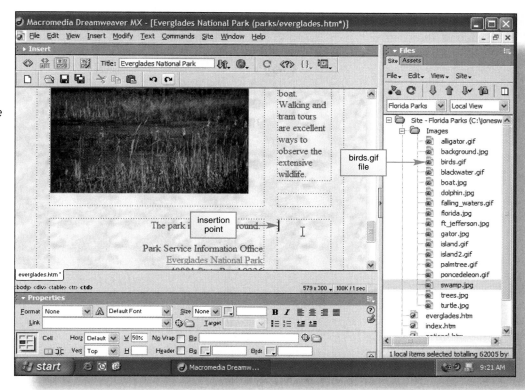

FIGURE 3-52

10 | **Drag the birds.gif file to the insertion point in row 3, column 2.**

The birds.gif image is displayed in the cell (Figure 3-53). The cell expands to accommodate the image. The insertion point is blinking to the right of the image.

FIGURE 3-53

Dreamweaver MX

11 Click the birds.gif image to select it. Click the Alt box. Type **Florida birds** and then press the ENTER key.

The Alt text is entered (Figure 3-54).

FIGURE 3-54

12 Scroll up. Click the cell in row 2, column 2 and then drag to select this cell and the cell in row 3, column 2.

The two cells are selected (Figure 3-55).

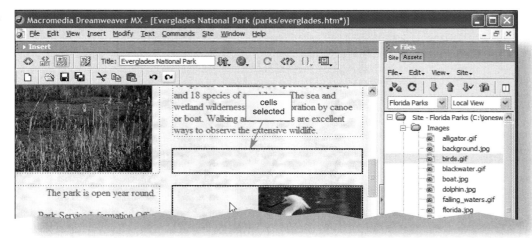

FIGURE 3-55

13 Click the Merge Cells button.

The two cells are merged and the top border of the newly merged cell moves up (Figure 3-56).

FIGURE 3-56

14 Click the Save button on the Document toolbar and then press the F12 key to view the page in your browser.

The Florida Everglades page displays in the browser (Figure 3-57).

15 Close the browser window and then close the Site panel and the Everglades National Park Web page.

FIGURE 3-57

Creating the Biscayne National Park Web Page

You used the Untitled-1 default page that displayed when you started Dreamweaver to begin creating the Everglades page. To create the Biscayne National Park Web page, you open a new Untitled Document window. You start by applying a color scheme and the background image. This is the same color scheme and background image you used for the Florida Parks Web site in Projects 1 and 2.

TO ADD A COLOR SCHEME AND BACKGROUND IMAGE TO THE BISCAYNE NATIONAL PARK WEB PAGE

1 Open a new Untitled window. Apply the settings in Table 3-1 on page DW 3.10 to add the color scheme and then click the OK button in the Set Color Scheme Command dialog box.

2 Apply the settings in Table 3-1 to add the background image. Click the OK button in the Page Properties dialog box.

3 Click the Save button on the Standard toolbar and save the Web page in the parks folder. Type biscayne for the file name.

The background image is applied to the Biscayne National Park page (Figure 3-58).

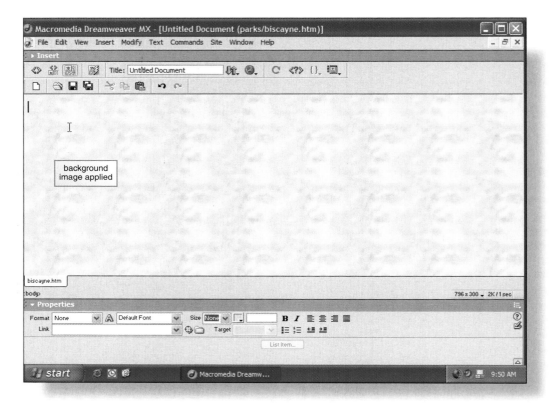

FIGURE 3-58

Next, you will insert and center a 3-row, 2-column table. Then you will add the page title — Biscayne National Park. Perform the following steps to insert and center the table and to add the title.

TO INSERT AND CENTER A TABLE

1 Click the Align Center button in the Property inspector.

2 If necessary, expand the Insert bar and then click the Layout tab. Click the Insert Table button.

3 In the Insert Table dialog box, change the following settings: Rows 3, Cell Padding 10, Columns 2, Cell Spacing 2, W 90 Percent, and Border 4. Press the OK button to insert the table.

4 Title the page Biscayne National Park.

5 Click the expand/collapse arrow to collapse the Insert bar.

6 Click the Save button on the Standard toolbar.

The centered table is added to the Web page (Figure 3-59). The Web page is saved in the parks folder.

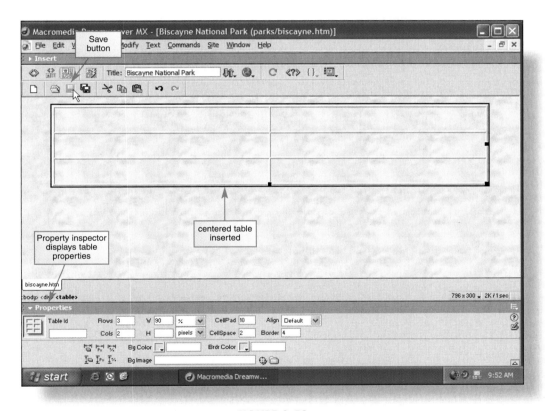

FIGURE 3-59

An understanding of HTML and how it relates to a table and to parts of a table provides you with the ability to select a table and table components and to modify a table through the code. Merging and varying the span of columns (as you did in the Everglades National Park page) and merging and varying the span of rows is helpful for grouping information, adding emphasis, or deleting empty cells. When you merge two cells in a row, you are spanning a column. Continuing with the <TABLE> example on page DW 3.19 and spanning the two cells in row 1, the HTML tags would be <TD COLSPAN="2">First cellSecond cell</TD>. When you merge two cells in a column, you are spanning a row. The attribute ROWSPAN would replace COLSPAN in the above example. Understanding COLSPAN and ROWSPAN will help you determine when and if two columns or two rows have been merged.

For the Everglades National Park page, you entered a heading outside the table and links to the other pages in a second table. For the Biscayne National Park page, you will merge the cells in row 1 and then merge the cells in row 3. You will enter a heading in row 1 and then enter text for the links to the home page and other national parks in row 3. Perform the following steps to merge the cells in row 1 and merge the cells in row 3.

TO MERGE CELLS IN ROWS 1 AND 3

1 Click row 1, column 1 and drag to select row 1.

2 Click the Merge Cells button in the Property inspector.

3 Click row 3, column 1 and drag to select row 3.

4 Click the Merge Cells button in the Property inspector.

The cells in row 1 are merged into one column and the cells in row 3 are merged into one column (Figure 3-60).

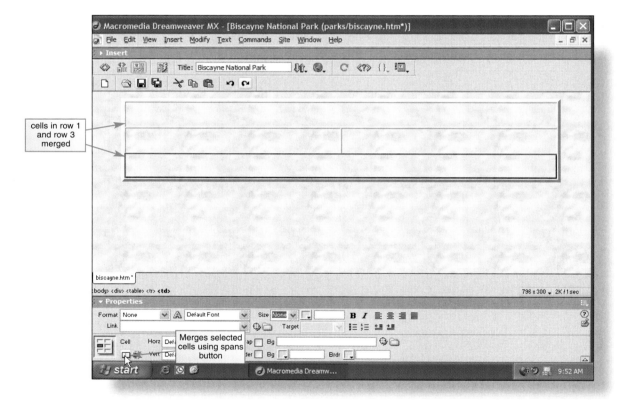

FIGURE 3-60

Next, you will add and center a heading. Complete the following steps to add and center the heading in row 1.

To Add a Heading to Row 1

1 **Click row 1 and then click the Align Center button in the Property inspector.**

The insertion point is aligned in the middle of the row (Figure 3-61).

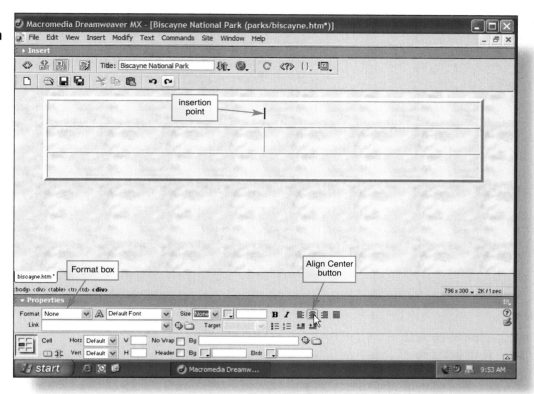

FIGURE 3-61

2 **Type** Biscayne National Park **and then use the Format pop-up menu to apply Heading 1.**

The heading is centered in row 1 and Heading 1 is applied to the text (Figure 3-62).

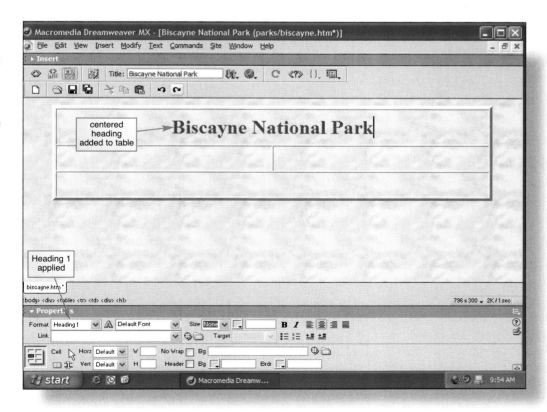

FIGURE 3-62

3 **Click row 3 and then click the Align Center button in the Property inspector.**

The insertion point is centered in row 3 (Figure 3-63).

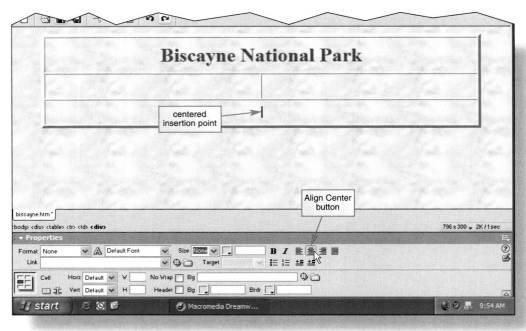

FIGURE 3-63

4 **Type** Home **and then press the SPACEBAR. Press SHIFT+| (VERTICAL BAR) and then press the SPACEBAR. Type** Everglades National Park **and then press the SPACEBAR. Press SHIFT+| and then press the SPACEBAR. Type** Dry Tortugas National Park **as the last link text.**

The text for the links is centered in the row (Figure 3-64).

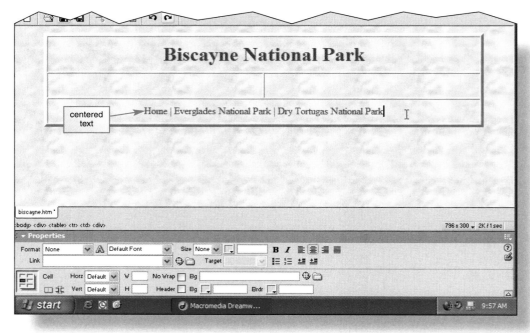

FIGURE 3-64

Splitting and Merging Cells

Tables in a traditional sense generally are thought of as having an internal **symmetry**; that is, cells of the same size form neatly arranged columns and rows. On a Web page, however, by varying the size of a cell, you can use tables to create an asymmetrical arrangement. This design option allows for more visual variation on a Web page. In a three-column table, for example, you could specify the first column as 20 percent and the second and third columns as 40 percent each. Depending on the number of columns, hundreds of variation percentages can be applied. In the Biscayne National Park page, you adjust the width for columns 1 and 2 and then change the vertical alignment to Top within both columns. Perform the following steps to adjust the width and change the vertical spacing.

More About

Column Width

In addition to using the Property inspector to change the width or height of a column, you also can change cell widths and heights directly in the HTML code.

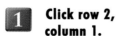 **To Adjust the Column Width**

1 **Click row 2, column 1.**

The insertion point is located in row 2, column 1 (Figure 3-65).

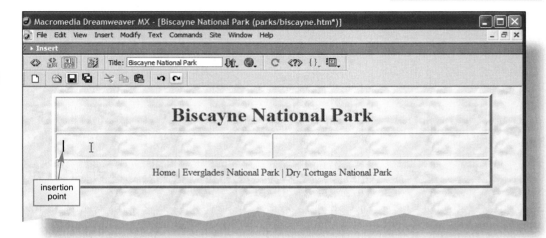

FIGURE 3-65

2 **Click the W box in the Property inspector. Type** 40% **and then press the ENTER key. Click row 2, column 2. Click the W box in the Property inspector. Type** 60% **and then press the ENTER key.**

Column 1 is decreased in size to reflect the new percentage and column 2 is increased in size to reflect the new percentage (Figure 3-66).

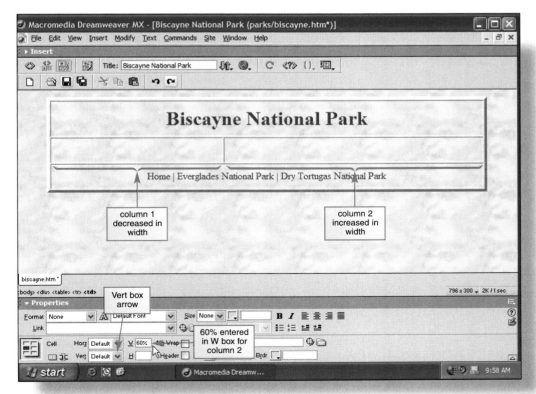

FIGURE 3-66

3 Select row 2, columns 1 and 2. Click the Vert box arrow in the Property inspector and then select Top from the Vert pop-up menu.

Top is selected in the Vert box (Figure 3-67).

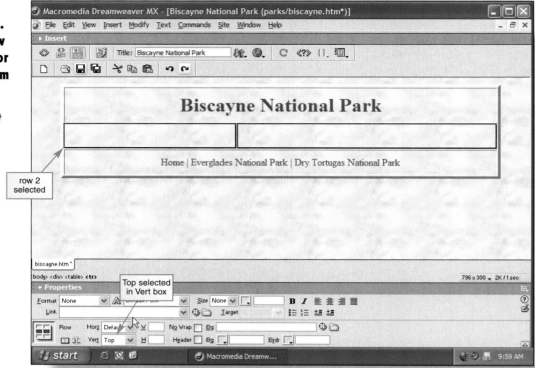

FIGURE 3-67

Now you will add the text and images to row 2, columns 1 and 2. Table 3-4 contains the text for the Biscayne National Park Web page.

Inserting Images into a Table

In Macromedia Dreamweaver MX, you can work in Design view or Code view to insert images in a document.

Table 3-4	Biscayne National Park Web Page Text
SECTION	*TEXT FOR BISCAYNE NATIONAL PARK WEB PAGE*
Part 1	Located off the eastern coast of Florida, the 180,000-acre Biscayne National Park is less than an hour's drive from Miami. The park originally was established as a national monument in 1968. It became a national park in 1980, specifically to protect the incredible diversity of mammals, birds, fish, and plants.<ENTER><ENTER>
Part 2	Park Service Information Office: Biscayne National Park P. O. Box 1369 Homestead, FL 33090<ENTER> E-mail: Biscayne National Park
Part 3	More than 95 percent of the park is underwater and includes mangrove swamps, coral reefs, and the waters of Biscayne Bay. The remaining 5 percent includes 44 islands that form an 18-nautical mile north-south chain. In this watery paradise, one can find more than 200 varieties of fish, which inhabit the coral reefs. Starfish, sponges, soft corals, and other marine plants and animals live and thrive in Biscayne Bay.<ENTER>
Part 4	Biscayne National Park is best explored with snorkels or scuba gear. For those not quite so adventurous, glass-bottom boat trips and canoe rentals are available.<ENTER>

To Add Text and Images to the Biscayne National Park Web Page

1 **Press F8 to display the Site panel. If necessary, click the plus (+) sign to the left of Images to display the image files. Click row 2, column 1.**

The insertion point is positioned in row 2, column 1 and the Site panel is displayed (Figure 3-68). The island.gif image will be inserted at the location of the insertion point.

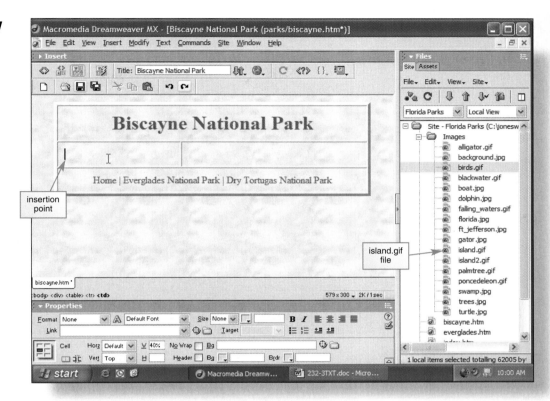

FIGURE 3-68

2 **Drag the island.gif image to the insertion point in row 2, column 1.**

The island.gif image is displayed in row 2, column 1. The insertion point is blinking to the right of the image (Figure 3-69).

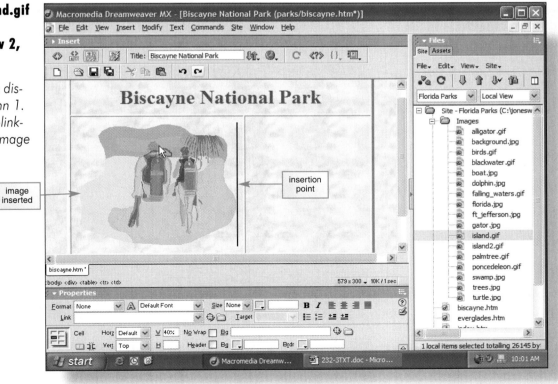

FIGURE 3-69

3 Press the ENTER key and then type the text of Part 1 in Table 3-4 on page DW 3.48. Press the ENTER key two times after you type the text.

The text is entered as shown in Figure 3-70.

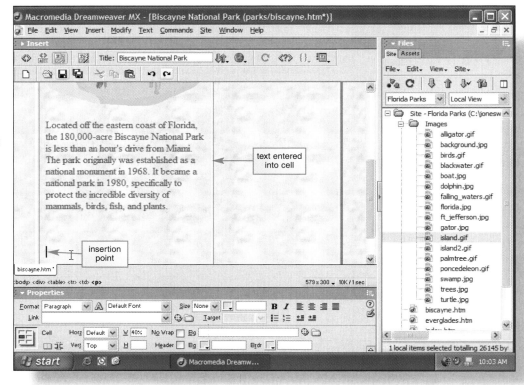

FIGURE 3-70

4 Type the text of Part 2 in Table 3-4. Insert line breaks and press the ENTER key as indicated in Table 3-4.

The text is entered as shown in Figure 3-71.

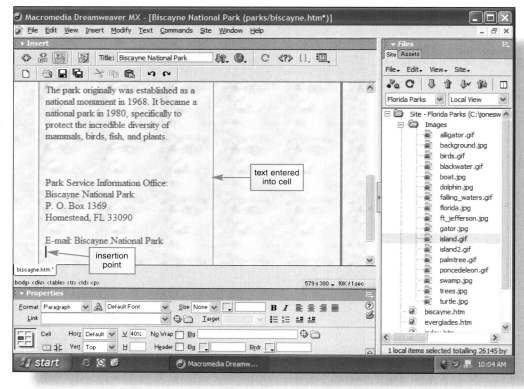

FIGURE 3-71

5 **Scroll up and click row 2, column 2.**

The insertion point is positioned in row 2, column 2 (Figure 3-72).

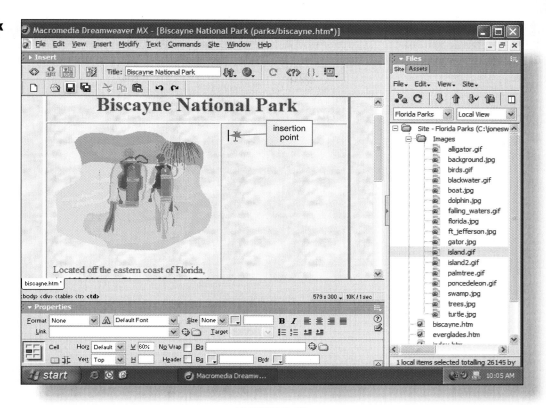

FIGURE 3-72

6 **Type the text of Part 3 in Table 3-4.**

The text is entered as shown in Figure 3-73. The palmtree.gif image will be inserted at the location of the insertion point.

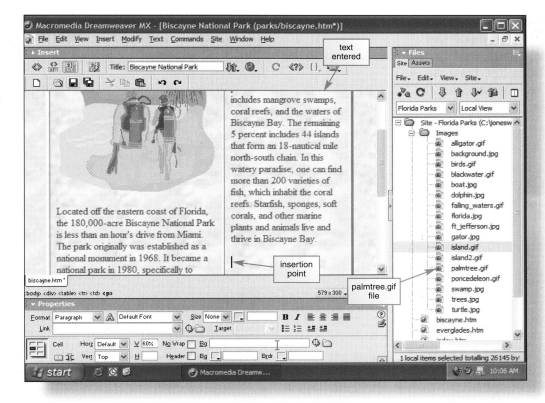

FIGURE 3-73

7 **Drag the palmtree.gif image to the insertion point.**

The palmtree.gif image is inserted into the cell. The insertion point is blinking to the right of the image (Figure 3-74).

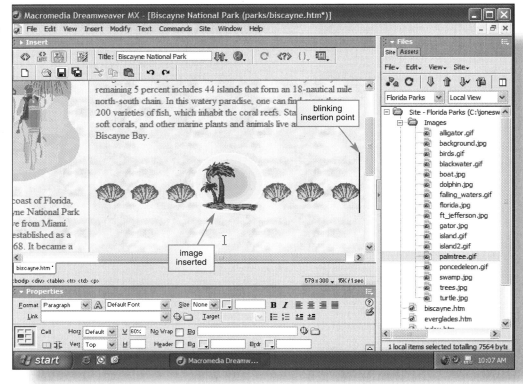

FIGURE 3-74

8 **Press the ENTER key and then type the text of Part 4 in Table 3-4. Press the ENTER key after entering the text.**

The text is entered as shown in Figure 3-75. The island2.gif image will be inserted at the location of the insertion point.

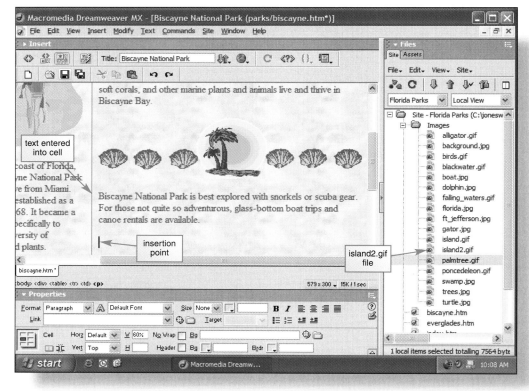

FIGURE 3-75

9 **Drag the island2.gif image to the insertion point. Click the image to select it. Double-click the W box in the Property inspector. Type** 375 **as the new value. Double-click the H box and then type** 220 **as the new value. Click the Align Center button. Type** island **for the Alt text.**

The image is inserted into the cell, resized, and centered (Figure 3-76).

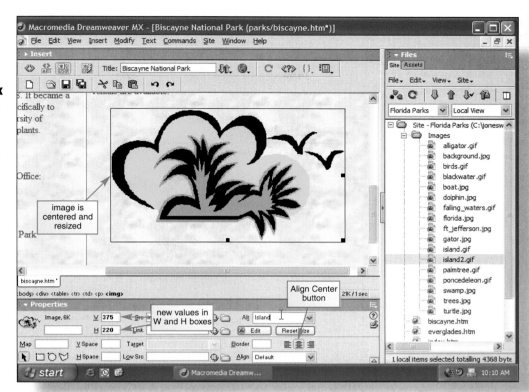

FIGURE 3-76

Adding a Border and a Border Color

A **border** is the width, in pixels, of the table border. The purpose of most tables in a Web page is to provide a structure for the positioning of text and images. When creating a table within Dreamweaver, therefore, the default border is 0 (zero) or no border. Adding a border to a Web page, however, transforms the table into a graphical element within itself. Depending on the content, a border can become a visual cue for the reader by separating content. A border is applied to the full table. You cannot apply a border to an individual cell unless the table consists of only one cell.

When you created the table for the Biscayne National Park Web page, you specified a border size of 4. By default, borders are gray, but the border color can be changed. Using the color picker, you can apply a color of your choice. Although you cannot apply a border to an individual cell, you can apply a border color to a single cell or to a range of cells.

Background images and background color work the same for a table as they do for a Web page. The image or color, however, is contained within the table and does not affect the rest of the page. Background color (unlike borders) and images can be applied to a single cell or to a range of cells. Perform the steps on the next two pages to add a border color to the table and a background color to a merged cell.

More *About*

Borders

A border can help separate content within a table. Borders are especially useful if the table includes information that contains data that must be read across a row or down a column.

Dreamweaver MX

Steps **To Add Border Color and Cell Background Color**

1 Click <table> in the tag selector and then click the Brdr Color box arrow in the Property inspector. Point to row 9, column 2.

The table is selected and the Continuous Tone color palette is displayed (Figure 3-77).

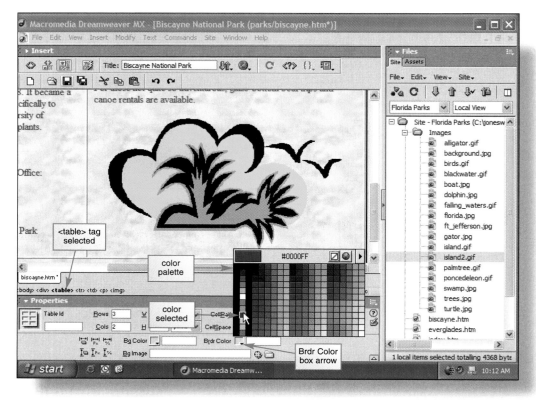

FIGURE 3-77

2 Click row 9, column 2 to select the blue color, hexadecimal #0000FF.

A shade of blue is applied to the border (Figure 3-78).

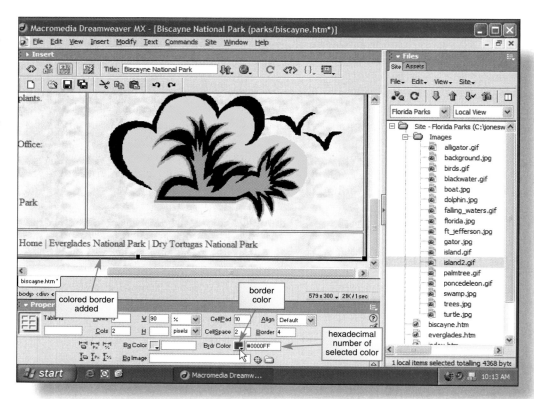

FIGURE 3-78

3 If necessary, scroll up and left. Click anywhere in row 1. Click the Bg Color box arrow. If necessary, select the Color Cubes palette and then point to the second column from the right and fourth row from the bottom — hexadecimal color #FFCC66.

The color palette displays the selected background (Figure 3-79).

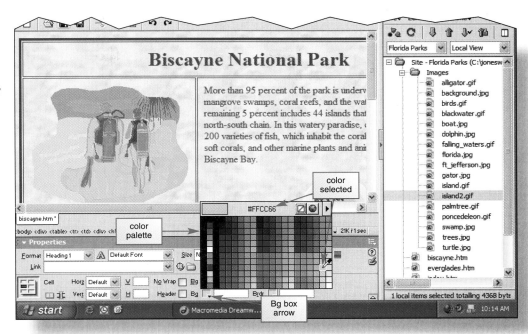

FIGURE 3-79

4 Click the mouse pointer.

The palette is closed and the background color is applied to the row (Figure 3-80).

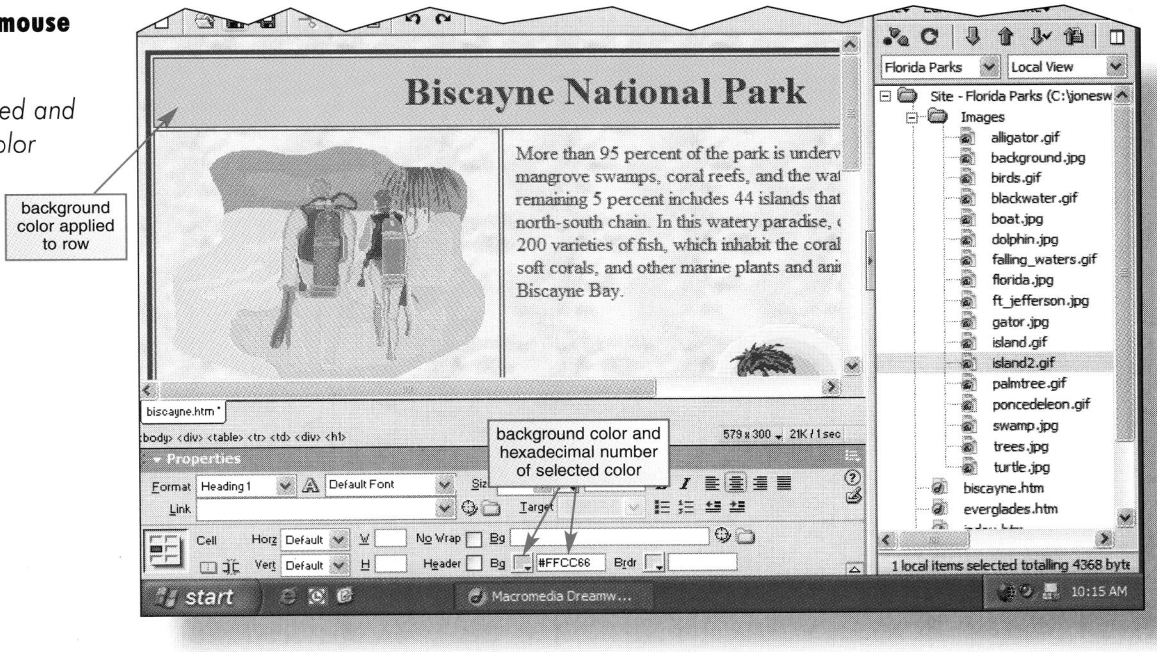

FIGURE 3-80

Your last task for the Biscayne National Park page is to spell check, add links, and save the page. Perform the steps on the next page to spell check, add the absolute, relative, and e-mail links to the Biscayne National Park page, and then save the Web page.

TO ADD LINKS TO AND SPELL CHECK THE BISCAYNE NATIONAL PARK PAGE

1 Scroll down select the first instance of Biscayne National Park in the address in row 2, column 1. Type `http://www.nps.gov/bisc/` in the Link box.

2 Select the second instance of Biscayne National Park. Click Insert on the menu bar and then click Email Link. Type `biscayne@parks.gov` in the E-Mail text box. Click the OK button in the Email Link dialog box.

3 Double-click Home in row 3 and then type `index.htm` in the Link box.

4 Select Everglades National Park and then type `everglades.htm` in the Link box.

5 Select Dry Tortugas National Park and then type `dry_tortugas.htm` in the Link box.

6 Click the Save button on the Document toolbar.

7 Check spelling.

8 Press the F12 key to view the Web page in the browser as shown in Figure 3-81. Close the browser and then close the Web page. If necessary, save any changes.

In the browser, the Biscayne National Park page is displayed as shown in Figure 3-81.

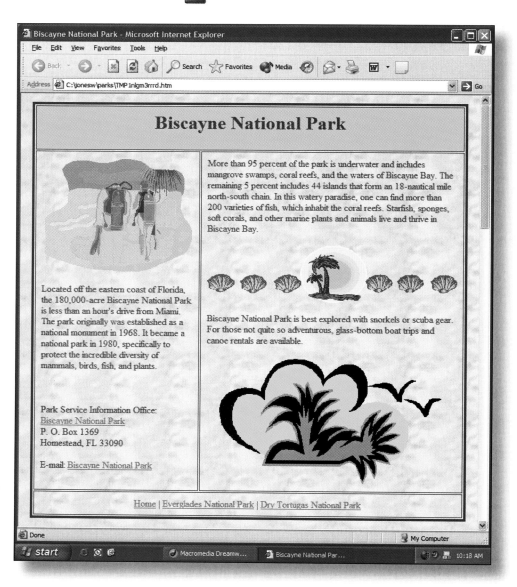

FIGURE 3-81

Layout View

Tables created in Standard view are useful for creating Web pages that are simple in format or contain tabular data. A second option for creating tables in Dreamweaver is the Layout view. Layout view provides more flexibility than Standard view. In Layout view, you draw your own table and cells. When using Layout view, you are creating the framework for the entire table. The layout can be as simple or as complex as you want.

Layout view is a tool unique to Dreamweaver. Terms such as layout view and layout cell do not exist in HTML. When you draw a **layout table**, Dreamweaver creates an HTML table. When you draw a **layout cell**, Dreamweaver creates a tag (<TD>) in the table. When a cell is drawn in a table, it stays within the row-and-column grid as it does in Standard view. Cells cannot overlap, but they can span rows and columns. When you draw cells of different widths and different heights, Dreamweaver creates additional cells in the HTML table. These cells are displayed with a gray background.

You can use Layout view to modify the structure of an existing page created in Standard view. Layout view, however, provides the greatest advantage when designing the page from the start. As you draw the table and/or cells in Layout view, Dreamweaver creates the code. If you draw a layout cell first, a layout table is inserted automatically to serve as a container for the layout cell. A layout cell cannot exist outside of a layout table. You can create your page using one layout table with several layout cells contained within the table or you can have multiple layout tables. Using multiple layout tables isolates parts of your layout so that one section is not affected by another. For example, the cell size within a table can affect the other cells in the same row and column. Using multiple tables eliminates this problem.

When you draw a table in Layout view, the table is outlined in green. A tab labeled Layout Table is displayed at the top of each table. Clicking the tab selects the table. When you complete your page design for the Dry Tortugas National Park, it will look similar to Figure 3-82 on the next page.

Perform the following steps to add a new page, add a background image, and prepare the work area of the page.

TO ADD A COLOR SCHEME AND BACKGROUND IMAGE TO THE DRY TORTUGAS NATIONAL PARK WEB PAGE

1 Open a new Document window. Apply the settings in Table 3-1 on page DW 3.10 to add the color scheme and then click the OK button in the Set Color Scheme Command dialog box.

2 Apply the settings in Table 3-1 to add the background image. Click the OK button in the Page Properties dialog box.

3 Type Dry Tortugas National Park for the title.

4 Click the Save button on the Standard toolbar and save the Web page in the parks folder. Type dry_tortugas for the file name.

Using Visual Guides

Dreamweaver provides three types of visual guides to help you design documents and project how the page will appear in a browser: ruler, tracing image, and grid.

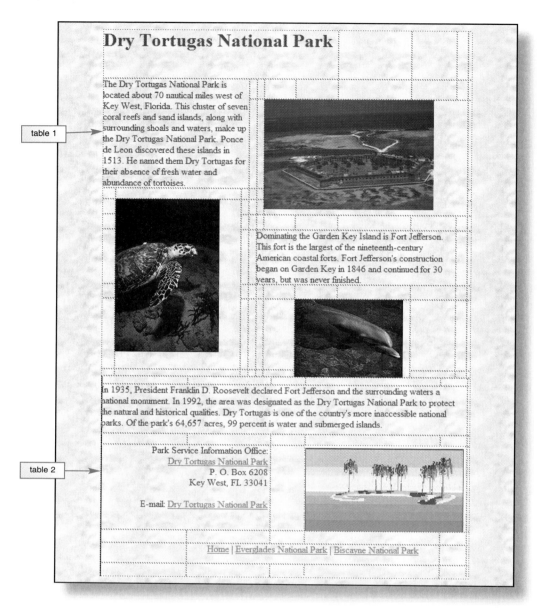

table 1

table 2

FIGURE 3-82

RULER   Provides a visual cue for positioning and resizing layers or tables.

TRACING IMAGE   Used as the page background to duplicate a design.

GRID   Provides precise positioning and resizing of layers.

You will use the ruler to help approximate cell width and height and cell location within a table. Then, you will make final adjustments to the cells and table using settings in the Property inspector. Perform the following steps to display the ruler in the Document window.

More About

The Grid Feature

Dreamweaver's grid feature allows for precise positioning. Options include changing the grid square size and specifying that table and cell edges snap to the grid edges. To turn on the grid, click View on the menu bar, point to Grid, and then click Show Grid on the Grid submenu.

Steps | **To Display the Ruler**

1 **Click View on the menu bar, point to Rulers, and then point to Show on the Rulers submenu.**

Dreamweaver displays the View menu and the Rulers submenu (Figure 3-83).

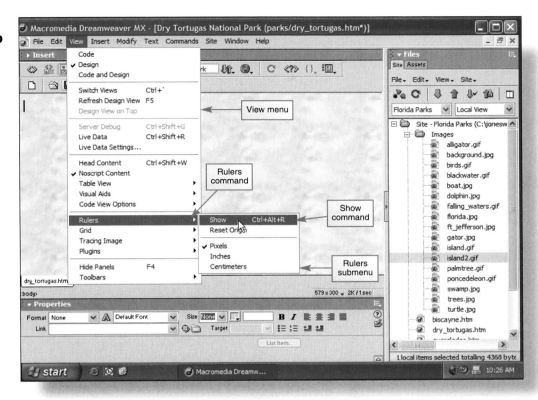

FIGURE 3-83

2 **Click Show. Expand the Insert bar. If necessary, click the Layout tab in the Insert bar.**

The ruler is displayed at the top and left margins of the Document window (Figure 3-84). Measurements are in pixels.

3 **Right-click the Files title bar and then click the Close Panel Group command. Click the Property inspector expander arrow.**

The lower pane of the Property inspector collapses.

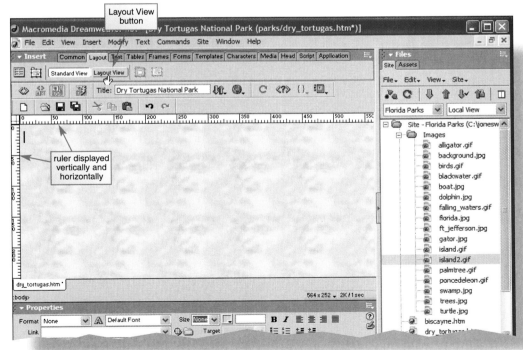

FIGURE 3-84

Creating a Layout Table for the Dry Tortugas National Park Web Page

You begin creating the Dry Tortugas National Park page by drawing a table. This is one of two tables you will create for the Dry Tortugas National Park page. In the first table, you will create six cells: one cell to hold the heading, two cells to hold text content, and three cells to hold images. The second table is below the first. This table will contain four cells: a cell to hold informational content, a cell to hold address and contact information, a cell to hold an image, and a cell to contain links to the home page and the other two national park pages.

Your next task is to draw the first layout table. This table has an approximate width of 620 pixels and an approximate height of 575–590 pixels. Perform the following steps to create the layout table.

 To Create the First Layout Table

1 **Click the Layout View button. Point to the OK button.**

The Getting Started in Layout View dialog box is displayed (Figure 3-85). The dialog box contains help information on how the layout feature works. The dialog box may not display if the Don't show me this message again box previously was checked.

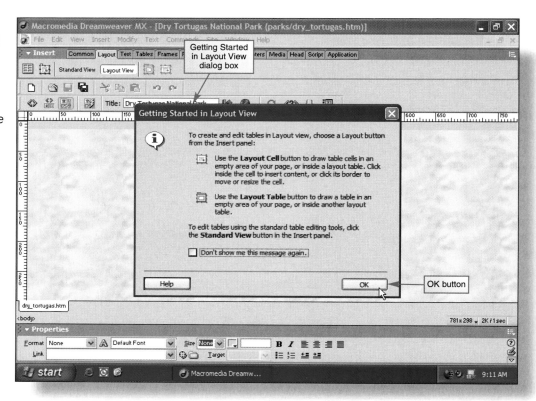

FIGURE 3-85

2 Read the information in the Getting Started in Layout View dialog box and then click the OK button. Move the mouse pointer to the Document window.

The mouse pointer changes to a plus sign, which indicates you can draw a table (Figure 3-86).

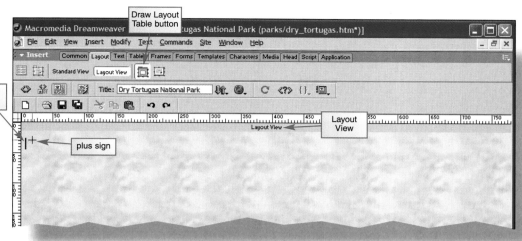

FIGURE 3-86

3 Position the mouse pointer in the upper-left corner of the Document window. Use the ruler as a guide and drag to draw a table with a width of approximately 600 pixels and a height of approximately 575 pixels. Scroll to the top of the page.

The table is added to the Document window and is outlined in green. The Property inspector changes to reflect the table in Layout view (Figure 3-87). The Layout Table tab is displayed at the top of the table and the table width displays in the column header area. The table displays with a gray background.

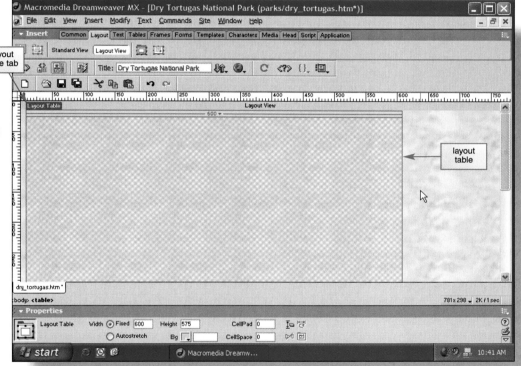

FIGURE 3-87

Layout Table and Layout Cell Properties

When a layout table is selected, the Property inspector displays properties related to the layout table. Some properties, such as width and height, background color, cell padding and cell spacing, are the same as those for a table in Standard view. The following describes the properties unique to the table in Layout view (Figure 3-88 on the next page).

FIXED Sets the table to a fixed width.

AUTOSTRETCH The rightmost column of the table stretches to fill the browser window width. The column header area for an autostretch column displays a wavy line instead of a number. If the layout includes an autostretch column, the layout always fills the entire width of the browser window.

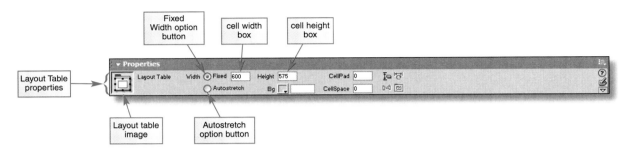

FIGURE 3-88

If the table is not the correct width or height or needs other modifications, adjustments can be made through the Width and Height properties of the Property inspector.

The next step is to add a cell that will contain the table heading and the five cells that will contain text and images. The heading is aligned left at the top of the table. Perform the following steps to add layout cells and a table heading cell to the table.

To Add Layout Cells

1 If necessary, make any adjustments in the Property inspector Width and Height boxes. Click the Draw Layout Cell button on the Layout tab.

The status bar indicates the function of the button (Figure 3-89).

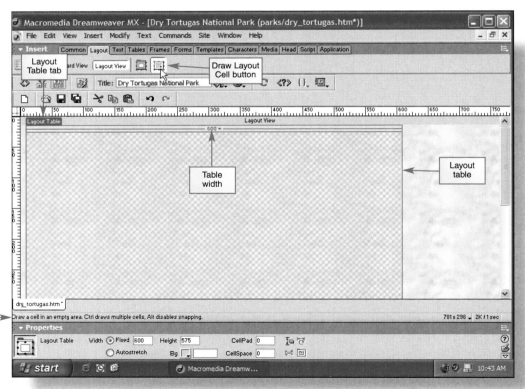

FIGURE 3-89

2 **Click the upper-left corner of the layout table and drag to draw a cell with an approximate width of 425 and an approximate height of 85. Click the blue outline of the cell to select it and make any necessary width and height adjustments in the Property inspector Width and Height boxes.**

A layout cell is created in the upper-left corner of the layout table. The cell is displayed in the table with a blue outline (Figure 3-90). The handles on the borders indicate the cell is selected.

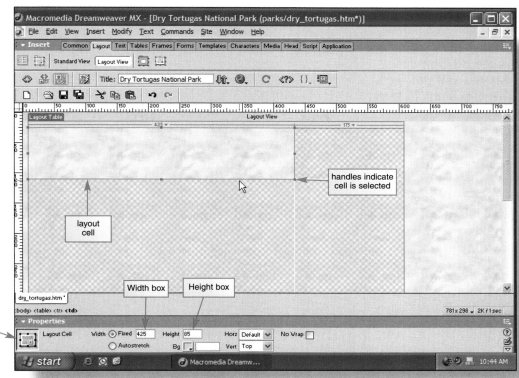

FIGURE 3-90

3 **Click the cell and type** Dry Tortugas National Park. **Apply Heading 1 to the text. Point to the Draw Layout Cell button.**

The heading is inserted into the cell and Heading 1 is applied to the text (Figure 3-91). Text properties are displayed in the Property inspector.

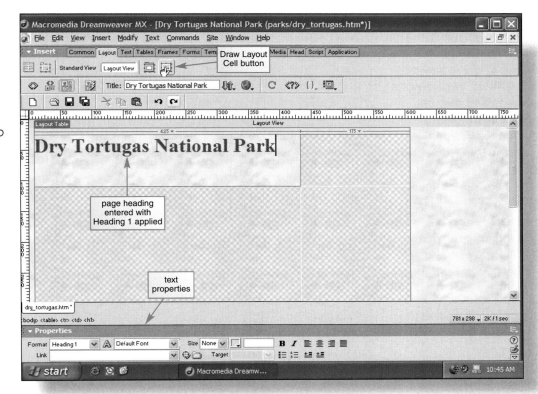

FIGURE 3-91

4 Click the Draw Layout Cell button. Click to the left and below the first cell and then draw a cell with an approximate width of 250 and an approximate height of 190 as shown in Figure 3-92. Click the blue outline of the cell to select it and make any necessary width and height adjustments in the Property inspector Width and Height boxes.

The second cell is added to the table and is selected (Figure 3-92). This cell will contain text.

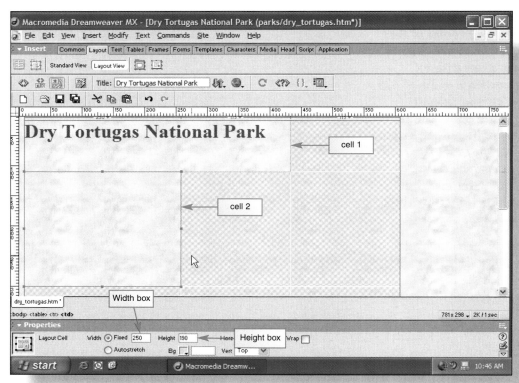

FIGURE 3-92

5 Click the Draw Layout Cell button and then draw a cell to the right of the second cell with an approximate width of 290 and an approximate height of 200 as shown in Figure 3-93. If necessary, scroll to view the entire cell. Click the blue outline of the cell to select it and make any necessary width and height adjustments in the Property inspector Width and Height boxes.

The third cell is added to the table and is selected (Figure 3-93). This cell will contain an image.

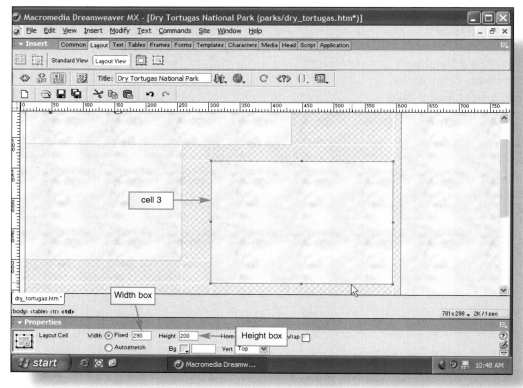

FIGURE 3-93

6 Scroll down and then click the Draw Layout Cell button. Click approximately 20 pixels below the second cell and about 20 pixels to the right of the table border. Draw a cell with a width of approximately 180 and a height of approximately 275 as shown in Figure 3-94. Click the blue outline of the cell to select it and make any necessary width and height adjustments in the Property inspector Width and Height boxes.

The fourth cell is added to the table and is selected (Figure 3-94). The cell will contain an image.

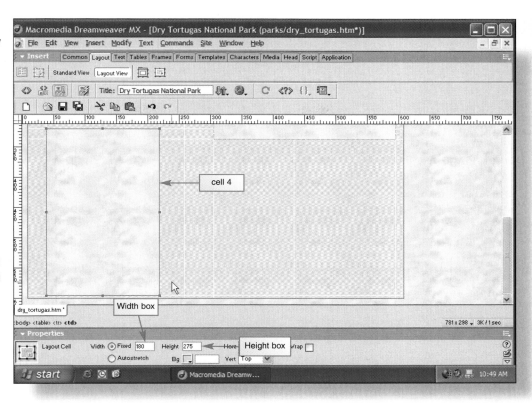

FIGURE 3-94

7 Click the Draw Layout Cell button. Click 20 pixels below and 50 pixels to the left of the third cell and draw a cell with a width of approximately 300 and a height of approximately 75 as shown in Figure 3-95. Click the blue outline of the cell to select it and make any necessary width and height adjustments in the Property inspector Width and Height boxes.

The fifth cell is added to the table and is selected (Figure 3-95). The cell will contain text.

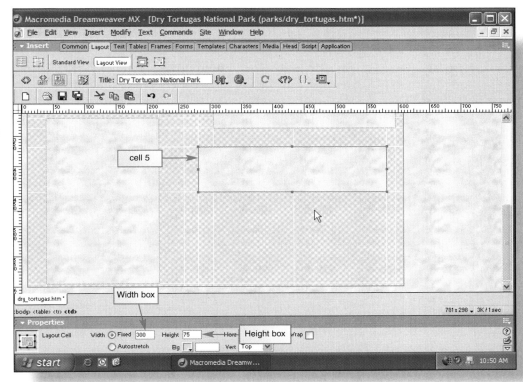

FIGURE 3-95

8 **Click the Draw Layout Cell button. Click about 20 pixels below and about 50 pixels to the right of the fifth cell and draw a cell with a width of approximately 185 and a height of approximately 135 as shown in Figure 3-96. Click the blue outline of the cell to select it and make any necessary width and height adjustments in the Property inspector Width and Height boxes.**

The sixth cell is added to the table and is selected (Figure 3-96). The cell will contain an image.

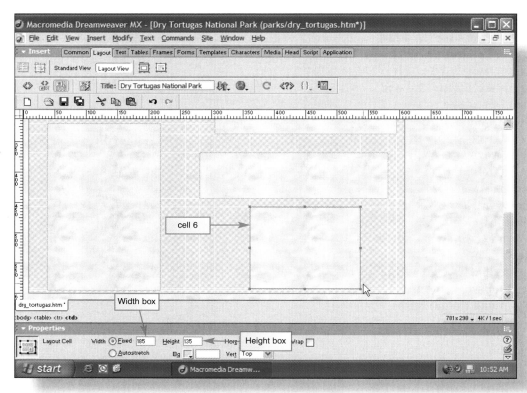

FIGURE 3-96

Adding Content and Images to the Cells

Adding text content and images to layout cells is similar to adding content and images to cells in a Standard view table. The only place content can be inserted in a layout table is in a layout cell. When Dreamweaver creates a layout cell, it automatically assigns a vertical alignment of Top. You have the same options as you did in Standard view to change the alignment to Middle, Bottom, or Baseline. When you insert an image into a layout cell, all the properties in the Property inspector that were available for images in Standard view also are available in Layout view.

Next, you will enter and format the text for the first table for the Dry Tortugas National Park Web page. The text is entered into the layout cells just as you entered it in the cells in the Standard view table. Then you will display the Site panel and drag images into the cells. Table 3-5 contains the text for the Dry Tortugas National Park Web page.

Layout Cells

To delete a layout cell, click the edge of the cell to select it, and then press the DELETE key. The space is replaced with noneditable cells.

TABLE 3-5	Dry Tortugas National Park Web Page Text
SECTION	TEXT FOR DRY TORTUGAS NATIONAL PARK WEB PAGE
Part 1	The Dry Tortugas National Park is located about 70 nautical miles west of Key West, Florida. This cluster of seven coral reefs and sand islands, along with surrounding shoals and waters, make up the Dry Tortugas National Park. Ponce de Leon discovered these islands in 1513. He named them Dry Tortugas for their absence of fresh water and abundance of tortoises.
Part 2	Dominating the Garden Key Island is Fort Jefferson. This fort is the largest of the nineteenth-century American coastal forts. Fort Jefferson's construction began on Garden Key in 1846 and continued for 30 years, but was never finished.
Part 3	In 1935, President Franklin D. Roosevelt declared Fort Jefferson and the surrounding waters a national monument. In 1992, the area was designated as the Dry Tortugas National Park to protect the natural and historical qualities. Dry Tortugas is one of the country's more inaccessible national parks. Of the park's 64,657 acres, 99 percent is water and submerged islands.
Part 4	Park Service Information Office: Dry Tortugas National Park P. O. Box 6208 Key West, FL 33041 <ENTER> E-mail: Dry Tortugas National Park <ENTER>
Part 5	Home | Everglades National Park | Biscayne National Park

More About

Positioning Images

The Property inspector contains two different sets of tools for positioning images. The top panel of the Property inspector lets you change the alignment of the image itself. The bottom panel of the Property inspector contains tools that change the cell's alignment settings.

To Add Text and Images to Table 1 of the Dry Tortugas National Park Web Page

1 **Scroll to the top of the Document window. Click the second cell and type the text of Part 1 in Table 3-5.**

The text is entered (Figure 3-97).

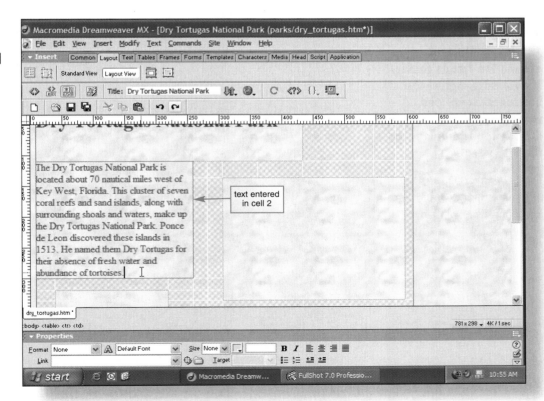

FIGURE 3-97

2 Scroll down and click the fifth cell you added. Type the text of Part 2 in Table 3-5.

The text is entered (Figure 3-98).

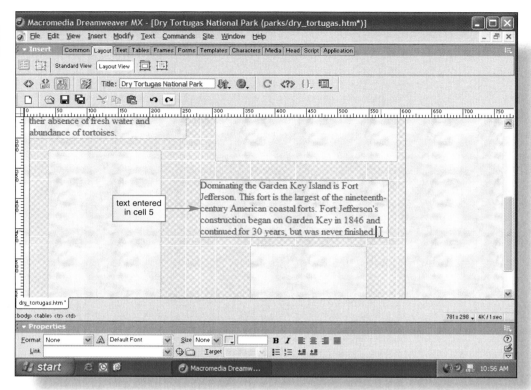

FIGURE 3-98

3 Scroll up and click the third cell. Press the F8 key to display the Site panel. If necessary, expand the Image folder. If necessary, adjust the horizontal scroll and vertical scroll bars to display the file names in the Site panel.

The insertion point is blinking in the third cell and the Site panel is displayed (Figure 3-99).

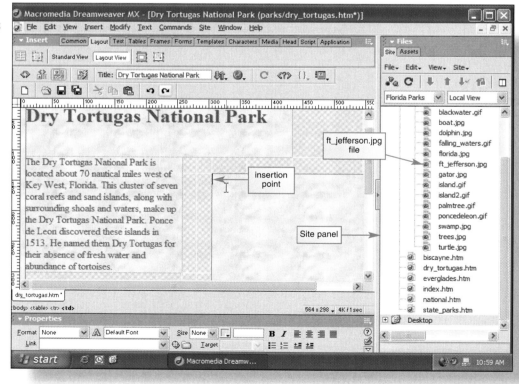

FIGURE 3-99

4 **Drag the ft_jefferson.jpg file to the insertion point.**

The image is displayed in the cell (Figure 3-100). The insertion point is blinking to the right of the image.

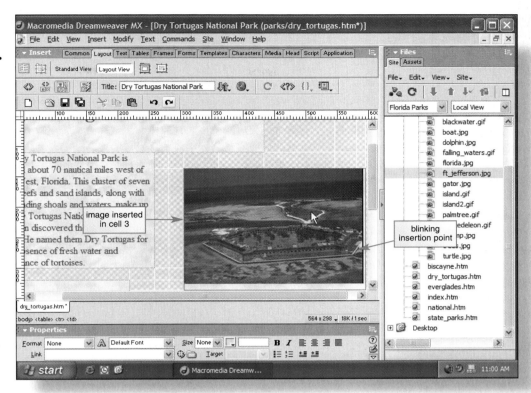

FIGURE 3-100

5 **Scroll down and click the fourth cell. Drag the turtle.jpg image to the cell.**

The turtle image is displayed in the cell (Figure 3-101). The insertion point is blinking to the right of the image.

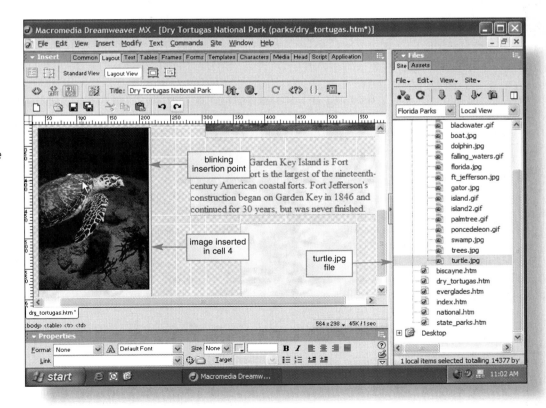

FIGURE 3-101

6 Click the sixth cell and then drag the dolphin.jpg image to the cell.

The dolphin image is displayed (Figure 3-102). The insertion point is blinking to the right of the image.

7 Scroll up and then click the ft_jefferson image in cell 3. Type Ft. Jefferson in the Alt box in the Property inspector. Click outside the image to deselect it. Repeat these steps for the other two images: type Turtle for the turtle image and Dolphin for the dolphin image.

8 Click the Save button on the Standard toolbar.

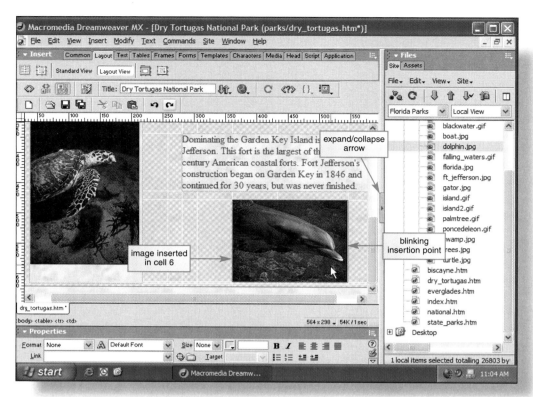

FIGURE 3-102

Adding a Second Table to the Dry Tortugas National Park Web Page

The second table in the Dry Tortugas National Park Web page will go immediately below the first table. This table will contain four cells. Three of the cells will contain text and the fourth cell will contain an image.

Layout Tables

For more information about Dreamweaver MX layout tables, visit the Dreamweaver MX More About Web page (scsite.com/dreamweavermx/more.htm) and then click Dreamweaver MX Layout Tables.

To Add a Second Table to the Dry Tortugas National Park Web Page

1 **Click the Site panel expand/ collapse arrow. If necessary, scroll down. Click the Draw Layout Table button on Layout tab and then position the mouse pointer outside the lower-right border of the first table.**

The mouse pointer changes to a plus sign and is positioned to the right and lower border of the first table (Figure 3-103).

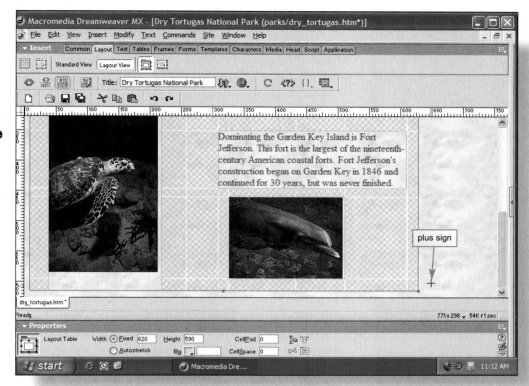

FIGURE 3-103

2 **Drag to the left to create a table with an approximate width of 620 and an approximate height of 350 as shown in Figure 3-104. Make any necessary width and height adjustments in the Property inspector.**

The new table is inserted into the Document window (Figure 3-104).

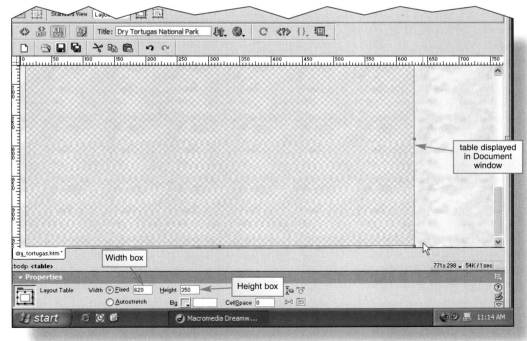

FIGURE 3-104

The next task is to add the cells to the table. Perform the following steps to add the four cells.

1 If necessary, scroll up. Click the Draw Cell Layout button on the Layout tab and then position the insertion point about 10 pixels below the top of the table. Draw a cell with an approximate width of 615 pixels and an approximate height of 85 pixels. Select the cell and make any necessary adjustments to the width and height in the Property inspector.

2 Click the Draw Cell Layout button and draw a second cell about 5–10 pixels below the first cell with an approximate width of 285 and an approximate height of 150. Select the cell and make any necessary adjustments to the width and height in the Property inspector.

3 Click the Draw Cell Layout button and draw a third cell to the right of the second cell and about 5–10 pixels below cell 1 with an approximate width of 275 and an approximate height of 130. Select the cell and make any necessary adjustments to the width and height in the Property inspector.

4 Click the Draw Cell Layout button and draw a fourth cell about 10 pixels below the second cell and about 100 pixels from the left border with an approximate width of 425 and an approximate height of 35. Select the cell and make any necessary adjustments to the width and height in the Property inspector.

5 Scroll the page to view the tables and cells as shown in Figure 3-105.

An overview of the tables and cells in the Dry Tortugas Document window is shown in Figure 3-105.

Next, you will add content to the cells in table 2. Three of the cells will contain text and one of the cells will contain an image. Two of the text cells will contain links. Complete the following steps to add text and the image to the cells and to create the links for table 2. Figure 3-82 on page DW 3.58 shows the completed project.

1 Click cell 1 and type the text from Part 3 in Table 3-5 on page DW 3.67 into the cell.

2 Click cell 2 and type the text from Part 4 in Table 3-5 into the cell.

3 Click cell 4 and type the text from Part 5 in Table 3-5 into the cell.

4 Select the text in cell 2 and then click the Align Right button in the Property inspector.

5 Select the first instance of Dry Tortugas National Park in cell 2. Type `http://www.nps.gov/dry_tort/` in the Link box to create an absolute link.

6 Select the second instance of Dry Tortugas National Park. Click Insert on the menu bar and then click Email Link. When the Email Link dialog box is displayed, type `dry_tortugas@parks.gov` for the e-mail address. Click the OK button.

7 Select the text in cell 4 and then click the Align Center button in the Property inspector.

8 Select Home in cell 4 in the second table (last cell in the table). Type `index.htm` in the Link box to create the relative link.

9 Select Everglades National Park. Type `everglades.htm` in the Link box to create the relative link.

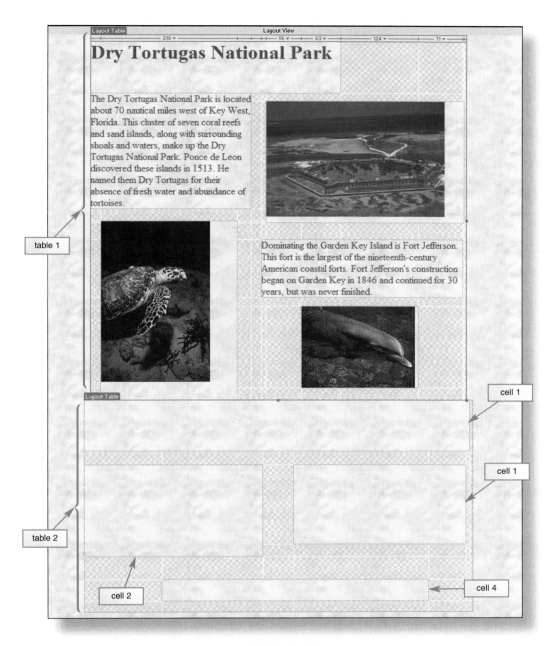

FIGURE 3-105

10　Select Biscayne National Park. Type biscayne.htm in the Link box to create the relative link.

11　Click the expand/collapse arrow on the Site panel. Drag the trees.jpg image to the third cell. Click the image and then drag a handle to resize the image to fit the cell. Click anywhere outside the cell to deselect it.

12　Click the Save button in the Standard toolbar.

13　Collapse the Site panel (Figure 3-106 on the next page).

The table is displayed as shown in Figure 3-106.

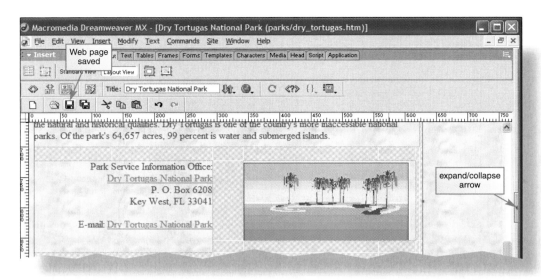

FIGURE 3-106

Centering the Table in Standard View

Layout view does not provide all the features that are provided for a table in Standard view. For example, you cannot select a number of rows or select a number of columns when creating Web pages in Layout view, and you cannot center a table when in Layout view. To access these features requires that the table be displayed in Standard view. Your next task is to center the two tables. Each table in the Document window must be centered separately. Perform the following steps to display the Web page in Standard view and to center the tables.

Steps **To Center a Table Created in Layout View**

1 **Click the Standard View button on the Layout tab. If necessary, click in a cell in the second table. Point to the <table> tag in the tag selector.**

The table is displayed in Standard view (Figure 3-107).

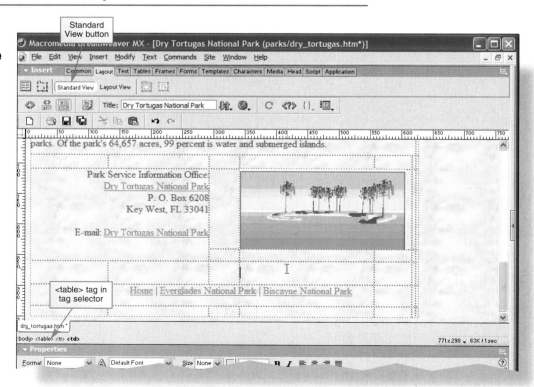

FIGURE 3-107

2 Click the <table> tag. Click the Align box arrow in the Property inspector and then click Center.

The second table is selected and centered in the Document window (Figure 3-108).

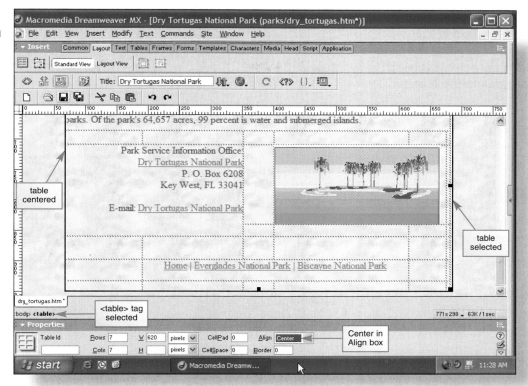

FIGURE 3-108

3 Scroll to the top and then click any cell in the first table. Click the <table> tag in the tag selector. Click the Align box arrow and select Center.

The first table is centered in the Document window (Figure 3-109).

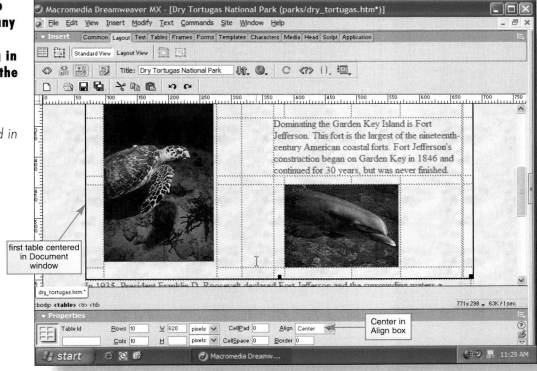

FIGURE 3-109

4 **Click the Save button in the Standard toolbar and then press the F12 key to view the page in the browser.**

The Web page displays centered in the browser (Figure 3-110)

5 **Close the browser and then close the Dry Tortugas page in Dreamweaver.**

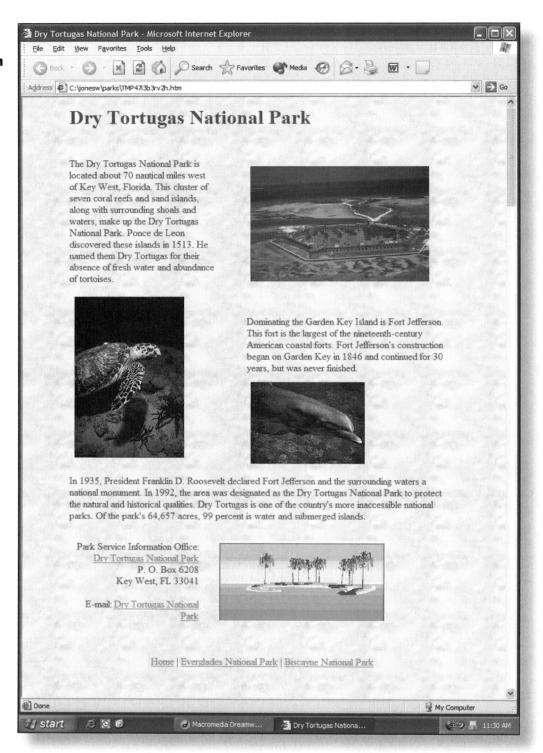

FIGURE 3-110

Head Content

HTML files consist of two main sections: the head section and the body section. The head section is one of the more important sections of a Web page. A standard HTML page contains a <head> tag and a <body> tag. Contained within the head section is site and page information. With the exception of the title, the information contained in the head does not display in the browser. Some of the information contained in the head is accessed by the browser and other information is accessed by other programs such as search engines and server software. In Figure 3-111, the head content of the Everglades page is displayed. The title and the default meta tag are the only pieces of information currently contained between the start <head> and end </head> tags.

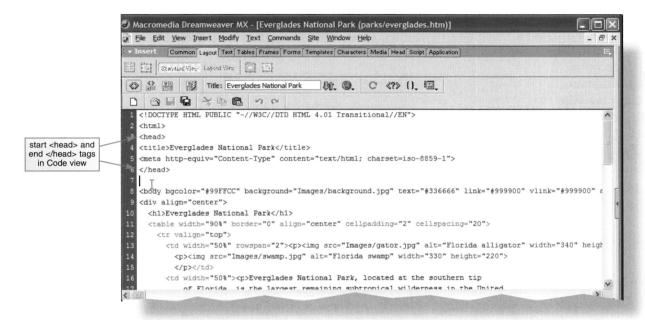

start <head> and
end </head> tags
in Code view

FIGURE 3-111

Head Content Elements

Dreamweaver makes it easy to add content to the head section by providing the Head tab in the Insert bar. The Head tab contains the following elements that can be added to your Web page.

META A <meta> tag contains information about the current document. This information is used by servers, browsers and search engines. HTML documents can have as many <meta> tags as needed, but each item uses a different set of tags.

KEYWORDS Keywords is a list of words that someone would type into a search engine search field.

DESCRIPTION The description contains a sentence or two that can be used in a search engine's results page.

REFRESH The <refresh> tag is processed by the browser to reload the page or load a new page after a specified amount of time has elapsed.

More About

Head Content

Meta tags are information inserted into the head content area of Web pages. The meta description tag allows you to influence the description of a page in the search engines that support the tag. For more information about meta tags, visit the Dreamweaver MX More About Web page (scsite.com/ dreamweavermx/ more.htm) and then click Dreamweaver MX Meta tags.

BASE The base tag sets the base URL to provide an absolute link and/or a link target that the browser can use to resolve link conflicts.

LINK The link element defines a relationship between the current document and another file. This is not the same as a link in the Document window.

Keywords, descriptions, and refresh settings are special-use cases of the meta tag. Complete the following steps to add keywords and a description to the Everglades National Park page.

Steps **To Add Keywords and a Description**

1 **Press the F8 key to display the Site panel and double-click everglades.htm to open the Everglades National Park page. Close the Site panel. Point to the Head tab in the insert bar (Figure 3-112).**

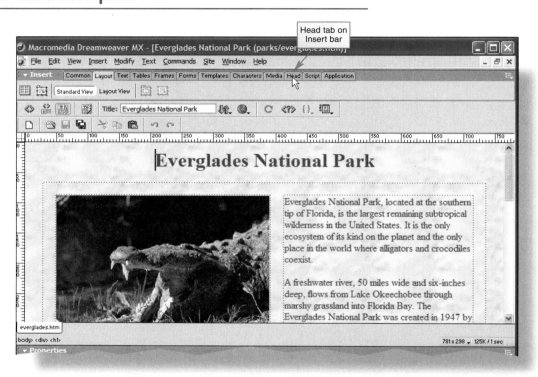

FIGURE 3-112

2 **Click the Head tab.**

The buttons on the Head tab are displayed (Figure 3-113).

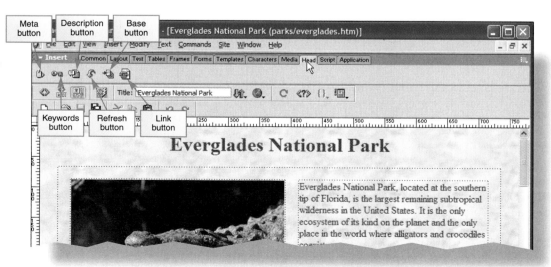

FIGURE 3-113

3 Click the Keywords button on the Head tab. Type the following keywords in the Keywords text box. Separate each keyword with a comma: parks, Florida, national parks, state parks **and then point to the OK button.**

Keywords are added to the Keywords dialog box (Figure 3-114). When a search is done with a search engine for any of the keywords, the Web site address will be displayed in the browser search results.

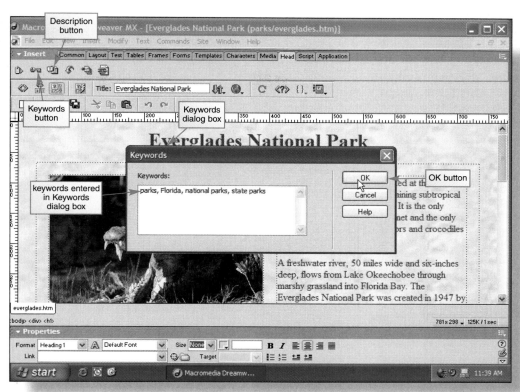

FIGURE 3-114

4 Click the OK button and then click the Description button on the Head tab. Type A Web site featuring Florida state and national parks **in the Description text box and then point to the OK button.**

The Description dialog box is displayed as shown in Figure 3-115.

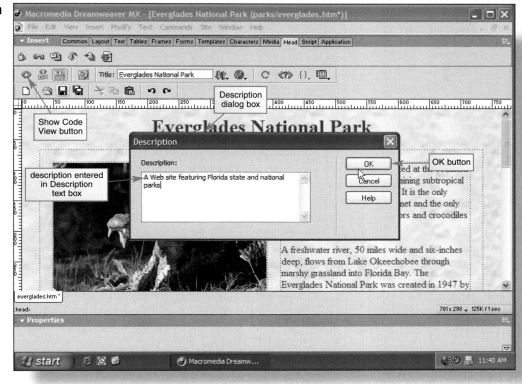

FIGURE 3-115

Dreamweaver MX

5 Click the OK button and then click the **Show Code View** button on the Document toolbar. Point to the Show Design View button.

The keywords and description that you entered are displayed in Code view (Figure 3-116).

6 Click the Show Design View button on the Document toolbar and then click the Save button on the Standard toolbar.

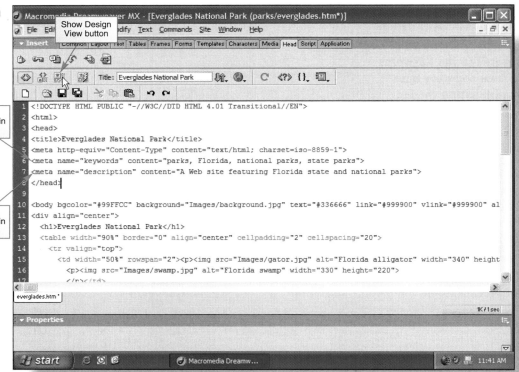

FIGURE 3-116

Other Ways

1. Click Show Code View button on Document toolbar, type keywords code in code window

Publishing a Web Site

In Project 1 you defined a local site, and in Projects 1, 2, and 3, you added Web pages to the local site. This local site resides on your computer's hard disk, a network drive, or possibly a Zip disk. You can view the organization of all files and folders in your site through the Site panel.

To prepare a Web site and make it available for others to view requires that you **publish** your site by putting it on a Web server for public access. A **Web server** is an Internet- or intranet-connected computer that delivers, or *serves up*, Web pages. You **upload** files to a folder on a server and **download** files to a folder in the Site panel. Generally, when Web site designers publish to a folder on a Web site, they do so by using a file transfer (FTP) program such as WS_FTP or Cute FTP. Dreamweaver, however, includes built-in support that enables you to connect and transfer your local site to a Web server without requiring an additional program. To publish to a Web server requires that you have access to a Web server.

Publishing and maintaining your site using Dreamweaver involves the following steps:

1. Use the Site Definition Wizard to enter the FTP information.
2. Specify the Web server to which you want to publish your Web site.
3. Connect to the Web server and upload the files.
4. Synchronize the local and remote sites.

Your school or company may have a server that you can use to upload your Web site. Free Web hosting services such as those provided by Angelfire, Tripod, or GeoCities are other options. These services, as well as many other hosting services, also offer low-cost Web hosting from approximately $3.95 to $9.95 a month. The FreeSite.com contains a list of free and inexpensive hosting services, and FreeWebspace.net provides a PowerSearch form for free and low-cost hosting. Table 3-6 contains a list of Web hosting services. Appendix D contains step-by-step instructions on publishing a Web site to a remote folder.

Table 3-6 Web Site Hosting Services		
NAME	*WEB SITE*	*COST*
Angelfire®	angelfire.lycos.com	Free (ad supported); starting at $4.95 monthly ad free
Yahoo! GeoCities	geocities.yahoo.com	Free (ad supported); starting at $4.95 monthly ad free
Tripod®	tripod.lycos.com/	Free (ad supported); starting at $4.95 monthly ad free
The FreeSite.com	thefreesite.com/Free_Web_Space	A list of free and inexpensive hosting sites
FreeWebspace.net	freewebspace.net	A searchable guide for free Web space

For an updated list of Web site hosting services, visit the Macromedia Dreamweaver Web page (scsite.com/dreamweavermx) and then click Web Hosting. If required by your instructor, publish the Florida Parks Web site to a remote server by following the steps in Appendix D.

With your work completed, you are ready to quit Dreamweaver.

Quitting Dreamweaver

After you add pages to your Web site and add the head content, Project 3 is complete. To close the Web site, quit Dreamweaver MX, and return control to Windows, perform the following step.

TO CLOSE THE WEB SITE AND QUIT DREAMWEAVER

1 Click the Close button on the right corner of the Dreamweaver title bar.

The Dreamweaver window, the Document window, and Florida Parks Web site all close. If you have unsaved changes, Dreamweaver will prompt you to save the changes. Clicking the Yes button in the Dreamweaver MX dialog box saves the changes.

> **More About**
>
> **Publishing Your Florida Parks Web Site**
>
> Appendix D contains step-by-step instructions on publishing the Florida Parks Web site.

CASE PERSPECTIVE SUMMARY

As planned, your team finished designing the three pages for the Florida Parks Web site. Using tables to help with the layout enabled you to design the pages better. Joan obtained server space for your Web site and you used Dreamweaver to define, connect, and upload the Web site. Then, you used Dreamweaver's synchronization feature. All team members agree that this feature will become more important as you continue to expand the site. You shared with Joan and Will the importance of adding head content to all Web pages. Everyone agrees that adding the new pages made the Web site more impressive.

Project Summary

Project 3 introduced you to tables and to Web page design using tables. You created three Web pages, using the Standard view for two pages and the Layout view for the third page. You merged and split cells and learned how to add text and images to the tables. Next, you added a border color and cell background color. Finally, you added head content to one of the Web pages.

What You Should Know

Having completed this project, you now should be able to perform the tasks in Table 3-6.

Table 3-7	Project 3 What You Should Know	
TASK NUMBER	**TASK**	**PAGE NUMBER**
1	Start Dreamweaver and Close Open Panels	DW 3.08
2	Copy Data Files to the Parks Web Site	DW 3.09
3	Add a Color Scheme and Background Image to the Everglades National Park Web Page	DW 3.10
4	Insert and Format the Heading	DW 3.11
5	Display the Insert Bar and Select the Layout Category	DW 3.12
6	Insert a Table Using Standard View	DW 3.13
7	Select and Center a Table	DW 3.21
8	Change Vertical Alignment from Middle to Top	DW 3.23
9	Specify Column Width	DW 3.24
10	Add Everglades National Park Text	DW 3.25
11	Add a Second Table to the Everglades National Park Web Page	DW 3.27
12	Adjust the Table Width	DW 3.30
13	Add Links to the Everglades National Park Page	DW 3.31
14	Merge Two Cells	DW 3.34
15	Add Images to a Standard View Table	DW 3.35
16	Add a Color Scheme and Background Image to the Biscayne National Park Web Page	DW 3.42
17	Insert and Center a Table	DW 3.43
18	Merge Cells in Rows 1 and 3	DW 3.44
19	Add a Heading to Row 1	DW 3.45
20	Adjust the Column Width	DW 3.47
21	Add Text and Images to the Biscayne National Park Web Page	DW 3.49
22	Add Border Color and Cell Background Color	DW 3.54
23	Add Links to and Spell Check the Biscayne National Park Page	DW 3.56
24	Add a Color Scheme and Background Image to the Dry Tortugas National Park Web Page	DW 3.57
25	Display the Ruler	DW 3.59
26	Create the First Layout Table	DW 3.60
27	Add Layout Cells	DW 3.62
28	Add Text and Images to Table 1 of the Dry Tortugas National Park Web Page	DW 3.67
29	Add a Second Table to the Dry Tortugas National Park Web Page	DW 3.71
30	Add the Four Cells to the Dry Tortugas National Park Web Page	DW 3.72
31	Add Content to Table 2 of the Dry Tortugas National Park Page	DW 3.72
32	Center a Table Created in Layout View	DW 3.74
33	Add Keywords and a Description	DW 3.78
34	Close the Web Site and Quit Dreamweaver	DW 3.81

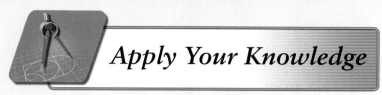

Apply Your Knowledge

1 Modifying the B & B Lawn Service Web

Instructions: Start Dreamweaver. If the panels display, press the F4 key to close all panels. See the inside back cover of this book for instructions for downloading the Data Disk or see your instructor for information on accessing the files in this book.

The B & B Lawn Service Web site currently contains four pages. You will add a fifth page with a table created using Standard View. You use the Untitled-1 window that displays when you start Dreamweaver. The new Web page will include a 7-row, 3-column centered table with a list of services, how often the services are scheduled, and the price of each service. You merge one of the rows and then add and center an image in the row. A border color is applied to the entire table and the first row has a background color applied. Keywords and a description are added. You then add a link to the home page, save the page, and upload the Web site to a Web server. The new page added to the Web site is shown in Figure 3-117. Software and hardware settings determine how a Web page is displayed in a browser. Your Web page may display differently than the one in Figure 3-117. For a selection of images and backgrounds, visit the Dreamweaver MX Media Web page (scsite.com/dreamweavermx/media) and then click Media below Project 3.

Appendix D contains instructions for uploading your local site to a remote site.

1. Display the Insert bar, Property inspector, Standard toolbar, and Site panel. Select Lawn Service from the Site pop-up menu in the Site panel.
2. Use Dreamweaver's integrated file browser to copy the triming.gif image from the Data Files to your /lawn/Images folder.

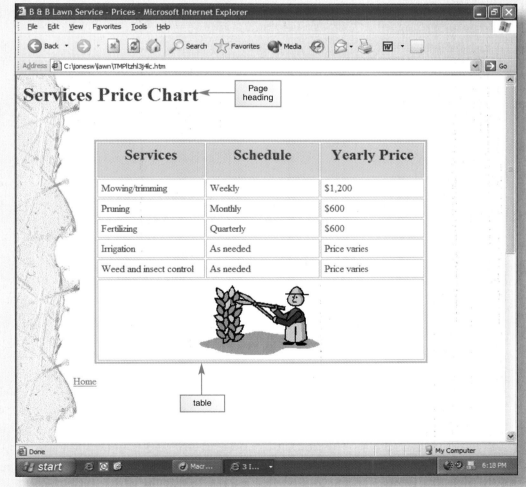

FIGURE 3-117

(continued)

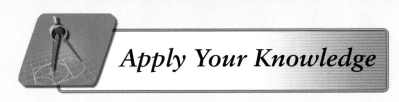

Apply Your Knowledge

Modifying the B & B Lawn Service Web *(continued)*

3. Apply the color scheme you added in Project 1 (Green background and Brown, Yellow, Red text and links). Use the Page Properties dialog box to add the background.gif image and to change the Links color to #CC3333 (Color Cubes palette, row 8 from the top and column 11 from the left).

4. Click the upper-left corner of the Document window. Type Services Price Chart and then apply Heading 1 to the text. Press the ENTER key and then click the Layout tab on the Insert bar. If necessary, click the Standard View button and then click the Insert Table button on the Layout tab. Type the following data in the Insert Table dialog box: 7 for Rows, 5 for Cell Padding, 3 for Columns, 2 for Cell Spacing, 70 for Width, and 3 for Border.

5. Type the text as shown in Table 3-8. Press the TAB key to move from cell to cell.

Table 3-8 Lawn Services Price Chart		
SERVICES	*SCHEDULE*	*YEARLY PRICE*
Mowing/trimming	Weekly	$1,200
Pruning	Monthly	$600
Fertilizing	Quarterly	$600
Irrigation	As needed	Price varies
Weed and insect control	As needed	Price varies

6. Click anywhere in row 1 and then click the <tr> tag in the tag selector to select row 1. Apply Heading 2 and center the heading. Click the Bg box in the Property inspector and apply background color #FF9900 (Color Cubes palette, row 7 from the top and column 3 from the right).

7. Click anywhere in row 7 in the table and then click the <tr> tag in the tag selector to select row 7. Click the Merge Cells button and then click the Align Center button in the Property inspector. With the insertion point in the middle of the merged row 7, drag the triming.gif image to the insertion point. Select the image and then type Tree trimming for the Alt text.

8. Click the <table> tag in the tag selector and then apply border color #FF9900 (Color Cubes palette, row 7 from the top and column 3 from the right). Center the table.

9. Position the insertion point outside the table by clicking to the right of the table. Press the ENTER key and then click the Text Indent button two times. Type Home and then create a relative link to the index.htm file.

10. Click the Head tab on the Insert bar and then click the Keyword button. When the Keyword dialog box is displayed, type lawn service, price schedule, your name in the Keywords text box and then click the OK button. Click the Description button. When the Description dialog box is displayed, type B & B Lawn Service price schedule in the Description text box, and then click the OK button.

11. Title the page B & B Lawn Service - Prices. Check spelling. Save the Web page and name it prices.

12. Print a copy of the page if required by your instructor. Close the Lawn Service Web site. Close Dreamweaver.

1 Adding a Page with a Table to the CandleDust Web Site

Problem: Publicity from the Web site has generated several requests for examples of Mary Stewart's candles. Mary has asked you to add a page to the site that shows some of her creations and the price of each candle. The Web page will have a link to the home page and will be named products. The new page is shown in Figure 3-118. Appendix D contains instructions for uploading your local site to a remote site. For a selection of images and backgrounds, visit the Dreamweaver MX Media Web page (scsite.com/dreamweavermx/media) and then click Media below Project 3.

Instructions: Perform the following tasks:

1. Start Dreamweaver. If necessary, press F4 to close the open panels. Display the Insert bar, Property inspector, Standard toolbar, and Site panel. Select CandleDust from the Site pop-up menu in the Site panel.

2. Use Dreamweaver's integrated file browser to copy the six images (candle3.gif through candle8.gif) from the Data Files to your /candle/Images folder.

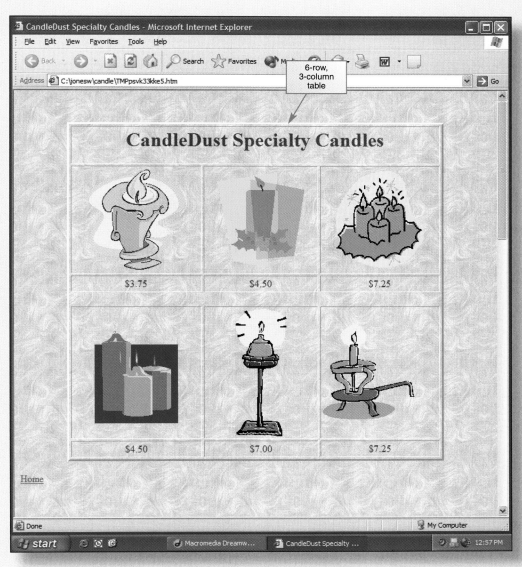

FIGURE 3-118

(continued)

In the Lab

Adding a Page with a Table to the CandleDust Web Site *(continued)*

3. Apply the color scheme you added in Project 1 (Purple background and Blue,Purple,Green text and links). Use the Page Properties dialog box to add the background.gif image. Title the page CandleDust Specialty Candles and save the page as products.

4. Click the upper left corner of the page and then press the ENTER key.

5. If necessary, click the Insert bar's Layout tab, the Standard View button, and then the Insert Table button. Enter the following data in the Insert Table dialog box: 6 for Rows, 3 for Cell Padding, 3 for Columns, 3 for Cell Spacing, 80 for Width, and 3 for Border. Center the table.

6. Merge the three cells in row 1 into one cell. Click the Align Center button in the Property inspector and then type CandleDust Specialty Candles for the heading. Apply Heading 1 to the text heading.

7. Click column 1, row 2 and then drag to select all cells in rows 2 through 6. Click the Align Center button, click the Vert box arrow, and then select Middle. Select column 1, rows 2 through 6. Click the Width box and type 33% as the new width. Repeat this step for column 2, rows 2 through 6, and column 3, rows 2 through 6.

8. Click column 1, row 2 and drag candle3.gif to the insertion point. Repeat this step dragging candle4.gif to column 2, row 2, and candle5.gif to column 3, row 2.

9. Type the following information in row 3: $3.75 in column 1, $4.50 in column 2, and $7.25 in column 3.

10. Merge the three cells in row 4.

11. Click column 1, row 5 and drag candle6.gif to the insertion point. Repeat this step dragging candle7.gif to column 2, row 5, and candle8.gif to column 3, row 5.

12. Type the following information in row 6: $4.50 in column 1, $7.00 in column 2, and $7.25 in column 3.

13. Click outside of the table to the right and then press the ENTER key. Type Home and create a link from the products page to the index.htm page.

14. Save the products page and then view your page in your browser. Verify that your link works. Save the page. Print a copy of the Web page if required and hand it in to your instructor. Close your browser. Close Dreamweaver.

In the Lab

2 Adding a Table Page to the Credit Web Site

Problem: The Credit Protection Web site has become very popular. Marcy receives numerous e-mail messages requesting that the Web site be expanded. Several messages have included a request to provide some hints and tips about how to save money. Marcy asks you to create a new page for the Web site so she can share some of this information. Figure 3-119a shows the table layout, and the Web page is shown in Figure 1-119b on the next page. Appendix D contains instructions for uploading your local site to a remote site. For a selection of images and backgrounds, visit the Dreamweaver MX Media Web page (scsite.com/dreamweavermx/media) and then click Media below Project 3.

Instructions: Perform the following tasks:

1. Start Dreamweaver. Display the Insert bar, Property inspector, Standard toolbar, and Site panel. Select Credit Protection from the Site pop-up menu in the Site panel.
2. Apply the color scheme you added in Project 1 (Yellow background and Green,Blue,Purple text and links) and then add the background image. Title the page Tips and Hints and then save the page with the file name saving.

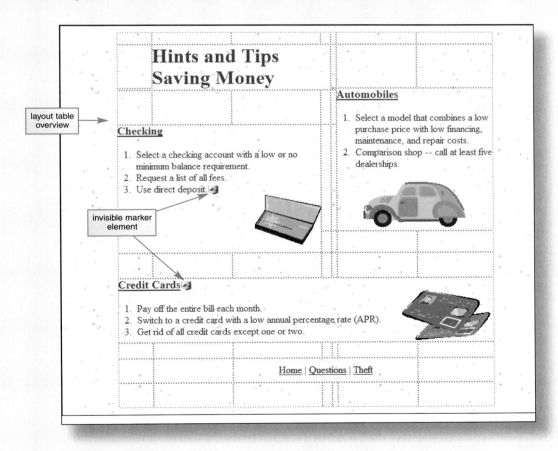

(a) Table Layout

FIGURE 3-119

(continued)

In the Lab

Adding a Table Page to the Credit Web Site *(continued)*

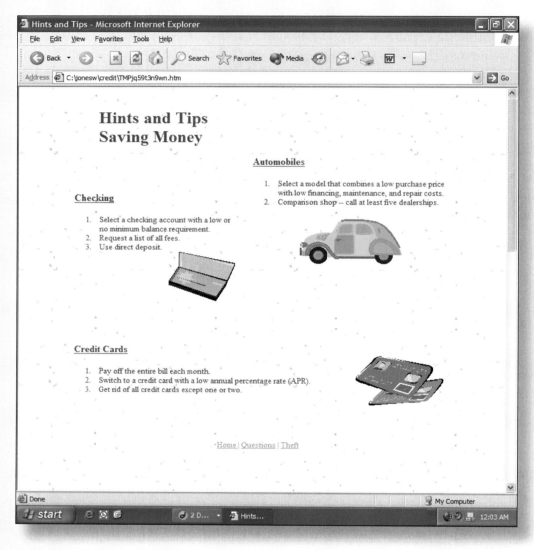

(b) Web Page

FIGURE 3-119 *(continued)*

3. Use Dreamweaver's integrated file browser to copy the three images (car.gif, check.gif, and credit_card.gif) from the Data Files to your /credit/Images folder. Display the ruler. Click the Insert bar's Layout tab and then click the Layout View button.

4. Click the Draw Layout Table button on the Layout tab and then create a table with a fixed width of approximately 600 and a height of approximately 615 pixels.

5. Use Figure 3-119a on the previous page as a guide and draw the five layout cells. Use Table 3-9 for widths and heights.

In the Lab

Table 3-9	Credit Protection Cell Layout Guide				
NUMBER	*CELL NAME*	*W*	*H*	*IMAGE ALT TEXT*	*IMAGE NAME*
1	Heading	285	75	None	None
2	Checking	325	210	Checking Account	check.gif
3	Automobiles	250	235	Car	car.gif
4	Credit Cards	600	105	Credit Cards	credit_card.gif
5	Links	295	40	None	None

6. Use Figure 3-119a as a reference and type the text into each of the layout cells. Apply Heading 1 to the text in the first cell. Apply Heading 3 to the headings in cells 2 through 4 and then underline the headings.

7. Insert the images into the cells. Refer to the invisible element marker in Figure 3-119a as the insertion point for the images in cells 2 and 4. For cell 3, press the ENTER key after item 2 and then click the Align Center button in the Property inspector. Drag the car.gif to the insertion point.

8. Add relative links to the three text items in cell 5.

9. Click the Standard View button on the Layout tab, select the table, and then center the table.

10. Click the Head tab in the Insert bar and then click the Description button. Click the Keyword button and then type credit, money, tips, checking, saving, your name in the Keywords dialog box. Click the Description button and then type Tips and hints on how to save money in the Description dialog box. Save the Web page as saving.

11. View the Web site in your browser and verify that your links work. Close the browser. If required, print a copy for your instructor.

3 Adding a Table Page to the Plant City Web Site

Problem: In his job as a member of the Plant City marketing group, Juan Benito has been exploring the city's history. On a recent tour, Juan discovered that the city contains many well-preserved historic homes. He would like to feature some of these homes on the Web site and has requested that you add a new page to the Plant City Web site. You elect to use a layout table to create this page. Figure 3-120a shows the layout table, and the Web page is displayed in 3-120b. Appendix D contains instructions for uploading your local site to a remote site. For a selection of images and backgrounds, visit the Dreamweaver MX Media Web page (scsite.com/dreamweavermx/media) and then click Media below Project 3.

Instructions: Perform the following tasks:

1. Start Dreamweaver. Display the Insert bar, Property inspector, Standard toolbar, and Site panel. Select Plant City from the Site pop-up menu in the Site panel.

2. Add the background image border you added in Project 2. Title the page Plant City, Florida - Historic Homes and then save the page with the file name homes.

(continued)

In the Lab

Adding a Table Page to the Plant City Web Site *(continued)*

3. Use Dreamweaver's integrated file browser to copy the four images (house01.gif through house04.gif) from the Data Files to your /city/Images folder. Display the ruler. Click the Insert bar's Layout tab and then click the Layout View button.

4. Create a layout table with a fixed width of approximately 650 and a height of approximately 675 pixels.

5. Use Figure 3-120a as a guide and draw the 10 layout cells. Use Table 3-10 on page DW 3.92 for widths, heights, and file names.

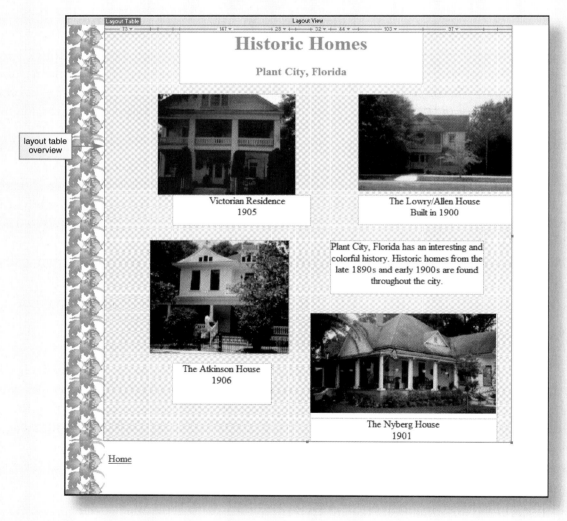

(a) Table Layout

FIGURE 3-120

In the Lab

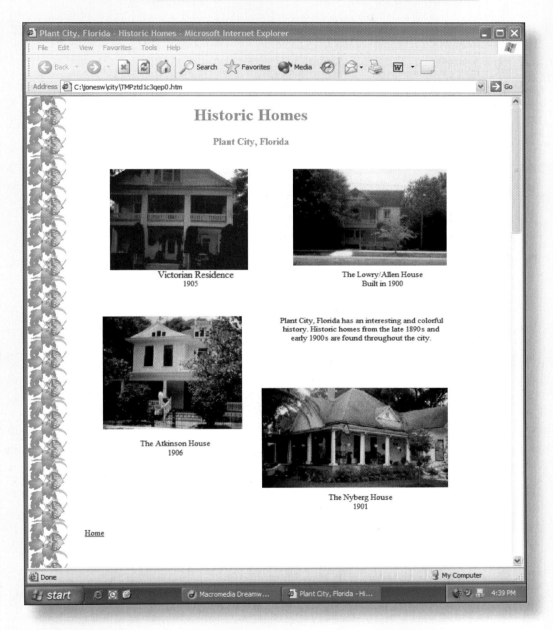

(b) Web Page

FIGURE 3-120 (continued)

(continued)

In the Lab

Adding a Table Page to the Plant City Web Site *(continued)*

Table 3-10	Plant City Cell Layout Guide				
NUMBER	*CELL NAME*	*W*	*H*	*IMAGE ALT TEXT*	*FILE NAME*
1	Heading	390	85	None	None
2	Victorian House	220	160	Victorian House	house01.gif
3	Text	220	50	None	None
4	Atkinson House	225	190	Atkinson House	house02.gif
5	Text	160	70	None	None
6	Lowry/Allen House	245	160	Lowry/Allen House	house03.gif
7	Text	245	50	None	None
8	Text	245	90	None	None
9	Nyberg House	300	170	Nyberg House	house04.gif
10	Text	300	40	None	None

6. Use Figure 3-120a on page DW 3.90 as a reference and type the text into each of the layout cells. Apply Heading 1 to the first line of text in the first cell and Heading 3 to the second line of text.
7. Insert the images into the cells. Refer to Table 3-10 for the image file names.
8. Click the Standard View button on the Layout tab, select the table, and then center the table.
9. Click the Keywords button, and then type Plant City, Florida, homes, history, your name in the Keywords dialog box. Click the Description button and then type A tour of Plant City, Florida historic homes in the Description dialog box.
10. View the Web site in your browser. Close the browser. If required, print a copy for your instructor.

Cases and Places

The difficulty of these case studies varies:
▶ are the least difficult; ▶▶ are more difficult; and ▶▶▶ are the most difficult.

1 ▶ The sports Web site has become very popular. Several of your friends have suggested that you add a statistics page. You agree that this is a good idea. Create the new page. Using the Internet or other resources, find statistics about your selected sport. Add a background image to the page and use Standard view to insert a table that contains your statistical information. Add an appropriate heading to the table and an appropriate title for the page. Create a link to the home page. Save the page in your sports Web site. For a selection of images and backgrounds, visit the Dreamweaver MX Media Web page (scsite.com/dreamweavermx/media) and then click Media below Project 3.

2 ▶ Modify your hobby Web site. Expand the topic and add an additional page with a table created in Standard view. The table should contain a minimum of three rows, three columns, and a 2-pixel border. Include information in the table about your hobby. Include a minimum of two images in the table. Merge one of the rows or one of the columns and add a border color. Add a background image to the page and give your page a title. Create a link to the home page. Save the page in your hobby Web site. For a selection of images and backgrounds, visit the Dreamweaver MX Media Web page (scsite.com/dreamweavermx/media) and then click Media below Project 3.

3 ▶▶ Modify your favorite type of music Web site by adding a new page. The new page should contain a table with three columns and four rows created in Standard view. Merge one of the rows and add a background color to the row. Add at least two images to your table. Center the images in the cell. View your Web pages in your browser. Give your page a title and save the page in your music subfolder. Appendix D contains instructions for uploading your local site to a remote site. For a selection of images and backgrounds, visit the Dreamweaver MX Media Web page (scsite.com/dreamweavermx/media) and then click Media below Project 3.

4 ▶▶ Your running for office campaign is going well. You want to add a new page to the Web site to include pictures and text listing some of your outstanding achievements. Apply a color scheme and a background image to the page. Draw a layout table with a minimum of four layout cells. Include your picture in one of the cells. Add an appropriate title, keywords, and a description to the page. Center the table. Save the page in the office subfolder and then view the page in your browser. Appendix D contains instructions for uploading your local site to a remote site. For a selection of images and backgrounds, visit the Dreamweaver MX Media Web page (scsite.com/dreamweavermx/media) and then click Media below Project 3.

Cases and Places

5 ▶▶▶ The students at your school are requesting more information about the student trips. Add another page to the student trips Web site. Add a heading and format it appropriately. Draw a layout table with a minimum of six layout cells. Include an image in three of the cells and text describing the three possible school trip destinations in the other three cells. Format the text and center the table. Center the images in each of three cells and add Alt text for each. Add a title, keywords, meta tags, and a description. Save the page and view it in your browser. Appendix D contains instructions for uploading your local site to a remote site. For a selection of images and backgrounds, visit the Dreamweaver MX Media Web page (scsite.com/dreamweavermx/media) and then click Media below Project 3.

Macromedia Dreamweaver MX

PROJECT

Page Layout
with Frames

O B J E C T I V E S

You will have mastered the material in this project when you can:

- Describe the advantages and disadvantages of using frames on a Web page
- Describe frameset layout and properties
- Create a frameset and frames
- Define frames and describe how they work
- Delete a frame
- Set the properties for a frame and for a frameset
- Apply and modify the properties of a frame
- Add static content to a frame using the main content frame
- Add Flash buttons as navigation elements
- Save the frame and frameset

Macromedia Dreamweaver MX

Page Layout with Frames

CASE PERSPECTIVE

The Florida Parks Web site is very popular and is receiving numerous hits each day. Will received 43 e-mail messages last week asking for more general information about Florida State Parks. The messages included questions such as the cost to visit a park, accessibility options, whether pets are allowed, and so on. Will shares the e-mail messages with you and Joan and explains that answering these messages is very time-consuming. He asks if either of you have any suggestions or solutions for how he can respond in a more efficient way.

Joan suggests that adding additional pages to the existing Web site could be one solution. Everyone agrees that this is a good idea, but Will expresses concern that the main Web site focuses on different parks and this is a more general topic. You suggest that a new Web site be created and that it be a subsection of the main Web site. Joan further suggests that frames be used to keep this Web site compact and easy to navigate. The team agrees that this is the best solution and that a framed Web site containing general information about Florida parks is a good addition.

Introduction

You learned in Project 3 that you can use tables to control the arrangement or layout of items on a Web page. Frames are another layout option and a unique way to design the presentation of your Web pages and Web sites. This project focuses on creating a Web site using frames and examines the advantages and disadvantages of using a framed Web site.

Web designers use frames to present information in a more flexible and useful fashion. A **frame** is an area that acts as an independent browser window and acts independently of other regions in the window. Using frames, a Web page is divided into multiple, scrollable regions, or panes; and each frame contains its own source document. For instance, you could have four different HTML documents displaying in a single window.

When pages in a Web site share many of the same links and images, creating and maintaining these links for each page involves considerable duplication. With frames, you can create a Web page to display the common links in one frame and display the linked target Web pages in another frame. Some typical uses of frames include displaying a navigation bar consisting of links in one frame and displaying the corresponding Web pages in another; placing a number of images in one frame and displaying the accompanying descriptions and details in another; and placing a list of vocabulary words in one frame and displaying their definitions in another.

With frames, a Web page designer can place elements the user always should see, such as navigation buttons and title graphics, in static frames that do not change. As the user navigates the site, the static frame's contents remain fixed, even as

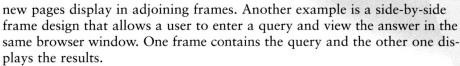

new pages display in adjoining frames. Another example is a side-by-side frame design that allows a user to enter a query and view the answer in the same browser window. One frame contains the query and the other one displays the results.

Although most Web browsers support frames, some Web site visitors may have older browsers that do not support frames or may prefer a no-frames version. Developers of sites that use frames often create an alternative set of pages without frames to display to those users.

Project Four — Florida Parks Web Page Layout with Frames

In this project, you learn to use frames to create and display general information for a new local site that will be a subsection of the Florida Parks Web site.

The frameset, which is an HTML file that defines the layout and properties of a set of frames, will display three frames. The top frame is a single-row, one-column static frame that contains a title graphic. The second row contains two columns with a left frame and a right frame. The left frame is the navigate frame and contains Flash buttons that link to content files. The right frame is the main frame, which will display the linked content files. When a visitor clicks one of the buttons in the left frame, related park information is displayed in the right frame. The navigate frame contains five buttons. Clicking any of the first four buttons displays the associated page in the right frame (Figures 4-1a, 4-1b, 4-1c, and 4-1d on pages DW 4.04 and DW 4.05). The Home button breaks out of the frames and returns to the main Florida Parks Web site index page.

Borders separate the frames. The right frame is scrollable and contains a scroll bar. Each button in the navigate frame contains text to meet Web design accessibility standards.

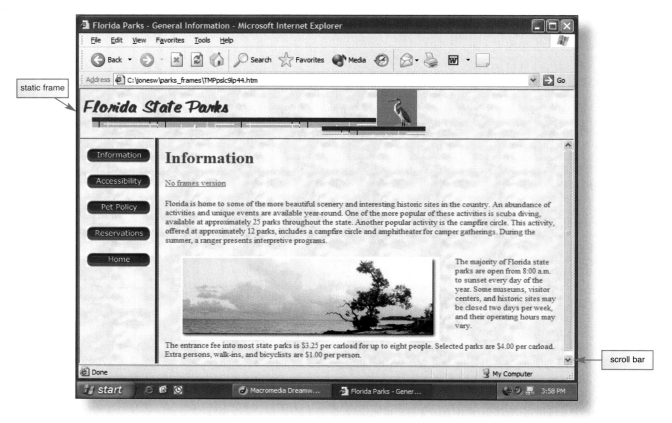

(a) Information Frame

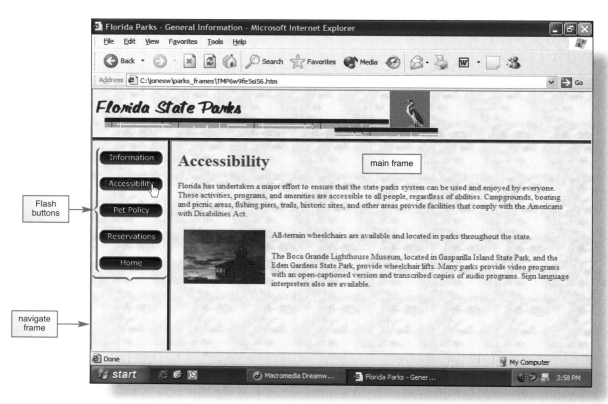

(b) Accessibility Frame

FIGURE 4-1

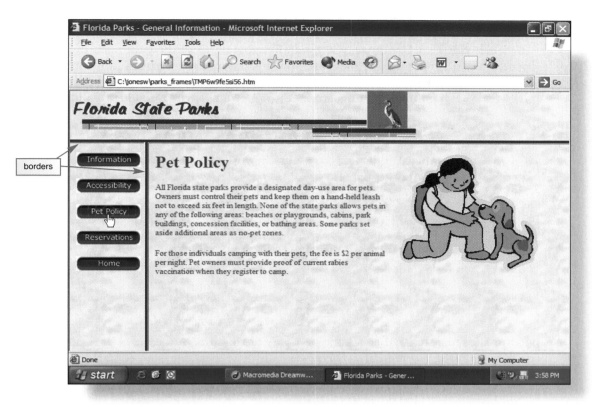

(c) Pet Policy Frame

(d) Reservations Frame

FIGURE 4-1 (*continued*)

Starting Dreamweaver and Closing Open Panels

When you start Dreamweaver, generally most or all of the panels are displayed by default. Closing unused panels provides uncluttered workspace in the Document window. Closing unused open panels allows you to organize your workspace and gives you the maximum window space in the Dreamweaver Document window.

TO START DREAMWEAVER AND CLOSE OPEN PANELS

1 Start Dreamweaver. If necessary, maximize the Document window. Press the F4 key to close all open panels.

2 Press the F8 key to display the Site panel.

3 If necessary, use the View menu to display the Standard toolbar.

4 Use the Window menu to display the Property inspector.

Workspace Organization

Creating a separate local site is the best way to organize and control the number of pages within the Florida Parks Web site. This new, local site, named Parks_Frames, will be linked later to the main Florida Parks Web site. Before you begin these steps, verify with your instructor whether you are to complete the section on publishing to a remote server. You will need this information in Step 5 when you create a local site. After creating your local site, you will use the Dreamweaver integrated file browser to copy Project 4 data files. Perform the following steps to create a local site.

TO CREATE A LOCAL SITE

1 Click Site on the menu bar and then click New Site to display the Site Definition dialog box. If necessary, click the Basic tab.

2 Type Parks_Frames in the What would you like to name your site? text box and then click the Next button to display the Editing Files, Part 2 options.

3 If necessary, click No, I do not want to use a server technology and then click the Next button to display the Editing Files, Part 3 options.

4 If necessary, click Edit local copies on my machine, then upload to server when ready (recommended). If necessary, change the Where on your computer do you want to store your files? path to C:\ or the location designated by your instructor. Click the Folder icon to the right of the Where do you want to store your files? text box. Create a new folder under C:\jonesw and name it Parks_Frames so the path will be C:\jonesw\Parks_Frames. Click the Next button to display the Sharing Files options.

5 Click the How do you connect to your remote server? box arrow. Verify with your instructor if you are to select None or if you are to complete the information on publishing to a remote server. Appendix D contains information on how to publish your site to a remote server. If you are to publish to a remote server, follow the instructions in Appendix D. Otherwise, select None. Click the Next button to display the Sharing Files, Part 2 options.

6 If necessary, click No, do not enable check in and check out (this is displayed only if you selected instructions to publish to a remote site). Click the Next button to display the Summary options.

7 Verify that the Summary options are correct and then click the Done button to return to Dreamweaver.

The new Parks_Frames site is created (Figure 4-2).

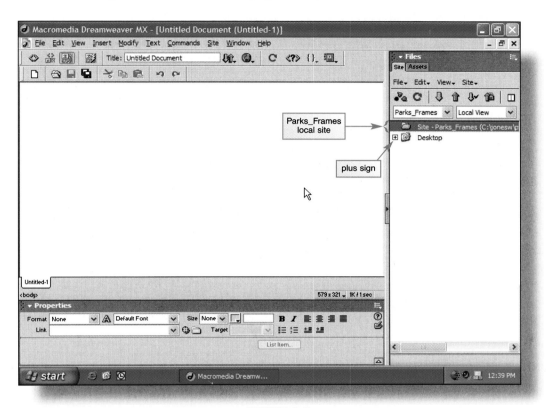

FIGURE 4-2

The frames Web site you create in this project requires additional HTML documents and images. These documents and images need to be copied from the Data Files folder to the Parks_Frames Web site.

Copying Data Files to the Local Web Site

Your Data Disk contains HTML documents, an Images folder, and a no_frames folder for Project 4. These four HTML documents and the Images and no_frames folders are located in the Proj04 folder. You use Dreamweaver's integrated file browser to copy the Project 4 documents and images to the Parks_Frames folder.

The Data Files folder for this project is stored on Local Disk (C:). The location on your computer may be different. If necessary, verify with your instructor the location of the Data Files folder. Complete the following steps to copy the files and folders to the C:\jonesw\Parks_Frames local root folder.

TO COPY DATA FILES TO THE PARKS_FRAMES WEB SITE

1 Click the plus sign (+) to the left of the Desktop icon in the Site panel. Click the plus sign to the left of the My Computer icon and then navigate through the file hierarchy to the Data Files folder as you did in Project 2 on pages DW 2.09 – 2.14.

2 Click the plus sign to the left of the Proj04 folder and then click the plus sign to the left of the Parks_Frames folder.

3 Click the Images folder.

4 Hold down the SHIFT key, click the no_frames folder, and then click reservations.htm (or the last file if your list is sorted in a different order).

5 Copy the Images and no_frames folders and the four HTML documents using Copy and Paste on the context menu to the C:\jonesw\Parks_Frames local root folder.

6 Click the minus sign to the left of the Desktop icon to collapse the file list.

The Project 4 HTML documents, Images folder, and no_frames folder are pasted into the Parks_Frames local root folder (Figure 4-3).

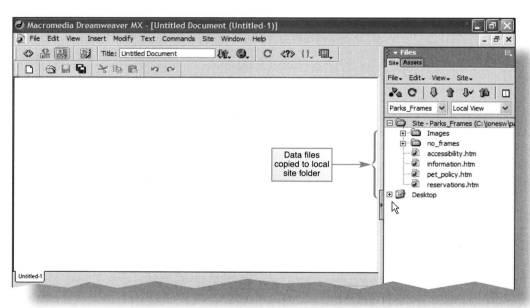

Frames versus Tables

When creating your page design, you may be confused when deciding between frames or tables. Frames are used more frequently for navigation but can be difficult to create and implement. For more information about frames versus tables, visit the Dreamweaver MX More About Web page (scsite.com/ dreamweavermx/ more.htm) and then click Frames versus Tables.

FIGURE 4-3

Advantages and Disadvantages of Frames

Frames became a standard on Web pages with the release of Netscape Navigator 2.0 and were added to the HTML specification with HTML 4.0. After being added to the standard, they experienced immediate popularity and became widely used as a design tool. Designing with frames, however, can be challenging. The complexity of designing with frames is particularly difficult for inexperienced Web site authors. As a result, poorly designed frame-based Web sites became fairly common. This resulted in a controversy among Web site developers and users regarding the value and use of frames for Web site development.

When frames are well designed and used for specific purposes, however, they can be very useful. Some advantages of using frames include the following:

- Navigation-related graphics do not have to be reloaded for every page in the Web site.
- Each frame can have its own scroll bar, permitting the visitor to scroll the frames independently.
- Static content remains fixed.
- Content and navigation can be separated from each other in a clear way.

Users who dislike frames generally have encountered sites that use frames poorly or unnecessarily. Or, they may dislike frames for some of the following disadvantages:

- Frames are difficult to bookmark or to add to favorites.
- Some browsers do not provide good frame support.
- Frames may be difficult to navigate for visitors with disabilities.
- Printing may be a problem.
- Pages that are displayed in the main frame are displayed in a smaller window than when displayed in a full browser window.

Several of the disadvantages, however, are compensated for in the more recent versions of the major browsers. When viewing a frame-based site in a browser, right-clicking in a particular frame displays a context menu with a number of commands, including Add to Favorites, View Source, and Print. Selecting the Print command displays the Print dialog box that includes options to print just the selected frame, to print all frames individually, to print as laid out on the screen, to print all linked documents, and to print a table of links.

Frameset and Frame Basics

Creating a framed Web site is more complex than creating a Web page without frames. The <BODY> tag is not used to create a framed page. Instead, a **frameset** defines the layout of the frames when displayed on the screen. A frameset requires a combination of two HTML tags: <FRAMESET> and <FRAME>. Most Web site developers also include the <NOFRAMES> tag for those users whose browsers do not support frames or for those who prefer a no-frames version. Dreamweaver automatically includes the <NOFRAMES> tag when the frameset is created.

Frameset Layout

Frames on a page function independently of one another. A separate HTML document is loaded into each frame. To create a framed Web page requires an accompanying file called a frameset. The frameset is an underlying HTML document that defines the layout and properties of a set of frames and then displays navigation elements, title graphics, content documents, and so on inside the defined frames.

Compare the frameset to a sectioned box, such as a desk drawer organizer. Each section of the box is designed to hold a specific item such as pens, pencils, paper clips, and so on. The design of each section of the box determines what should be placed within that section. The frameset works in a similar way. The <FRAME> tags within the frameset provide information to the browser about what a set of frames displays and what documents are displayed in the frames. Some frames may contain static documents such as title graphics, while the content in other frames changes based on the provided navigation options.

More About

Designing with Frames

Many Web sites consist of a narrow left frame and a wide right frame. The navigation links are displayed in the left frame and the site's main content is displayed on the right. Other site designs may split the window vertically. The site's title and navigation links appear in a narrow top frame and the main content appears in a wider lower frame. For more information about frame design, visit the Dreamweaver MX More About Web page (scsite.com/ dreamweavermx/ more.htm) and then click Frame Design.

Creating the Frameset

Dreamweaver provides two methods for creating a frameset: you can design it or you can use a predefined frameset. You design a frameset in the following way:

- Display a new Document window.
- Click Modify on the menu bar, select Frameset, and then select Split Frame Left, Split Frame Right, Split Frame Up, or Split Frame Down on the Frameset submenu.

To split the frame into smaller sections, use one of the following methods:

- Click the frame and then select Split Frame Left, Split Frame Right, Split Frame Up, or Split Frame Down on the Frameset submenu.
- To split a frame or set of frames vertically or horizontally, drag a frame border from the edge of the Design view into the middle of the Design view.
- To split a frame using a frame border that is not at the edge of the Design view, press the ALT key and then drag a frame border.
- To divide a frame into four frames, drag a frame border from one of the corners of the Design view into the middle of a frame.

Figure 4-4 contains an example of a frameset created using the Split Frame Left command. The Frames panel (discussed later in this project) is displayed on the right side of the screen. Notice that (no name) appears in both frames.

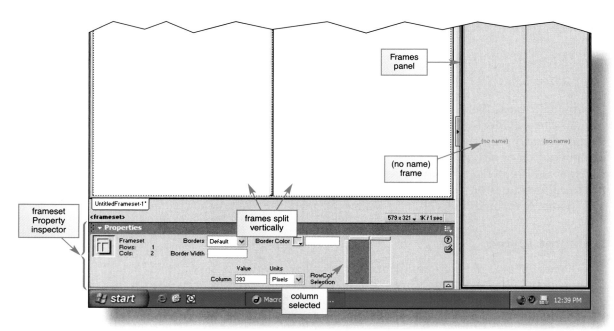

FIGURE 4-4

The second method for creating a frameset in Dreamweaver is to use a predefined frameset. A **predefined frameset** provides a visual representation of how the framed window will display. You can use a predefined frameset as a starting point and then modify the frameset using one or more of the options listed previously for splitting frames or you can use the predefined frameset without modifications.

Dreamweaver provides two methods to create the predefined frameset: the Frames category of the Insert bar and the New Document dialog box. The Insert bar Frames category generally is used to create a predefined frameset and, at the same time, display an existing document in one of the frames. The New Document dialog box is used to create a new empty predefined frameset.

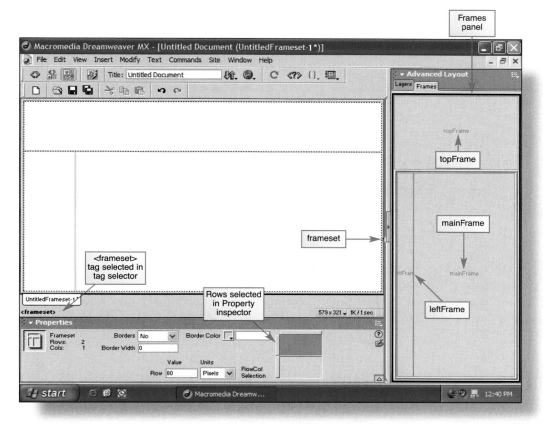

FIGURE 4-5

In this project, you use the New Document dialog box to create a predefined nested frameset, such as the one shown in Figure 4-5. Notice, in Figure 4-5, that Dreamweaver names the frames in the Frames panel: topFrame, leftFrame, and mainFrame. The primary frameset is selected as indicated by the <frameset> tag in the tag selector and the dark border surrounding the frame in the Frames panel. In the Property inspector, rows are selected.

A frameset inside another frameset is called a **nested frameset**. Most framesets contain nested framesets, and most Web pages that use frames use nested frames. The majority of the predefined framesets in Dreamweaver also use nesting. A single frameset file can contain multiple nested framesets. Any set of frames in which different numbers of frames are in different rows or columns creates a nested frameset.

The most common frame layout has one frame in the top row and two frames in the second row. Generally, the top frame contains a title graphic or logo. The left frame in the second row usually is a navigate frame and the right frame generally is the main frame that displays the linked content. In this example, the second row is the nested frameset. As shown in Figure 4-6 on the next page, the tag selector displays a second <frameset> tag and the dark border surrounds the second row. In the Property inspector, Columns is selected.

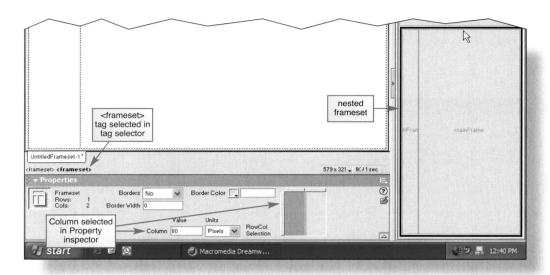

FIGURE 4-6

You copied the images necessary to begin creating the new framed Web site to the parks_frames local root folder in the Site panel. You begin the project by using a visual aid to make the frame borders visible in the Document window. Then you create, name, and save the frameset. Complete the following steps to display the frame borders.

Steps **To Display Frame Borders**

1 Click View on the menu bar, point to Visual Aids, and then point to Frame Borders on the Visual Aids submenu (Figure 4-7).

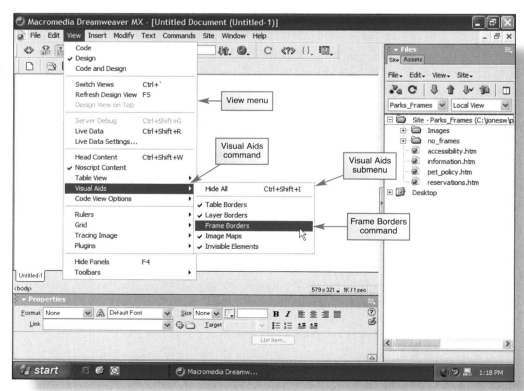

FIGURE 4-7

2 **Click Frame Borders.**

Frame borders are turned on (Figure 4-8). An outline of the frame borders will be displayed in the Document window when the frameset is created.

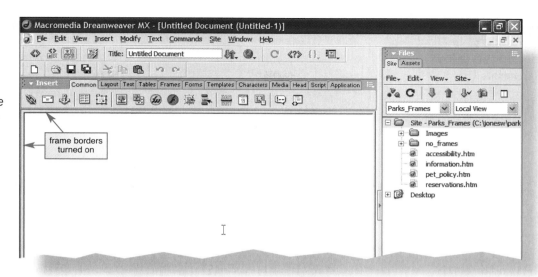

frame borders turned on

FIGURE 4-8

Other Ways

1. On Insert menu click Frames, select frameset

With the frame borders turned on, the next step is to create the frameset. Complete the following steps to create the frameset.

Steps **To Create the Frameset**

1 **Close the Untitled-1 window. Click File on the menu bar and then click New. If necessary, click the General tab. Point to Framesets in the Category list.**

The New Document dialog box is displayed (Figure 4-9).

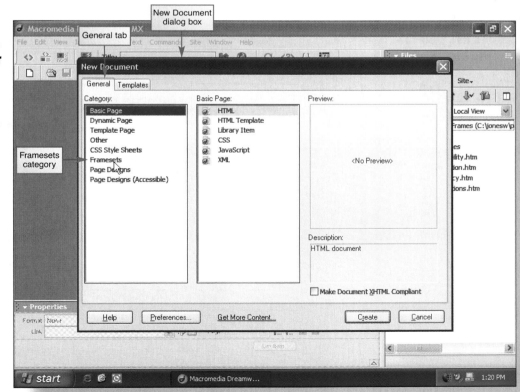

New Document dialog box

General tab

Framesets category

FIGURE 4-9

2 **Click Framesets. Point to Fixed Top, Nested Left in the Framesets list.**

The Framesets category is displayed within the New Document dialog box. The Framesets category contains fifteen predefined framesets. The Fixed Bottom frameset is selected, as indicated by the preview and description displayed in the right pane (Figure 4-10). Your selection might be different.

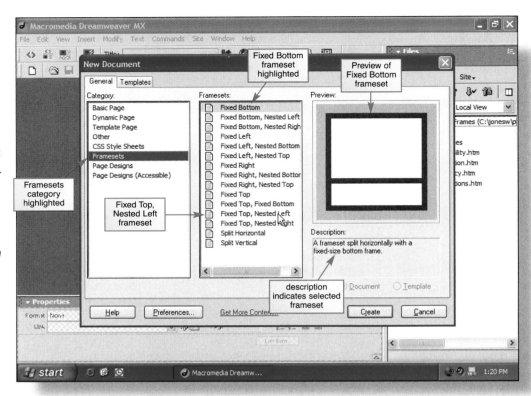

FIGURE 4-10

3 **Click Fixed Top, Nested Left in the Framesets list. Point to the Create button.**

The Fixed Top, Nested Left frameset is selected. A preview and description of the selected frameset is displayed in the right pane (Figure 4-11).

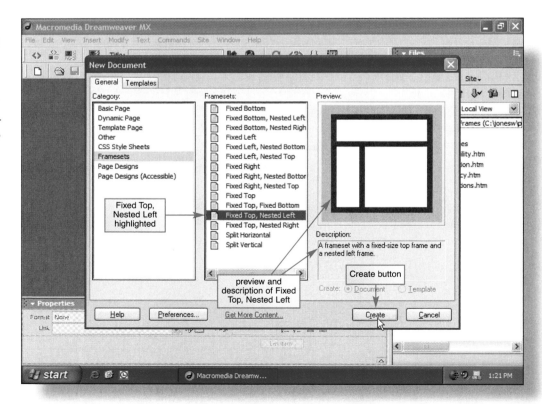

FIGURE 4-11

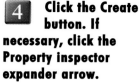

4 **Click the Create button. If necessary, click the Property inspector expander arrow.**

The UntitledFrameset-1 displays in the Document window (Figure 4-12). The dotted border around the frameset indicates that the frameset is selected. The Property inspector displays attributes relevant to the frameset. The tag selector displays the <frameset> tag. The UntitledFrameset-1 tab may display a different number on your computer.

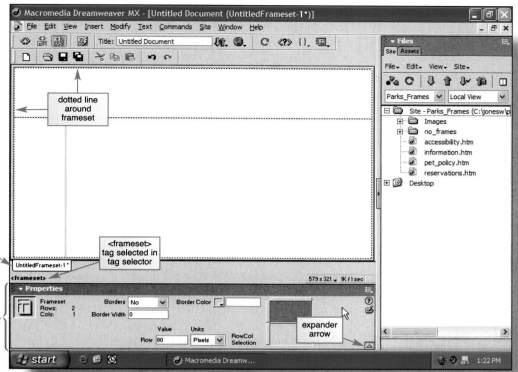

FIGURE 4-12

Frameset Properties

Similar to many other objects in Dreamweaver, the frameset also has its own Property inspector that displays when a frameset is selected. This Property inspector displays frameset properties when a frameset is selected in the Document window. Clicking the expander arrow in the lower-right corner expands the Property inspector to show additional attributes.

Dreamweaver determines the default attributes used for each predefined frameset. These default attributes are applied automatically to each frame. In the Fixed Top, Nested Left example, the mainFrame default is no borders, no scroll bars, and no resizing of frames in the browser. Using the Property inspector, however, these attributes are changed easily and additional attributes can be applied. The following section describes the frameset-related features of the Property inspector (Figure 4-13). The Property inspector for frames is discussed later in this project.

More About

Inserting a Predefined Frameset

Dreamweaver's predefined framesets make it easy for you to select the type of frameset you want to create. To insert a predefined frameset, the Dreamweaver Document window must be open in Design view.

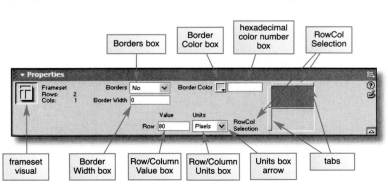

FIGURE 4-13

FRAMESET VISUAL A visual representation of a frameset is displayed in the upper-left corner of the Property inspector. This visual is generated automatically and cannot be altered through the Property inspector.

BORDERS **Borders** determines if borders should appear around frames when the document is viewed in a browser. Clicking the Border box arrow to the right of the Borders box displays three options: Yes, No, and Default. Selecting Yes causes borders to display around the frames when the Web page is viewed in a browser. Selecting No causes borders not to display in the browser. Selecting Default allows the user's browser to determine how borders are displayed.

BORDER WIDTH In the **Border Width** box, a number specifies a width for all the borders in the frameset.

BORDER COLOR Use the color box to select a **Border Color**, or type the hexadecimal value for a color in the related text box.

FRAMESET COLUMN SIZES AND ROW SIZES The **RowCol Selection** box on the right side of the Property inspector is a visual representation of the frameset. On the top and left sides of the box are tabs. Click a tab on the left side of the RowCol Selection area to select a row, or click a tab on the top to select a column. When the row is selected, you enter a height for the selected row. When a column is selected, you enter a width for the selected column. When you click the **Units** box arrow, three options are displayed: Pixels, Percent, and Relative. Table 4-1 contains information about these three size options.

In Figures 4-12 and 4-13 on page DW 4.15, the RowCol Selection in the Property inspector contains rows only, which can be confusing because the Document window (Figure 4-12) displays two columns in row 2. Recall, however, that this frameset contains a nested frameset. If the nested frameset is selected, then the Property inspector displays two columns instead of two rows in the RowCol Selection area.

Table 4-1	Frameset Row and Column Size Measurements
UNIT	**RESULT**
Pixels	Sets the size of the row or column to an absolute value. This option is the best choice for a frame that always should be the same size, such as a title frame or navigate frame.
Percent	A percentage-based frame stretches and shrinks based on the width of a browser window. Frames with Units set to Percent are allocated space after frames with Units set to Pixels, but before frames with Units set to Relative.
Relative	Relative specifies that the selected column or row be allocated the leftover space after pixels and percent frames have had space allocated; the remaining space is divided proportionally among the frames with sizes set to Relative.

Selecting and Naming Frames and the Frameset

Selecting framesets and frames can be somewhat complex. Dreamweaver provides two basic ways to select a frame or frameset: select the frame or frameset directly in the Document window or use the Frames panel.

Selecting Framesets and Frames in the Document Window

In the Document window, clicking a frame border selects the frameset that contains the frame. When a frameset is selected, all the borders of the frames within the frameset are outlined with a dotted border. To select a frame in the Document window, hold down the ALT key and click inside the frame. When a frame is selected, its borders are outlined with a dotted border.

Displaying the Frames Panel

The easiest method to select a frame or frameset is to use the Frames panel. In the Frames panel, clicking within a frame or on a frame border selects that frame. Clicking the frameset border selects the frameset. The following steps display the Frames panel.

Steps | To Display the Frames Panel

1 Click Window on the menu bar, point to Others, and then point to Frames (Figure 4-14).

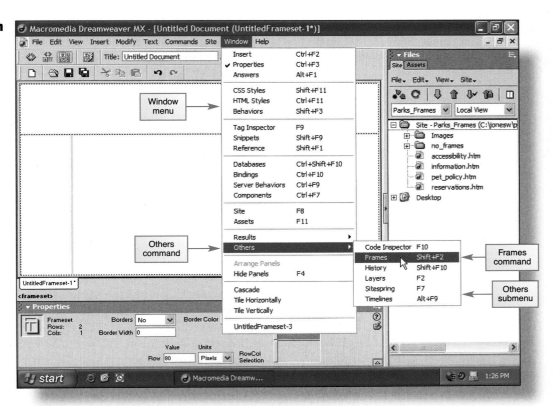

FIGURE 4-14

2 **Click Frames.**

The Advanced Layout panel group is displayed and the Frames tab is selected (Figure 4-15). A dark border appears around the frameset in the Frames panel. The <frameset> tag is displayed in the tag selector, indicating the frameset is selected. Each frameset within the Frames panel has a name: topFrame, leftFrame, and mainFrame. Dreamweaver automatically names these frames.

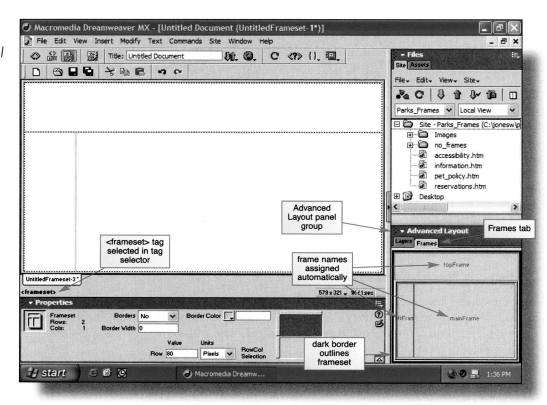

FIGURE 4-15

Other Ways

1. Press SHIFT+F2

Naming and Saving the Frameset

The frameset and the frame documents must be saved before you can preview framed pages in a browser. When you use visual tools in Dreamweaver to create a set of frames, each new document that appears in a frame is given a default file name. As indicated earlier in this project, when you create a frameset using a predefined frameset, the frames are given names such as topFrame, leftFrame, and so on in the Frames panel. These are not the default names Dreamweaver uses, however, when you select one of the Save commands. Instead, the first frameset file is named UntitledFrameset-1, while the first document in a frame is named UntitledFrame-1, and so on. You can use the default names to save the frameset and frames, but you might find it less confusing if you provide meaningful names to the frameset and the frames. Frames and framesets also should be given titles. You add a title to a frame or frameset the same way you added a title to previous HTML documents: through the Page Properties dialog box or by typing the title in the Title text box on the Document toolbar. In this project, you use the same title for all the framesets and frames: Florida Parks – General Information.

Dreamweaver provides several options for saving your documents. You can save each frameset file and framed document individually, or you can save the frameset file and all documents appearing in frames at once. In this project, you save the frameset and each frame separately. The frameset is named index. Complete the following steps to name and save the frameset.

Steps **To Name and Save the Frameset**

1 **Verify that <frameset> is selected in the tag selector. Select Untitled Document in the Title text box on the Document toolbar and then type** Florida Parks - General Information **for the title.**

The Florida Parks – General Information title is displayed in the Title text box (Figure 4-16).

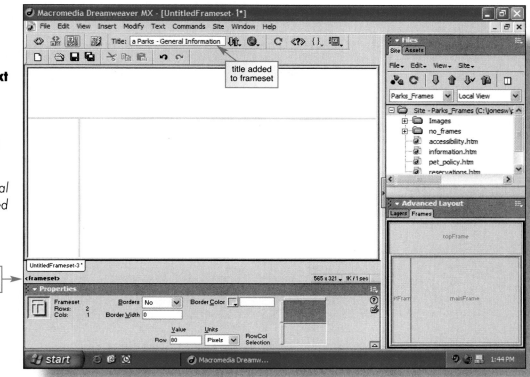

FIGURE 4-16

2 **If the <frameset> is not selected, click the outside border of the frameset in the Frames panel. Click File on the menu bar and then point to Save Frameset As (Figure 4-17).**

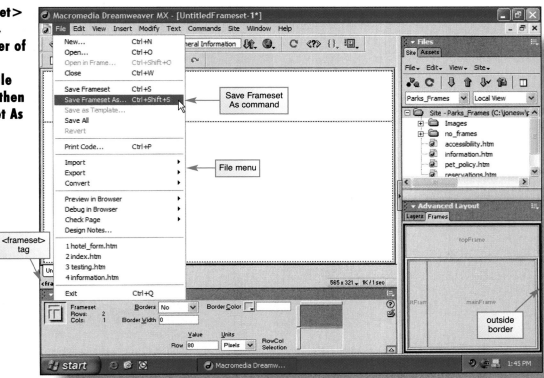

FIGURE 4-17

3 | **Click Save Frameset As.**

The Save As dialog box is displayed (Figure 4-18). If necessary, navigate to the root folder, parks_frames, so that it is displayed in the Save in box. The default file name UntitledFrameset-1.htm is displayed in the File name text box and the blinking insertion point is at the end of the file name. The number in the file name on your computer may be a number other than 1.

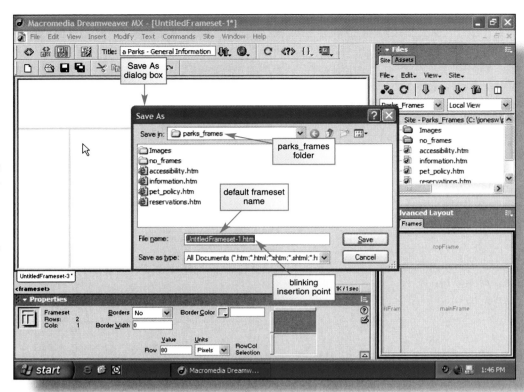

FIGURE 4-18

4 | **Type** index **and then point to the Save button in the Save As dialog box.**

The index file name is displayed in the File name text box (Figure 4-19).

Removing a Frameset

You can remove a frame by dragging its borders. You cannot, however, remove a frameset entirely by dragging borders. To remove a frameset, close the Document window in which it is displayed. If the frameset file has been saved, delete the file.

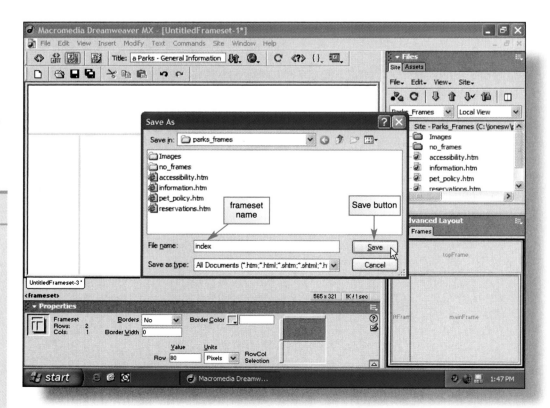

FIGURE 4-19

5 **Click the Save button.**

The frameset is saved in the parks_frames root folder (Figure 4-20).

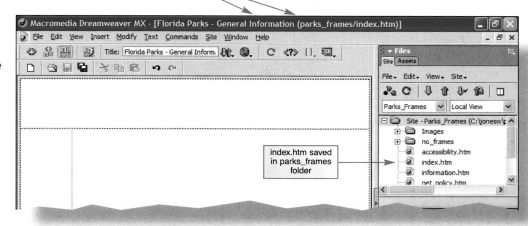

FIGURE 4-20

Selecting a Frame

To make changes to the properties of a frame, you first select the frame. You can select a frame in the Document window or by using the Frames panel. When you select a frame, a dotted border appears around the frame in both the Frames panel and the Document window's Design view. Placing the insertion point in a document that is displayed in a frame is not the same as selecting a frame.

Deleting a Frame

Deleting a frame is simple. Drag a frame border off the page or to the edge of the frameset. If the frame contains unsaved content in a document in a frame that is being removed, Dreamweaver prompts you to save the document. After a frame is deleted, you will not be able to undo this action.

Frames Properties

Like other objects in Dreamweaver, a frame also has a specific Property inspector. When you select a frame within the Document window or in the Frames panel, the Property inspector displays frame properties. Clicking the expander arrow in the lower-right corner expands the Property inspector to show additional attributes.

When a frame is selected, the default attributes are applied automatically. Using the Property inspector, however, you easily can change these attributes and apply additional attributes. The following section describes the frame-related features of the Property inspector (Figure 4-21).

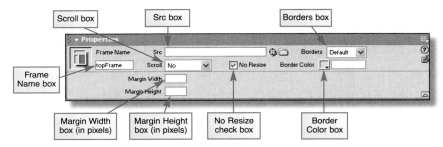

FIGURE 4-21

FRAME NAME The **Frame Name** is used by a link's target attribute or by a script to refer to the frame. A frame name must be a single word and must start with a letter (not a numeral). An underscore (_) is allowed, but hyphens (-), periods (.), and spaces cannot be used. Frame names are case-sensitive.

SRC The **Src** box specifies the source document to display in the frame.

SCROLL The **Scroll** box specifies whether scroll bars appear in the frame. Setting this option to Default allows each browser to use its default value of Auto. Scroll bars display only when needed to display the full contents of the current frame.

NO RESIZE The **No Resize** check box specifies whether the user can change the frame size by dragging the frame borders.

BORDERS The **Borders** box displays or hides the borders of the current frame when it is viewed in a browser. Choosing a Borders option for a frame overrides the frameset border settings. Most browsers default to showing borders unless the parent frameset has Borders set to No.

BORDER COLOR The **Border Color** box specifies a color for the frame borders. The selected color applies to all borders that touch the frame, and overrides the specified border color of the frameset.

MARGIN WIDTH The **Margin Width** box sets the width in pixels of the space between the frame borders and the content.

MARGIN HEIGHT The **Margin Height** box sets the height in pixels of the space between the frame borders and the content.

Naming and Saving the Frames

The frameset that you created contains three frames. These three frames need to be named and saved. When naming and saving a frame, remember that a frame is not a file. A frame contains a document. You can use the default name of UntitledFrame-xx.htm to save the frame, but providing meaningful names to frames causes less confusion. In this project, the topFrame is named title, the leftFrame is named navigate, and the rightFrame is named main. Frames are saved with an .htm extension. Complete the following steps to name the three frames.

Steps **To Name and Save the Three Frames**

1 **Click the topFrame in the Document window.**

The insertion point is displayed in the topFrame (Figure 4-22). The UntitledFrame number may be different on your computer.

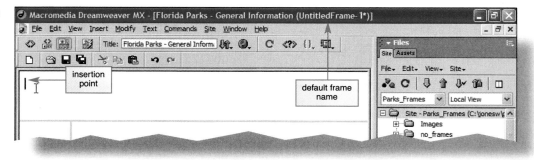

FIGURE 4-22

2 Click File on the menu bar and then point to Save Frame As (Figure 4-23).

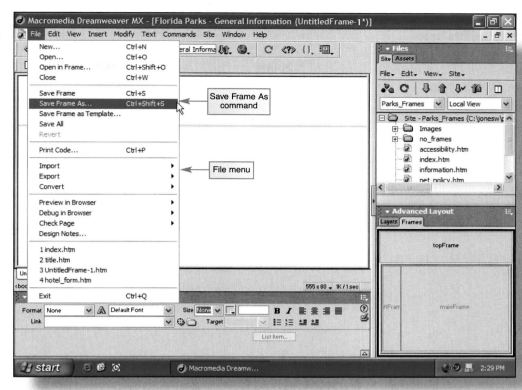

FIGURE 4-23

3 Click Save Frame As.

The Save As dialog box is displayed (Figure 4-24). The root folder, parks_frames, is displayed in the Save in box. The default name, UntitledFrame-1.htm, is displayed in the File name text box, and the insertion point is at the end of the file name. The number in the file name on your computer may be different.

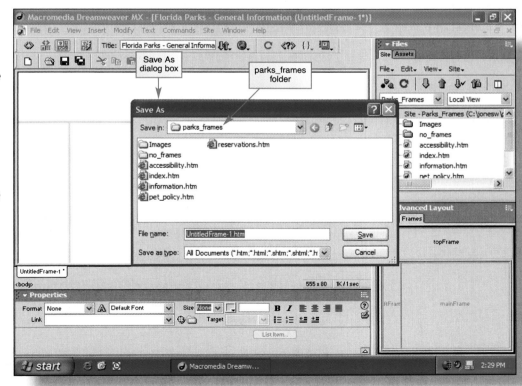

FIGURE 4-24

4 Type title in the File name text box and then point to the Save button in the Save As dialog box (Figure 4-25).

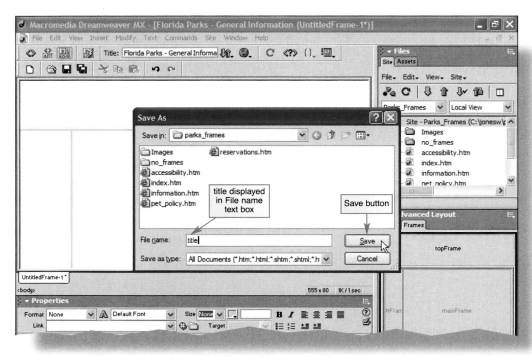

FIGURE 4-25

5 Click the Save button, and then scroll down in the Site panel.

The frame is saved as title and is displayed in the Site panel (Figure 4-26). The file name also is displayed on the frame tab and the title bar.

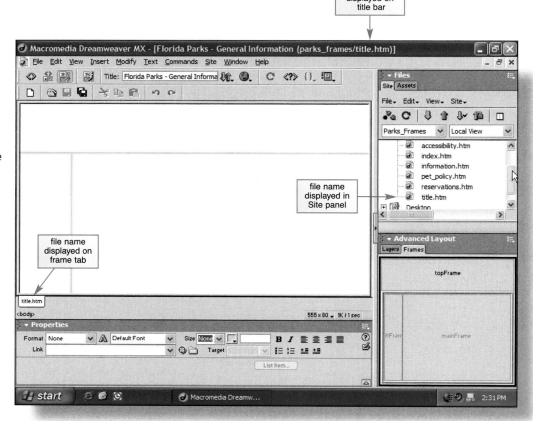

FIGURE 4-26

You save the other two frames the same way in which you saved the title frame. Complete the following steps to save the other two frames: navigate and main.

TO SAVE THE NAVIGATE AND MAIN FRAMES

1 Click the left frame in row 2, click File on the menu bar, and then click Save Frame As.

2 In the Save As dialog box, type `navigate` in the File name text box, and then click the Save button.

3 Click the right frame in row 2. Click File on the menu bar, and then click Save Frame As.

4 In the Save As dialog box, type `main` in the File name text box, and then click the Save button. If necessary, scroll down in the Site panel.

The navigate.htm and main.htm file names are displayed in the Site panel (Figure 4-27).

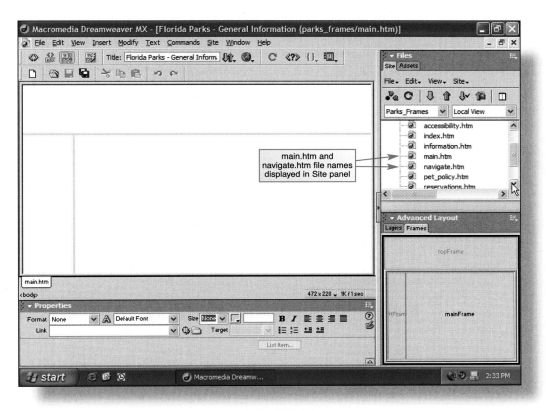

FIGURE 4-27

Formatting the Frames

Backgrounds, text, tables, images, and other elements can be added to the frame in a similar manner to the way in which they are added to a regular Document window. You add the same background to each of the frames that you used in the main Florida Parks Web site you developed in Projects 1 through 3. The title frame also contains a title graphic, and the navigate frame will contain buttons to load content into the main frame.

The Title Frame

One of the advantages of frames is that they can reduce the amount of duplicate information on each page, thus saving download time. A title image, for instance, can be inserted into a frame and remains static as new content is viewed in the main frame. Complete the following steps to apply a background image to the title frame and to give the frame a title.

Steps **To Add a Background Image to the Title Frame**

1 **Click the title frame (topFrame) in the Document window. Click Modify on the menu bar and then click Page Properties. Point to the Browse button.**

The Page Properties dialog box is displayed (Figure 4-28).

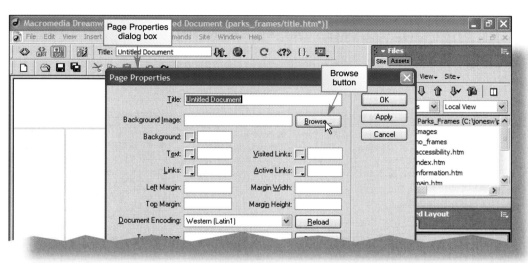

FIGURE 4-28

2 **Click the Browse button. If necessary, double-click the Images folder, and then click the background.jpg file. Point to the OK button in the Select Image Source dialog box.**

The Select Image Source dialog box is displayed (Figure 4-29). The background.jpg file is highlighted.

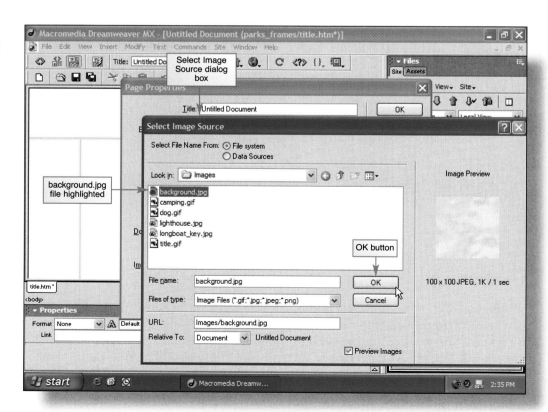

FIGURE 4-29

3 Click the OK button.

The path and background.jpg are displayed in the Background Image box in the Page Properties dialog box (Figure 4-30).

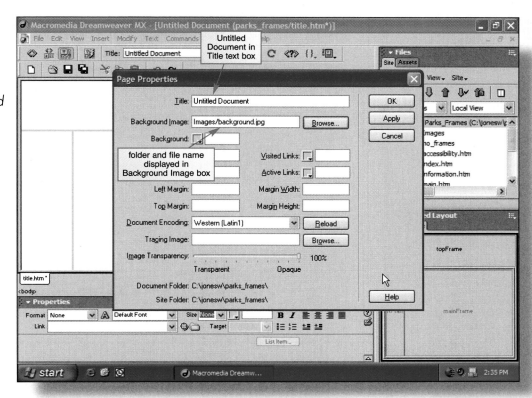

FIGURE 4-30

4 Select Untitled Document in the Title text box in the Page Properties dialog box. Type Florida Parks – General Information in the Title text box. Point to the OK button.

The Title text box contains Florida Parks – General Information (Figure 4-31).

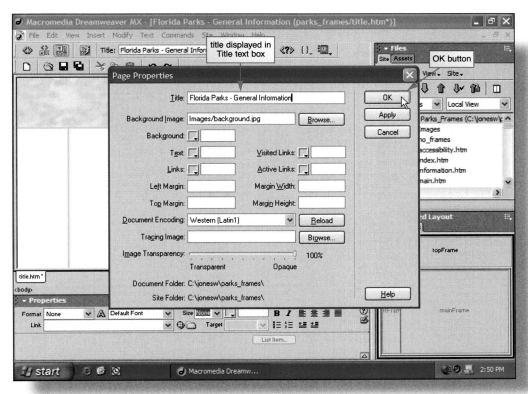

FIGURE 4-31

5 **Click the OK button.**

The background image is applied to the topFrame, and the title is displayed in the Title text box on the Document toolbar and on the title bar (Figure 4-32).

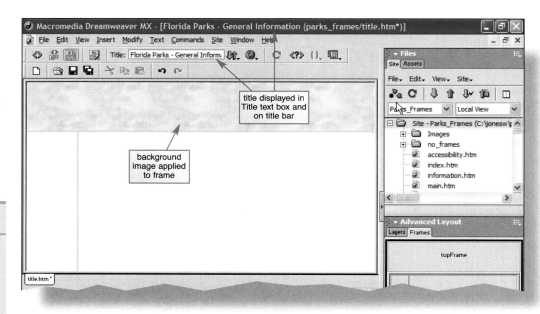

FIGURE 4-32

Adding an Image to the Title Frame

The next step is to add an image to the title frame and then adjust the margin height so the image will display correctly when viewed in a browser. Placing a 0 in the Margin Height box assures that the image will display properly when viewed in a browser. After making these changes, you will need to resave the frame.

 To Add a Title Image to the Title Frame

1 **If necessary, scroll in the Site panel to view the Images folder. Click the plus sign to the left of the Images folder and then click title.gif.**

The Images folder expands and title.gif is selected (Figure 4-33).

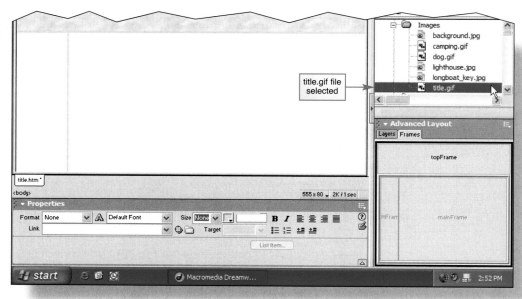

FIGURE 4-33

2 Drag the title.gif image to the title frame. Point to the Save button on the Standard toolbar.

The title.gif image is displayed in the title.htm frame (Figure 4-34). The insertion point is blinking to the right of the image.

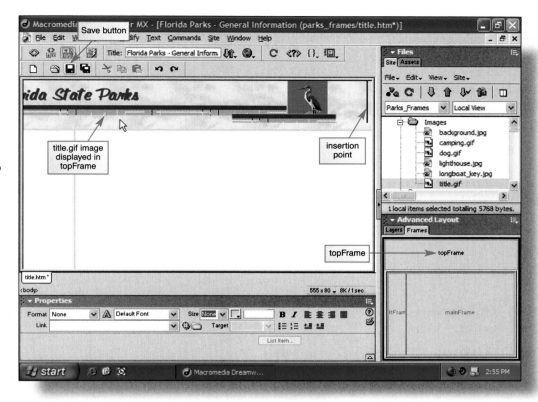

FIGURE 4-34

3 Click the Save button and then click the topFrame in the Frames panel.

The title.htm (topFrame) frame is selected. The Property inspector displays Frame attributes (Figure 4-35).

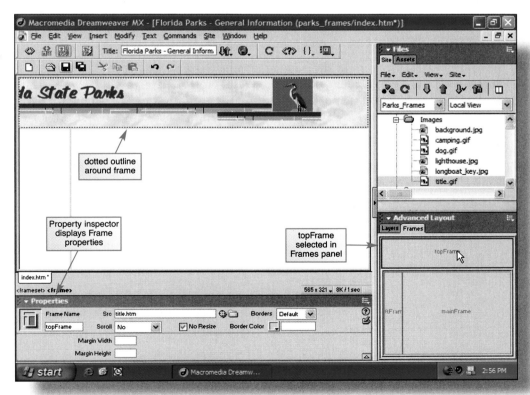

FIGURE 4-35

4 **Click the Margin Height box in the Property inspector. Type** 0 **and then press the ENTER key. Point to the Save button on the Standard toolbar.**

The Margin Height value is changed to 0 (Figure 4-36). No changes are evident in the Document window. Changing the Margin Height affects how the image is displayed in the browser.

5 **Click the Save button.**

The title.htm file is saved within the index frameset.

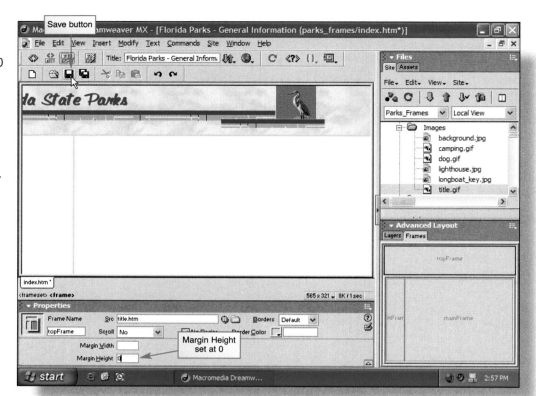

FIGURE 4-36

Setting a Frame Property

Frames and Framesets can have different property settings. Setting a frame property overrides the setting for that property in a frameset.

The Navigate Frame

In the navigate frame (leftFrame), buttons provide links to each of the four content pages and to the Florida Parks main Web site. The main frame (mainFrame) uses most of the display area and shows the content of the page. To display another page in the main frame, simply click another button in the navigate frame. To display this content in the main frame requires that text or image links be added to one of the frames. Image links with text in the form of Flash buttons will be inserted into the navigate frame. First, however, you add the background image and title to the frame.

TO ADD A BACKGROUND IMAGE AND A FRAME TITLE TO THE NAVIGATE FRAME

1 Click the navigate (leftFrame) frame in the Document window.

2 Click Modify on the menu bar and then click Page Properties.

3 Click the Browse button, select the background.jpg image, and then click the OK button in the Select Image Source dialog box.

4 Drag to select Untitled Document in the Title text box in the Page Properties dialog box. Type Florida Parks - General Information as the title.

5 Click the OK button.

The title is added and the background image is applied to the navigate frame (Figure 4-37). The insertion point is blinking in the navigate frame.

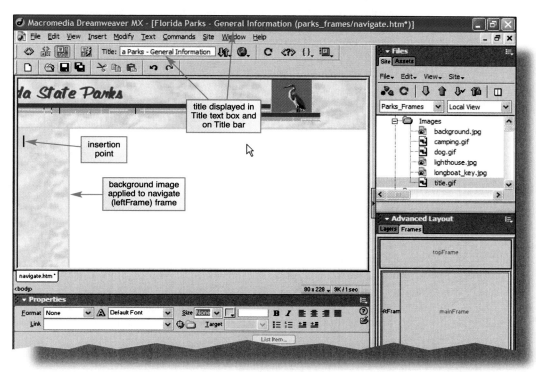

FIGURE 4-37

Inserting Flash Buttons into the Navigate Frame

The Macromedia Flash program is used to develop vector-based graphics and animations. To create the graphics and animations in most instances requires that the Flash program be installed on your computer. Dreamweaver, however, comes with Flash objects that you can use without having this program. You can use these objects to create Flash buttons and Flash text and then insert the objects into your Dreamweaver document.

Flash can generate three different types of file types, as follows:

FLASH FILE (.FLA) This is the source file for any project and is created in the Flash program. To open a .fla file requires the Flash program. Using Flash, you then can export the .fla file as a .swf or .swt file that can be viewed in a browser.

FLASH MOVIE FILE (.SWF) This is a compressed version of the Flash (.fla) file, optimized for viewing on the Web. The .swf file can be played back in browsers and previewed in Dreamweaver, but cannot be edited in Flash. This is the type of file you create when using the Flash button and text objects in Dreamweaver.

FLASH TEMPLATE FILE (.SWT) This file type enables you to modify and replace information in a Flash movie file. The Flash button object uses .swt files.

The Flash Player is available as both a Netscape Navigator plug-in and an ActiveX control for Microsoft Internet Explorer, and it is incorporated in the latest versions of Netscape Navigator, Microsoft Internet Explorer, and the America Online browser. When the Flash button is saved in Dreamweaver, it has a .swf extension. This is a compressed version of a Flash source file and is optimized for viewing on the Web. This file can be played back in browsers and previewed in Dreamweaver. When a Flash object is selected, the Property inspector displays properties specific to the Flash object. The following section describes the Flash-related features of the Property inspector (Figure 4-38 on the next page).

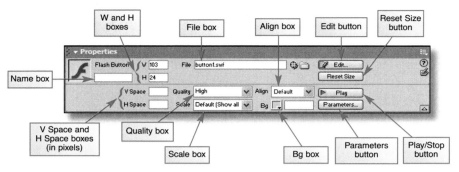

FIGURE 4-38

NAME   The **Name** box specifies the Flash button name that identifies the button for scripting. It is not necessary to enter a name.

W AND H   The **W** and **H** boxes indicate the width and height of the object in pixels. You also can specify the width and height as a percentage. The % sign must follow the value without a space (for example, 3%).

FILE   The **File** box contains the path to the Flash object file and the file name.

EDIT   Clicking the **Edit** button displays the Insert Flash button dialog box or related dialog box if the object is other than a button.

RESET SIZE   The **Reset Size** button resets the selected button to the original size.

V SPACE AND H SPACE   The **V Space** and **H Space** boxes specify the number of pixels of white space above, below, and on both sides of the button.

QUALITY   The **Quality** box contains options that set the quality parameter for the object and embed tags that define the button. The options are High, Low, Auto Low, and Auto High. **Low** emphasizes speed over appearance, whereas **High** favors appearance over speed. **Auto Low** emphasizes speed at first, but improves appearance when possible. **Auto High** emphasizes both qualities at first, but sacrifices appearance for speed, if necessary.

SCALE   The **Scale** box options define how the button (movie) is displayed within the area defined for the movie by the width and height values. The options are Default (Show all), No Border, and Exact Fit.

ALIGN   The **Align** box options define how the object is aligned on the page. The align options are the same as those for images discussed in Project 2.

BG   The **Bg** color box contains a palette of colors you can use to specify a background color for the object. The color also is represented by the hexadecimal value in the adjacent box.

PLAY/STOP   The **Play/Stop** button lets you preview the Flash object in the Document window. Click the green Play button to see the object in Play mode; click the red Stop button to stop the movie.

PARAMETERS   The **Parameters** button opens a dialog box for entering additional parameters. These values are for special parameters defined for Shockwave and Flash movies, ActiveX controls, Navigator plug-ins, and Java applets.

You insert five Flash buttons into the navigate frame. The first four of these buttons display content in the main frame. This content is generated from the four HTML documents you copied from the Data Files folder. The four documents (information, accessibility, pet_policy, and reservations) are formatted and the background image has been added to each one. Perform the following steps to insert the first Flash button into the navigate (leftFrame) frame.

Steps **To Insert a Flash Button into the Navigate Frame**

1 **Click Insert on the menu bar, point to Interactive Images, and then point to Flash Button.**

The Insert menu is displayed and Flash Button is highlighted on the Interactive Images submenu (Figure 4-39).

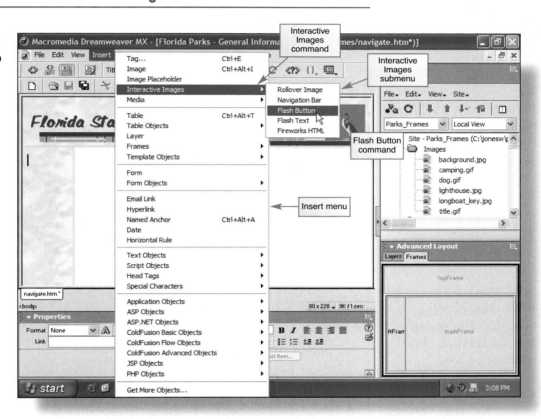

FIGURE 4-39

2 **Click Flash Button. Point to Blue Warper in the Style list.**

The Insert Flash Button dialog box is displayed (Figure 4-40).

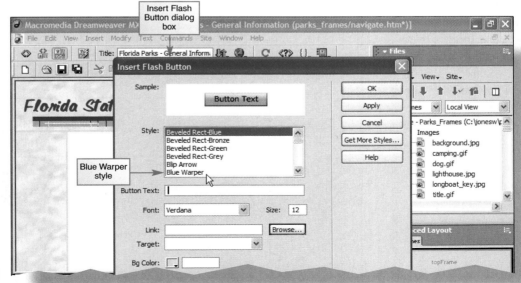

FIGURE 4-40

3 Click Blue Warper. Click the Button Text text box and then type Information as the text to display on the first button. Double-click the Size box and then type 12 as the new value. Point to the Browse button to the right of the Link box.

The Blue Warper button sample is displayed in the Sample area, Information is displayed in the Button Text text box, and the font size is changed to 12 (Figure 4-41).

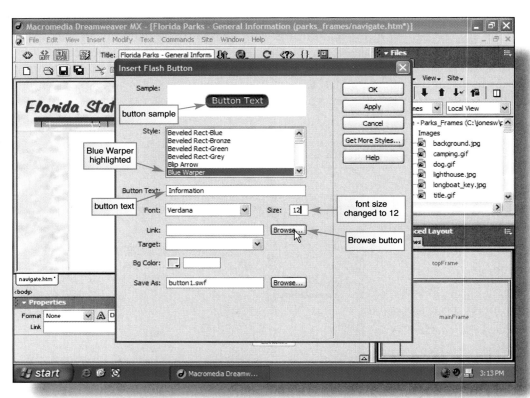

FIGURE 4-41

4 Click the Browse button. When the Select File dialog box is displayed, click information.htm. Verify that Document is displayed in the Relative To box, and then point to the OK button.

The Select File dialog box is displayed (Figure 4-42). The parks_frames folder is displayed in the Look in box. The information.htm file is selected and information.htm is displayed in the File name text box and the URL box.

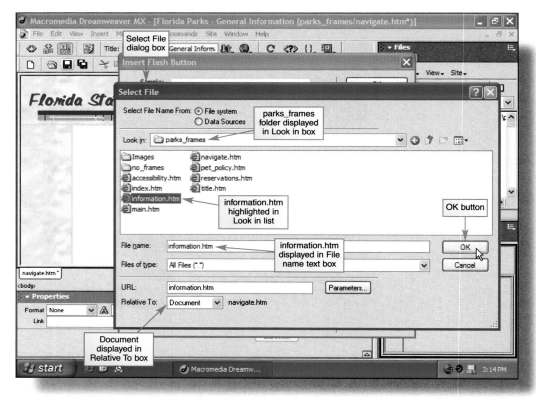

FIGURE 4-42

5 Click the OK button in the Select File dialog box. Point to the Target box arrow.

The information.htm link is displayed in the Link box in the Insert Flash Button dialog box (Figure 4-43).

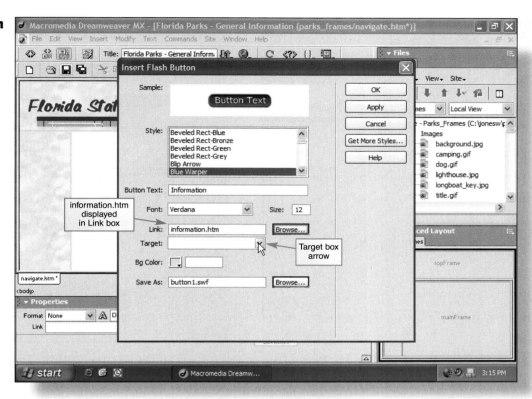

FIGURE 4-43

6 Click the Target box arrow and then point to mainFrame.

The mainFrame target is highlighted (Figure 4-44).

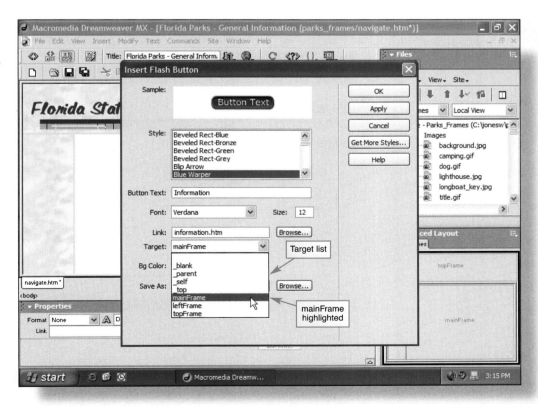

FIGURE 4-44

7 **Click mainFrame and then point to the OK button.**

The mainFrame frame is selected as the Target frame (Figure 4-45).

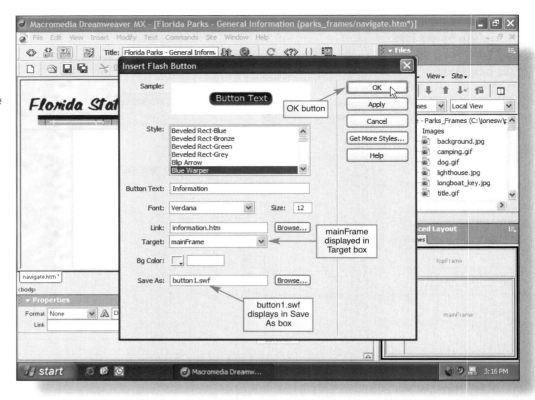

FIGURE 4-45

8 **Click the OK button to insert the Flash button.**

The Flash button is inserted into the navigate frame and is selected (Figure 4-46). The navigate frame is not wide enough to display the entire button. Later in this project, you will learn how to adjust the width of the frame so the whole button is displayed.

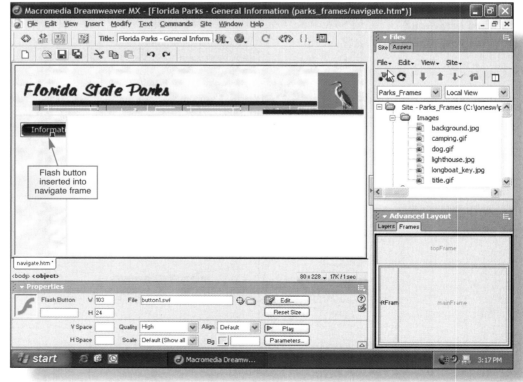

FIGURE 4-46

9 **Click below the button to deselect it and then press the ENTER key.**

A blank line space is inserted between the button and the insertion point (Figure 4-47).

FIGURE 4-47

Inserting the Remaining Buttons

You insert the Accessibility, Pet Policy, and Reservations buttons using the same steps you used to add the Information button. Complete the following steps to insert the Accessibility button.

TO INSERT THE ACCESSIBILITY BUTTON

1 Click Insert on the menu bar, point to Interactive Images, and then click Flash Button on the Interactive Images submenu.

2 Click Blue Warper.

3 Click the Button Text text box. Type `Accessibility` as the button text.

4 Change the font size to 12.

5 Click the Browse button, click accessibility.htm, and then click the OK button in the Select File dialog box.

6 Click the Target box arrow and then select mainFrame.

7 Click the OK button to insert the Accessibility button into the navigate frame.

8 Click below the button and then press the ENTER key.

The Accessibility button is inserted into the navigate frame, and a blank line is inserted below the button (Figure 4-48).

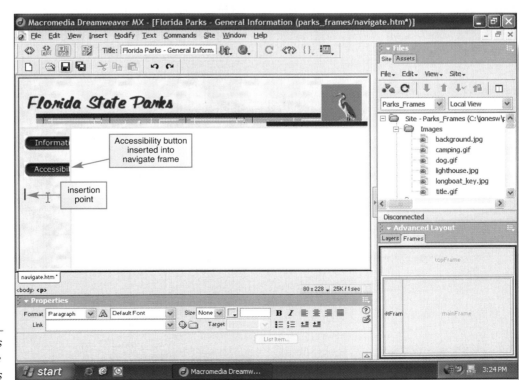

FIGURE 4-48

Complete the following steps to add the Pet Policy button.

TO INSERT THE PET POLICY BUTTON

1 Click Insert on the menu bar, point to Interactive Images, and then click Flash Button on the Interactive Images submenu.

2 Click Blue Warper. Click the Button Text text box. Type Pet Policy as the button name. Change the font size to 12.

3 Click the Browse button, click pet_policy.htm, and then click the OK button in the Select File dialog box.

4 Click the Target box arrow and then select mainFrame.

5 Click the OK button to insert the Pet Policy button into the navigate frame.

6 Click below the button and then press the ENTER key.

You have inserted the first three buttons. Complete the following steps to insert the Reservations button.

TO INSERT THE RESERVATIONS BUTTON

1 Click Insert on the menu bar, point to Interactive Images, and then click Flash Button on the Interactive Images submenu.

2 Click Blue Warper. Click the Button Text text box. Type Reservations as the button text. Change the font size to 12.

3 Click the Browse button, click reservations.htm, and then click the OK button in the Select File dialog box.

4 Click the Target box arrow and then select mainFrame.

5 Click the OK button to insert the Reservations button into the navigate frame.

6 Click below the button and then press the ENTER key.

7 Click the Save button on the Standard toolbar.

The first four buttons are inserted (Figure 4-49). The navigate.htm frame is saved.

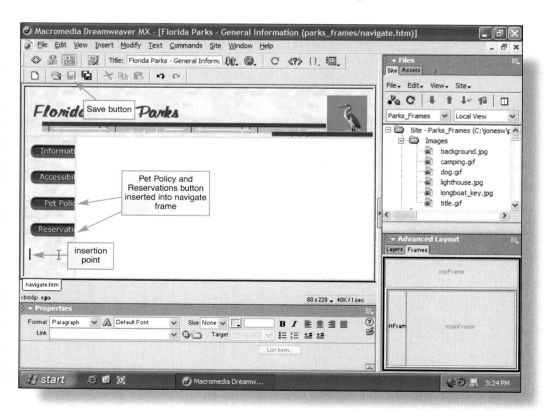

FIGURE 4-49

The last button to be added to the navigate frame is the Home button. When clicked, this button will cause the main index page of the Florida Parks Web site to display on the screen. Thus far, the target for your links has been the mainFrame. Other possible targets within the same frameset include leftFrame and topFrame. Targets outside the frameset include _blank, _parent, _self, and _top. The following section describes these targets.

▶ The **_blank** target opens the linked document in a new browser window, leaving the current window untouched.
▶ The **_parent** target opens the linked document in the parent frameset of the frame the link appears in, replacing the entire frameset.
▶ The **_self** target opens the link in the current frame, replacing the content in that frame.
▶ The **_top** target opens the linked document in the current browser window, replacing all frames.

To create the Home button, you use an absolute link. If you published the main Florida Parks Web site to a remote server in a previous project, use the remote server Web site address for the Index page as the link. Otherwise, use the path to the location of the C:/yourname/parks/index.htm folder. To further create this link, you select _blank as the target. Selecting this option opens the linked document in a new browser window, leaving the current window untouched. Complete the following steps to create a link to the main Web site index page.

Steps **To Insert the Home Button**

1 **Click Insert on the menu bar, point to Interactive Images, and then click Flash Button on the Interactive Images submenu. Click Blue Warper. Click the Button Text text box and then type** Home **as the button text. Change the font size to 12.**

Home is displayed in the Button Text text box and the font size is changed to 12 (Figure 4-50).

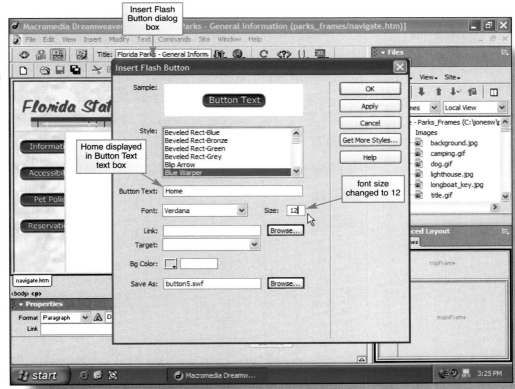

FIGURE 4-50

2 If you are linking to a remote server, copy and paste the URL to the main Florida Parks Web site into the Link box. If you are linking to the C:/jonesw/parks/index.htm folder, type the path in the Link box in the Property inspector. Point to the Target box arrow.

The path to the index.htm file for the main Florida Parks Web site appears in the Link box (Figure 4-51).

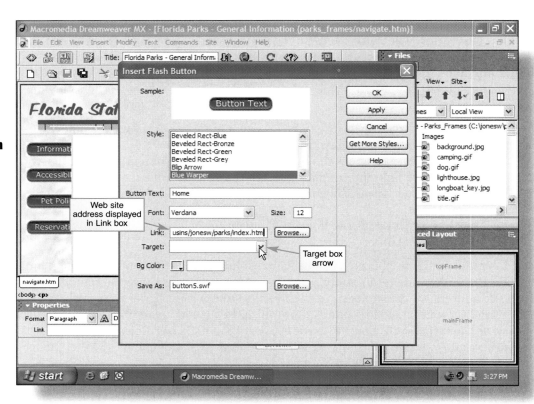

FIGURE 4-51

3 Click the Target box arrow and then select _blank in the list. Point to the OK button.

The Target box displays _blank (Figure 4-52).

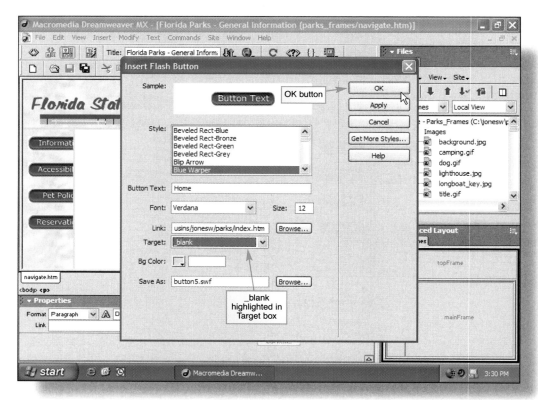

FIGURE 4-52

4 **Click the OK button and then click the Save button on the Standard toolbar.**

The five buttons are added to the navigate frame (Figure 4-53), and the navigate frame is saved.

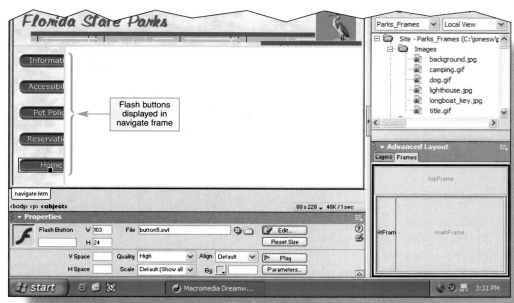

FIGURE 4-53

Adjusting Column Width

The Flash buttons are only partially displayed in the navigate frame. You can adjust the size of the button or you can adjust the column width. In this project, you adjust the column width and use pixels as the measurement for the width. Using pixels ensures that the column width does not change when displayed in a browser. The navigate frame is in the nested frameset. You can adjust the column width by dragging the right border of the frame or you can adjust the column width through the Property inspector. To adjust the column width through the Property inspector, first you must select the nested frameset. Complete the following steps to select the nested frameset and to adjust the column width of the navigate frame.

 To Adjust the Column Width

1 **Click the border surrounding the leftFrame and the mainFrame in the Frames panel.**

The nested frameset is selected. A second <frameset> tag is selected in the tag selector. The Property inspector for the frameset is displayed (Figure 4-54).

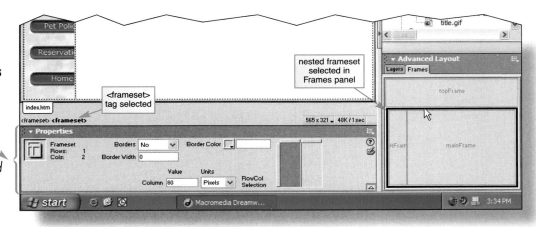

FIGURE 4-54

2 If necessary, click the tab on the first column in the Property inspector. Double-click the Column Value box, type 120, and then press the ENTER key.

The column width is expanded to 120 pixels (Figure 4-55).

3 Click the Save button on the Standard toolbar to save the navigate frame and the changes to the frameset.

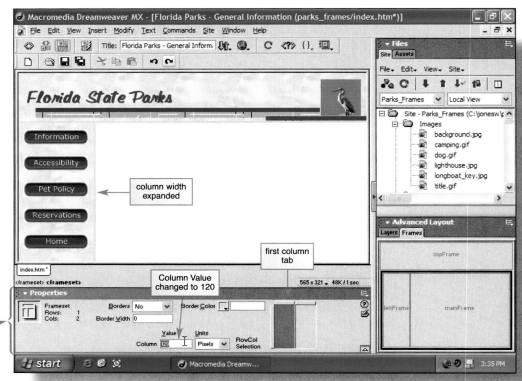

FIGURE 4-55

The Main Content Frame

The main content frame is where the content is displayed when one of the Flash navigation buttons is clicked. The four content pages are information, accessibility, pet policy, and reservations. First, you need to add the background image and title to the mainFrame page.

TO ADD A BACKGROUND IMAGE AND FRAME TITLE TO THE MAIN CONTENT FRAME

1 Click the main frame (mainFrame) in the Document window.

2 Click Modify on the menu bar and then click Page Properties.

3 Click the Browse button to the right of the Background Image box, select the background.jpg image, and then click the OK button in the Select Image Source dialog box.

4 Drag to select Untitled Document in the Title text box in the Page Properties dialog box. Type Florida Parks - General Information as the title.

5 Click the OK button.

6 Click the Save button on the Standard toolbar.

The background image is applied to the mainFrame (Figure 4-56). The insertion point is blinking in the main frame.

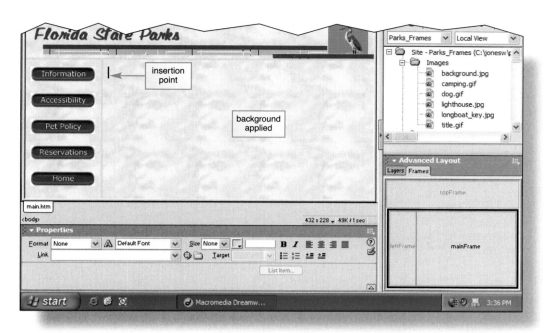

FIGURE 4-56

More *About*

Editing Framesets

Frame names appear only when you are editing a document within a frameset. When you edit a document in its own Document window, outside of the frameset, frame names do not appear in the Target pop-up menu.

Linking and Targeting

You created the links and targets for the navigation buttons when you created the buttons. To display default content in the main frame, however, requires that content be added in a manner similar to adding the title graphic and navigate frames content. The default content is the information.htm file. Complete the following steps to add the default content to the main frame.

 To Link and Target the Default Content

1 **Click the mainFrame in the Frames panel.**

A dotted border appears around the mainFrame in the Document window. The Frames Property inspector is displayed (Figure 4-57).

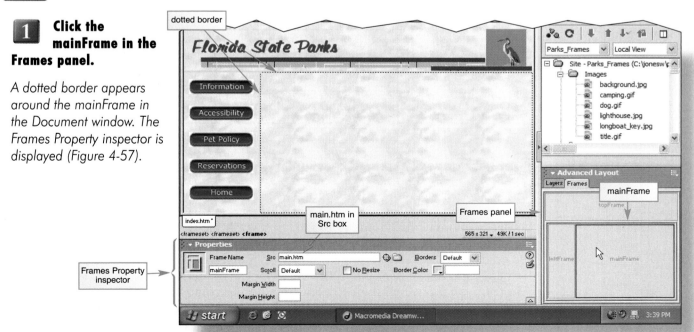

FIGURE 4-57

2 **Double-click main.htm in the Src box in the Property inspector.**

The text main.htm is high-lighted in the Src box (Figure 4-58).

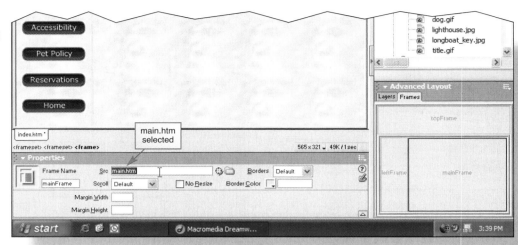

FIGURE 4-58

3 **Type** information.htm **and then press the ENTER key.**

The contents of the information.htm file are displayed in the main frame (Figure 4-59). Vertical and horizontal scroll bars are displayed in the main frame.

4 **Click File on the Menu bar and then click Save All.**

The framesets and frames are saved.

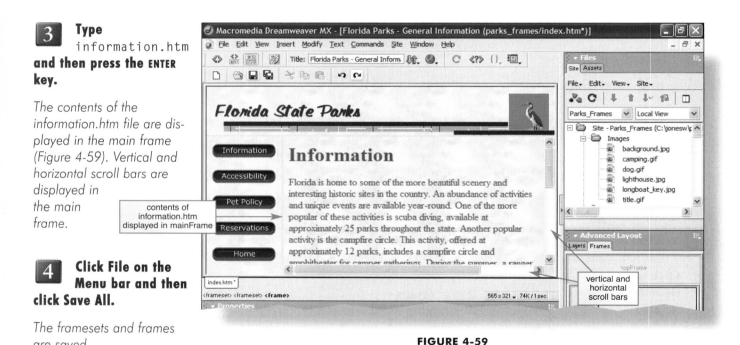

FIGURE 4-59

Adding a Border and Border Color to the Framesets

The **Borders** feature in the Property inspector determines whether borders should appear around frames when the document is viewed in a browser. You can add a border to an individual frame or to the frameset. If the frameset contains one or more nested framesets, then each nested frameset must be selected and the border added to the nested frameset. The **Border Width** specifies a width for all the borders in the frameset, and the **Border Color** sets a color for the borders. Border colors and widths selected in an individual frame override the border color and border width of the frameset properties. Use the color picker to select a color, or type the hexadecimal value for a color. Complete the following steps to add a border and border color to the main frameset. If your screen setting is greater than 800 × 600, the scroll bars may not display.

Steps | **To Add a Border and Border Color to the Main Frameset**

1 **Click the border around the outer frameset in the Frames panel. Point to the Borders box arrow in the Property inspector.**

A dark border surrounds the entire frame in the Frames panel and a dotted border surrounds the frameset and frames in the Document window (Figure 4-60). The Property inspector for the frameset is displayed and <frameset> is displayed in bold in the tag selector.

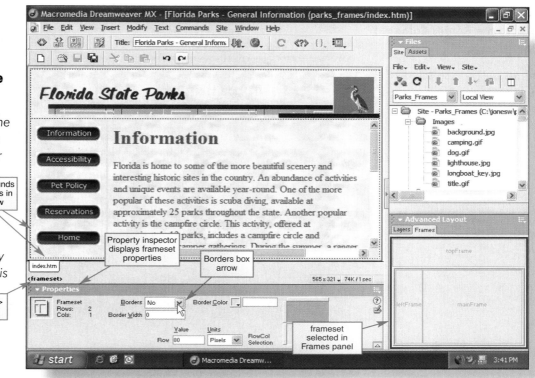

FIGURE 4-60

2 **Click the Borders box arrow and then point to Yes in the Borders list.**

The Borders list is displayed and the mouse pointer points to Yes (Figure 4-61).

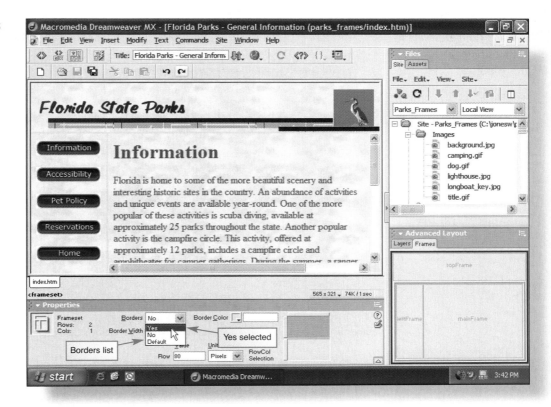

FIGURE 4-61

3 Click Yes. Double-click the Border Width box. Type 4 and then press the ENTER key. Point to the Border Color box.

The Yes option is selected in the Borders box and the border width is changed to 4 (Figure 4-62).

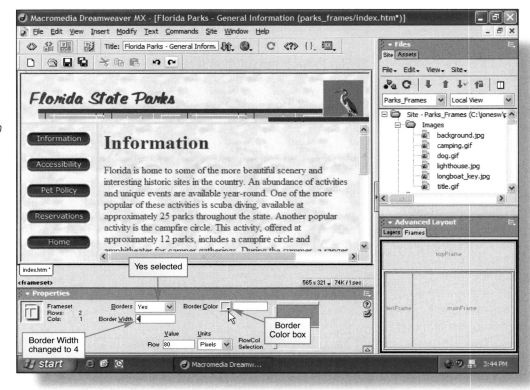

FIGURE 4-62

4 Click the Border Color box and then point to column 2, row 9.

The mouse pointer points to a shade of blue (#0000FF) (Figure 4-63).

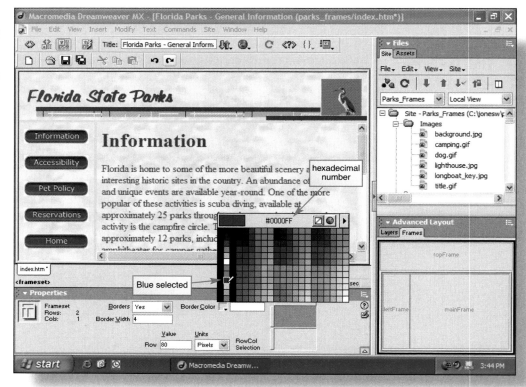

FIGURE 4-63

5 **Click to select the blue color.**

The border color is applied to the frameset (Figure 4-64). The border color, however, is not applied to the nested frameset.

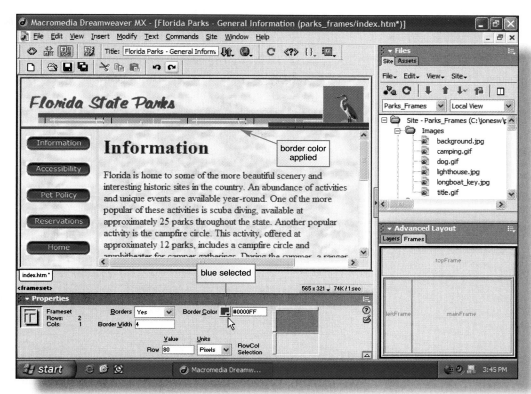

FIGURE 4-64

6 **Click the border surrounding the leftFrame (navigate frame) and the mainFrame in the Frames panel.**

The nested frameset is selected (Figure 4-65). The nested <frameset> tag is displayed in bold in the tag selector.

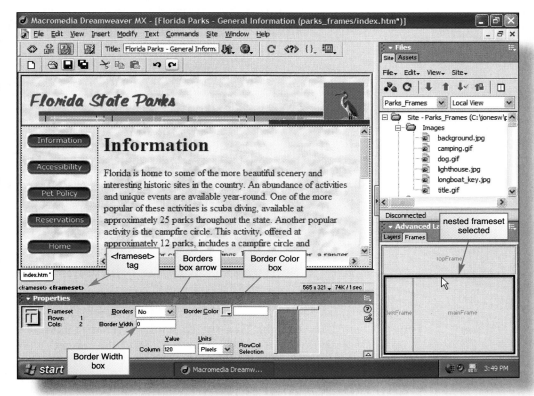

FIGURE 4-65

More About

Pros and Cons of Using Frames

Frames have advantages and disadvantages. Web designers and Web site visitors generally love or hate frames. For more information about this controversy, visit the Dreamweaver MX More About Web page (scsite.com/ dreamweavermx/ more.htm) and then click Pros and Cons of Using Frames.

Applying the Border and Border Color to the Nested Frameset

The steps to apply the border color to the border of the nested frameset are the same as those to apply the border color to the outside frameset. Complete the following steps to apply the border color to the nested frameset.

TO APPLY THE BORDER AND BORDER COLOR TO THE NESTED FRAMESET

1. Click the Borders box arrow in the Property inspector and then click Yes in the Borders list.

2. Double-click the Border Width box. Type 4 and then press the ENTER key.

3. Click the Border Color box and then click column 2, row 9.

4. Click the File menu and then click Save All.

The border color is applied to the nested frameset in Step 3 (Figure 4-66). The frames and the framesets for the Web site are saved.

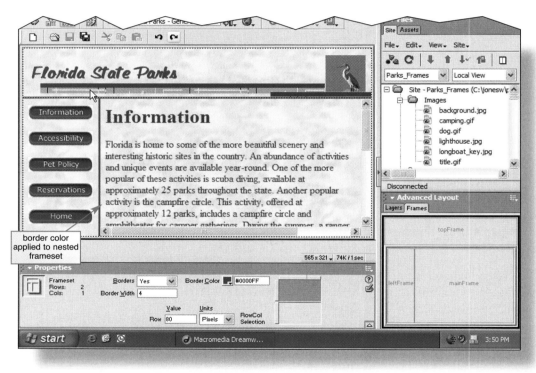

FIGURE 4-66

Adding a No-Frames Link to the Information Page

When you created the predefined frameset at the beginning of this project, Deamweaver automatically included a <noframes> tag within the HTML code. If a visitor accesses the Web site with a browser that does not support frames, then the <noframes> code takes him or her out of the framed Web site into a non-framed version of the Web site. Still, other visitors with browsers that support frames may prefer a no-frames version. A no-frames version was included in the Project 4 data files you copied to the parks_frames Web site. To access the no-frames version requires that a link be created and a target designated to the no-frames version. This link is added to the information.htm page. Complete the following steps to add a no-frames link.

To Add a No-Frames Link

1 **Position the insertion point at the end of the Information heading and then press the ENTER key.**

A blank line is inserted below the heading (Figure 4-67).

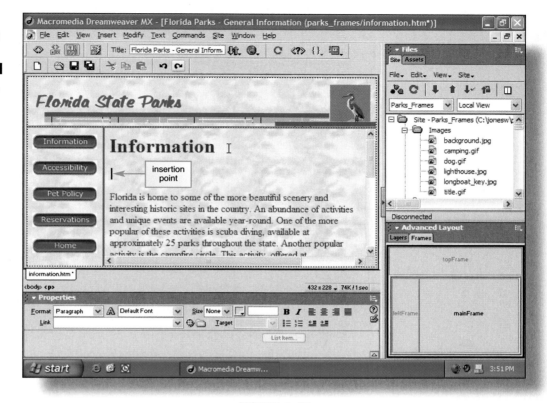

FIGURE 4-67

2 **Type** No frames version **as the text for the link.**

The text, No frames version, is displayed in the information.htm Document window (Figure 4-68).

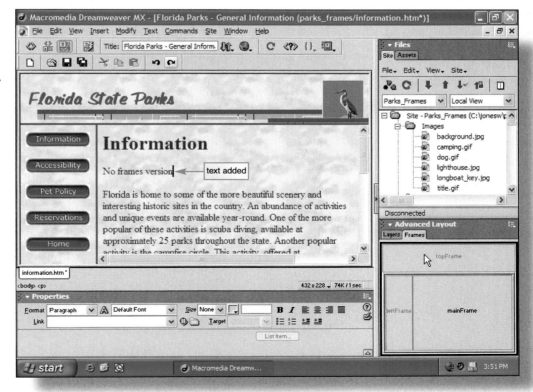

FIGURE 4-68

3 Select the text, No frames version.

The text, No frames version, is selected (Figure 4-69).

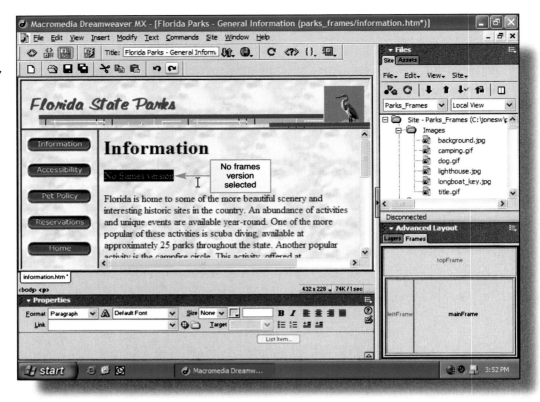

FIGURE 4-69

4 If necessary, scroll in the Site panel to display the no_frames folder. Click the plus sign to the left of the no_frames folder and then click the information.htm file.

The no_frames folder is open and the information.htm file is selected (Figure 4-70).

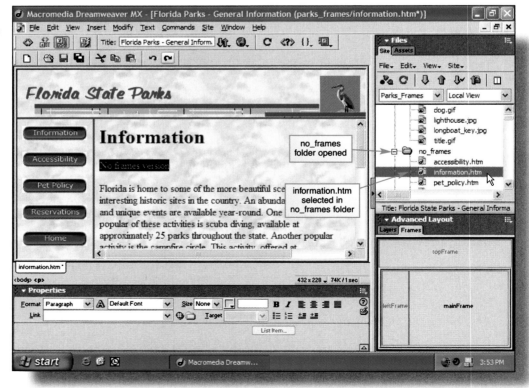

FIGURE 4-70

5 Drag the information.htm file to the Link box in the Property inspector and then press the ENTER key.

The link no_frames/ information.htm is displayed in the Link box (Figure 4-71).

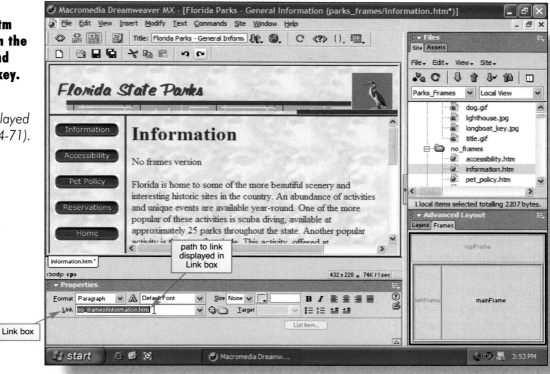

FIGURE 4-71

6 Click the Target box arrow and select _top. Click the Save button on the Standard toolbar.

The link has been established for the no_frames version and the file is saved (Figure 4-72).

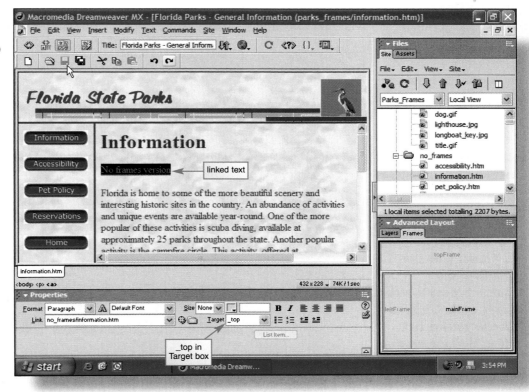

FIGURE 4-72

7 **Open the Florida Parks Web site, select the index.htm page, scroll to the bottom of the page, and then click to the right of the Florida Environmental Information link. Hold down the SHIFT key and then press the ENTER key. Type** General Information **and then create a link from the text, General Information, to the index.htm file in the Parks_Frames Web site. If you are publishing to a remote site, copy and paste the Florida Parks Web site address into the Link box. If you are saving your work to a local computer or server, use the Browse for File icon in the Property inspector to create the link path. Click the Save button on the Standard toolbar.**

The link is created (Figure 4-73). Your link may be different depending on the location of your Web site.

8 **If instructed to do so, upload your Web sites to a remote server. Press the F12 key to preview the Florida Parks index.htm page in the browser. Click the General Information link to display the Parks_Frames Web site. Click each of the navigation buttons to verify that they work. Click the No frames version link and then click the browser Back button to return to the framed version.**

The framed Web site is displayed in the browser (Figure 7-74).

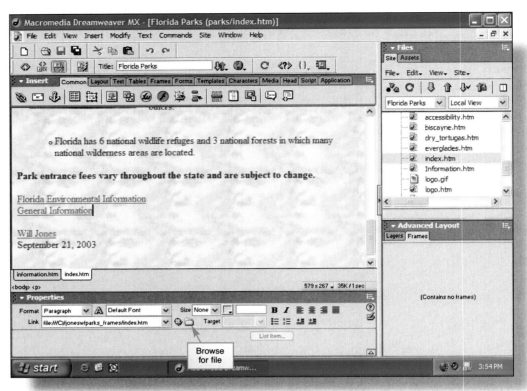

FIGURE 4-73

FIGURE 4-74 (a)

9 If instructed to do so, right-click in each frame, print a copy of each frame, and hand in the copies to your instructor. Close the browser.

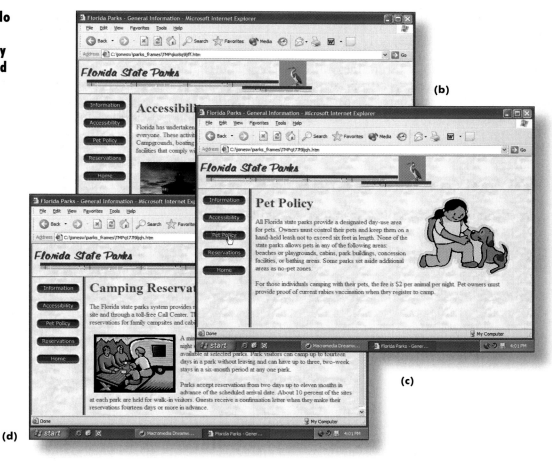

(b)

(c)

(d)

FIGURE 4-74 (continued)

Quitting Dreamweaver

After you have created your framed Web site, verified that the navigation works, and uploaded it to a remote server, Project 4 is complete. To close the Web site, quit Dreamweaver MX, and return control to Windows, perform the following step.

TO CLOSE THE WEB SITE AND QUIT DREAMWEAVER

1 Click the Close button on the right corner of the Dreamweaver title bar.

The Dreamweaver window, the Document window, and the Parks_Frames Web site all close. If you have unsaved changes, Dreamweaver will prompt you to save the changes. Clicking the Yes button in the Dreamweaver MX dialog box saves the changes.

CASE PERSPECTIVE SUMMARY

As planned, your team finished designing the framed Web site as a subsection to the Florida Parks main Web site. Using frames to help with the layout enabled you to design the pages better and present the general information in an easy-to-navigate fashion. You shared with Joan and Will the importance of including a no-frames version. Everyone agrees that the addition of the new framed Web site will help answer the general questions being asked by many of the main Web site visitors.

Project Summary

Project 4 introduced you to frames and to Web page design using frames. You created a framed Web site that included two framesets – one a nested frameset. You named the framesets and the frames and modified the frameset and frame properties. You added navigation links in the form of Flash buttons to display content in the main frame. Finally, you added a link for a no frames version of the Web site for those visitors who do not want to use frames.

What You Should Know

Having completed this project, you now should be able to perform the tasks in Table 4-2.

Table 4-2 Project 4 What You Should Know		
TASK NUMBER	**TASK**	**PAGE NUMBER**
1	Start Dreamweaver and Close Open Panels	DW 4.06
2	Create a Local Site	DW 4.06
3	Copy Data Files to the Parks_Frames Web Site	DW 4.08
4	Display Frame Borders	DW 4.12
5	Create the Frameset	DW 4.13
6	Display the Frames Panel	DW 4.17
7	Name and Save the Frameset	DW 4.19
8	Name and Save the Three Frames	DW 4.22
9	Save the Navigate and Main Frames	DW 4.25
10	Add a Background Image to the Title Frame	DW 4.26
11	Add a Title Image to the Title Frame	DW 4.28
12	Add a Background Image and a Frame Title to the Navigate Frame	DW 4.30
13	Insert a Flash Button into the Navigate Frame	DW 4.33

TASK NUMBER	**TASK**	**PAGE NUMBER**
14	Insert the Accessibility Button	DW 4.37
15	Insert the Pet Policy Button	DW 4.38
16	Insert the Reservations Button	DW 4.38
17	Insert the Home Button	DW 4.39
18	Adjust the Column Width	DW 4.41
19	Add a Background Image and Frame Title to the Main Content Frame	DW 4.42
20	Link and Target the Default Content	DW 4.43
21	Add a Border and Border Color to the Main Frameset	DW 4.45
22	Apply the Border and Border Color to the Nested Frameset	DW 4.48
23	Add a No-Frames Link	DW 4.49
24	Close the Web Site and Quit Dreamweaver	DW 4.53

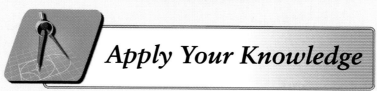

Apply Your Knowledge

1 Creating a Framed Web Site for B & B Lawn Service

Instructions: Start Dreamweaver. If the panels display, press the F4 key to close all panels. See the inside back cover of this book for instructions for downloading the Data Disk or see your instructor for information on accessing the files in this book.

B & B Lawn Service recently started selling lawn mowers and other lawn equipment and would like to investigate the possibility of selling this equipment on the Internet. Its goal is to start with a framed Web site displaying four of the more popular lawn mowers. The Web site will contain five pages: the index page and a page describing each of the four lawn mowers. The frameset will contain three frames: topFrame, mainFrame, and bottomFrame. The top frame (named title) displays the title, the middle frame displays the linked content, and the bottom frame contains the navigation text, as shown in Figure 4-75. Appendix D contains instructions for uploading your local site to a remote server. For an updated list of links, visit the Dreamweaver MX Links Web page (scsite.com/dreamweavermx/links) and then click Project 4 Links.

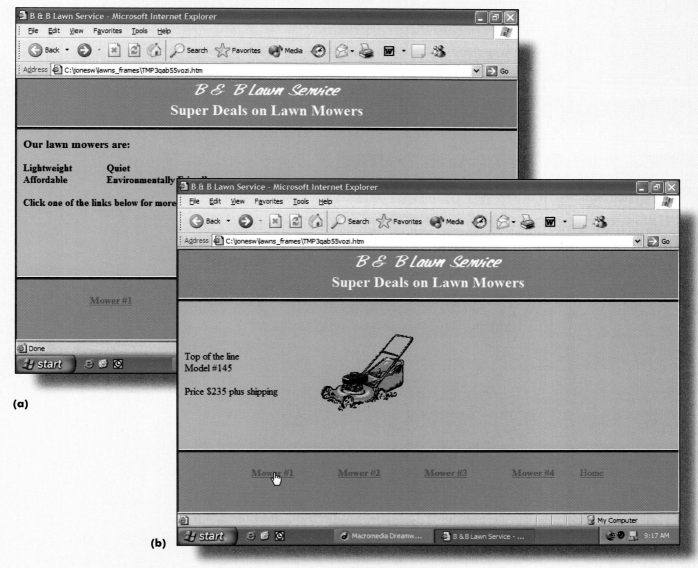

(a)

(b)

FIGURE 4-75   *(continued)*

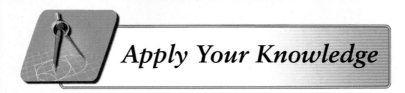

Apply Your Knowledge

Creating a Framed Web Site for B & B Lawn Service *(continued)*

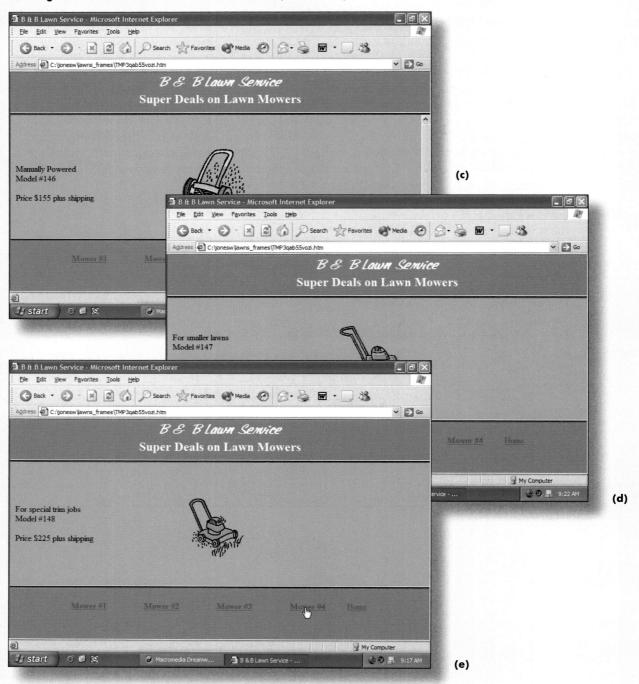

FIGURE 4-75 *(continued)*

1. Display the Property inspector, Standard toolbar, Site panel, and Frames panel.
2. Create a new Web site. Name the Web site Lawn Service Frames. Store your Web site in a new folder called lawn_frames. The path will be C:/yourname/lawn_frames.

Apply Your Knowledge

3. Close the Untitled-1 page that displayed when you started Dreamweaver. Click File on the menu bar, click New, and then click Framesets on the New dialog box. Select Fixed Top, Fixed Bottom and then click the Create button to create the frameset.

4. Use Dreamweaver's integrated file browser to copy files and the Images folder from the Data Files to your lawn_frames local root folder.

5. If necessary, select the frameset. Drag to select Untitled Document in the Title text box on the Document menu bar. Type B & B Lawn Service. Save the frameset as index in the lawn_frames local root folder.

6. Click the topFrame, click Modify on the menu bar, and then click Page Properties. In the Title text box type B & B Lawn Service. In the Background hexadecimal box, type #3399FF and then click the OK button.

7. Drag the title.gif to the topFrame and then center the title.gif file. Click the topFrame in the Frames panel to display the Frames Property inspector. Click the Margin Height text box and then type 0. Click the topFrame in the Document window and then save the topFrame. Use title for the frame name.

8. Click the mainFrame, click Modify on the menu bar, and then click Page Properties. Type B & B Lawn Service in the Title text box. In the Background hexadecimal box, type #66CCFF and then click the OK button. Save the mainFrame. Use main for the file name.

9. Click the mainFrame in the Frames panel and then double-click main.htm in the Src text box in the Property inspector.

10. Type content.htm, press the ENTER key, and then click the Save button.

11. Click the bottomFrame. Click Modify on the menu bar, and then click Page Properties. Type B & B Lawn Service in the Title text box. In the Background hexadecimal box, type #3399FF and then click the OK button. Save the frame as navigation in the lawn_frames local root folder.

12. Create a one-row, five-column table in the navigate frame. Use 0 for the Cell Padding, Cell Spacing, and Border, and use 95 Percent for the Width. Center the table. Type Mower #1 in column 1, type Mower #2 in column 2, type Mower #3 in column 3, type Mower #4 in column 4, and type Home in column 5.

13. Select the text Mower #1 in column 1. Drag the file mower01.htm from the Site panel to the Link box in the Property inspector. Click the Target box arrow and select mainFrame.

14. Repeat step 13 for columns 2, 3, and 4, dragging the related files (mower02.htm through mower04.htm) to the Link box. Select mainFrame as the target for each of these.

15. Select Home in the fifth column and drag content.htm to the Link box. Select mainFrame as the target.

16. Select the frameset in the Frames panel.

17. Click the Borders arrow in the Property inspector and change Default to Yes. Double-click the Border Width box and type 2. Click the Border Color hexadecimal box and then type #000000 for the color black. Click File on the menu bar and then click Save All. If instructed to do so, upload your Web sites to a remote server.

18. Open the Lawn Service Web site, select the index.htm page, scroll to the bottom of the page, and then click to the right of the Ecological Lawn Maintenance link. Hold down the shift key and then press the ENTER key. Type Lawn mowers for sale and then create a link from the text, Lawn mowers for sale, to the index.htm file in the Lawn Service Frames Web site. If you are publishing to a remote site, copy and paste the Lawn Service Frame Web site address into the Link box. If you are saving your work to a local computer or server, use the Browse for File icon in the Property inspector to create the link path. Click the Save button on the Standard toolbar. If instructed to do so, upload your Web site changes to a remote server.

19. Press the F12 key to view the Lawn Service index.htm page in your browser. Click the Lawn Mowers for sale link to display the Lawn Service Frames Web site. Click each of the navigation buttons to verify that they work. Print copies of each frame if instructed to do so.

In the Lab

1 Adding a Framed Web Page to CandleDust

Problem: Mary has received several e-mails asking how to make candles. She has some specialty recipes for votive and pillar candles and would like to put these online. Mary has requested that you add a left and right framed page to the CandleDust site. The navigation will be Flash buttons in the left frame. The recipe formulas will be displayed in the right frame. The left frame also will contain a link to the CandleDust home page. The framed Web site is shown in Figure 4-76. For an updated list of links, visit the Dreamweaver MX Links Web page (scsite.com/dreamweavermx/links) and then click Project 4 Links.

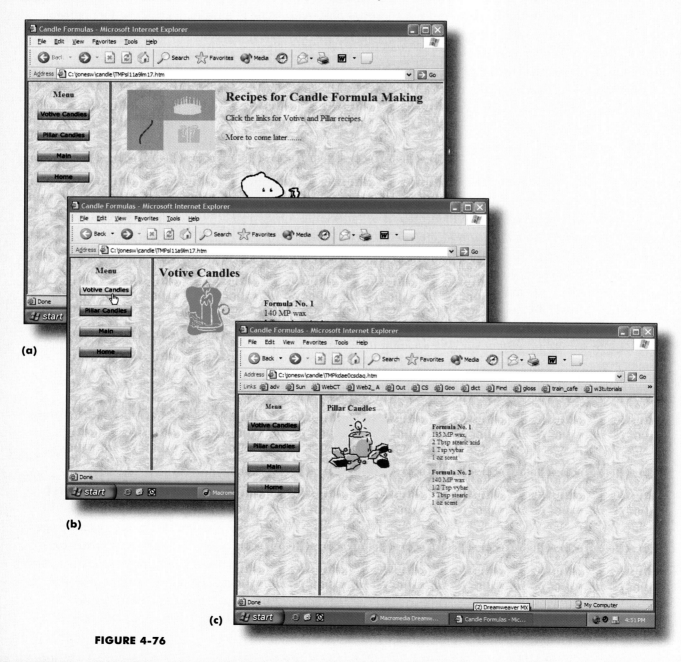

FIGURE 4-76

In the Lab

Instructions: Perform the following tasks:

1. Start Dreamweaver. If necessary, press the F4 key to close the open panels. Display the Property inspector, Standard toolbar, Site panel, and Frames panel. Select CandleDust from the Site pop-up menu in the Site panel.

2. Use Dreamweaver's integrated file browser to copy the images to the Images folder and the files from the Data Files to your /candle folder.

3. Create a predefined frameset. Use the Split Vertical frameset. Add the title Candle Formulas to the frameset. Save the frameset as recipes.htm in the CandleDust root folder.

4. Click the leftFrame and add the color scheme you added in Project 1: (Purple background and Blue,Purple,Green text and links). Add the background.jpg image and add the title Candle Formulas to the frame. Save the frame as navigate in the CandleDust root folder.

5. Click the mainFrame and repeat step 4 to add the background image and color scheme. Title the frame Candle Formulas. Save the frame as main in the CandleDust root folder.

6. Click the mainFrame in the Frames panel.

7. Double-click main.htm in the Src text box in the Property Inspector, type content.htm, and then click the Save All button.

8. Click the leftFrame. Type Menu and then center the text. Press the ENTER key.

9. Click Insert on the menu bar, point to Interactive Images, and then click Flash Button on the Interactive Images submenu. Select the Beveled Rect-bronze button.

10. Type Votive Candles for the Button Text. Select votive.htm for the Link and mainFrame for the target.

11. Click below the first button and then press the ENTER key. Repeat step 9 to create another button.

12. For the Button Text, type Pillar Candles and then select pillar.htm for the link and mainFrame for the target.

13. Click below the second button and then press the ENTER key. Repeat step 9 to create another button.

14. For the Button Text, type Main and then select main.htm for the link and mainFrame for the target.

15. Click under the third button and then press the ENTER key. Repeat step 9 to create another button.

16. For the Button Text, type Home and then select index.htm for the link and _blank for the target.

17. Click File on the menu bar and then click Save All.

18. Open the index.htm page. Scroll to the bottom of the page and add a relative link, Recipes, to the recipes.htm frames page. Click the Save button.

19. Press the F12 key to view the index page and then click the link to the Recipes framed page. Test each button. Print copies of each frame if instructed to do so. Upload the Web Site to a remote server if instructed to do so.

In the Lab

2 Creating a Framed Layout for the Credit Protection Web Site

Problem: The Credit Protection Web site has become very popular. Marcy recently received several e-mails asking for suggestions on how to spend money wisely. Marcy asks you to create a new Web site with frames so she can share some of this information. The framed Web site is shown in Figure 4-77. For an updated list of links, visit the Dreamweaver MX Links Web page (scsite.com/dreamweavermx/links) and then click Project 4 Links.

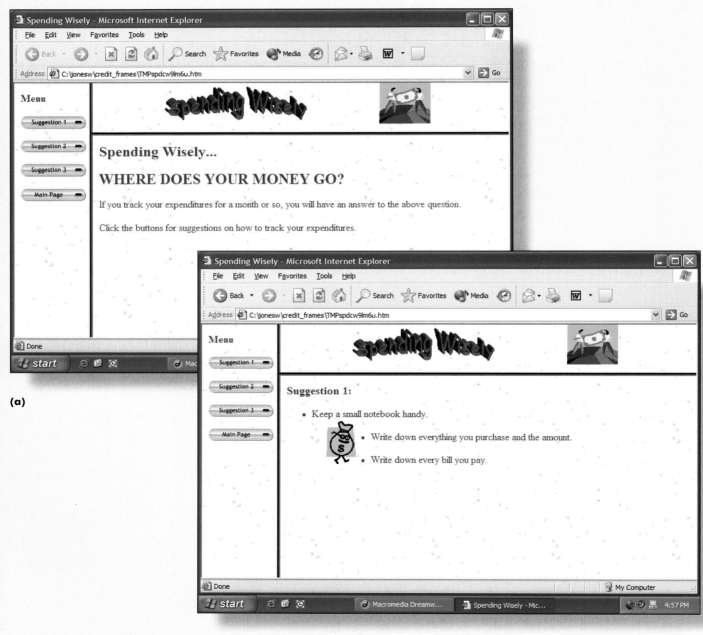

FIGURE 4-77

In the Lab

Instructions: Perform the following tasks:

1. Start Dreamweaver. Display the Property inspector, Standard toolbar, Site panel, and Frames panel.
2. Create a new Web site. Name the Web site Credit Frames and create a folder named credit_frames. The path will be C:/yourname/credit_frames.
3. Use Dreamweaver's integrated file browser to copy the Images folder and files from the Data Files folder to the credit_frames Web site.
4. Create a predefined frameset. Use the Fixed Left, Nested Top frameset. Drag to select Untitled Document in the Title text box on the Document toolbar and then type Spending Wisely. Save the frameset as index in the credit_frames local root folder.

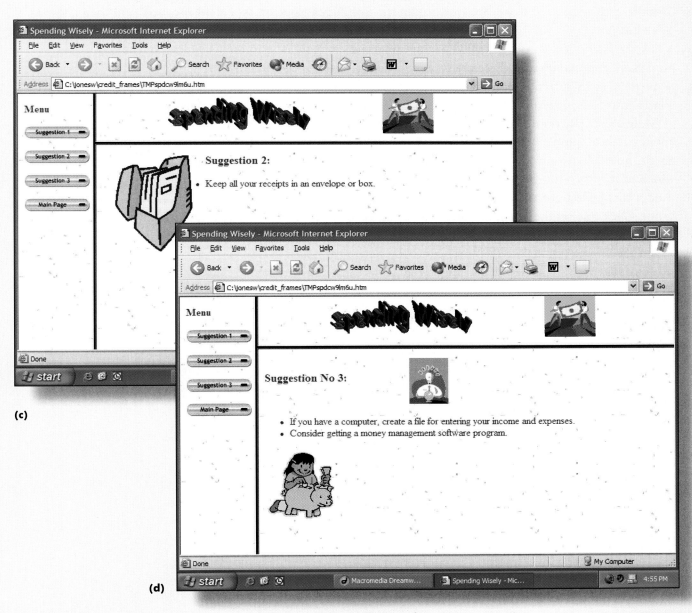

(c)

(d)

FIGURE 4-77 (continued)

(continued)

DW 4.62   Project 4   Page Layout with Frames

Dreamweaver MX

In the Lab

Creating a Framed Layout for the Credit Protection Web Site *(continued)*

5. Click the topFrame. Apply the Yellow color scheme with the Green,Blue,Purple text and links. Apply the background.jpg image and add the Spending Wisely title. Title the frame Spending Wisely. Save the frame as title. Create a one-row, two-column table in the title frame (topFrame). Drag title01.gif to the first column and title02.gif to the second column. Adjust the table size so that the images display proportionally. Select the topFrame in the frames panel and add a margin height of 0. Save the title frame.

6. Click the mainFrame. Apply the same background and color scheme to the mainFrame as you did to the title frame. Title the frame Spending Wisely and save the frame as main.htm.

7. Click the mainFrame in the Frames panel.

8. Double-click main.htm in the Src text box in the Property Inspector, type content.htm, and then click the Save button.

9. Click the leftFrame. Apply the same background and color scheme to the leftFrame as you did to the topFrame and mainFrame. Title the frame Spending Wisely.

10. Type Menu at the top of the leftFrame. Press the ENTER key. Add four Flash buttons. The text for the first Flash button is Suggestion 1, for the second is Suggestion 2, for the third is Suggestion 3, and for the fourth is Main Page. Use the Chrome Bar button with a font size of 10. The links for buttons 1, 2, and 3 are money01.htm, money02.htm, and money03.htm. The link for the Main Page button is content.htm. The target for all four buttons is the mainFrame. Adjust the width of the leftFrame to accommodate the button size and then save the leftFrame as navigate.

11. Add a three-pixel border to both the outer and nested framesets. Use hexadecimal #330000 for the border color. Click File on the menu bar and then click Save All. If instructed to do so, upload your Web site to a remote server.

12. Open the Credit Protection Web site, select the index.htm page, and scroll to the bottom of the page. Insert a blank line above your name and then type Spending Wisely. Create a link from the text, Spending Wisely, to the index.htm file in the Credit Frames Web site. If you are publishing to a remote site, copy and paste the Credit Frames Web site address into the Link box. If you are saving your work to a local computer or server, use the Browse for File icon in the Property inspector to create the link path. Click the Save button on the Standard toolbar.

13. If instructed to do so, upload your Web site changes to a remote server. Press the F12 key to view the Credit Protection index.htm page in your browser. Click the Spending Wisely link to display the Credit Frames Web site. Click each of the navigation buttons to verify that they work. Print copies of each frame if instructed to do so.

In the Lab

3 Adding a Framed Page to the Plant City Web Site

Problem: The mayor has requested that Juan Benito further enhance the Plant City Web site and has suggested that an employment section be added. Juan agrees that this is an excellent idea and meets with you to discuss this new addition. You suggest that a framed-based section be added to the main Web site. Juan supports the idea and provides you with the information to begin creating the site. The Web site is displayed in Figure 4-78. For an updated list of links, visit the Dreamweaver MX Links Web page (scsite.com/dreamweavermx/links) and then click Project 4 Links.

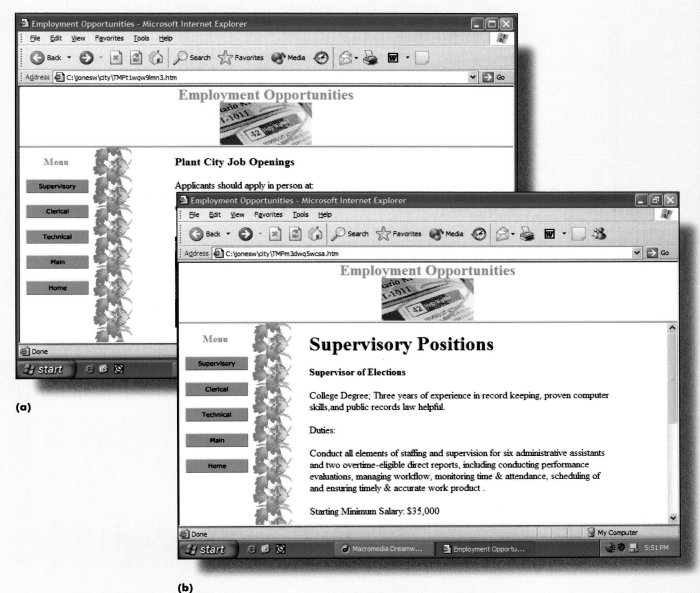

(a)

(b)

FIGURE 4-78

(continued)

In the Lab

Adding a Framed Page to the Plant City Web Site *(continued)*

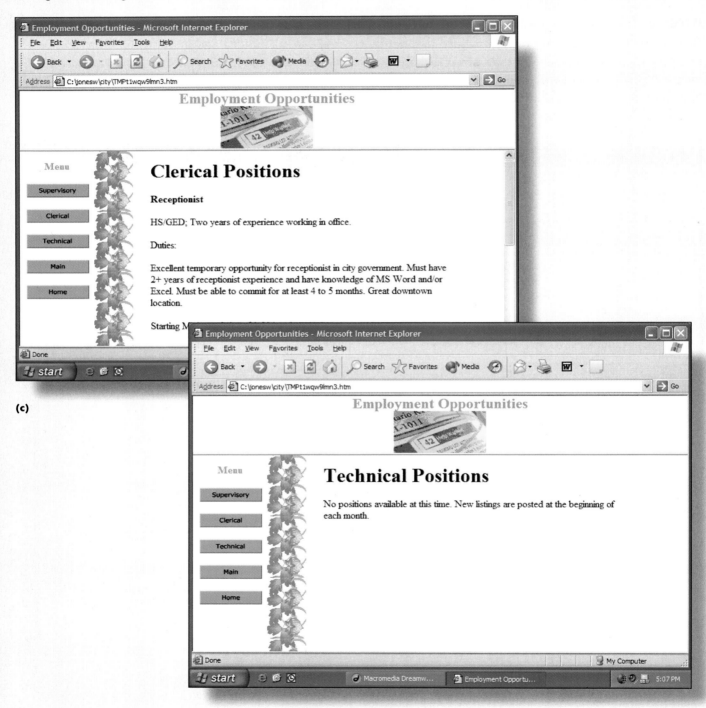

(c)

(d)

FIGURE 4-78 (continued)

In the Lab

Instructions: Perform the following tasks:

1. Start Dreamweaver. Display the Property inspector, Standard toolbar, Site panel, and Frames Panel. Select Plant City in the Site pop-up menu in the Site panel.

2. Use Dreamweaver's integrated file browser to copy the images to your /city/Images folder and the files from the Data Files folder to your /city folder.

3. Create a predefined frameset. Use the Fixed Top, Nested Left frameset. Type Employment Opportunities in the Title text box on the Document toolbar. Save the frameset as employment in the city local root folder.

4. Click the topFrame. Type Employment Opportunities and then center the text. Apply red as the text color and Heading 2 as the style. Drag the help_wanted.gif to the center point under the Employment Opportunities text. Select the topFrame and add a margin height of 0. Save the topFrame as title.

5. Click the mainFrame. Apply the border background to the mainFrame. Save the frame as main.

6. Click the mainFrame in the Frames panel.

7. Double-click main.htm in the Src text box in the Property Inspector, and drag content.htm to the Src text box. Click the File menu and then click Save All.

8. Click the leftFrame. Type Menu at the top of the leftFrame. Center the text and apply red for the text color. Press the ENTER key.

9. Add five Flash buttons. The text for the first Flash button is Supervisory, for the second is Clerical, for the third is Technical, for the fourth is Main, and for the fifth is Home. Use the Generic-Ruby button with a font size of 10. The document links for the first four buttons are the same names as the buttons. The target for all buttons, except for the Home button, is the mainFrame. The link for the Home button is index.htm, and the target is _blank. Adjust the width of the leftFrame to accommodate the button size and then save the leftFrame as navigate.

10. Select the frameset and apply a two-pixel red border. Click File on the menu bar and then click Save All.

11. Open the index.htm page. Scroll to the bottom of the page and add a relative link to the employment.htm frames page. Click the Save button. If instructed to do so, upload your Web site changes to a remote server.

12. Press the F12 key to view the Web site in your browser. Click the Employment link. Test each button. Print copies of each frame if instructed to do so.

Cases and Places

The difficulty of these case studies varies:
▶ are the least difficult; ▶▶ are more difficult; and ▶▶▶ are the most difficult.

1 ▶ Your sports Web site has become very popular. You have decided to add two pages showing uniform types for football and baseball. To show these, you will use a right and left frame. The left frame will contain the name or the link. When the user clicks the link, a picture of the uniform type will display in the right frame. Add a background image to the pages and add a title to each page. Create a link to the home page. Save the page in your sports Web site.

2 ▶ Modify your hobby Web site by adding a two-framed Web page. The left frame should contain three navigation links. Use buttons or text. The first link loads general information about your hobby into the content frame. The second link loads a page with an introductory paragraph and a minimum of three links to other related Web sites. The third link displays the index page in a separate window. Create a link to your home page. Add a four-pixel border to the frame. Upload to a remote site if instructed to do so.

3 ▶▶ Create a new site for your music hobby. Name the site music_frames. Select one of the predefined framesets. Add three pages of content and a title graphic. Use buttons or text in the navigate frame to access and display the content pages in the main frame. Name your frames and framesets and add titles to all frames. Add a background to all frames. Upload the entire Web site to a remote site.

4 ▶▶ Your campaign for political office is doing terrific. Create a new Web site and name it office_frames. Use a predefined frameset. Create three content pages with information highlighting at least three major accomplishments over the past 12 months. Create a static title frame and add your logo to this frame. Create a navigate frame using Flash buttons – one of each for the content pages. Add a three-pixel border to the frame. Upload the framed Web site to a remote server.

5 ▶▶▶ The student trips Web site is receiving hundreds of hits each day, and the student government officers have selected three possible sites to visit. Create a trip_frames Web site using a predefined frameset. Create four content pages: one with general information and the other three highlighting the three possible student trip locations. Include at least one image on each of the content pages. Create a static title frame and a navigate frame. Add a background image to all frames. Create a link to the home page to break out of the framed Web site. Upload the framed Web site to a remote server.

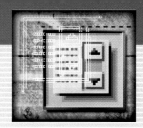

Macromedia Dreamweaver MX

PROJECT

Forms

You will have mastered the material in this project when you can:

O B J E C T I V E S

- Discuss form processing
- Describe the difference between client-side and server-side form processing
- Create a form
- Discuss form design
- Insert a table into a form
- Describe form objects
- Describe and add text fields and text areas to a form
- Describe and add check boxes and radio buttons to a form
- Describe and add lists and menus to a form
- Describe and add form buttons to a form
- Describe form accessibility options
- Apply behaviors to a form
- View and test a form

Macromedia Dreamweaver MX

Forms

CASE PERSPECTIVE

Each day the Florida Parks Web site receives increasingly more hits. Even though the Web site has been expanded, Will is receiving numerous e-mail messages asking questions about the parks. Many of the messages request information about hotel accommodations. Will meets with you and Joan and asks for suggestions. Joan is involved with a group of friends who coordinate the Florida National Parks Volunteer Association. The members suggest to Joan that they could add a form to their Web site to provide hotel information for the three national parks. The volunteer group puts together a daily, weekly, and monthly newsletter and will provide an option for requesting a newsletter. The group members further suggest that the form Web page contain a link to the main Florida Parks Web site.

The team agrees that this is a good idea and that interactive forms with links to the main Florida Parks Web site will enhance and add significantly to their effort to share their affection for Florida's great outdoors.

Introduction

Forms enable the Web page designer to provide visitors with dynamic information and to obtain and process information and feedback from the person viewing the Web page. Web forms are a highly versatile tool and are used for tasks such as surveys, guest books, order forms, tests, automated response, user questions, reservations, and so on. As you complete the activities in this project, you will find that forms are one of the more important sources of interactivity on the Web and are one of the standard tools for the Web page designer.

Project Five — Creating and Using Interactive Forms

In this project, you will learn to create forms and to add form fields to the forms. You will modify two Web pages — a general information page and a hotel reservations form page. The general information page, sponsored by the Florida National Parks Volunteer Association, is shown in Figure 5-1a. This Web page contains a small form at the bottom of the page that provides the viewer an opportunity to subscribe to a free newsletter. The viewer links from within the text contained on the page to a named anchor embedded in the form code. Also contained on the page is a relative link to the Hotel Reservations Form, shown in Figure 5-1b, and an absolute link to the main Florida Parks Web site. The hotel reservations form page contains a request for a hotel reservation at one of the three national parks and provides a jump menu to the Web site for each of the three parks.

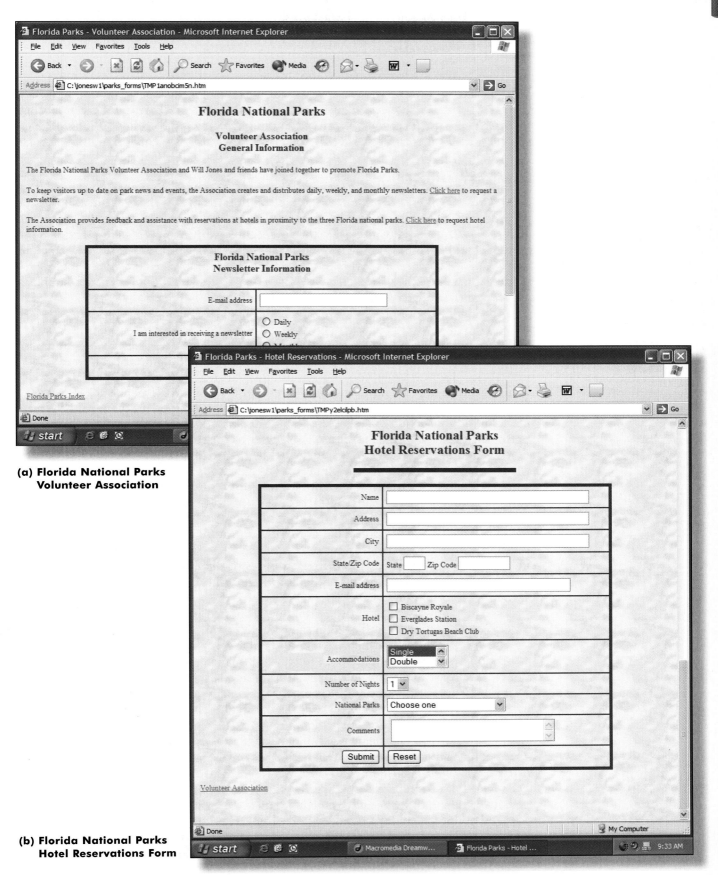

**(a) Florida National Parks
Volunteer Association**

**(b) Florida National Parks
Hotel Reservations Form**

FIGURE 5-1

Understanding How Forms Work

Forms are interactive elements that provide a way for the Web site visitor to interact with the site. A form provides a method for a user to give feedback, submit an order for merchandise or services, request information, and so on. Forms are created using HTML tags. Each form must have a beginning <FORM> and ending </FORM> tag. You cannot nest forms. Each HTML document, however, may contain multiple forms.

Form Processing

A form provides a common way to collect data from a Web site visitor. Forms do not process data. Forms require a script in order for the form input data to be processed. Such scripts are generally a text file that is executed within an application and usually are written in Perl, VBScript, JavaScript, Java, or C++. They reside on a server. Therefore, they are called **server-side scripts**. Other server-side technologies include Macromedia ColdFusion, ASP, ASP.NET, PHP, and JavaServer Pages (JSP). Some type of database application typically supports these technologies.

A common way to process form data is through a **Common Gateway Interface (CGI)** script. When a browser collects data, the data is sent to a Hypertext Transfer Protocol (HTTP) server (gateway) specified in the HTML form. The server starts a program, also specified in the HTML form, that can process the collected data. The gateway can process the input however you choose. It may return customized HTML based on the user's input, log the input to a file, or e-mail the input to someone.

The **<FORM> tag** includes parameters that allow you to specify a path to the server-side script or application that processes the form data and indicate which HTTP method to use when transmitting data from the browser to the server. The two HTTP methods are GET and POST. The **GET method** sends the data with a URL. This method is not widely used because it places a limitation on the amount and format of the data that is transmitted to the application. Another limitation of the GET method is that the information being sent is visible in the browser's Address bar. The **POST method** is more efficient because it sends the data to the application as standard input with no limits. The POST method can send much more information than the typical GET method. With POST, the information is not sent with the URL, so the data is invisible to the site visitor. Both of these methods are attributes of the <FORM> tag.

As an example, when a user enters information into a form and clicks the Submit button, the information is sent to the server, where the server-side script or application processes it. The server responds by sending requested information back to the user, or performing some action based on the content of the form.

The specifics of setting up scripts and database applications are beyond the scope of this book. Another option exists, however, in which a form can be set up to send data to an e-mail address. The e-mail action is not 100 percent reliable and may not work if your Internet connection has extensive security parameters. In some instances, submitting a mailto form results in just a blank mail message being displayed. Nothing is harmed when this happens, but no data is attached and sent with the message. Additionally, some browsers display a warning message whenever a form button using mailto is pressed. This book uses the e-mail action, however, because this is the action more widely available for most students and users. On the other hand, your instructor may have server-side scripting available. Verify with your instructor the action you are to use.

Between the <FORM> and </FORM> tags are the tags that create the body of the form and collect the data. These tags are <INPUT>, <SELECT>, and <TEXTAREA>. The most widely used is the **<INPUT> tag**, which collects data from check boxes, radio buttons, single-line text fields, form/image buttons, and passwords. The **<SELECT> tag** is used with list and pop-up menu boxes. The **<TEXTAREA>** tag collects the data from multiline text fields.

More About

Form Processing

Forms can contain form objects that enable user interaction and allow you to interact with or gather information from visitors to a Web site. After the data is collected from the user, it is submitted to a server for processing or e-mailed to a designated e-mail address. For more information about form processing, visit the Dreamweaver MX More About Web page (scsite.com/ dreamweavermx/ more.htm) and then click Form Processing.

Starting Dreamweaver and Closing Open Panels

When you start Dreamweaver, generally most or all of the panels are displayed by default. Closing unused panels provides uncluttered workspace in the Document window. To organize your workspace, you close the unused open panels. This gives you the maximum window space in the Dreamweaver Document window.

TO START DREAMWEAVER AND CLOSE OPEN PANELS

1 Start Dreamweaver. If necessary, maximize the Document window. Press the F4 key to close all open panels.

2 Press the F8 key to display the Site panel.

3 If necessary, use the View menu to display the Standard toolbar.

4 Use the Window menu to display the Property inspector and the Insert bar.

Workspace Organization

You begin this project by creating a new local site. Creating a local site better organizes and controls the number of pages within the site. Later, you will link this site, named Parks_Forms, to and from the main Florida Parks Web site. Before beginning these steps, verify with your instructor if you are to complete the section on publishing to a remote server. You will need this information in Step 5 when you create a local site. After creating your local site, you use the Dreamweaver integrated file browser to copy Project 5 data files. Perform the following steps to create a local site.

TO CREATE A LOCAL SITE

1 Click Site on the menu bar and then click New Site to display the Site Definition dialog box. If necessary, select the Basic tab.

2 Type Parks_Forms in the What would you like to name your site? text box and then click the Next button to display the Editing Files, Part 2 options.

3 Click No, I do not want to use a server technology and then click the Next button to display the Editing Files, Part 3 options.

4 If necessary, click Edit local copies on my machine, then upload to server when ready (recommended). If necessary, change the Where on your computer do you want to store your files? path to C:\ or the location designated by your instructor. Click the folder icon to the right of the Where do you want to store your files? text box. Create a new folder under C:\jonesw and name it parks_forms so that the path will be C:\jonesw\parks_ forms. Click the Next button to display the Sharing Files options.

5 Click the How do you connect to your remote server? box arrow. Verify with your instructor if you are to select None or if you are to complete the information on publishing to a remote server. Appendix D contains information on how to publish your site to a remote server. If you are to publish to a remote server, follow the instructions in Appendix D. Otherwise, select None. Click the Next button to display the Sharing Files, Part 2 options.

6 If necessary, click No, do not enable check in and check out (displays only if you selected instructions to publish to a remote site). Click the Next button to display the Summary options.

7 Verify that the Summary options are correct, click the Done button to return to Dreamweaver, and then click the Done button in the Edit Sites dialog box.

The new Parks_Forms site is created (Figure 5-2).

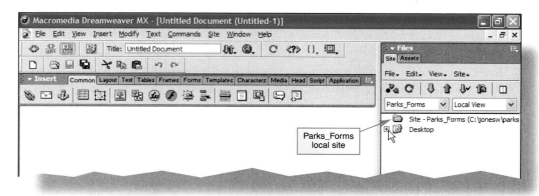

FIGURE 5-2

The Parks Forms Web site you create in this project requires additional HTML documents and images. The documents and images need to be copied from the Data Files to the parks_forms local root folder.

Copying Data Files to the Local Web Site

Your Data Disk contains two HTML documents and an Images folder for Project 5. The HTML documents and the Images folder are located in the Proj05 folder. You use Dreamweaver's integrated file browser to copy the Project 5 documents and Images folder to the parks_forms folder.

The Data Files folder for this project is stored on Local Disk (C:). The location on your computer may be different. If necessary, verify with your instructor the location of the Data Files folder. Complete the following steps to copy the files and folders to the C:\jonesw\parks_forms local root folder.

TO COPY DATA FILES TO THE PARKS_FORMS WEB SITE

1 Click the plus sign (+) to the left of the Desktop icon in the Site panel. Click the plus sign to the left of the My Computer icon and then navigate through the file hierarchy to the Data Files folder as you did in Project 2.

2 Click the plus sign to the left of the Data files folder. Click the plus sign to the left of the Proj05 folder and then click the plus sign to the left of the parks_forms folder.

3 Click the Images folder.

4 Hold down the SHIFT key and then click volunteer.htm or the last file in the list.

5 Copy the Images folder and the HTML documents using Copy and Paste on the context menu to the C:\jonesw\parks_forms local root folder.

6 Click the minus sign to the left of the Desktop icon to collapse the file list.

The Project 5 HTML documents and the Images folder are pasted into the parks_forms local root folder (Figure 5-3).

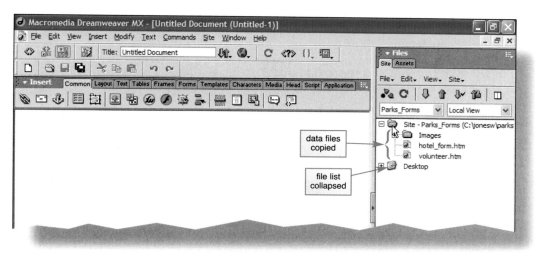

FIGURE 5-3

Form Design

Consistency in Web pages ties the Web site together. Using the same color scheme and background image on all pages within the site is one way to achieve consistency. The Parks_Forms site is a separate site, but will be linked to the main Florida Parks site at a later time. It is even more important, therefore, to continue with the same background and color scheme. The background and color scheme have been added to the two HTML documents you copied from the Data Files folder.

You open the hotel_form.htm document and then insert, center, and format a page heading. Then, you add a page title and save the Web page. Perform the following steps to open the document and to insert and format the heading.

TO INSERT AND FORMAT THE HEADING

1 Close the Untitled-1 Document window and then double-click hotel_form.htm in the Site panel.

2 Click Modify on the menu bar and then click Page Properties. Title the page Florida Parks – Hotel Reservations.

3 Click the Document window and type Florida National Parks for the heading and then press SHIFT + ENTER to insert a line break. Type Hotel Reservations Form for the second heading line.

4 Drag to select both lines of text, apply Heading 1, and then click the Align Center button in the Property inspector.

5 Click outside the selected text and then press the ENTER key.

6 Drag the line.gif image from the Site panel Images folder to the insertion point in the Document window and then press the ENTER key.

7 Click the Align Left button.

8 Click View on the menu bar, point to Visual Aids, and then, if necessary, click to enable Invisible Elements.

9 Click the Save button on the Standard toolbar.

10 Right-click the Files panel group title bar and then click Close Panel Group on the context menu.

The heading is centered and formatted and the title is added (Figure 5-4). The Web page is saved in the folder.

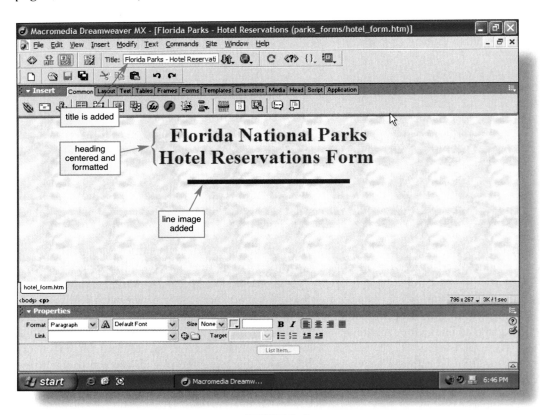

FIGURE 5-4

Forms and Web Pages

Web page designers create forms consisting of a collection of input fields so users can obtain useful information and can enter data. When the user clicks the form Send or Submit button, the data is processed with a server-side script or is sent to a specified e-mail address. A typical form, such as the one created in this project, is composed of form objects. A **form object** can be a text box, check box, radio buttons, list, menu, and other buttons. Form objects are discussed in more detail later in this project.

Inserting a Form

Inserting a form is accomplished in the same manner as inserting a table or any other object in Dreamweaver. Simply position the insertion point where you want the form to start and then click the Form button on the Forms tab. Dreamweaver inserts the <FORM> tags into the source code and then displays a dotted red outline to represent the form in Design view. You cannot resize a form by dragging the borders. The form expands as objects are inserted into the form.

When viewed in a browser, the form outline does not display; therefore, no border exists to turn on or off. Complete the following steps to insert a form into the hotel_form.htm page.

Dreamweaver and Forms

Dreamweaver makes it easy to add forms to your Web pages. The Insert bar contains all of the traditional form objects. When the object is entered into the form, Dreamweaver creates the JavaScript necessary for processing the form. For more information about Dreamweaver and forms, visit the Dreamweaver MX More About Web page (scsite.com/ dreamweavermx/ more.htm) and then click Dreamweaver and Forms.

 **To Insert a Form**

1 **Click the Forms tab in the Insert bar and then point to the Form button (Figure 5-5)**

FIGURE 5-5

2 **Click the Form button. If the dotted red outline is not displayed, click View on the menu bar, click Visual Aids, and then click Invisible Elements.**

The form is inserted into the Document window and is indicated by a dotted red outline. The Form Property inspector is displayed (Figure 5-6). The insertion point is blinking inside the dotted red outline.

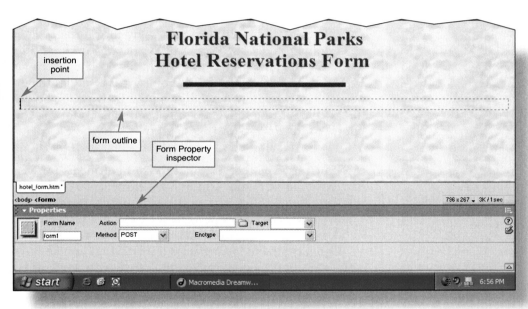

FIGURE 5-6

Property Inspector Form Properties

As you have seen, the Property inspector options change depending on the selected object. The following section describes the form-related features of the Property inspector shown in Figure 5-7.

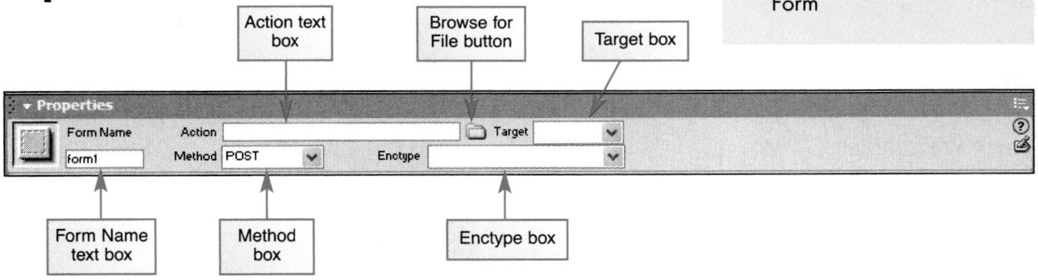

FIGURE 5-7

Other Ways

1. On Insert menu click Form

FORM NAME Naming a form makes it posible to reference or control the form with a scripting language, such as JavaScript, VBScript, or other languages.

The GET Method

Do not use the GET method to send long forms. URLs are limited to 8,192 characters. If the amount of data sent is too large, data will be truncated, leading to unexpected or failed processing results.

Interactive Forms

The mailto:link is the easiest method for e-mailing form data. Generally, however, it is not recommended because many browsers do not recognize an e-mail address as a form's Action. Furthermore, even if the browser accepts this attribute, the user's system and mail configuration may prevent this strategy from working. For more information about interactive forms, visit the Dreamweaver MX More About Web page (scsite.com/ dreamweavermx/ more.htm) and then click Interactive Forms.

ACTION Contains the mailto address or specifies the URL to the dynamic page or script that will process the form.

TARGET Specifies a window or frame in which to display the data after processing if a script designates that a new page displays. The four targets are _blank, _parent, _self, and _top. The **_blank** target opens the referenced link (or processed data) in a new browser window, leaving the current window untouched. The _blank target is the one most often used with a jump menu, discussed later in this project. The three other targets are mostly using with framesets. Project 4 contains a discussion of these three targets.

METHOD Indicates the method with which the form data is transferred to the server. The three options are **POST**, which embeds the form data in the HTTP request; **GET**, which appends the value to the URL requesting the page; and **Default**, which uses the browser's default setting to send the form data to the server. Generally, the default is the GET method. Methods were discussed earlier in this project.

ENCTYPE Specifies a **MIME (Multipurpose Internet Mail Extensions)** type for the data being submitted to the server so the server software will know how to interpret the data. The default is application/x-www-form-urlencode and typically is used in conjunction with the POST method. This default automatically encodes the form response with non-alphanumeric characters in hexadecimal format. The multipart/form-data MIME type is used with a form object that enables the user to upload a file. You can select one of these two values from the Enctype list box or manually enter a value in the Enctype list box. The text/plain value is useful for e-mail replies, but is not an option in the Enctype list box and must be entered manually. This value enables the data to be transmitted in a readable format instead of one long string of data.

When naming the form and the form elements (discussed later in this project), use names that identify the form or form element. Be consistent with your naming conventions and do not use spaces or other special characters, except the underscore. This project uses lowercase letters to name the form and form elements. If you are using server-side scripting, be aware of and avoid reserved words that exist in the scripting language.

Complete the following steps to name the form and to set the other form properties, including using the mailto: action. Verify with your instructor that this is the correct action and that the form data is not to be processed with a server-side script.

Steps To Set the Form Properties

1 **Double-click the Form Name text box in the Property inspector. Type** hotel_form **and then press the TAB key.**

The form is named (Figure 5-8). The insertion point is blinking in the Action text box.

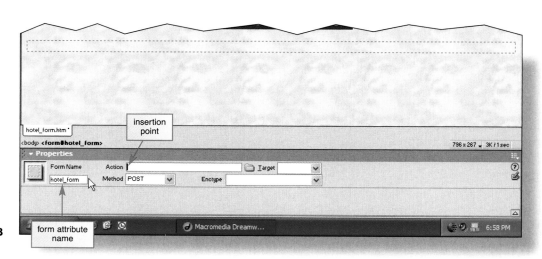

FIGURE 5-8

2 Type `mailto: wjones@parks .com` **(use your own e-mail address).**

Your e-mail address is displayed in the Action text box (Figure 5-9).

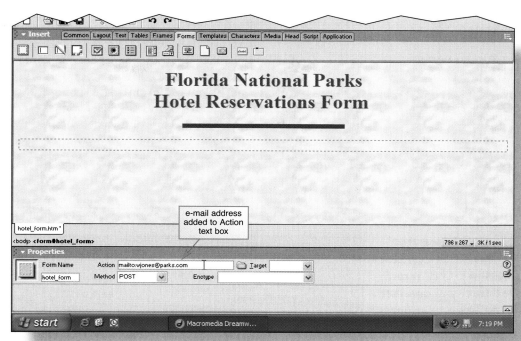

FIGURE 5-9

3 **Click the Target box arrow, select _self, and then press the TAB key.**

The insertion point moves to the Enctype text box (Figure 5-10).

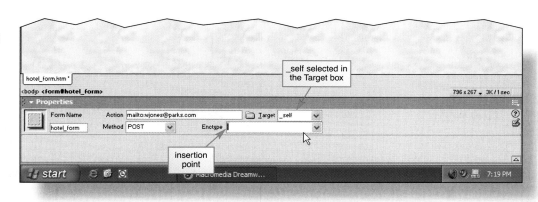

FIGURE 5-10

4 Type `text/plain` **and then press the ENTER key.**

The Enctype text box displays the text/plain text (Figure 5-11).

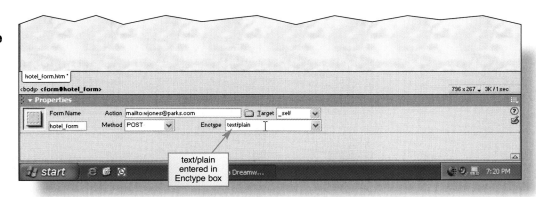

FIGURE 5-11

More About

Naming Forms

A form does not need a name to work, but a name is helpful if you use a Dreamweaver behavior or JavaScript to interact with the form.

Inserting a Table into a Form

Adding and lining up labels within a form sometimes can be a problem. The text field width for labels is measured in **monospace**, meaning that each character has the same width. Regular fonts, however, are not monospaced; they are proportional. Two options to solve this problem are preformatted text and tables. To align labels properly using preformatted text requires the insertion of extra spaces. Using tables and text alignment, therefore, is a faster and easier method to use when creating a form.

Complete the following steps to add a 2-column, 11-row table to the form.

Steps **To Insert a Table into a Form**

1 **Click inside the form (the dotted red outline). Click Insert on the menu bar and then point to Table.**

The insertion point is blinking inside the form (Figure 5-12).

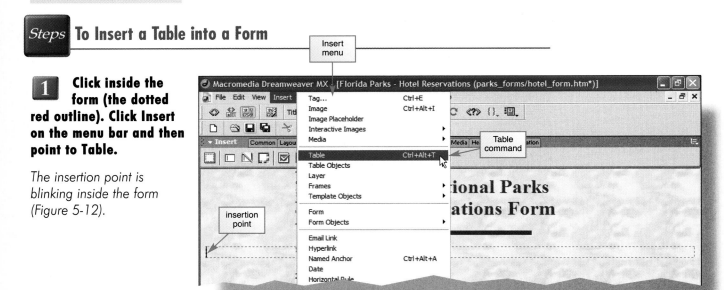

FIGURE 5-12

2 **Click Table.**

The Insert Table dialog box is displayed (Figure 5-13). The Insert Table dialog box on your computer most likely will display different values than those contained in Figure 5-13.

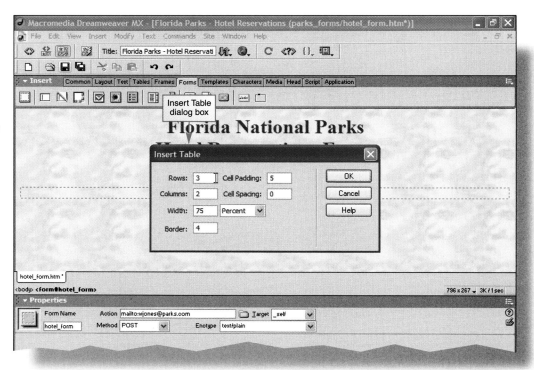

FIGURE 5-13

3 Type the following values in the table: **Rows** – 11, **Cell Padding** – 5, **Columns** – 2, **Cell Spacing** – 0, **Width** – 75 **Percent, and Border** – 4. **Point to the OK button.**

The Insert Table dialog box displays the new values (Figure 5-14).

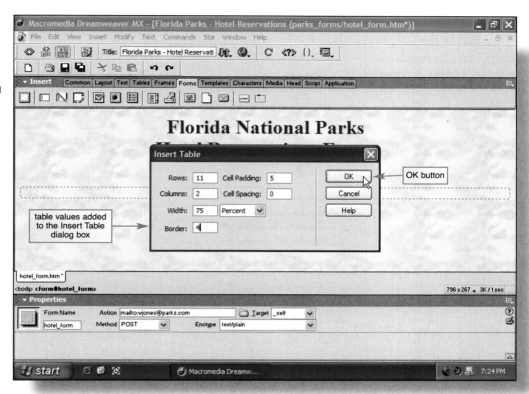

FIGURE 5-14

4 Click the OK button.

The table is inserted into the form outline (Figure 5-15). The <table> tag is selected in the tag selector and the table properties are displayed in the Property inspector.

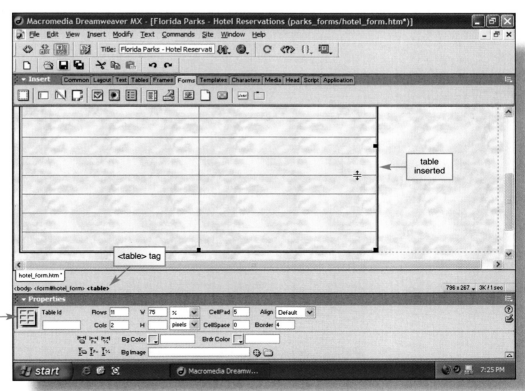

FIGURE 5-15

5 **Click the Align box arrow in the Property Inspector and then select Center.**

The table is centered within the form outline (Figure 5-16).

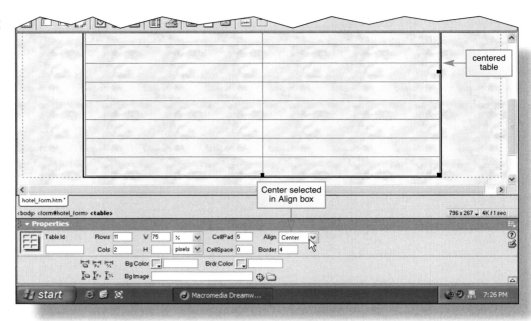

FIGURE 5-16

Other Ways

1. Click Table button on Common tab in Insert bar

Formatting the Table within the Form

Adding formatting creates a more attractive form. Formatting includes changing column width, aligning the text for the labels in column 1 to the right, and changing the border color to match the text color by typing the hexadecimal number. Complete the following steps to add these formatting changes.

Steps **To Format the Form**

1 **If necessary, scroll up, click column 1, row 1, and then drag to select column 1. Click the W text box, type 35% and then press the ENTER key. Point to the Align Right button.**

The column width is set to 35% (Figure 5-17).

FIGURE 5-17

2 **Click the Align Right button in the Property inspector.**

No noticeable changes are displayed in the column. When text is entered into the table cells in column 1, however, the text will align to the right.

3 **Click the <table> tag in the tag selector. Click the Brdr Color hexadecimal text box. Type** #336666 **and then press the ENTER key.**

The table is selected, the Table Property inspector is displayed, and the form border color is changed to match the text color (Figure 5-18).

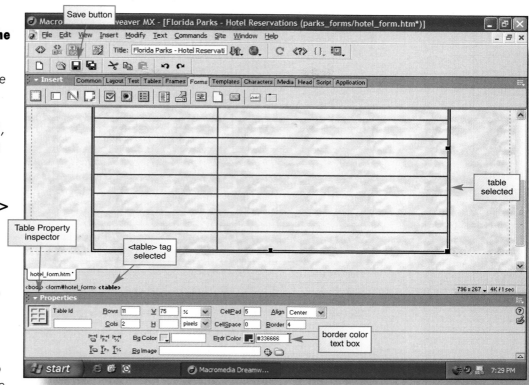

FIGURE 5-18

4 **Click the Save button on the Standard toolbar.**

The form is saved.

Form Objects

In Dreamweaver, data is entered through form input types called **form objects**. After you add the form to your Web page, you begin creating the form by adding form objects. Forms can contain various objects that enable user interaction and are the mechanisms that allow users to input data. Examples of form objects are text fields, check boxes, radio buttons, and so on. Each form object should have a unique name except radio buttons within the same group. In this instance, the radio buttons should share the same name.

The two steps used to insert a form field in a Web page are (1) to add the form field and any accompanying descriptive text, and (2) to modify the properties of the form object. All Dreamweaver form objects are available through the Insert bar Forms tab. Table 5-1 on the next page lists the button names and descriptions available on the Forms tab (Figure 5-19 on the next page).

Table 5-1 Buttons on the Forms Insert Bar	
BUTTON NAME	**DESCRIPTION**
Form	Inserts a form into the Document window
Text Field	Accepts any type of alphanumeric text entry
Hidden Field	Stores information entered by a user and then uses that data within the site database
Textarea	Provides a multi-line text entry field
Checkbox	Allows multiple responses within a single group of options and permits the user to select as many options as apply
Radio Button	Represents an exclusive choice; only one item in a group of buttons can be selected
Radio Group	Represents a group of radio buttons
List/Menu	List displays option values within a scrolling list that allows users to select multiple options; Menu displays the option values in a pop-up menu that allows users to select only a single item
Jump Menu	Special form of a pop-up menu that lets the viewer link to another document or file
Image Field	Creates custom, graphical buttons
File Field	Allows users to browse to a file on their computers and upload the file as form data
Button	Performs actions when clicked; standard Submit and Reset buttons send data to the server and clear the form fields
Label	Provides a way to associate structurally the text label for a field with the field
Fieldset	Container tag for a logical group of form elements

More About

Adding Form Tags

If you attempt to insert a form object without first creating the form, Dreamweaver will display the message, Add form tags? Choose Yes to let Dreamweaver create form tags for the object.

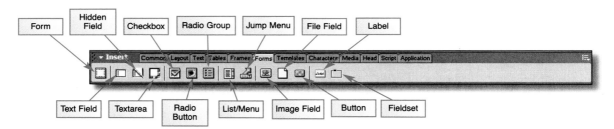

FIGURE 5-19

Text Fields

A **text field** is a form object in which users enter a response. Forms support three types of text fields: single-line, multiple-line, and password. Input into a text field can consist of alphanumeric and punctuation characters. When you insert a text field into a form, the TextField Property inspector is displayed (Figure 5-20).

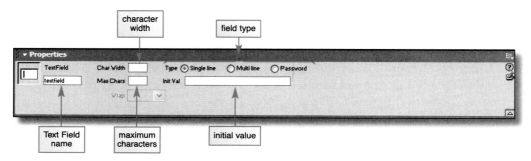

FIGURE 5-20

The following section describes the text field attributes for a single-line and password form. The multiple-line attributes are described later in this project.

TEXTFIELD   Assigns a unique name to the form object.

CHAR WIDTH   Specifies the maximum number of characters that can be displayed in the field.

MAX CHAR   Specifies the maximum number of characters that can be entered into the field.

TYPE   Designates the field as a single-line, multiple-line, or password field.

INIT VAL   Assigns the value displayed in the field when the form first loads.

Typically, a **single-line text field** provides for a single word or short phrase response. A **password text field** is a single-line text box that contains special characters. When a user types in a password field, the entered text is replaced by asterisks or bullets as a security precaution. Passwords sent to a server using a password field are not encrypted and can be intercepted and read as alphanumeric text. For this reason, you should always provide encryption for data you want to keep secure. A multiple-line text field provides for a text area in which to enter a response. The Property inspector for a **multiple-line text field** contains some minor differences than that shown in Figure 5-20. A multiple-line text field is discussed later in this project.

Inserting Text in a Form

You will notice as you insert form objects in a Web page that typically they contain no text label. **Labels** identify the type of data to be entered into the text field form object. Adding a descriptive label to the form that indicates the type of information requested provides a visual cue to the Web site visitor about the type of data to be typed into the text box. Inserting text in a form is as simple as positioning the insertion point and then typing.

Single-Line Text Fields

In the TextField Property inspector, you enter a unique name for each text field in the form. Server-side scripts use this name to process the data. If you use the mailto: option, the name is contained within the data in the e-mail that is sent to your e-mail address. Recall that form object names cannot contain spaces or special characters other than an underscore and that form names are case-sensitive.

The Char Width field default setting is 20 characters. You can change the default, however, by typing in another number. If the Char Width is left as the 20-character default and a user enters 50 characters, the text scrolls to the right and only 20 of those characters are displayed in the text field. Even though the characters are not displayed, they are recognized by the field object and will be sent to the server for processing or contained within the data if mailto: is used.

Entering a value into the Max Chars field defines the size limit and is used to validate the form. If a user exceeds the limit, an alert is sounded. If the Max Chars field is left blank, users can enter any amount of text.

To display a default text value in a field, type the default text in the Init Value field. When the form displays in the browser, this text displays. Complete the following steps to add name, address, and e-mail single-line text boxes to the Hotel Reservations form.

 To Add Descriptive Text and Single-Line Text Fields to the Hotel Reservations Form

1 **If necessary, scroll up and then click column 1, row 1.**

The insertion point is aligned to the right in the cell (Figure 5-21).

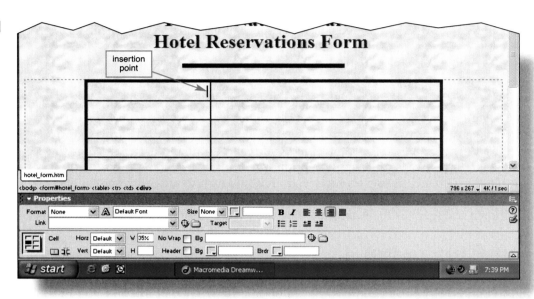

FIGURE 5-21

2 **Type** Name **for the text, press the TAB key, and then point to the Text Field button on the Forms tab.**

The insertion point is displayed in row 1, column 2 (Figure 5-22).

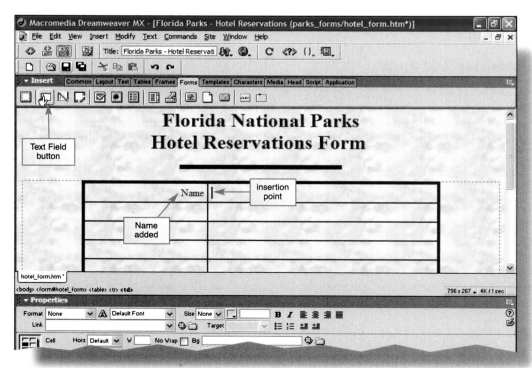

FIGURE 5-22

3 Click the Text Field button.

A text field form object is inserted into the table (Figure 5-23). The Property inspector displays properties relative to the text field.

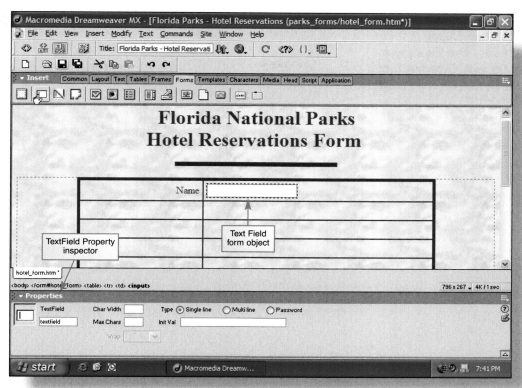

FIGURE 5-23

4 Double-click the TextField text box in the Property inspector, type name and then press the TAB key. Type 50 in the Char Width text box and then press the TAB key. If necessary, click Single line.

The text field expands to a character width of 50 (Figure 5-24).

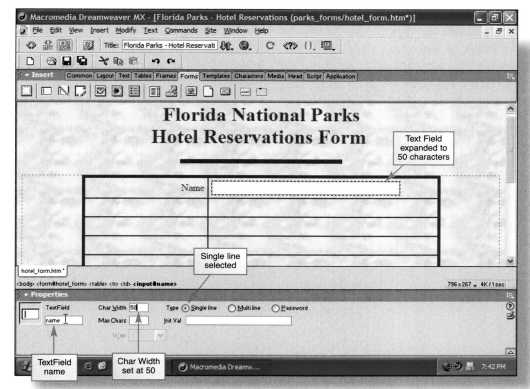

FIGURE 5-24

5 **Click column 1, row 2, type** Address**, and then press the TAB key. Click the Text Field button on the Forms tab.**

The Address text is displayed in column 1, row 2, and the text field form object is inserted into the table (Figure 5-25). The Property inspector displays TextField properties.

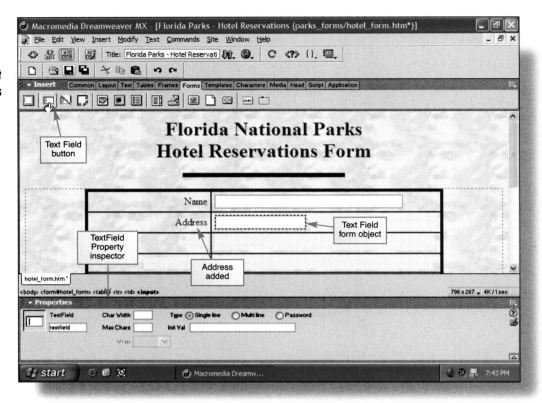

FIGURE 5-25

6 **Double-click the TextField text box in the Property inspector, type** address**, and then press the TAB key. Type** 50 **in the Char Width text box and then press the TAB key. If necessary, click Single line.**

The text field expands to a character width of 50 (Figure 5-26).

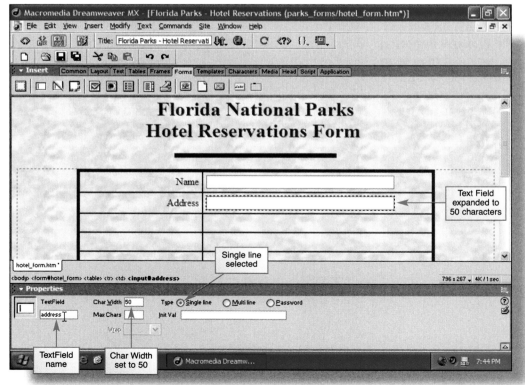

FIGURE 5-26

7 Click column 1, row 3, and then type City. Click the Text Field button on the Forms tab. Type city for the TextField name. Type 50 in the Char Width box and then press the TAB key. Ensure Single line is selected.

City is displayed in column 1, row 3. The text field expands to a character width of 50 (Figure 5-27).

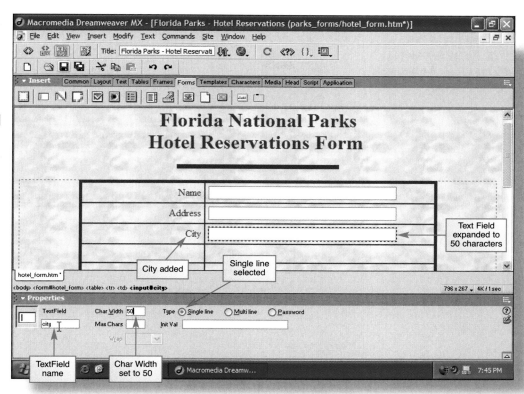

FIGURE 5-27

8 Click column 1, row 4. Type State/Zip Code as the label and then press the TAB key.

State/Zip Code is displayed in column 1, row 4, and the insertion point is blinking in column 2, row 4 (Figure 5-28).

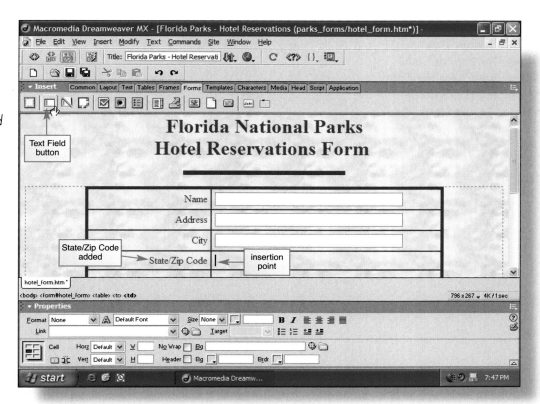

FIGURE 5-28

9 Type `State` and then press the **SPACEBAR**. Point to the Text Field button on the Forms tab.

The descriptive text for State is displayed (Figure 5-29).

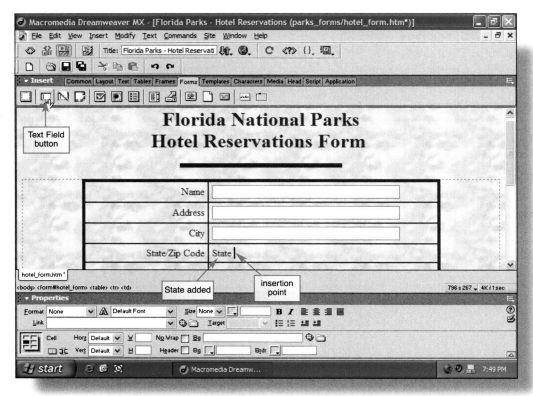

FIGURE 5-29

10 Click the Text Field button. Type `state` for the TextField name. Type `2` for the Char Width and Max Chars values. Ensure Single line is selected.

The TextField name is displayed as state, and Char Width and Max Chars are set to 2 (Figure 5-30).

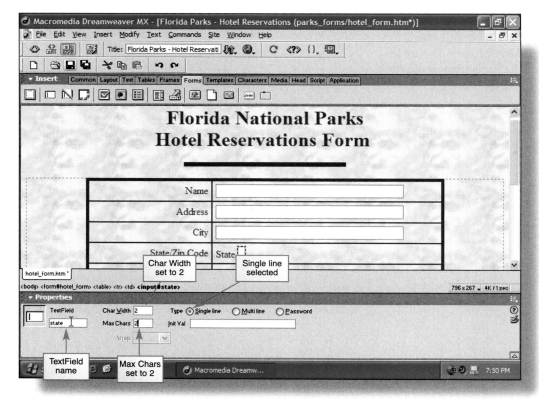

FIGURE 5-30

11 Click to the right of the State form object and then press the **SPACEBAR.** Type Zip Code and then press the **SPACEBAR.** Click the Text Field button on the Forms tab. Type zip for the TextField name. Type 10 for the Char Width and Max Chars values and then press the **TAB** key. Ensure Single line is selected.

Zip Code is displayed as the text. The Char Width and Max Chars are set to 10 (Figure 5-31).

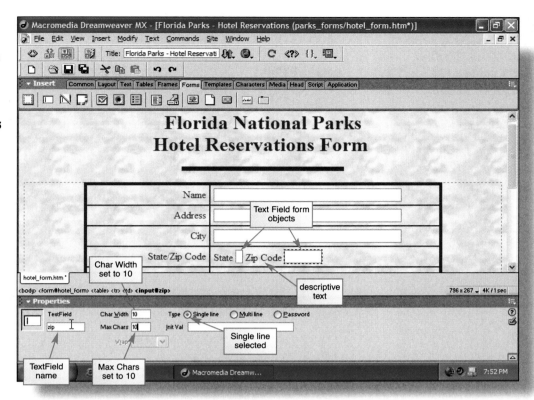

FIGURE 5-31

12 If necessary, scroll down. Click column 1, row 5, and then type E-mail address. Press the **TAB** key and then click the Text Field button on the Forms tab.

The descriptive text for the e-mail address is displayed and the text field form is added to the document (Figure 5-32).

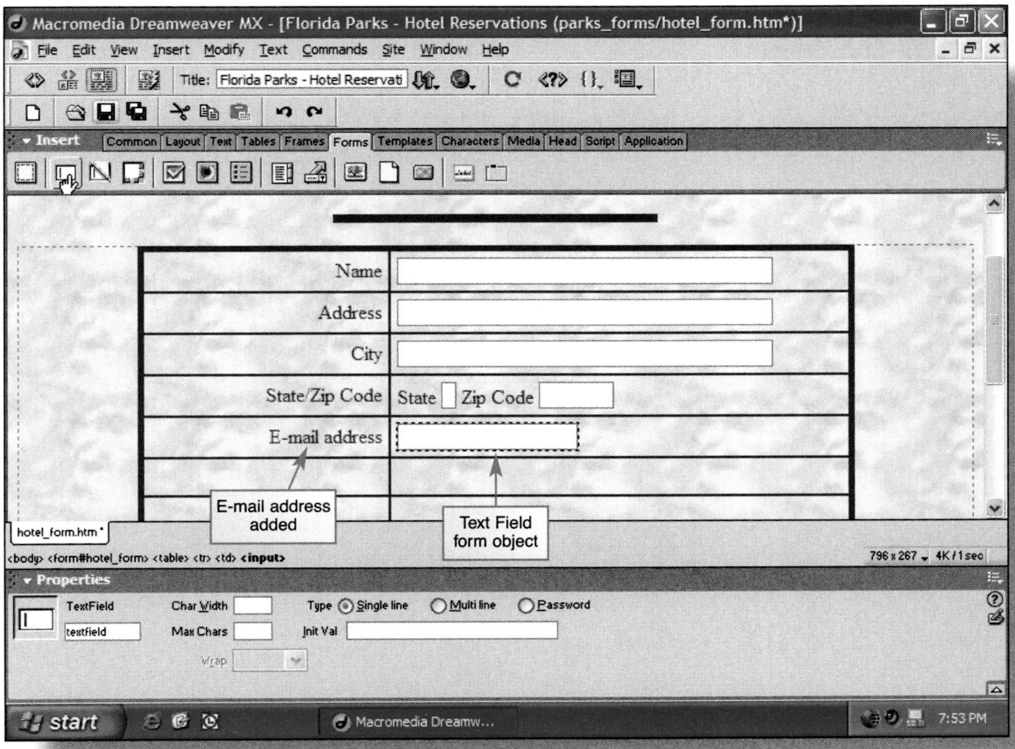

FIGURE 5-32

13 Type email **for the TextField name. Type** 45 **for the Char Width value and then press the ENTER key. Ensure Single line is selected.**

The text field is named and the size of text box form is adjusted (Figure 5-33).

14 **Click the Save button on the Standard toolbar.**

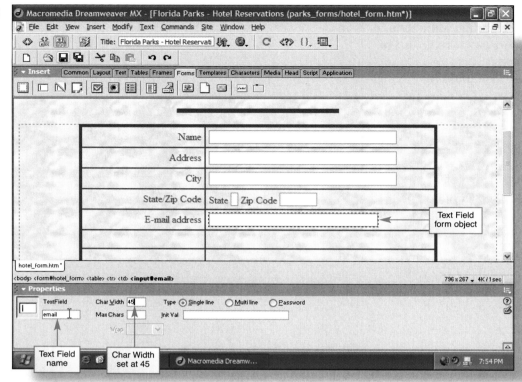

FIGURE 5-33

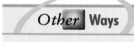

Other Ways

1. On Insert menu point to Form Object, click Text Field

Check Boxes

Check boxes allow the Web user to click a box to toggle a value to either yes or no. They frequently are used to enable the visitor to select as many of the listed options as desired. Figure 5-34 displays the Property inspector for a check box. Similar to a text field, each check box should have a unique name. The Checked Value text box contains the information you want to send to the script or to include in the mailto information to identify the data. For the Initial State, the default is Unchecked. Click Checked if you want an option to appear selected when the form first loads in the browser. Complete the following steps to add three check boxes to the Hotel Reservations form.

Figure 5-34

1 **Click column 1, row 6, type** Hotels **and then press the TAB key. Click the Checkbox button on the Forms tab.**

Hotels is displayed for the descriptive text and a check box is added to the form (Figure 5-35). The Property inspector changes to display the Checkbox properties.

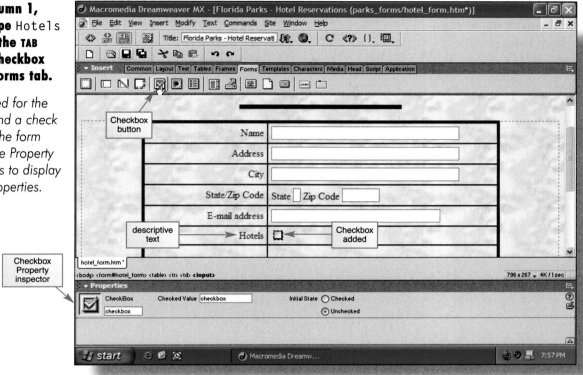

FIGURE 5-35

2 **Type** hotel1 **for the CheckBox name. Press the TAB key and then type** biscayne **in the Checked Value text box.**

The properties for the first check box are displayed (Figure 5-36).

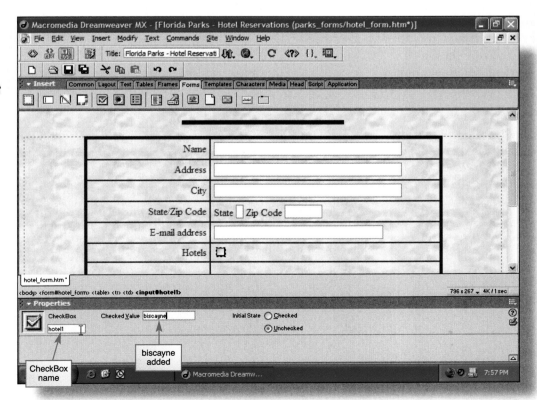

FIGURE 5-36

3 Click to the right of the check box form object and then press SHIFT + ENTER to add a line break. Point to the Checkbox button on the Forms tab.

The insertion point is below the first check box (Figure 5-37).

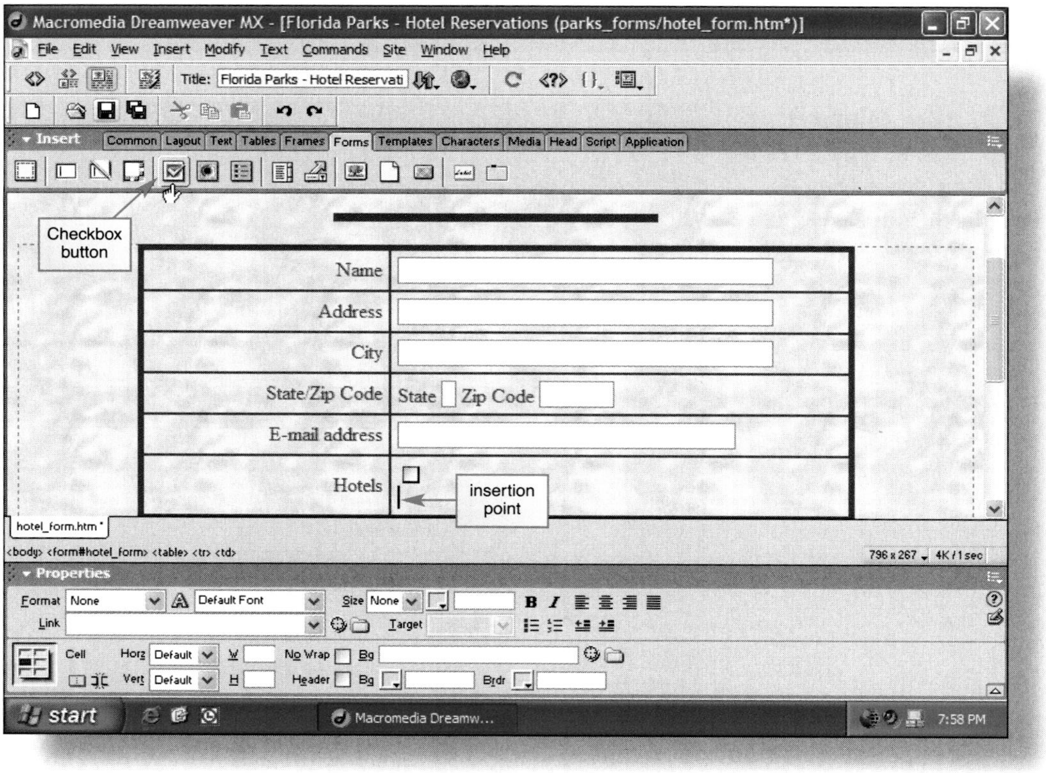

FIGURE 5-37

4 Click the Checkbox button. Type hotel2 for the CheckBox name. Press the TAB key and then type everglades in the Checked Value text box. Press the ENTER key.

The second check box is added to the form and the properties for the second check box are displayed (Figure 5-38).

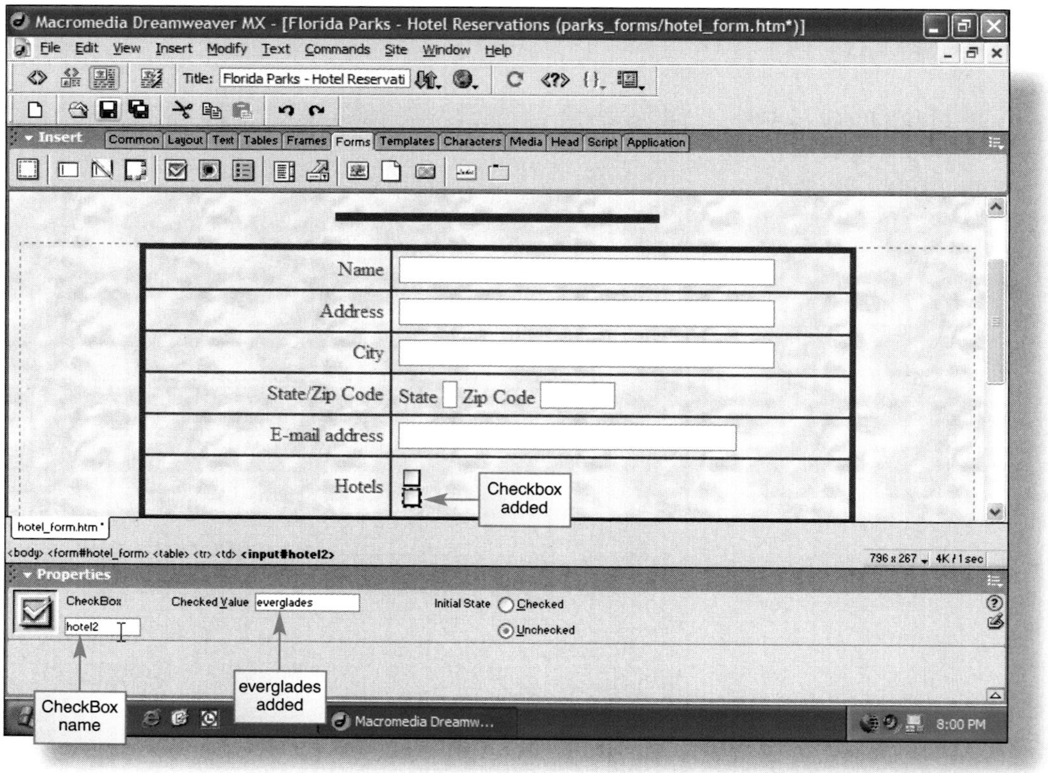

FIGURE 5-38

5 **Click to the right of the second check box, press SHIFT + ENTER to add a line break, and then click the Checkbox button on the Forms tab.**

The third check box is added (Figure 5-39).

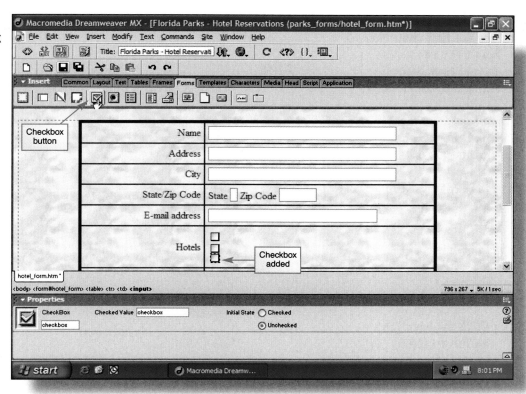

FIGURE 5-39

6 **Type hotel3 for the CheckBox name. Press the TAB key and then type dry_tortugas in the Checked Value text box.**

The properties for the third check box are displayed (Figure 5-40).

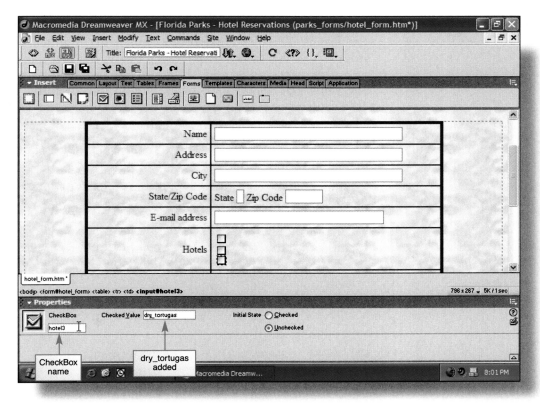

FIGURE 5-40

7 **Click to the right of the first check box. Type** Biscayne Royale **and then press the DOWN ARROW key. Type** Everglades Station **for the descriptive text for the second check box, press the DOWN ARROW key, and then type** Dry Tortugas Beach Club **as the text for the third check box.**

The descriptive text is entered for all three check boxes (Figure 5-41).

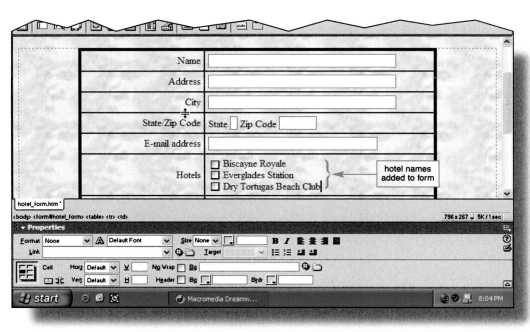

FIGURE 5-41

8 **Click the Save button on the Standard toolbar.**

List/Menu

Another way to provide form field options to your Web site visitor is with lists and menus. These options provide many choices within a limited space. A **list** provides a scroll bar with up and down arrows that lets a user scroll the list, whereas a menu contains a pop-up list. Multiple selections can be made from a list. Users can select only one item from a menu. The menu is discussed later in this project. Figure 5-42 illustrates the Property inspector for a list.

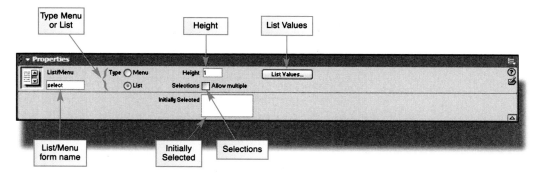

Figure 5-42

LIST/MENU Assigns a name to the list or menu.

TYPE Designates if the form object is a pop-up menu or a scrolling list.

HEIGHT Specifies the number of lines that display in the form; default is 1.

SELECTIONS Designates if the user can select more than one option; not available with Menu.

LIST VALUES Opens the List Values dialog box.

INITIALLY SELECTED Contains a list of available items from which the user can select.

As with all other form objects, the list should be named. You control the height of the list by specifying a number in the Height box. You can elect to show one item at a time or show the entire list. If you display the entire list, the scroll bar does not display. Clicking the Selections check box allows the user to make multiple selections. Clicking the List Values button opens the List Values dialog box so you can add and remove items in the list. These added items are displayed in the Initially Selected text box. The List Values dialog box lets you add items to a list or pop-up menu. Each item in the list has a label and a value. The label represents the text that appears in the list and the value is sent to the processing application if the item is selected. If no value is specified, the label is sent to the processing application instead.

Complete the following steps to add a scrolling list to the Hotel Reservations form.

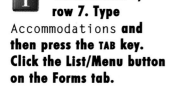

To Create a Scrolling List

1 **Click column 1, row 7. Type** Accommodations **and then press the TAB key. Click the List/Menu button on the Forms tab.**

The text label Accommodations is entered and the List/Menu form object is inserted. The Property inspector displays the List/Menu properties (Figure 5-43).

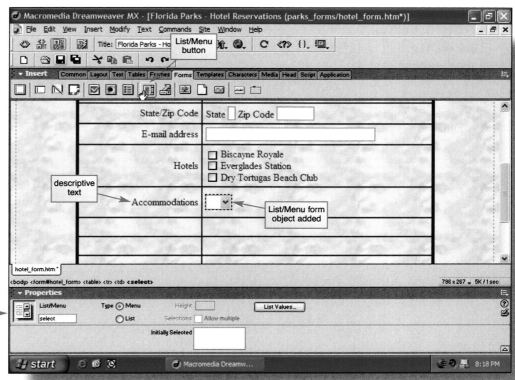

FIGURE 5-43

2 **Type** accommodations **for the List/Menu name. Click List in the Type options. Type** 2 **in the Height box. Click the Selections check box to allow multiple selections. Point to the List Values button.**

The list is named, the height is set to 2, and Allow multiple selections is selected (Figure 5-44).

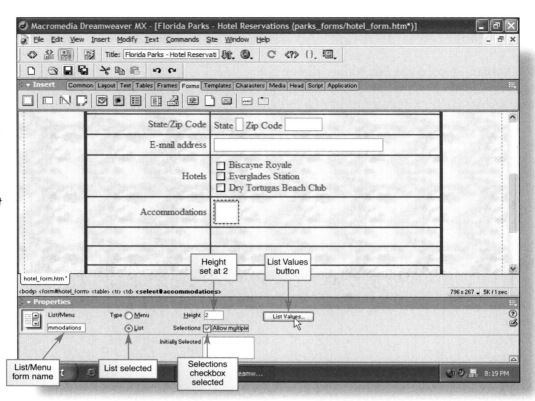

FIGURE 5-44

3 **Click the List Values button.**

The List Values dialog box is displayed (Figure 5-45). The insertion point is blinking in the Item Label box.

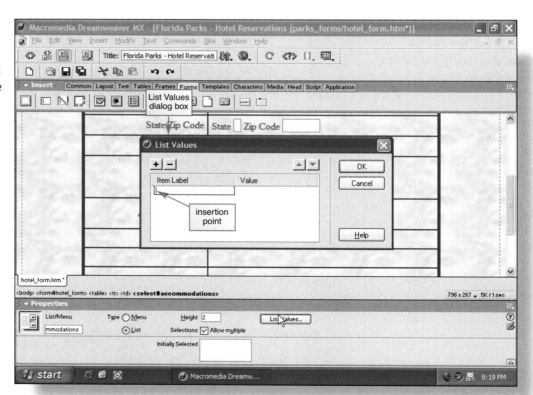

FIGURE 5-45

4 **Type** Single **as the first Item Label, press the TAB key, and then type** single **as the Value. Press the TAB key.**

A second line is added to the Item Label list (Figure 5-46).

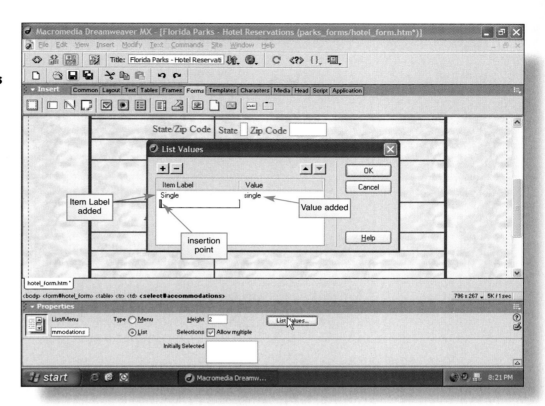

FIGURE 5-46

5 **Type** Double **as the second Item Label. Type** double **as the Value and then press the TAB key. Type** Suite **as the third Item Label. Type** suite **as the Value and then press the TAB key. Type** Luxury Suite **as the fourth Item Label. Type** luxury_suite **as the Value and then point to the OK button.**

The items for the List Menu are added to the List Values dialog box (Figure 5-47).

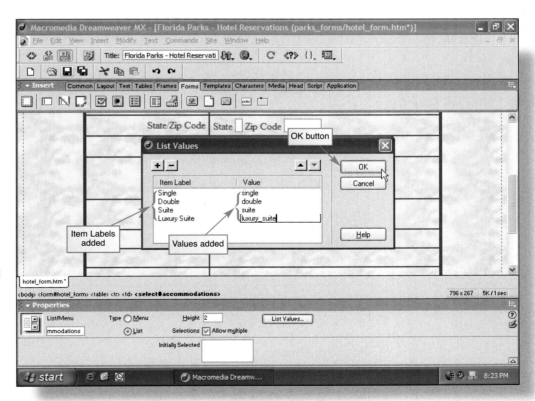

FIGURE 5-47

6 Click the OK button.

The list is displayed in the Initially Selected box in the Property inspector (Figure 5-48).

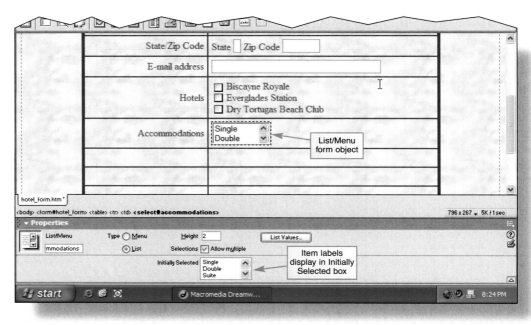

FIGURE 5-48

7 Click Single in the Initially Selected box in the Property inspector.

Single is designated as the default item in the list (Figure 5-49).

8 Click the Save button on the Standard toolbar.

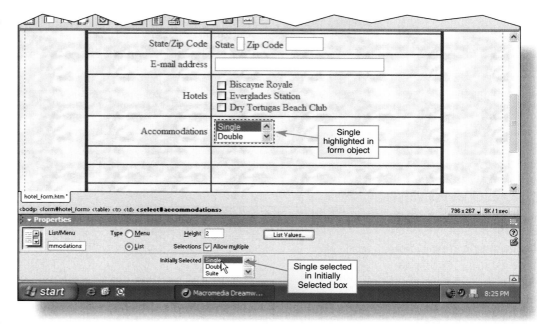

FIGURE 5-49

1. On Insert menu point to Form Object, click List/Menu

Pop-Up Menus

You can offer your Web site visitors a range of choices by using a pop-up menu. This type of menu (also called a drop-down menu) lets a user select a single item from a list of many options. **Pop-up menus** are useful when you have a limited amount of space because it occupies only a single line of vertical space in the form. Only one option choice is visible when the menu form object is displayed in the browser.

Clicking a down arrow displays the entire list. The user then clicks one of the menu items to make a choice. The following steps create a pop-up menu.

Steps To Create a Pop-Up Menu

1 **If necessary, scroll down and then click column 1, row 8. Type** Number of Nights **and then press the TAB key. Click the List/Menu button on the Forms tab.**

The descriptive text for the pop-up menu is added to the form and the List/Menu form object is displayed. The Property inspector changes to reflect the selected form object (Figure 5-50).

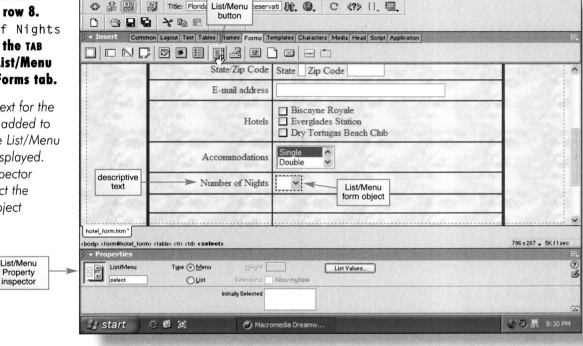

FIGURE 5-50

2 **Type** nights **in the List/Menu text box to name the pop-up menu. Point to the List Values button.**

The pop-up menu is named (Figure 5-51).

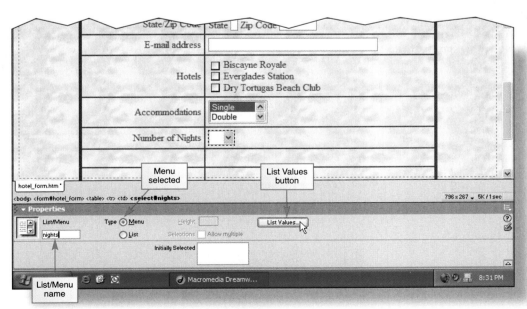

FIGURE 5-51

3 Click the List Values button. In the List Values dialog box, type 1 for the Item Label, press the TAB key, and then type 1 for the Value. Press the TAB key.

The List Values dialog box is displayed (Figure 5-52). The Item Labels and Values are entered.

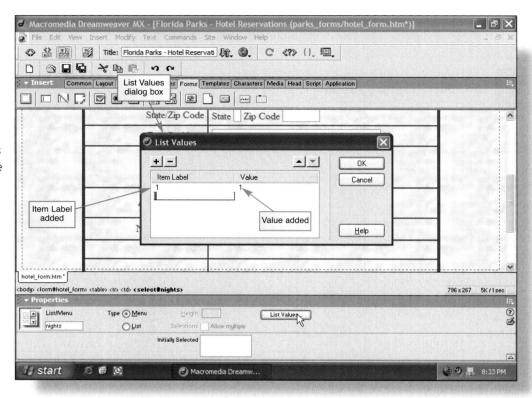

FIGURE 5-52

4 Repeat Step 3 in the List Values dialog box, incrementing the number each time by 1 in the Item Label and Value fields, until the number 7 is added to the Item Label field and the Value field. Point to the OK button.

The List Values dialog box displays Item Label and Value field numbers through 7. (Figure 5-53).

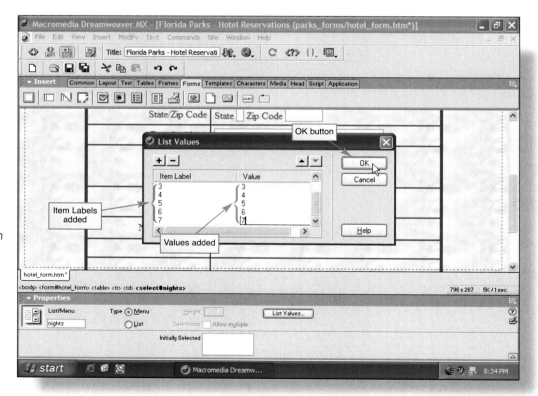

FIGURE 5-53

5 **Click the OK button.**

The numbers are displayed in the Initially Selected text box (Figure 5-54).

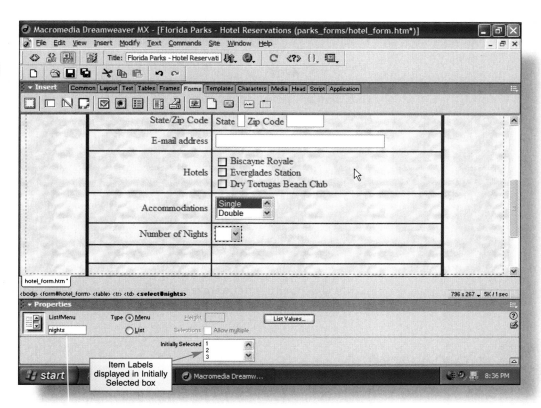

FIGURE 5-54

6 **Click the number 1 in the Initially Selected box in the Property inspector.**

The number 1 is displayed in the pop-up menu form object as the default value (Figure 5-55).

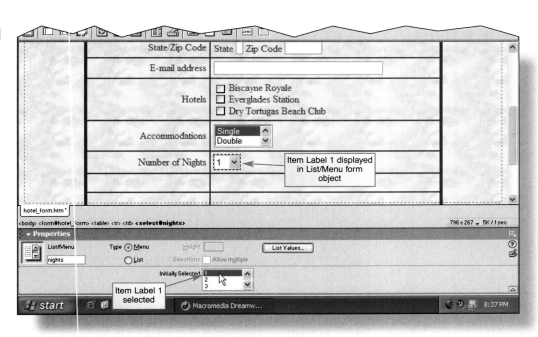

FIGURE 5-55

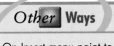

Other Ways

1. On Insert menu point to Form Object, click List/Menu

Jump Menus

A **jump menu** is a special type of pop-up menu that provides options that link to documents or files. You can create links to documents in your Web site, links to documents on other Web sites, e-mail links, links to graphics, or links to any file type that can be opened in a browser. A jump menu can contain three basic components:

▶ An optional menu selection prompt. This could be a category description for the menu items or instructions, such as Choose one.

▶ A required list of linked menu items. When the user chooses an option, a linked document or file is opened.

▶ An optional Go button. With a Go button, the user makes a selection from the menu and the new page loads when the Go button is clicked. Without a Go button, the new page loads as soon as the user makes a selection from the menu.

The following steps add a jump menu with a link to each of the three national parks. The menu will contain a Choose one selection prompt and the linked Web site will open in the main window.

To Insert a Jump Menu

1 Click column 1, row 9, type Links, and then press the TAB key. Point to the Jump Menu button on the Forms tab.

The text for the Jump Menu is inserted in the form (Figure 5-56).

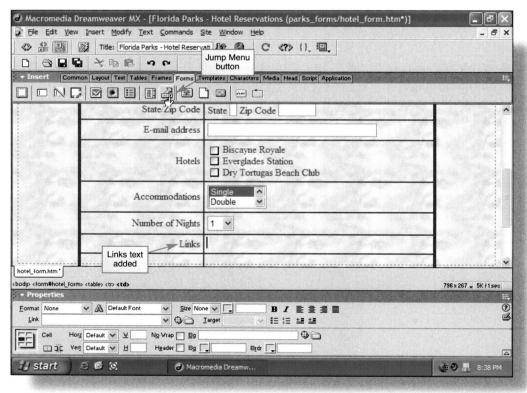

FIGURE 5-56

2 **Click the Jump Menu button. Type** Choose one **in the Text text box and then point to the plus (+) button.**

The Insert Jump Menu dialog box is displayed (Figure 5-57). Choose one is added as the first menu item in the Text text box.

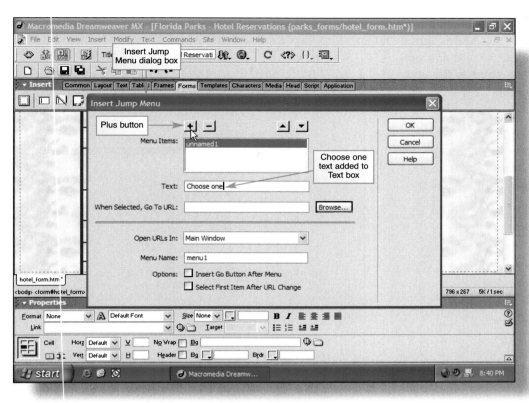

FIGURE 5-57

3 **Click the plus button and then double-click the Text text box. Type** Biscayne National Park **as the text for the second menu item and then press the TAB key.**

Biscayne National Park is added as the text for the second menu item (Figure 5-58). The insertion point is blinking in the When Selected, Go To URL text box.

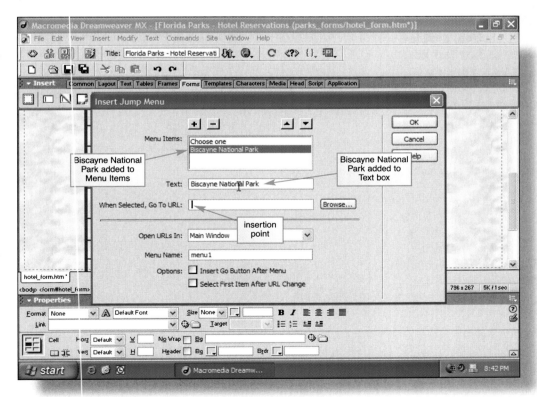

FIGURE 5-58

4 **Type** http://
www.nps.gov/
bisc/index.htm **and
then point to the plus
button.**

The URL for the Biscayne
National Park is added to
the Insert Jump Menu dia-
log box (Figure 5-59).

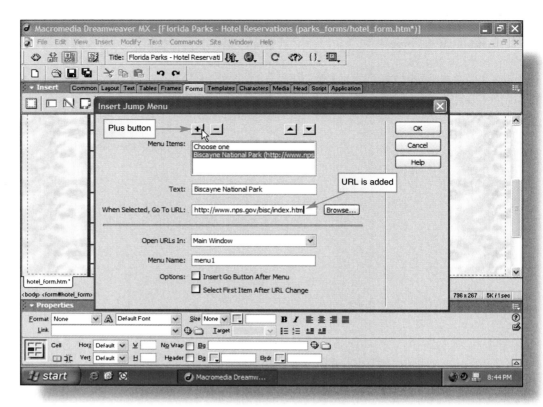

FIGURE 5-59

5 **Click the plus
button, double-
click the Text text box,
type** Dry Tortugas
National Park, **and
then press the TAB
key. Type** http://
www.nps.gov/drto/
index.htm **and then
point to the plus button.**

Dry Tortugas National Park
is added as the third menu
item and the URL for the
Dry Tortugas National
Park is added to the Insert
Jump Menu dialog box
(Figure 5-60).

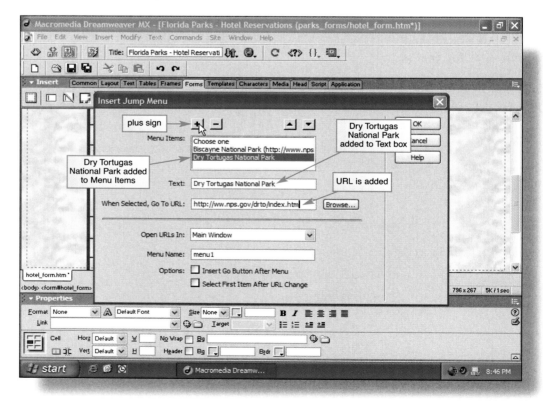

FIGURE 5-60

6 Click the plus button, double-click the Text text box, type Everglades National Park, and then press the TAB key. Type http:// www.nps.gov/ever/ index.htm and then click Select First Item After URL Change to select the check box. Point to the OK button.

Everglades National Park is added as the fourth menu item, and the URL for the Everglades National Park is added to the Insert Jump Menu dialog box (Figure 5-61). The Select First Item After URL Change check box is selected.

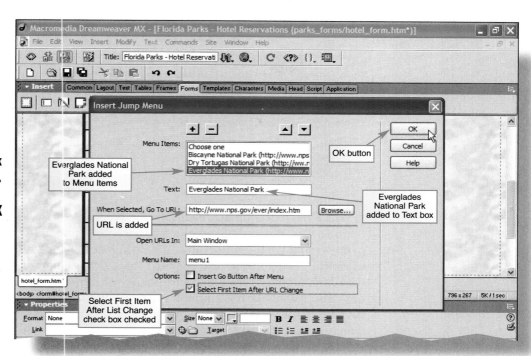

FIGURE 5-61

7 Click the OK button.

The Jump Menu is added to the form and is completed (Figure 5-62).

8 Click the Save button on the Standard toolbar.

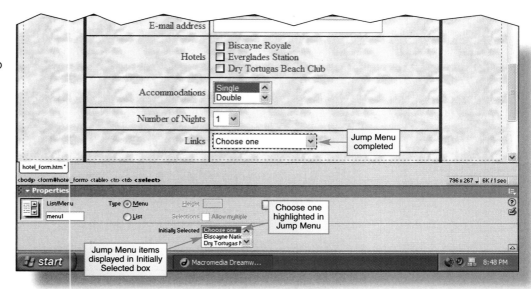

FIGURE 5-62

TextArea Text Fields

Earlier in this project, you added several single-line text fields to the Hotel Reservations form. You create a **text area form object** by adding a multiple-line text field. The Property inspector settings are similar to single-line text fields except in the multiple-line text field you can specify the maximum number of lines the user can enter and specify the wrap attributes. The Property inspector for a TextField textarea is shown in Figure 5-63.

Other Ways

1. On Insert menu point to Form Object, click Jump Menu

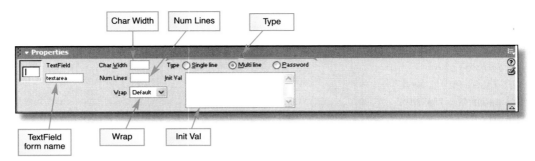

FIGURE 5-63

The Wrap pop-up menu enables the Web page designer to select one of four options: Off, Default, Virtual, or Physical. Selecting **Off** or **Default** prevents the text from wrapping to the next line and requires that the user press the ENTER key to move the insertion point to the next line. **Virtual** limits word wrap to the text area. If the user's input exceeds the right boundary of the text area, the text wraps to the next line. When data is submitted for processing, however, it is submitted as one string of data. **Physical** sets word wrap in the text area and applies it to the data when it is submitted for processing.

An initial value is added to the Init Val box. When the user clicks the box, this initial value is highlighted and then deleted when the user begins to enter text. Use the multiple-line text field to provide a comments text area in your Hotel Reservations form. Use the following steps to add a multiple-line text field to provide a comments text area in your Hotel Reservations form.

 To Add a TextArea Text Field

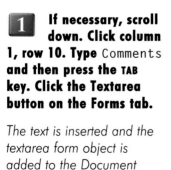

1 If necessary, scroll down. Click column 1, row 10. Type Comments and then press the TAB key. Click the Textarea button on the Forms tab.

The text is inserted and the textarea form object is added to the Document window (Figure 5-64).

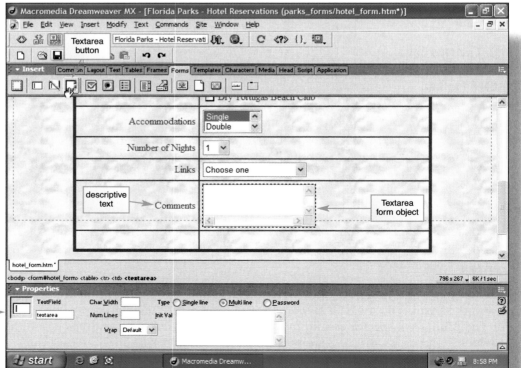

FIGURE 5-64

2 **Type** comments **as the name for the TextField. Press the TAB key and type** 50 **for the Char Width. Press the TAB key and type** 4 **for the Num Lines. Click the Init Val box, type** Please add your comments **and then click the Save button on the Standard toolbar.**

The form is named, the character width and number of lines are set, and an initial value is entered (Figure 5-65).

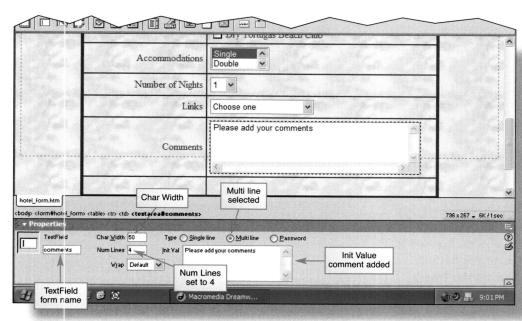

FIGURE 5-65

Form Buttons

Form buttons control form operations. HTML provides three basic types of buttons: Submit, Reset, and Command. Submit and Reset buttons are standard features of almost every form. When the user presses the **Submit button,** the data entered into a form is sent to a server for processing or forwarded to an e-mail address. In some instances, the data is edited by JavaScript or other code prior to processing. The **Reset button** clears all the fields in the form. You also can assign other processing tasks that you have defined in a script to a **Command button.** For example, a Command button might calculate the total cost of a hotel room for a week. Command buttons require that additional code be added using Code View. The Button Name Property inspector is displayed in Figure 5-66.

Other Ways

1. On Insert menu point to Form Object, click Textarea

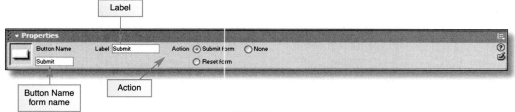

FIGURE 5-66

BUTTON NAME Assigns a name to the button. Submit and Reset are reserved names.

SUBMIT BUTTON Tells the form to submit the form data to the processing application or script or send the data to an e-mail address.

RESET BUTTON Tells the form to reset all the form fields to their original values.

LABEL Determines the text that appears on the button.

ACTION Determines what happens when the button is clicked and how the data is to be processed. Form processing was discussed earlier in this project. The three processing options are to submit the contents of the form, to clear the contents of the form, or to do nothing.

The following steps add the Submit and Reset buttons to the Hotel Reservations form.

Steps **To Add the Submit and Reset Buttons**

1 **If necessary, scroll down and then click column 1, row 11. Point to the Button button on the Forms tab (Figure 5-67).**

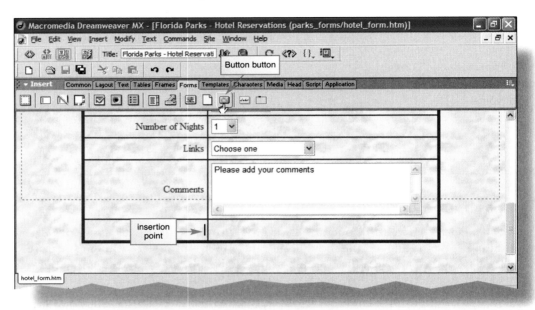

FIGURE 5-67

2 **Click the Button button.**

The Submit button form object is added to the form and the Property inspector displays the Submit button attributes (Figure 5-68).

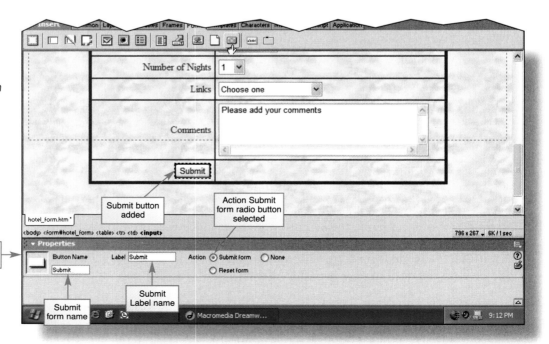

FIGURE 5-68

3 Press the TAB key and then click the **Button** button on the **Forms** tab.

The Submit button form object is added to the form and the Property inspector displays the Submit button attributes (Figure 5-69).

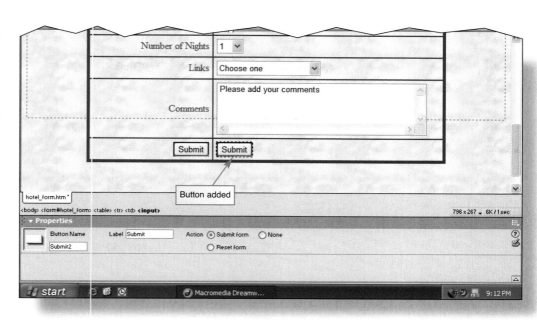

FIGURE 5-69

4 Type Reset as the **Button Name** name and then press the TAB key. Type Reset in the **Label** text box and then click **Reset form** in the **Action** area.

The button is renamed Reset and Reset form is selected (Figure 5-70).

5 Click the **Save** button on the **Standard toolbar.**

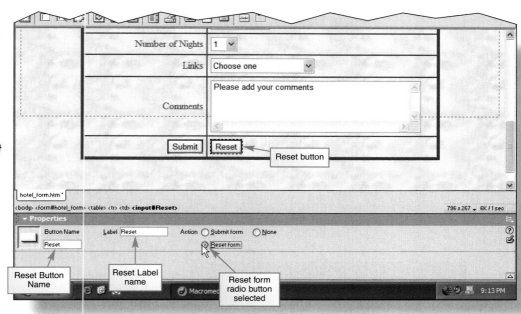

FIGURE 5-70

Radio Buttons and Radio Button Groups

Radio buttons provide a set of options from which the user can select only one button. Clicking a second button automatically deselects the first choice. Each button in a form consists of a radio button and a corresponding descriptive label. In Dreamweaver, you can insert radio buttons one at a time or insert a radio button group. When you insert an individual radio button, the Property inspector in Figure 5-71 on page DW 5.44 is displayed. In the Property inspector's RadioButton text box, type a descriptive name. If you are inserting individual radio buttons to create a group, you must label each

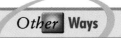
Other **Ways**

1. On Insert menu point to Form Object, click Button

More About

Customizing Forms

Some organizations develop a template form for use throughout their Web sites. The Web site developer uses the template to design a custom form for a particular need. For more information about customizing Dreamweaver forms, visit the Dreamweaver MX More About Web page (scsite.com/dreamweavermx/more.htm) and then click Customizing Forms.

button. In the Checked Value text box, enter the value you want sent to the server-side script or application when a user selects this radio button. For Initial State, click Checked if you want an option to appear selected when the form first loads in the browser.

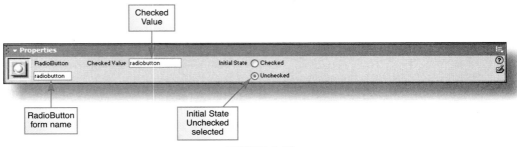

FIGURE 5-71

A radio button group is the most commonly used option. If you are adding multiple radio buttons to a form, each set of radio buttons must have a unique name. When you click the Radio Group button on the Forms tab, the Radio Group dialog box is displayed (see DW 5.48).

Form Objects, the Label Button, and Accessibility

So far, when you added a form object to a page, you also added descriptive text to identify the object. Traditionally, this is the way most Web page authors label form objects. The current HTML specifications, however, provide the <LABEL> tag. This tag adds functionality to the form object by associating the descriptive text for the form object directly with that object. This is particularly helpful for those users of speech-based browsers.

The Forms Insert bar contains a Label button. To add a label, select the form object to which you want to associate the label, and then click the Label button. When you click the Radio button, for instance, and then click the Label button, Code View is displayed. The label is manually typed between the <LABEL> and </LABEL> tags. Likewise, Dreamweaver does not provide a Property inspector for labels, so any editing of labels is done in Code View.

Manual editing of the <LABEL> tag can be time-consuming and error-prone, but Dreamweaver provides an alternative with the Accessibility options for form objects. When the Accessibility option for form objects is enabled, Dreamweaver displays the Input Tag Accessibility Attributes dialog box (Figure 5-72). Table 5-2 contains a description of the options in this dialog box. Recall that Accessibility options are turned on through Preferences. In the Preferences dialog box, click the Accessibility category and then click the check box for Form Objects. Appendix B contains an expanded discussion of accessibility options.

FIGURE 5-72

Table 5-2 Input Tag Accessibility Attributes

ATTRIBUTE NAME	DESCRIPTION
Label	The descriptive text that identifies the form object.
Style	Provides three options for the <label> tag. *Wrap with Label Tag* wraps a label tag around the form item. *Attach Label Tag using 'for' Attribute* allows the user to associate a label with a form element, even if the two are in different table cells. *No Label Tag* turns off the accessibility option.
Position	Determines the placement of the label text in relation to the form object — before or after the form object.
Access Key	Selects the form object in the browser using a keyboard shortcut (one letter). This key is used in combination with the CTRL key (Windows) to access the object.
Tab Index	Specifies the order in which the form objects are selected when pressing the TAB key. The tab order goes from lowest to highest numbers.

Adding a Form to the Volunteer.htm Page

The next step is to add a form and radio button group form field to the volunteer.htm Web page. Informational text has been added and the background image has been applied to this data file. You open the file and then add a form containing an e-mail form object and a radio button group.

Complete the following steps to open the volunteer.htm Web page.

TO OPEN THE VOLUNTEER.HTM WEB PAGE

1 Press the F8 key to display the Site panel.

2 Double-click volunteer.htm in the Site panel.

3 Right-click the Files panel group title bar and then click Close Panel Group on the context menu.

The volunteer.htm file is displayed in the Document window (Figure 5-73).

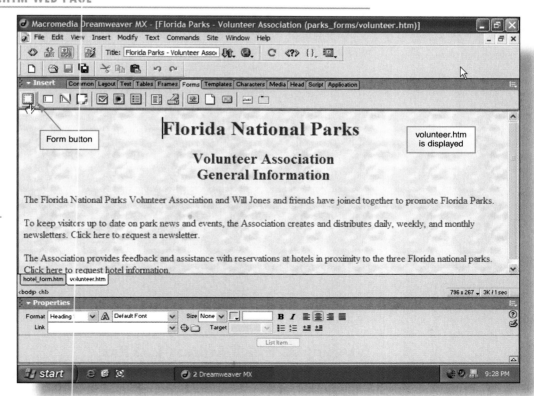

FIGURE 5-73

Complete the following steps to add a form and a table to the volunteer.htm Web page.

TO ADD A FORM AND TABLE TO THE VOLUNTEER WEB PAGE

1 If necessary, scroll down and then position the insertion point at the end of the last line of text. Press the ENTER key.

2 Click the Form button on the Forms tab.

3 In the Property inspector, type newsletter for the form Name. Type mailto:wjones@parks.com in the Action text box (use your e-mail address). Select _self on the Target pop-up menu, type text/plain in the Enctype box, and then press the ENTER key.

4 Click inside the form in the Document window. Click Insert on the menu bar and then click the Table command.

5 Create a 2-column, 4-row table, with a cell padding of 5, a width of 75%, and a border of 4.

6 Click the Align pop-up menu in the Property inspector and center the table.

7 Enter #336666 in the Brdr Color text box and then press the ENTER key.

8 Select row 1 and merge the cells.

9 Click row 1 and type Florida National Parks and then press SHIFT + ENTER to insert a line break.

10 Type Newsletter Information and then select the two lines of text.

11 Apply Heading 2 and then center the heading.

12 Select column 1, rows 2 through 4, and then click the Align Right button in the Property inspector.

13 Click the Save button on the Standard toolbar.

The form and table are added to the volunteer.htm page (Figure 5-74).

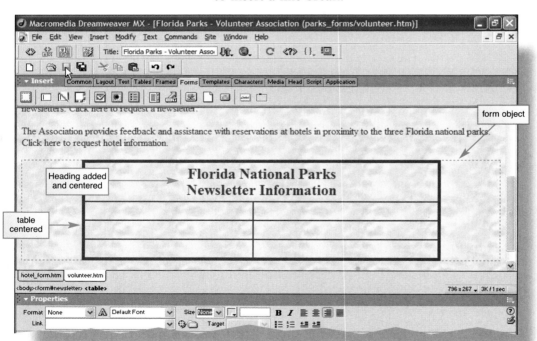

FIGURE 5-74

Inserting an E-Mail Address Text Box

Descriptive text for the e-mail address and a single-line text field for user input are added to row 2. Complete the following steps to add the e-mail address and single-line text form object.

TO INSERT A SINGLE-LINE TEXT BOX

1 Click column 1, row 2, type E-mail address, and then press the TAB key.

2 Click the Text Field button on the Forms tab.

3 Double-click the TextField text box in the Property inspector. Type email and then press the TAB key.

4 Type 30 and then press the TAB key.

The descriptive text and text form object for the e-mail address are added to the form (Figure 5-75). A character width of 30 is set.

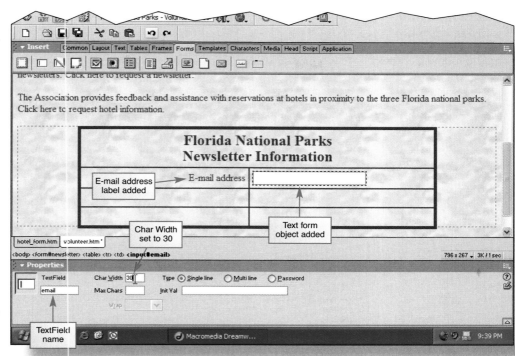

FIGURE 5-75

Radio Groups

When adding multiple radio buttons to a form, the **Radio Group** form object is the fastest and easiest method to use. Complete the following steps to add labels and a Radio Group to the Newsletter Information form.

To Add a Radio Group

1 Click column 1, row 3. Type I am interested in receiving a newsletter **and then press the TAB key. Point to the Radio Group button on the Forms tab.**

The text is added (Figure 5-76).

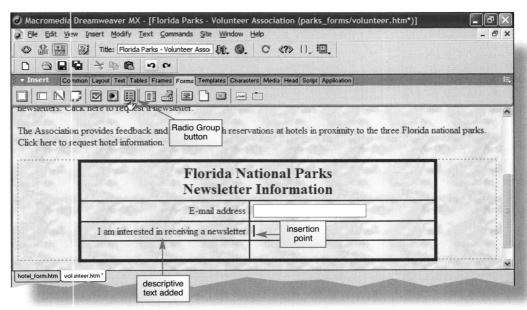

FIGURE 5-76

2 **Click the Radio Group button.**

The Radio Group dialog box is displayed (Figure 5-77). The insertion point is blinking in the Name text box.

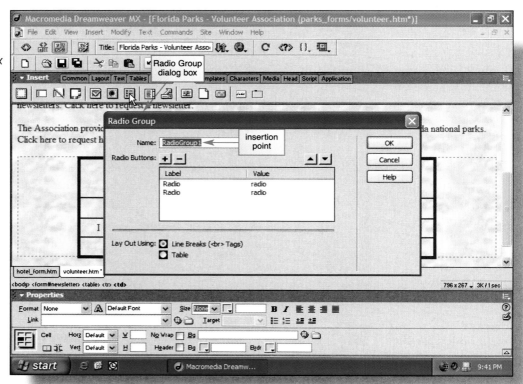

FIGURE 5-77

3 **Type** newsletter **and then click the first instance of Radio in the Label field.**

The Radio label is selected (Figure 5-78).

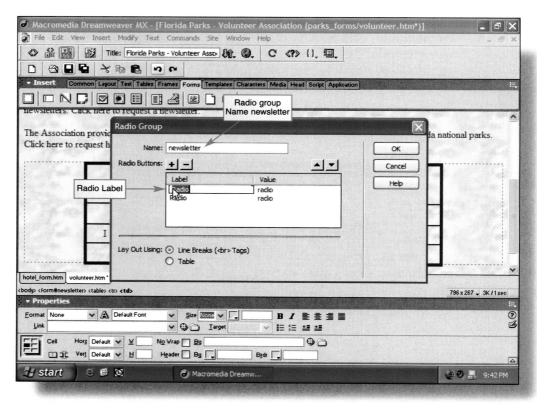

FIGURE 5-78

4 Type Daily as the
Label and then
press the TAB key. Type
daily as the Value.

*The Label and Value are
entered (Figure 5-79).*

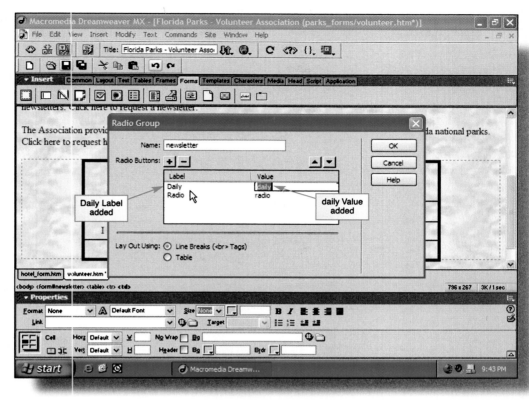

FIGURE 5-79

5 Press the TAB key,
type Weekly, and
then press the TAB key.
Type weekly and then
point to the plus button.

*The Label and Value are
entered (Figure 5-80).*

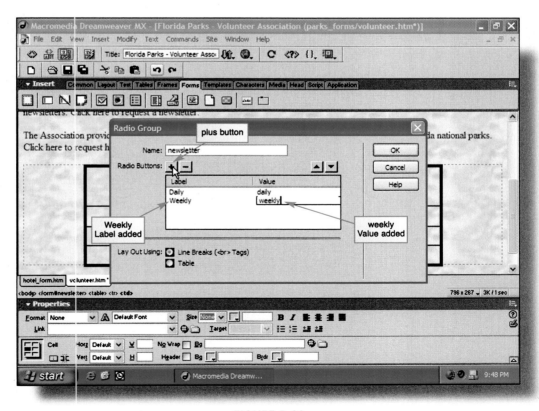

FIGURE 5-80

6 Click the plus button, click Radio in the Label field, type `Monthly`, and then press the TAB key. Type `monthly` and then, if necessary, click the Lay Out Using Line Breaks (
 Tags) radio button. Point to the OK button.

The text Monthly is entered for the Label and monthly is entered for the Value (Figure 5-81).

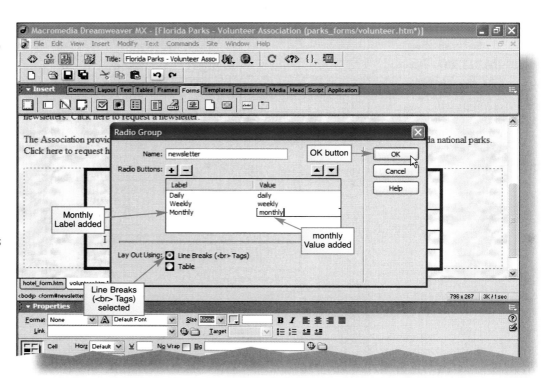

FIGURE 5-81

7 Click the OK button.

The radio group and labels are inserted into the form (Figure 5-82).

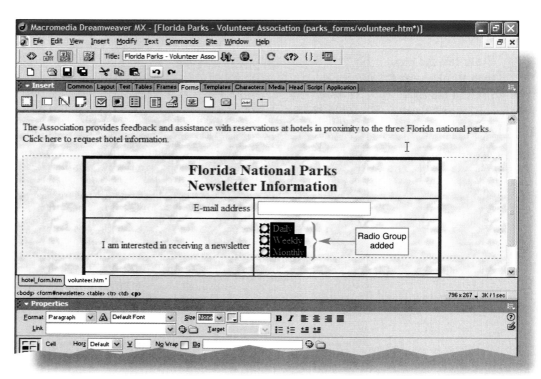

FIGURE 5-82

Other Ways

1. On Insert menu point to Form Object, click Radio Group

The final step is to add the Submit and Reset buttons to the form. Complete the following steps to add these two buttons.

TO ADD THE SUBMIT AND RESET BUTTONS TO THE VOLUNTEER FORM

1 If necessary, scroll down. Click column 1, row 4 and then click the Button button on the Forms tab.

2 Click column 2, row 4 and then click the Button button on the Forms tab.

3 Type Reset as the ButtonName name and then press the TAB key.

4 Type Reset in the Label text box and then click Reset form in the Action area.

5 Click the Save button on the Standard toolbar.

The properties are set and the Submit and Reset buttons are added to the form (Figure 5-83).

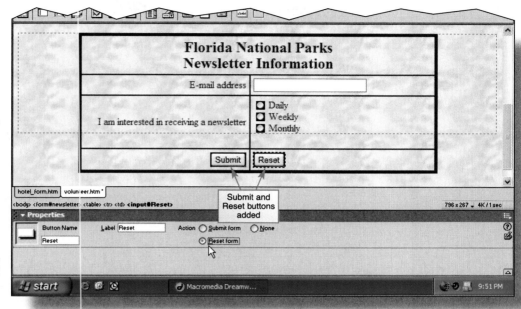

FIGURE 5-83

Adding Links

Project 2 discussed the different types of links, including relative, absolute, named anchors, and e-mail links. Complete the following steps to add links to the volunteer.htm and hotel_form.htm Web pages.

TO ADD LINKS TO THE VOLUNTEER AND HOTEL FORM WEB PAGES

1 Click to the right of the Florida National Parks heading in the radio buttons form.

2 Click Insert on the menu bar and then click Named Anchor. Name the anchor newsletter.

3 If necessary, scroll up. Select the text, Click Here, in the second paragraph, second sentence. Type #newsletter in the Link box in the Property inspector.

4 Select the text, Click Here, in the third paragraph, third sentence. Type hotel_form.htm in the Link box.

5 Scroll down, click below the form, type Florida Parks Index, and then select the text you just typed.

6 Click the Link box in the Property inspector. If you publish your Web sites, type the absolute link to the Florida Parks index page. Otherwise, type the full path to the location of the Florida Parks index page on your computer. If necessary, check with your instructor for the full path information.

7 Click the Save button on the Standard toolbar.

8 Click the hotel_form tab and then, if necessary, scroll to the bottom of the form. Type Volunteer Association and then select the text you just typed. Type volunteer.htm in the Property inspector Link box.

9 Click the Save button on the Standard toolbar. Figures 5-84a and 5-84b on the next page display the whole form for both pages.

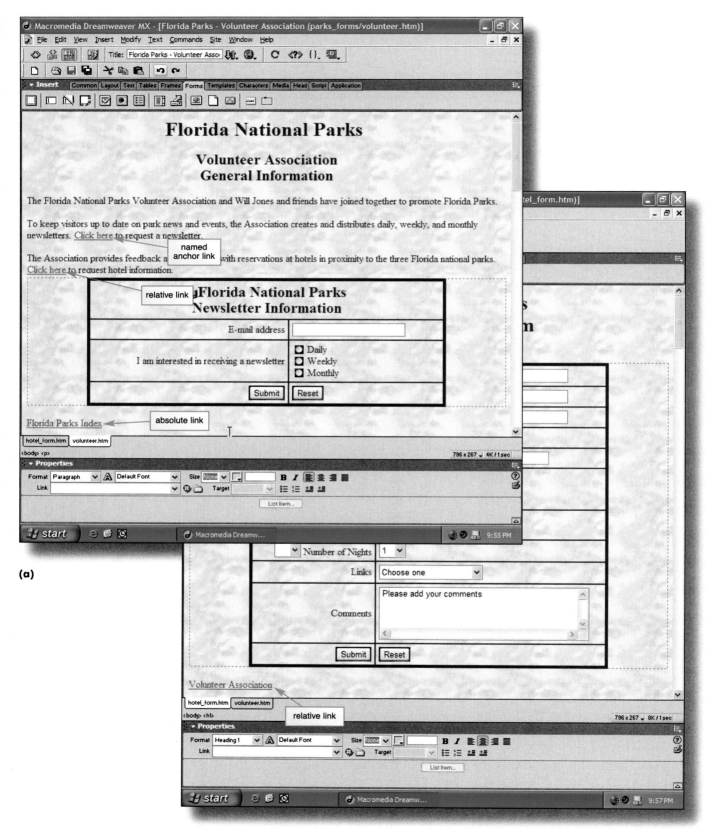

(a)

(b)

FIGURES 5-84

Behaviors

A **behavior** is a combination of an event and an action. Behaviors are attached to a specific element on the Web page. The element can be a table, an image, a link, a form, a form object, and so on. When a behavior is initiated, Dreamweaver uses JavaScript to write the code. **JavaScript** is a scripting language written as a text file. After a behavior is attached to a page element, and when the event specified occurs for that element, the browser calls the action (the JavaScript code) that is associated with that event. A scripting language, such as JavaScript, provides flexibility, interaction, and power to any Web site.

Using Behaviors with Forms

To create this type of user interaction with almost any other software program requires that you write the JavaScript. When you attach a behavior in Dreamweaver, however, the JavaScript is produced and inserted into the code for you. Dreamweaver provides two form-related behaviors: the Validate Form and Set Text of Text Field. These behaviors are available only if a text field has been inserted into the form.

The **Validate Form** behavior verifies that the user has entered data into each designated field. The form is checked when the user clicks the Submit button. If omissions or other errors occur, a Microsoft Internet Explorer dialog box is displayed. The errors must then be corrected before the form can be submitted successfully.

The **Set Text of Text Field** action replaces the content of a form's text field with the content you specify when creating the behavior. For example, this could be used to insert the current date. The Behavior panel is displayed in Figure 5-85. Complete the following steps to add the Validate Form behavior to the Hotel Reservations form.

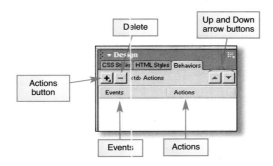

Figure 5-85

More About

Form Validation

Additional form validation behaviors can be added to Dreamweaver by downloading and installing the JavaScript Integration Kit for Flash 5 from the Macromedia Exchange. This extension contains several advanced form validations that check field entries such as credit card numbers, Zip codes, and dates. For more information about form validation, visit the Dreamweaver MX More About Web page (scsite.com/dreamweavermx/more.htm) and then click Form Validation.

Steps To Add the Validate Form Behavior

1 If necessary, click the hotel_form.htm tab. Click Window on the menu bar and then point to Behaviors.

The Window menu is displayed (Figure 5-86).

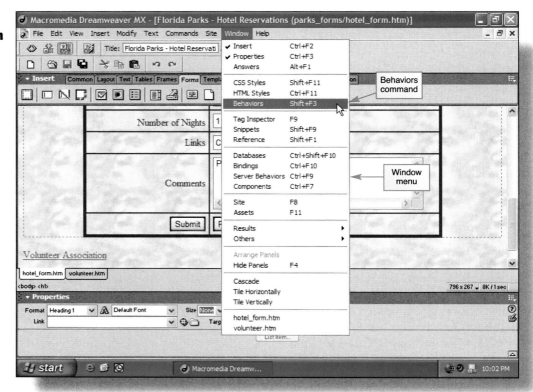

FIGURE 5-86

2 Click Behaviors.

The Behaviors panel is displayed (Figure 5-87).

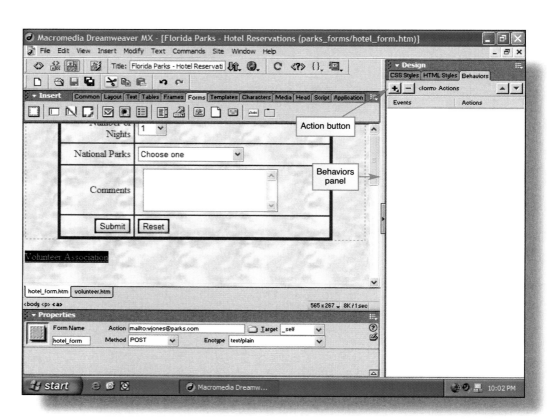

FIGURE 5-87

3 Click anywhere inside the form and then click Forms#hotel_form in the tag selector. Click the Actions button in the Behaviors panel and then point to Validate Form on the pop-up menu.

The form is selected (Figure 5-88).

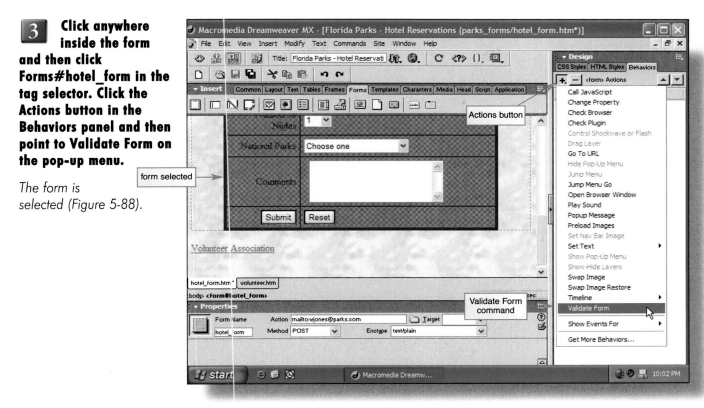

FIGURE 5-88

4 Click Validate Form.

The Validate Form dialog box is displayed (Figure 5-89). Each of the text fields in the hotel_form.htm document is listed in the Named Fields list. The text "name" in form "hotel_form" field is highlighted and the Anything Radio button is selected.

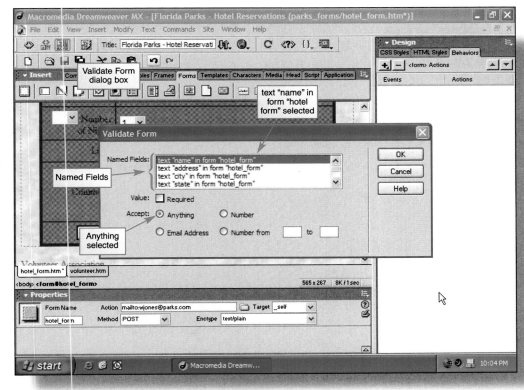

FIGURE 5-89

5 **Click Value (Required).**

The Value check box (Required) is selected for the "name" field. An (R) is inserted to the right of the field name (Figure 5-90).

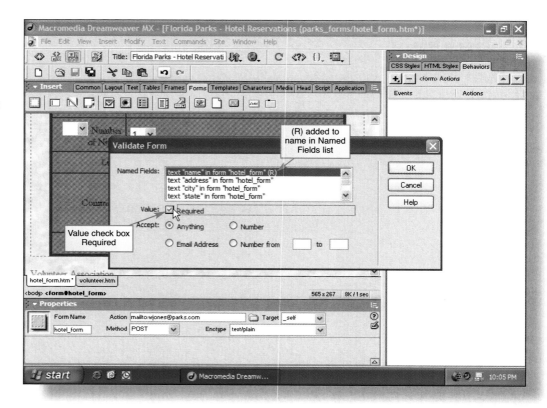

FIGURE 5-90

6 **Click the text "address" in form "hotel_form" field and then click Value (Required) for the address field.**

The Value check box (Required) is selected for the "address" field. An (R) is inserted to the right of the field name (Figure 5-91).

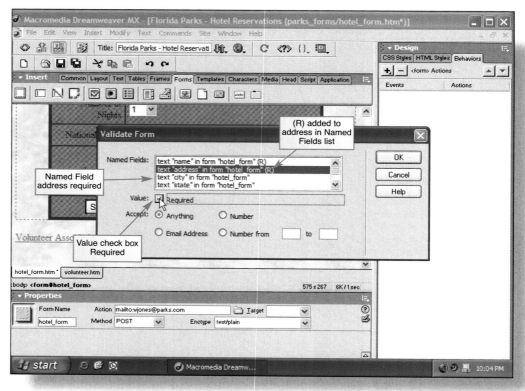

FIGURE 5-91

7 **Repeat Step 6 for the city, state, and zip fields.**

The Value check box (Required) is selected for the "city", "state", and "zip" fields. An (R) is inserted to the right of the field names (Figure 5-92).

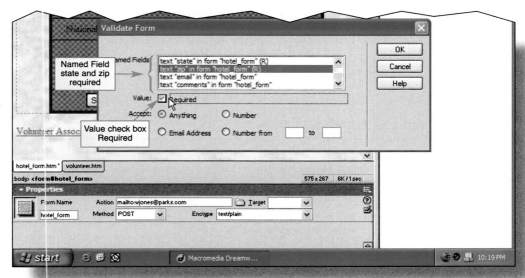

FIGURE 5-92

8 **Click the text "email" in the form "hotel_form" field. Click Value (Required) and Email Address. Point to the OK button.**

The Value check box (Required) and the Email Address radio button are selected (Figure 5-93).

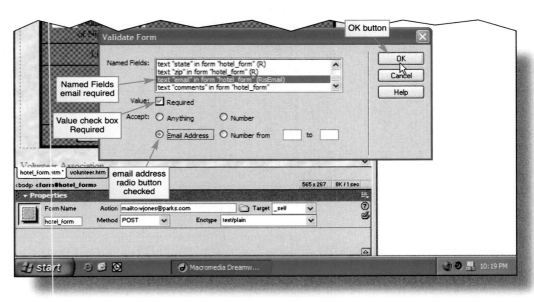

FIGURE 5-93

9 **Click the OK button. Click the Save button on the Standard toolbar.**

The added Events and Actions are displayed in the Behaviors panel. No visible changes are evident in the Document window (Figure 5-94).

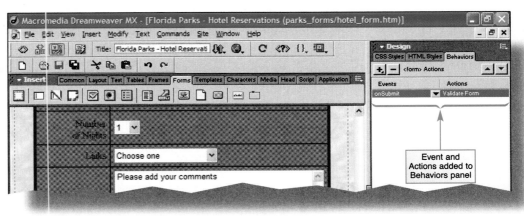

FIGURE 5-94

Dreamweaver MX

Viewing and Testing the Forms

To ensure that the forms objects work correctly, they are viewed through the browser and each of the form objects is tested. Complete the following steps to view and test the hotel_form and volunteer form.

 To View and Test the Hotel Form

1 **Press the F12 key.**

The hotel_form.htm is displayed in the browser (Figure 5-95).

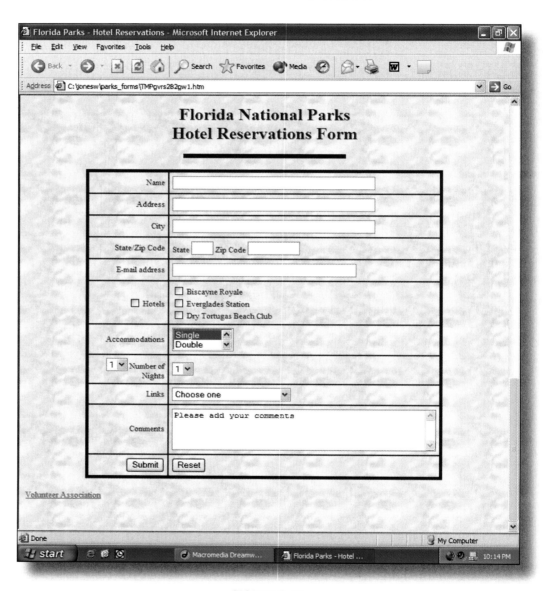

FIGURE 5-95

2 Complete the form, typing data in each field, and then press the Submit button.

A Microsoft Internet Explorer dialog box is displayed (Figure 5-96).

3 Click the OK button.

The form is processed and the data is e-mailed to you. In some instances, your e-mail message may not include the data attachment. This is determined by the e-mail program, server, and security set up on the computer.

4 Close the browser and return to Dreamweaver.

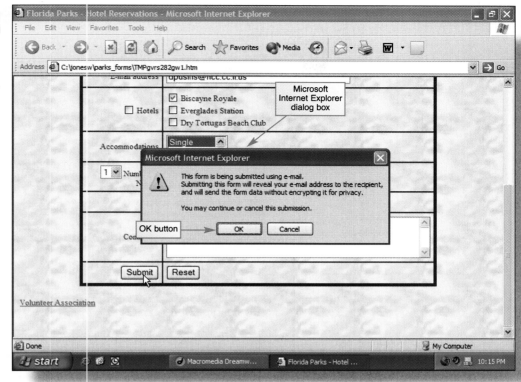

FIGURE 5-96

Complete the following steps to view and test the volunteer.htm form.

TO VIEW AND TEST THE VOLUNTEER FORM

1 Click the volunteer.htm tab and then press the F12 key.

2 Click the E-mail address form object and type your e-mail address.

3 Click the Weekly radio button and then click the Submit button. Click the OK button in the Microsoft Internet Explorer dialog box to e-mail the data.

4 Close the browser and return to Dreamweaver.

5 If instructed to do so, upload your Web site to a remote server. Appendix D contains information on uploading to a remote server. A remote folder is required before you can upload to a remote server. Generally, the remote folder is defined by the Web server administrator or your instructor.

Figure 5-97 shows the Volunteer Association page as it displays in the browser in Step 1.

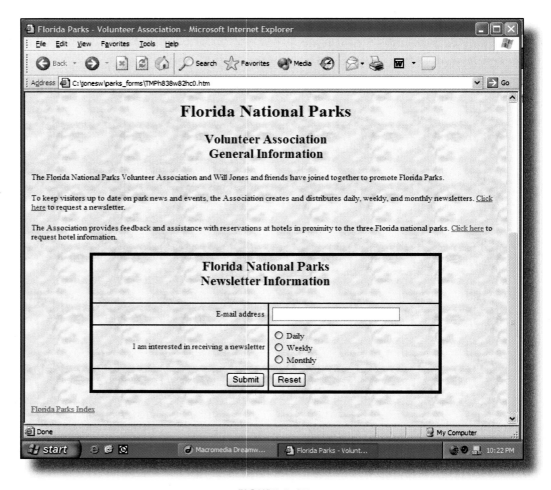

FIGURE 5-97

The last step is to create a link from the Florida Parks Web site to the Volunteer Association General Information Web page.

TO CREATE A LINK FROM THE FLORIDA PARKS INDEX PAGE TO THE VOLUNTEER ASSOCIATION WEB PAGE

1. Open the Florida Parks Web site, select the index.htm page, scroll to the bottom of the page, and then click to the right of the General Information link. Hold down the SHIFT key and then press the ENTER key.

2. Type Florida Parks Volunteer Association and then create a link from the text Florida Parks Volunteer Association to the volunteer.htm file in the Parks_Forms Web site.

3. If you are publishing to a remote site, copy and paste the Volunteer Association Web site address into the Link box. If you are saving your work to a local computer or server, use the Browse for File icon in the Property inspector to create the link path. Click the Save button on the Standard toolbar.

4　Press the F12 key to preview the Florida Parks index.htm page in the browser. Click the Florida Parks Volunteer Association link to display the Volunteer Association Web page. Click each of the links to verify that they work.

5　If instructed to do so, print a copy of each Web page and hand in to your instructor. Close the browser.

Quitting Dreamweaver

After you have created your forms, tested and verified that the forms work, and uploaded the Web site to a remote server, Project 5 is complete. To close the Web site, quit Dreamweaver MX, and return control to Windows, perform the following step.

TO CLOSE THE WEB SITE AND QUIT DREAMWEAVER

1　Click the Close button on the upper-right corner of the Dreamweaver title bar.

The Dreamweaver window, the Document windows, and Parks_Forms Web site all close. If you have unsaved changes, Dreamweaver will prompt you to save the changes. Clicking the Yes button in the Dreamweaver MX dialog box saves the changes.

CASE PERSPECTIVE SUMMARY

As planned, your team finished creating the forms for the Florida National Parks Volunteer Association. This Web site will become a subsection to the Florida Parks main Web site. Your partnership with the Florida Parks Volunteer Association and the feedback you receive from the forms will help with the promotion of the Florida Parks Web site. Everyone agrees that this is a good partnership and that the Web site will add interactivity and enable your group to serve your Web site visitors better.

Project Summary

Project 5 introduced you to forms and to Web page design using forms. You created two forms and added a table to both to format the form better. In the Hotel Reservations form, you added the following form objects: text fields, check boxes, a list and pop-up menu, a jump menu, a text area and Submit and Reset buttons, You added a text field, group radio buttons, and Submit and Reset button to the Newsletter Information form. You then used the Behaviors panel to attach the Validate form behavior to the hotel reservations form. Finally, you viewed and tested the forms in your browser.

What You Should Know

Having completed this project, you now should be able to perform the tasks in Table 5-3.

Table 5-3	Project 5 What You Should Know	
TASK NUMBER	**TASK**	**PAGE NUMBER**
1	Start Dreamweaver and Close Open Panels	DW 5.05
2	Create a Local Site	DW 5.05
3	Copy Data Files to the Parks_Forms Web Site	DW 5.06
4	Insert and Format the Heading	DW 5.07
5	Insert a Form	DW 5.09
6	Set the Form Properties	DW 5.10
7	Insert a Table into a Form	DW 5.12
8	Format the Form	DW 5.14
9	Add Descriptive Text and Single-Line Text Fields to the Hotel Reservations Form	DW 5.18
10	Add Check Boxes	DW 5.25
11	Create a Scrolling List	DW 5.29
12	Create a Pop-Up Menu	DW 5.33
13	Insert a Jump Menu	DW 5.36
14	Add a TextArea Text Field	DW 5.40
15	Add the Submit and Reset Buttons	DW 5.42
16	Open the Volunteer.htm Web Page	DW 5.45
17	Add a Form and Table to the Volunteer Web Page	DW 5.46
18	Insert a Single-Line Text Box	DW 5.47
19	Add a Radio Group	DW 5.47
20	Add the Submit and Reset Buttons to the Volunteer Form	DW 5.51
21	Add Links to the Volunteer and Hotel Form Web Pages	DW 5.51
22	Add the Validate Form Behavior	DW 5.54
23	View and Test the Hotel Form	DW 5.58
24	View and Test the Volunteer Form	DW 5.59
25	Create a Link from the Florida Parks Index Page to the Volunteer Association Web Page	DW 5.60
26	Close the Web Site and Quit Dreamweaver	DW 5.61

Apply Your Knowledge

1 Creating a Form for B & B Lawn Service

Instructions: Start Dreamweaver. If the panels display, press the F4 key to close all panels. See the inside back cover of this book for instructions for downloading the Data Disk or see your instructor for information on accessing the files in this book.

The B & B Lawn Service Web site currently contains five pages. You will add a sixth with a form containing a table. You copy a data file that contains the background image and color scheme. Then you add to this page a heading and a form with single-line text fields and text area fields, a list, Submit and Reset buttons, and a link to the B & B Lawn Service Index page. The new page added to the Web site is shown in Figure 5-98. Software and hardware settings determine how a Web page is displayed in a browser. Your Web page may display differently than the one shown in Figure 5-98. Appendix D contains instructions for uploading your local site to a remote server.

For a selection of images and backgrounds, visit the Dreamweaver MX Media Web page (scsite.com/dreamweavermx/media) and then click Media below Project 5.

1. Display the Property inspector, Standard toolbar, Site panel, and Insert bar. Select Lawn Service from the Site pop-up menu in the Site panel. Click the Forms tab in the Insert bar.
2. Use Dreamweaver's integrated file browser to copy the data file from the Data Files to your lawn local root folder.
3. Close the Untitled-1 page. Double-click services_form.htm to open the data file and then close the Site panel. Click the Title text box on the Document toolbar and then type B & B Lawn Service - Service Request Form.
4. Click the upper-left corner of the Document window. Type B & B Lawn Service and then press SHIFT + ENTER. Type Service Request and then press the ENTER key.
5. Apply Heading 2 and then center the two lines of text.
6. Click the Form button on the Forms tab. Double-click the Form Name text box in the Property inspector and then type services as the Form name. Click the Action text box and then type mailto: wjones@parks.com (use your e-mail address). Click the Target box arrow and select _self. Click the Enctype text box and then type text/plain as the text.

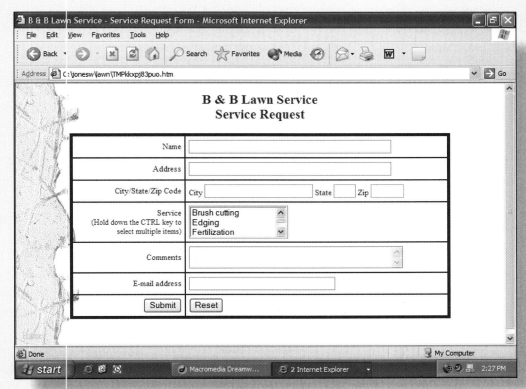

FIGURE 5-98

(continued)

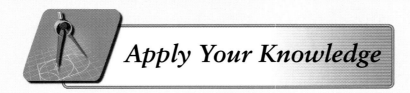

Apply Your Knowledge

Creating a Form for B & B Lawn Service *(continued)*

7. Click inside the form. Click Insert on the menu bar and then click Table. Insert a 7-row, 2-column table with a width of 80 percent, a cell padding of 5, and a border of 4.

8. If necessary, select the table. Click the Align box arrow in the Property inspector and then click Center.

9. Select column 1 and then click the Align Right button. Set the column W (width) at 30%. Select the table. Click the Brdr text box and then type #663333 for the border color.

10. Click column 1, row 1, type Name, and then press the TAB key.

11. Click the Text Field button on the Forms tab. Name the form object name. Press the TAB key and then type 50 for the Char Width.

12. Click column 1, row 2, type Address, and then press the TAB key. Insert a TextField form object in column 2, row 2. Name the form object address with a Char Width of 50.

13. Click column 1, row 3, type City/State/Zip Code, and then press the TAB key.

14. Type City and then press the SPACEBAR. Insert a TextField form object named city with a Char Width of 30. Click to the right of the text field and then press the SPACEBAR.

15. Type State and then press the SPACEBAR. Insert a TextField form object named state with a Char Width of 2. Click to the right of the text field and then press the SPACEBAR.

16. Type Zip and then press the SPACEBAR. Insert a TextField form object named zip with a Char Width of 5.

17. Click column 1, row 4, type service, and then press SHIFT+ENTER. Type (Hold down CTRL key to select multiple items).

18. Click column 2, row 4 and then click the List/Menu button on the Forms tab. Name the List/Menu form object service, click List in the Property inspector Type area, specify a height of 3, and then click the List Values button. Type each Item Label and Value as shown in Table 5-4. Press the TAB key to move from field to field.

19. Click the OK button, click column 1, row 5, type Comments and then press the TAB key. Insert a Textarea form object named field comments, with a Char Width of 40. Type 4 for the Num Lines.

21. Click column 1, row 6, type E-mail address and then press the TAB key. Insert a Text Field form object named email, with a Char Width of 35.

22. Click column 1, row 7 and then insert a Submit button. Click the TAB key and then insert a button named Reset. Name the Label Reset, and then click Reset form in the Action area.

23. Click Window on the menu bar and then click Behaviors. Click form#services in the tag selector and then click the Add button in the Behaviors panel. Click Validate Form on the Add menu.

24. In the Validate Form dialog box, click Value (Required) for all fields. In the Accept area, click Anything for all fields except the email field. For the email field, click Email Address. Click the OK button in the Validate Form dialog box and then close the Behaviors panel.

25. Click below the form. Add a link to the Index.htm page and change the text color to hexadecimal #663333. Click the Save button on the Standard toolbar. Display the browser. Input data into the form and then click the Submit button to test the form. Open the index.htm page and scroll down to the bottom of the page. Create a link to the services_form.htm page. Print a copy of the form if instructed to do so. Upload the form page and index page to the lawn Web site on a remote server if instructed to do so.

Table 5-4 Lawn Services List Values	
ITEM LABEL	**VALUE**
Brush cutting	brush
Edging	edging
Fertilization	fertilize
Mowing/Trimming	mowing
Irrigation	irrigate
Landscaping	landscape
Mulching	mulching
Pruning	pruning
Weed/Insect control	weed

In the Lab

1 Creating a Web Form for the CandleDust Web Site

Problem: Mary has decided she would like to conduct a survey to determine which candles her Web site visitors like best and their favorite place to burn the candles. She wants to include a comments section and provide a copy of the results to those visitors who are interested. To do the survey, she has requested that you add a form to the CandleDust site. The Data File contains the background and color scheme. The form is shown in Figure 5-99. Appendix D contains instructions for uploading your local site to a remote server. For a selection of images and backgrounds, visit the Dreamweaver MX Media Web page (scsite.com/dreamweavermx/media) and then click Media below Project 5.

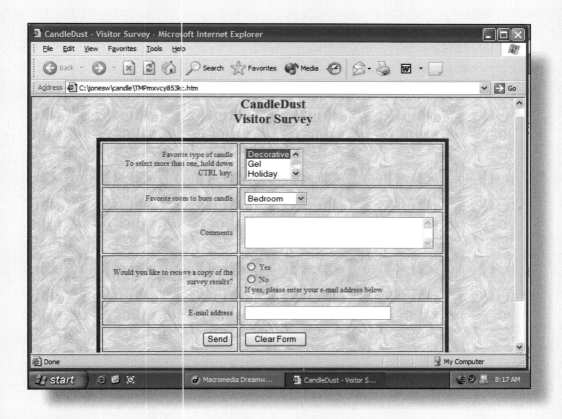

Instructions: Perform the following tasks:

1. Start Dreamweaver. If necessary, press F4 to close the open panels. Display the Property inspector, Standard toolbar, Site panel, and Insert bar. Select CandleDust from the Site pop-up menu in the Site panel.
2. Use Dreamweaver's integrated file browser to copy the file from the Data Files to your candle folder.
3. Close the Untitled-1 page. Double-click survey_form.htm to open the Data File and then close the Site panel. Click the Title box on the Document menu bar and then type CandleDust - Visitor Survey.
4. Click the upper-left corner of the Document window. Add and center the two-line heading, CandleDust and Visitor Survey. Apply Heading 1 to the heading. If necessary, click the Align Left button in the Property inspector.

(continued)

In the Lab

Creating a Web Form for the CandleDust Web Site *(continued)*

5. If necessary, click the Forms tab in the Insert bar and click the Form button. Name the form survey. Type `mailto:wjones@parks.com` (use your e-mail address) in the Action text box and then select _self in the Target box. Click the Enctype text box and then type `text/plain` as the text.

6. Click inside the form and then insert a table with the following attributes: 6 rows, 2 columns, width of 75%, cell padding of 7, cell spacing of 3, and a border of 6. Center the table in the form.

7. Click the Brdr Color text box and then type `#006666` for the border color. Select column 1 and then click the Align Right button.

8. Click column 1, row 1, type `Favorite type of candle`, and then enter a line break. Type `To select more than one, hold down CTRL key` and then press the TAB key.

9. Click the List/Menu button on the Forms tab. Name the List/Menu favorite, click List in the Type area, type 3 in the Height text box, and then click Selections to select Allow multiple.

10. Click the List Values button. Type each Item Label and Value as shown in Table 5-5. Press the TAB key to move from field to field.

11. Click column 1, row 2. Type `Favorite room to burn candle` and then click the TAB key. Click the List/Menu button on the Forms tab. Name the menu burn. If necessary, click Menu in the Type area, and then click the List Values button. Type each Item Label and Value as shown in Table 5-6. Press the TAB key to move from field to field.

12. Click column 1, row 3, type `Comments`, and then press the TAB key. Insert a Textarea form object named comments, with a Char Width of 40 and Num Lines of 6.

13. Click column 1, row 4. Type `Would you like to receive a copy of the survey results?` and then press the TAB key.

14. Insert a Radio Group form object named group results. Click the first instance of Radio below Label, type `Yes` for the Label and then press the TAB key. Type `yes` for the Value and then press the TAB key. Type `No` for the Label field, press the TAB key, and then type `no` for the Value. Click the OK button.

15. Position the insertion point to the right of No and then insert a line break. Type `If yes, please enter your e-mail address below` and then press the TAB key.

16. Type `E-mail address` and then press the TAB key. Insert a TextField form object named email and set a Char Width of 35.

17. Click column 1, row 6 and then insert a Button form object named Send. Type `Send` in the Label text box.

18. Click column 2, row 6 and then insert a Button form object named clear. Type `Clear Form` in the Label text box, and then click Reset form in the Action area.

19. Click below the form. Add a link to the Index.htm page. Click the Save button on the Standard toolbar. Press the F12 key to view the form in your browser. Input data into the form and then click the Submit button to test the form. Open the index.htm page and scroll down to the bottom of the page. Create a link to the survey_form.htm page. Print a copy of the form if instructed to do so. Upload the form page and index page to the candle Web Site on a remote server if instructed to do so.

Table 5-5	CandleDust List Values
ITEM LABEL	VALUE
Decorative	decorative
Gel	gel
Holiday	holiday
Pillar	pillar
Scented	scented
Texture	texture
Votive	votive

Table 5-6	CandleDust Menu Values
ITEM LABEL	VALUE
Bedroom	bedroom
Dining room	dining room
Bathroom	bathroom
Kitchen	kitchen

In the Lab

2 Creating a Form Page for the Credit Protection Web Site

Problem: Marcy recently received several e-mails asking for suggestions on how to spend money wisely. She has created three informational articles and would like to provide these articles to her Web site visitors. Marcy asks you to create a form so she can provide this information. The form is shown in Figure 5-100. Appendix D contains instructions for uploading your local site to a remote server. For a selection of images and backgrounds, visit the Dreamweaver MX Media Web page (scsite.com/dreamweavermx/media) and then click Media below Project 5.

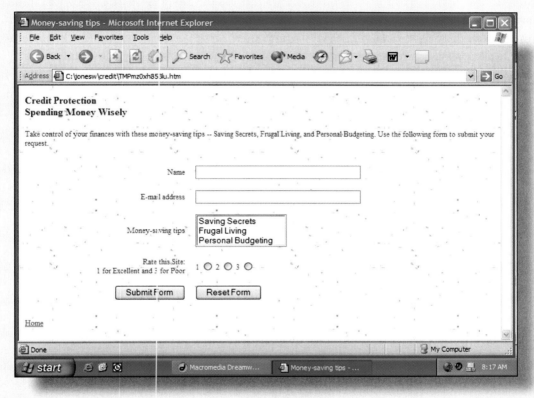

FIGURE 5-100

Instructions: Perform the following tasks:

1. Start Dreamweaver. Display the Property inspector, Standard toolbar, Site panel, and Insert bar.
2. Use Dreamweaver's integrated file browser to copy the Data File to the credit Web site.
3. Close the Untitled-1 page. Double-click tips_form.htm to open the Data File. Title the document Money-saving tips.
4. Click to the right of the last sentence and then press the ENTER key. If necessary, click the Forms tab in the Insert bar and then click the Form button. Name the form guest_comments. Type mailto:wjones@parks.com (use your e-mail address) in the Action text box and then select _self in the Target box. Click the Enctype text box and then type text/plain as the text.

(continued)

In the Lab

Creating a Form Page for the Credit Protection Web Site *(continued)*

5. Click inside the form and then insert a table with the following attributes: 5 rows, 2 columns, width of 75%, cell padding of 7, cell spacing of 3, and a border of 0. Center the table in the form.

6. Select column 1 and then click the Align Right button.

7. Click column 1, row 1, type Name, and then press the TAB key. In the Property inspector, type 6 for Num Lines. Add a TextField named name with a Char Width of 40.

8. Click column 1, row 2, type E-mail address, and then press the TAB key. Add a TextField named email with a Char Width of 40.

9. Click column 1, row 3, type Money-saving tips, and then press the TAB key. Insert a List/Menu form object named list with Type List, and a Height of 3. Click Selections to select Allow multiple.

10. Type each Item Label and Value as shown in Table 5-7. Press the TAB key to move from field to field.

11. Click column 1, row 4. Type Rate this site: 1 for Excellent and 3 for Poor and then press the TAB key. Type 1 and then press the SPACEBAR. Insert a Radio Button form object and then click to the right of the object. Press the SPACEBAR. Type 2 and then press the SPACEBAR. Insert a Radio Button form object and then click to the right of the object. Press the SPACEBAR. Type 3 and press the SPACEBAR. Insert a Radio Button form object. In the Property inspector, name each button and the Checked Value with the related number; that is, 1, 2, and 3.

12. Click column 1, row 5. Insert the Submit button and then press the TAB key. Insert another button, name the Label Reset Form, and then click Reset form in the Action area.

13. Add a link to the index page.

14. Click SHIFT + F3 to display the Behaviors panel. Click the Add button and validate the form.

15. Save the form and then view the form in your browser. Input data into the form and then click the Submit button to test the form. Open the index.htm page and scroll down to the bottom of the page. Create a link to the tips_form.htm page. Print a copy of the form if instructed to do so. Upload the form page and index page to the credit Web Site on a remote server if instructed to do so.

Table 5-7 Credit Protection List Values	
ITEM LABEL	*VALUE*
Saving Secrets	saving
Frugal Living	frugal
Personal Budgeting	budget

In the Lab

3 Creating a Guest Book Form for the Plant City Web Site

Problem: The Plant City Web site provides information about the city, but does not provide a means of response from your visitors. The mayor would like the visitors to comment on the Web site and the city and asks that you add a guest book to the site. The Web page is shown in Figure 5-101. Appendix D contains instructions for uploading your local site to a remote server. For a selection of images and backgrounds, visit the Dreamweaver MX Media Web page (scsite.com/dreamweavermx/media) and then click Media below Project 5.

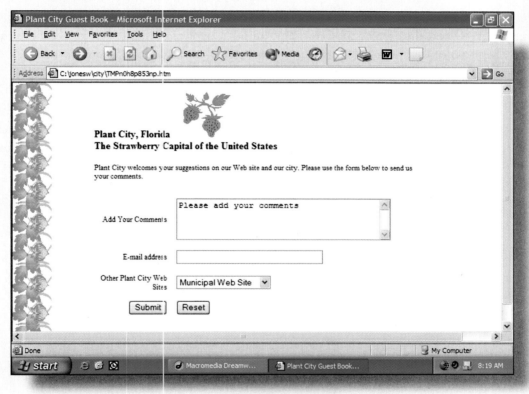

FIGURE 5-101

Instructions: Perform the following tasks:

1. Start Dreamweaver. Display the Property inspector, Standard toolbar, Site panel, and Insert bar.
2. Use Dreamweaver's integrated file browser to copy the data file to the city Web site.
3. Close the Untitled-1 page. Double-click guest_form.htm to open the Data File. Title the document Plant City Guest Book.
4. If necessary, click the Forms tab in the Insert bar. Insert a Form named guests. Type `mailto:wjones@parks.com` (use your e-mail address) in the Action text box and then select _self in the Target box. Click the Enctype text box and then type `text/plain` as the text.
5. Click inside the form and then insert a table with the following attributes: 4 rows, 2 columns, width of 75 percent, cell padding of 5, cell spacing of 5, and a border of 0. Center the table in the form.
6. Select column 1 and then click the Align Right button.

(continued)

In the Lab

Creating a Guest Book Form for the Plant City Web Site *(continued)*

7. Click column 1, row 1, type `Add Your Comments`, and then press the TAB key. Insert a TextArea form object named comments, with a Char Width of 40, Num of Lines 4, and the initial value, Please add your comments.

8. Click column 1, row 2, type `E-mail address`, and then press the TAB key. Insert a Text Field form object named email, with a Char Width of 35.

9. Click column 1, row 3, type `Other Plant City Web Sites`, and then press the TAB key. Insert a Jump Menu form object. Type the Text and URL as shown in Table 5-8. Press the TAB key to move from field to field.

10. Name the Jump Menu city.

11. Click column 1, row 4, and then insert the Select Button form object. Press the TAB key and then insert another Button form object named clear. Name the Label Reset, and then click Reset form.

12. Add a link to the Plant City Web site index page.

13. Click SHIFT + F3 to display the Behaviors panel. Click the Add button and validate the form.

14. Save the form and then view the form in your browser. Input data into the form and then click the Submit button to test the form. Open the index.htm page and scroll down to the bottom of the page. Create a link to the guest_form.htm page. Print a copy of the form if instructed to do so. Upload the form page and index page to the city Web Site on a remote server if instructed to do so.

Table 5-8	
TEXT	**WHEN SELECTED, GO TO URL**
Municipal Web Site	http://www.ci.plant-city.fl.us/
Community Director	http://www.plantcity.com/
Dinosaur World	http://www.dinoworld.net/florida.htm

Cases and Places

The difficulty of these case studies varies:
▶ are the least difficult; ▶▶ are more difficult; and ▶▶▶ are the most difficult.

1 ▶ Your sports Web site is receiving more hits each day. You have received many e-mails asking for statistics and other information. You decide to start a weekly newsletter and want to add a form so your visitors can subscribe to the newsletter. Add a background image to the page and add a title to the page. Insert a form and name the form appropriately. Next, add a table to your form. Include text fields for name and e-mail address and a text area for comments. Add descriptive text asking if the visitor would like to subscribe to the newsletter and then include a Radio Group with Yes and No options. Add Submit and Reset buttons. Create a link to and from the home page. Save the page in your sports Web site.

2 ▶ You would like to add some interactivity to your hobby Web site. You decide to do this by adding a survey. First, add a background image to the page and then add an appropriate title. Insert a form and then add a table to your form. Add a 4-pixel border to the form. Add a list form object that contains a list of hobbies. Ask your viewers to select their favorite hobby. Create an e-mail link for those visitors who would like a copy of your survey results. Add Submit and Reset buttons. Create a link to and from the home page. Upload to a remote site if instructed to do so.

3 ▶▶ Add an informational form to your music hobby Web site and then add a background to the page. Insert a form and a table. Include form objects for name, address, telephone number, and e-mail address. Include a menu with at least five choices and then add the Submit and Reset buttons. Rename the buttons. Fill in all relevant attributes in the Property inspector for each object. Create a link to and from the home page. Upload the page to a remote site.

4 ▶▶ Your campaign for political office is progressing well. Create a new Web site and name it office_form. Add two pages with forms to the new site. The first page should contain a form asking for opinions and comments about your political views. The second form should contain form objects requesting donations and campaign volunteers. Create a link to and from the home page. Upload the form Web site to a remote server.

5 ▶▶▶ Last week, the student government officers selected three possible vacation sites to visit. Now they would like to have a form page for students to provide feedback about each of the three sites. Create a page with introductory text and a form listing each of the three student trip locations. Provide form objects so the Web site visitors can vote on which trip they would like to take and provide feedback regarding number of days, minimum and maximum costs, and other related information. Create a link to and from the home page. Upload the form page to a remote server.

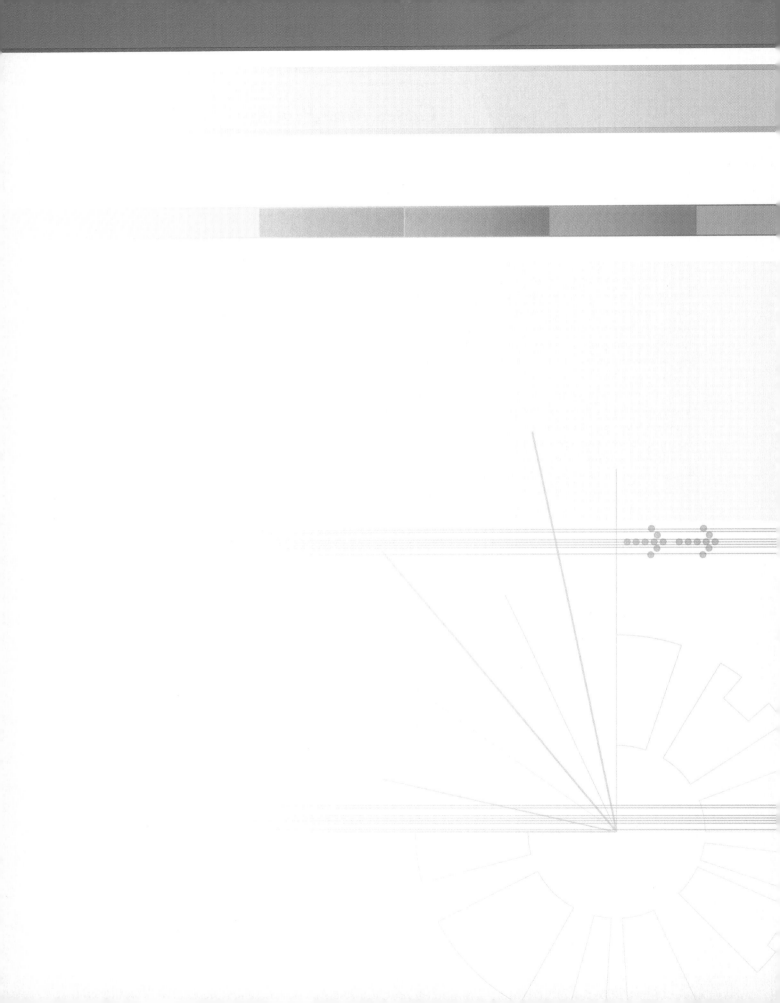

Macromedia Dreamweaver MX

Templates
and Style Sheets

You will have mastered the material in this project when you can:

- Describe a template
- Create a template
- Describe the different types of style sheets
- Create a Cascading Style Sheet
- Apply Cascading Style Sheet attributes to a template
- Create a Web page from a template
- Describe and use the Assets panel

Macromedia Dreamweaver MX

Templates and Style Sheets

The Florida Parks Web site offers visitors many interesting and informative Web pages. Will, however, would like to add additional enhancements to the site. He asks you and Joan for ideas and suggestions. After numerous discussions and the exchange of ideas, several proposals are put forward. One idea is to do a photo album page containing various images from several of the state parks. To add variety to the Web site, however, Joan suggests that a new Web page be developed that will spotlight a different park each month. Will expresses concern that changing this page each month will become quite a chore.

Joan explains that instead of redeveloping the entire page each month, the team can use a template. She also explains that style sheet attributes can be added to the template to provide consistency in the heading, park description, and display of images and links. All team members agree to add the Web page and develop a template.

Introduction

Project 6 introduces the addition of a Dreamweaver template to the Florida Parks Web site. Designing a Web site is a complex process that requires the author to make decisions about the structure of the site and the appearance and content of each Web page within the site. Templates are an important element of many Web sites and are used in a variety of ways. For example, a Web site developer can use a template to provide a basic framework for structured organization of the entire Web site. Or, an educational institution could have a template for faculty home pages. The faculty member supplies the content for the Web page. The template will take care of the rest of the job and display it in a format that promotes consistency between Web pages. Another example is the content within an e-commerce catalog page. Using a template, the content developer easily can add and delete new products, change prices, and make other modifications.

Project Six — Creating Templates and Style Sheets

In this project, you learn how to create a Dreamweaver template, create a style sheet, and then apply styles to the template. Using the template, you then create a Web page highlighting one of Florida's state parks.

First, you create a single page that has all the elements you want to include in your Web page and then you save the page as a template. After creating the template, you create the style sheet and then apply the style sheet attributes to the template. Next, you use the template, containing the style sheet attributes, to create a Web page featuring one of Florida's state parks — Bahia Honda State Park — shown in Figure 6-1. This Web page contains a logo and four designated regions that can be edited. These editable regions are as follows: a heading, a short description, and two tables. You use styles to apply font and color attributes to the heading and description and to apply fonts, font color attributes, a background, and a border to the two tables. The first table contains template cells for park images. You also will add a short description of each image. The second table contains cells for links. In this project you add a relative link to the Florida Parks home page and an absolute link to the Bahia Honda State Park Web site.

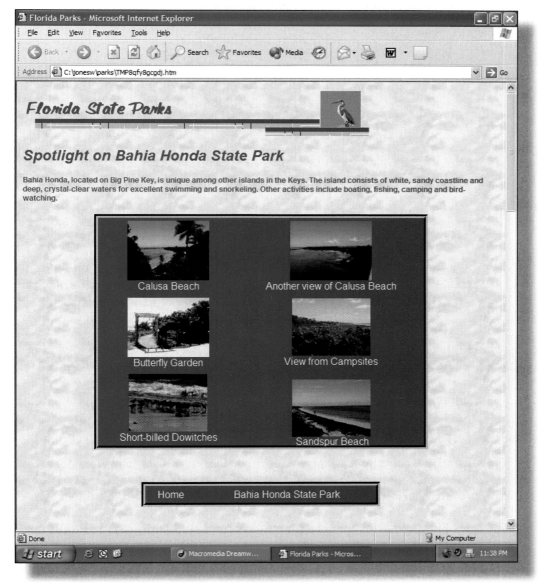

FIGURE 6-1

Workspace Organization

Organization and preparation lead to a more productive work setting. Successful Web developers prepare their Dreamweaver workspace to provide an effective work environment. As you learn to use additional Dreamweaver tools, including templates and style sheets, you will become even more proficient working in the Dreamweaver environment.

Starting Dreamweaver and Closing Open Panels

When you start Dreamweaver, generally most or all of the panels are displayed by default. Closing unused panels provides uncluttered workspace in the Document window. To organize your workspace, you close the unused open panels. This gives you the maximum window space in the Dreamweaver Document window.

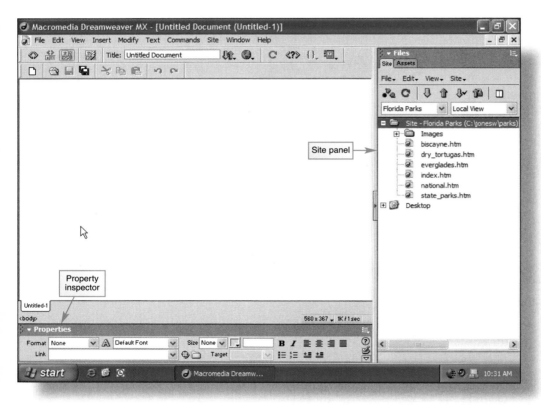

TO START DREAMWEAVER AND CLOSE OPEN PANELS

1 Start Dreamweaver. If necessary, maximize the Document window. Press the F4 key to close all open panels.

2 Press the F8 key to display the Site panel. Select the Florida Parks Web site.

3 If necessary, use the View menu to display the Standard toolbar.

4 Use the Window menu to display the Property inspector (Figure 6-2).

The Site panel and Property inspector are displayed (Figure 6-2).

FIGURE 6-2

Copying Data Files to the Local Web Site

Your Data Disk contains an Images folder for Project 6. The Images folder is located in the Proj06 folder. You use Dreamweaver's integrated file browser to copy the Project 6 images from the Data Disk Images folder to the Florida Parks Images folder.

The Data Files folder for this project is stored on Local Disk (C:). The location on your computer may be different. If necessary, verify with your instructor the location of the Data Files folder. Complete the following steps to copy the files and folders to the C:\jonesw\parks local root folder.

TO COPY DATA FILES TO THE FLORIDA PARKS WEB SITE

1 Click the plus sign (+) to the left of the Desktop icon in the Site panel. Click the plus sign to the left of the My Computer icon and then navigate through the file hierarchy to the Data Files folder as you did in Project 2 on pages DW 2.09 – 2.14.

2 Click the plus sign to the left of the Proj06 folder and then click the plus sign to the left of the parks folder.

3 Click the plus sign to the left of the Images folder.

4 Click butterfly_garden.jpg (or the first file in the list). Hold down the SHIFT key and then click sandspur_beach.jpg (or the last file in the folder if your files are sorted in a different order).

5 Copy the images to the jonesw/parks/Images folder using the Copy and Paste commands on the context menus, the result of which is shown in Figure 6-3.

6 Click the minus sign to the left of the Desktop icon to collapse the file list.

After completing step 5, the Project 6 images are pasted into the parks/Images local root folder. Figure 6-3 shows the expanded Images folder. Your images may be sorted in a different order.

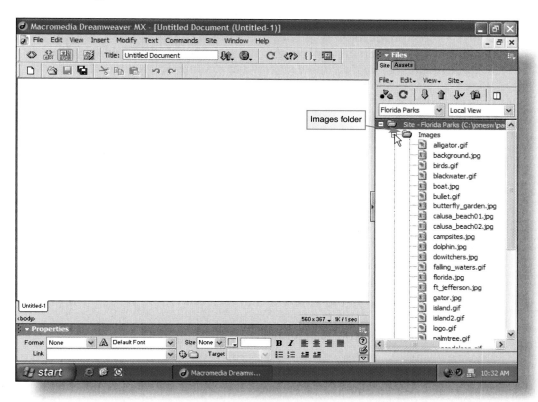

FIGURE 6-3

Understanding Templates

Templates exist in many forms. A stencil, for instance, is a type of template. Or, you may have used a template in Microsoft Office or other software applications to create documents with a repeated design. In Web site development with Dreamweaver, a **template** is a predesigned Web page that contains the definition of the appearance of the page, including items such as default font, font size, logos and images, backgrounds, and so on. A template provides an alternative to separately creating similar-type pages on your Web site. Instead, you create a basic layout and navigation system and use it as a template for each similar page. Template pages can function as a pattern for other pages, can save time, and can guarantee a consistent and standardized design.

Planning is an important element in creating a template. Organizing the information and deciding how to structure the template will make the template user-friendly and a more effective site-design tool. The first step is to determine the look of the page, including backgrounds, fonts, and logos. Other elements to consider are heading styles and the inclusion of links, tables, graphics, and other media.

The Dreamweaver Template

A **Dreamweaver template** is a special type of HTML document. When you create a template, Dreamweaver inserts special code into the template. A **template instance**, which is a Web page based on a template, looks identical to the template. The difference is, however, you can make changes only to designated parts of the page. The sections of the page to which you can make changes are called **editable regions**. An editable region can be any part of a page: a heading, a paragraph, a table, a table cell, and so on. You designate the editable regions when you design the template. Other parts of the page are locked.

One of the more powerful uses of templates within Dreamweaver is the ability it gives the developer to update multiple pages at once. After a new document is created from a template, it remains attached to the original template unless it is specifically separated. You can modify a template and immediately update the design in all documents on which it is based.

The purpose of the template created in this project is to use it as a foundation to spotlight a different park each month. Complete the following steps to begin the creation of the spotlight template page.

TO BEGIN CREATING THE SPOTLIGHT TEMPLATE PAGE
BY ADDING A BACKGROUND IMAGE AND TITLE

1 Click Modify on the menu bar and then click Page Properties. Click the Browse button to the right of the Background Image box.

2 If necessary, double-click the Images folder. Click background.jpg and then click the OK button in the Select Image Source dialog box.

3 Drag to select the text in the Title box and then type Florida Parks for the title.

4 Click the OK button in the Page Properties dialog box.

The background image and title are applied to the Spotlight template page (Figure 6-4). The insertion point is blinking at the top of the page.

Editable and Noneditable Regions

When a template is first created, Dreamweaver automatically locks most parts of the document. The title, however, is not locked. The template author defines which regions of a template-based document will be editable by inserting editable regions or editable parameters in the template. Dreamweaver supports four different types of regions in a template: editable regions, repeating regions, optional regions, and editable tag attributes. The following section describes these four regions.

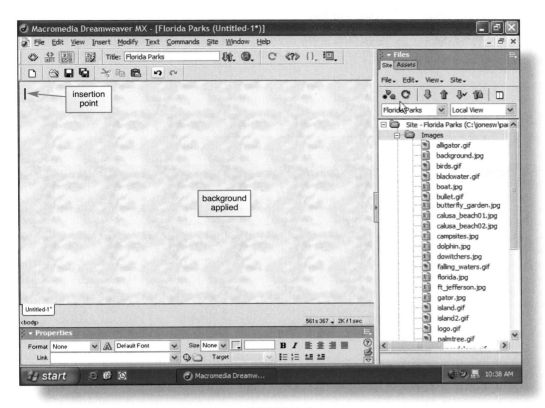

FIGURE 6-4

EDITABLE REGION An **editable region** is the basic building block of a template and is an unlocked region. A template author can define any area of a template as editable. This is a section a content developer can edit, and it can be a heading, a paragraph, a table, and so on. A template can have, and ususally does contain, multiple editable regions. For a template to be effective, it should contain at least one editable region; otherwise, pages based on the template cannot be edited.

REPEATING REGION A repeating region is a section in a document that is set to repeat. **Repeating regions** enable the template author to control the layout of regions that are repeated on a page. The two types of repeating regions are repeating table and repeating region. For instance, a list of catalog products may include a name, description, price, and picture in a single row. You can repeat the table row to allow the content developer to create an expanding list, thus enabling the template author to keep the design under their control. A repeating region is a section of a template that can be duplicated as often as desired in a template-based page. By default, the repeating region does not include an editable region, but the template author can insert an editable region into the repeating region. A repeating region generally is used with a table but also can be defined for other page elements.

OPTIONAL REGION An **optional region** lets the content developer show or hide content on a page-by-page basis. For example, the template author may want to include an optional region that would contain special promotional products.

EDITABLE TAG ATTRIBUTE An **editable tag attribute** lets the content developer unlock a tag attribute in a template and edit the tag in a template-based page. For instance, the template developer could unlock the table border attribute, but keep locked other attributes such as padding, spacing, and alignment.

More About

Design Notes

Using Design Notes, a Dreamweaver feature that allows you to generate your own notes, you can attach information about a template. The Design Notes can contain such data as the author's name, date of creation and/or modification, tips on using the template, and so on. For more information about Design Notes, visit the Dreamweaver MX More About Web page (scsite.com/ dreamweavermx/ more.htm) and then click Design Notes.

In the following steps, you add a logo image to the template. This logo is part of the template and is a noneditable item. When the content developer uses the template, the logo image will remain as is and cannot be deleted or aligned to another position.

Steps To Add the Logo Image to the Template

1 If necessary, scroll down to display the logo.gif image file (Figure 6-5).

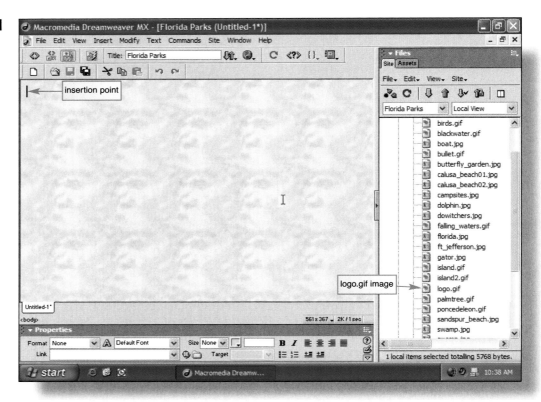

FIGURE 6-5

2 Drag the logo.gif image to the insertion point.

The logo.gif image is displayed in the Document window (Figure 6-6).

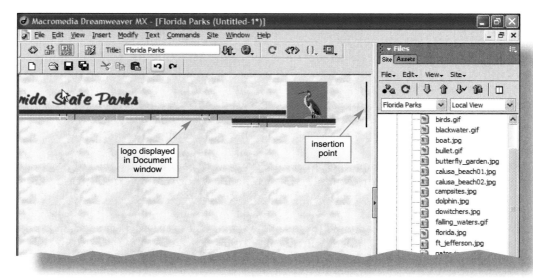

FIGURE 6-6

3 Press the ENTER key. If necessary, scroll up and then click the minus sign to the left of the Images folder in the Site panel.

The logo image is inserted and the Image folder is collapsed (Figure 6-7).

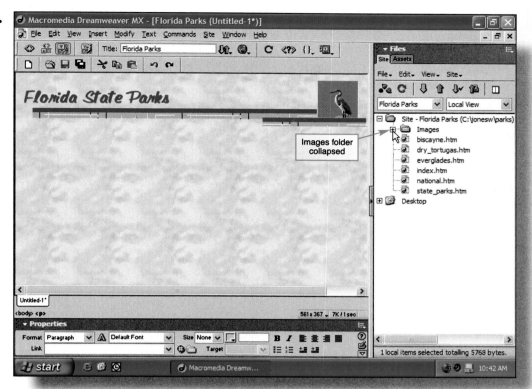

Images folder collapsed

FIGURE 6-7

Designing the Template

When creating a template, one of the best methods to use is to finalize a single page that includes all the elements in the template. Next, save the document as a template and then mark all of the editable regions. Consider the following when designing your basic page:

- Include as much content as possible. Structure and design will enable the content developer more quickly to produce a Web page based on the template.
- Use prompts in the editable regions to inform the content developer as to the type of content to be added to a particular region.
- Give your editable regions meaningful names.
- Use placeholders if possible, particularly for images.

In the next step, you add prompts for two editable regions to the template page. The prompt for the first editable region is the heading and includes instructions to add the park name; the instruction for the second editable region is a prompt to add a short description of the park.

Other Ways

1. On Insert menu click Image, select file name in Image Source dialog box, click OK button

Steps **To Add the Park Name and Park Description Prompt for the First Two Editable Regions**

1 **Click the Document window and then type** Spotlight on [name of state park] **as the heading prompt to be entered into the template. Point to the Format box arrow in the Property inspector.**

The heading text, Spotlight on [name of state park], appears in the Document window below the logo image (Figure 6-8).

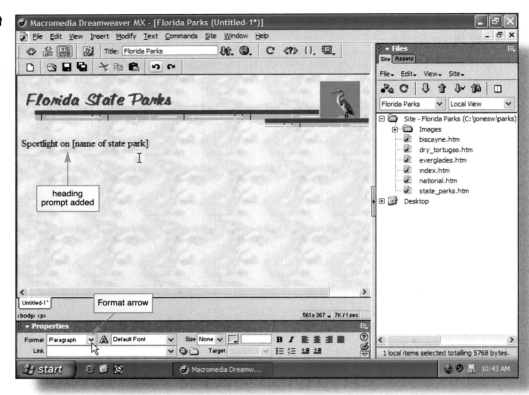

FIGURE 6-8

2 **Click the Format box arrow and apply Heading 2 to the heading prompt.**

Heading 2 is applied to the heading text prompt (Figure 6-9).

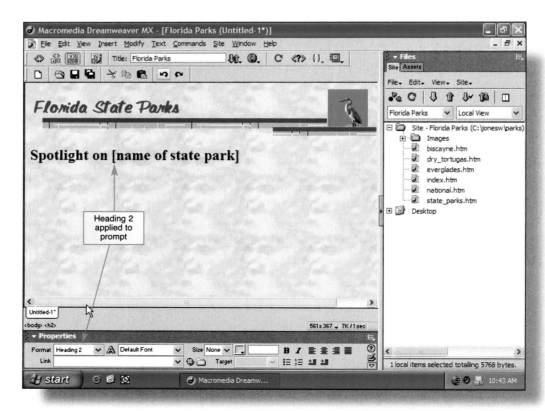

FIGURE 6-9

3 Press the ENTER key.

The insertion point is blinking at the left below the prompt (Figure 6-10).

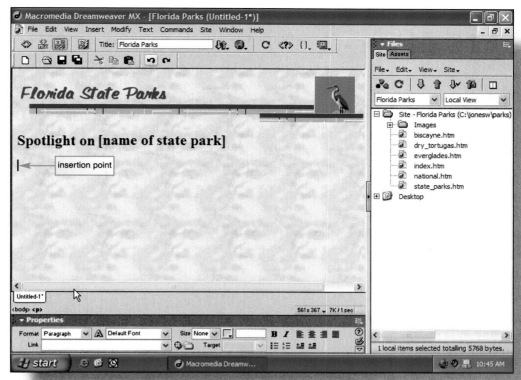

FIGURE 6-10

4 Type Add short description of park. **as a prompt for the second editable region and then press the ENTER key.**

The insertion point is blinking at the left below the description prompt (Figure 6-11).

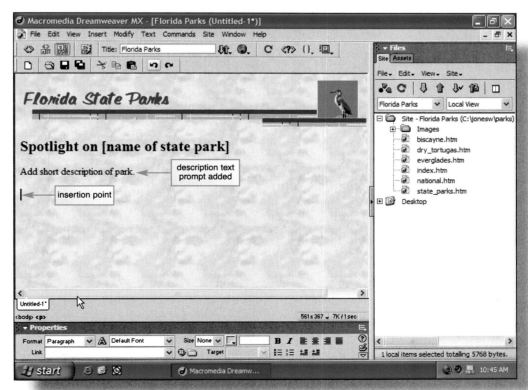

FIGURE 6-11

More About

Editable Tables

You can define an individual cell or an entire table as an editable region. You cannot, however, select several cells and define them as one editable region.

Adding Tables for Images and Links

The third editable region will consist of a one-row, two-column centered table that will contain centered images and a short description of the image immediately below each image. The table is editable, so depending on the park to be spotlighted and the number of available images, additional columns and rows can be added to the table as needed. A second table will become the fourth editable region. This one-row, two-column centered table will contain cells for a relative link to the Florida Parks index page and an absolute link to the Florida Department of Parks Bahia Honda State Park Web page. This second table also is editable, which will permit the content developer to add additional links as needed.

Complete the following steps to add the first table for the third editable region.

Steps To Add and Center a Table as the Third Editable Region

1 Click Insert on the menu bar and then click Table. Enter the following data in the Insert Table dialog box: 1 for Rows, 5 for Cell Padding, 2 for Columns, 0 for Cell Spacing, 70 Percent for Width, and 0 for Border. Point to the OK button.

The table data is entered (Figure 6-12).

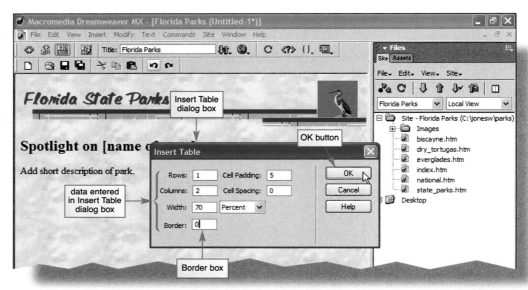

FIGURE 6-12

2 Click the OK button, click the Align box arrow in the Property inspector, and then click Center to center the table.

The table is centered in the Document window (Figure 6-13).

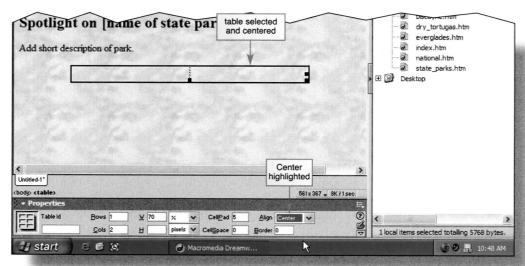

FIGURE 6-13

3 Click the left cell in the table and then drag to select both cells in the table. Point to the Property inspector expander arrow.

Both cells are selected (Figure 6-14).

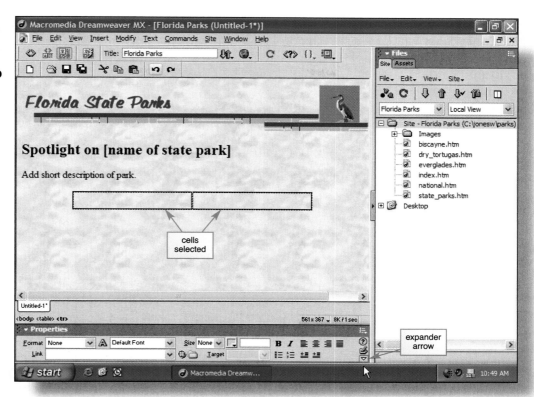

FIGURE 6-14

4 Click the Property inspector expander arrow. Click the Horz box arrow in the Property inspector and then click Center. Click the Vert box arrow and then click Middle.

The Property inspector is expanded and the attributes are added to the table cells (Figure 6-15). No changes are evident in the Document window at this time.

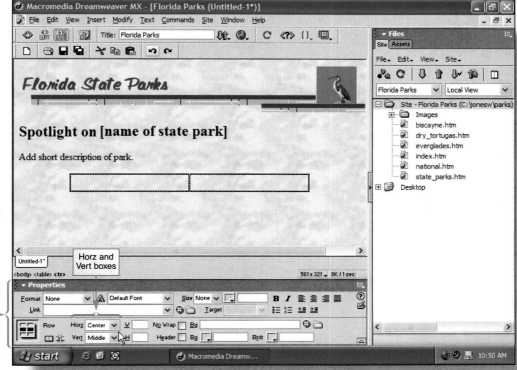

FIGURE 6-15

5 **Click the left cell in the table and then type** Add additional columns and rows as necessary. Add images and short description of image. **for the prompt.**

The prompt is entered into the left cell (Figure 6-16).

FIGURE 6-16

6 **Click the right cell. Click Insert on the menu bar and then point to Image Placeholder.**

The Insert menu is displayed and Image Placeholder is highlighted (Figure 6-17).

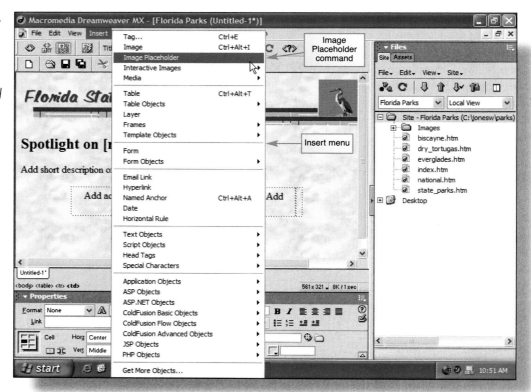

FIGURE 6-17

7 Click Image Placeholder. When the Image Placeholder dialog box is displayed, type add_image in the Name text box for the prompt and then press the TAB key. Type 64 for the Width and then point to the OK button.

The Image Placeholder dialog box is displayed. The prompt is added to the table cell. The width is changed to 64 (Figure 6-18).

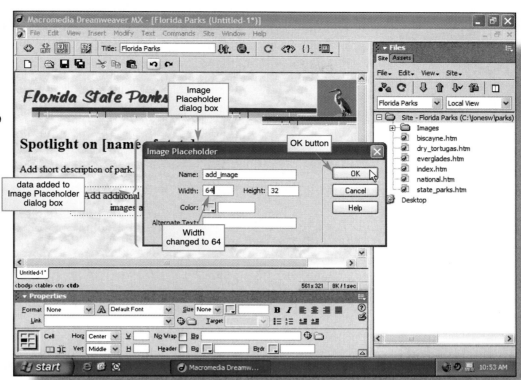

FIGURE 6-18

8 Click the OK button.

The image placeholder is added to the table cell (Figure 6-19).

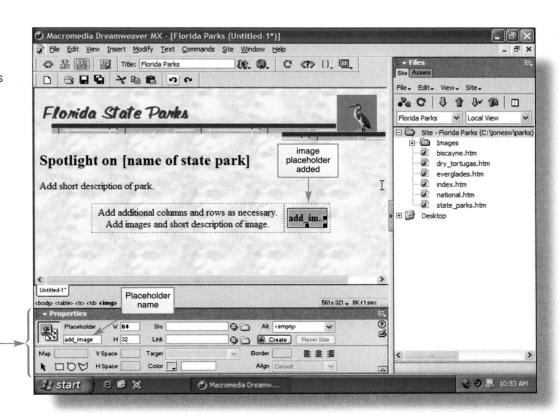

FIGURE 6-19

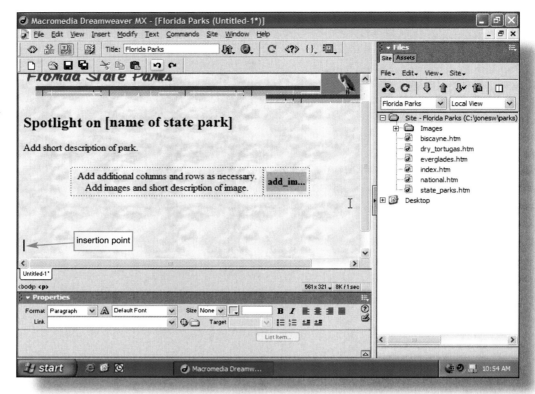

9 **Click to the right of the table and then press the ENTER key two times.**

The insertion point is blinking at the left margin below the table (Figure 6-20).

FIGURE 6-20

The second table will serve as a table for links. Complete the following steps to add the link table as the fourth editable region.

TO ADD AND CENTER A TABLE AS THE FOURTH EDITABLE REGION

1 Click Insert on the menu bar and then click Table to display the Insert Table dialog box.

2 Enter the following data in the Insert Table dialog box: 1 for Rows, 5 for Cell Padding, 2 for Columns, 0 for Cell Spacing, and 50 Percent for Width. Click the OK button.

3 Click the Align box arrow in the Property inspector, and center the table.

4 Click the left cell and then drag to select both cells in the table.

5 Click the Horz box arrow in the Property inspector and then click Center. Click the Vert box arrow and then click Middle.

6 Click the left cell and then type Add additional columns as necessary for links. as the prompt.

The second table is added and centered and a prompt is added to the table (Figure 6-21).

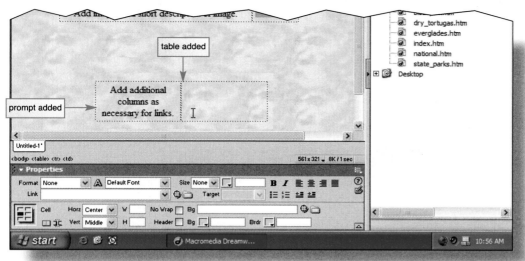

FIGURE 6-21

Creating and Saving a Template

Dreamweaver provides two methods to create a template: (1) create a template from an existing file, and (2) create a template from a new document page. To create a template from an existing file, you open the file, use the Save as Template command on the File menu, and then define the editable regions. In this project, you create a template from the new document Web page you have designed.

When the first template for a Web site is saved, Dreamweaver automatically creates a Templates folder at the Web site local root folder and then saves the template with a **.dwt extension** within that folder. Any additional templates added to the Web site are saved in the Templates folder.

Complete the following steps to save the Web page as a template and to have Dreamweaver create the Templates folder.

More About

Detaching a Page from a Template

To detach a page from a template, click Modify on the menu bar, point to Templates, and then click Detach from Template on the Templates submenu. The page becomes a regular document. Locked regions become editable.

 To Save the Web Page as a Template

1 **Click File on the menu bar and then point to Save as Template.**

The File menu is displayed and the Save as Template command is highlighted (Figure 6-22).

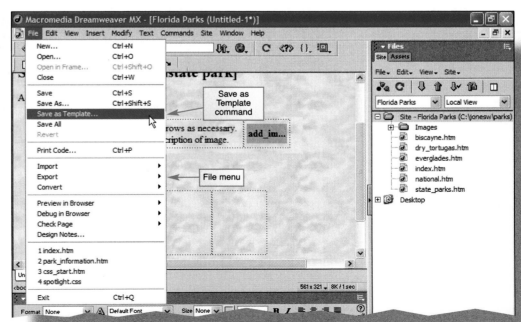

FIGURE 6-22

2 **Click Save as Template. Type** `spotlight_parks` **in the Save As text box and then point to the Save button in the Save As Template dialog box.**

The Save As Template dialog box is displayed (Figure 6-23). The spotlight_parks name is displayed in the Save As text box.

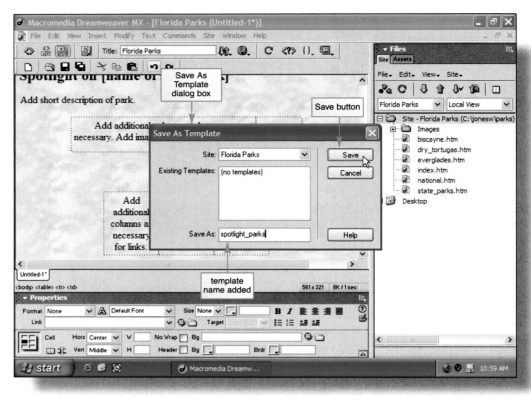

FIGURE 6-23

3 **Click the Save button.**

The template is saved. A Templates folder is created automatically in the Florida Parks Site panel (Figure 6-24).

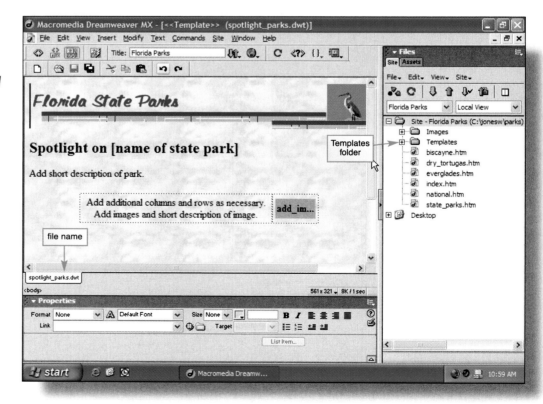

FIGURE 6-24

4 **Click the plus sign to the left of the Templates folder.**

The folder expands. The template name, spotlight_parks.dwt, is displayed in the Templates folder (Figure 6-25). The .dwt extension indicates it is a template file.

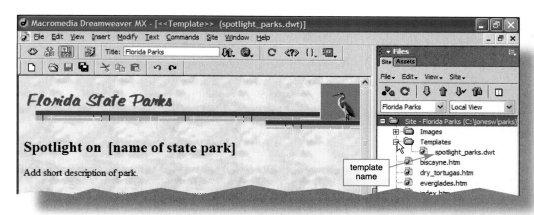

FIGURE 6-25

Other Ways

1 On File menu click New, click Template Page in Category list on General sheet, click Create button

Adding Editable Regions

As previously discussed on pages DW 6.06 – DW 6.07, Dreamweaver supports four different regions in a template: editable regions, repeating regions, optional regions, and editable tag attributes. All Dreamweaver region objects, along with other template-related objects, are available through the Templates tab in the Insert bar. Figure 6-26 shows the Insert bar with the Templates tab selected. Table 6-1 lists the button names and descriptions on the Templates tab.

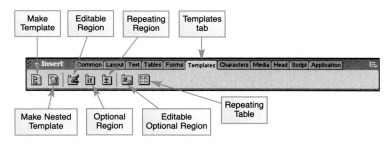

FIGURE 6-26

TABLE 6-1	Buttons on the Templates Insert Bar
BUTTON NAME	***DESCRIPTION***
Make Template	Displays the Save As Template dialog box; features in the dialog box include selecting a Web site in which to save the template, a list of existing templates, and a Save As box to name the template.
Make Nested Template	Creates a template whose design and editable regions are based on another template; useful for sites in which all pages share certain elements and subsections of those pages share a subset of page elements.
Editable Region	Creates an unlocked region; the basic building block of a template.
Optional Region	Designates a region that can be used to show or hide content on a page-by-page basis; use an optional region to set conditions for displaying content in a document.
Repeating Region	Creates a section of a template that can be duplicated as often as desired in a template-based page.
Editable Optional Region	Designates a region that can be used to show or hide content on a page-by-page basis.
Repeating Table	Defines a table and then defines the location of editable regions in each cell in the table.

Dreamweaver MX

Displaying the Templates Insert Bar

The Templates tab in the Insert bar is helpful when creating editable regions. Complete the following steps to display the Insert bar and the Templates tab.

 To Display the Insert Bar and Templates Tab

1 **Click Window on the menu bar and then click Insert. Point to the Templates tab in the Insert bar.**

The Insert bar is displayed (Figure 6-27).

FIGURE 6-27

2 **Click the Templates tab. Point to the expander arrow.**

The Templates bar is displayed (Figure 6-28).

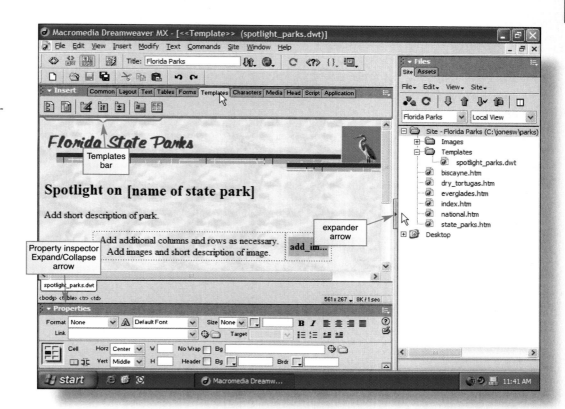

FIGURE 6-28

Marking Existing Content as an Editable Region

As discussed previously, an editable region is one that the content developer can change. Editable template regions control which areas of a template-based page can be edited. Each editable region must have a unique name. Dreamweaver uses the name to identify the editable region when entering new content or applying the template. Complete the following steps to make the heading an editable region.

To Create the First Editable Region

1 **Click the Site panel expander arrow and then click the Property inspector expand/collapse arrow. Click to the left of the heading prompt. Point to the <h2> tag in the tag selector.**

The Property inspector and Site panel are collapsed. The insertion point is blinking to the left of the heading text (Figure 6-29).

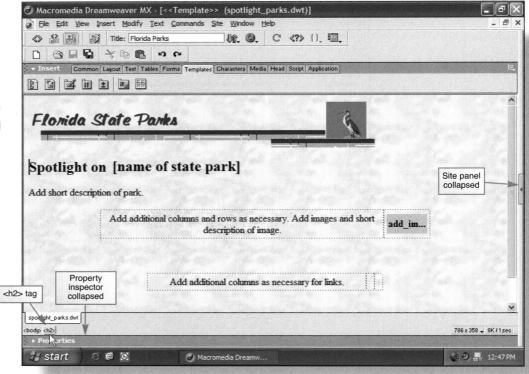

FIGURE 6-29

2 **Click the <h2> tag. Point to the Editable Region button on the Templates tab.**

The prompt for the title is highlighted and the <h2> tag is selected (Figure 6-30).

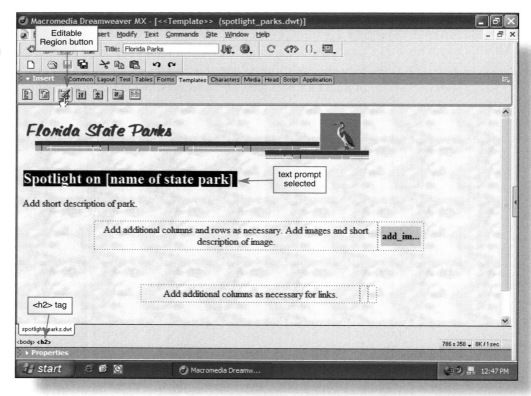

FIGURE 6-30

3 **Click the Editable Region button. Type** park_name **in the Name text box and then point to the OK button.**

The New Editable Region dialog box is displayed and park_name is typed in the Name text box (Figure 6-31).

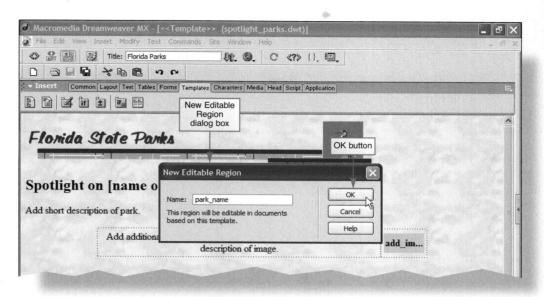

FIGURE 6-31

4 **Click the OK button.**

The editable region name is added. The editable region is enclosed in a highlighted rectangular outline in the template (Figure 6-32).

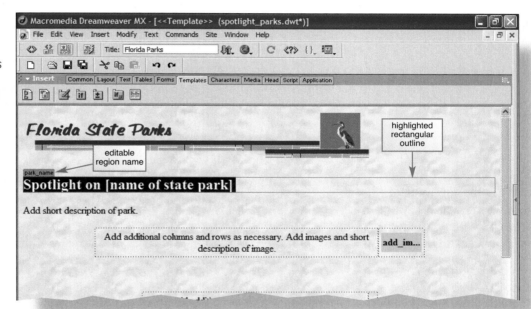

FIGURE 6-32

The second editable region that needs to be identified and given a name is the text area that will provide a short description of the featured park. Complete the following steps to make the park description section an editable region.

Other **Ways**

1. Click Document window, select content, on Insert menu point to Template Objects, click New Editable Region on Template Objects sub-menu

2. Click Document window, select content, right-click selected content, click New Editable Region on context menu

Steps **To Create the Second Editable Region**

1 **Click to the left of the prompt Add short description of park. in the Document window.**

The insertion point is blinking to the left of the prompt (Figure 6-33).

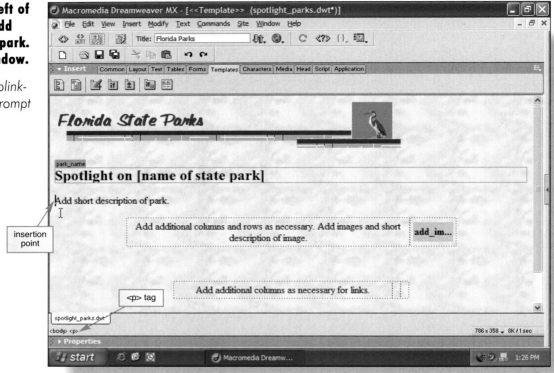

FIGURE 6-33

2 **Click the <p> tag in the tag selector and then click the Editable Region button on the Templates tab.**

The New Editable Region dialog box is displayed (Figure 6-34).

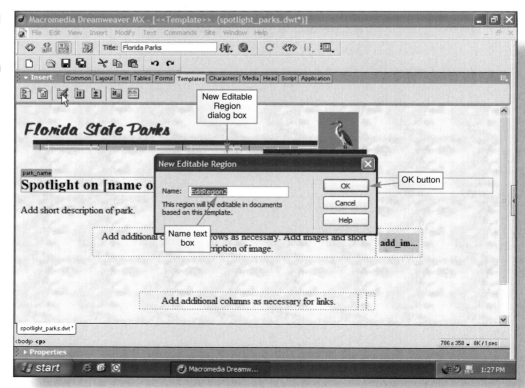

FIGURE 6-34

3 **Type** park_ description **in the Name text box and then click the OK button.**

The editable region name, park_description, is added. The editable region is enclosed in a highlighted rectangular outline in the template (Figure 6-35).

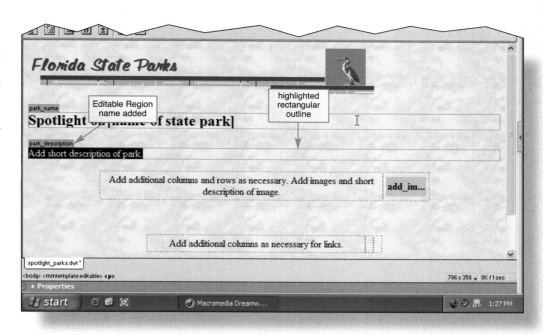

FIGURE 6-35

The third and fourth editable regions are the two tables that were added to the template. Complete the following steps to make both tables editable regions.

Steps **To Create the Third and Fourth Editable Regions**

1 **Click in the left cell of the first table and then click the <table> tag in the tag selector. Point to the Editable Region button.**

The table is selected (Figure 6-36).

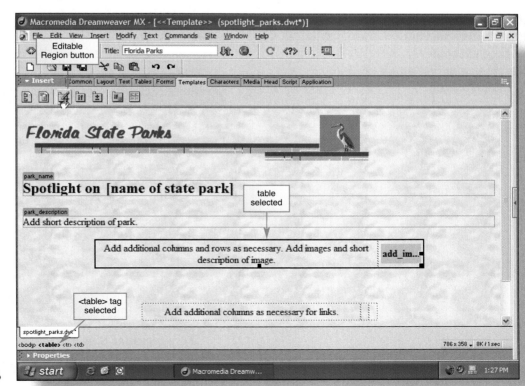

FIGURE 6-36

2 **Click the Editable Region button. When the New Editable Region dialog box is displayed, type** parks_images **in the Name text box, and then click the OK button.**

The editable region name, parks_images, is added. The editable region is enclosed in a highlighted rectangular outline in the template (Figure 6-37).

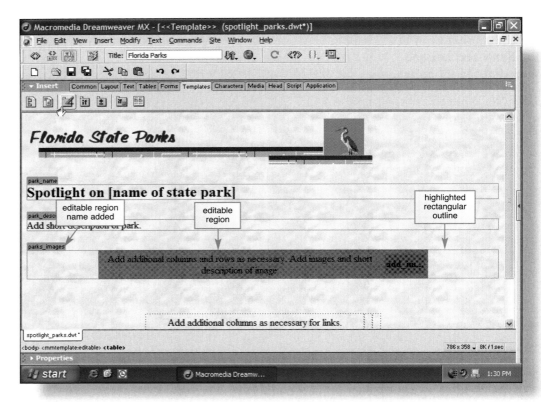

FIGURE 6-37

3 **If necessary, scroll down to display the second table, click in the left cell of the second table, click the <table> tag in the tag selector, and then click the Editable Region button on the Templates tab.**

The table is selected and the New Editable Region dialog box is displayed (Figure 6-38).

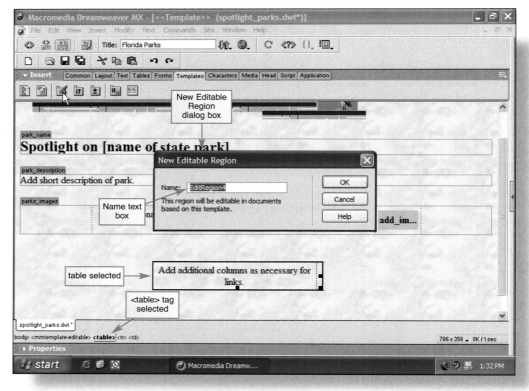

FIGURE 6-38

4 **Type links in the Name text box and then click the OK button.**

The editable region name, links, is added. The editable region is enclosed in a highlighted rectangular outline in the template (Figure 6-39).

5 **Click the Save button on the Standard toolbar.**

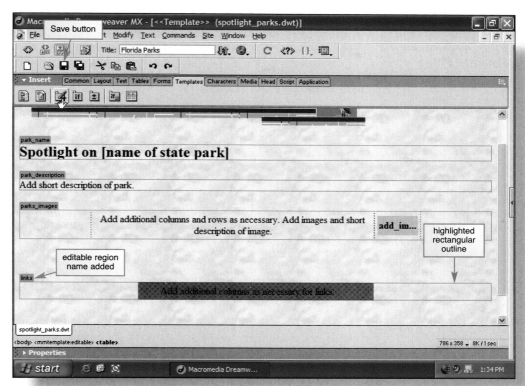

FIGURE 6-39

Introduction to Style Sheets

If you have used styles in a word processing program such as Microsoft Word, then the concept of styles within HTML and Dreamweaver will be familiar. A **style** is a rule describing how a specific object is formatted. A style sheet (discussed later in this section) is a file that contains a collection of these rules or styles.

Dreamweaver supports two types of styles: HTML styles and Cascading Style Sheets.

HTML Styles

Thus far, when you have formatted text, you selected the text in the Document window and then applied font attributes using the Property inspector. You selected and then formatted each text element individually: the heading, character, word, paragraph, or other. **HTML styles**, however, is a feature within Dreamweaver that a Web page developer can use to apply formatting options quickly and easily to text in a Web page. HTML styles use HTML tags such as the <font> and <b> tags to apply the formatting. Once you have created and saved an HTML style, you can apply it to any document in the Web site.

One advantage of HTML styles is that they consist only of font tags, and therefore display in just about all browsers, including Internet Explorer 3.0 and earlier versions. One of the main disadvantages of HTML styles, however, is that changes made to an HTML style are not updated automatically in the document. If a style is applied and then the style is modified, the style must be reapplied to the text to update the formatting. HTML styles are created through the HTML Styles panel.

More About

HTML Styles

Use the HTML Styles panel to record the HTML styles you use in your Web site, and then share them with other users, local sites, or remote sites. For more information about HTML Styles, visit the Dreamweaver MX More About Web page (scsite.com/ dreamweavermx/ more.htm) and then click HTML Styles.

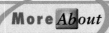

External Style Sheets

External style sheets are separate files and exist independently of any HTML pages within the Web site. Any and all Web pages within a Web site can access a common set of properties by linking to the same external style sheet. For more information about external style sheets, visit the Dreamweaver MX More About Web page (scsite.com/ dreamweavermx/ more.htm) and then click Style Sheets.

The HTML 4.0 specification released by the World Wide Web Consortium (W3C) in early 1998 discourages the use of HTML formatting tags in favor of Cascading Style Sheets (CSS). This project, therefore, focuses on Cascading Style Sheets.

Cascading Style Sheets

Cascading Style Sheets, also called **CSS** and **style sheets**, are a collection of formatting rules that control the appearance of content in a Web page. Cascading Style Sheets are the cornerstone of Dynamic HTML (DHTML). **DHTML** is an extension to HTML that enables a Web page to respond to user input without sending a request to the Web server. Compared with HTML styles, style sheets provide the Web site developer more precision and control over many aspects of page design. After creating a style, you can apply it instantly to text, margins, images, and other Web page elements. Some of the advantages of style sheets include the following:

1. Precise layout control
2. Smaller, faster downloading pages
3. Browser friendly — nonsupporting CSS browsers ignore the code
4. Updating all attached Web pages at one time

The capability of updating every element simultaneously with a certain style is one of the main benefits of style sheets. For example, suppose you create a text style defined as 24-point Times New Roman bold. Later you decide to change the text color to red. All elements formatted with that style instantly are displayed in red.

Conflicting Styles

The term **cascading** refers to the capability of applying multiple style sheets to the same Web page. When more than one style is applied to the same Web page, an order of preference is involved. Styles are used as described and applied in the following preference order:

1. An **external style sheet** is a single style sheet used to create uniform formatting and contains no HTML code. An external style sheet can be linked to any page within the Web site or imported into a Web site. Using the Import command creates an @import tag in the HTML code and references the URL where the published style sheet is located. This method does not work with Netscape Navigator.
2. An **internal** or **embedded style sheet** contains styles that apply to a specific page. The styles that apply to the page are embedded in the <HEAD> portion of the Web page.
3. A specified element within a page can have its own style.

In some instances, two styles will be applied to the same element. When this occurs, the browser displays all attributes of both styles unless an attribute conflict exists. For example, one style may specify Arial as the font and the other style may specify Times New Roman. When this happens, the browser displays the attribute of the style closest to the text.

The CSS Styles Panel

To develop a style sheet, you start with the **CSS Styles panel** (Figure 6-40), which is part of the Design panel group. Styles are created and controlled through the CSS Styles panel. Two radio buttons are located at the top of the panel: Apply Styles and Edit Styles. The Apply Styles list of styles will include only the list of custom styles, while the Edit Styles list of styles will show all styles used with that document, including the custom styles.

A **custom style** is a style you can create and name and specify all the attributes you want the style to include. The name of a custom style always begins with a period.

At the bottom of the CSS Styles panel are four buttons. These buttons are used for the following tasks:

1. The **Attach Style Sheet** button opens the Link External Style Sheet dialog box. Select an external style sheet to link to or import into your current document.
2. The **New CSS Style** button opens the New CSS Style dialog box. You use the New CSS Styles dialog to define a type of style.
3. The **Edit Style Sheet** button opens the CSS Style Definition dialog box. Edit any of the styles in the current document or in an external style sheet.
4. The **Delete CSS Style** button removes the selected style from the CSS Styles panel, and removes the formatting from any element to which it was applied.

Complete the following steps to display the Design panel group and the CSS Styles panel.

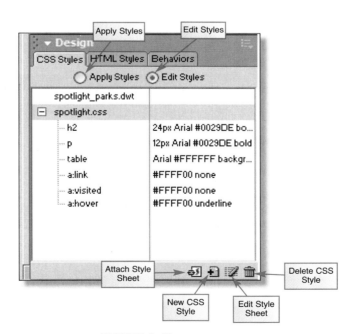

FIGURE 6-40

To Display the Design Panel Group

1 Scroll to the top of the Document window. Click the expander arrow to display the Site panel. Click Window on the menu bar and then point to CSS Styles.

The Site panel is expanded (Figure 6-41). The Window menu is displayed and the CSS Styles command is highlighted. The text in the Parks_images table on your screen may display on more or less than three lines.

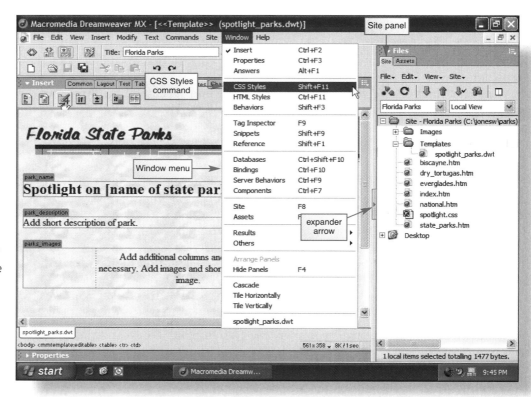

FIGURE 6-41

2 Click CSS Styles. If necessary, click the Apply Styles in the CSS Styles panel.

The Design panel group and the CSS Styles panel are displayed (Figure 6-42).

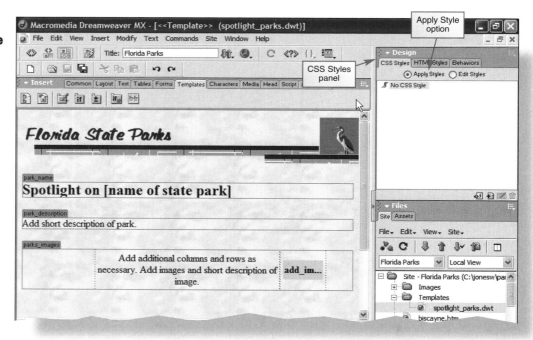

FIGURE 6-42

Other Ways

1 Press SHIFT + F11

Defining Style Attributes

Dreamweaver makes it easy to add style attributes to the style sheet. This is done through the CSS Style Definition dialog box (Figure 6-43). The Style Definition dialog box contains eight categories with more than 70 different CSS attributes. As you are defining a style, select the category to access the attributes for that category. Styles from more than one category can be applied to the same element. Tables 6-3 through 6-10 on pages DW 6.62 and DW 6.63 contain a description of each attribute in each of these eight categories.

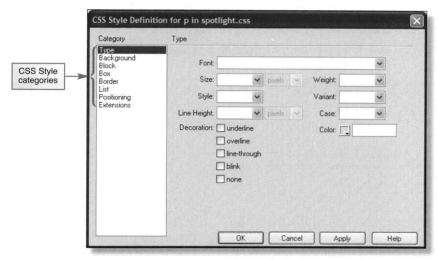

FIGURE 6-43

Adding a Style and Saving the Style Sheet

Recall that styles and style sheets are applied in a variety of formats: an external style sheet can be linked or imported to any number of Web pages, an embedded style sheet is contained within one Web page, or you can apply a style to a specific element within a Web page. The spotlight style sheet you create in the following steps is an external style sheet, which will be linked to the template page. Complete the following steps to create the heading style and then save the style sheet.

Steps **To Add a Style and Save the Style Sheet**

1 **Click to the left of the text in the park_name editable region and then click the <h2> tag in the tag selector. Point to the New CSS Style button in the CSS Styles panel.**

The heading is highlighted in the Document window (Figure 6-44).

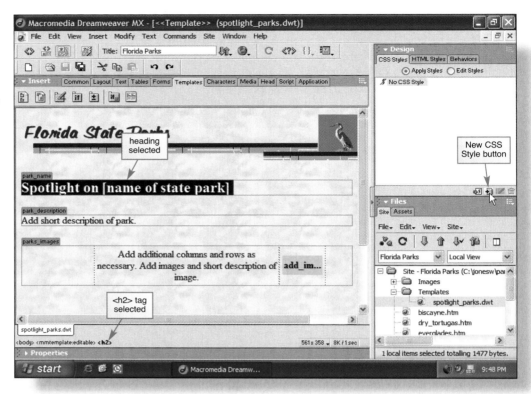

FIGURE 6-44

2 **Click the New CSS Style button. Click Redefine HTML Tag to select it. If necessary, click Define In (New Style Sheet File) to select it. Click the Tag box arrow and then click h2 in the list. Point to the OK button.**

The New CSS Style dialog box is displayed (Figure 6-45). The Type Redefine HTML Tag and Define In (New Style Sheet File) radio buttons are selected. The h2 tag is high-lighted in the Tag box.

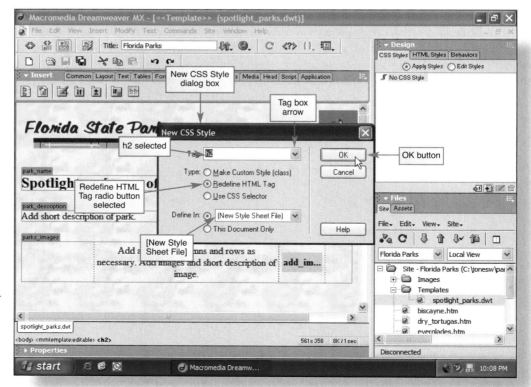

FIGURE 6-45

PROJECT 6

3 **Click the OK button. When the Save Style Sheet File As dialog box is displayed, point to the Save in box arrow.**

The Save Style Sheet File As dialog box is displayed (Figure 6-46). The Templates folder is displayed in the Save in box.

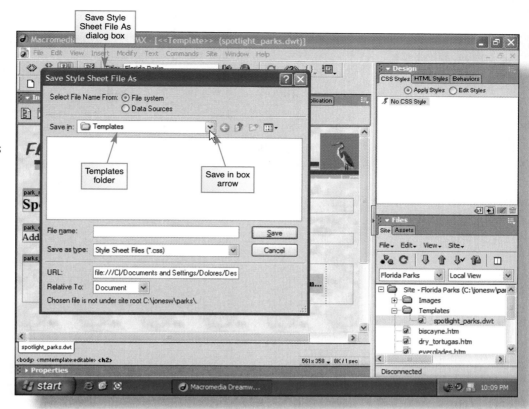

FIGURE 6-46

4 **Click the Save in text box arrow and then click the parks folder name. Click the File name text box and then type** spotlight **for the style sheet name. Point to the Save button in the Save Style Sheet File As dialog box.**

The parks folder is selected and is displayed in the Save in text box (Figure 6-47). The style sheet name spotlight is displayed in the File name text box.

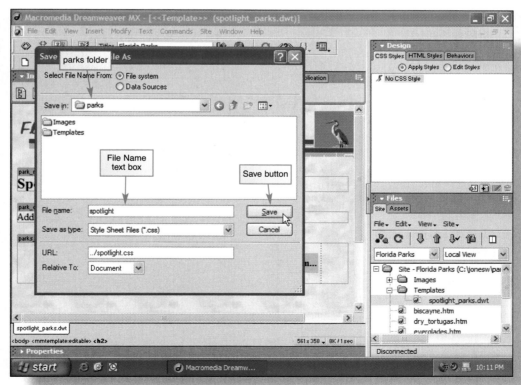

FIGURE 6-47

5 Click the Save button. When the CSS Style Definition dialog box is displayed, point to the Font box arrow.

The CSS Style Definition for h2 in spotlight.css dialog box is displayed. The Type Category is highlighted (Figure 6-48).

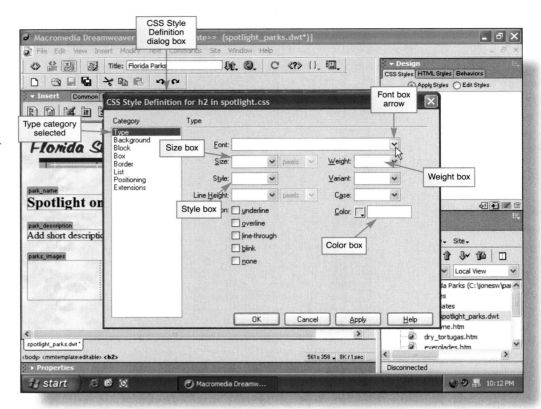

FIGURE 6-48

6 Click the Font box arrow, click Arial, Helvetica, sans-serif in the Font list, and then press the TAB key. Click the Size box arrow, click 24 in the Size list, and then press the TAB key two times. Click the Weight box arrow, click bolder, and then press the TAB key. Click the Style box arrow and then click italic. Click the Color text box, type #0029DE, and then press the TAB key. Point to the OK button.

The style definitions are entered as shown in Figure 6-49. The shade of blue in the Color box matches the blue color in the logo.

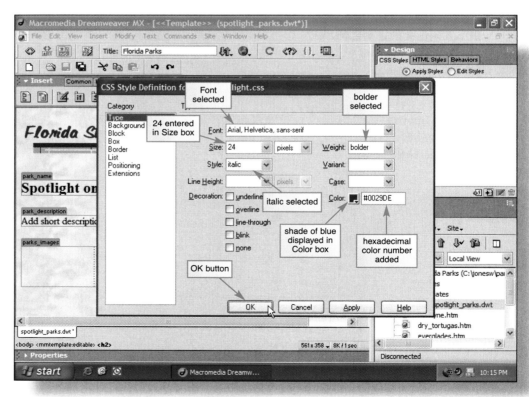

FIGURE 6-49

7 Click the OK button. If necessary, click Edit Styles in the CSS Styles panel and then click the plus sign to the left of the spotlight.css style in the CSS Styles panel.

The heading prompt in the Document window changes to reflect the new styles of the applied attributes. The new CSS style is displayed as h2 in the left pane of the CSS Styles panel and the style attributes display in the right (Figure 6-50). The Edit Styles option button is selected.

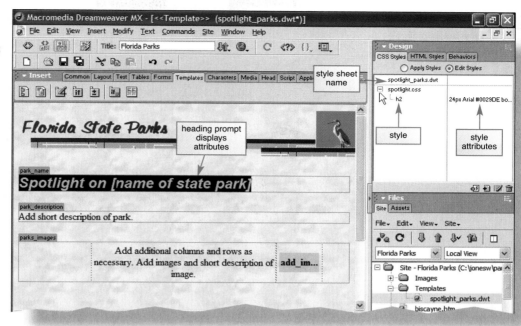

FIGURE 6-50

Next, you create a style for the paragraph text. Complete the following steps to redefine the HTML paragraph tag for the park_description editable region.

 To Create a Style for the Paragraph Text

1 Click to the left of the prompt Add short description of park, click the <p> tag in the tag selector, and then point to the New CSS Style button in the CSS Styles panel.

The prompt is highlighted (Figure 6-51).

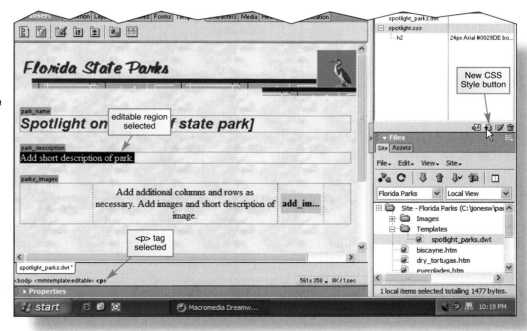

FIGURE 6-51

Dreamweaver MX

2 **Click the New CSS Style button in the CSS Styles panel. Point to the OK button.**

The New CSS Style dialog box is displayed. The p tag is highlighted in the Tag box and the spotlight.css is displayed in the Define In box (Figure 6-52).

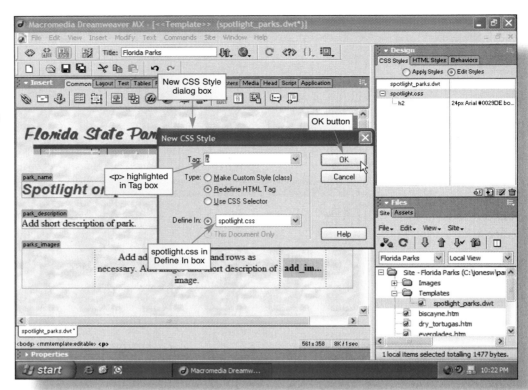

FIGURE 6-52

3 **Click the OK button. In the CSS Style Definition dialog box, point to the Font box arrow.**

The CSS Style Definition for p in spotlight.css dialog box is displayed (Figure 6-53.)

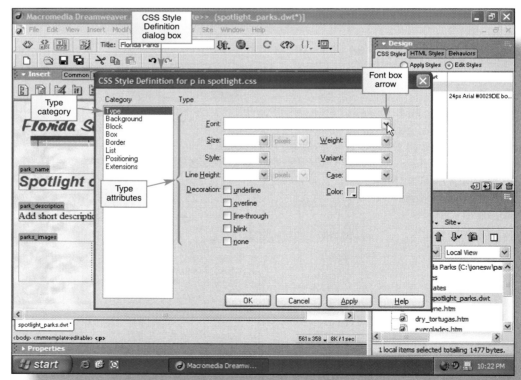

FIGURE 6-53

4 **Click the Font box arrow and then click Arial, Helvetica, sans-serif. Click the Size box arrow and then click 12. Click the Weight box arrow and then click bold. Click the Color text box and then type #0029DE for the color. Point to the OK button.**

The CSS Style Definition attributes for Type are added (Figure 6-54).

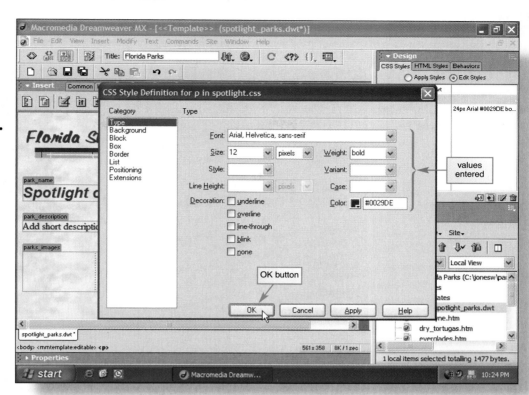

FIGURE 6-54

5 **Click the OK button.**

The text changes to reflect the new attributes. The new style is displayed as p in the CSS Styles panel (Figure 6-55).

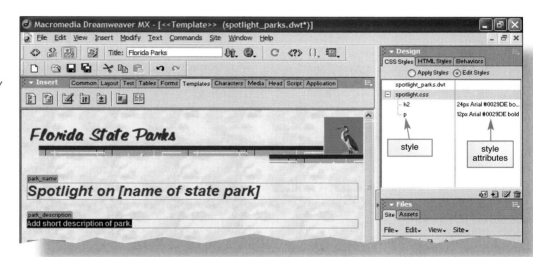

FIGURE 6-55

Adding a background, border, and text color to the tables is your next goal. To accomplish this, you use the Type, Background, and Border categories in the CSS Style Definition dialog box. In the steps on the following pages, you select a type font, a background color of blue, and a shade of green for the border to match the green color in the logo image.

Other Ways

1 Select content, right-click selected content, point to CSS Styles on context menu, click New CSS Style on CSS Style submenu

Steps To Add a Background, Border, and Text Color to a Table

1 **Click in the first cell of the parks_images table. Point to the <table> tag in the tag selector.**

The insertion point is blinking in the first cell of the parks_images table (Figure 6-56).

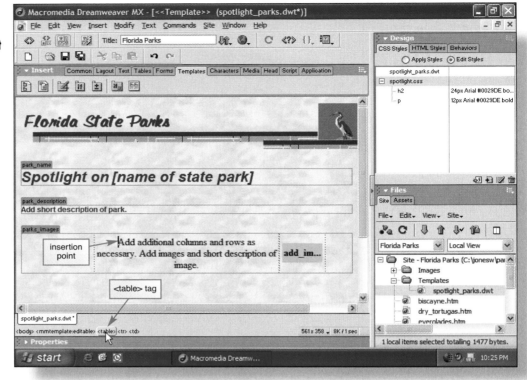

FIGURE 6-56

2 **Click the <table> tag in the tag selector. Point to the New CSS Style button in the CSS Styles panel.**

The table is selected (Figure 6-57).

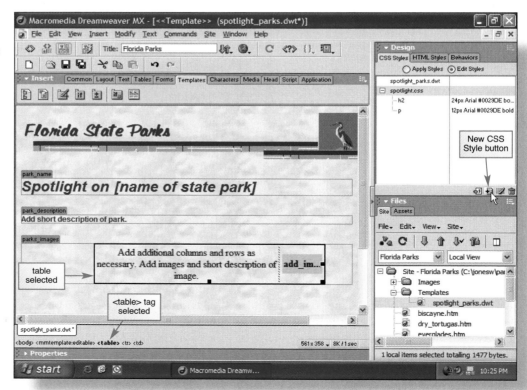

FIGURE 6-57

3 Click the New CSS Style button in the CSS Styles panel. Point to the OK button.

The New CSS Style dialog box is displayed (Figure 6-58). The table tag is highlighted in the Tag box, the Redefine HTML Tag radio button is selected, and spotlight.css is displayed in the Define In box.

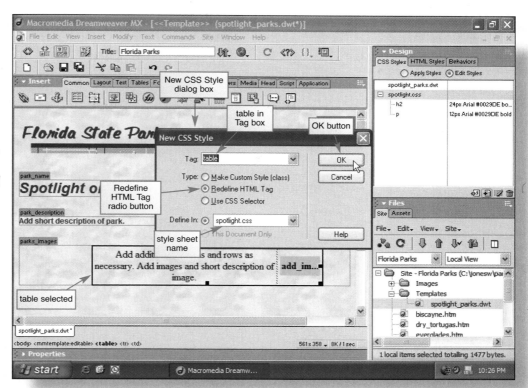

FIGURE 6-58

4 Click the OK button.

The CSS Style Definition for table in spotlight.css is displayed (Figure 6-59). The Type category is highlighted.

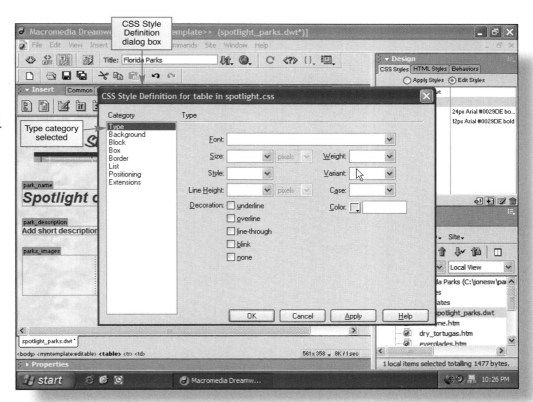

FIGURE 6-59

5 **Click the Font box arrow and then click Arial, Helvetica, sans-serif. Click the Color text box, type #FFFFFF, and then press the TAB key. Point to Background in the Category list.**

The font is displayed as Arial, Helvetica, sans-serif and the hexadecimal #FFFFFF is displayed in the Color text box (Figure 6-60).

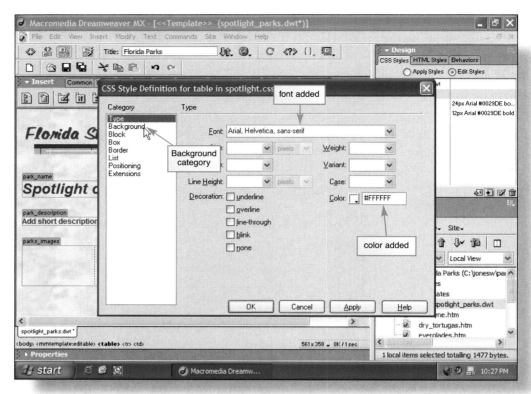

FIGURE 6-60

6 **Click Background.**

The Background category is highlighted and background attributes are displayed (Figure 6-61).

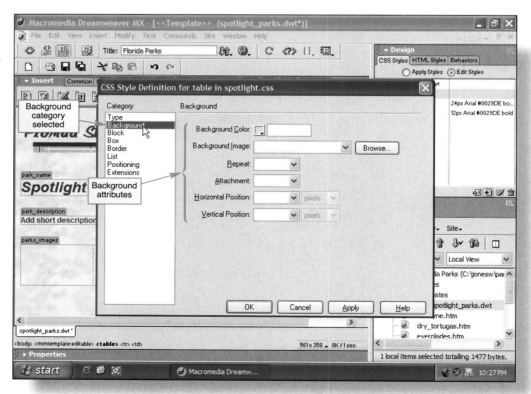

FIGURE 6-61

7 Click the
Background Color
text box, type #000099,
and then press the TAB
key. Point to Border in
the Category list.

*The Background Color is
displayed in the Background
Color box (Figure 6-62).*

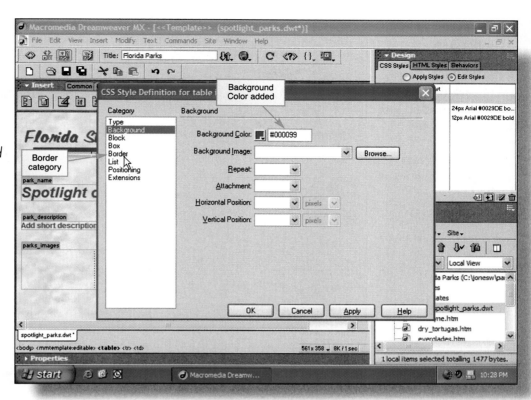

FIGURE 6-62

8 Click Border. Point
to the Top box
arrow in the Style area.

*The Border Category is
highlighted and Border
attribute boxes are dis-
played (Figure 6-63).*

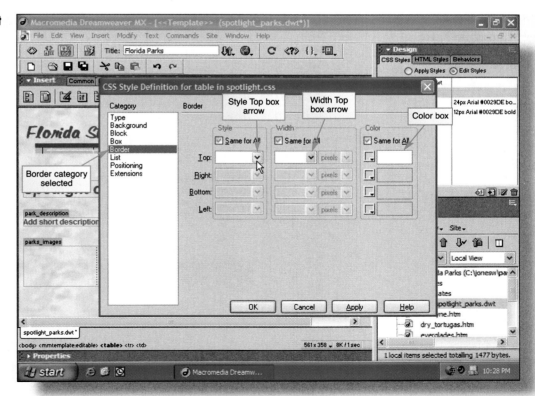

FIGURE 6-63

9 Click the Top box arrow and then click groove in the list. Click the Width box arrow and then click thick in the list. Click the Top text box in the Color area and then type #9CCE9C for the border color. Press the TAB key and then point to the OK button.

The attributes are defined and will apply to both tables (Figure 6-64).

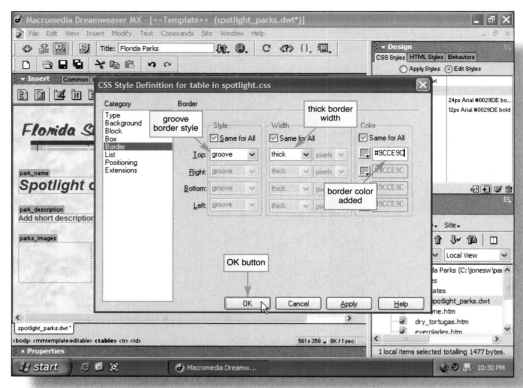

FIGURE 6-64

10 Click the OK button and then, if necessary, scroll down in the Document window to display both tables.

The attributes are added to both tables and the table style is added to the spotlight.css style sheet in the CSS Styles panel (Figure 6-65).

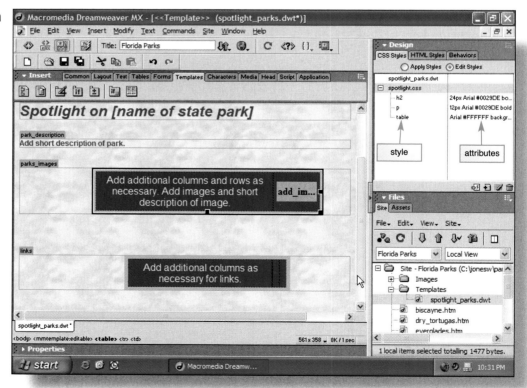

FIGURE 6-65

Style Sheets and Links

The background color and border attributes were applied to the links table when you applied the table attributes. Now you will add two links to the table — a relative link to the Florida Parks index Web page and an absolute link to the Florida Department of State Parks Web page. Style sheets provide new ways to display links, which enables the content developer to match the style of the rest of the Web page. For example, all of the attributes available in the Type category in the Style Definition dialog box also can be applied to links. When defining the style, four attributes are available: a:link, a:visited, a:hover, and a:active.

1. **a:link** defines the style of unvisited links.
2. **a:visited** defines the style of a link of Web sites that you have visited.
3. **a:hover** defines the style of a link when a mouse pointer moves over the link.
4. **a:active** defines the style of a clicked link.

Using the CSS Selector type and attributes from the Type category, the links will use yellow for the text color, but will not contain an underline when displayed in the browser. The check boxes within the **Decoration** attribute in the CSS Style Definition dialog box provide options to add an underline, overline, a line through the text, or make the text blink. The default setting for regular text is none. The default setting for links is underline. When you set the link attribute to none, you remove the underline from links. When the mouse pointer moves over the link, the underline is displayed. This indicates to the Web page visitor that a link is available. The Decoration attribute is supported by both browsers. Complete the following steps to add the links as they will display in the browser

More About

Browsers and Style Sheets

Microsoft Internet Explorer version 3 and Netscape Navigation version 4 were the first browsers to support style sheets. Newer versions of both browsers support style sheets, but still interpret some of the commands differently. View your Web pages in both browsers before publishing.

More About

Modifying Links

To make a link look like it is highlighted, use the Background category in the Style Definition dialog box and define a bright background color for the link. For more information about modifying links, visit the Dreamweaver MX More About Web page (scsite.com/dreamweavermx/more.htm) and then click Modifying Links.

To Modify the A:Link Attribute

1 **Select the links table. Click the New CSS Style button in the CSS Styles panel. Click Use CSS Selector, click the Selector box arrow, and then point to a:link.**

The New CSS Style dialog box is displayed and a:link is highlighted (Figure 6-66).

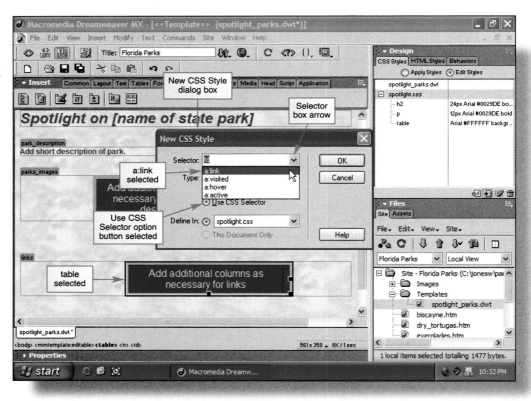

FIGURE 6-66

2 **Click a:link and then point to the OK button.**

The a:link attribute is displayed in the Selector box (Figure 6-67).

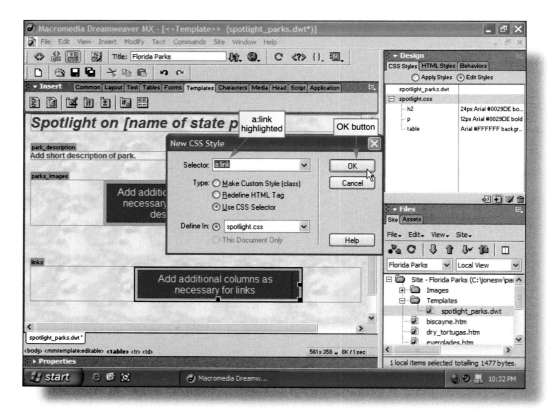

FIGURE 6-67

3 Click the OK button.

The CSS Style Definition for a:link in spotlight.css dialog box is displayed (Figure 6-68).

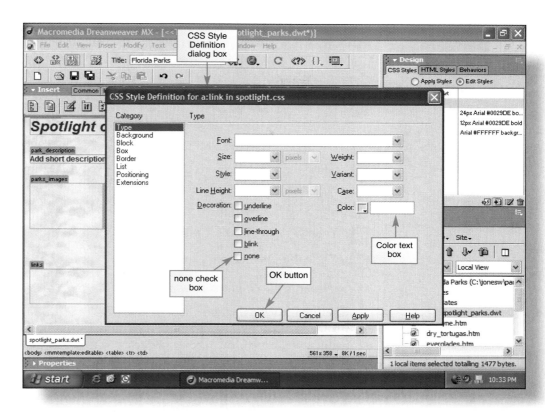

FIGURE 6-68

4 Click none to select the none Decoration attribute, click the Color text box, type #FFFFFF, and then click the OK button.

The a:link style is added to the spotlight.css style sheet (Figure 6-69). The link color is white.

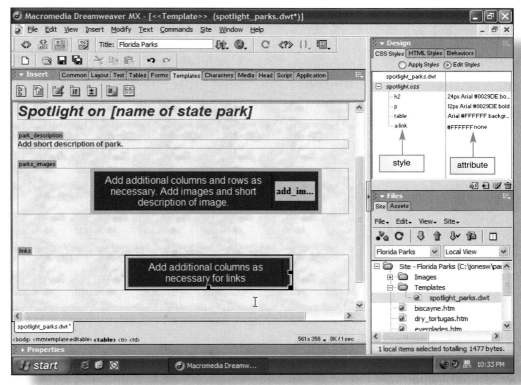

FIGURE 6-69

More About

Removing a Style Sheet Element

To remove a style from an element on a Web page, select the element and then click the No CSS Style button in the CSS Styles panel.

The link attribute is added to the template, and the next step is to add the visited attribute. After a Web site visitor clicks the link, it will display as yellow.

TO ADD THE A:VISITED ATTRIBUTE

1 Click the New CSS Style button in the CSS Styles panel to display the New CSS Style dialog box. If necessary, click Use CSS Selector as the Type option.

2 Click the Selector box arrow and then click a:visited.

3 Click the OK button to display the CSS Style Definition for a:visited in the spotlight.css dialog box.

4 Click none to select the none Decoration attribute.

5 Type #FFFF00 in the Color text box and then press the TAB key.

6 Click the OK button.

The a:visited style is added to the spotlight.css style sheet. (Figure 6-70)

The final attribute to be added is the a:hover attribute. Many Web site visitors are accustomed to having links identified by underlines. Because the links are designed to not include underlines, the **a:hover attribute** is applied to the link. Thus, when the mouse pointer moves over the link, an underline is displayed. The hover attribute is not displayed by all browsers. Complete the following steps to add the a:hover attribute.

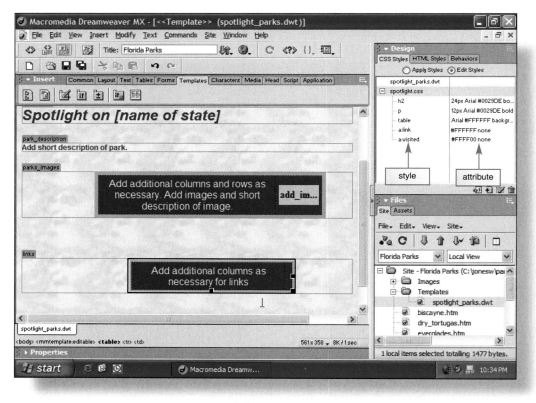

FIGURE 6-70

TO ADD THE A:HOVER ATTRIBUTE

1 Click the New CSS Style button in the CSS Styles panel to display the New CSS Style dialog box. If necessary, click Use CSS Selector.

2 Click the Selector box arrow and then click a:hover.

3 Click the OK button to display the CSS Style Definition for a:hover in the spotlight.css dialog box.

4 Click none to select the Decoration underline check box.

5 Type #FFFF00 in the Color text box and then press the TAB key.

6 Click the OK button and then click the Save button on the Standard toolbar (Figure 6-71 shows the spotlight_parks template after it is saved).

7 Close the spotlight_parks template.

The CSS styles are defined for the spotlight_parks template as shown in Figure 6-71 before closing the template.

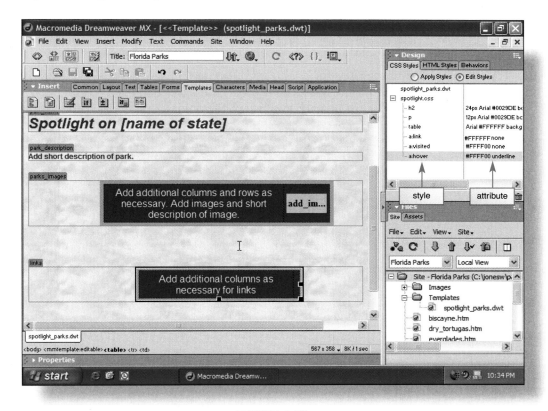

FIGURE 6-71

Style and Style Sheet Maintenance

After a style is created, it can be edited, deleted, or duplicated. You apply these commands through the CSS Styles panel. Click the Edit Styles radio button, right-click the style name to edit, delete, or duplicate, and then select the appropriate command on the context menu. You also can click the style name and then use the Delete CSS Style button to delete a style.

To edit a style sheet, right-click the style sheet name in the CSS Styles panel and then select the Edit command on the context menu. You also can click the style sheet name and then click the Edit Style Sheet button. To delete a style sheet, select the style sheet name and then click the Delete CSS Style button in the CSS Styles panel.

Creating the Web Page for the Bahia Honda State Park

The template is created and styles are added to the template. The next step is to open a basic page and then save the page as an HTML document.

TO CREATE THE BAHIA HONDA STATE PARK SPOTLIGHT WEB PAGE

1 Click File on the menu bar and then click New.

2 Click Basic Page in the New Document dialog box and then click the Create button.

3 Click the Save button on the Standard toolbar and save the page in the parks folder. Use bahia_park.htm as the file name.

The bahia_park document is saved in the parks folder (Figure 6-72).

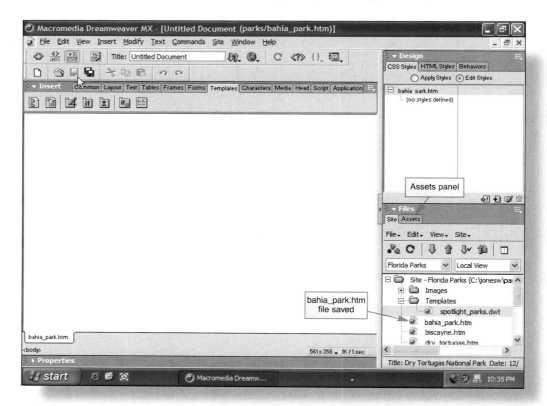

FIGURE 6-72

The Assets Panel

The **Assets panel**, which is part of the Files panel group (Figure 6-73), keeps track of and enables you to update easily objects that you use in a site. Objects may include images, Flash and Shockwave movies, URLs, templates, and so on. You can use the Assets panel in two ways: as an easily accessible list of the assets in your site (the Site list), or as a way to organize the assets that you use most frequently (the Favorites list). A local site must be defined and open before the assets display. To switch between asset types, click the buttons along the left side of the panel. The buttons in the Assets panel represent the following types of assets:

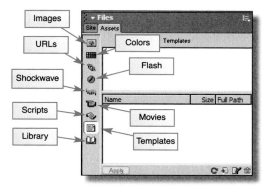

FIGURE 6-73

IMAGES These are image files in GIF, JPEG, or PNG formats.

COLORS The colors used in documents and style sheets in a Web site; these include text colors, background colors, and link colors. The colors added to the CSS file are not included in the Colors category site list.

URLS The external links in the selected Web site.

FLASH MOVIES Flash movies in any version of Macromedia Flash format. Files end with the .swf extension.

SHOCKWAVE MOVIES Shockwave movies in any version of Macromedia Shock format; created with Macromedia Director or Authorware programs.

MOVIES Movies in either Apple QuickTime or MPEG format.

SCRIPTS JavaScript and VBScript files contained within a Web site. Only independent script files are listed.

TEMPLATES Files that provide an easy way to reuse the same page layout on multiple pages.

LIBRARY Library items generally are small content elements, such as a navigation panel, that can be used on many pages within a Web site.

To apply a template to a document, you use the Assets panel. Complete the steps on the following pages to display the Assets panel and apply the template to the Bahia Honda State Park document.

Steps To Apply a Template to the Bahia Honda State Park Web Page

1 **Click the Assets panel tab in the Files group panel. If necessary, click the Templates button in the Assets panel. Point to the Apply button.**

The Assets panel is selected and the template is displayed in the Assets panel. The bahia_park.htm file name is displayed in the CSS Styles panel (Figure 6-74).

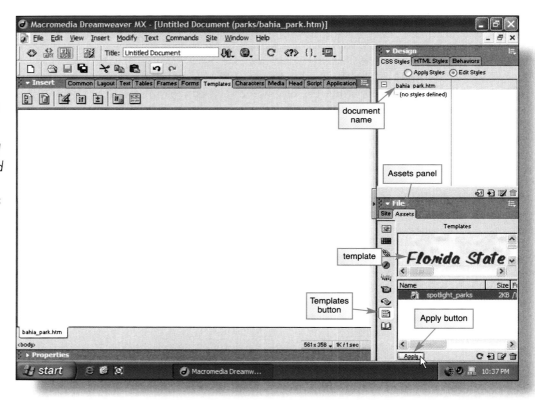

FIGURE 6-74

2 **Click the Apply button and then click the Site panel tab. If necessary, click the plus sign next to the spotlight.css in the CSS Styles panel to display the expanded styles.**

The template is applied to the bahia_park document. The spotlight.css is displayed in the CSS Styles panel (Figure 6-75). The template name, Template: spotlight_parks, is displayed in the upper-right corner of the Document window.

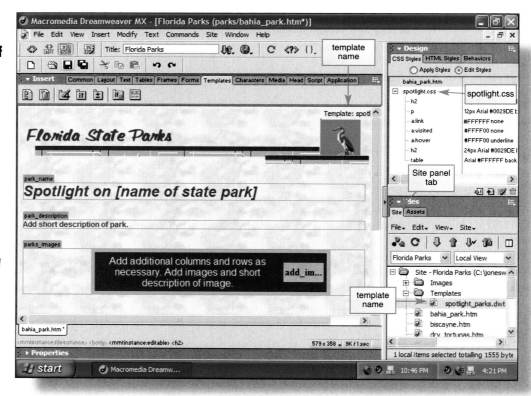

FIGURE 6-75

3 **Right-click the Design panel and close the panel group.**

The Design panel group is closed (Figure 6-76).

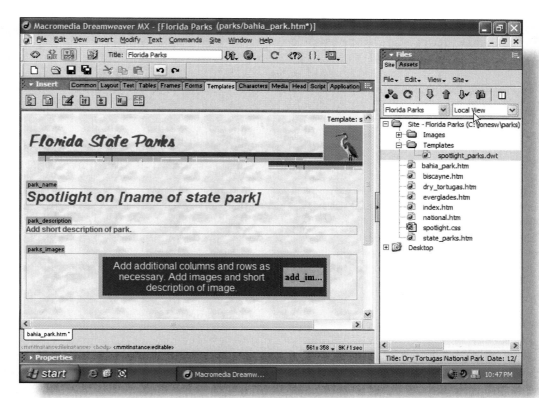

FIGURE 6-76

Other Ways

1. Click Document window, on Modify menu point to Templates, click Apply Template to Page on Templates submenu, select a template from list, click Select button

2. Click Document window, from Assets panel drag template to Document window

Now you use the template to create the Bahia Honda State Park Web page. You first add the name of the park and then add a short description of the park. Complete the following steps to add the park name and park description.

 To Add the Park Name and Park Description to the Bahia Honda State Park Web Page

1 **Select the text and brackets, [name of state park], in the park_name editable region.**

The text and brackets, [name of state park], are highlighted (Figure 6-77).

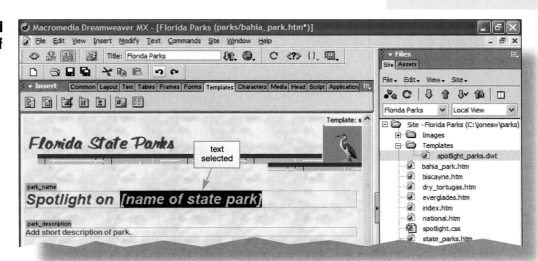

FIGURE 6-77

2 **Type** Bahia Honda State Park **as the park name.**

The park name — Bahia Honda State Park — is added to the bahia_park Web page (Figure 6-78).

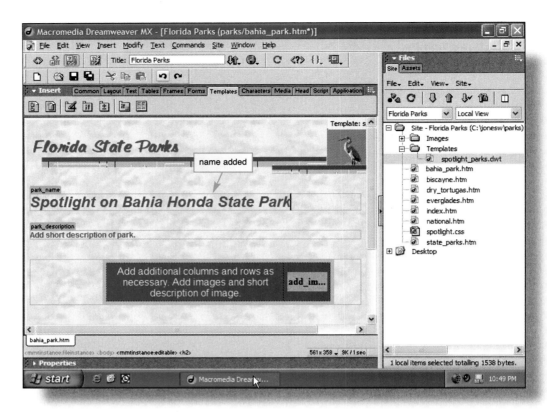

FIGURE 6-78

3 **Select the prompt Add short description of park. in the park description editable region. Type the following text:** Bahia Honda, located on Big Pine Key, is unique among other islands in the Keys. The island consists of white, sandy coastline and deep, crystal-clear waters for excellent swimming and snorkeling. Other activities include boating, fishing, camping, and bird-watching.

The description is added to the park_description editable region (Figure 6-79).

FIGURE 6-79

The Bahia Honda State Park page table will contain six images — three rows and two columns. The parks_images editable table contains one row and two columns. Complete the following steps to add two additional rows.

Steps **To Add Rows to the parks_images Table**

1 **Click in the left cell of the parks_images table. Click Modify on the menu bar, point to Table, and then point to Insert Rows or Columns.**

The Modify menu and Table submenu are displayed (Figure 6-80). The <table> tag is displayed in the tag selector.

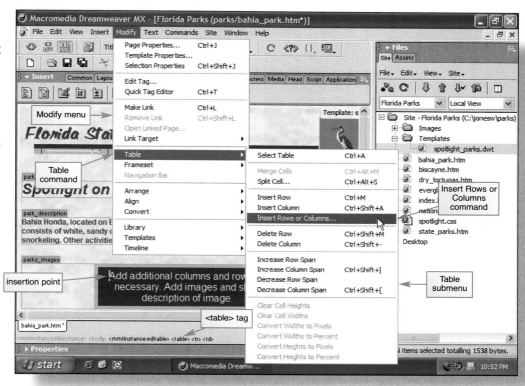

FIGURE 6-80

2 **Click Insert Rows or Columns.**

The Insert Rows or Columns dialog box is displayed (Figure 6-81). The number of rows may be different on your screen.

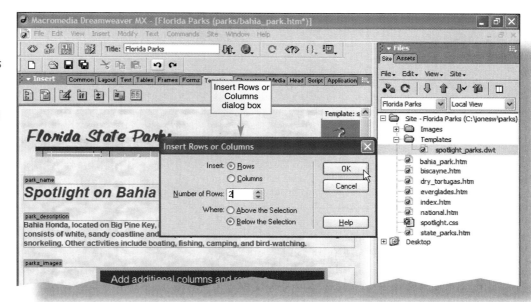

FIGURE 6-81

3 Double-click the Number of Rows text box and then type 2 for the number of rows. Point to the OK button.

The number of rows is changed to 2 (Figure 6-82).

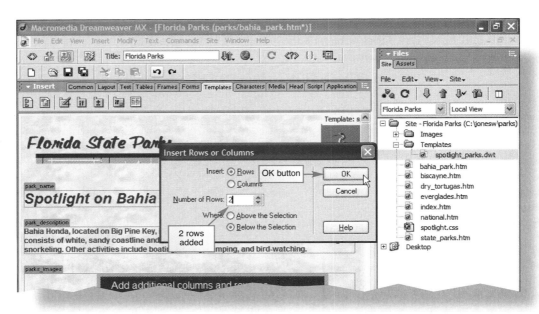

FIGURE 6-82

4 Click the OK button. Scroll down to display both tables.

The additional two rows are added to the parks_images table (Figure 6-83).

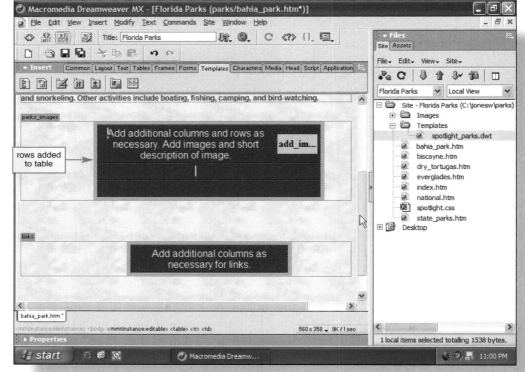

FIGURE 6-83

In the next sequence of steps, you add the six images and a short description of each image. To add the images, you drag the image from the Site panel to a table cell. You add a <br> tag by holding down the SHIFT key and pressing the ENTER key. Then you type the image description.

To Add Images to the parks_images Table

1 Select the text in row 1, column 1 of the parks_images table and then press the DELETE key.

The prompt is deleted from the cell (Figure 6-84).

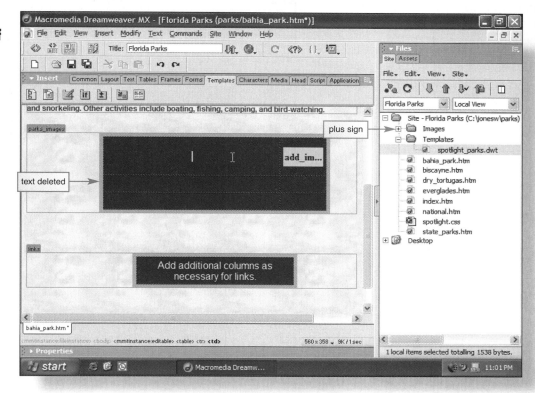

FIGURE 6-84

2 Click the plus sign to the left of the Images folder in the Site panel and then click calusa_beach01.jpg.

The file calusa_beach01.jpg is highlighted (Figure 6-85).

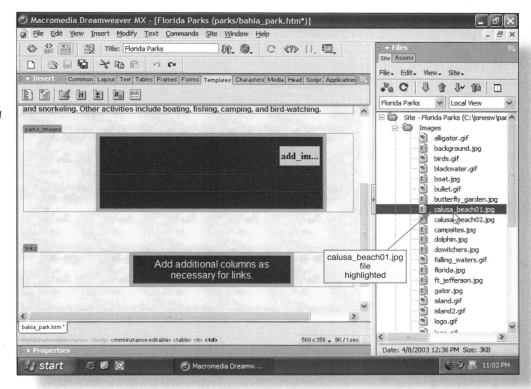

FIGURE 6-85

3 Drag the calusa_beach01.jpg image to row 1, column 1 of the parks_images table.

The image is displayed in the cell. The insertion point is blinking to the right of the image (Figure 6-86).

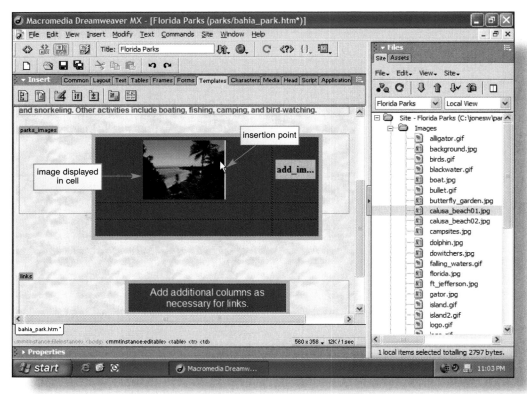

FIGURE 6-86

4 Hold down the SHIFT key and then press the ENTER key. Type Calusa Beach as the description.

The text, Calusa Beach, is added to the cell (Figure 6-87).

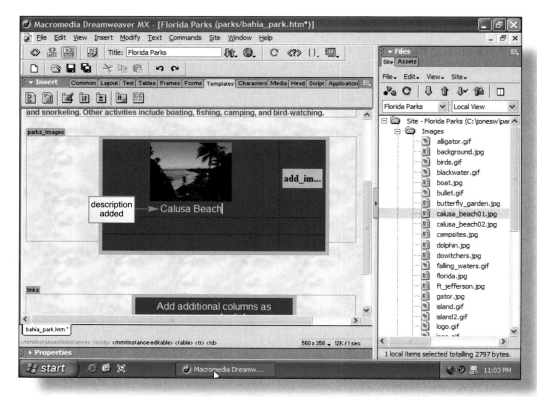

FIGURE 6-87

5 Press the TAB key to move the insertion point to row 1, column 2.

The image placeholder is selected (Figure 6-88).

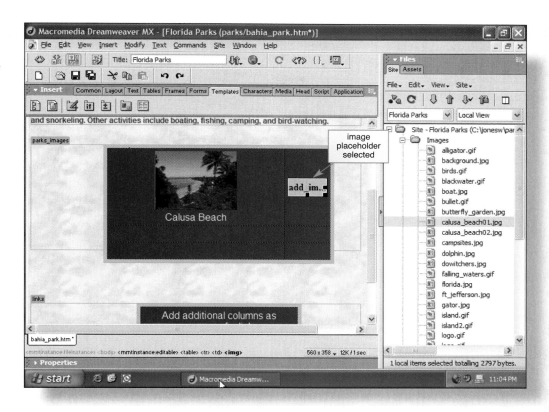

FIGURE 6-88

6 Press the DELETE key to delete the image placeholder and then drag the calusa_beach02.jpg image to the cell. Hold down the SHIFT key and then press the ENTER key. Type Another view of Calusa Beach as the description.

The image is displayed in the cell and the description is added below the image (Figure 6-89).

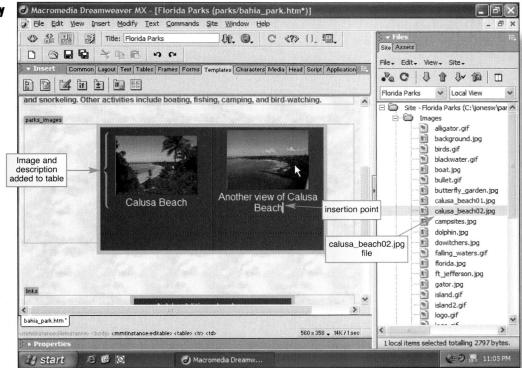

FIGURE 6-89

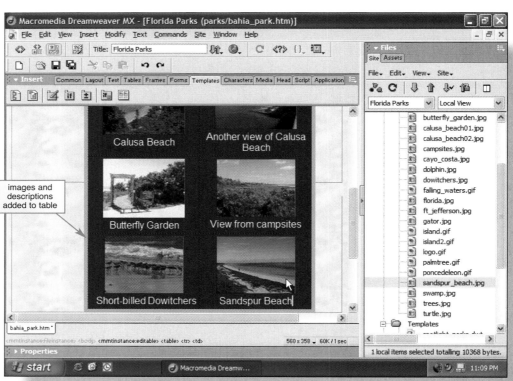

7 **Add the four other images and descriptions to the parks_images table as indicated in Table 6-2. Drag the image to the table cell, hold down SHIFT and then press the ENTER key, and then type the description. Press the TAB key to move from cell to cell.**

The images and descriptions are added to the park_description table (Figure 6-90).

FIGURE 6-90

Other Ways

1 Click table cell, on Insert menu click Image, select file name in Image Source dialog box, click OK button

Table 6-2	Park Images File Names and Descriptions	
CELL	**IMAGE**	**DESCRIPTION**
Row 2, Column 1	butterfly_garden.jpg	Butterfly Garden
Row 2, Column 2	campsites.jpg	View from campsites
Row 3, Column 1	dowitchers.jpg	Short-billed Dowitches
Row 3, Column 2	sandspur_beach.jpg	Sandspur Beach

To complete the Bahia Honda State Park Web page, you add two links in the links table. The first link is a relative link to the Florida Parks index page. The second link is an absolute link to the Department of Florida State Parks Bahia Honda State Park Web page.

Steps To Add Links to the Links Table

1 Scroll down to display the links table. Select the text in the left cell of the links table and then press the **DELETE** key. Point to the Property inspector expand/collapse arrow.

The text is deleted from the cell (Figure 6-91).

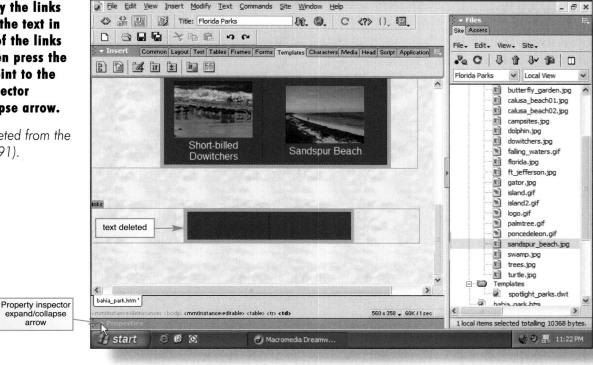

FIGURE 6-91

2 Click the Property inspector expand/collapse arrow. Type Home for the text link in the left cell and then select the text. Click the Link text box in the Property inspector and then type index.htm as the link text.

The link to the home page is added and centered in the cell (Figure 6-92).

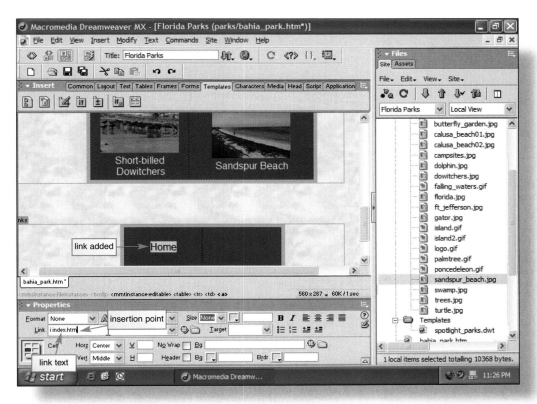

FIGURE 6-92

3 Click the right cell in the links table. **Type** Bahia Honda State Park **as the text for the link and then select the text. Click the Link text box in the Property inspector and then type** http://www.dep.state.fl.us/parks/district5/bahiahonda/index.asp **as the link text.**

The text is displayed in the table and the link is added to the Link text box (Figure 6-93).

4 Click the Save button on the Standard toolbar.

The bahia_park Web page is saved.

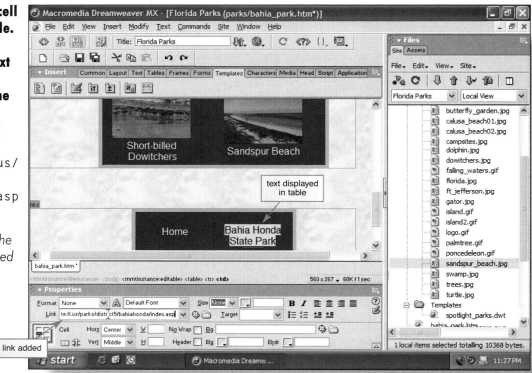

FIGURE 6-93

You complete the updating of the Florida Parks Web site by adding a link from the Index page to the Bahia Honda State Park page.

TO ADD A LINK FROM THE INDEX PAGE TO THE BAHIA HONDA STATE PARK PAGE

1 Open the Index page.

2 Scroll to the bottom of the page and then click to the right of the Florida Parks Volunteer Association link. Verify that the <a> tag does not appear in the tag selector. Hold down the SHIFT key and then press the ENTER key.

3 Type Featured Park as the link text.

4 Select the text and then type bahia_park.htm in the Property inspector Link text box.

5 Click the Save button on the Standard toolbar.

6 Press the F12 key to preview the Index page in the browser. Scroll down and then click the Featured Park link to view the Bahia Honda State Park Web page as shown in Figure 6-94.

7 Verify that the Bahia Honda State Park links work.

8 If instructed to do so, print a copy of the Bahia Honda State Park Web page and hand it in to your instructor. Close the browser.

The Bahia Honda State Park Web page is displayed in the browser after completing step 6 (Figure 6-94).

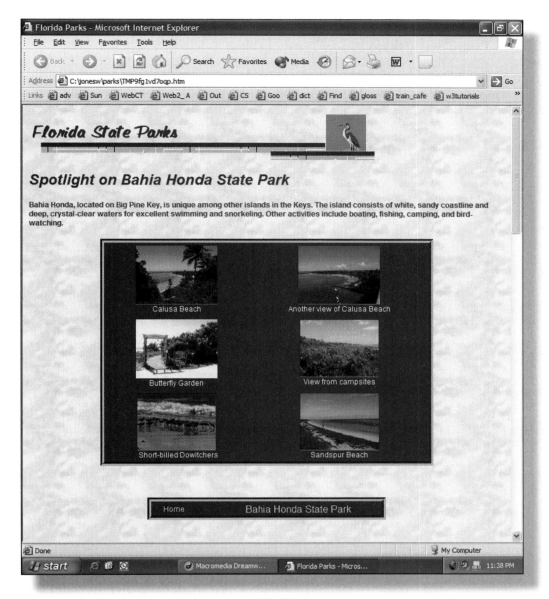

FIGURE 6-94

Quitting Dreamweaver

After you created your Web page based on a template with applied styles, tested and verified that the links work, and uploaded the Web site to a remote server, Project 6 is complete. To close the Web site, quit Dreamweaver MX, and return control to Windows, perform the following step.

TO CLOSE THE WEB SITE AND QUIT DREAMWEAVER

1 Click the Close button on the upper-right corner of the Dreamweaver title bar.

The Dreamweaver window, the Document window, and the Parks Web site all close. If you have unsaved changes, Dreamweaver will prompt you to save the changes. Clicking the Yes button in the Dreamweaver MX dialog box saves the changes.

CSS Style Definition Category Descriptions

The following tables list the attributes and descriptions of the eight categories available through the CSS Style Definition dialog box. Not all browsers support all properties; browser support is indicated in the Description column for most properties as supported by both browsers. Both browsers refers to Internet Explorer and Netscape.

Table 6-3   Type Style Properties

ATTRIBUTES	DESCRIPTION
Font	Sets the font family for the style; supported by both browsers.
Size	Defines the size of the text. Enter or select a number and then select a unit of measurement. Pixels prevent the Web site visitor from adjusting the text size in their Web browser; supported by both browsers.
Weight	Defines the thickness of the font. Thirteen different choices are available; normal and bold are the most common and work in all browsers that support CSS.
Style	Specifies normal, italic, or oblique as the font style; supported by both browsers.
Variant	Specifies small-caps or normal. Dreamweaver does not display this attribute in the Document window; not supported by Netscape.
Line Height	Refers to the amount of space between lines of text; also called leading. Normal allows the line height for the font size to be calculated automatically; supported by both browsers.
Case	Capitalizes the first letter of each word in the selection or sets the text to all uppercase or lowercase; supported by both browsers.
Decoration	Adds an underline, overline, or line-through to the text, or makes the text blink; supported by both browsers.
Color	Sets the text color; supported by both browsers.

Table 6-4   Background Style Properties

ATTRIBUTES	DESCRIPTION
Background Color	Sets the background color for an element — a character, a word, a paragraph, or even the Web page itself; supported by both browsers.
Background Image	Adds a background image to either a Web page or a table; supported by both browsers.
Repeat	Repeats the background image; supported by both browsers.
Attachment	Determines whether the background image is fixed at its original position or scrolls along with the content; not supported by Netscape.
Horizontal and Vertical Positions	Specifies a position for selected text or other Web page elements; can be used to align a background image to the center of the page, both vertically and horizontally, or align the element relative to the Document window; not supported by Netscape.

Table 6-5   Block Style Properties

ATTRIBUTES	DESCRIPTION
Word Spacing	Sets the spacing between words; not displayed in the Document window. The bigger the number, the more space between the words; supported by both browsers.
Letter Spacing	Sets the spacing between letters or characters; supported by both browsers.
Vertical Alignment	Specifies the vertical alignment of the element to which it is applied; displayed in Document window only when applied to an image; supported by both browsers.
Text Align	Sets the text alignment with the element; supported by both browsers.
Text Indent	Specifies the amount of space the first line of text is indented; supported by both browsers.
Whitespace	Determines how the browser displays extra white space; supported by Netscape and Internet Explorer 5.5.
Display	Specifies whether an element is displayed and if so how it is displayed; suppported by both browsers.

Table 6-6   Box Style Properties

ATTRIBUTES	DESCRIPTION
Width and Height	Sets the width and height of an element; supported by both browsers.
Float	Sets which side other elements, such as text, layers, tables and so on, will float around an element; supported by both browsers.
Clear	Prevents an element from wrapping around an object with a right or left float; supported by both browsers.
Padding	Specifies the amount of space between the content of an element and its border or margin if there is no border; supported by both browsers.
Margin	Specifies the amount of space between the border of an element or the padding if there is no border and another element; supported by both browsers.
Same for All (Padding and Margin)	Sets the same padding or margin attributes to the Top, Right, Bottom, and Left of the element to which it is applied; supported by both browsers.

Table 6-7   Border Style Properties

ATTRIBUTES	DESCRIPTION
Style	Sets the style appearance of the border. Appearance may be rendered differently in browsers; supported by both browsers.
Width	Sets the thickness of the element; supported by both browsers.
Color	Sets the color of the border; supported by both browsers.
Same For All	Applies the same style, thickness, or color to the Top, Bottom, Right and Left of the element to which is it is applied; supported by both browsers.

Table 6-8   List Style Properties

ATTRIBUTES	DESCRIPTION
Type	Sets the appearance of bullets or numbers; supported by both browsers.
Bullet Image	Specifies a custom image for the bullet; supported by both browsers.
Position	Sets whether list item text wraps and indents (outside) or whether the text wraps to the left margin (inside); supported by both browsers.

Table 6-9   Positioning Style Properties (Used with Layers)

ATTRIBUTES	DESCRIPTION
Type	Determines how the browser should position the element (absolute, relative, or static); supported by both browsers.
Visibility	Determines the initial display condition of the layer; supported by both browsers.
Width	Sets the width of the layer; supported by both browsers.
Z-Index	Determines the stacking order of the layer; supported by both browsers.
Height	Sets the height of the layer; supported by both browsers.
Placement	Specifies the location and size of the layer (Left, Top, Right, and Bottom); supported by both browsers.
Clip	Defines the part of the layer that is visible (Left, Top, Right, and Bottom); supported by both browsers.

Table 6-10   Extensions Style Properties

ATTRIBUTES	DESCRIPTION
Page Break	Creates a page break during printing either before or after the object controlled by the style; supported by both browsers.
Visual Effect (Cursor and Filter)	Cursor changes the pointer image when the pointer is over the object controlled by the style; supported by both browsers. Filter applies special effects to the object controlled by the style; supported by both browsers.

CASE PERSPECTIVE SUMMARY

As envisioned, your team has completed designing a template page and added the page to the Florida Parks Web site. Using tables to help with the layout, editable regions were added to the page. Other parts of the page remain locked to provide consistency with the design and static elements. You used a style sheet and applied styles to various parts of the page, including the text and tables. The images table was designed as an editable region and can be expanded as needed to add any number of images. You will update this page on a monthly basis to spotlight a different Florida state park. Everyone agrees that a template page and a spotlight feature will enhance the Web site.

Project Summary

Project 6 introduced you to templates and style sheets. You created a template, added editable regions, applied styles to the template, and then saved the template. Next, you applied the template to a blank document and added text and images. You used the Assets panel and the CSS Styles panel to complete these tasks.

What You Should Know

Having completed this project, you now should be able to perform the tasks in Table 6-11.

Table 6-11 Project 6 What You Should Know

TASK NUMBER	TASK	PAGE NUMBER
1	Start Dreamweaver and Close Open Panels	DW 6.04
2	Copy Data Files to the Florida Parks Web Site	DW 6.05
3	Begin Creating the Spotlight Template Page by Adding a Background Image and Title	DW 6.06
4	Add the Logo Image to the Template	DW 6.08
5	Add the Park Name and Park Description Prompt for the First Two Editable Regions	DW 6.10
6	Add and Center a Table as the Third Editable Region	DW 6.12
7	Add and Center a Table as the Fourth Editable Region	DW 6.16
8	Save the Web Page as a Template	DW 6.17
9	Display the Insert Bar and Templates Tab	DW 6.20
10	Create the First Editable Region	DW 6.22
11	Create the Second Editable Region	DW 6.24
12	Create the Third and Fourth Editable Regions	DW 6.25
13	Display the Design Panel Group	DW 6.30

TASK NUMBER	TASK	PAGE NUMBER
14	Add a Style and Save the Style Sheet	DW 6.32
15	Create a Style for the Paragraph Text	DW 6.35
16	Add a Background, Border, and Text Color to a Table	DW 6.38
17	Modify the A:Link Attribute	DW 6.44
18	Add the A:Visited Attribute	DW 6.46
19	Add the A:Hover Attribute	DW 6.47
20	Create the Bahia Honda State Park Spotlight Web Page	DW 6.48
21	Apply a Template to the Bahia Honda State Park Web Page	DW 6.50
22	Add the Park Name and Park Description to the Bahia Honda State Park Web Page	DW 6.51
23	Add Rows to the parks_images Table	DW 6.53
24	Add Images to the parks_images Table	DW 6.55
25	Add Links to the Links Table	DW 6.59
26	Add a Link from the Index Page to the Bahia Honda State Park Page	DW 6.60
27	Close the Web Site and Quit Dreamweaver	DW 6.61

Apply Your Knowledge

1 Creating a Template and Style Sheet for B & B Lawn Service

Instructions: Start Dreamweaver. If the panels display, press the F4 key to close all panels. See the inside back cover of this book for instructions for downloading the Data Disk or see your instructor for information on accessing the files in this book.

The proprietors of B & B Lawn Service Web site would like to add a page to their Web site that features native plants for different areas of the county. They want something that is modified easily, so a template is used. To create this template and then add styles, you copy six images from the Data Files folder to the Lawn Service Web site Images folder. You begin the process by creating a template, then defining styles. When this is completed, you apply this template to a new blank page and then create a page for Florida native plants. Finally, you add a link to the Florida Parks Index home page. The template is shown in Figure 6-95a and the Web page in Figure 6-95b on the next page. Software and hardware settings determine how a Web page is displayed in a browser. Your Web page may display differently than the ones shown in Figure 6-95a and 6-95b. Appendix D contains instructions for uploading your local site to a remote server.

For a selection of images and backgrounds, visit the Dreamweaver MX Media Web page (scsite.com/dreamweavermx/media) and then click Media below Project 6.

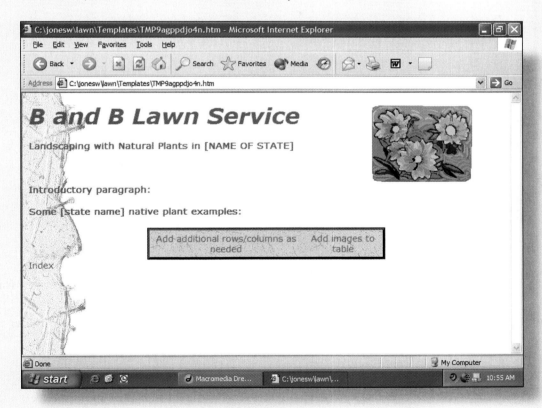

FIGURE 6-95a

(continued)

Apply Your Knowledge

Creating a Template and Style Sheet for B & B Lawn Service *(continued)*

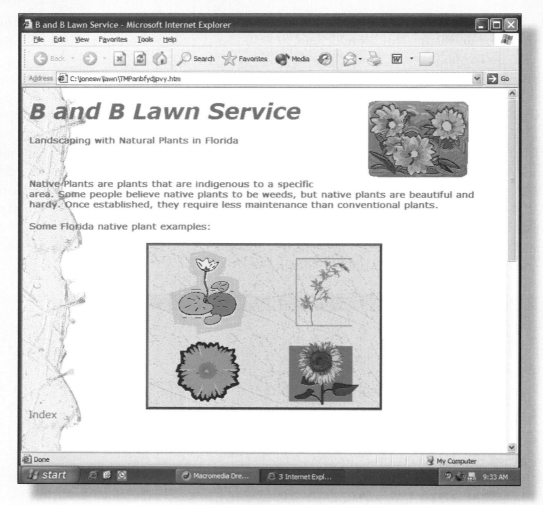

FIGURE 6-95b

1. Display the Property inspector, Standard toolbar, Site panel, and Insert bar. Select Lawn Service from the Site pop-up menu in the Site panel. Click the Templates tab in the Insert bar.
2. Use Dreamweaver's integrated file browser to copy the data file from the Data Files Images folder to your lawn Images folder.
3. To create the template, click Modify on the menu bar and then click Page Properties. Type B & B Lawn Service for the Web page title and apply the background.gif image.
4. In the Document window, type B & B Lawn Service. Apply Heading 1 and then press the ENTER key.
5. Type Landscaping with Natural Plants in [NAME OF STATE]. and then press the ENTER key.
6. Type Introductory paragraph: and then press the ENTER key.
7. Type Some [name of state] native plant examples: and then press the ENTER key.
8. Insert a one-row, two-column table with a width of 50 percent, cell padding of 5, and Align Center the table.

Apply Your Knowledge

9. If necessary, click the Property inspector expander arrow to expand the Property inspector. Drag the background_table.gif file to the Bg Image text box. Click to the right of the table and then press the ENTER key.

10. Type Index and then select the text. Drag the index.htm file name to the Property inspector Link box. Click File on the menu bar and then click Save as Template. Use plants for the template name.

11. Drag the logo.gif image to the right of the heading. Set V Space of 4 and H Space of 50. Type Landscaping for the Alt tag. Press the ENTER key.

12. Use the Editable Regions button on the Templates tab to create the five editable regions as indicated in Table 6-12. (Click to the left of each region.)

13. Click CSS Styles on the Window menu to display the CSS Styles panel.

14. Click anywhere in the heading B & B Lawn Service and then click the New CSS Style button in the CSS Styles panel. In the New CSS Style dialog box, verify that <h1> is selected in the Tag box, Redefine HTML Tag is the Type, and Define In This Document Only is selected, and then click the OK button. Save the style sheet as plants.dwt. In the CSS Style Definition dialog box, set the following values in the Type category: Verdana, Arial, Helvetica, sans-serif for Font; 36 pixels for Size; bolder for Weight; oblique for Style; and #996600 for Color. Click the OK button.

Table 6-12 B & B Lawn Service Editable Regions	
REGION TEXT	*REGION NAME*
Landscaping with Natural Plants in [NAME OF STATE]	subtitle
Introductory paragraph:	introductory_paragraph
Some [state name] native plant examples:	example
The table	table_images
Index	links

15. Click anywhere in the first paragraph prompt — Landscaping with Natural Plants in [name of state] — and then click the <p> tag in the tag selector. Click the New CSS Style button in the CSS Styles panel. In the New CSS Style dialog box, verify that p is selected in the Tag box, Redefine HTML Tag is the Type, and Define In [This Document Only] is selected. Set the following values in the Type category: Verdana, Arial, Helvetica, sans-serif for the Font; 14 pixels for the Size; 600 for Weight; and #996633 for Color. Click the OK button.

16. Click anywhere in the table and then click the <table> tag in the tag selector. Click the New CSS Style button in the CSS Styles panel. In the New CSS Style dialog, verify that Table is selected in the Tag box, Redefine HTML Tag is the type, and Define In [This Document Only] is selected. Set the following values in the Type category: Verdana, Aria, Helvetica, sans-serif for the Font; 14 pixels for the Size; #996600 for Color; and none for Decoration. Set the following values in the Border category: Outset for Style and #996633 for Color. Click row 1, column 1 and then type: Add additional rows/columns as needed and then click row 1, column 2. Type Add images to table.

17. Select the text Index and then click the New CSS Style button in the CSS Styles panel. In the New CSS Style dialog box, click Use CSS Selector for Type, and Define In [This Document Only]. Click the Selector arrow and then click a:link. Set the following values in the Type category: Verdana, Arial, Helvetica, sans-serif for the Font; 16 pixels for the Size; and #996633 for Color. Click the OK button, and then save and close the template.

18. Open a new Basic Page Document window and save the page as native_plants.htm in the lawn folder.

19. Click the Assets tab in the Files panel group and then click the Templates button. Click the Apply button to apply the template to the native_plants.htm page.

(continued)

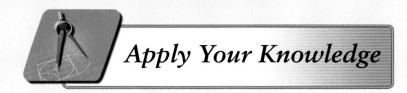

Apply Your Knowledge

Creating a Template and Style Sheet for B & B Lawn Service *(continued)*

20. Use Table 6-13 as a guide to add content to each of the editable regions as shown in this table. Title the document Native Plants.

21. Save the Document. Open the index.htm file. Scroll to the bottom of the page and then click to the right of the Lawn mowers for sale link. Insert a line break and then type `Native Plants` for the link text. Add a link to the native_plants.htm page.

22. Press the F12 key to view the page in your browser. Click the Native Plants link. Print a copy of the template and Web page if instructed to do so. Upload the page to the lawn Web Site on a remote server if instructed to do so.

Table 6-13 B & B Lawn Service Page Content	
REGION TEXT	*REGION NAME*
Landscaping with Natural Plants in <u>Florida</u>	subtitle
Native Plants are plants that are indigenous to a specific area. Some people believe native plants to be weeds, but native plants are beautiful and hardy. Once established, they require less maintenance than conventional plants.	introductory_paragraph
Some <u>Florida</u> native plant examples:	example
Row 1, column 1: plant01.gif	table_images
Row 1, column 2: plant02.gif	
Row 2, column 1: plant03.gif	
Row 2, column 2: plant04.gif	
Add link to index.htm	links

In the Lab

1 Creating a Template for the CandleDust Web Site

Problem: The CandleDust Web site is receiving a large number of hits every day, and Mary is receiving increasingly more orders each day. She foresees a time when she will need to expand the Web site and is considering a standard design for her pages. Mary is not sure exactly how a template works within a Web site and has requested that you put together an example. You know that she has been considering beeswax for candle making, so you decide to create the page using this topic. The template is shown in Figure 6-96a and the example in Figure 6-96b on the next page. Appendix D contains instructions for uploading your local site to a remote server. For a selection of images and backgrounds, visit the Dreamweaver MX Media Web page (scsite.com/dreamweavermx/media) and then click Media below Project 6.

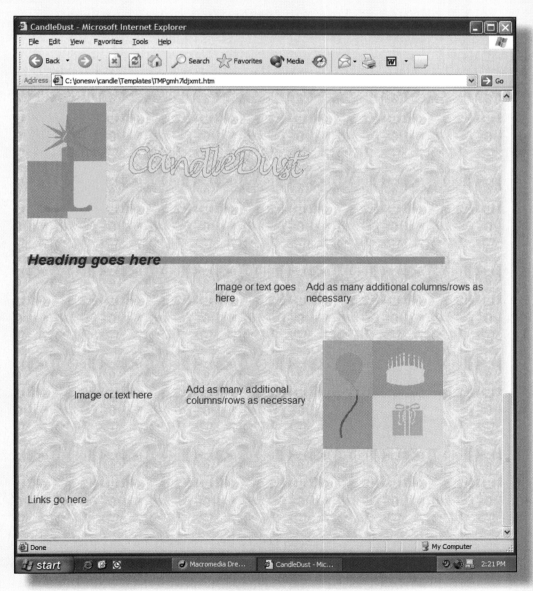

FIGURE 6-96a

(continued)

In the Lab

Creating a Template for the CandleDust Web Site *(continued)*

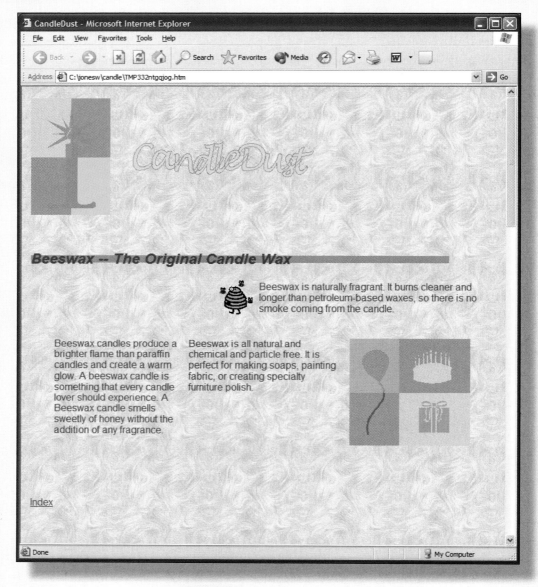

FIGURE 6-96b

Instructions: Perform the following tasks:

1. Start Dreamweaver. If necessary, press F4 to close the open panels. Display the Property inspector, Standard toolbar, Site panel, and Insert bar. Select CandleDust from the Site pop-up menu in the Site panel.

2. Use Dreamweaver's integrated file browser to copy the Image files from the Data Files to your Images candle folder.

3. Apply the color scheme you added in Project 1 (Purple background, and Blue,Purple,Green text and links). Use the Page Properties dialog box to add the background.gif image to the page.

In the Lab

4. Create a one-row, two-column table. This is a noneditable table. Select the table cells and set the alignment to middle. Drag the candle1.gif to the first cell and then type `logo_image` for the Alt tag. Drag the logo.gif to the second cell and type `logo` for the Alt tag.

5. Click to the right of the table and then press the ENTER key. Type `Heading goes here` and apply Heading 1 to the text. Press the ENTER key.

6. Add a one-row, two-column table with a width of 60 percent and cell padding of 5. Align the table to the right. Select the table cells and set Vert to Middle. In the first cell, type `Image or text goes here` as the text prompt, and in the second cell, type `Add as many additional columns/rows as necessary` as the text prompt. Click to the right of the table and then press the ENTER key.

7. Add a second table with one row and three columns. Use a width of 80 percent and cell padding of 5. Center the table. In the first cell, type `Image or text goes here` as the prompt, and in the second cell, type `Add as many additional columns/rows as necessary` as the prompt. Drag candle02.gif to the third cell. Click outside the table and then press the ENTER key.

8. Insert a third table — a one-row, one-column table with a width of 60 percent and cell padding of 5. Select the cells and set Vert to Middle. Type `Links go here` in the table cell. Save the template as primary.

9. Create four editable regions in the template — the first with the heading and then the three tables. Name the heading editable region heading, name the first table text_image01, the second table text_image02, and the third table links.

10. Click anywhere in the heading prompt and then click the <H1> tag in the tag selector. Click the New CSS Style button in the CSS Styles panel. If necessary, click Redefine HTML Tag as the Type, and Define In [New Style Sheet File]. If necessary, click the Tag arrow and then click h1. Name the CSS example in the Type category, set the Font to Geneva, Arial, Helvetica, sans-serif; the Size to 24; Style to italic; and the Weight to bolder. Click the Background category and then type #CC9966 for the Background Color. Save and then close the style sheet.

11. Open a new Document window and then click the Assets tab in the Files panel group. Apply the template to the new Document window. Title the page CandleDust.

12. Type `Beeswax -- The Original Candle Wax` in the heading editable region.

13. Drag the bee.gif image to the left cell in the first editable table — text_image01. In the right cell of the first table, type `Beeswax is naturally fragrant. It burns cleaner and longer than petroleum-based waxes, so there is no smoke coming from the candle.`

14. Click the left cell of the second table and then type `Beeswax candles produce a brighter flame than paraffin candles and create a warm glow. A beeswax candle is something that every candle lover should experience. A beeswax candle smells sweetly of honey without the addition of any fragrance.` Click the center cell of the second table and then type `Beeswax is all natural and chemical and particle free. It is perfect for making soaps, painting fabric, or creating specialty furniture polish.` Drag the candle2.gif image to the right cell.

15. Click the Links table, type `Index`, and then drag the index.htm file to the Link text box in the Property inspector. Save the page as beeswax.htm.

16. Open the index.htm file. Scroll to the bottom of the page and then click to the right of the Candle making Recipes link. Insert a line break and then type `Beeswax Candlemaking` for the link text. Create a link to the beeswax.htm page.

17. Press the F12 key to view the page in your browser. Click the Beeswax Candle making link. Print a copy of the template and Web page if instructed to do so. Upload the page to the candle Web Site on a remote server if instructed to do so.

In the Lab

2 Creating a Template for the Credit Protection Web Site

Problem: Marcy has decided to add additional Web pages emphasizing the ABCs of Credit. She would like to have a uniform format for these pages and has asked you to create a template. She has provided you with content for the first one of these pages. The template is shown in Figure 6-97a and the Web page in Figure 6-97b. Appendix D contains instructions for uploading your local site to a remote server. For a selection of images and backgrounds, visit the Dreamweaver MX Media Web page (scsite.com/dreamweavermx/media) and then click Media below Project 6.

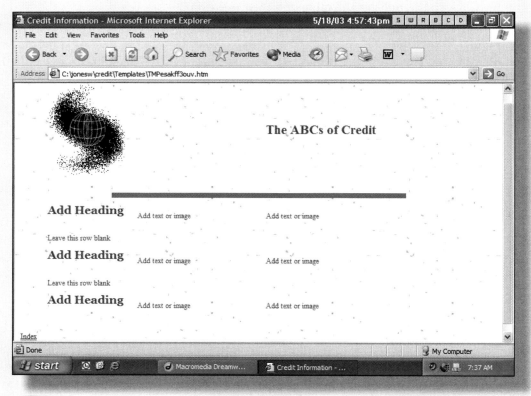

FIGURE 6-97a

In the Lab

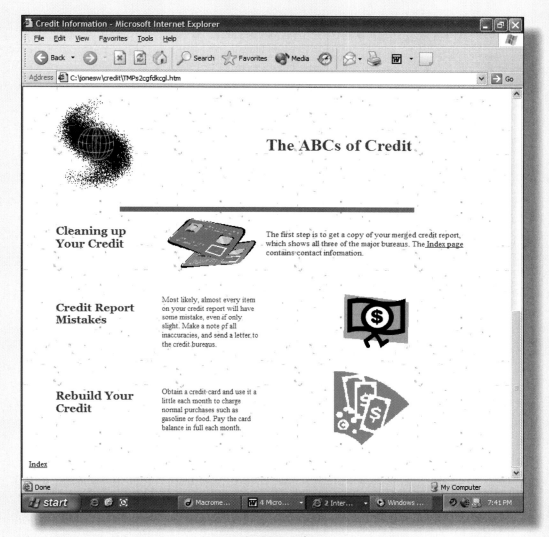

FIGURE 6-97b

Instructions: Perform the following tasks:

1. Start Dreamweaver. Display the Property inspector, Standard toolbar, Site panel, and Insert bar. Click the Templates tab in the Insert bar.
2. Use Dreamweaver's integrated file browser to copy the Data File to the credit Web site. Apply the background.jpg image and the color scheme you added in Project 1 (Yellow background and Green,Blue,Purple text and links). Title the page Credit Information.
3. Insert a seven-row, three-column table with a width of 90 percent, cell padding of 5, and then center the table. Drag the logo.gif image to the first cell in the first row. Merge the last two cells in row 1. Type The ABCs of Credit in the merged cells.
4. Merge all three cells in row 2. Click row 2, drag the line.gif image to the merged row, and then click the Center button in the Property inspector.

(continued)

In the Lab

Creating a Template for the Credit Protection Web Site *(continued)*

5. Merge all three cells in row 4 and and then type `Leave this row blank` in those merged cells. Repeat this instruction in row 6.

6. Click row 3, column 1, type `Add Heading` and then apply Heading 2 to this text. Repeat this instruction in column 1, rows 5 and 7.

7. Click row 3, column 2, type `Add text or image`, and then copy this text. Paste the text into row 3, columns 2 and 3; row 5, columns 2 and 3; and row 7, columns 2 and 3.

8. Click outside of the table, press the ENTER key, and then type `Index`. Create a link from this text to the index.htm page.

9. Click the <table> tag in the tag selector and then click the Editable Region button on the Template tab. Name the editable region table_credit. Save the template as credit.

10. Open the Styles panel and then click the Add CSS Style button. Name the style sheet credit_info. Apply the following attributes in the Type category: Georgia, Times New Roman, Times, serif for Font; 18 for Size; and bold for Weight. Click the Save button and close the template.

11. Open a new Document window and save it as credit_info.htm. Click the Assets panel tab, and then click the Apply button. Delete the text Leave this row blank from all cells.

12. Select the text in row 3, column 1, type `Cleaning up Your Credit` and then click row 3, column 3. Type `The first step is to get a copy of your merged credit report, which shows all three of the major bureaus. The Index page contains contact information.` Select the text Index page and add a link to the credit Index page. Click row 3, column 2, and drag credit_card.gif to the cell.

13. Select the text in row 5, column 1, type `Credit Report Mistakes`, and then click row 5, column 2. Type `Most likely, almost every item on your credit report will have some mistake, even if only slight. Make a note of all inaccuracies, and send a letter to the credit bureaus.` Click row 5, column 3 and then drag the money3.gif image to the cell.

14. Click row 7, column 1, type `Rebuild Your Credit`, and then click row 7, column 2. Type `Obtain a credit card and use it a little each month to charge normal purchases such as gasoline or food. Pay the card balance in full each month.` Click row 7, column 3 and then drag the rebuild.gif image to the cell.

15. Save the document. Open the index.htm file. Scroll to the bottom of the page and then click to the right of the Spending Wisely link. Insert a line break and then type `Credit Information` for the link text. Create a link to the credit_info.htm page. Press the ENTER key and save the page.

16. Press the F12 key to view the page in your browser. Click the Credit Information link. Print a copy of the template and Web page if instructed to do so. Upload the page to the credit Web site on a remote server if instructed to do so.

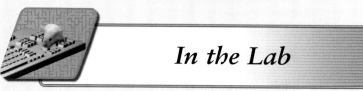

In the Lab

3   Creating a Template for the Plant City Web Site

Problem: The Plant City Web site provides information about the city, but provides very little information about activities. The mayor wants to let visitors know about upcoming attractions and events. She wants the page to have a structured format and would like it to be changed easily. You will use a template to accomplish this task. The template is shown in Figure 6-98a and the Web page is shown in Figure 6-98b on the next page.

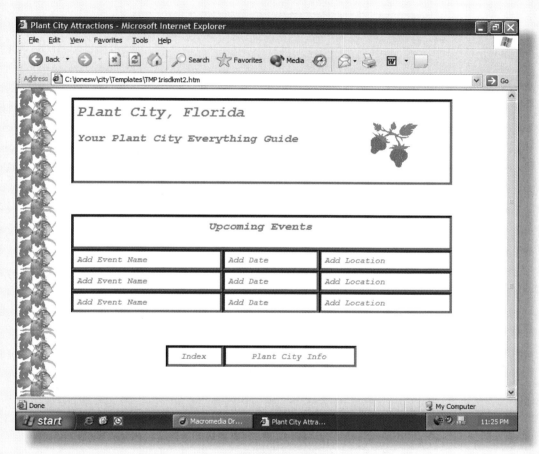

FIGURE 6-98a

(continued)

In the Lab

Creating a Template for the Plant City Web Site *(continued)*

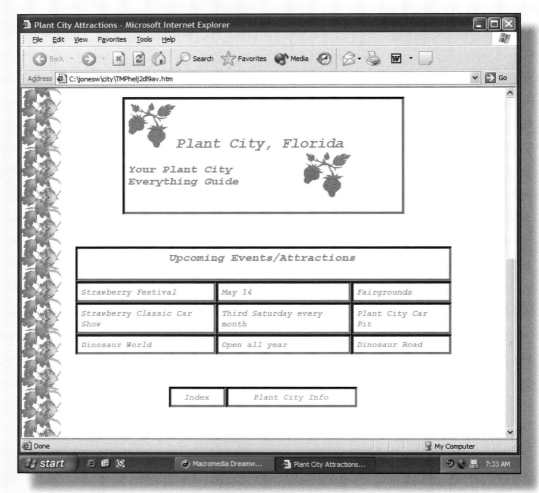

FIGURE 6-98a

Instructions: Perform the following tasks:

1. Start Dreamweaver. Display the Property inspector, Standard toolbar, Site panel, and Insert bar. No data files are required for this exercise.
2. Add a one-row, three-column table with the following attributes: Width of 60 percent, cell padding of 5. Use Center alignment.
3. Add a second table — 4 rows and 3 columns. Use a width of 80 percent, cell padding of 5, and center alignment.
4. Add a third table — one row and two columns. Use a width of 40 percent, cell padding of 3, and center alignment.
5. Click the first table and then type Plant City, Florida. Add Heading 1 to the text. Press the ENTER key, type Your Plant City Everything Guide, and apply Heading 2 to the text.
6. Drag the strawberry01.gif to the left of Plant City, Florida and then left-align. Drag the same image (strawberry01.gif) to the right of Plant City, Florida and then right-align. Add a H Space of 75 to the image.

In the Lab

7. Click the left cell of the second table and then merge all three cells. Type `Upcoming Events/Attractions` and then set Horz as Center. Apply Heading 2 to the text.
8. Click row 2, column 1, type `Add Event Name`, and then add this same text to rows 3 and 4, column 1.
9. Click row 2, column 2, type `Add Date`, and add this same text to rows 3 and 4, column 2.
10. Click row 2, column 3, type `Add Location`, and add this same text to rows 3 and 4, column 3.
11. Click the heading in the first table. Open the CSS Styles panel and then click the New CSS Style button. In the CSS Style dialog box, verify that <h1> is selected in the Tag box, Redefine HTML Tag is the Type, Define In [New Style Sheet File] is selected, and then click the OK button. Add the following attributes: "Courier New", Courier, mono for the font; 24 for the Size; bolder for the Weight; oblique for the Style; and #FF0000 for the Color. Click none to select the none Decoration attribute.
12. Click the second heading in the first table. Add a style with the following attributes: "Courier New", Courier, mono for the font; 18 for the Size, bold for the Weight; italic for the Style; and #FF0000 for the color.
13. Click row 2, column 1 in the second table. Click <td> in the tag selector and then click the New CSS Style button. Add the following attributes: "Courier New", Courier, mono for the font; 14 for the Size; normal for the Weight; oblique for the Style; and #FF0000 for the Color. Click the Border category and select Inset for the Style. Add #FF0000 for the Color. Click the OK button.
14. Click the first cell in the third table and then type `Index`. Select the text Index and create a link to the Plant City Web site index page. Click the second cell and then type `Plant City Info`. Create a link from this text to www.plantcity.org. Click the <table> tag in the tag selector. Click the New CSS Style button and then click Use CSS Selector. Add the following attributes for the a:link: "Courier New", Courier, mono for the Font; 12 for the Size; normal for the Weight; oblique for the Style; and #FF0000 for the Color. Click none to select the none Decoration attribute.
15. For the a:visited link, add #FF0066 for the Color and none for the Decoration. Save and close the template. Use events for the template name.
16. Open a new Document window and apply the template. Add the data in Table 6-14 to the second table for the Upcoming Events.
17. Save the document and use events for the file name. Open the index.htm file. Scroll to the bottom of the page and then click to the right of the Employment link. Insert a line break and then type `Events` for the link text. Create a link to the events.htm page.
18. Press the F12 key to view the page in your browser. Click the Events link. Print a copy of the template and Web page if instructed to do so. Upload the page to the city Web Site on a remote server if instructed to do so.

Table 6-14		
LEFT CELL	*MIDDLE CELL*	*RIGHT CELL*
Strawberry Festival	May 14	Fairgrounds
Strawberry Classic Car Show	Third Saturday every month	Plant City Car Pit
Dinosaur World	Open all year	Dinosaur Road

Cases and Places

The difficulty of these case studies varies:
▶ are the least difficult; ▶▶ are more difficult; and ▶▶▶ are the most difficult.

1 ▶   Your sports Web site has become very popular. You have received many e-mails asking for statistics and other information. You decide to add a Web page that will contain statistics and will be updated on a weekly basis. Add a background image to the page and add a title to the page. Create the template using tables. Add descriptive prompts and then create editable regions. Add styles to the headings and text. Then create a page, apply the template, and save the page in your sports Web site. Create a link to and from the home page. For a selection of images and backgrounds, visit the Dreamweaver MX Media Web page (scsite.com/dreamweavermx/media) and then click Media below Project 6.

2 ▶   You have decided to add a do-it-yourself section to your hobby Web site and want to use a consistent format and look for the page. You decide to use a template to create this new section. Create the template using a logo, tables, and links. Add descriptive prompts to the editable regions and apply styles to enhance the text and text size. Create the first do-it-yourself Web page and apply the template. Create a link to and from the home page. Upload to a remote server if instructed to do so. For a selection of images and backgrounds, visit the Dreamweaver MX Media Web page (scsite.com/dreamweavermx/media) and then click Media below Project 6.

3 ▶▶   Create a template for your music hobby Web site and then add a background to the page. Insert logos, tables, and other appropriate elements. Add a background image to a table. Apply a border to the table. Use the CSS Styles panel and apply styles to the elements on the page. Create a new Web page featuring a new topic for your Web site and apply the template. Create a link to and from the home page. Upload the page to a remote server if instructed to do so. For a selection of images and backgrounds, visit the Dreamweaver MX Media Web page (scsite.com/dreamweavermx/media) and then click Media below Project 6.

4 ▶▶   Your campaign for political office is progressing well and you are one of the top-two candidates. You have decided to add a new section to your Web site featuring your campaign supporters. To provide consistency and control, you use a template for this site. After completing the template, attach styles. Next, create two new pages for the site and then apply the template. Create a link to and from the home page. Upload the new pages to a remote server if instructed to do so. For a selection of images and backgrounds, visit the Dreamweaver MX Media Web page (scsite.com/dreamweavermx/media) and then click Media below Project 6.

5 ▶▶▶ Create a template for the three vacation sites previously selected. Include headings, tables, links, and graphics. Add appropriate styles, including styles from the Type, Background, and Border categories. Include at least two images and a logo on the page. Create the three vacation site Web pages and apply the template. Create links to and from the home page. Upload the new pages to a remote server if instructed to do so. For a selection of images and backgrounds, visit the Dreamweaver MX Media Web page (scsite.com/dreamweavermx/media) and then click Media below Project 6.

Macromedia Dreamweaver MX

PROJECT

Layers, Image Maps, and Navigation Bars

You will have mastered the material in this project when you can:

O B J E C T I V E S

- Explain the concept of layers
- Insert, select, resize, and move a layer
- Name a layer
- Align layers
- Describe an image map
- Create an image map
- Add and edit behaviors
- Describe a navigation bar
- Create a navigation bar
- Insert a Date object

Macromedia Dreamweaver MX

Layers, Image Maps, and Navigation Bars

PROJECT

Will Jones recently attended a business workshop and was fascinated by some of the Web sites demonstrated by other workshop attendees. He particularly was impressed with some of the options offered through the utilization of layers and behaviors. He describes to you and Joan some of the features of layers, including flexibility and precise positioning. Will is most impressed, however, with the concept of adding behaviors to show and hide different objects on a Web page.

Another feature that Will specifically liked on some of the demonstrated Web sites was a navigation bar. He felt this gave the Web page a more professional look. You and Joan both agree that these would be good additions to the Web site. Web page visitors have been inquiring about some of the more popular parks throughout the state. Joan thinks that a new page could be added to the Web site using layers to display some of the parks receiving large numbers of visitors. She further suggests that you develop a navigation bar and add it to the index page. Everyone agrees that these are both good suggestions, and you are eager to get started with these modifications and additions.

Introduction

Project 7 introduces three unique Dreamweaver features: layers, image maps, and navigation bars. Web developers have long dreamed of being able to position graphics, text, and other HTML objects at specific pixel coordinates. Tables provide some placement control, but not absolute precision. Layers, however, can be positioned anywhere on the page. They remain in the same position relative to the top and left margins of the window regardless of how a user resizes the browser window.

An image map is an image that is divided into regions, called hotspots. When a user clicks a hotspot, an assigned action occurs. You can create multiple hotspots in the image, and you can have more than one image map on a single Web page.

The third feature introduced in this project is the navigation bar. Navigation bars often provide an easy way to move among pages and files on a site. The linking elements within a navigation bar can consist of text, images, and/or a combination of text and images. As you complete the activities in this project, you will find that adding these features to a Web page provide interactivity and excitement.

Project Seven — Creating Layers, Image Maps, and Navigation Bars for a Web Page

In this project, you learn how to use and apply three favorite Dreamweaver tools to the Florida Parks Web site. You begin the project by adding a new page to the Web site containing interactive layers and an image map (Figure 7-1a). Four separate layers are added to the page and images then are embedded in each of the layers. One of the layers contains a Florida map, which serves as the image map. Clicking different spots on the image

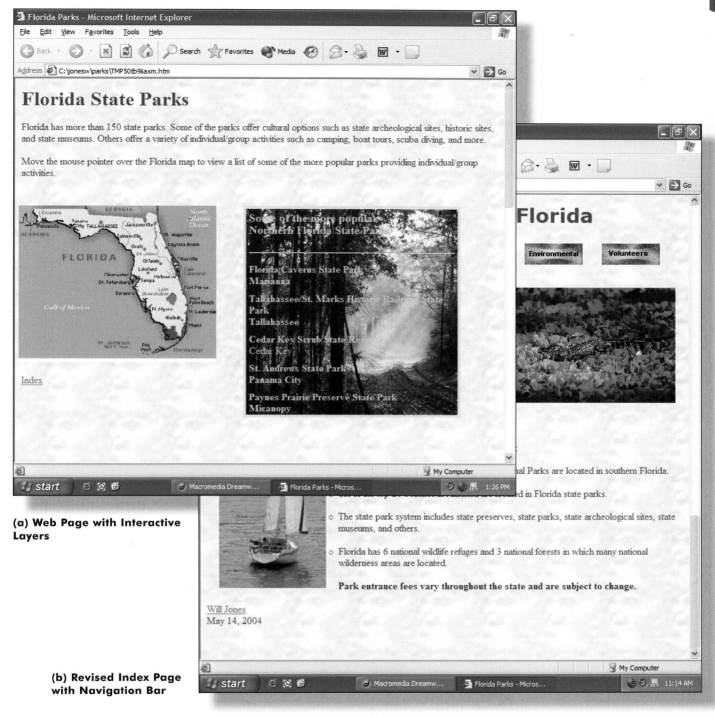

(a) Web Page with Interactive Layers

(b) Revised Index Page with Navigation Bar

FIGURE 7-1

map displays a list of some of the favorite state parks in north, central, and south Florida. Next, you revise the Index page by deleting the existing links and adding a navigation bar (Figure 7-1b). The navigation bar adds a more professional look by bringing all of the links together in one location at the top of the Web page. When the mouse pointer moves over an image link within the navigation bar, the image changes color to indicate that this is an active link. Each image also has alternate text to address accessibility issues.

Workspace Organization

Organization and preparation lead to a more productive work setting. Successful Web developers prepare their Dreamweaver workspace to provide an effective work environment. As you learn to use additional Dreamweaver tools, including layers, image maps, and navigation bars, you will become even more proficient working in the Dreamweaver environment.

Starting Dreamweaver and Closing Open Panels

When you start Dreamweaver, generally most or all of the panels are displayed by default. Closing unused panels provides uncluttered workspace in the Document window. To organize your workspace, you close the unused open panels. This gives you the maximum window space in the Dreamweaver Document window. Start Dreamweaver and close open panels using the following steps.

TO START DREAMWEAVER AND CLOSE OPEN PANELS

1 Start Dreamweaver. If necessary, maximize the Document window. Press the F4 key to close all open panels.

2 Press the F8 key to display the Site panel. Select the Florida Parks Web site.

3 If necessary, use the View menu to display the Standard toolbar.

4 Use the Window menu to display the Property inspector and the Insert bar (Figure 7-2).

The Site panel, Insert bar, and Property inspector are displayed (Figure 7-2).

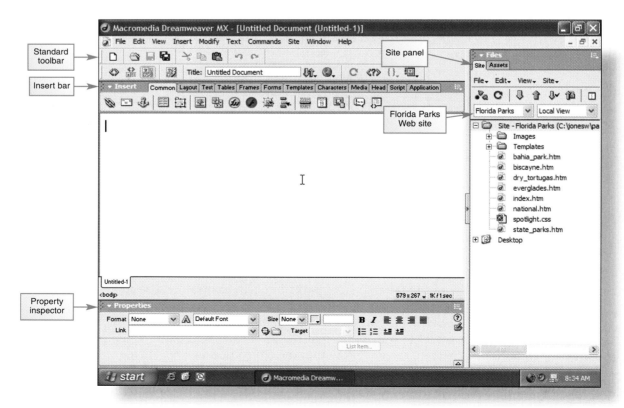

FIGURE 7-2

Copying Data Files to the Local Web Site

Your Data Disk contains an Images folder and a data file for Project 7. The Images folder and data file are located in the Proj07 folder. You use Dreamweaver's integrated file browser to copy the Project 7 images and data file to the Florida Parks folder.

The Data Files folder for this project is stored on Local Disk (C:). The location on your computer may be different. If necessary, verify with your instructor the location of the Data Files folder. Complete the following steps to copy the data file and images to the C:\jonesw\parks local root folder using the same procedure as in previous projects.

TO COPY DATA FILES TO THE FLORIDA PARKS WEB SITE

1 Click the plus sign (+) to the left of the Desktop icon in the Site panel. Click the plus sign to the left of the My Computer icon and then navigate through the file hierarchy to the Data Files folder as you did in Project 2 on pages DW 2.09–14.

2 Click the plus sign to the left of the Proj07 folder and then click the plus sign to the left of the parks folder.

3 Click the plus sign to the left of the Images folder.

4 Click central.jpg (or the first file in the list). Hold down the SHIFT key and then click volunbutton02.gif (or the last file in the folder if your files are sorted in a different order).

5 Copy the images to the jonesw/parks/Images folder using the Copy and Paste commands on the context menus, the result of which is shown in Figure 7-3.

6 Copy the state_park_activities.htm file to the jonesw/parks folder.

7 Click the minus sign to the left of the Desktop icon to collapse the file list.

After completing step 6, the Project 7 images are pasted into the parks/Images local root folder, and the data file is copied into the /parks folder. Figure 7-3 shows the expanded Images folder. Your images may be sorted in a different order.

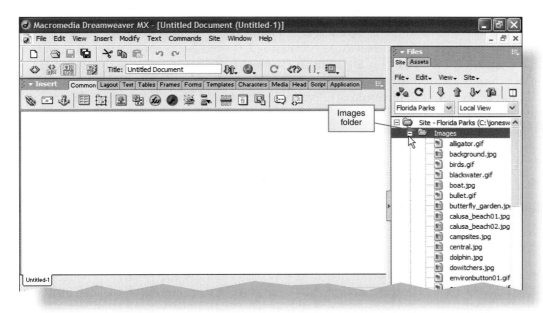

FIGURE 7-3

Understanding Layers

A **layer** is similar to a table — it is a container that holds other types of content such as images, text, form objects, and even other layers (nested layers). Anything you can put in an HTML document, you also can put in a layer. Layers can be stacked on top of one another, placed side by side, or overlapped. They easily can be moved, dragged, or resized. Web site developers use layers for page layout much as they use tables for page layout. A layer, however, provides more flexibility than a table because it can be placed in an exact spot anywhere on the page with pixel-perfect precision. It remains in this position (relative to the top and left margins of the page) regardless of how the Web page visitor resizes the browser window or views the text size. This is called **absolute positioning** and is possible because layers are positioned using a standard x-, y-, and z-coordinate system, similar to what you would use to create a graph on graph paper. Instead of having the point of origin in the bottom-left corner, however, the x and y coordinates correspond to a layer's top and left positions within the page. The z coordinate, also called the **z-index**, determines a layer's stacking order when more than one layer is added to a page.

Layers and DHTML

Layers are a component of dynamic HTML. **Dynamic HTML** (**DHTML**) is an extension of HTML and gives Web page developers the capability of precisely positioning objects on the Web page. DHTML combines layers, Cascading Style Sheets (CSS), and JavaScript coding, enabling the creation of dynamic page elements. Additionally, because a layer uses both DHTML and CSS, it offers a wide range of flexibility and control. Some possible effects you can accomplish using DHTML are as follows:

- Add images that are hidden from view and then display them when a user clicks a button or hotspot
- Create pop-up menus
- Position objects side by side
- Drag and drop objects
- Create animations
- Provide feedback to right and wrong answers

A disadvantage of using layers is that older browsers do not support layers. Internet Explorer 4.0 and Netscape Navigator 4.0 (and later) support layers under the original W3C **Cascading Style Sheets-Positioning** (**CSS-P**) specifications. Browsers older than 4.0 ignore the layer code and display the content in the normal flow of the page (no absolute positioning). Even though current browsers support layers, Internet Explorer and Netscape Navigator implement DHMTL differently, and, therefore, some discrepancy in the display of layers exists. Navigator 4.0 in particular has a difficult time with layers and often displays them incorrectly. Dreamweaver, however, contains a Netscape 4 Resize Fix option available through the Layers category in the Preferences dialog box.

Dreamweaver provides three options for creating layers: the Draw Layer button located on both the Common and Layout tabs in the Insert bar and the layer option available through the CSS Styles panel. In this project, you use the Draw Layer button on the Common tab in the Insert bar and modify attributes through the Layer Property inspector. Displaying Dreamweaver's layout tools such as the ruler or the grid helps with precise positioning. In this project, you use the ruler.

Complete the following steps to open the state_park_activities.htm page and to display the ruler.

Steps ## To Open the Florida State Parks Activities Page and Display the Ruler

1 **Close the Untitled-1 page that displayed when you started Dreamweaver. Scroll down in the Site panel to display the list of .htm files.**

2 **Double-click the state_park_activities.htm file.**

The state_park_activities .htm file opens in the Document window (Figure 7-4). The insertion point is blinking at the top of the page to the left of the heading.

FIGURE 7-4

3 **Click View on the menu bar, point to Rulers, and then point to Show on the Rulers submenu.**

The View menu and Rulers submenu are displayed (Figure 7-5).

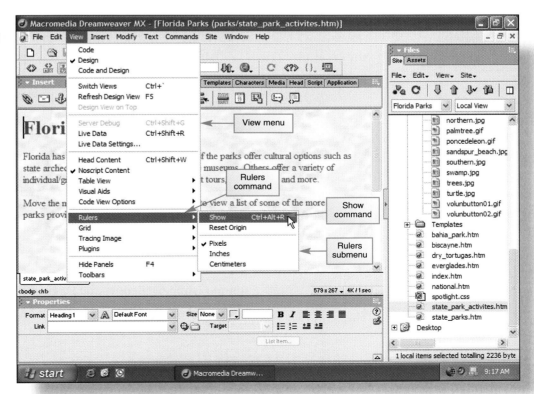

FIGURE 7-5

4 **Click Show.**

Dreamweaver displays the rulers in the Document window (Figure 7-6). The ruler-origin icon is displayed in the upper-left corner where the rulers meet in the Document window.

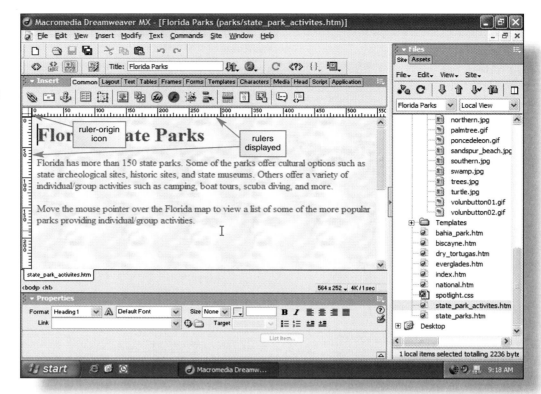

FIGURE 7-6

Layer Property Inspector

When you insert a layer into a Web page and the layer is selected, Dreamweaver displays the Layer Property inspector (Figure 7-7). The following section describes the layer properties available through the Layer Property inspector.

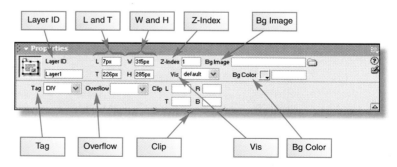

FIGURE 7-7

LAYER ID Assigns a unique name to identify the layer in the Layers panel and in JavaScript code. Layer names must start with a letter and can contain only standard alphanumeric characters.

L AND T Specify the position of the layer's top-left corner relative to the top-left corner of the page, or of the parent layer if nested. A nested layer (child layer) is a layer whose code is contained in another layer. Nesting often is used to group layers together. A nested layer moves with its parent layer and can be set to inherit visibility from its parent. (Parent and child layers are discussed in more detail in the section on Nesting, Overlapping, and Stacking Layers later in this project.)

W AND H Specify the width and height of the layer in Design view. If the content of the layer exceeds the specified size, the bottom edge of the layer stretches to accommodate the content. When the layer appears in a browser, the bottom edge does not stretch unless the Overflow property is set to visible. The default unit for position and size is pixels (px). Other units include pc (picas), pt (points), in (inches), mm (millimeters), cm (centimeters), or % (percentage of the parent layer's corresponding value). The abbreviations must follow the value without a space: for example, 3mm indicates 3 millimeters.

Z-INDEX Determines the stacking order of the layer. In a browser, higher-numbered layers appear in front of lower-numbered layers. Values can be positive or negative. Stacking order can be changed through the Layers panel.

VIS Specifies whether the layer initially is visible or not. The following options are available:

- ▶ **default** does not specify a visibility property. When no visibility is specified, most browsers default to inherit.
- ▶ **inherit** uses the visibility property of the layer's parent.
- ▶ **visible** displays the layer contents, regardless of the parent's value.
- ▶ **hidden** hides the layer contents, regardless of the parent's value. Note that hidden layers created with ilayer (a tag unique to Netscape Navigator) still take up the same space as if they were visible.

BG IMAGE Specifies a background image for the layer.

BG COLOR Specifies a background color for the layer. Leave this option blank to specify a transparent background.

TAG Specifies the HTML tag used to define the layer. The two selections are DIV and SPAN. By default, Dreamweaver creates layers using the DIV tag.

OVERFLOW Works with the DIV and SPAN tags only and controls how layers appear in a browser when the content exceeds the layer's specified size. The following options are available:

- ▶ **visible** indicates that the extra content appears in the layer.
- ▶ **hidden** specifies that extra content is not displayed in the browser.
- ▶ **scroll** specifies that the browser should add scroll bars to the layer whether or not they are needed.
- ▶ **auto** causes the browser to display scroll bars for the layer only when when the layer's contents exceed its boundaries.

CLIP Defines the visible area of a layer. Specify left, top, right, and bottom coordinates to define a rectangle in the coordinate space of the layer (counting from the top-left corner of the layer). The layer is *clipped* so that only the specified rectangle is visible.

More *About*

<DIV> versus <SPAN> Tags

The difference between the <DIV> and <SPAN> tags is that those browsers that do not support layers place extra line breaks before and after the <DIV> tag. In most cases, it is better for layer content to appear in a paragraph of its own in browsers that do not support layers. Therefore, in most cases it is better to use <DIV> than <SPAN>.

More *About*

Ruler

You can change the ruler unit of measurement from the default pixels to inches or centimeters by right-clicking anywhere on the ruler and then selecting a different unit of measurement on the context menu.

Next, you use the ruler as a visual guide and create a layer that will be a container for the Florida map image. When you draw the layer in the Document window, a rectangular image appears, representing the layer. (If the layer borders do not display in the Document window, they can be turned on through the View menu.) The rectangular image, however, does not display when viewed in a browser. The content of what is contained within the layer is displayed in the browser.

The default rulers appear on the left and top borders of the Document window, marked in pixels. The **ruler origin** is the 0 point, or the location on the page where the horizontal and vertical lines meet and read 0. The 0 point is represented by the **ruler-origin icon** located in the Document window when in Design view and rulers are displayed (see Figure 7-6 on page DW 7.08). Generally, this is the upper-left corner of the Document window.

Using a ruler as a drawing guideline can be somewhat difficult to manage. To make measuring easier, you can move the 0 point anywhere within the Document window. To move the 0 point, move the mouse pointer to the upper-left corner where the vertical and horizontal lines meet and then click and drag the cross hairs to the desired location. When you move the 0 point, the cross hairs are displayed in the Document window and follow the mouse pointer. The mouse pointer position is indicated with a dotted line on both the vertical and horizontal ruler lines.

Relocating the 0 point does not affect the page content. You can relocate the 0 point as many times as necessary. Reset the ruler origin by right-clicking anywhere on the ruler and then selecting Reset Origin on the context menu. Complete the following steps to create, select, and drag a layer.

Steps **To Create, Select, and Drag a Layer for the Florida Map Image**

1 **Click below the last line of text in the Document window. Click the ruler-origin icon and drag to the insertion point. If necessary, click the Common tab in the Insert bar and then point to the Draw Layer button.**

The insertion point is blinking below the last line of text in the Document window (Notice that the cross hair increases in size as you drag.) The vertical ruler 0 point is to the left of the insertion point (Figure 7-8).

FIGURE 7-8

2 **Click the Draw Layer button on the Common tab in the Insert bar and then move the pointer to the insertion point.**

The layer pointer is displayed in the Document window (Figure 7-9).

FIGURE 7-9

3 **Using the rulers as a guide, draw a layer approximately 315 pixels wide and 285 pixels high as shown in Figure 7-10. If the layer outline does not appear in the Document window, click View on the menu bar, point to Visual Aids, and then click Layer Borders on the Visual Aids submenu.**

The layer is displayed in the Document window. Most likely, the layer overlaps some of the text (Figure 7-10). Your measurements and layer position are approximate and most likely will not match those in Figure 7-10. You will have an opportunity to adjust the size and position later in this project.

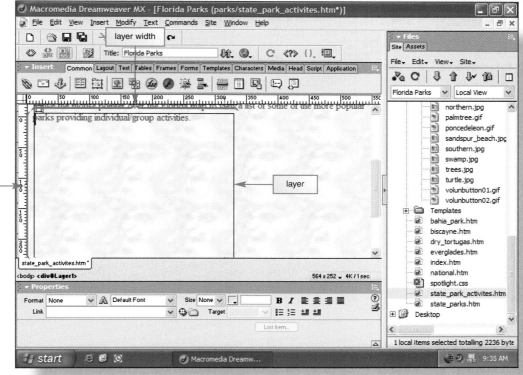

FIGURE 7-10

4 **Move the mouse pointer over any border of the layer outline and then click the border.**

The layer is selected as indicated by the resize handles that appear around the layer (Figure 7-11). The mouse pointer changes to a four-headed arrow when positioned on a border indicating that the layer can be moved. Dreamweaver displays the Layer Property inspector. The L (left) and T (top) attributes indicate the position of the layer's top-left corner relative to the top-left corner of the page. Your measurements and layer position are approximate and most likely will not match those in Figure 7-11. You will have an opportunity to adjust the size and position later in this project.

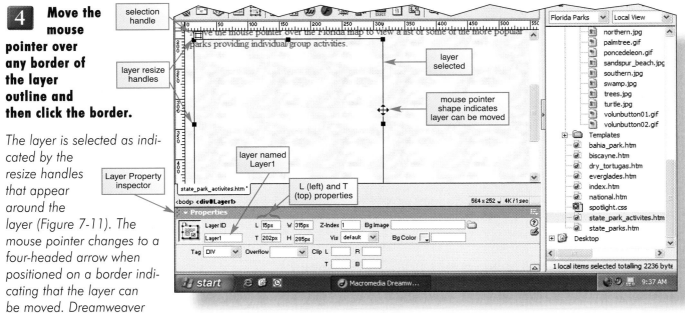

FIGURE 7-11

5 **Use the ruler as a visual guide, and drag the border of the layer downward until it is about 25 pixels below the text.**

The layer is displayed in its new position (Figure 7-12). The L and T attributes indicate the layer's new position. Your measurements and layer position are approximate and most likely will not match those in Figure 7-12. You will have an opportunity to adjust the size and position later in this project.

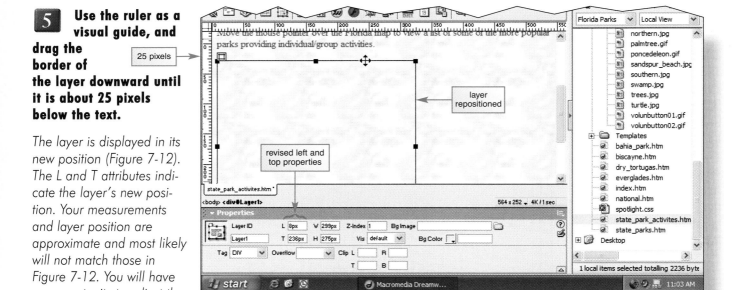

FIGURE 7-12

6 **Right-click anywhere on the rulers and select Reset Origin on the context menu.**

The vertical 0 point returns to its original position.

Other **Ways**

1. On Insert menu click Layer

In addition to moving a layer by positioning the mouse pointer on a layer border, you also can drag the **selection handle** that appears above the layer in the upper-left corner (see Figure 7-11).

The Layer-Code Marker

When you insert a layer, a **layer-code marker** appears in the Document window. This small yellow square indicates that a layer is on the page. The Invisible Elements option must be turned on for the layer-code marker to display. When the Invisible Elements option is turned on, the elements on the page in the Document window may appear to shift position. These markers, however, are not displayed in the browser. When you view the page in your browser, the layers and other objects are displayed in the correct positions.

The layer-code marker is similar in appearance to the invisible element marker that displayed when you inserted images into a Web page in Project 2. In Project 2, dragging the invisible element marker to another position in the Document window also moved the image to another position. Normally, the position of HTML objects in the Document window and in the browser is determined by their order in the HTML source code. They are displayed in a top-to-bottom sequence that mirrors their order in the source code.

Dragging or moving the layer-code marker, however, generally does not reposition the layer and has no effect on the way a Web page displays the layer in a browser. When you move a layer-code marker, you are not moving the layer; instead, you are repositioning the layer's code in the HTML of the page. Moving a layer-code marker, therefore, can affect how the code is interpreted and the order in which the layer content is loaded. It is possible to have a layer's content displayed at the top of the Web page while the source code is at the end of the page.

If your Web page contains tables, do not drag the layer-code marker into a table cell. This can cause display problems in some browsers. You can drag a layer, however, to overlap a table or make a label display so that it appears to be inside the table cell as long as the layer-code marker itself is not in the table cell. When you use the Draw Layer button to create the layer, Dreamweaver will not put the code into a table cell. Complete the following steps to view and move the layer-code marker.

 To View and Move the Layer-Code Marker

1 **Scroll to the top of the Document window.**

The layer-code marker is selected because the layer is selected (Figure 7-13).

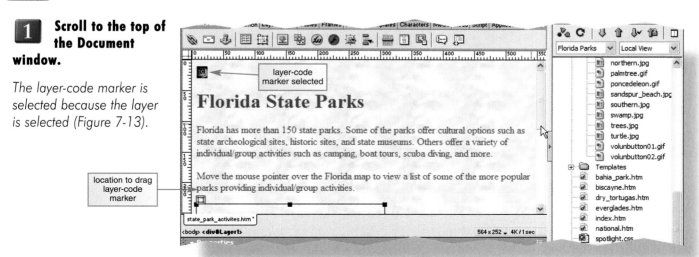

FIGURE 7-13

2 **Drag the layer-code marker to the top of the layer. If the paragraph splits when moving the layer-code marker, click the Undo button on the Standard toolbar and then move it again.**

The layer-code marker is moved so that it appears above the layer. The layer is still in the same position as indicated by the L and T attributes in the Property inspector (Figure 7-14). The position on your screen and the L and T attributes most likely will be different from those in Figure 7-14. You will adjust these later in this project.

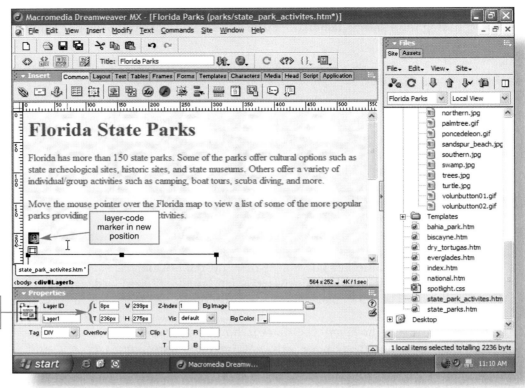

FIGURE 7-14

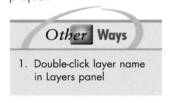

Other Ways

1. Double-click layer name in Layers panel

The Layers Panel

The **Layers panel,** part of the Advanced Layout group, is helpful in managing the layers in your document. Use the Layers panel to prevent overlaps, to change the visibility of layers, to nest or stack layers, and to select one or more layers. All layers on the Web page are listed in the panel. The panel contains three columns: Visibility, Name, and Z-Index. The Visibility column uses eye icons. A **closed-eye icon** indicates a layer is hidden; an **open-eye icon** indicates the layer is visible. The absence of an eye icon indicates that the layer is in its default state — that it is showing, but not defined as showing in the HTML code. The middle column displays the names of the layers. Clicking a layer name in the Layers panel is another way to select a layer. In the Z-Index column, layers are displayed in order of z-index. The first created layer appears at the bottom of the list, and the most recently created layer at the top of the list. Nested layers are displayed as indented names connected to parent layers (discussed later in this project). The Prevent Overlaps check box, when clicked, prevents layers from overlapping. When the Prevent Overlaps option is on, a layer cannot be created in front of, moved or resized over, or nested within, an existing layer.

The following step illustrates how to display the Layers panel.

TO DISPLAY THE LAYERS PANEL

1 Press the F2 key to display the Layers Panel.

The Layers panel is displayed (Figure 7-15). The Layers panel on your screen may be in a different location.

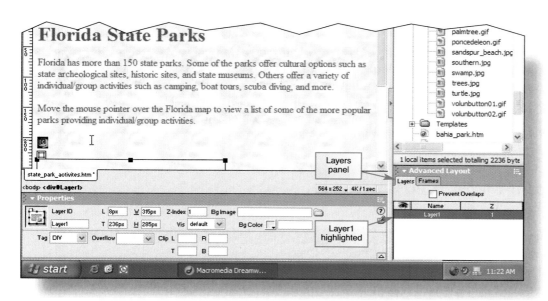

FIGURE 7-15

The next step is to rename the layer, to adjust the layer width and height properties, and to specify the layer visibility using the Property inspector. Complete the following step to make these property changes.

 To Name the Layer and Adjust the Layer Properties

1 **Double-click the Layer ID text box in the Property inspector and then type flmaplayer as the layer name. If necessary, double-click the W box and change the width to 315px, then double-click the H box and change the height to 285px. Click the Vis box arrow and then click visible. Click the Overflow box arrow and then click hidden.**

The property changes for the flmaplayer layer are made in the Property inspector. The flmaplayer name appears in the Layers panel with the open-eye icon indicating the layer is visible (Figure 7-16).

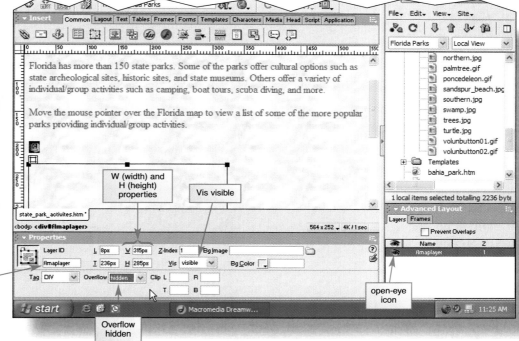

FIGURE 7-16

Adding Objects to Layers

As indicated previously, a layer is a container that can hold objects. The objects can be anything that can be added to an HTML page and include such items as images, text, form objects, and even other layers (nested layers). Objects, including images, can be inserted into layers through the Insert menu. Images also can be dragged from the Site panel onto the layer. Complete the following steps to add the Florida map image to the flmaplayer layer.

Steps To Add an Image to the flmaplayer Layer

1 If necessary, scroll in the Site panel and then locate the florida_map.jpg image (Figure 7-17).

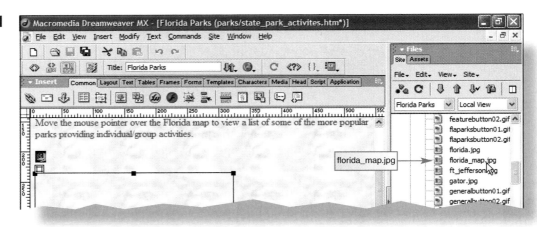

FIGURE 7-17

2 Drag the florida_map.jpg image onto the layer.

The Florida map image is selected and displayed in the layer. The Property inspector no longer displays layer properties (Figure 7-18).

3 Click the Save button on the Standard toolbar.

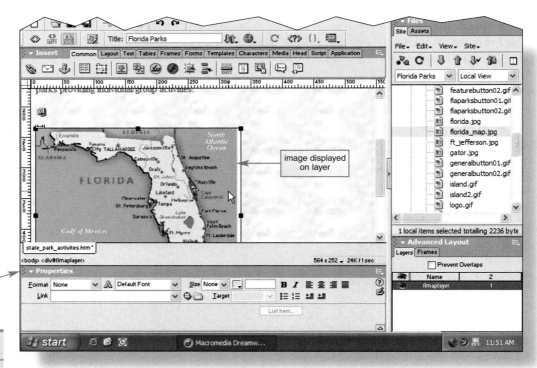

Other Ways

1. On Insert menu click Image, select file name in Image Source dialog box, click OK button

FIGURE 7-18

Nesting, Overlapping, and Stacking Layers

Several methods are available to manage and manipulate layers. They can be nested, overlapped, or stacked one on top of another.

Nesting is used to group layers. This process also is referred to as creating a parent-child relation. A nested layer, also called a **child layer**, is similar in concept to a nested table or a nested frame. A nested layer, however, does not necessarily mean that one layer resides within another layer. Rather, it means that the HTML code for one layer is written inside the code for another layer. The nested layer can be displayed anywhere on the page. It does not even have to touch the **parent layer**, which is the layer containing the code for the other layers. The primary advantage of nested layers is that the parent layer controls the behavior of its child layers. If the parent layer is moved on the screen, the nested layers move with it. Additionally, if you hide the parent layer, you also hide the nested layers. In the Layers panel, nested layers are indented below the parent layer.

To create a nested layer, draw the layer inside an existing layer while holding down the CTRL key. To un-nest a nested layer, drag the layer-code marker to a different location in the Document window, or, in the Layers panel, drag the nested layer to an empty spot.

Layers also can overlap and/or be stacked one on top of another. Layers that float on top of each other have a **stacking order**. In the HTML source code, the stacking order, or **z-index**, of the layers is determined by the order in which they are created. The first layer you draw is 1, the second is 2, and so on. The layer with the highest number appears on top or in front of layers with lower numbers. Stacking layers provides opportunities for techniques such as hiding and displaying layers and/or parts of a layer, creating draggable layers, and creating animation.

Two different methods are available through the Layers panel to change the z-index for a layer and set which layer appears in front of or behind another layer. First, you can click the layer name and then drag it up or down in the list. A line appears, indicating where the layer will be placed. The second method is to click the number of the layer you want to change in the Z column and then type a higher number to move the layer up or a lower number to move the layer down in the stacking order. After you change the z-index, Dreamweaver automatically rearranges the layers from highest to lowest, with the highest number on top. You also can turn off the overlapping feature in the Layers panel. When the Prevent Overlaps check box is selected, layers cannot be overlapped or stacked.

Complete the steps on the next pages to draw three stacked layers, one on top of the other. The placement of the layers in Figures 7-19 through 7-28 is approximate. Later in this project, you align and position the layers.

More *About*

Converting Layers to Tables

Absolute positioning is the more common and widely used CSS positioning method. Dreamweaver uses this method. Two other methods, however, are available: static positioning and relative positioning. **Relative** places the layer using the coordinates entered in the Placement boxes relative to object's position in the text flow of the document. This option is not displayed in the Document window. **Static** places the layer at its location in the text flow.

More *About*

Z-Index

The term z-index comes from the coordinate system used in algebra. The z-index is the third coordinate that works with x and y and is required to describe three-dimensional space.

To Create Stacked Layers

1 Click the expander arrow to collapse the Site panel. Point to the ruler-origin icon.

The Site panel is collapsed (Figure 7-19).

FIGURE 7-19

2 Click the ruler-origin icon and drag about 25 pixels to the right of the flmaplayer layer. Click the Draw Layer button in the Insert bar and then use the ruler as a visual guide to draw a layer measuring approximately 350px in width and 325px in height to the right of the flmaplayer layer.

The layer is drawn and appears to the right of the flmaplayer layer (Figure 7-20).

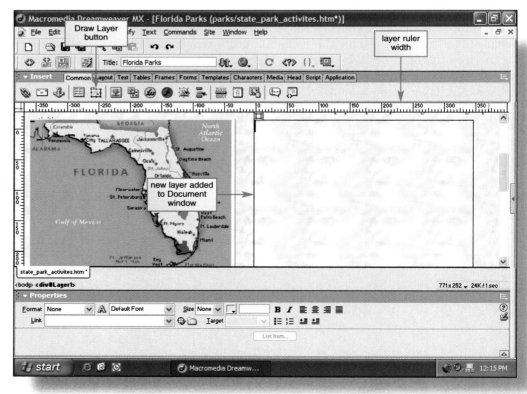

FIGURE 7-20

3 **Right-click anywhere on the ruler and then click Reset Origin on the context menu. Move the mouse pointer over any border of the layer outline and then click the border. Double-click the Layer ID text box and then type northfllayer for the layer name. If necessary, change the W to 350px and the H to 325px in the Property inspector. Click the Vis box arrow and then click hidden. Click the Overflow box arrow and then click hidden.**

The properties for the northfllayer layer are added and are displayed in the Property inspector. The 0 origin point for the ruler is reset to 0 (Figure 7-21). You will align the T and L properties later in this project.

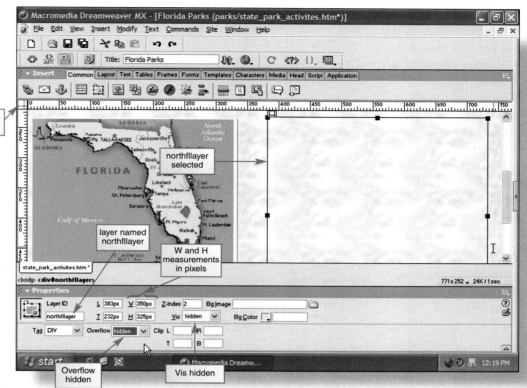

FIGURE 7-21

4 **Click the Draw Layer button in the Insert bar and then draw a second layer directly on top of the northfllayer layer. Add and modify the following properties in the Property inspector: Layer ID – cenfllayer; W – 350px, H – 325px; Vis – hidden; and Overflow – hidden.**

The properties are modified and added for the cenfllayer layer and are displayed in the Property inspector (Figure 7-22). You will align the T and L properties later in this project.

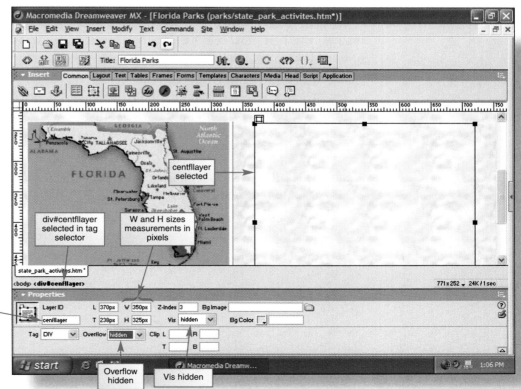

FIGURE 7-22

5 **Click the Draw Layer button in the Insert bar and then draw a third layer on top of the cenfllayer. Add and modify the following attributes in the Property inspector: Layer ID — southfllayer; W — 350px, H — 325px; Vis — hidden; and Overflow — hidden. Point to the Site panel expander arrow.**

The properties are added and modified for the southfllayer layer and are displayed in the Property inspector (Figure 7-23). You will align the T and L properties later in this project.

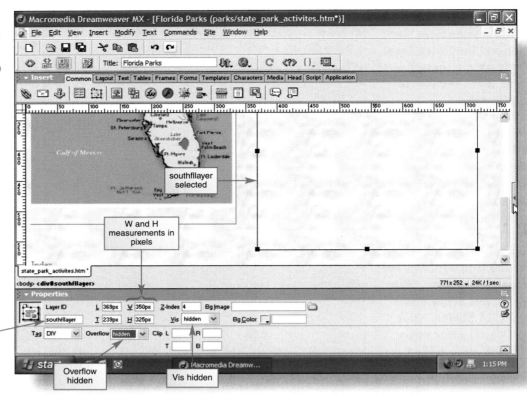

FIGURE 7-23

Selecting Layers

The next step is to add images to each of the layers, but before you add the images, you first must select the correct layer. Dreamweaver provides the following options for selecting layers.

▶ Click the name of the layer in the Layers panel.
▶ Click a layer's selection handle. If the selection handle is not visible, click anywhere inside the layer to make the handle visible.
▶ Click a layer's border.
▶ Press CTRL+SHIFT. If multiple layers are selected, this deselects all other layers and selects only the one that you clicked.
▶ Click the layer-code marker (in Design view) that represents the layer's location in the HTML code.

When layers are stacked, the easiest way to select a layer is to click the name in the Layers panel. Complete the following steps to select layers and add images to each layer.

To Select Layers and Add Images

1 **Click the expander arrow to expand the Site panel. If necessary, close any other open panel groups.**

The Files and Advanced Layout panel groups are displayed. The southfllayer layer is highlighted in the Layers panel and selected in the Document window. Closed-eye icons are displayed to the left of the three hidden layers. An open-eye icon displays to the left of the flmaplayer layer (Figure 7-24).

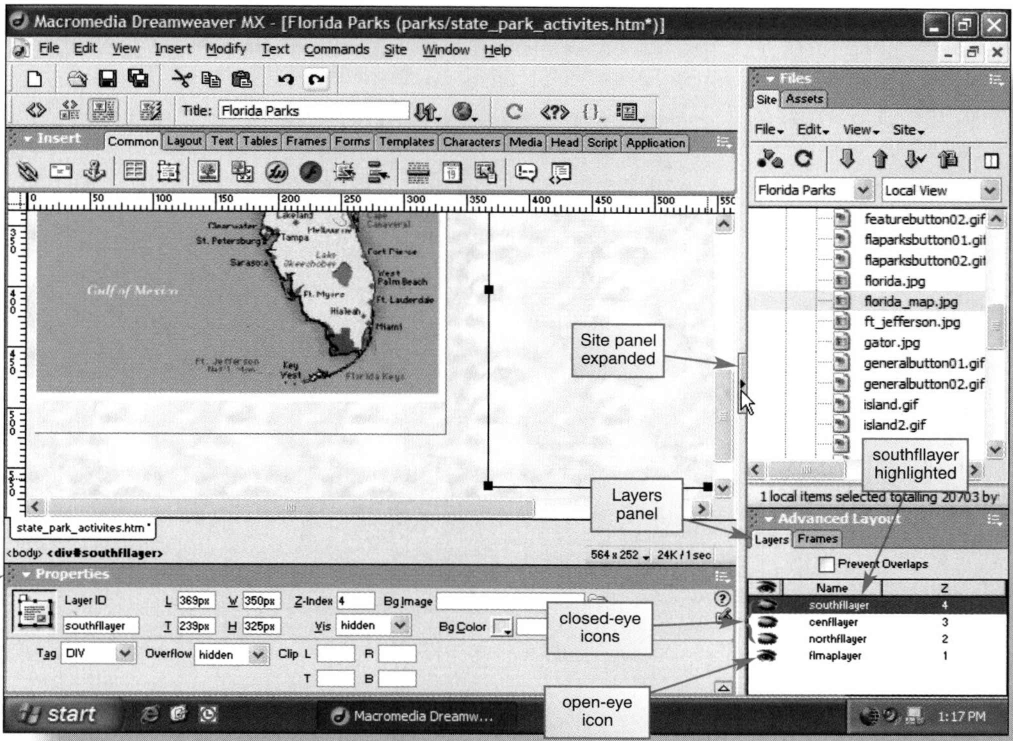

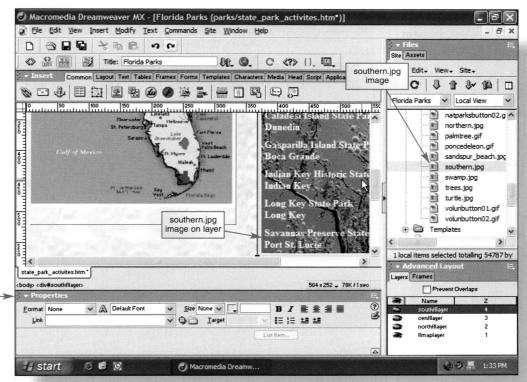

FIGURE 7-24

2 **Scroll in the Site panel and locate the southern.jpg file. Drag the southern.jpg image onto the southfllayer layer.**

The southern.jpg image is displayed in the southfllayer layer. The Layer Property inspector no longer is displayed (Figure 7-25).

FIGURE 7-25

3 Click cenfllayer in the Layers panel.

The cenfllayer is highlighted in the Layers panel and selected in the Document window. The Layer Property inspector is displayed (Figure 7-26).

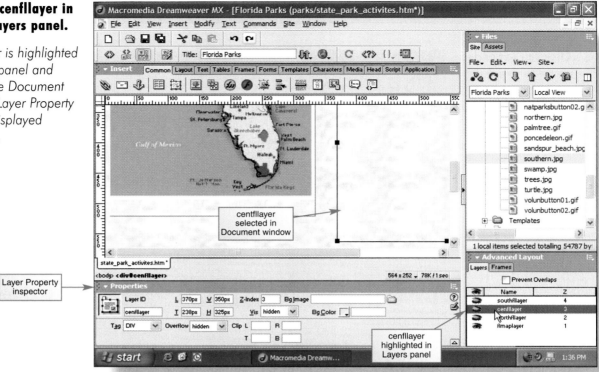

FIGURE 7-26

4 If necessary, scroll up in the Site panel and locate the central.jpg file. Drag the central.jpg image onto the cenfllayer layer.

The central.jpg image is displayed in the cenfllayer layer. The Layer Property inspector no longer is displayed (Figure 7-27).

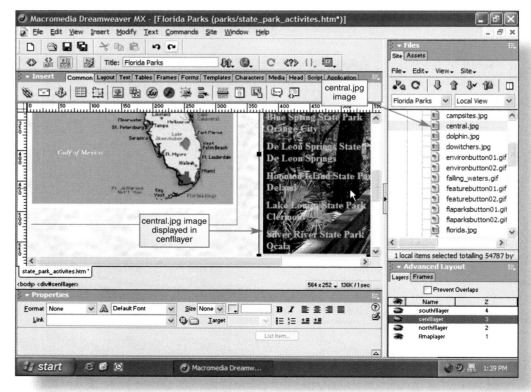

FIGURE 7-27

5 **Click the northfllayer layer in the Layers panel. Locate the northern.jpg image in the Site panel and drag the image onto the northfllayer layer.**

The northern.jpg image is displayed in the northfllayer layer. The Layer Property inspector no longer is displayed (Figure 7-28).

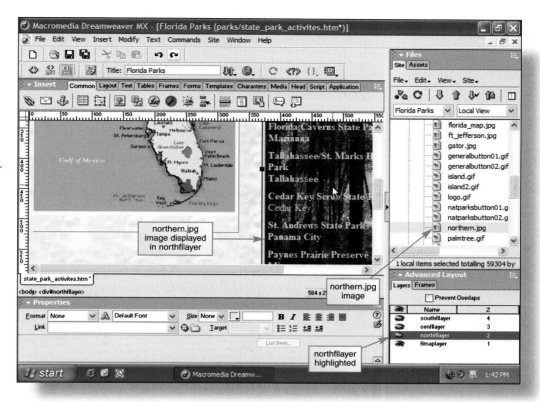

FIGURE 7-28

Image Maps

Image maps are an exciting and interesting way to liven up your Web site. An **image map** is an image that has one or more hotspots placed on top of it. A **hotspot** is a designated area on the map that the user clicks to cause an action to occur. You can create a hotspot on an image map to link to different parts of the same Web page, to link to other Web pages within the Web site or outside the Web site, or to display content within a hidden layer.

Two types of image maps exist: server-side and client-side. The way in which **map data** is stored and interpreted depends on the type of map. Map data is the description in HTML code of the mapped regions or hotspots within the image. A Web server interprets the code or map data for **server-side maps**. When a visitor to a Web page clicks a hotspot in a server-side image map, the browser transfers data to a program running on a Web server for processing. The code for **client-side maps** is stored as part of the Web page HTML code. The Web browser, therefore, interprets the code for client-side maps. When a visitor to a Web page clicks a hotspot in a client-side image map, the browser processes the HTML code without interacting with the Web server. The code for client-side maps is processed faster because it does not have to be sent to a server.

You can add both client-side image maps and server-side image maps to the same document in Dreamweaver. Browsers that support both types of image maps give priority to client-side image maps. When you create an image map in the Document window, Dreamweaver automatically creates the code for client-side image maps. To include a server-side image map in a document, you must write the appropriate HTML code in Code view. In this project you create a client-side image map.

More About

Image Maps

Image maps are images with hotspots that are clickable. When the Web site visitor clicks the hotspot, the visitor is transferred to other Web pages or activates a behavior. For more information about image maps, visit the Dreamweaver MX More About Web page (scsite.com/dreamweavermx/more.htm) and then click Image Maps.

Creating a Client-Side Image Map

The first step in creating the image map is to place the image on the Web page. In this project, the image is the Florida map. Earlier in this project, you placed the image onto the flmaplayer layer. It is not necessary to place an image onto a layer to create an image map. You can insert the image anywhere on the page just as you previously have inserted images in earlier projects. Placing the image in a layer, however, provides absolute positioning. Using this method, you can be assured that the image map will display properly in all browsers supporting CSS-P.

When you create an image map and add a hotspot, you are creating an area that is clickable on the image. To define a hotspot, use one of three shapes: a rectangle, a circle (or oval), or a polygon. Select the tool you want to use and then drag the pointer over the image to create the hotspot. Use the **Rectangular Hotspot Tool** to create a rectangular shaped hotspot. Use the **Oval Hotspot Tool** to define an oval or circular hotspot area. Use the **Polygon Hotspot Tool** to define an irregularly shaped hotspot. Click the **Pointer Hotspot Tool** (arrow) to close the polygon shape.

When an image is selected, the Property inspector for images is displayed. The Map name text box and hotpot tools are available in the lower portion of the Property inspector (Figure 7-29a).

The **Map name** and the **hotspot tools** allow you to label and create a client-side image map. The other properties in the Image Property inspector are described in Project 2 on page DW 2.29.

FIGURE 7-29

After you create a hotspot, Dreamweaver displays the Property inspector for a hotspot (Figure 7-29b). If you are linking to other locations within the same Web page or to Web pages outside of your existing Web site, the link or URL is inserted into the Link text box. On the Target pop-up menu, choose the window in which the file should open in the Target field. If the Web site contains frames, a list of the frame names is contained on the pop-up menu. You also can select from the reserved target names: _blank, _parent, _self, and _top. See page DW 4-39 in Project 4 for a discussion about these target names. The target option is not available unless the selected hotspot contains a link.

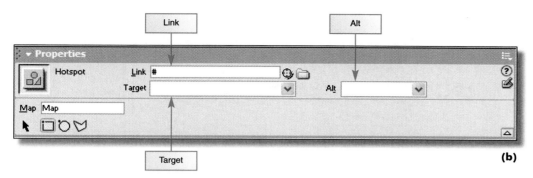

FIGURE 7-29 (continued)

In this image map, you will not link to another Web site or Web page. Instead, you add behaviors to the hotspots to link to and to display hidden layers. Behaviors are discussed later in this project. Clicking the top third of the Florida map displays an image listing some of the more popular parks in north Florida, clicking the middle portion of the map displays an image listing some of the more popular parks in central Florida, and clicking the lower third of the map displays an image listing some of the more popular parks in south Florida.

Earlier in this project, you used the View menu to select Visual Aids, and then verified that Layer Borders was selected. This same menu also contains an Image Maps command. To see a visual of the hotspot on the image, the Image Map command must be active. To verify that the Image Maps command is selected and to create three rectangular hotspots on the Florida Map image, complete the following steps.

 To Create Hotspots on the Florida Map Image

1 If necessary, scroll up to display the top of the flmaplayer layer. Click the florida_map image in the flmaplayer layer. Point to the Rectangular Hotspot Tool in the Property inspector.

The florida_map image is selected. The Image Property inspector is displayed (Figure 7-30).

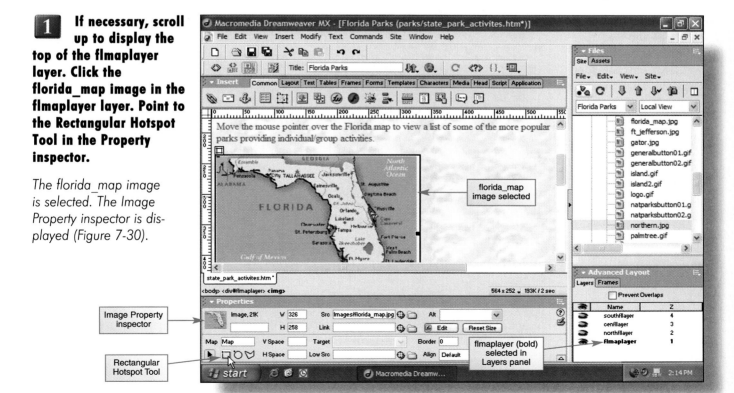

FIGURE 7-30

2 **Click the Rectangular Hotspot Tool and then move the cross hair pointer to the upper-left corner of the florida_map image.**

The cross hair pointer is located in the upper-left corner of the florida_map.jpg image (Figure 7-31).

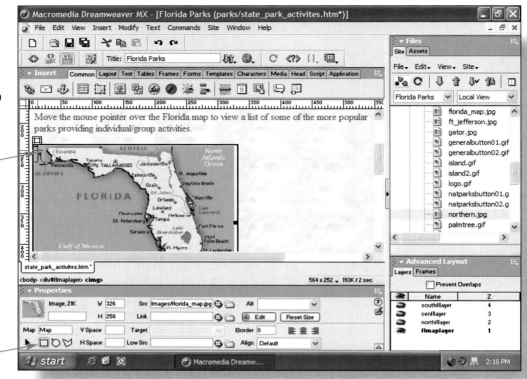

FIGURE 7-31

3 **Drag to draw a rectangle encompassing approximately the top third of the florida_map.jpg image. If the rectangular hotspot does not appear, click View on the menu bar, point to Visual Aids, and then click Image Maps on the Visual Aids submenu.**

A rectangular hotspot is drawn on the florida_map .jpg image (Figure 7-32). Dreamweaver displays the Hotspot Property inspector.

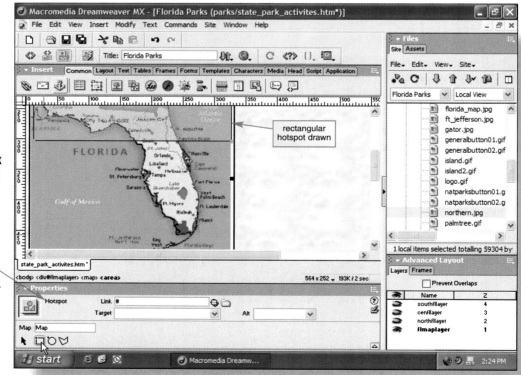

FIGURE 7-32

4 Draw two more hotspots on the image. Drag the cross hair pointer over the middle third of the image and then over the lower third of the image.

The second and third hotspots are drawn in the middle and lower thirds of the florida_map.jpg image (Figure 7-33).

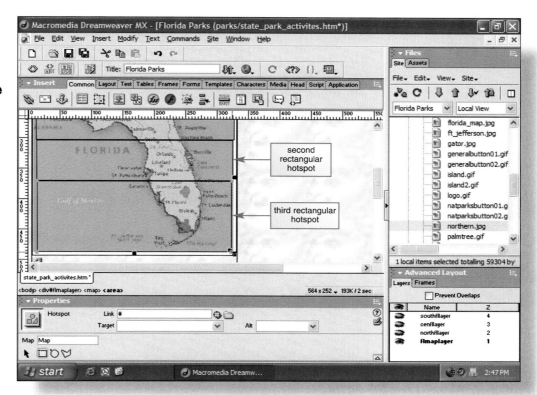

FIGURE 7-33

Behaviors

In Project 4, you learned about using behaviors with forms. Recall that a **behavior** is a combination of an event and an action. Behaviors are attached to a specific element on the Web page. The element can be a table, an image, a link, a form, a form object, and even a hotspot on an image map. Some of the actions you can attach to hotspots (or other elements) include Show Pop-Up Menu, Play Sound, Drag Layer, Swap Image, Show-Hide Layers, and so on.

Dreamweaver contains three standard events designed expressly for working with layers: Drag Layer, Set Text of Layer, and Show-Hide Layers. **Drag Layer** is used to set up an interactive process in which the user can drag or rearrange elements of the design. **Set Text of Layer** is used to change a layer's content dynamically; using this action, the user can swap the content of one layer for a new content. **Show-Hide Layers** is used to make visible and to hide a layer and the layer's content.

Actions to invoke these events are **onMouseOut**, which initiates whatever action is associated with the event when the mouse is moved out of an object; **onMouseOver**, which initiates whatever action is associated with the event when the mouse is moved over the object; and **onClick**, which initiates whatever action is associated with the event when the object is clicked. These actions are selected through the Behaviors panel. The default is onMouseOver. To change the action for an event, click the existing event in the Behaviors panel. An arrow is displayed to the right of the event listing the three actions. Click the arrow to display a pop-up menu and to select another action: onClick, onMouseOut, or onMouseOver.

More About

Behaviors

Use Dreamweaver behaviors to allow visitors to interact with a Web page. Simply specify the action and the event that triggers that action. For more information about behaviors, visit the Dreamweaver MX More About Web page (scsite. com/dreamweavermx/ more.htm) and then click Behaviors.

Adding Behaviors

Selecting a hotspot and then clicking the Actions (+) pop-up menu in the Behaviors panel displays a menu of actions that can be attached to the hotspot. When you choose an action on this menu, Dreamweaver displays a dialog box in which you can specify parameters for the action. In this project, you use the Show-Hide Layers action.

Complete the following steps to attach the Show-Hide Layers action to each of the three image map hotspots.

Steps | **To Add the Show-Hide Layers Action to the Image Map Hotspots**

1 | Press SHIFT+F3 to display the Design group. If necessary, click the Behaviors tab.

The Design group is displayed and the Behaviors panel is selected (Figure 7-34).

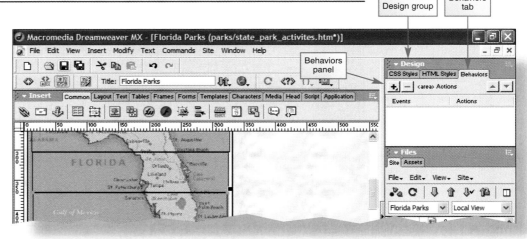

FIGURE 7-34

2 | If necessary, scroll up and then click the top rectangular hotspot on the florida_map.jpg image.

The top rectangular hotspot is selected on the florida_map.jpg image (Figure 7-35).

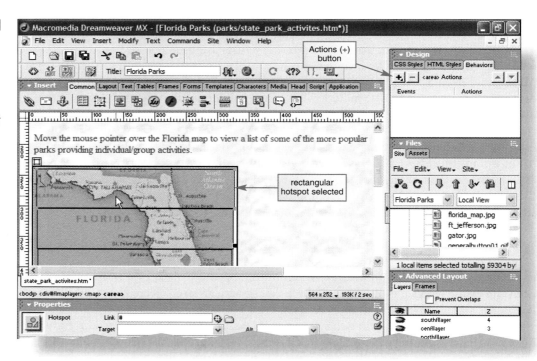

FIGURE 7-35

3 **Click the Actions (+) button to display the Actions pop-up menu in the Behaviors panel. Point to Show-Hide Layers.**

Dreamweaver displays the Actions pop-up menu and the Show-Hide Layers command is highlighted (Figure 7-36).

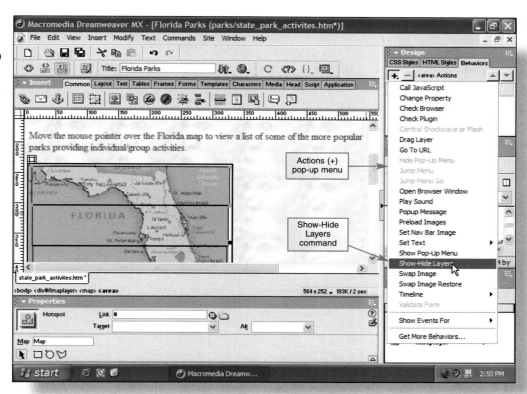

FIGURE 7-36

4 **Click Show-Hide Layers. If necessary, click layer "cenfllayer" in the Named Layers list. Point to the Hide button.**

Dreamweaver displays the Show-Hide Layers dialog box for the top layer (Figure 7-37). The order of the layers in your dialog box may be different.

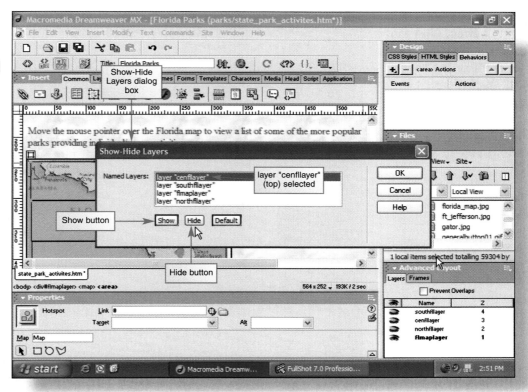

FIGURE 7-37

5 Click the Hide button. Click layer "southfllayer" and then click the Hide button. Click layer "flmaplayer" and then click the Show button. Click layer "northfllayer" and then click the Show button. Point to the OK button.

The Show-Hide Layers actions are added to each of the layers (Figure 7-38).

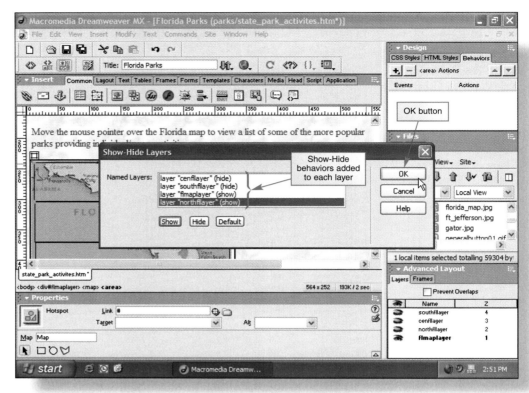

FIGURE 7-38

6 Click the OK button. Click the middle hotspot on the florida_map.jpg image, click the Actions (+) button in the Behaviors panel, and then click Show-Hide Layers on the Actions pop-up menu.

The middle hotspot is selected in the florida_ map.jpg image. Dreamweaver displays the Show-Hide Layers dialog box for the middle layer (Figure 7-39). The order of the layers in your dialog box may be different.

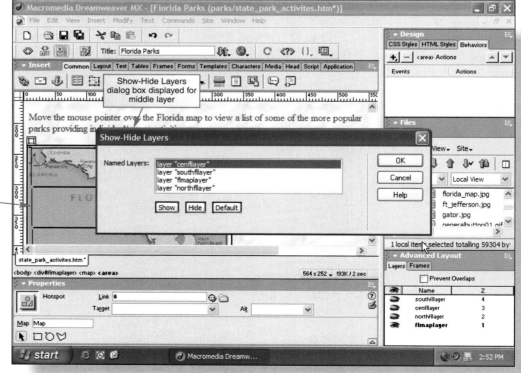

FIGURE 7-39

7 **If necessary, click layer "cenfllayer" and then click the Show button. Click layer "southfllayer" and then click the Hide button. Click layer "flmaplayer" and then click the Show button. Click layer "northfllayer" and then click the Hide button. Point to the OK button.**

The Show-Hide behaviors are added to each of the layers (Figure 7-40).

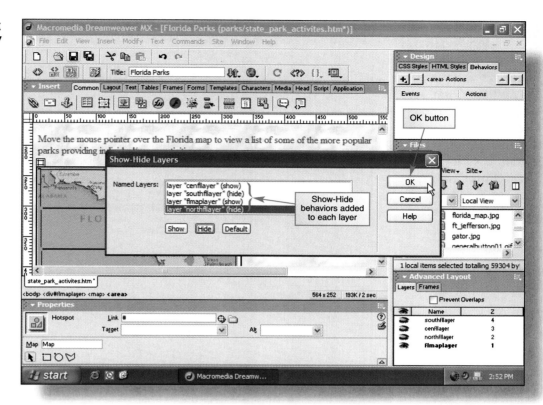

FIGURE 7-40

8 **Click the OK button. If necessary, scroll down in the Document window and then click the bottom hotspot on the florida_map.jpg image. Click the Actions (+) button in the Behaviors panel, and then click Show-Hide Layers on the Actions pop-up menu.**

The bottom hotspot is selected in the florida_map.jpg image. Dreamweaver displays the Show-Hide Layers dialog box for the bottom layer (Figure 7-41). The order of the layers in your dialog box may be different.

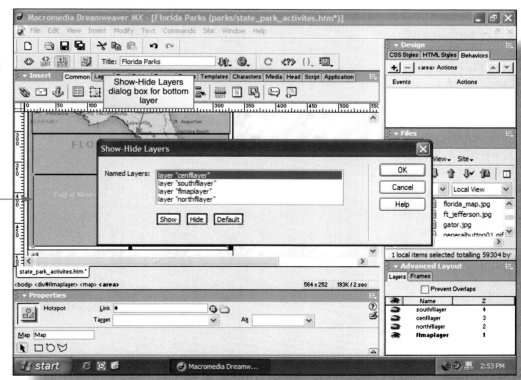

FIGURE 7-41

9 If necessary, click layer "cenfllayer" and then click the Hide button. Click layer "southfllayer" and then click the Show button. Click layer "flmaplayer" and then click the Show button. Click layer "northfllayer" and then click the Hide button. Point to the OK button.

The Show-Hide Layers actions are added to each of the layers (Figure 7-42).

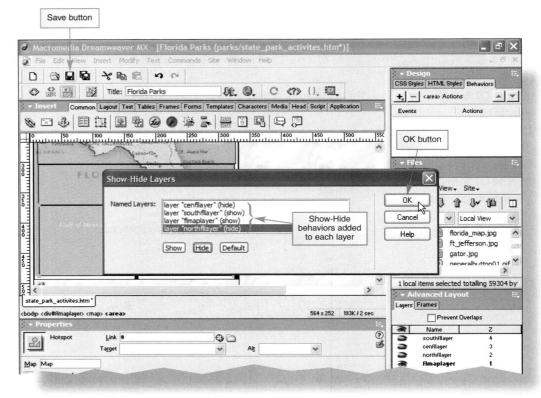

FIGURE 7-42

10 Click the OK button. Click the Save button on the Standard toolbar and then press the F12 key to display the Web page in the browser. If necessary, maximize the browser window. Move the mouse pointer over the hotspots on the florida_map.jpg image to display each of the hidden layers.

As you move the mouse pointer over each hotspot on the Florida map image, the image maps appear to the right. The layer with the image for Northern Florida State Parks is displayed (Figure 7-43).

11 Close the browser window and return to Dreamweaver.

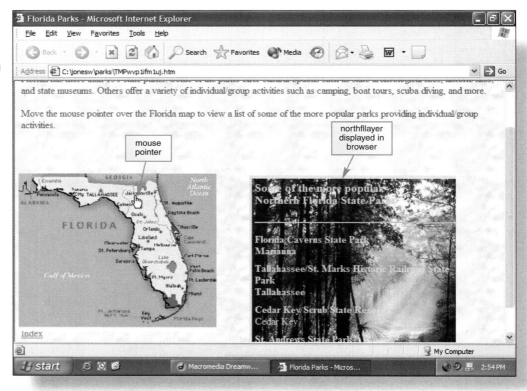

FIGURE 7-43

Positioning Layers

You may have noticed when you displayed the Florida map image and the images in the browser that quite a bit of space appeared between the images and the paragraph above the images. You can position a layer anywhere on the page. In some instances, to eliminate extra space, it is necessary to drag the image over existing text. Even though the text is covered in the Document window, it is displayed correctly in the browser. This sometimes can be a trial-and-error process. You can select and drag the layer by the selection handle or you can move the layer pixel by pixel by selecting the image, holding down the SHIFT key, and then pressing one of the arrow keys.

Complete the following steps to position the flmaplayer layer.

More About

Positioning Layers

Control the absolute positioning of layers on a Web page by setting five attributes: Left, Top, Width, Height, and Z-index. For more information about positioning layers, visit the Dreamweaver MX More About Web page (scsite.com/dreamweavermx/more.htm) and then click Positioning Layers.

Steps **To Adjust Layer Placement**

1 **Click flmaplayer in the Layers panel and then, if necessary, scroll up in the Document window to display the top of the flmaplayer layer. Move the mouse pointer over the selection handle.**

The Layer Property inspector is displayed. The flmaplayer layer is highlighted in the Layers panel, and the mouse pointer is positioned over the selection handle of the flmaplayer layer in the Document window (Figure 7-44). The Layer properties may be different on your screen than those in Figure 7-44. You will adjust the T and L properties later in this project.

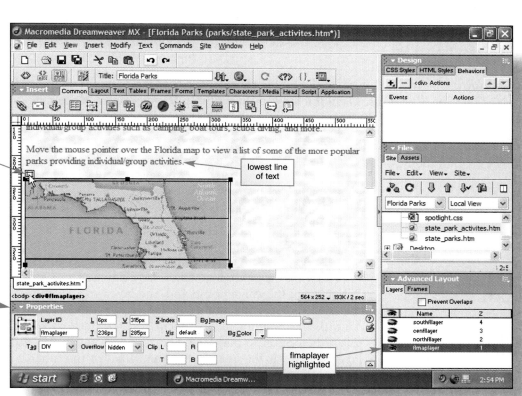

FIGURE 7-44

2 Drag the image up until it covers the lowest line of text. To ensure that the browser can display it in the best position, hold down the SHIFT key and then press the UP ARROW key.

The flmaplayer layer is moved up in the Document window and overlaps part of the text (Figure 7-45). The text will not be overlapped when displayed in the browser.

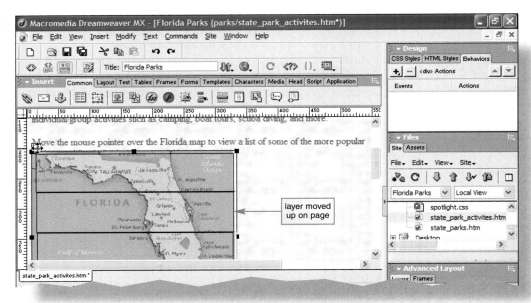

FIGURE 7-45

3 Press the F12 key to view the Web page in the browser. Verify that none of the text is covered and that the image is positioned nicely within the Web page. Close the browser to return to Dreamweaver. Make any necessary adjustments in the Document window to adjust the placement of the flmaplayer layer.

Selecting, Aligning, and Resizing Multiple Layers

Dreamweaver contains yet another command that you can use to lay out your Web page: the **Align command**. This command, accessed through the Modify menu, lets you align layers to their left, right, top, or bottom edges. The Align command also provides an option to make the width and/or height of selected layers the same. When using the Align command, the layer you select last controls the alignment selection. For instance, you first select northfllayer, then cenfllayer, and finally southfllayer. Alignment placement is determined by southfllayer. Likewise, if you select the option to make the width and/or height of selected layers the same, the last layer selected is the one used as the value for the other layers.

To align two or more layers, you first must select the layers. To select multiple layers, in the Layers panel, you select one layer, hold down the SHIFT key, and then click the other layers you want to align. A second method for selecting multiple layers is to click the border of one layer, hold down the SHIFT key, and then click the border of any other layers. When multiple layers are selected, the handles of the last selected layer are highlighted in black. The resize handles of the other layers are highlighted in white.

Layers do not have to be stacked or overlapped to be aligned. The three layers you are going to align, however, are stacked one on top of the other. Thus, the best method for selecting the three layers is through the Layers panel.

The final steps for this Web page are to use the Align command to align the top of the three hidden layers with the flmaplayer layer, make the three hidden layers the same height and width, and then align the three layers to the left. Finally, you add a link from the state_parks Web page to this new state_parks_activities page. Complete the following steps to complete the alignment options and to add the link.

 **To Select and Align Multiple Layers**

1 **Hold down the SHIFT key and select all four layers in the Layers panel. Point to Modify on the menu bar.**

All four layers are selected in the Layers panel. The Property inspector for Multiple Layers is displayed (Figure 7-46).

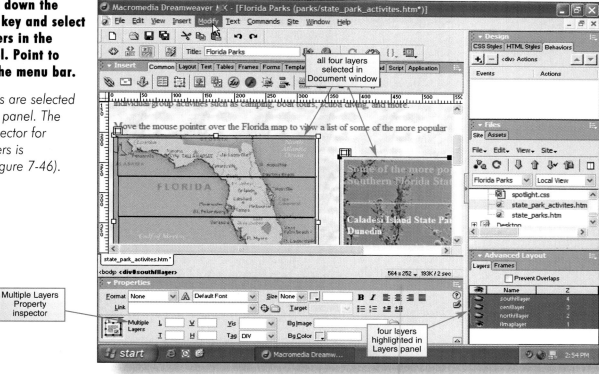

FIGURE 7-46

2 **Click Modify on the menu bar, point to Align, and then point to Top on the Align submenu.**

The Modify menu and Align submenu are displayed (Figure 7-47).

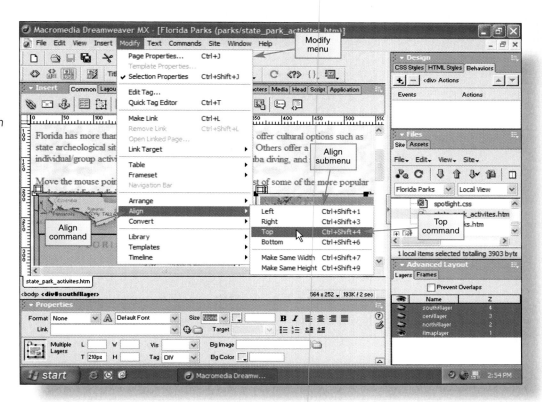

FIGURE 7-47

3 **Click Top.**

All four layers are aligned at the top (Figure 7-48).

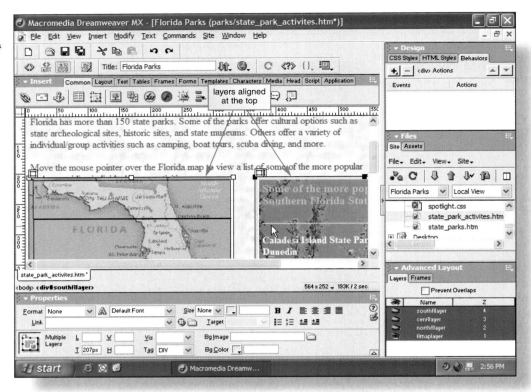

FIGURE 7-48

4 **Hold down the SHIFT key and then click flmaplayer in the Layers panel.**

The flmaplayer layer is deselected (Figure 7-49). The other three layers are still selected.

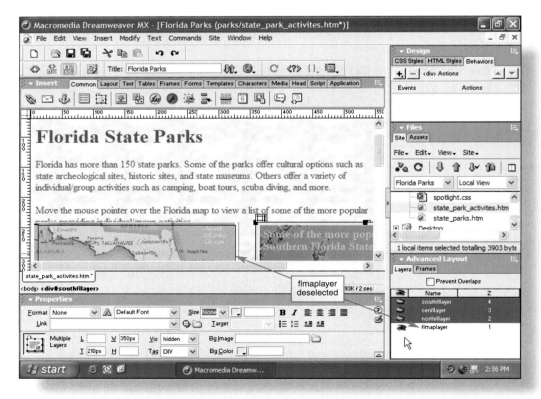

FIGURE 7-49

5 Click Modify on the menu bar, point to Align, and then click Left on the Align submenu. Click Modify on the menu bar, point to Align, and then click Make Same Width on the Align submenu. Click Modify on the menu bar, point to Align, and then click Make Same Height on the Align submenu.

The three stacked layers are aligned at the left and are now the same width and height. No apparent changes appear in the Document window.

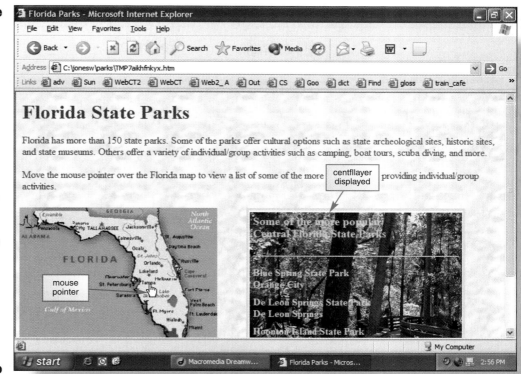

FIGURE 7-50

6 Press the F12 key to view the Web page in your browser. Move the mouse pointer over the Florida map to verify that the images display and that they are aligned properly.

The browser is displayed (Figure 7-50). The mouse pointer is over the middle portion of the Florida map and the image for Central Florida is displayed.

7 Close the browser and return to Dreamweaver. Click View on the menu bar, point to Rulers, and then click Show on the Rulers submenu to hide the rulers.

8 Open the state_parks.htm file and scroll to the bottom of the page. Click below the last image. Type Popular state parks throughout Florida, create a link to the state_parks_activities file, and then save the state_parks file. Press F12 to view the Web page and test the link. Close the browser and then close the state_parks.htm page.

The Netscape Resize Fix

The Netscape 4 browser has a known compatibility problem that causes layers to lose their positioning coordinates when a visitor resizes a browser window. Dreamweaver provides a fix for this through the Preferences dialog box by adding JavaScript code that forces the page to reload each time the browser window is resized, thus reassigning the layers to the correct position. Complete the steps on the next page to set the fix.

Steps **To Set the Netscape Resize Fix**

1 **Click Edit on the menu bar and then click Preferences. Click the Layers category and then click the Netscape 4 Compatibility Add Resize Fix when Inserting Layer check box to select it. If necessary, click the Nest when Created Within a Layer check box to select it. Point to the OK button.**

The Netscape 4 Compatibility Add Resize Fix when Inserting Layer check box is selected (Figure 7-51).

2 **Click the OK button. Click the Save button on the Standard toolbar and then close the state_parks_activities page.**

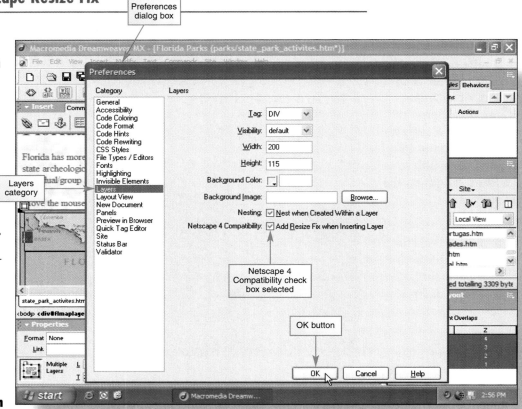

FIGURE 7-51

The Navigation Bar and Date Object

In earlier projects, you used text to add links to your Web pages. In Project 4, when you developed the frames Web site, you created a type of navigation bar with Flash buttons. Dreamweaver provides another quick-and-easy method to provide navigation: a navigation bar. A **navigation bar** (or **nav bar**) is a set of interactive buttons that the Web site visitor uses as links to other Web pages or Web sites or other frames. Many Web site developers consider a navigation bar to be a convenient, customized alternative to a browser's Back and Forward buttons.

Dreamweaver also provides the **Date object**, which inserts the current date in a format of your preference and provides the option of updating the date (with or without the time) whenever you save the file. You open the existing index.htm page, delete the existing links, and then insert a navigation bar to replace these links. Additionally, you delete the static date and replace it with the Date object.

Complete the following steps to open and prepare the index.htm page for the navigation bar and Date object.

Steps **To Open and Prepare the Index Page**

1 **Double-click index.htm in the Site panel to open the index.htm file. If necessary, close the Insert bar and the Property inspector.**

Dreamweaver displays the index.htm page in the Document window (Figure 7-52).

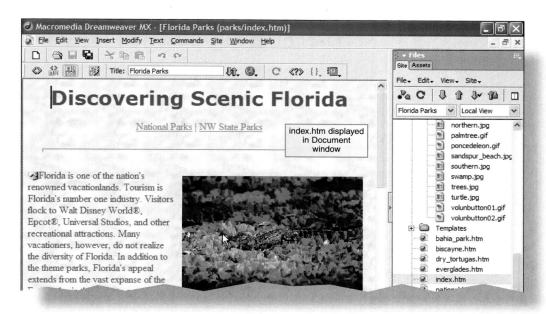

FIGURE 7-52

The Date Object

The index page contains six links — two at the top of the page and four at the bottom of the page. The first step in modifying the index page is to delete these six links.

To further update the page, you remove the static date placed at the bottom of the page and replace it with a new format using the Dreamweaver Date object. To edit the date format after it has been inserted, display the Property inspector, click the formatted text, and then select Edit Date Format in the Property inspector. Perform the following steps to delete the exisiting links and insert the Date object.

Steps **To Delete Existing Links and Insert the Date Object**

1 **Move the insertion point to the left of the two links at the top of the index.htm page and then drag to select the links and the horizontal line.**

The two links and horizontal line are selected (Figure 7-53).

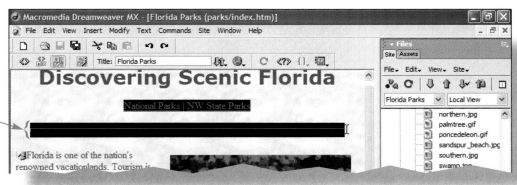

FIGURE 7-53

2 Press the DELETE key to remove the two links and the horizontal line.

The links and horizontal line are deleted (Figure 7-54).

FIGURE 7-54

3 Scroll to the end of the page to display the remaining four links.

The four remaining links are displayed (Figure 7-55).

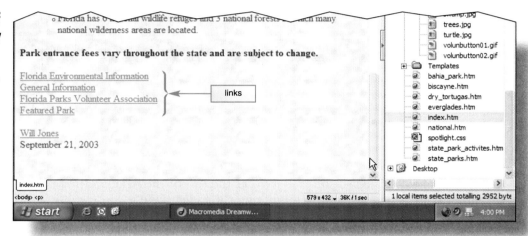

FIGURE 7-55

4 Move the insertion point to the left of the first link (Florida Environmental Information) and then select all four links.

All four links are selected (Figure 7-56).

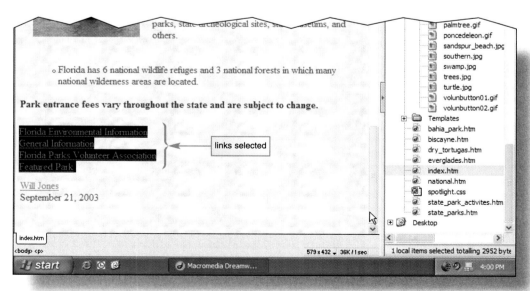

FIGURE 7-56

5 Press the DELETE key to remove the four links. If necessary, press the DELETE key one more time to remove the blank line between your name and the last line of the text.

The links and blank line space are deleted (Figure 7-57).

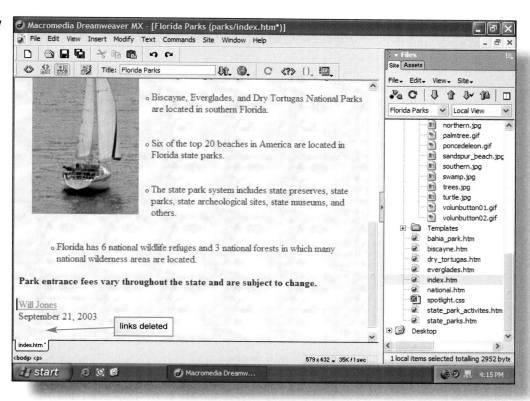

FIGURE 7-57

6 Select the date below your e-mail address link and then press the DELETE key. Point to Insert on the menu bar.

The date is deleted. The insertion point is blinking below your linked e-mail address (Figure 7-58).

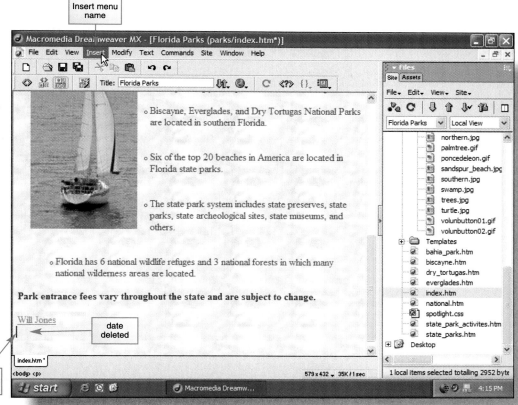

FIGURE 7-58

7 **Click Insert on the menu bar and then point to Date.**

The Insert menu is displayed (Figure 7-59).

FIGURE 7-59

8 **Click Date.**

Dreamweaver displays the Insert Date dialog box. The March 7, 1974 Date Format is selected (Figure 7-60). The dates and times shown in the Insert Date dialog box neither are the current date nor reflect the dates/times that visitors will see when they display your site. They are examples only of the way you want to display this information.

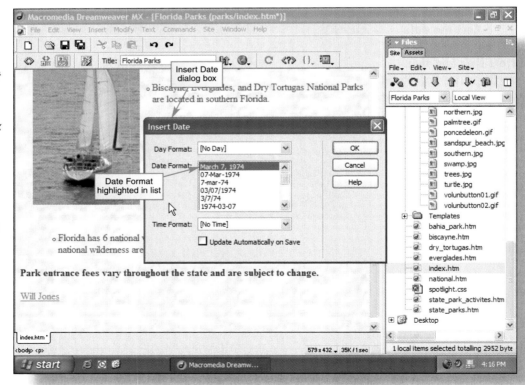

FIGURE 7-60

9 **Click the Update Automatically on Save check box and then point to the OK button.**

The Update Automatically on Save check box is selected (Figure 7-61).

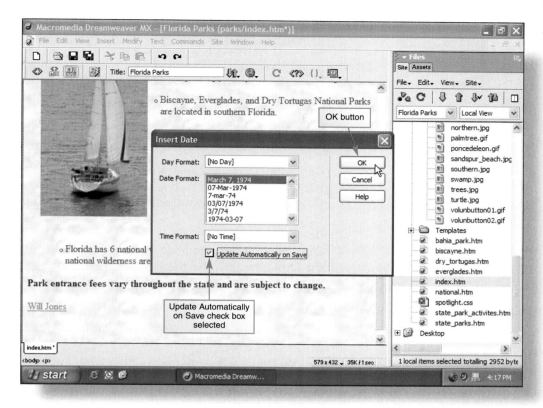

FIGURE 7-61

10 **Click the OK button. Point to the Save button on the Standard toolbar.**

The current date is inserted (Figure 7-62). The date on your Web page will be different from that displayed in Figure 7-62.

11 **Click the Save button.**

Other Ways

1. Click Common tab in Insert bar, click the Date button on Common tab, select Date Format in Insert Date dialog box, click OK button

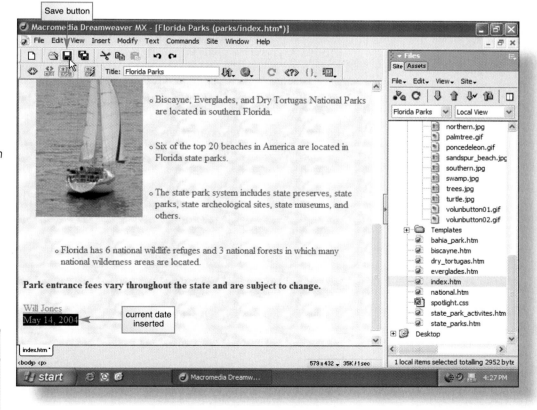

FIGURE 7-62

Creating a Navigation Bar

You create a navigation bar using icon or button elements. Each element is a little different shape or a different color. An element in a navigation bar is called a **rollover** if animation takes place when you move the mouse pointer over the element or click the element. The original image is swapped out for a different one, thus creating a simple animation.

Each element in a Dreamweaver navigation bar can have up to four different states. It is not necessary, however, to include images for all four states.

- **Up**: the image that displays when the visitor has not clicked or interacted with the element.
- **Over**: the image that appears when the mouse pointer is moved over the Up image.
- **Down**: the image that appears after the element is clicked.
- **Over While Down**: the image that appears when the pointer is rolled over the Down image after the element is clicked.

Dreamweaver also provides several features that contribute to the versatility of the navigation bar. Some of these features are:

- The navigation bar can be placed within a table or directly integrated into the HTML code.
- An Alternative Text text box is available for nongraphical browsers and as an accessibility option.
- You can copy the navigation bar to other Web pages.
- A Preload check box is available; select Preload Images to download the images when the page loads.
- Check the Show Down Image to display the selected element initially in its Down state when the page is displayed instead of its default Up state.

Modifying a navigation bar is easy. After you create the navigation bar, you can add images to or remove them from the navigation bar by using the Navigation Bar command on the Modify menu. You can use this command to change an image or set of images, to change which file opens when an element is clicked, to select a different window or frame in which to open a file, and to reorder the images. The following steps create the navigation bar.

To Create the Navigation Bar

1 Scroll up to the top of the page in the Document window and then click below the heading. Click Insert on the menu bar, point to Interactive Images, and then point to Navigation Bar on the Interactive Images submenu.

The Insert menu and Interactive Images submenu are displayed (Figure 7-63).

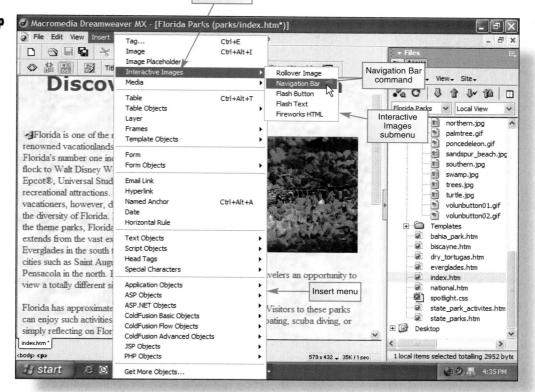

FIGURE 7-63

2 Click Navigation Bar.

Dreamweaver displays the Insert Navigation Bar dialog box (Figure 7-64). The insertion point is blinking in the Element Name text box.

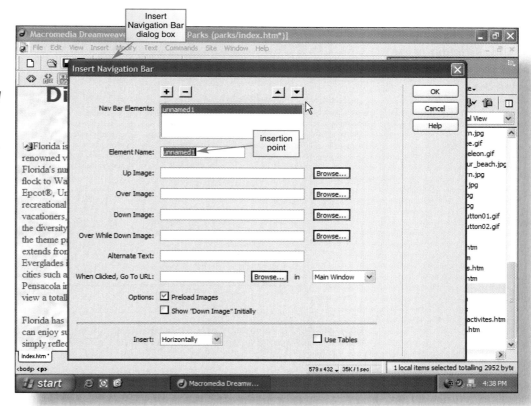

FIGURE 7-64

3 **Type**
FloridaParks in
the Element Name text
box. If necessary, click
Use Tables to select the
check box and then point
to the Browse button for
the Up Image text box.

FloridaParks is displayed
in the Element Name text
box and the Use Tables
check box is selected
(Figure 7-65).

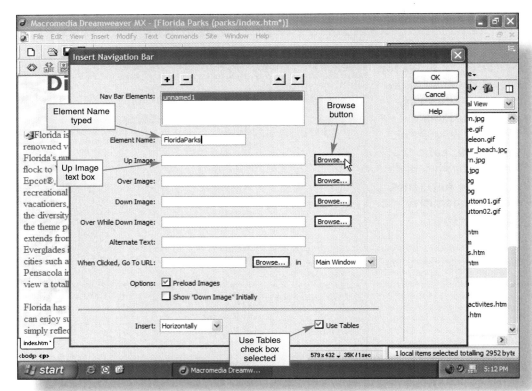

FIGURE 7-65

4 **Click the Browse**
button to the right
of the Up Image text box.
If necessary, double-click
the Images folder in the
Select Image Source
dialog box.

Dreamweaver displays the
Select Image Source dialog
box (Figure 7-66).

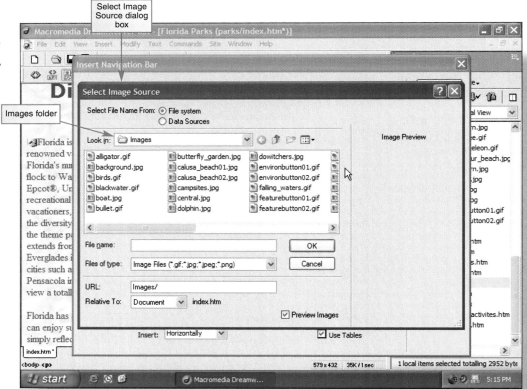

FIGURE 7-66

5 Scroll to the right and then click the flaparksbutton01.gif file. Point to the OK button.

The flaparksbutton01.gif image is highlighted (Figure 7-67). The Image Preview area shows how the button will look.

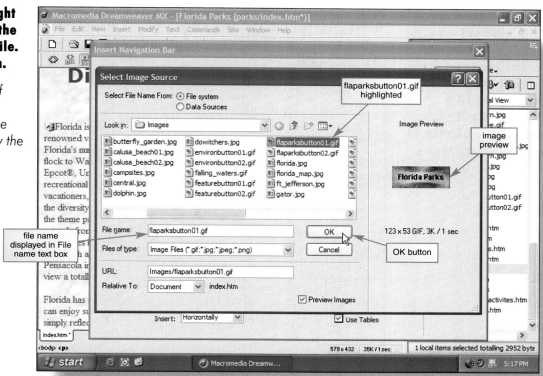

FIGURE 7-67

6 Click the OK button in the Select Image Source dialog box and then point to the Browse button to the right of the Over Image text box.

The path to the flaparksbutton01.gif image is inserted into the Up Image text box (Figure 7-68).

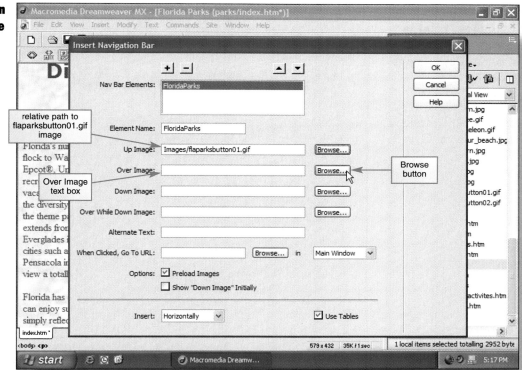

FIGURE 7-68

7 **Click the Browse button to the right of the Over Image text box, scroll to the right in the Select Image dialog box, and then click flaparksbutton02.gif. Point to the OK button in the Select Image Source dialog box.**

The flaparksbutton02.gif file is selected (Figure 7-69).

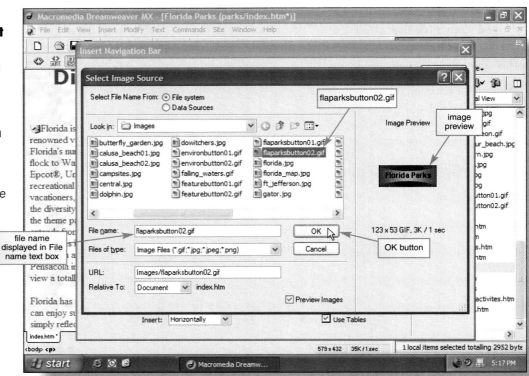

FIGURE 7-69

8 **Click the OK button. Point to the Browse button to the right of the Down Image text box.**

The path to the flaparksbutton02.gif image is inserted into the Over Image text box (Figure 7-70).

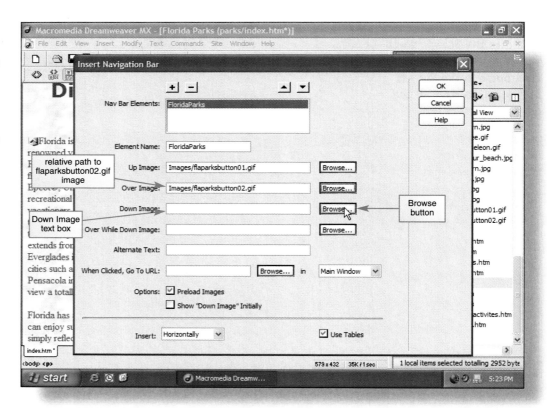

FIGURE 7-70

9 **Click the Browse button to the right of the Down Image text box. Scroll to the right in the Select Image dialog box, click flaparksbutton02.gif, and then click the OK button.**

The path to the flaparksbutton02.gif image is inserted into the Down Image text box (Figure 7-71).

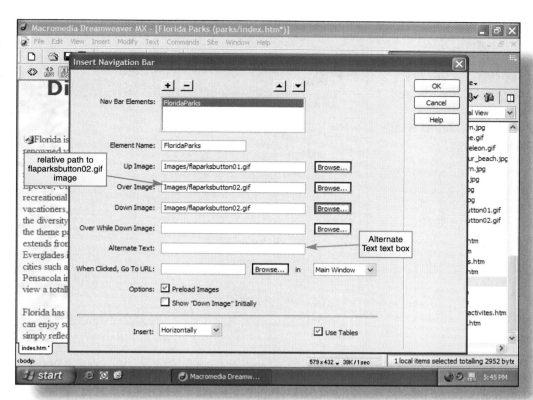

FIGURE 7-71

10 **Click the Alternate Text text box and then type** Florida Parks **as the alternate text. Point to the Browse button to the right of the When Clicked, Go To URL text box.**

Florida Parks is displayed in the Alternate Text text box (Figure 7-72).

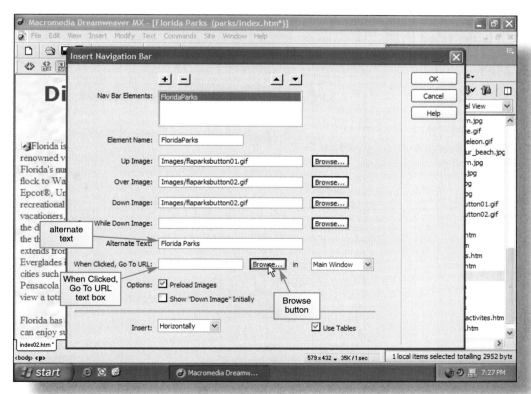

FIGURE 7-72

11 **Click the Browse button. If necessary, navigate to the parks folder. Click the state_parks.htm file and then point to the OK button in the Select HTML file dialog box.**

Dreamweaver displays the Select HTML file dialog box (Figure 7-73). The state_parks.htm file is highlighted.

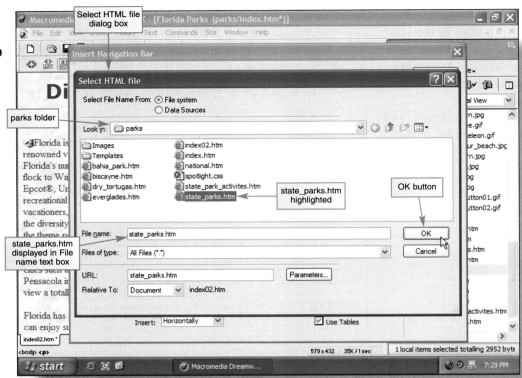

FIGURE 7-73

12 **Click the OK button in the Select HTML file dialog box. Point to the Add Item button.**

The link to the state_parks.htm file is displayed in the When Clicked, Go To URL text box (Figure 7-74).

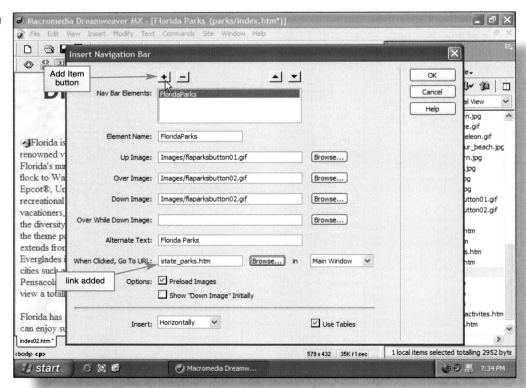

FIGURE 7-74

13 **Click the Add Item button.**

The data for the first button for the navigation bar is added and the Modify Navigation Bar dialog box is ready for the next button (Figure 7-75).

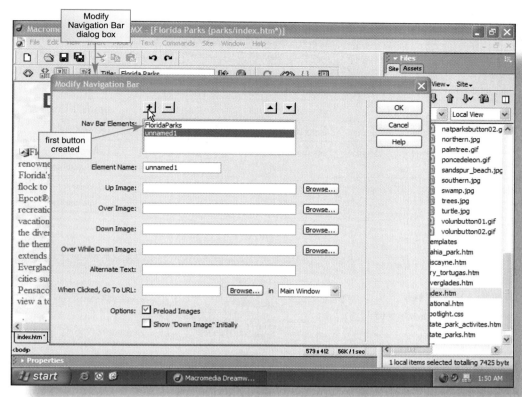

FIGURE 7-75

14 **Repeat Steps 2 through 13 to add the other five buttons using the data in Table 7-1 on the next page. For links that contain jonesw, replace jonesw with your name and/or folder name.**

15 **Click the OK button.**

The navigation bar is created and is inserted into the Document window (Figure 7-76).

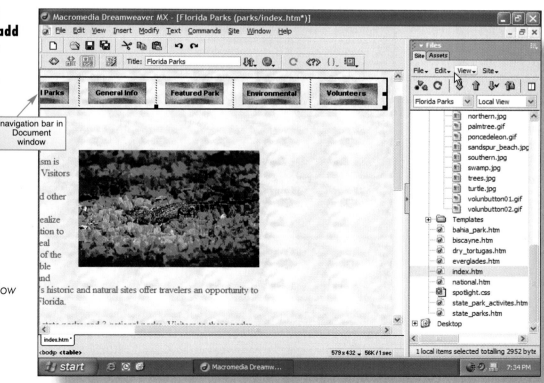

FIGURE 7-76

Table 7-1 Navigation Bar Buttons

ELEMENT NAME	UP IMAGE	OVER IMAGE	DOWN IMAGE	ALTERNATE TEXT	URL
NationalParks	natparksbutton01.gif	natparksbutton02.gif	natparksbutton02.gif	National Parks link	national.htm
GenInfo	generalbutton01.gif	generalbutton02.gif	generalbutton02.gif	General Information	C:/jonesw/parks_frames/index.htm
FeaturedPark	featurebutton01.gif	featurebutton02.gif	featurebutton02.gif	Featured Park	bahia_park.htm
Environmental	environbutton01.gif	environbutton02.gif	environbutton02.gif	Environmental Information	http://www.dep.state.fl.us/
Volunteer	volunbutton01.gif	volunbutton02.gif	volunbutton02.gif	Volunteer Information	C:/jonesw/parks_forms/volunteer.htm

16 Press the F12 key to view the navigation bar in the browser and test each one of the links.

The navigation bar is displayed in the browser window (Figure 7-77).

17 If instructed to do so, print a copy of the state_park_activities page and the revised index page, hand them in to your instructor, and upload the revised Web pages to a server. Close the browser and then click the Save button on the Standard toolbar.

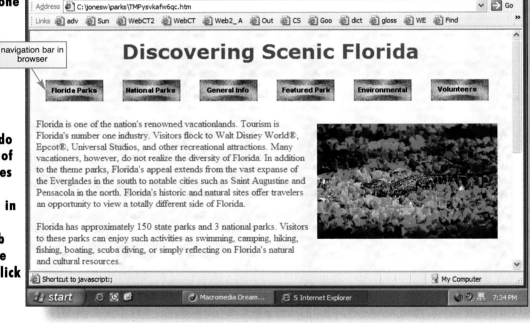

navigation bar in browser

FIGURE 7-77

Other Ways

1. Click Common tab in Insert bar, click the Navigation button on Common tab, select and add properties in Insert Navigation Bar dialog box, click OK button

Quitting Dreamweaver

After you added a new page with layers and an image map and modified the index page by adding a Date object and a navigation bar, Project 7 is complete. To close the Web site, quit Dreamweaver MX, and return control to Windows, perform the following step.

TO CLOSE THE WEB SITE AND QUIT DREAMWEAVER

1 Click the Close button on the upper-right corner of the Dreamweaver title bar.

The Dreamweaver window, the Document window, and the Parks Web site all close.

CASE PERSPECTIVE SUMMARY

As envisioned, your team has created and added a new page to the Web site. This page, the state_parks_activities page, contains four layers, three of which are hidden and stacked on top of each other. Each layer contains an image. An image map was overlaid on the Florida map image and behaviors were added to display the hidden image when a visitor clicks the mouse pointer on the image.

Additionally, the index page was modified by deleting existing links and replacing those links with an animated navigation bar. The Date object also was added to the index page, so that the current date will display when visitors view the page in a browser.

Project Summary

Project 7 introduced you to layers, image maps, navigation bars, and the Date object. You added single layers and stacked layers. You selected and aligned several layers. Next, you created an image map and then added hotspots that displayed hidden layers. Then, you modified the existing index page by deleting links and replacing those links with a navigation bar. You also inserted a Date object on the index page.

What You Should Know

Having completed this project, you now should be able to perform the tasks in Table 7-2.

Table 7-2	Project 7 What You Should Know	
TASK NUMBER	**TASK**	**PAGE NUMBER**
1	Start Dreamweaver and Close Open Panels	DW 7.04
2	Copy Data Files to the Florida Parks Web Site	DW 7.05
3	Open the Florida State Parks Activities Page and Display the Ruler	DW 7.07
4	Create, Select, and Drag a Layer for the Florida Map Image	DW 7.10
5	View and Move the Layer-Code Marker	DW 7.13
6	Display the Layers Panel	DW 7.14
7	Name the Layer and Adjust the Layer Properties	DW 7.15
8	Add an Image to the flmaplayer Layer	DW 7.16
9	Create Stacked Layers	DW 7.18

TASK NUMBER	**TASK**	**PAGE NUMBER**
10	Select Layers and Add Images	DW 7.21
11	Create Hotspots on the Florida Map Image	DW 7.25
12	Add the Show-Hide Layers Action to the Image Map Hotspots	DW 7.28
13	Adjust Layer Placement	DW 7.33
14	Select and Align Multiple Layers	DW 7.35
15	Set the Netscape Resize Fix	DW 7.38
16	Open and Prepare the Index Page	DW 7.39
17	Delete Existing Links and Insert the Date Object	DW 7.39
18	Create the Navigation Bar	DW 7.45
19	Close the Web Site and Quit Dreamweaver	DW 7.53

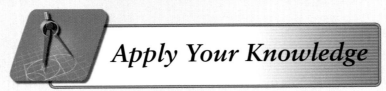

Apply Your Knowledge

1 Adding Layers to the B & B Lawn Service

Instructions: Start Dreamweaver. If the panels display, press the F4 key to close all panels. See the inside back cover of this book for instructions for downloading the Data Disk or see your instructor for information on accessing the files in this book.

The proprietors of the B & B Lawn Service Web site would like to make some additions to their Web site. First, they would like to add a navigation bar to the main page. Second, they would like to have an additional informational page that provides tree-pruning tips. You begin the process by adding a navigation bar to the index page. Next, you open a data file and add layers to show some tree-pruning procedures. You use the onMouseOver action instead of the onClick action to display the procedures. The modified index page and the new tree-pruning page are shown in Figures 7-78a and 7-78b. Software and hardware settings determine how a Web page is displayed in a browser. Your Web page may display differently than the ones shown in Figure 7-78a and 7-78b. Figure 7-78b shows the topping layer. Appendix D contains instructions for uploading your local site to a remote server.

For a selection of images and backgrounds, visit the Dreamweaver MX Media Web page (scsite.com/ dreamweavermx/media) and then click Media below Project 7.

1. Display the Property inspector, Standard toolbar, and Site panel. Select Lawn Service on the Site pop-up menu in the Site panel. Display the rulers. Close the Untitled-1 page.

2. Delete the services.htm page from the Lawn Service Web site (you will replace this page). Use Dreamweaver's integrated file browser to copy the data files and the images from the Data Files folder to your lawn folder and lawn Images folder. The file, services.htm, is contained within the data files. This is simply an updated page with a link to the new tree-pruning page. You will not need to make any changes to this page.

3. Open the index.htm page. Scroll to the bottom of the page and delete the three links — Ecological Lawn Maintenance, Lawn mowers for sale, and Native Plants. If necessary, press the DELETE key to delete extra line spaces.

4. Scroll to the top of the page and delete the horizontal rule. If you delete the extra line space, press the ENTER key.

5. Click Insert on the menu bar, point to Interactive Images, and then click Navigation Bar on the Interactive Images submenu. If necessary, click the Align Center button. Verify that Preload Images is selected, that Horizontally is selected, and that the Use Tables check box is selected on the Insert Navigation Bar dialog box.

6. Type Ecology as the element name. Click the Browse button to the right of the Up Image text box. Navigate to the jonesw/lawn/Images folder, click ecol01.gif, and then click the OK button. Click the Browse button to the right of the Over Image text box. Click ecol02.gif, and then click the OK button. Click the Browse button to the right of the Down Image text box, click ecol02.gif, and then click the OK button. Click the Alternate Text text box and then type Ecological Information. Click the When Clicked, Go To URL text box and then type http://www.eap.mcgill.ca/Publications/EAP68.htm for the linked text.

7. Click the Add button. Type Mowers for the element name. Click the Browse button to the right of the Up Image text box, click mower01.gif, and then click the OK button. Click the Browse button to the right of the Over Image text box, click mower02.gif, and then click the OK button. Click the Browse button to the right of the Down Image text box, click mower02.gif, and then click the OK button. Type Lawn mowers for sale in the Alternate Text text box. Click the When Clicked, Go To URL text box and then type C:/jonesw/lawn_frames/index.htm (or the appropriate path in your Web site).

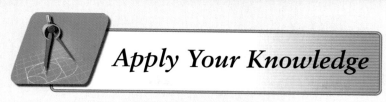

Apply Your Knowledge

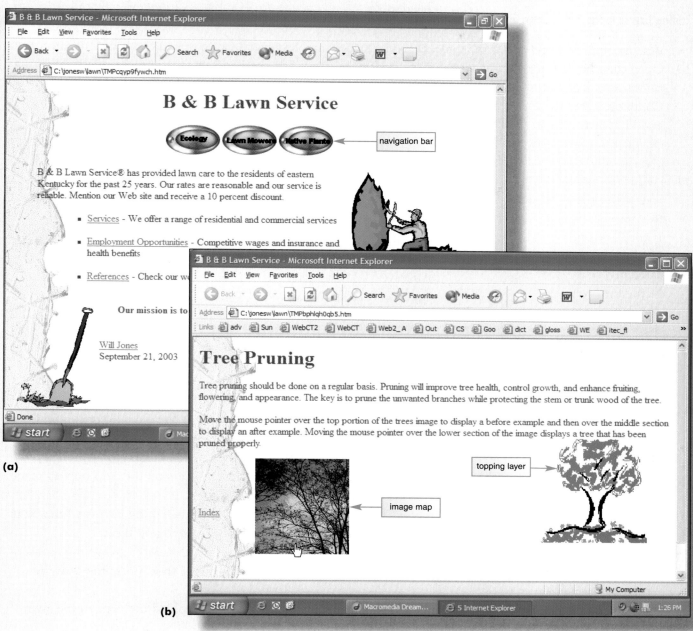

(a)

(b)

FIGURE 7-78

8. Click the Add button. Type NativePlants for the element name. Click the Browse button to the right of the Up Image text box and then click plants01.gif. Click the Browse button to the right of the Over Image text box and then click plants02.gif. Click the Browse button to the right of the Down Image text box and then click plants02.gif. Type Native Plants in the Alternate Text text box. Click the When Clicked, Go To URL text box and then type native_plants.htm (or the appropriate path in your Web site). Click the OK button.

(continued)

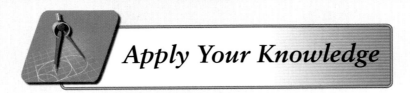

Apply Your Knowledge

Adding Layers to the B & B Lawn Service *(continued)*

9. If necessary, select and center the table. Press the F12 key and test each link. Save and close the index.htm page.

10. Open the tree_pruning.htm page and then display the Insert bar, the Layers panel, and the rulers. Click the ruler-origin icon and drag about 25 pixels below the last paragraph. Click the Draw Layer button on the Common tab in the Insert bar and draw a layer approximately 150 by 150 pixels. Make any necessary W and H adjustments in the Property inspector. Type map in the Layer ID text box. Click the TAB key and change the L property to 100px. Click the TAB key again and change the T property to 200px. Click the Overflow box arrow and then click hidden. Drag the trees.gif image onto the layer.

11. Add three more layers. Use the ruler to approximate the L and T position on the page as indicated in Table 7-3. Name the layers and drag images onto each layer,

Table 7-3	Layer Properties				
LAYER ID	*L AND T PROPERTIES*	*W AND H PROPERTIES*	*VIS PROPERTY*	*OVERFLOW PROPERTY*	*IMAGE*
before	380px 200px	160px 170px	hidden	hidden	before.gif
after	500px 250px	180px 200px	hidden	hidden	after.gif
topping	550px 165px	175px 170px	hidden	hidden	topping.gif

using the data as indicated in the table. Make any other necessary adjustments in the Property inspector.

12. Add three rectangular hotspots to the trees.gif image. Each hotspot should cover about one-third of the image. Display the Behaviors panel. Select the first hotspot, click the Actions button in the Behaviors panel, and then click Show-Hide Layers on the Actions pop-up menu. In the Show-Hide Layers dialog box, show layer "map" and layer "before". Hide layer "after" and layer "topping". Click the second hotspot and then click the Actions button in the Behaviors panel. Click Show-Hide Layers on the Actions pop-up menu. Show layer "map" and layer "after". Hide layer "before" and layer "topping". Click the third hotspot, click the Actions button in the Behaviors panel, and then click Show-Hide Layers on the Add pop-up menu. Show layer "map" and layer "topping". Hide layer "before" and layer "after".

13. Click the first hotspot and then click the onClick event in the Behaviors panel. Click the arrow to the right of the event and then click onMouseOver. Repeat this procedure for hotspots two and three.

14. Click the Save button and then press the F12 key to view the Web page in your browser. Move the mouse pointer over the map image and verify that each layer is displayed in its proper spot. Close the browser to return to Dreamweaver.

15. Print a copy of the index and tree-pruning Web pages if instructed to do so. Upload the page to the lawn Web Site on a remote server if instructed to do so.

In the Lab

1 Creating a New Index Page for the CandleDust Web Site

Problem: The CandleDust Web site has become very popular. Mary would like to redesign the index page and give it a more professional look. She has requested that you help her with this project by adding a navigation bar, rearranging some of the text by using layers, adding an automatic Date object so the current date is displayed on the page, and aligning existing layers. You agree to help her. The revised Web page is shown in Figure 7-79. Appendix D contains instructions for uploading your local site to a remote server. For a selection of images and backgrounds, visit the Dreamweaver MX Media Web page (scsite.com/dreamweavermx/media) and then click Media below Project 7.

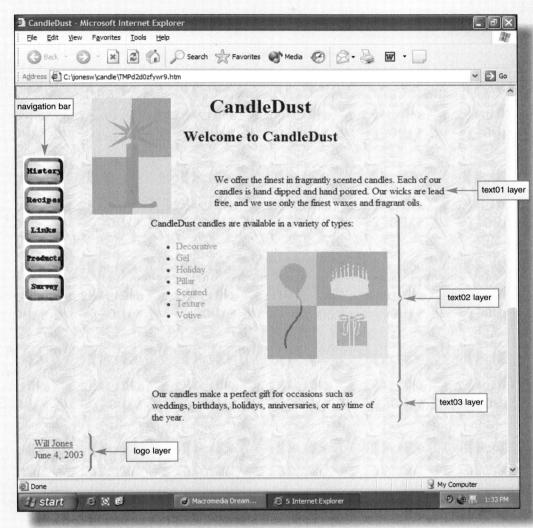

FIGURE 7-79

Instructions: Perform the following tasks:

1. Start Dreamweaver. If necessary, press F4 to close the open panels. Display the Property inspector, Standard toolbar, Site panel, Insert bar, and Layers panel. Display the rulers. Close the Untitled-1 document. Select CandleDust on the Site pop-up menu in the Site panel.
2. Use Dreamweaver's integrated file browser to copy the data files and the images from the Data Files folder to your candle folder and candle Images folder. The data files contain a file named index01.htm. You will revise this file and then save it as index.htm
3. Open the index01.htm file. This file contains three visible layers — text01, text02, and text03.
4. The first task is to add a vertical navigation bar with five links. Click below and to the left of the heading. Click Insert on the menu bar, point to Interactive Images, and then click Navigation Bar on the Interactive Images submenu. Verify that Preload Images is selected, that Vertically is selected, and that the Use Tables check box is selected.

(continued)

In the Lab

Creating a New Index Page for the CandleDust Web Site *(continued)*

5. Use the data in Table 7-4 to complete the Insert Navigation Bar dialog box.

Table 7-4	Navigation Bar Data				
ELEMENT NAME	**UP IMAGE**	**OVER IMAGE**	**DOWN IMAGE**	**ALTERNATE TEXT**	**WHEN CLICKED, GO TO URL**
History	history01.gif	history02.gif	history02.gif	Company history	history.htm
Recipes	recipes01.gif	recipes02.gif	recipes02.gif	Candle-making recipes	recipes.htm
Instructions	links01.gif	links02.gif	links02.gif	Instruction links	http://candleandsoap.about.com/ cs/candlemaking1/
Products	products01.gif	products02.gif	products02.gif	Products for sale	products.htm
Survey	survey01.gif	survey02.gif	survey02.gif	Survey	survey_form.htm

6. After all data is entered, click the OK button to insert the navigation bar.

7. Next, you add a layer for the logo. Display the rulers and then move the ruler-origin point about 120px to the left and approximately 20px from the top. Click the Draw Layer button in the Insert bar and then draw a layer with an approximate width of 120px and height of 145px. The layer most likely will overlap the heading. Make any necessary adjustments in the Property inspector. Name the layer logo. Click the Vis box arrow and then click visible. Drag the candle1.gif image onto the layer. Right-click anywhere on the rulers and select Reset Origin on the context menu.

8. Next, you add three new layers for the text data contained on the page and a fifth layer for your e-mail address and date at the end of the page. Cut and paste the text from the Web page into the layers. Table 7-5 contains the data for the layers.

9. Click in the date layer, type your name, and then select your name. Add an e-mail link to your name and then press SHIFT+ENTER to insert a line break. Click Insert on the menu bar and then click Date. Select the first option in the Insert Date dialog box. Click the Update Automatically on Save check box and then click the OK button.

10. Select the text02 layer in the Layers panel. Hold down the SHIFT key and select the text03 layer. Click Modify on the menu bar, click Align, and then click Left to align both layers to the left. Click the File menu and then click Save As. Type index.htm in the Save As dialog box. Click the Yes button in response to the Macromedia alert dialog box. The Web page is saved as index.htm.

11. Press the F12 key to view the page in your browser. Click each of the links in the navigation bar to verify that they work. Print a copy of the Web page if instructed to do so. Upload the page to the candle Web Site on a remote server if instructed to do so.

In the Lab

Table 7-5	Layer Properties				
LAYER ID	L AND T PROPERTIES	W AND H PROPERTIES	VIS PROPERTY	OVERFLOW PROPERTY	IMAGE/TEXT
text01	15px 145px	385px 40px	visible	visible	We offer the finest in fragrantly scented candles. Each of our candles is hand dipped and hand poured. Our wicks are lead free, and we use only the finest waxes and fragrant oils.
text02	215px 220px	380px 80px	visible	visible	CandleDust candles are available in a variety of types: • Decorative • Gel • Holiday • Pillar • Scented • Texture • Votive
text03	215px 500px	370px 60px	visible	visible	Our candles make a perfect gift for occasions such as weddings, birthdays, holidays, anniversaries, or any time of the year.
date	25px 580px	155px 65px	visible	visible	Your name and date object

2 Modifying the Questions Web Page for the Credit Protection Web Site

Problem: Marcy would like to add more interaction to the Credit Protection Web site and has asked you for ideas. You suggest that the questions.htm page could be revised so when the question is clicked, the answer to the question is displayed. Marcy likes your suggestion and you agree to revise the page. The revised page is shown in Figure 7-80 and shows one of the answers after the question is clicked. Appendix D contains instructions for uploading your local site to a remote server. For a selection of images and backgrounds, visit the Dreamweaver MX Media Web page (scsite.com/dreamweavermx/media) and then click Media below Project 7.

Instructions: Perform the following tasks:

1. Start Dreamweaver. Display the Property inspector, Standard toolbar, Site panel, Layers panel, Behaviors panel, and Insert bar.
2. Use Dreamweaver's integrated file browser to copy the data file and the images from the Data Files folder to your credit folder and credit Images folder. The data files contain a file named questions01.htm. You will revise this file and then save it as questions.htm.
3. Open the questions01.htm file. Position the insertion point below the horizontal line, type Wondering about your credit? Click any of the following questions to find some answers., and then press the ENTER key.
4. Click the Draw Layer button in the Insert bar and use the rulers as a guide to draw a layer with the following properties: Layer ID – questions; L 25px, T 195px; W 305px, H 220px; click the Vis box arrow and then click visible. Drag the questions.gif from the Site panel onto the questions layer.

(continued)

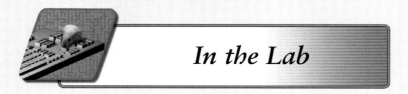

In the Lab

Modifying the Questions Web Page for the Credit Protection Web Site *(continued)*

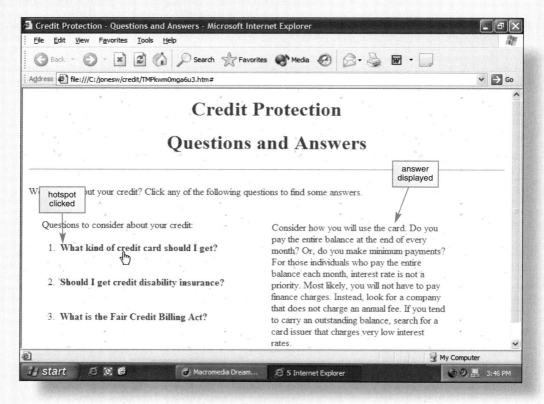

FIGURE 7-80

5. Draw three more layers. Use the rulers as a guide to draw the lawers. Use Table 7-6 for the properties for each layer. After you create each layer, type the text as listed under the text column.

6. Select the questions image and then draw a rectangular hotspot over the first question. With the hotspot selected, click the Actions button in the Behaviors panel and then click Show-Hide Layers on the Actions pop-up menu. Show layer "questions" and layer "quest01". Hide layers "quest02" and "quest03". Use the default onClick event.

7. Draw a second rectangular hotspot over the second question. With the hotspot selected, click the Actions button in the Behaviors panel and then click Show-Hide Layers on the Actions pop-up menu. Show layer "questions" and layer "quest02". Hide layers "quest01" and "quest03". Use the default onClick event.

8. Draw a third rectangular hotspot over the third question. With the hotspot selected, click the Actions button in the Behaviors panel and then click Show-Hide Layers on the Actions pop-up menu. Show layer "questions" and layer "quest03". Hide layers "quest01" and "quest02". Use the default onClick event.

9. Click File on the menu bar and then click Save As. Type `questions.htm` in the Save As dialog box. Click the Yes button in response to the Macromedia alert dialog box. The Web page is saved as questions.htm.

10. Press the F12 key to view the page in your browser. Click each of the hotspots to verify that they work correctly. Print a copy of the Web page if instructed to do so. Upload the page to the credit Web site on a remote server if instructed to do so.

In the Lab

Table 7-6	Layer Properties			
LAYER ID	**L/T IN PX**	**W/H IN PX**	**VIS**	**TEXT**
quest01	400/200	280/205	hidden	Consider how you will use the card. Do you pay the entire balance at the end of every month? Or, do you make minimum payments? For those individuals who pay the entire balance each month, interest rate is not a priority. Most likely, you will not have to pay finance charges. Instead, look for a company that does not charge an annual fee. If you tend to carry an outstanding balance, search for a card issuer that charges very low interest rates.
quest02	400/255	275/145	hidden	Credit disability insurance pays off your credit card bills if you become unable to work. Many credit card and direct mail companies offer this type of insurance. The insurance is generally very expensive. If you are in good health, a broader policy would probably be a better option.
quest03	400/300	285/160	hidden	The Fair Credit Billing Act is a federal law that determines how billing errors and disputes involving credit and charge cards are handled. If you check the back of your monthly statement, generally you will find information about this process. If the company violates any provision of the law, you can sue to recover any damages.

3 Creating a Layered Page for the Plant City Web Site

Problem: Juan wants to add some interactivity to the Plant City Web site. You suggest to Juan that a navigation bar on the index page would be a good addition and that a different layout for the recipes page would enhance the overall site. Juan likes your ideas, and you are ready to get started. The revised pages are shown in Figures 7-81a and Figure 7-81b.

1. Start Dreamweaver. Display the Property inspector, Standard toolbar, Site panel, and Insert bar.
2. Use Dreamweaver's integrated file browser to copy the images from the Data Files folder to your city Images folder.
3. Open the index.htm page. Delete the links at the end of the page and then select and delete the horizontal rule at the top of the page. Click below heading 2, The Strawberry Capital of the United States. If necessary, center the insertion point.

(continued)

In the Lab

Creating a Layered Page for the Plant City Web Site *(continued)*

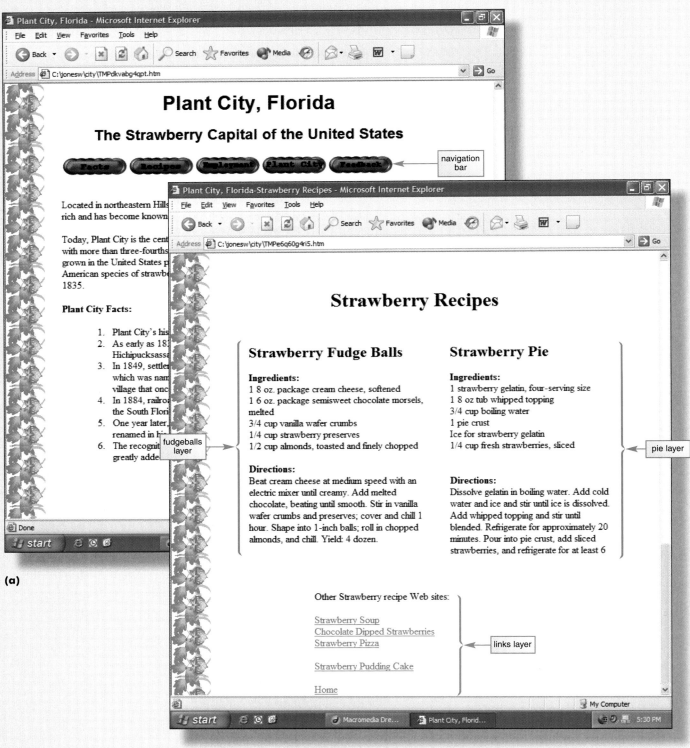

(a)

(b)

FIGURE 7-81

In the Lab

4. Click the Insert menu, point to Interactive Images, and then click Navigation Bar on the Interactive Images submenu. In the Insert Navigation Bar dialog box, verify that Horizontally and Use Tables are selected. Use the data in Table 7-7 to create the Navigation Bar.

Table 7-7	Data for Navigation Bar				
ELEMENT NAME	UP IMAGE	OVER IMAGE	DOWN IMAGE	ALTERNATE TEXT	WHEN CLICKED, GO TO URL
Facts	facts01.gif	facts02.gif	facts02.gif	Plant City facts	facts.htm
Recipes	recipes01.gif	recipes02.gif	recipes02.gif	Strawberry recipes	recipes.htm
Employment	employ01.gif	employ02.gif	employ02.gif	Employment	employment.htm
Plant City	pc01.gif	pc02.gif	pc02.gif	Plant City city Web site	http://www.ci.plant-city.fl.us/
Feedback	feedback01.gif	feedback02.gif	feedback02.gif	feedback form	guest_form.htm

5. After inserting the Navigation bar, press the F12 key and verify that the navigation bar links work. Click the Save button on the Standard toolbar and then close the index.htm page.

6. Open the recipes.htm Web page. Select and delete the two horizontal rules on the page. Select and cut the first recipe (Strawberry Fudge Balls). Display the rulers and then move the origin point about 125px to the right and down about 150px. Draw a layer with the following properties: Layer ID – fudgeballs; L – 125px, T – 150px; W – 295px, H – 335px; Vis – Visible.

7. Click in the layer and then click the Paste button on the Standard toolbar to paste the recipe into the layer.

8. Click to the right of the fudgeballs layer and draw a second layer with the following properties: Layer ID – pie; L – 455px, T – 150px; W – 295px, H – 335px; Vis – Visible.

9. Select and cut the Strawberry Pie recipe and then paste it into the layer.

10. Click below the first two layers and then draw a third layer with the following properties: Layer ID – links; L – 230px, T – 525px; W – 295px, H – 335px; Vis – Visible. Cut and paste the Other Strawberry recipe Web sites text and the links into this layer.

11. Press the F12 key to view the page in your browser. Print a copy of the Web page if instructed to do so. Upload the page to the city Web site on a remote server if instructed to do so. For a selection of images and backgrounds, visit the Dreamweaver MX Media Web page (scsite.com/dreamweavermx/media) and then click Media below Project 7.

Cases and Places

The difficulty of these case studies varies:
▶ are the least difficult; ▶▶ are more difficult; and ▶▶▶ are the most difficult.

1   ▶   You would like to add some interactivity to your sports Web site. You have looked at some other Web sites and are impressed with navigation bars. You decide to modify the index page and add a navigation bar to your sports Web site. You also decide to add the Date object so the date will be updated automatically when you save the page. Create a navigation bar for your sports site. Determine if a vertical or horizontal bar will best fit your needs. Then insert the Date object at the end of the page.

2   ▶   Your hobby Web page has become very popular and you want to give it a more professional look. One object you can add is a navigation bar. Determine if a vertical or horizontal bar will best suit your particular Web page. Next, use layers to create a new layout for one of your pages. Determine which page in your Web site you will revise and then add at least four layers to the page. Name each layer and place it appropriately on the page. Add images and/or text to the layers. Upload to a remote site if instructed to do so.

3   ▶▶   You are receiving a lot of e-mail about what a great Web site you have for your music hobby. You decide to make it more interactive by adding a navigation bar on the index page, adding a layer with an image map, and then adding two additional layers. Create the navigation bar and then create the three layers — the first one with the image map and the other two displaying images related to your music site. Add hotspots to your image map to show and hide the two images. Upload the revised pages to a remote site.

4   ▶▶   Polls indicate that you are the favorite to win your political campaign. You want to add a new page to the site that will provide some interactivity and give the page a professional look. Add a navigation bar to the index page. Next, add another page with additional text information and then add a layer for an image map. Add at least two additional layers with pictures of yourself campaigning. Add hotspots to the image map to hide and show the pictures. Upload the revised and new pages to a remote server.

5   ▶▶▶   The student trips Web site still is receiving numerous hits, and the debate about which location for the trip is continuing. Add a new page to the Web site. Include a navigation bar that will link to various Web sites providing information about three different possible vacation spots. Then, add at least four layers to the Web site. The first layer will contain a map of the United States. The other three layers will contain pictures of possible trip locations. Add hotspots to the image map on the individual states and then add the Show-Hide Layers action. Upload the new pages to a remote server.

Macromedia Dreamweaver MX

Animation and Behaviors

You will have mastered the material in this project when you can:

OBJECTIVES

- Describe a timeline
- Describe the Timelines panel
- Create a nonlinear timeline
- Add a behavior to a layer
- Add a play button to a timeline
- Create a linear timeline
- Add a layer to a timeline
- Show and hide a layer
- Play an animation

Macromedia Dreamweaver MX

Animation and Behaviors

CASE PERSPECTIVE

Adding interactivity to Web pages makes visiting and surfing Web sites interesting. Will Jones thinks it would be a good idea to add some animation to the Parks Web site. Now that he understands how to use layers and behaviors, he wants to add animation using these Dreamweaver features. He comes to you for help in utilizing these more advanced concepts. You explain that Dreamweaver provides the capability of adding animation by using layers through the Timelines panel.

The next decision is where within the Web site to add the animation and what will be the focus of the animated page. Joan suggests that this be a project similar to the spotlight page previously added to the site. Instead of a static page, however, the Web page will contain a slide show where the viewer controls the display of images of various state parks. Joan further suggests that a second page be added to the site. The second page would contain a map focused on one part of the state and include the names and locations of the parks. The map would contain an image such as a motor home that moves across the northwest part of the state from park to park. Everyone on the team agrees that both of these pages would be a great addition to the site.

Introduction

In Project 7, you applied some simple animation techniques when you learned about layers and behaviors and how to show and hide layers. Project 8 continues with the layer feature and introduces the integration of layers and timelines using the Dreamweaver Timelines panel. You can use timelines in three ways:

- To alter a layer's position, size, visibility, and depth
- To apply Dreamweaver's JavaScript behaviors
- To change the source for any image and replace it with another

Using this feature, the layers and images can be manipulated over time. Thus, adding layers and applying behaviors to the layers within a timeline provide the Web site designer the ability to add interactivity and animation to a Web site.

A **timeline** is similar to a strip of movie film. Just like movies, animation requires movement and time. A timeline is made up of frames. Each **frame** represents a moment in time, similar to that in a movie or video. A collection of frames makes a timeline. The Web site developer also can control the speed of the timeline or how fast the frames play. The default is 15 **fps**, or frames per second. If you decrease the number of fps, the animation takes longer to play; increase the number of fps and the animation plays faster.

Because timelines depend on layers, they require version 4 or later browsers. Some features work only in Internet Explorer. Only layers and images can be added to the Dreamweaver Timeline, and only layers can be positioned. Using the timeline feature to add animation is a valuable tool that captures the interest of Web site visitors.

Project Eight — Creating Timeline Animation

In this project, you learn how to use Dreamweaver's Timelines panel and to add animation to the Florida Parks Web site. You begin the project by adding a new page to the Web site containing a map of northwest Florida (Figure 8-1a). A layer is added to the page and an image of a motor coach is embedded in the layer. Clicking a Forward button on the page moves the motor coach image over the map from one park location to another. This animation is created by dragging the image to create a nonlinear **animation path**. Dreamweaver automatically records the path, but does not record the timing of the drag operation. You specify these movements through the **Timelines panel**. Therefore, you can take your time to make sure that the path is what you want.

The second page added to the Web site is a slide show presentation (Figure 8-1b on the next page). The Web site visitor controls the display of the slide show by clicking a Forward button. The six slides within the slide show correspond to the park names displayed on the northwest Florida map and the motor coach path you create for the first page. You create this second animation using a linear, or straight-line, animation technique.

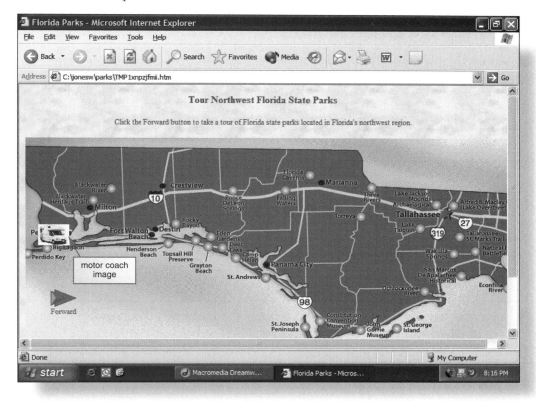

(a) Map Web Page

FIGURE 8-1

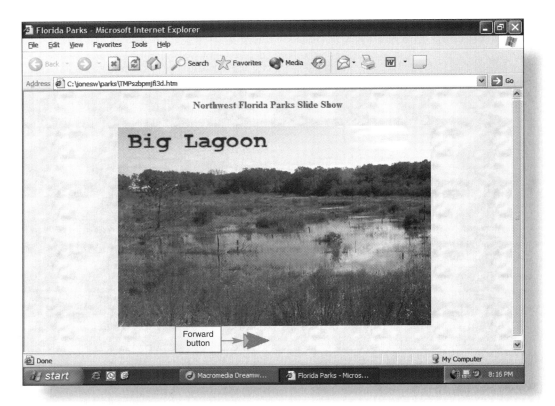

(b) Slide Show Web Page

FIGURE 8-1 *(continued)*

Workspace Organization

Organization and preparation lead to a more productive work setting. Successful Web site developers prepare their Dreamweaver workspace to provide an efficient work environment. As you learn to use additional Dreamweaver tools, including layers and the Timelines panel, you will become even more proficient working in the Dreamweaver environment.

Starting Dreamweaver and Closing Open Panels

When you start Dreamweaver, generally most or all of the panels are displayed by default. Closing unused panels provides uncluttered workspace in the Document window. To organize your workspace, you close the unused open panels. This gives you the maximum window space in the Dreamweaver Document window. Start Dreamweaver and close open panels using the following steps.

TO START DREAMWEAVER AND CLOSE OPEN PANELS

1 Start Dreamweaver. If necessary, maximize the Document window. Press the F4 key to close all open panels.

2 Press the F8 key to display the Site panel. Select the Florida Parks Web site. Press the F2 key to display the Layers panel.

3 If necessary, use the View menu to display the Standard toolbar.

4 Use the Window menu to display the Property inspector (Figure 8-2).

The Site panel, Layers panel, Standard toolbar, and Property inspector are displayed (Figure 8-2).

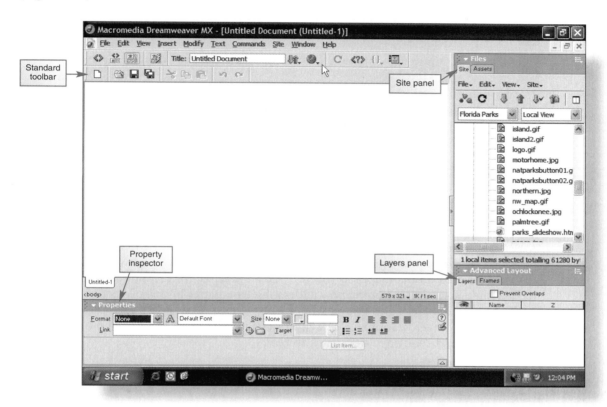

FIGURE 8-2

Copying Data Files to the Local Web Site

Your Data Disk contains an Images folder and two data files for Project 8. The Images folder and data files are located in the Proj08 folder. You use Dreamweaver's integrated file browser to copy the Project 8 images and the data files to the Florida Parks folder.

The Data Files folder for this project is stored on Local Disk (C:). The location on your computer may be different. If necessary, verify with your instructor the location of the Data Files folder. Complete the following steps to copy the files and folder to the C:\jonesw\parks local root folder using the same procedure as in previous projects.

TO COPY DATA FILES TO THE FLORIDA PARKS WEB SITE

1 Click the plus sign (+) to the left of the Desktop icon in the Site panel. Click the plus sign to the left of the My Computer icon and then navigate through the file hierarchy to the Data Files folder as you did in Project 2 on pages DW 2.09–14.

2 Click the plus sign to the left of the Proj08 folder and then click the plus sign to the left of the parks folder.

> **3** Click the plus sign to the left of the Images folder.
>
> **4** Click big_lagoon.jpg (or the first file in the list). Hold down the SHIFT key and then click wakulla.gif (or the last file in the folder if your files are sorted in a different order).
>
> **5** Copy the images to the jonesw/parks/Images folder using the Copy and Paste commands on the context menu.
>
> **6** Copy the slideshow.htm and tour.htm files to the jonesw/parks folder.
>
> **7** Click the minus sign to the left of the Desktop icon to collapse the file list.

After completing step 6, the Project 8 images are pasted into the parks/Images local root folder, and the two data files are copied into the /parks folder.

Preparing the Web Page

Creating an animation in Dreamweaver requires some Document window preparation before creating the actual animation. To prepare the Web page requires that images and a layer be added.

To begin the preparation for the tour.htm page, you first add a map of northwest Florida. The map contains the name and location of each park. Highways and roadways are marked on the map and will provide a guideline for creating a nonlinear animation path. Creating the animation path is discussed later in this project. Animations are built around images and layers, which requires that a layer be added to the map and within that layer is an image of a motor coach. The layer and image move along the highways and roadways from park to park.

Steps To Add the NW Florida Map Image and Layer

1 Close the Untitled-1 document. Open the tour.htm document. If necessary, click below the introductory paragraph.

The tour.htm page is displayed in the Document window and the insertion point is centered below the introductory paragraph (Figure 8-3).

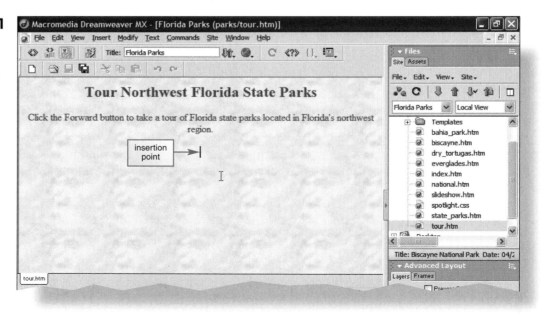

FIGURE 8-3

2 Open the Images folder, drag the nw_map.gif to the Document window insertion point, and then click the image to select it. Click the Alt box in the Image Property inspector and then type NW Florida map as the alternate text.

The nw_map image is displayed and selected. The Property inspector for images is displayed (Figure 8-4). The Alt box contains the text, NW Florida map.

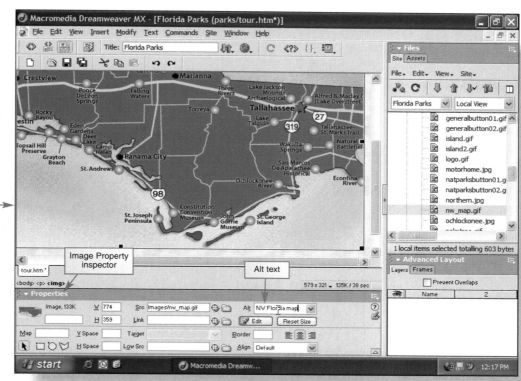

FIGURE 8-4

3 Close the Property inspector. Click Insert on the menu bar and then click Layer. If necessary, use the Document window horizontal scroll bar to scroll to the left.

A layer is added to the Document window and Layer1 is displayed in the Layers panel (Figure 8-5).

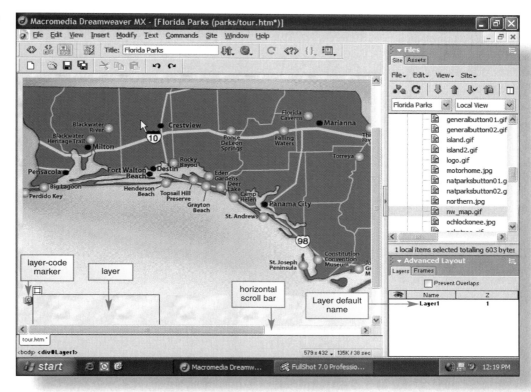

FIGURE 8-5

4 Double-click the Layer1 name in the Layers panel. Type motortour for the layer name and then press the ENTER key.

Layer1 is now named motortour and the layer is selected (Figure 8-6).

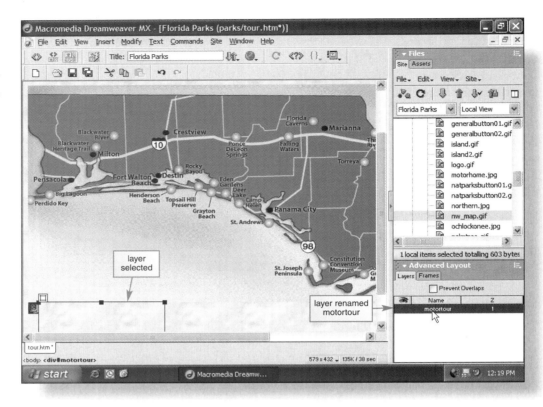

FIGURE 8-6

5 Click the motortour layer selection handle and drag the layer so that it is placed above Big Lagoon on the map.

The motortour layer is displayed on the map (Figure 8-7).

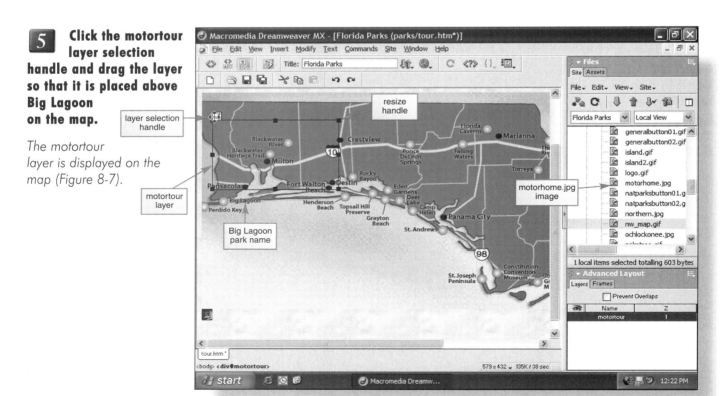

FIGURE 8-7

6 Click inside the motortour layer and then drag the motorhome image from the Site panel onto the layer. Point to the expander arrow on the Files panel group.

The motorhome image is displayed in the layer (Figure 8-8).

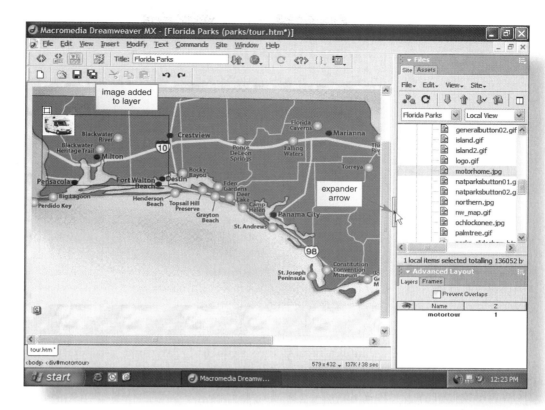

FIGURE 8-8

7 Click the expander arrow to collapse the Files panel group and then click a resize handle on the motortour layer. Resize the layer to fit the motorhome image. Click the layer selection handle and then drag the layer so that it is placed above and in close proximity to the Big Lagoon park name.

The Files panel group is collapsed, and the layer is resized and placed close to the Big Lagoon park name (Figure 8-9).

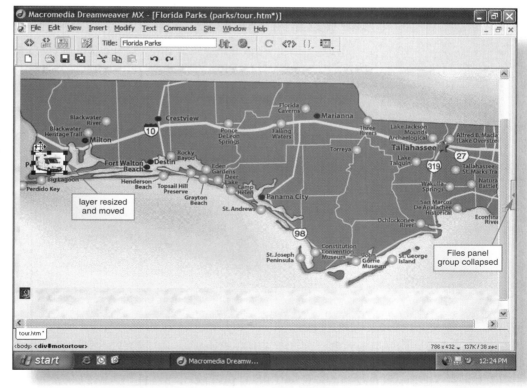

FIGURE 8-9

Other Ways

1. On Window menu click Insert, click Draw Layer button on Layout tab

Introduction to Timelines

Timelines use dynamic HTML (DHTML) to change the position of a layer or the source of an image over time or to call behavior actions automatically after the page has loaded. (See page DW 7.06 for a detailed discussion of DHTML.) The timeline is the critical component for creating animation in a Web page. This Dreamweaver feature lets the Web site developer create animations that do not require plug-ins, ActiveX controls, or Java. As the Web site developer, you can choose to control the animation or you can add controls that let the Web site visitor control the animation.

Timeline Features

A timeline is composed of a series of frames. A **frame** is one cell or one point of time in a timeline. The total number of frames in the timeline determines the length of the presentation. You can create multiple animations on a Web page. The animations all can be contained within one timeline or spread out over several timelines. A single timeline can contain up to 32 individual layers.

As you create the animation, Dreamweaver converts the timeline commands into JavaScript and thus creates the animation. Layers and images are the only objects that can be added to a timeline. Anything you add to a layer, however, can be animated, whether it is text, images, forms, tables or other objects. A basic animation moves from one point on the timeline to another. Any animation created in the timeline must have a start and stop point. These start and stop points are marked on the timeline by small circles and are called **keyframes**. Keyframes are discussed in more detail throughout this project.

The Timelines Panel

The Web site developer uses the **Timelines panel** to create animation. The Timelines panel resembles a spreadsheet somewhat, showing units of time as columns and animated objects as rows. Figure 8-10a shows an overall view of the Timelines panel and Figure 8-10b shows a view of the playback options and command buttons for viewing the animation.

The following section describes the Timelines panel (Figure 8-10a).

Timelines

To display a list of commands that can be applied to timelines, click the Timelines panel menu button. For more information about timelines, visit the Dreamweaver MX More About Web page (scsite.com/dreamweavermx/more.htm) and then click Timelines.

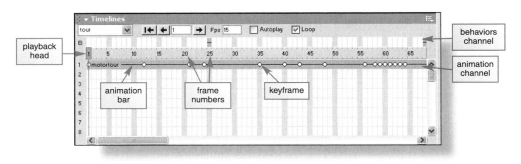

(a) Timelines Panel

FIGURE 8-10

ANIMATION BAR The animation bar shows the duration of each object's animation. A single row can include multiple bars representing different objects. Different bars cannot control the same object in the same frame.

ANIMATION CHANNEL The animation channel contains the bars for animating layers and images.

BEHAVIORS CHANNEL The behaviors channel executes behaviors along a channel at a particular frame in the timeline.

FRAME A frame is one cell or one point of time in a timeline. The total number of frames in the timeline determines the length of the presentation.

FRAME NUMBERS The frame numbers indicate the sequential numbering of frames. The number between the Back and Play buttons is the current frame number. The Web site developer controls the duration of animation by setting the total number of frames and the number of frames per second (fps). The default setting is 15 frames per second.

KEYFRAME A keyframe contains specific properties (such as position) for an object; small circles indicate keyframes.

PLAYBACK HEAD The playback head indicates which frame of the timeline currently is displayed in the Document window.

TIMELINE POP-UP MENU The Timeline pop-up menu contains names of a document's recent timelines; the Timeline pop-up menu text box displays which of the document's timelines currently appears in the Timelines panel.

The timeline contains several playback options and command buttons. You can use the command buttons to preview and control an animation in the Document window. The following section describes the playback options and command buttons (Figure 8-10b) within the Timelines panel. The buttons are similar to the controls on a VCR.

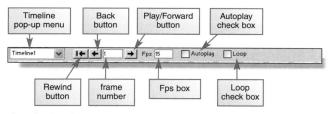

(b) Playback Options

FIGURE 8-10 (continued)

AUTOPLAY When checked, a timeline begins playing automatically when the current page loads in a browser. Autoplay attaches a behavior to the page's body tag that executes the Play Timeline action when the page loads.

BACK The Back button moves the playback head one frame to the left. Play the timeline backward by clicking the Back button and holding down the mouse button.

LOOP When the Loop check box is selected, the current timeline loops indefinitely while the page is open in a browser. Loop inserts the Go to Timeline Frame behavior in the behaviors channel after the last frame of the animation.

PLAY/FORWARD The Play/Forward button moves the playback head one frame to the right. Play the timeline forward by clicking the Play button and holding down the mouse button.

REWIND The Rewind button moves the playback head to the first frame in the timeline.

Nonlinear Animations

The most common kind of timeline animation involves moving a layer along a path. Using layers and the Timelines panel, you can create linear, or straight-line, animations and nonlinear animations. A **nonlinear animation** is one that does not follow a straight path. Creating a linear, or straight-line, animation is discussed later in this project.

To create a layer with a complex path for a nonlinear animation, it is easier to drag the layer rather than creating individual keyframes. Earlier in this project, you added a northwest Florida map image to the tours Web page, added and resized a layer, and then added the motorhome image to the layer. The object of the animation is to create a path where the motorhome image moves to the right across the page via the path, then up and then back to the left to its original position. The roadways and highways are used as a guideline for this animated movement.

To create this animation, you drag the layer containing the motorhome image. This is a freeform exercise, so the path on which you drag the image will vary somewhat from the path as shown in Figure 8-16(a–f) on pages DW 8.15–8.16.

Complete the following steps to add the nonlinear animation path to the tours.htm Web page. As you are creating this animation, you will find it necessary to expand and collapse the Timelines panel and the Files panel group to provide maximum Document window visibility. You also will find that at times you will have to scroll horizontally and vertically within the Document window to redisplay the motorhome image. When dragging this image, a thin grey line will indicate the path you are creating. Recall that Dreamweaver automatically records the path, but does not record the timing of the drag operation. You control the timing through the Timelines panel.

 Steps **To Create a Nonlinear Animation**

1 Press ALT+F9 to display the Timelines Panel. If necessary, click the Timelines panel expand/ collapse arrow to expand the Timeline. Point to the Timeline pop-up menu text box.

The Timelines panel is displayed (Figure 8-11).

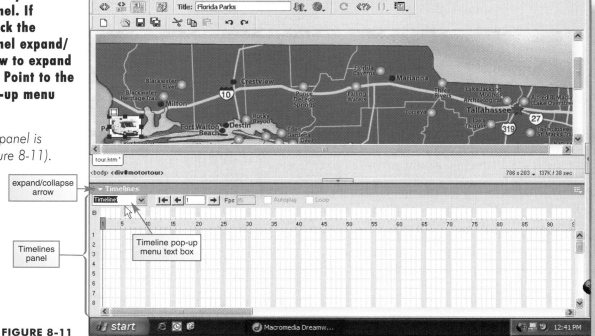

expand/collapse arrow

Timelines panel

Timeline pop-up menu text box

FIGURE 8-11

2 **Click the Timeline text box, and then delete the default name. Type** tour **for the timeline name, and then press the TAB key.**

The timeline is renamed tour (Figure 8-12).

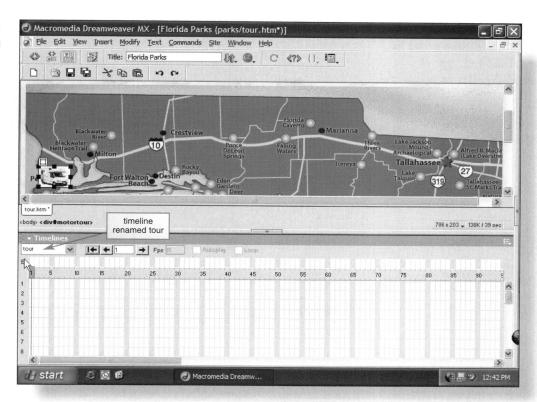

FIGURE 8-12

3 **If necessary, select the motortour layer in the Document window and then right-click the selected motortour layer. Point to Record Path on the context menu.**

The motortour layer is selected and the context menu is displayed (Figure 8-13).

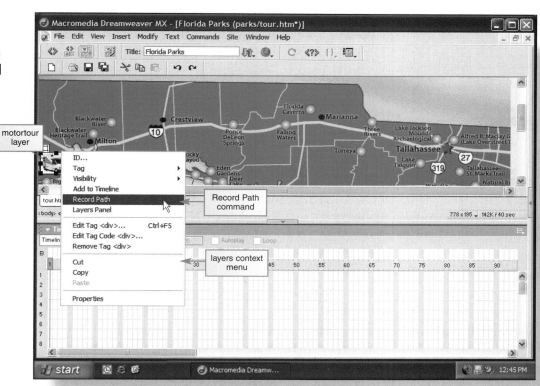

FIGURE 8-13

4 **Click Record Path and then point to the Timelines panel expand/collapse arrow.**

The motortour layer is selected and the Record Path command is active (Figure 8-14).

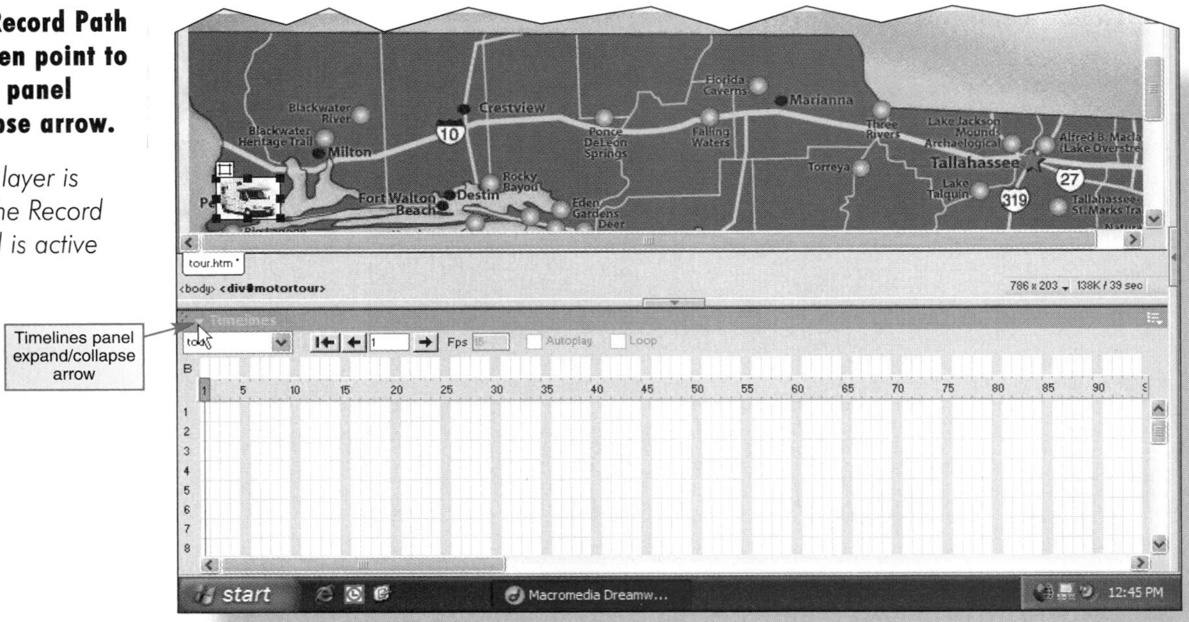

Timelines panel expand/collapse arrow

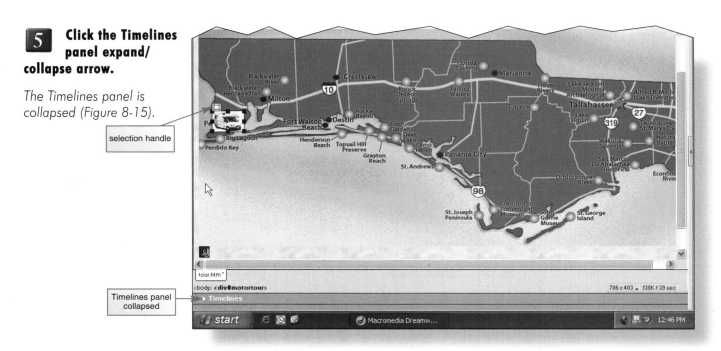

FIGURE 8-14

5 **Click the Timelines panel expand/collapse arrow.**

The Timelines panel is collapsed (Figure 8-15).

selection handle

Timelines panel collapsed

FIGURE 8-15

6 Click the motortour layer selection handle and then drag it east (right) on Highway 98 to Rocky Bayou, then to St. George Island, north (up) to Highway 319 and Wakulla Springs, north and then west (left) on Highway 10 to Three Rivers, continuing west to Ponce DeLeon Springs, and ending back at Big Lagoon. Do not release the mouse button while dragging. Figures 8-16a through 8-16f on pages DW 8.15 and 8.16 show the motortour layer as it is being dragged to each of the park sites. If a Dreamweaver dialog box displays, read the information and then click the OK button.

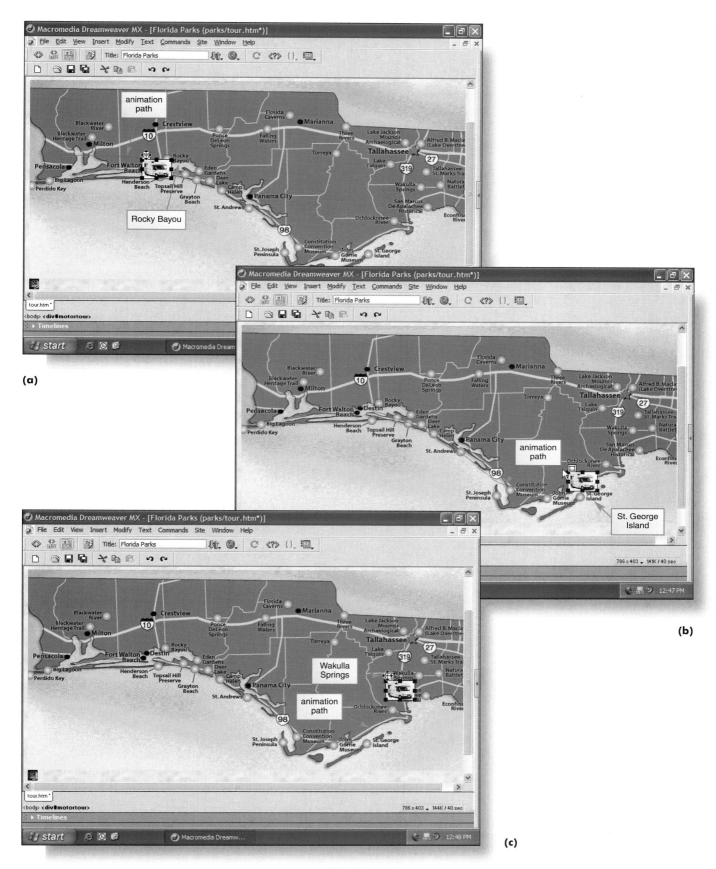

(a)

(b)

(c)

FIGURE 8-16

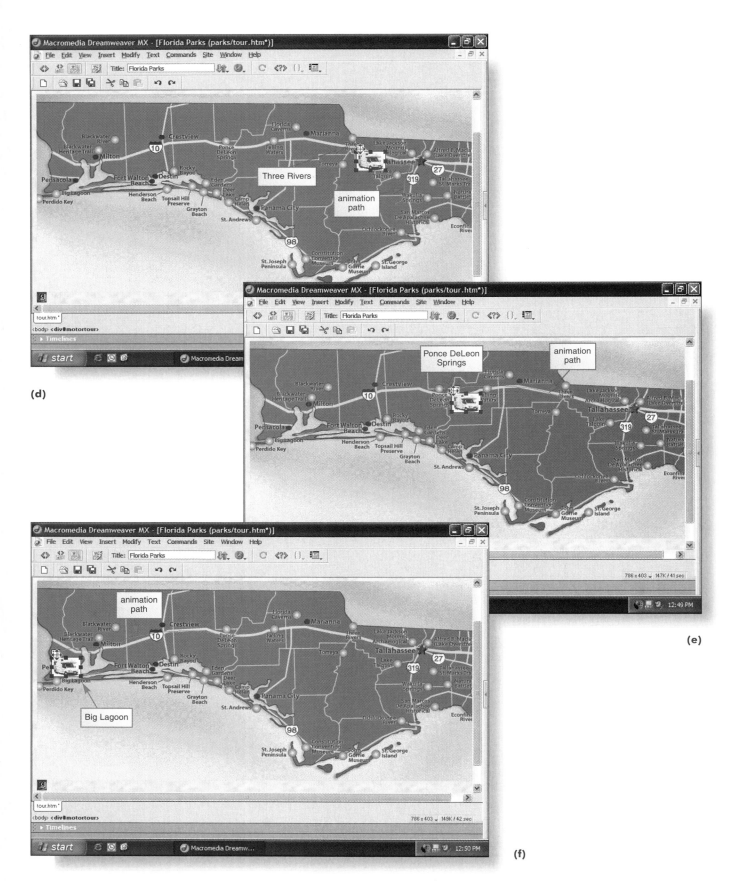

FIGURE 8-16 *(continued)*

7 **Click the Timelines panel expand/collapse arrow to expand the Timelines panel. Point to the Autoplay check box in the Timelines panel.**

A timeline has been added to the animation channel in the Timelines panel. A thin grey line on the image map shows the image drag path (Figure 8-17). The timeline is selected in the animation channel. Several keyframes are added to the timeline. These keyframes were added when you hesitated or dragged the timeline in a nonlinear line. The timeline on your screen will be somewhat different and the keyframes will be in different frames. Viewing the entire timeline requires that you scroll to the right in the Timelines panel.

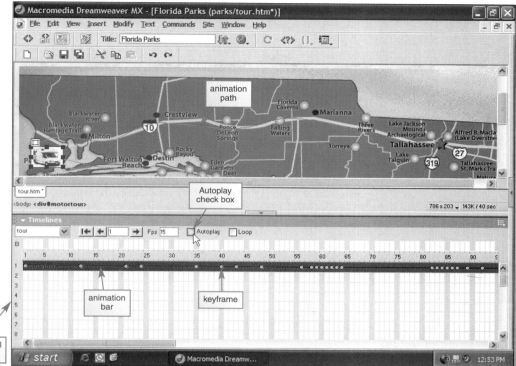

FIGURE 8-17

8 **Click the Autoplay check box. If a Dreamweaver dialog box is displayed, read the information, and then click the OK button. Click the Save button on the Standard toolbar. Press the F12 key to view the animation in your browser. Close the browser and return to Dreamweaver.**

The motorhome image travels across the map and returns to its original position.

Editing a Timeline

As you are creating a timeline, occasionally you will need to edit different features. The following provides editing information for frames, timelines, behaviors, and animation channels.

- To add or remove frames in the timeline, click the frame, right-click the timeline, and then click Remove Frame or Add Frame on the context menu.
- To remove or rename a timeline, click the timeline to select it, right-click the timeline, and then click Remove Timeline or Rename Timeline on the context menu.
- To remove a behavior from the Timelines panel, right-click the behavior in the behaviors channel and then click Remove Behavior on the context menu.
- To remove a keyframe, select the keyframe and then press SHIFT+F6.
- To remove an animation channel, select it in the Timelines panel, right-click the animation channel, and then click Delete on the context menu.

Other Ways

1. On Window menu point to Others, click Timelines on Others submenu to display Timelines panel

Adding Behaviors to the Timeline

In Project 7, you learned about behaviors and how to add behaviors to show and hide objects. These behaviors are ready-to-use Dreamweaver-created JavaScript functions. The available functions vary based on the selected object. You also can add behaviors to your timeline animations. Examples of behaviors you can add to a timeline include sound, pop-up messages, showing and hiding layers, starting and stopping timelines, and other events. To add a pop-up message, for example, select the object, click the Actions (+) button in the Behaviors panel, and then click Popup Message. Type the message in the Popup Message dialog box and then click the OK button.

Complete the following steps to add Stop Timeline behaviors to the tour timeline. You add a Stop Timeline behavior at each of the six parks listed in the previous steps. Keep in mind that this is a freeform exercise and that the frame numbers in the Timelines panel in the following figures most likely will not match those on your screen.

Steps To Add the Stop Timeline Behavior

1 If necessary, scroll down in the Document window so that the Rocky Bayou park name is displayed. If necessary, click the motortour layer so that the selection handle is displayed. Click frame 25 in the animation channel to move the motortour layer so that it is close to the Rocky Bayou park name. If necessary, click other frame numbers until the motortour layer is in close proximity to the Rocky Bayou park name. Use the Document window vertical scroll bar as necessary to reposition the image so that the motortour layer is displayed.

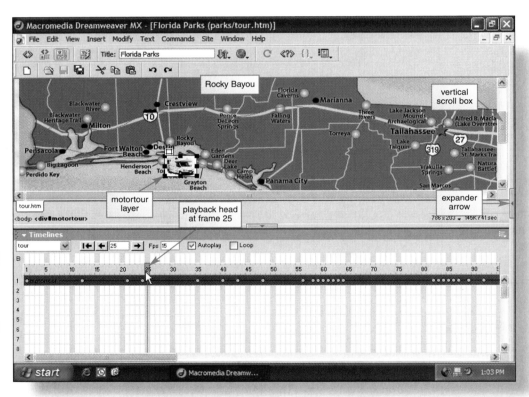

FIGURE 8-18

The motortour layer moves based on the selected frame number and is positioned in close proximity to the Rocky Bayou park name. The playback head is in frame 25 in the animation channel (Figure 8-18). The location of the motortour layer and the frame number on your screen most likely will be different.

2 Click the Files panel group expander arrow and then, if necessary, press SHIFT+F3 to display the Design panel group and the Behaviors panel. Point to the frame number in the timeline behaviors channel that is the same number as the one in the animation channel on your screen. In Figure 8-19, this is frame 25. Most likely the frame number on your screen will be a different number.

The Files panel group is expanded and the Behaviors panel is displayed (Figure 8-19).

FIGURE 8-19

3 Click frame 25 (or your selected frame) in the behaviors channel and then point to the Actions (+) button in the Behaviors panel.

Frame 25 is selected in the behaviors channel (Figure 8-20). Most likely the frame number on your screen will be different.

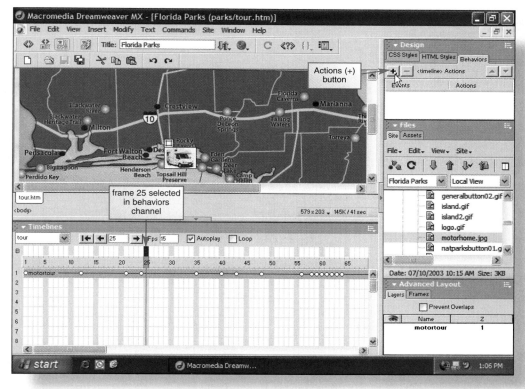

FIGURE 8-20

4 Click the Actions (+) button, point to Timeline on the Actions pop-up menu and then point to Stop Timeline on the Timeline submenu.

The Actions pop-up menu is displayed and the Stop Timeline command is selected (Figure 8-21).

FIGURE 8-21

5 Click Stop Timeline. In the Stop Timeline dialog box, click the Stop Timeline box arrow and then point to tour.

The Stop Timeline dialog box is displayed and tour is highlighted (Figure 8-22).

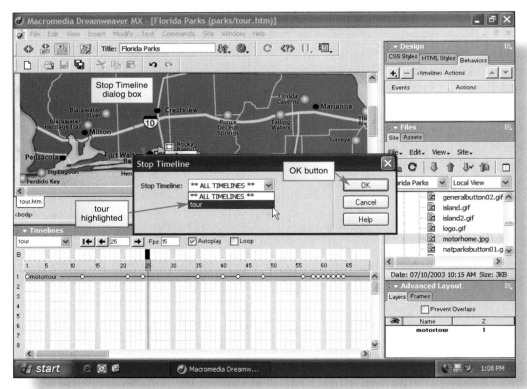

FIGURE 8-22

6 **Click tour and then click the OK button.**

The Stop Time behavior is added to the Behaviors panel and a minus sign is displayed in frame 25 in the behaviors channel (Figure 8-23). Most likely the frame number for the behaviors channel on your screen will be different.

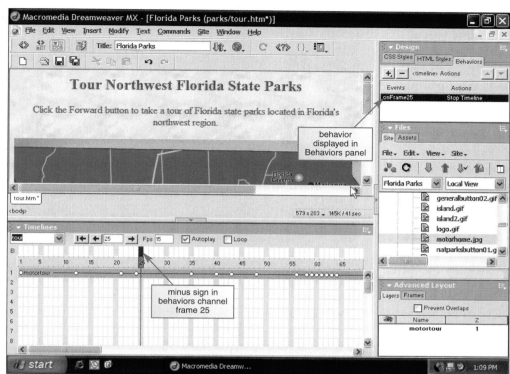

FIGURE 8-23

7 **Click the Files panel group** expander arrow to collapse the Site panel. Scroll down in the Document window to display the motortour layer and the St. George Island park name. Click frame 68 in the animation channel to move the motortour layer so that it is close to the St. George park name. Use the vertical scroll bar as needed to reposition the image so that the motortour layer and St. George park name are displayed. If necessary, click other frame numbers until the motortour layer is in close proximity to the St. George park name on your screen.

The motortour layer is positioned in close proximity to the St. George Island park name (Figure 8-24).

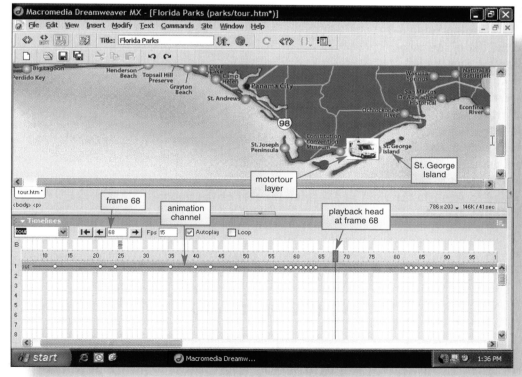

FIGURE 8-24

8 Click the Files panel group expander arrow. If necessary, scroll to the right in the Timelines panel. Click frame 68 (or your selected frame) in the behaviors channel and then click the Actions (+) button in the Behaviors panel. Click Timeline and then click Stop Timeline. Click the Stop Timeline box arrow, click tour, and then click the OK button.

The Stop Timeline behavior is added to the Behaviors panel and a minus sign is displayed in frame 68 (or your selected frame) in the behaviors channel (Figure 8-25).

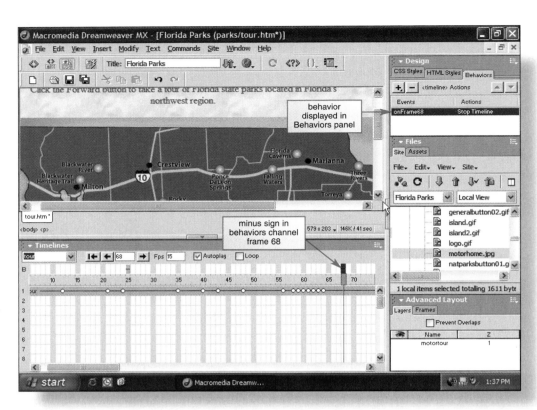

FIGURE 8-25

9 Repeat Steps 7 and 8 using Table 8-1 for the list of the other four park names and the approximate frame number to stop the motortour layer. Modify the frame numbers to fit your timeline. Use the horizontal scroll bar in the Timelines panel as needed to scroll to the right and display the rest of the animation bar in the animation channel.

Table 8-1 Park Names and Frame Numbers	
PARK NAMES	**APPROXIMATE FRAME NUMBER**
Wakulla Springs	Frame 89
Three Rivers	Frame 112
Ponce DeLeon Springs	Frame 136
Big Lagoon	Frame 175

The Stop Timeline behavior is added to each frame close to one of the designated park names.

Controlling the Timeline

With the Stop Timeline behaviors added to the timeline, a method is needed to start the timeline and move from park to park. This is done by adding another layer, adding an image to that layer, and then adding the Start Timeline behavior to the image. Complete the following steps to add the Forward button and the Start Timeline behavior to the tours.htm Web page.

Steps | **To Add a Forward Button**

1 **Click the Timelines expander arrow to collapse the Timelines panel. Use the vertical and horizontal scroll bars to scroll as necessary in the Document window. Click to the right of the layer-code marker, click Insert on the menu bar, and then click Layer.**

A new layer and new layer code-marker are inserted into the Document window (Figure 8-26).

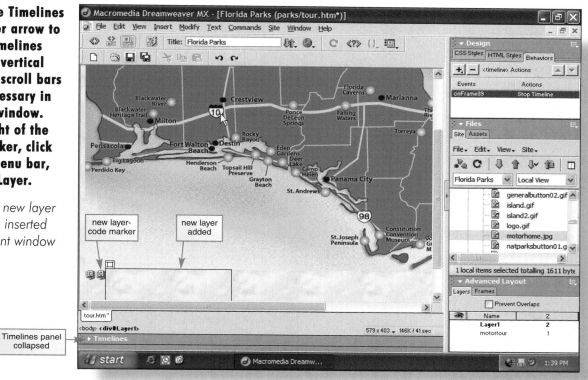

FIGURE 8-26

2 **Double-click the Layer1 name in the Layers panel and rename the layer forward. Click the forward layer selection handle and drag the layer up and onto the nw_map image as shown in Figure 8-27.**

The layer is renamed forward and is displayed on the nw_map image.

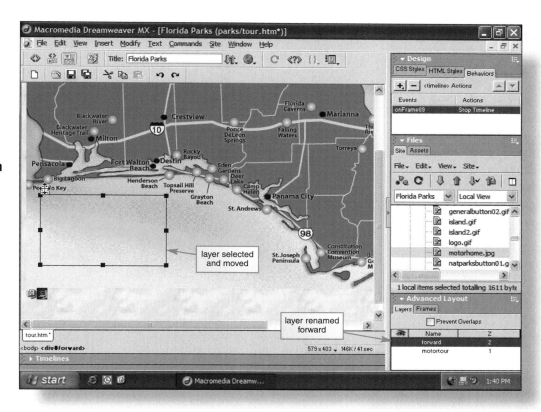

FIGURE 8-27

3 If necessary, open the Images folder in the Site panel and then drag the forward.gif image onto the forward layer. Hold down the SHIFT key and then press the ENTER key. If necessary, click in the layer and then type Forward as the text.

The forward image is displayed in the forward layer (Figure 8-28). The image is named forward.

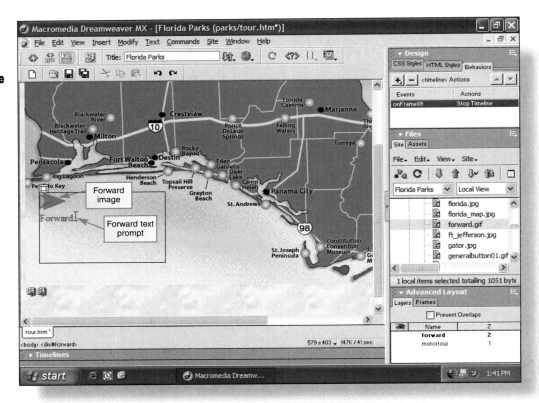

FIGURE 8-28

4 Click a resize handle on the forward layer and then resize the layer around the image. Press CTRL+F3 to display the Property inspector. Set L at 50 and T at 335. Click the Property inspector expand/collapse arrow to collapse the Property inspector; if necessary, scroll down to view the forward layer and image.

The forward layer is resized and the forward layer is selected (Figure 8-29).

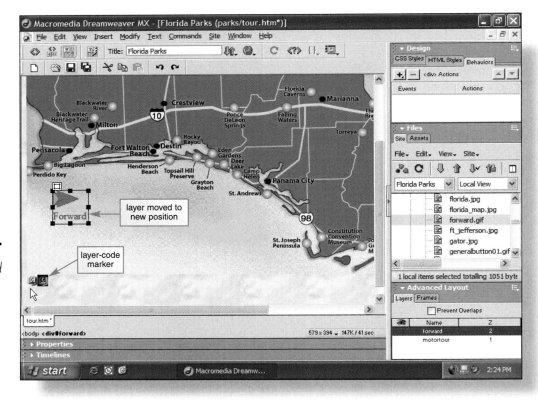

FIGURE 8-29

5 Click the forward image. Click the Actions (+) button in the Behaviors panel, click Timeline, and then click Play Timeline. Click the OK button in the Play Timeline dialog box.

The onMouseOver event and the Play Timeline action are added to the Behaviors panel (Figure 8-30). If the onClick event is displayed instead of the onMouseOver event, see page 8.26.

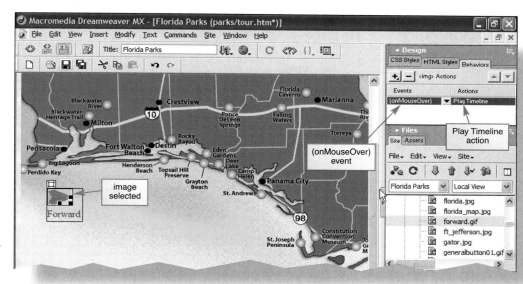

FIGURE 8-30

6 Click the Timelines panel expand/collapse arrow to expand the Timelines panel. Click the Loop check box. If a dialog box displays, read the information, and then click the OK button.

The behavior for the Loop action is added to the Behaviors panel (Figure 8-31). Most likely, the Events frame number in the Behaviors panel on your screen will be different.

7 Press the F12 key to view the animation in your browser. Move the mouse pointer over and then off the Forward button to move the motorhome image along the animation path. Close the browser and return to Dreamweaver.

The motorhome image moves along the animation path and returns to the Big Lagoon starting point.

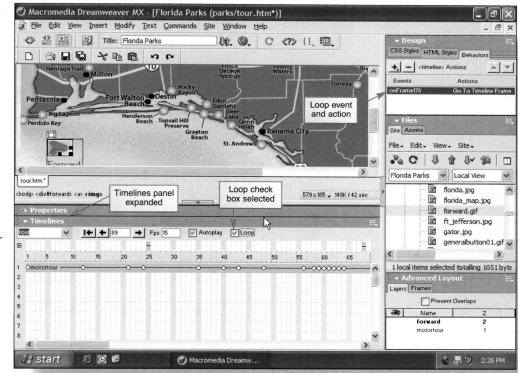

FIGURE 8-31

Animation Speeds

Slow down an animation by increasing the length of the animation bar. Click the last keyframe on the bar and drag right. To speed up an animation, decrease the length of the animation bar.

Changing the onMouseOver Behavior to onClick Behavior

In Project 7, you learned about the onMouseOver and onClick events. When you applied the Show-Hide Layers behavior in Project 7, the onClick action was the default action. With the Play Timeline event, however, the default is onMouseOver. Dreamweaver generally does not provide a drop-down option, such as those with the Show-Hide Layers behavior, to change this from onMouseOver to onClick. In certain instances, however, special features may have been activated within Dreamweaver and the onClick Event is available. If so, then you will not need to complete the next set of steps. To change this event requires that it be changed within the code. To locate and change this event easily, you use Dreamweaver's Find and Replace dialog box. Complete the following steps to change the onMouseOver behavior to onClick.

Steps **To Change the onMouseOver Behavior to the onClick Behavior**

1 **Click the expand/ collapse arrow for the Timelines panel to collapse the Timelines panel. Click the forward.gif image in the forward layer. Point to the Show Code View button on the Document toolbar.**

The Timelines panel is collapsed (Figure 8-32).

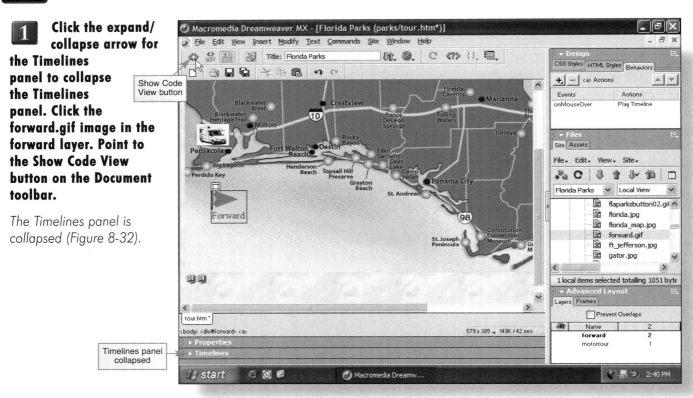

FIGURE 8-32

2 **Click the Show Code View button.**

The Dreamweaver Code View window is displayed (Figure 8-33). Your window most likely will show a different view of the code than that in Figure 8-33.

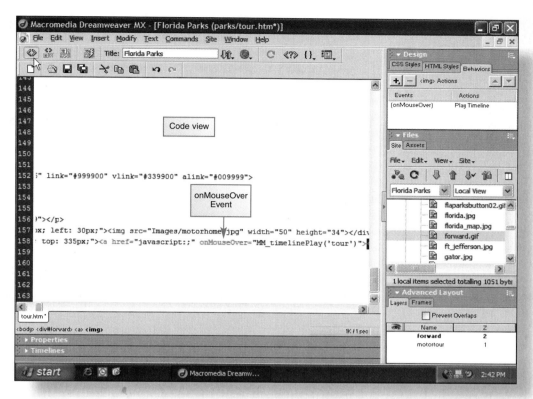

FIGURE 8-33

3 **Press CTRL+F.**

The Find and Replace dialog box is displayed (Figure 8-34). Most likely, the text in the Search For text box will be different on your screen.

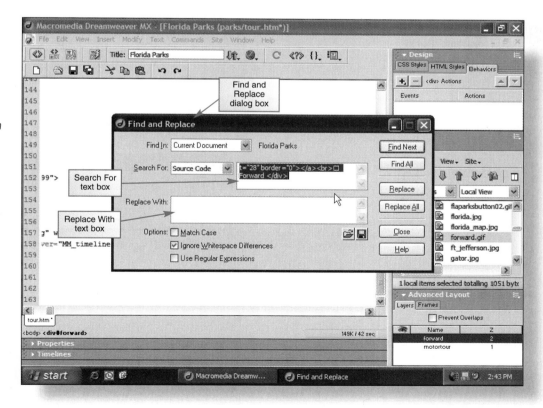

FIGURE 8-34

4 **Type** onMouseOver **in the Search For text box. Press the TAB key and then type** onClick **in the Replace With text box. Point to the Replace All button.**

The onMouseOver behavior is displayed in the Search For text box and the onClick behavior is displayed in the Replace With text box (Figure 8-35).

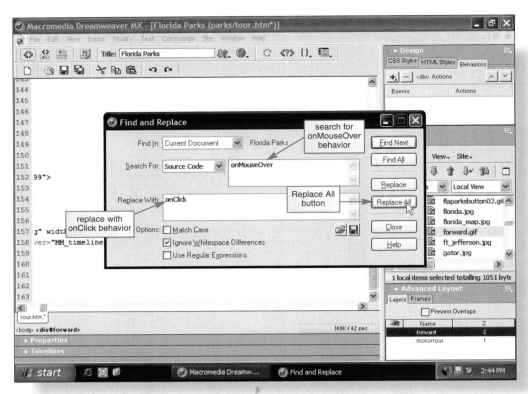

FIGURE 8-35

5 **Click the Replace All button. Point to the OK button.**

A Macromedia Dreamweaver MX dialog box is displayed indicating 1 item found and 1 item replaced (Figure 8-36). Code displays in green when it is changed manually.

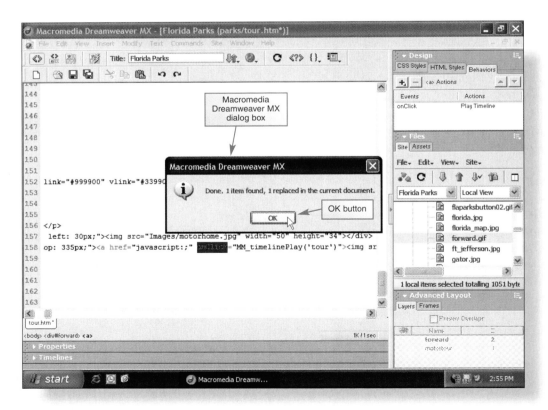

FIGURE 8-36

6 Click the OK button. Review the code in highlighted green text and then click the Show Design View button on the Document toolbar.

The event in the Behaviors panel is changed to onClick (Figure 8-37).

7 Press F12 to view the Web page in the browser. Click the Forward button to move the motorhome image from park location to park location. Close the browser.

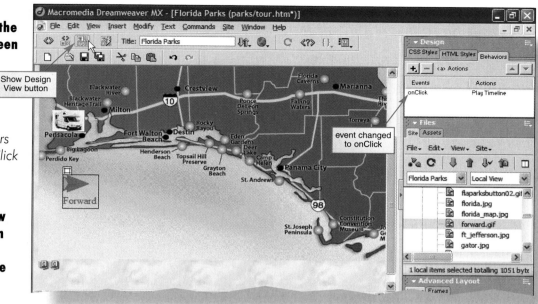

FIGURE 8-37

To integrate the Web page into the parks Web site, create a link to the state_parks.htm page. Later in this project, you create a link from the state_parks.htm to this page (tour.htm) and to the slideshow.htm page you create next.

TO ADD A LINK TO THE STATE_PARKS.HTM PAGE

1 Expand the Property inspector.

2 Scroll to the bottom of the Document window and then click to the right of the second layer-code marker.

3 Press the ENTER key. Type `Florida State Parks` as the link text and then press the ENTER key.

4 Select the text, Florida State Parks, and then drag state_parks.htm to the Link text box (Figure 8-38 on the next page). Press the ENTER key.

5 Press the F12 key to view the image in your browser. Test the link, and then close the browser.

6 Click the Save button on the Standard toolbar and then close the tour.htm document.

The link is added to Web page and is displayed in the Link text box as described in Step 4 (Figure 8-38).

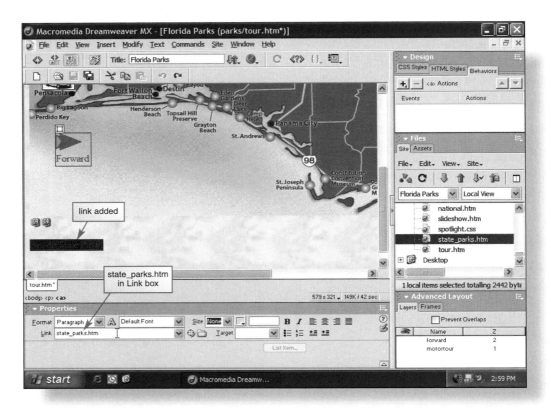

FIGURE 8-38

Linear, or Straight-Line, Path Animations

With the animation using a nonlinear path created, your next objective is to create a slide show using a **linear**, or **straight-line**, **path animation**. You accomplish this primarily through the Timelines panel by adding keyframes at various points along the timelines. As discussed previously, keyframes are marked on the timeline by small circles. A keyframe is the main tool for controlling an animation. Using a keyframe, you can change the properties of an object in a timeline. In this exercise, you change the Show-Hide properties.

The slide show contains six layers — one for each image of the six state parks the motor home visited on its tour of northwest Florida. You use the Show-Hide behavior to display and hide the slides. All images are the same size and use absolute positioning. The Web site visitor cycles through the images by clicking a Forward button. The image sequence loops and the Forward button returns the visitor to the beginning slide at the end of the loop.

To begin creating your slide show, you add six layers and six images. The images are positioned on top of each other and each is aligned to the same coordinates. Using same-sized images and absolute positioning provides for a smooth transition between slides and keeps the user's attention focused on a single spot. Complete the following steps to create the layers and add images to each layer.

Steps **To Add the First Layer and Image**

1 **Open slideshow.htm. If necessary, display the Property inspector and collapse the Design panel group. If necessary, click below the heading and then click the Align Left button in the Property inspector.**

The slideshow page is displayed in the Document window. The insertion point is at the left in the Document window (Figure 8-39). The Site and Layers panels are displayed and the Design panel group is collapsed.

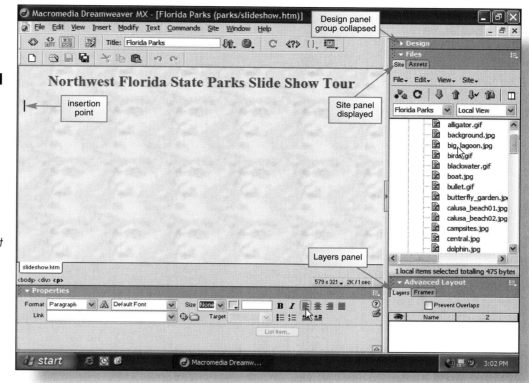

FIGURE 8-39

2 **Click Insert on the menu bar and then click Layer. Scroll to display the big_lagoon.jpg file in the Site panel. Click inside the layer.**

A layer is inserted into the Document window. The layer-code marker is displayed in the upper-left corner (Figure 8-40).

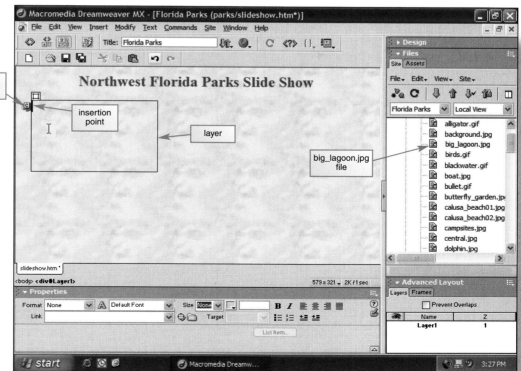

FIGURE 8-40

3 Drag the big_lagoon.jpg image onto the layer. Point to the Layer1 name in the Layers panel.

The Big Lagoon image is displayed in Layer1 (Figure 8-41).

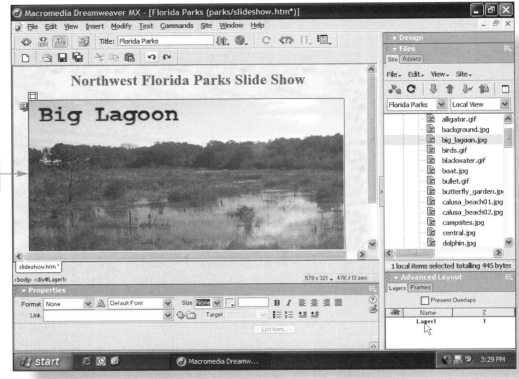

FIGURE 8-41

4 Click the Layer1 name in the Layers panel.

The Layer1 name is selected in the Layers panel and the Property inspector for layers is displayed (Figure 8-42).

FIGURE 8-42

5 In the Property inspector, add the following attributes: Layer ID — biglagoon; L — 150; and T — 60.

The properties are added for the biglagoon layer and the Layer1 name is changed to biglagoon in the Layers panel (Figure 8-43).

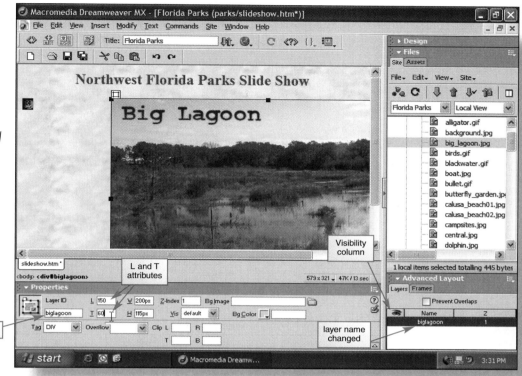

FIGURE 8-43

6 Click the Visibility column to the left of the layer biglagoon in the Layers panel until a closed-eye icon is displayed. If necessary, click the Document window to hide the layer and image.

The closed-eye icon is displayed (Figure 8-44). Later in this project, you will change this closed-eye icon to the open-eye icon.

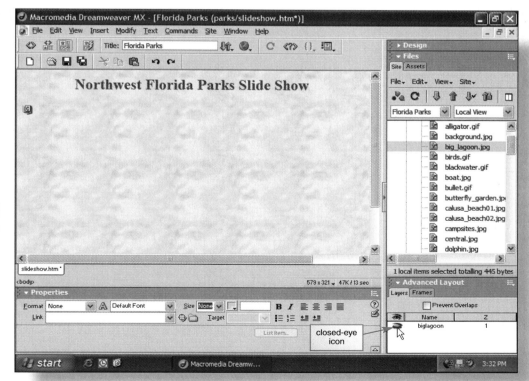

FIGURE 8-44

More About

Slide Shows

When creating a slide show, make all the images the same size to create smooth transitions. Most browsers running on average computer systems cannot display animations at rates faster than 15 fps. For more information about slide shows, visit the Dreamweaver MX More About Web page (scsite. com/dreamweavermx/ more.htm) and then click Slide Shows.

The first layer and image for the slide show have been added to the Document window. Next, you add five more layers, add an image to each layer, and then change the properties for each of the layers.

Steps **To Add the Next Five Layers and Images**

1 **Click Insert on the menu bar, click Layer, and then drag the rocky_bayou.jpg image onto the layer.**

Layer1 is added to the Layers panel. The Rocky Bayou image is displayed in the Document window (Figure 8-45).

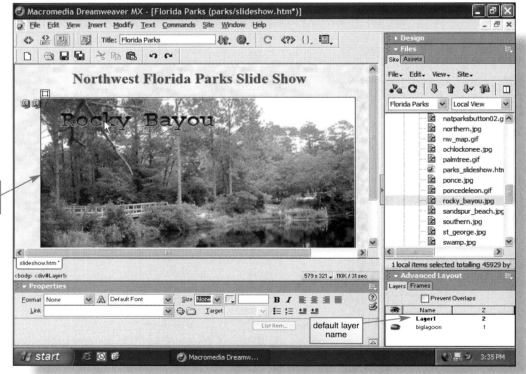

FIGURE 8-45

2 Select the Layer1 name in the Layers panel. Add the following attributes in the Layers Property inspector: LayerID — rockybayou; L — 150 and T — 60.

The properties are added for the Rocky Bayou layer and the layer name is changed to rockybayou in the Layers panel (Figure 8-46).

3 Click the Visibility column to the left of the rockybayou layer in the Layers panel until a closed-eye icon is displayed. If necessary, click the Document window to hide the layer and image.

The closed-eye icon is displayed for the rockybayou layer in the Layers panel. The rockybayou image no longer appears in the Document window.

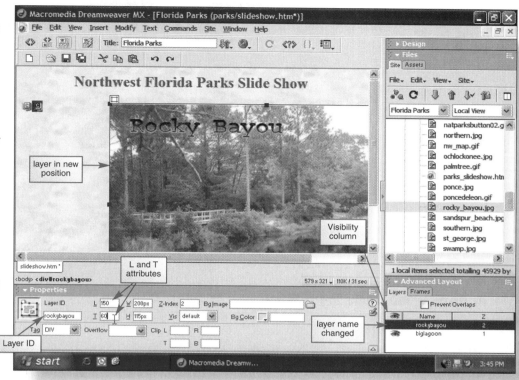

FIGURE 8-46

4 Four more layers are to be added for the slide show preparation. Repeat steps 1 through 3 to add the next four layers. Table 8-2 on the next page contains the attributes for each layer. Apply the closed-icon icon to all of the layers. If necessary, scroll to the left to view the six layer-code markers in the upper-left corner.

All six layers are added and are hidden (Figure 8-47).

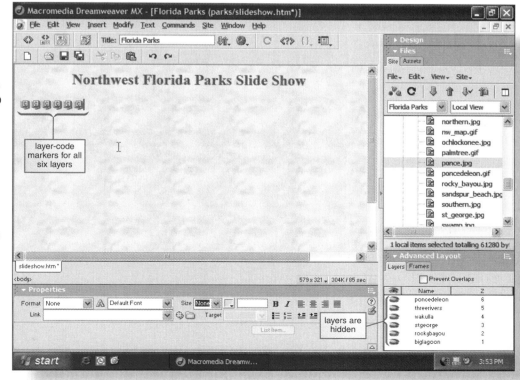

FIGURE 8-47

5 **Click the Save button on the Standard toolbar.**

The slideshow.htm file is saved.

Table 8-2   Layer Attributes

IMAGE NAME	LAYER ID	L AND T
st_george.jpg	stgeorge	150 and 60
wakulla.jpg	wakulla	150 and 60
three_rivers.jpg	threerivers	150 and 60
ponce.jpg	poncedeleon	150 and 60

Next, you display the Timelines panel and then name the timeline. Recall that the Timelines panel shows how the properties of layers and images change over time. Complete the following steps to accomplish this task.

Steps **To Display and Name the Timeline**

1 **Collapse the Property inspector. Press ALT+F9 to display the Timelines panel.**

The Timelines panel is displayed and the Property inspector collapsed (Figure 8-48).

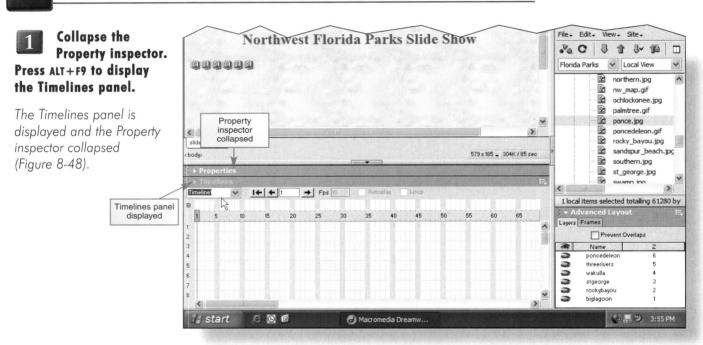

FIGURE 8-48

2 **Click the Timeline pop-up menu text box. Delete the default text entry, type** slideshow, **and then press the TAB key.**

The timeline is named and the name is displayed in the Timeline pop-up menu text box (Figure 8-49).

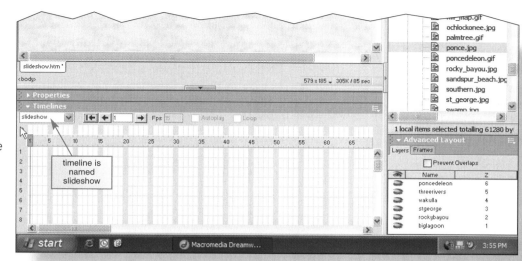

FIGURE 8-49

Adding Layers to a Timeline

The next step is to add the six layers to the timeline. The timeline for each layer is on a separate animation channel. Complete the following steps to add the six layers to the timeline.

Steps **To Add the Layers to the Timeline**

1 **Click the biglagoon layer in the Layers panel.**

The biglagoon layer is selected in the Layers panel and the layer-code marker in the Document window is highlighted. The Big Lagoon image is displayed in the Document window (Figure 8-50).

FIGURE 8-50

2 **Drag the biglagoon layer-code marker to animation channel 1, frame 1, in the Timelines panel. If a Dreamweaver dialog box is displayed, read the information and then click the OK button.**

The biglagoon layer is displayed and highlighted in animation channel 1 (Figure 8-51).

FIGURE 8-51

3 **Click the rockybayou layer in the Layers panel.**

The rockybayou layer is selected in the Layers panel and the rockybayou layer-code marker is selected in the Document window (Figure 8-52).

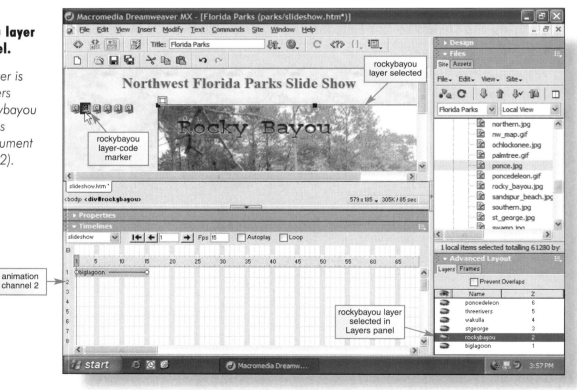

FIGURE 8-52

4 Drag the Rocky Bayou layer-code marker to animation channel 2, frame 1, in the Timelines panel. Click the OK button.

The rockybayou layer is displayed and highlighted in animation channel 2 (Figure 8-53).

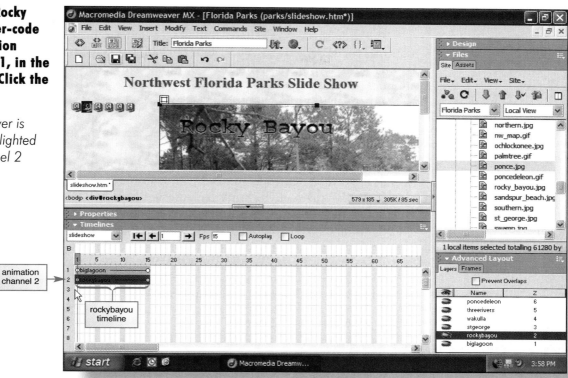

FIGURE 8-53

5 Repeat Steps 3 and 4, selecting and dragging the remaining four layers to the Timelines panel: the stgeorge layer to animation channel 3, the wakulla layer to animation channel 4, the threerivers layer to animation channel 5, and the poncedeleon layer to animation channel 6.

All six layers are displayed in the Timelines panel. The poncedeleon timeline is highlighted (Figure 8-54).

Other Ways

1. Right-click layer, click Add to Timeline on context menu

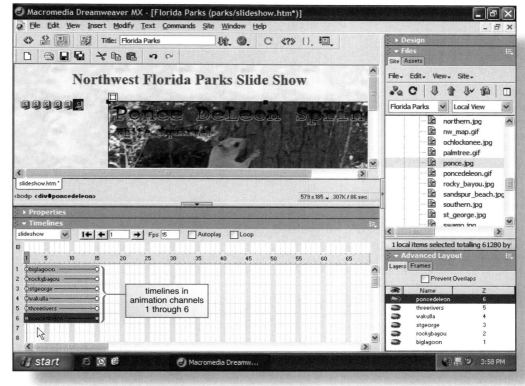

FIGURE 8-54

Adjusting the Number of Frames

The slide show is not a self-running animation. Instead, the Web site user controls the slide show by clicking a button. Thus, the time, or fps, is not relevant. The number of frames within each of the timelines, therefore, can be set to a minimum. Keyframes are added to the timeline to show and hide each layer and a pause added between the show and hide events. The pause is added through the behaviors channel. Because fps is not relevant, and to create the most efficient slide show, the number of frames for each timeline is set at the lowest number required to create the slide show.

As discussed, a keyframe is required to hide and then show each of the six images within the layers. Keyframe number 3, for instance, is used to hide the biglagoon layer and to display the rockybayou layer. Another keyframe is required to stop the display of each of the layers, and an ending keyframe is required. Therefore, to determine the minimum number of frames, multiply the number of images in your sequence by 2 and then add 1. In this instance, the slide show contains six slides, which makes the number of required frames 13. You adjust the number of frames by dragging the last keyframe for each of the timelines to the left. Complete the following steps to adjust the number of keyframes for each timeline.

More About

Timing

Animations do not have to start at the beginning of a timeline. For example, if you want the animation to begin five seconds after a page has loaded, use 15 fps and set the behavior on frame 60 of the timeline.

Steps To Adjust the Number of Frames

1 **Click the keyframe at frame 15 in the biglagoon animation bar in the Timelines panel.**

The playback head moves to frame 15 and the keyframe circle is highlighted (Figure 8-55).

FIGURE 8-55

2 **Drag the keyframe to frame 13.**

The playback head moves to frame 13 (Figure 8-56).

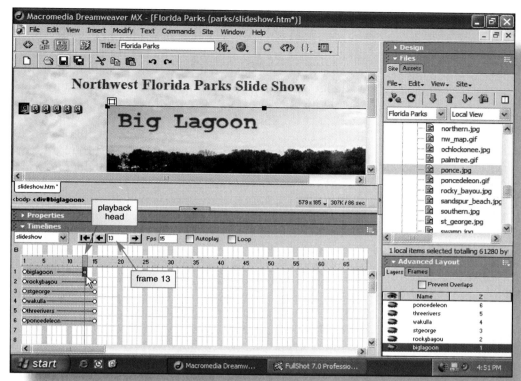

FIGURE 8-56

3 **Repeat Steps 1 and 2 for the other five layers.**

All six timelines are adjusted to 13 frames (Figure 8-57).

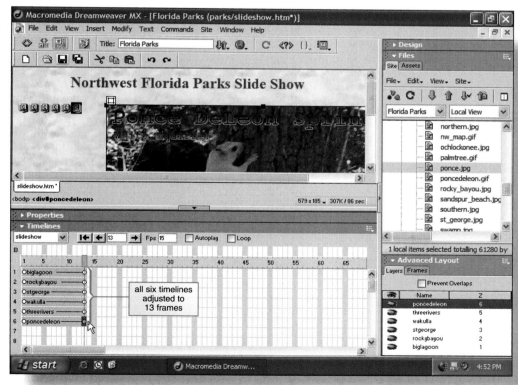

FIGURE 8-57

Frame Rate

The actual frame rate depends on the user's system.

More About

Animation Sequences

After you have an animation sequence that you like, you can copy it and paste it into another area of the current timeline, into another timeline in the same document, or into a timeline in another document. You also can copy and paste multiple sequences at once.

Adding Keyframes to Show and Hide Layers

Recall that a keyframe represents frames for which you define properties for the timeline. A start and stop keyframe automatically is added to the beginning and end of each timeline. You can use keyframes to change an object's position or to show and hide layers. As the slide show plays, for instance, the layers are displayed and then hidden.

When using keyframes to show and hide layers as within a slide show, visualize the keyframes as a stairstep approach. To display the slide show, a layer is turned on and then turned off. When the layer is turned off, the next layer is turned on, and so on. The slide show starts with the biglagoon layer displayed at frame 1 and the other five layers hidden. Showing and hiding layers is accomplished through the Visibility column in the Layers panel using the open-eye and closed-eye icons. Therefore, for the biglagoon timeline, the keyframe at frame 1 shows the layer (open-eye icon in the Layers panel). The keyframes at frame 1 for the other five layers shows the closed-eye icon. To hide the biglagoon layer and to show the rockybayou layer, the keyframe at frame 3 for biglagoon is a closed-eye icon (hides the layer) and the keyframe at frame 3 for the rockybayou layer is an open-eye icon. When the biglagoon layer is hidden, the next layer (the rockybayou layer) is displayed. Continuing with the slide show, the keyframe at frame 5 for the rockybayou layer is a closed-eye icon and the keyframe at frame 5 for the stgeorge layer displays the open-eye icon, and so on. When one layer is hidden, the next one is turned on. In between hiding and showing a layer, a behavior is added to the even-numbered frames to stop the slide show. Clicking the Play button resumes the slide show presentation.

In the following steps, keyframes are added to the timeline to show and hide layers. When the timeline is executed, and a keyframe is encountered, then the visibility of the selected layer is turned on or off. Complete the following steps to add keyframes to show or hide a selected layer. The keyframes are added at odd-numbered frames for each of the timelines.

Steps **To Add Keyframes to Show and Hide Layers**

1 **Click the biglagoon timeline in the Timelines panel at frame 1. Drag the playback head to frame 1 and then click the biglagoon Visibility column in the Layers panel until an open-eye icon is displayed. Verify that the biglagoon timeline still is selected. Drag the playback head to frame 3.**

The playback head is in frame 3 and the biglagoon timeline is selected (Figure 8-58). The open-eye icon for keyframe 1 displays the first slide when the slide show opens in the browser window.

FIGURE 8-58

2 **Click the biglagoon timeline at frame 3. Press the F6 key to add the keyframe and then click the Visibility column for the biglagoon layer until the closed-eye icon is displayed.**

A keyframe is added to the biglagoon layer at frame 3. This keyframe setting hides the biglagoon layer (Figure 8-59).

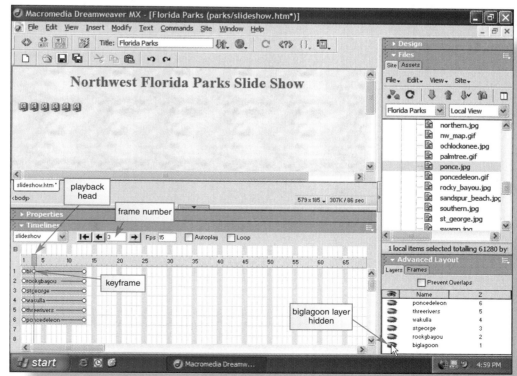

FIGURE 8-59

3 Click the rockybayou timeline at frame 3 in the Timelines panel. Press the **F6** key. Click the Visibility column for the rockybayou layer in the Layers panel until an open-eye icon displays.

The open-eye icon is displayed to the left of the rockybayou layer in the Layers panel. A keyframe is added to the rockybayou timeline at frame 3 (Figure 8-60). This keyframe setting shows the image during the slide show presentation.

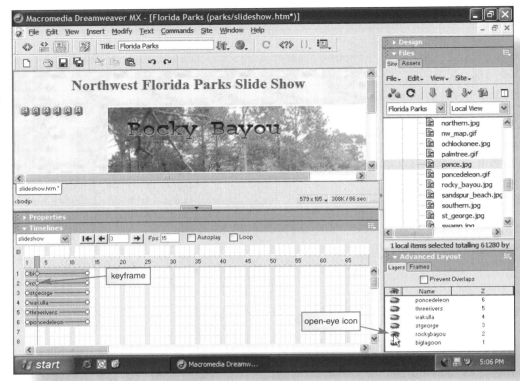

FIGURE 8-60

4 Drag the playback head to frame 5. Click the rockybayou timeline at frame 5 in the Timelines panel.

The rockybayou timeline is selected in the Timelines panel (Figure 8-61)

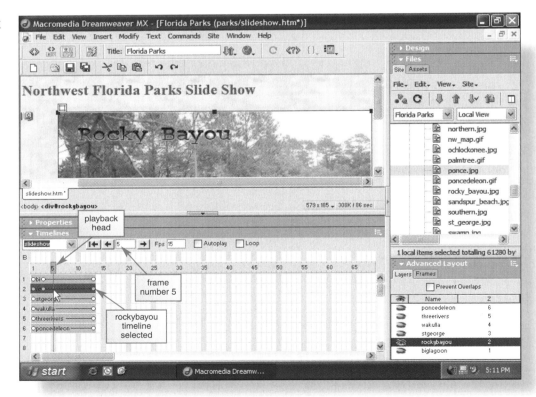

FIGURE 8-61

5 Press the **F6** key. Click the Visibility column in the Layers panel for the rockybayou layer until the closed-eye icon is displayed.

A keyframe is added to the rockybayou timeline at frame 5 (Figure 8-62). This keyframe setting hides the image during the slide show presentation.

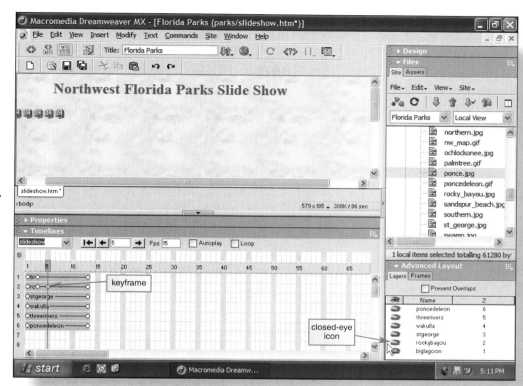

FIGURE 8-62

6 Click the stgeorge timeline at frame 5 in the Timelines panel.

The stgeorge timeline is selected at frame 5 (Figure 8-63).

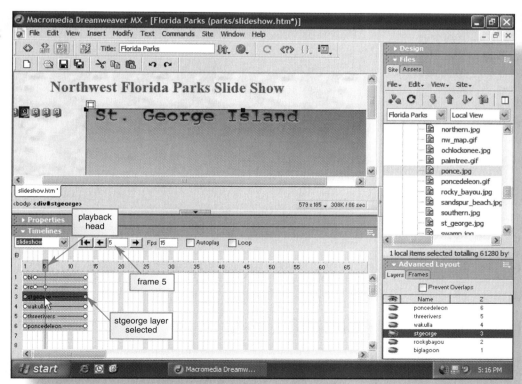

FIGURE 8-63

7 Press the F6 key. Click the Visibility column in the Layers panel for the stgeorge layer until the open-eye icon is displayed.

A keyframe is added to the stgeorge timeline at frame 5 (Figure 8-64). This keyframe setting shows the image during the slide show presentation.

FIGURE 8-64

8 Click frame 7 in the stgeorge timeline in the Timelines panel and then press the F6 key. Click the Visibility column in the Layers panel until the closed-eye icon is displayed.

A keyframe is added to the stgeorge timeline at frame 7 (Figure 8-65). This keyframe setting hides the image during the slide show presentation.

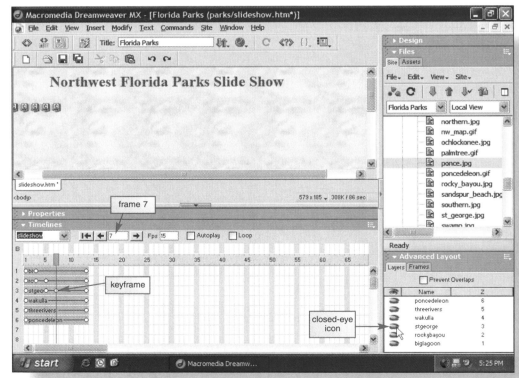

FIGURE 8-65

9 Click frame 7 in the wakulla timeline in the Timelines panel and then press the F6 key. Click the Visibility column in the wakulla layer in the Layers panel until an open-eye icon is displayed.

A keyframe is added to the wakulla timeline at frame 7 (Figure 8-66). This keyframe setting shows the image during the slide show presentation.

FIGURE 8-66

10 Click the wakulla timeline at frame 9 in the Timelines panel and then press the F6 key. Click the Visibility column in the wakulla layer in the Layers panel until a closed-eye icon is displayed.

A keyframe is added to the wakulla timeline at frame 9 (Figure 8-67). This keyframe setting hides the image during the slide show presentation.

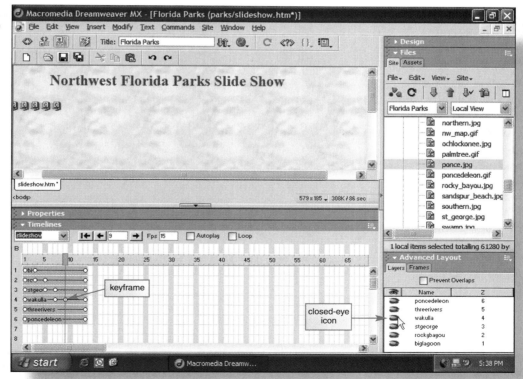

FIGURE 8-67

11 Click the threerivers timeline in the Timelines panel at frame 9 and then press the F6 key. Click the Visibility column in the threerivers layer in the Layers panel until an open-eye icon is displayed.

A keyframe is added to the threerivers layer at frame 9 (Figure 8-68). This keyframe setting shows the image during the slide show presentation.

FIGURE 8-68

12 Click the threerivers timeline at frame 11 in the Timelines panel and then press the F6 key. Click the Visibility column in the threerivers layer in the Layers panel until a closed-eye icon is displayed.

A keyframe is added to the threerivers layer at frame 11 (Figure 8-69). This keyframe setting hides the image during the slide show presentation.

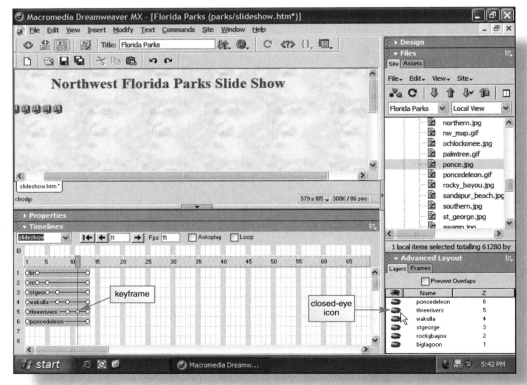

FIGURE 8-69

13 **Click the poncedeleon timeline at frame 11 in the Timelines panel and then press the F6 key. Click the Visibility column in the poncedeleon layer in the Layers panel until the open-eye icon is displayed.**

A keyframe is added to the poncedeleon layer at frame 11 (Figure 8-70). This keyframe setting shows the image during the slide show presentation.

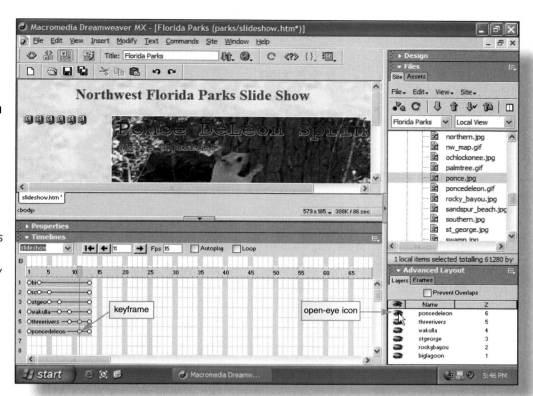

FIGURE 8-70

14 **Click the poncedeleon timeline at frame 13 in the Timelines panel. If necessary, click the Visibility column in the poncedeleon layer in the Layers panel until the closed-eye icon is displayed.**

This keyframe setting hides the image during the slide show presentation (Figure 8-71). The closed-eye icon is displayed for all six layers at this point.

FIGURE 8-71

15 **Click the keyframe in frame 13 in the biglagoon timeline in the Timelines panel. Click the Visibility column in the biglagoon layer in the Layers panel until the open-eye icon is displayed. Click the Save button on the Standard toolbar. Point to the Autoplay check box in the Timelines panel.**

The visibility setting is added to keyframe 13 of the biglagoon layer and the file is saved (Figure 8-72). This keyframe setting redisplays the first image at the end of the slide show presentation so that the viewer is not left with a blank screen.

FIGURE 8-72

16 **Click the Autoplay check box in the Timelines panel. If a Dreamweaver dialog box is displayed, read the information and then click the OK button. Press the F12 key to view the presentation in your browser.**

The presentation cycles through quickly. It ends with the first image (Big Lagoon) (Figure 8-73).

17 **Close the browser window and return to Dreamweaver.**

Other Ways

1. Click a frame, on Modify menu point to Timeline, click Add Keyframe on Timeline submenu

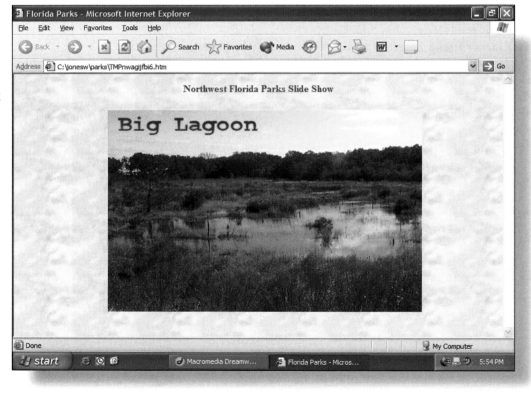

FIGURE 8-73

Using Behaviors to Pause the Slides

The next step is to add a pause between each slide. Adding a pause stops the timeline from playing. Adding pauses between slides is accomplished through the Timelines panel behaviors channel. Simply click the frame number in the behaviors channel and apply the Stop Timeline behavior. The Stop Timeline behavior is added to even-numbered frames. The Play Timeline behavior is added through the Forward button. You add the Forward button later in this project. Complete the following steps to add the pauses.

Steps | **To Use Behaviors to Pause between Slides**

1 Click the Design panel expand/collapse arrow to display the Behaviors panel. Click frame 2 in the behaviors channel in the Timelines panel. Point to the Actions (+) button in the Behaviors panel.

The Behaviors panel is displayed and frame 2 in the behaviors channel is highlighted (Figure 8-74).

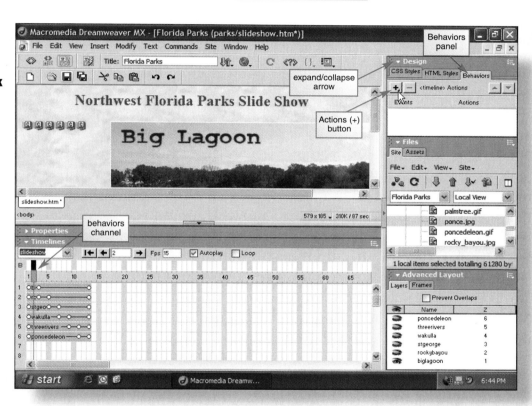

FIGURE 8-74

2 **Click the Actions (+) button in the Behaviors panel, point to Timeline, and then point to Stop Timeline.**

The Actions pop-up menu is displayed (Figure 8-75).

FIGURE 8-75

3 **Click Stop Timeline. Click the Stop Timeline box arrow and then point to slideshow.**

The Stop Timeline dialog box is displayed and slideshow is selected (Figure 8-76).

FIGURE 8-76

Apply Your Knowledge

Creating a Slide Show for B & B Lawn Service *(continued)*

1. Display the Property inspector, Standard toolbar, Site panel, and Layers panel. Select Lawn Service from the Site pop-up menu in the Site panel.
2. Use Dreamweaver's integrated file browser to copy the six images from the Data Files Images folder to your lawn Images folder and the data file to your lawn folder. Close the Untitled window. Open the slideshow.htm file and then click below the introductory paragraph.
3. Click Insert on the menu bar and then click Layer.
4. Drag slide01.gif image onto the layer. Click the layer selection handle to select the layer and to display the Layers Property inspector. Add the following attributes to the Property inspector: Layer ID — slide01, L — 250, and T — 175.
5. Click the Visibility column for the slide01 layer in the Layers panel until the closed-eye icon is displayed.
6. Use the data in Table 8-4 and repeat steps 3 through 5 to add the next four layers to the Web page and to add images to the layers.

Table 8-4	Slide Data			
SLIDE IMAGE	**LAYER ID**	**L**	**T**	**EYE ICON**
slide02	slide02	250	175	closed
slide03	slide03	250	175	closed
slide04	slide04	250	175	closed
slide05	slide05	250	175	closed

7. Click the Property inspector expand/collapse arrow to collapse the panel and then press ALT+F9 to display the Timelines panel. Select the text in the Timelines pop-up menu textbox and then type flowers to name the timeline.
8. Drag the layer-code marker for the slide01 layer to animation channel 1 in the Timelines panel. Drag the layer-code marker for the slide02 layer to animation channel 2 and so on until all five layers have been added to the Timelines panel. If a Dreamweaver dialog box displays, read the information and then click the OK button.
9. Drag the keyframe at the end of each timeline to change the number of frames to 11.
10. Click keyframe 1 in the slide01 timeline in the animation bar of the Timelines panel and change the closed-eye icon in the Layers panel to open. Click the slide01 timeline at frame 3. Press the F6 key to add a keyframe and then click the Visibility column in the Layers panel to display a closed-eye icon.
11. Click slide02 timeline at frame 3 in the Timelines panel. Press the F6 key to add a keyframe and then click the Visibility column in the Layers panel to display an open-eye icon. Click the slide02 timeline at frame 5 in the Timelines panel. Press the F6 key to add a keyframe and then click the Visibility column in the Layers panel to display a closed-eye icon.
12. Click the slide03 timeline at frame 5 in the Timelines panel. Press the F6 key to add a keyframe and then click the Visibility column in the Layers panel to display an open-eye icon. Click the slide03 timeline at frame 7 in the animation bar. Press the F6 key to add a keyframe and then click the Visibility column in the Layers panel to display a closed-eye icon.

(continued)

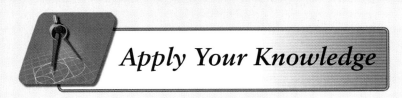

Apply Your Knowledge

Creating a Slide Show for B & B Lawn Service *(continued)*

13. Click the slide04 timeline at frame 7 in the Timelines panel. Press the F6 key to add a keyframe and then click the Visibility column in the Layers panel to display an open-eye icon. Click the slide04 timeline at frame 9 in the Timelines panel. Press the F6 key to add a keyframe and then click the Visibility column in the Layers panel to display a closed-eye icon.

14. Click the slide05 timeline at frame 9 in the Timelines panel. Press the F6 key to add a keyframe and then click the Visibility column in the Layers panel to display an open-eye icon. Click the slide05 timeline at frame 11 in the Timelines panel. Press the F6 key to add a keyframe and then click the Visibility column in the Layers panel to display a closed-eye icon.

15. Click the slide01 timeline at frame 11 in the Timelines panel. Press the F6 key to add a keyframe and then click the Visibility column in the Layers panel to display an open-eye icon.

16. Use the playback options in the Timelines panel to play the animation in the Document window. Verify that the open and closed-eye icons are correct. When playing the animation to verify the icons, only one open-eye icon should display and this is the icon for the layer currently displayed. All other icons in the Layers Visibility column should be closed.

17. Press SHIFT+F3 to display the Design panel group and the Behaviors panel.

18. Click frame 2 in the behaviors channel, click the Actions (+) button in the Behaviors panel, and then add the Stop Timeline behavior.

19. Repeat step 18 and add the Stop Timeline behavior to frames 4, 6, 8, and 10 in the Timelines panel behaviors channel. Click the Autoplay check box and the Loop check box. Collapse the Timelines panel.

20. Insert another layer in the Document window. Drag the start_button.gif image to the layer and resize the layer around the image.

21. Expand the Property inspector; if necessary, select the layer, and then add the following attributes: Layer ID — start, L — 350, and T — 350.

22. Select the start_button image within the layer and then click the Actions (+) button in the Behaviors panel. Apply the Play Timeline behavior.

23. Click the Show Code View button on the Standard toolbar in the Document window and then press CTRL+F. Type onMouseOver in the Search For text box and then type onClick in the Replace With text box. Click the Replace All button. Click the Show Design View button on the Standard toolbar.

24. Press the F12 key to view the slide show in your browser. Click the Start button to move from slide to slide. Close the browser.

25. If necessary, scroll to the bottom of the page and then type Services as the link text. Select Services and change the text color to red. With the text still selected, create a link to services.htm. Save the Document. Open services.htm. Select the text, Landscaping, and create a link to the slideshow.htm page. Save the services.htm page.

26. Press the F12 key to view the page in your browser. Click the landscaping link. Print a copy of the slideshow.htm page if instructed to do so. Upload the page to the lawn Web Site on a remote server if instructed to do so.

27. Quit Dreamweaver.

In the Lab

1 The CandleDust Web Site

Problem: Mary would like to add a Web page with some interactivity to the CandleDust Web site. She wants to advertise a sale for some of her special candles. You suggest a page where the special for-sale candles are displayed one by one on the same page. The first candle appears in the upper left of the screen, below the heading; the second in the middle of the screen; and the third on the right side of the screen. Mary likes this idea, and you agree to create the page. As you are completing this exercise, expand and collapse the panels as necessary. Because this is a freeform exercise, the placement on your screen is approximate. For a selection of images and backgrounds, visit the Dreamweaver MX Media Web page (scsite.com/dreamweavermx/media) and then click Media below Project 8.

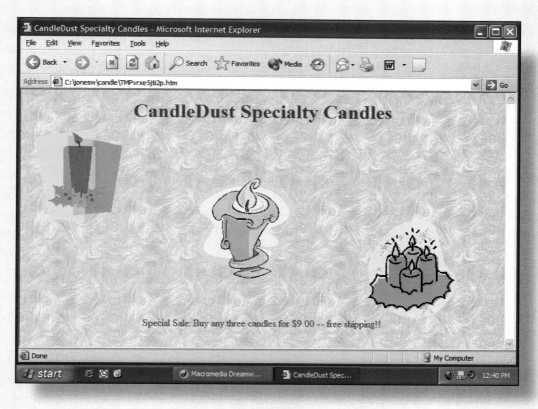

FIGURE 8-85

Instructions: Perform the following tasks:

1. Start Dreamweaver. If necessary, press F4 to close the open panels. Display the Property inspector, Standard toolbar, Site panel, Timelines panel, and Layers panel. Select CandleDust on the Site pop-up menu in the Site panel. Copy the data file to the candles folder. Open candlesale.htm. Closed the Untitled window.
2. Show rulers using the View menu. If necessary, move the insertion point to the left margin below the heading. Insert a layer. Drag candle3.gif onto the layer and then resize the layer to fit the image.

(continued)

In the Lab

The CandleDust Web Site *(continued)*

3. In the Timelines panel, name the timeline candlesale. Double-click Layer1 in the Layers panel and rename the layer sale01. Click the layer-code marker and drag it to frame 1, animation channel 1, in the Timelines panel. The candle will display in this location, so there is no need to drag it.

4. Insert a second layer and then drag candle4.gif onto the layer. Resize the layer to fit the image. Double-click Layer1 in the Layers panel and rename the layer sale02.

5. Verify that the playback head is in frame 1 in the Timelines panel. If necessary, select the layer and then right-click the selection handle. Click Record Path on the context menu, and then, using the rulers as a guide, drag the layer and image downward about 50 pixels and to the right approximately 300 pixels. The timeline for the sale02 layer is displayed in the timeline in animation channel 2.

6. Insert a third layer and then drag candle5.gif onto the layer. Resize the layer to fit the image. Double-click Layer1 in the Layers panel and rename the layer sale03.

7. Move the playback head to frame 1 in the Timelines panel. If necessary, select the layer and then right-click the selection handle. Click Record Path on the context menu, and then using the rulers as a guide, drag the layer and image downward around 75 pixels and to the left approximately 500 pixels. The timeline for the sale03 layer is displayed in the timeline in animation channel 3.

8. Move the playback head to frame 1 and click the keyframe for sale01. Click the Visibility column in the Layers panel until an open-eye icon displays. Click the keyframe in frame 1 for the sale02 layer and then click the Visibility column in the Layers panel until a closed-eye icon displays. Click the keyframe in frame 1 for the sale03 layer and then click the Visibility column in the Layers panel until a closed-eye icon displays. For frame 1, sale01 has an open-eye icon and sale02 and sale03 have closed-eye icons.

9. Click the ending keyframe for sale01. The frame number will be somewhere around 15. If necessary, click the Visibility column for sale01 until an open-eye icon is displayed. Click the same frame number (somewhere around 15) in the sale02 animation channel. Press the F6 key to add a keyframe. Click the Visibility column for sale02 until an open-eye icon is displayed.

10. Click the ending keyframe for sale02, and, if necessary, change the eye icon to an open-eye icon.

11. Click the ending keyframe for sale03, and, if necessary, change the eye icon to an open-eye icon. All three layers should display open-eye icons.

12. Click the Autoplay check box in the Timelines panel.

13. Press the F12 key to view the page in your browser. If necessary, close the browser and make any necessary adjustments to your animated Web page. Print a copy of the Web page if instructed to do so. Upload the page to the lawn Web Site on a remote server if instructed to do so.

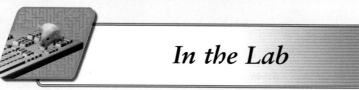

In the Lab

2 Creating a Slide Show for the Credit Protection Web Site

Problem: Marcy recently gave a PowerPoint presentation on stock market investing. She has received several requests asking for a copy of her presentation. To accommodate the requests, she would like to add this presentation to the Web site. Marcy saved each slide as a jpg image and has asked if you can create a Web page with the slide show images. You assure her you can create the slide show. The first screen is shown in Figure 8-86. As you are completing this exercise, expand and collapse the panels as necessary. Appendix D contains instructions for uploading your local site to a remote server. For a selection of images and backgrounds, visit the Dreamweaver MX Media Web page (scsite.com/dreamweavermx/media) and then click Media below Project 8.

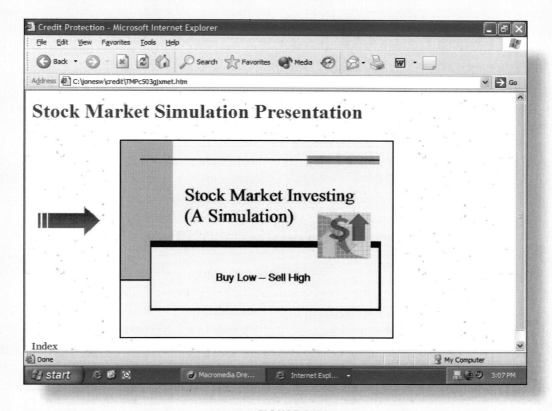

FIGURE 8-86

Instructions: Perform the following tasks:

1. Start Dreamweaver. Display the Property inspector, Standard toolbar, Site panel, Layers panel, and Timelines panel. Close the Untitled page. Collapse the Timelines panel.
2. Select Credit Protection on the Site pop-up menu in the Site panel. Use Dreamweaver's integrated file browser to copy the data file and images to the credit Web site. Open credit_slides.htm.
3. If necessary, move the insertion point to the left margin below the heading. Insert a layer. Drag slide1.jpg onto the layer.

(continued)

In the Lab

Creating a Slide Show for the Credit Protection Web Site *(continued)*

4. Click Layer1 in the Layers panel to select the layer. Click the Visibility column in the Layers panel until the closed-eye icon is displayed. In the Layers Property inspector, add the Layer ID as stock01, and set L to 150 and T to 80. Click the layer-code marker and drag it to frame 1, animation channel 1 in the Timelines panel. Name the timeline stockmarket.

5. Insert three more layers. Use the data in Table 8-5 to create the layers and to add the images for each layer.

6. Drag the layer-code marker for the slide2 layer to animation channel 2, the layer-code marker for the slide3 layer to animation channel 3, and the layer-code marker for the slide4 layer to animation channel 4.

Table 8-5	Slide Data			
SLIDE IMAGE	LAYER ID	L	T	EYE ICON
slide2.jpg	stock02	150	80	closed
slide3.jpg	stock03	150	80	closed
slide4.jpg	stock04	150	80	closed

7. Drag the keyframe at the end of each timeline to change the number of frames to 9.

8. Click keyframe 01 in the stock02 animation bar of the Timelines panel and change the eye icon in the Layers panel to open. The closed-eye icon should be displayed in the Layers panel for the other three layers.

9. Click the stock01 animation bar at frame 3. Press the F6 key to add a keyframe and change the eye icon in the Layers panel to a closed eye.

10. Click the stock02 animation bar at frame 3. Press the F6 key to add a keyframe and, if necessary, change the eye icon in the Layers panel to an open eye.

11. Click the stock02 animation bar at frame 5. Press the F6 key to add a keyframe and change the eye icon in the Layers panel to a closed eye.

12. Click the stock03 animation bar at frame 5. Press the F6 key to add a keyframe and change the eye icon in the Layers panel to an open eye. Click the stock03 animation bar at frame 7. Press the F6 key to add a keyframe and change the eye icon in the Layers panel to a closed eye.

13. Click the stock04 animation bar at frame 7. Press the F6 key to add a keyframe and change the eye icon in the Layers panel to an open eye. Click the stock04 animation bar at frame 9. Press the F6 key to add a keyframe and change the eye icon in the Layers panel to a closed eye.

14. Click the stock01 animation bar at frame 9 and then change the eye icon in the Layers panel to an open eye.

15. Click frame 2 in the behaviors channel in the Timelines panel. Click the Actions (+) button in the behaviors channel and add the Stop Timeline behavior.

16. Repeat step 15 for frames 4, 6, and 8.

17. Create another layer and drag the next.jpg image onto the layer. Set the following properties in the Layers property inspector: Layer ID — next; L — 20; T — 190. Select the image and then click the Actions (+) button in the Behaviors panel. Apply the Play Timeline command. Access Code View in the Document window, and then, if necessary, use the Find and Replace command to change the onMouseOver behavior to onClick.

18. Click the Autoplay and Loop check boxes.

19. Save the document. Press the F12 key to view the page in your browser. Click the Next button and review the slide show. Print a copy of the Web page if instructed to do so. Upload the page to the credit Web site on a remote server if instructed to do so.

In the Lab

3 Creating an Animation Page for the Plant City Web Site

Problem: Juan wants to add some animation to the Plant City Web site. You suggest to Juan that an animated map through the city and around the outlying areas would enhance the overall site. Juan likes your ideas, and you are ready to get started. As you are completing this exercise, expand and collapse the panels as necessary. The Web page with the map is shown in Figure 8-87.

Instructions: Perform the following tasks:

1. Start Dreamweaver. Display the Property inspector, Standard toolbar, Site panel, Timelines panel, and Layers panel. Select Plant City from the Site pop-up menu.

2. Use Dreamweaver's integrated file browser to copy the data file and the images from the Data Files folder to your city Images folder. Open tour.htm.

3. Insert a layer and then drag the map.gif image onto the layer. Select the layer and apply the following properties in the

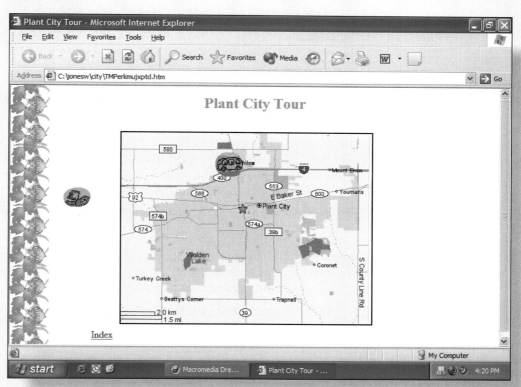

FIGURE 8-87

Layers property inspector: Layer ID — map; L — 175; T — 75.

4. Insert a second layer and then drag the bus.gif image onto the map layer. Resize the layer to accommodate the size of the bus.gif. image. Double-click Layer1 in the Layers panel and name the layer bus. Drag the bus.image layer onto the map and place the image near the top and to the left of Shilow. Right-click the bus layer and then click Select Record Path on the context menu.

5. Drag the image down and to the left to Highway 92 and then down to Turkey Creek. From Turkey Creek, drag to the right to Beatty's Corner and then to Trapnell. Drag up to Plant City and Baker Street, to the right to Youmans, up to Mount Enon, and then back to Shilow.

6. Name the timeline tour and then add Stop Timeline behaviors at frames near Turkey Creek, Trapnell, Plant City, Mount Enon, and Shilow.

7. Insert another layer. Drag the go.gif button onto the layer and resize the layer to accommodate the image size. Apply the following properties to the layer: layer ID — go; L — 85; T — 170. Click the image, click the Actions (+) button in the Behaviors panel, and apply the Play Timeline command.

(continued)

In the Lab

Creating an Animation Page for the Plant City Web Site *(continued)*

8. Click the Autoplay and Loop check boxes.
9. Press the F12 key to view the page in your browser. Print a copy of the Web page if instructed to do so. Upload the page to the city Web site on a remote server if instructed to do so.

Cases and Places

The difficulty of these case studies varies:
▶ are the least difficult; ▶▶ are more difficult; and ▶▶▶ are the most difficult.

1 ▶ Your sports Web site is receiving more hits each day. You decide to add a slide show page highlighting some of the more popular players. Add a background image to the page and add a title to the page. Insert three layers and add images to the layers. Use the Timelines panel and Autoplay to create the slide show. Create a link to and from the home page. Save the page in your sports Web site.

2 ▶ You would like to add some interactivity to your hobby Web site. You decide to do this by adding an animation. First, add a background image to the page and then add an appropriate title. Insert four layers and four images. All images should be the same size. Create a Forward button to advance the show from slide to slide. Create a link to and from your home page. Upload to a remote site if instructed to do so.

3 ▶▶ Add a new page to your music hobby Web site and then add a background to the page. Add a large image that contains images of five musical instruments, musicians, or other applicable musical features. Add a layer and an image that will move from instrument to instrument (or other musical feature). Use Dreamweaver's Record a Path command to move the image from instrument to instrument using the Timelines Autoplay feature. Create a link to and from your home page. Upload the page to a remote site.

4 ▶▶ Your campaign for political office is doing terrific. Create a new Web page and name it campaign_trail. Add an appropriate background and tile. Next, add a map image showing locations you recently have visited. Add a layer and then add your picture to the layer. Use Dreamweaver's Record a Path command and drag the layer from location to location. Add a Forward button. Add Play Timeline and Stop Timeline behaviors where appropriate. Create a link to and from your index page. Upload the revised Web site to a remote server.

5 ▶▶▶ Recently, the student government officers selected three possible vacation sites to visit. Create a slide show showing two images from each of these vacation sites. All images should be the same size. Use the T and L properties within the Layers Property inspector to center the layers. Add Stop Timeline and Play Timeline behaviors where appropriate. Add another layer with a Forward button. Create a link to and from the index page. Upload the slide show to a remote server.

Macromedia Dreamweaver MX

Media Objects

You will have mastered the material in this project when you can:

OBJECTIVES

- Describe media objects
- Insert Flash text into a Web page
- Insert a Flash movie into a Web page
- Add a sound link to a Web page
- Embed a sound file in a Web page
- Insert a video into a Web page
- Check for plug-ins
- Describe Shockwave and how to insert a Shockwave movie into a Web page
- Describe a Java applet and how to insert an applet into a Web page

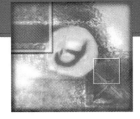

Macromedia Dreamweaver MX

Media Objects

C A S E   P E R S P E C T I V E

After visiting other Web sites for new ideas for the Florida Parks Web site, Will Jones has found that many Web sites start with a splash page, which adds visual appeal and interest for visitors. Generally, splash pages contain videos, audio, and/or other media. This is an element that the Florida Parks Web site does not include. Will asks how involved it would be to add a splash page to the Web site. You explain to Will that this involves some technical issues, but that Dreamweaver provides the capability of easily adding these types of features.

Will brings the team together to make the next determination: the content of the splash page. Joan suggests that some Flash text be added, a link to a sound file, and a Flash movie and also suggests that the state_parks.htm page be modified. The state parks page would contain an embedded sound file and a video file. The video, titled Technosaurus, focuses on technology changes.

With the addition of these media objects, the Web site culminates with the best features that Dreamweaver has to offer. Will and Joan are grateful to you for your guidance and assistance that have made the development of their site possible.

Introduction

Media objects, also called **multimedia**, are files that can be displayed or executed within HTML documents, or in a stand-alone fashion. Examples include graphics such as GIFs and JPEGs, video, audio, Flash objects (SWF), Shockwave objects (DIR or DCR), PDFs (Adobe's Portable Document Format), Java applets, and other objects that can be viewed through a browser using a helper application or using a plug-in. A **helper application** is a program such as the Flash player or Shockwave viewer. These two examples are Macromedia programs and are handled easily through Dreamweaver. A **plug-in** is a program application that is installed on your computer and used to view plug-in programs through the Web browser. Once installed, its function is integrated into the HTML file and the Web browser generally recognizes the plug-in application.

Project Nine — Designing with Interactive Media

In this project, you learn how to add interactive media to a Web page. Interactive media, or multimedia, is not suitable for all Web sites. Most likely, you have visited Web sites that contained so many bits and pieces of multimedia that instead of being a constructive part of the site, they were detrimental to the Web experience. Therefore, when adding this type of element to your Web page, you need to consider the value of each element and how it will enhance or detract from your site.

Consider the following guidelines for adding interactive media to your Web site:

▶ Use it for entertainment
▶ Assist Web site visitors with navigation

- Direct attention to certain elements
- Provide feedback
- Illustrate and/or demonstrate a particular element or part of the Web page

In this project, you learn to add interactive media to the Florida Parks Web site. You add a splash page that will contain Flash text, a Flash movie, and a linked sound file. A **splash page** generally consists of a default home page that displays the Web site logo or some other Web site promotion. Many splash pages use various types of interactive media — from Flash movies to animated graphics — and are good mood setters. After one or two visits to the splash page, however, the frequent Web site visitor most likely would prefer to skip the page and move on to the main Web site. Therefore, a link is added that, when clicked, will take the visitor directly to the Web site's index page. The splash page with the link is shown in Figure 9-1a.

Next, you add an embedded sound and a video to the state_parks.htm page (Figure 9-1b on the next page). These two elements use the Windows Media Player as the application helper to display the media within the browser window.

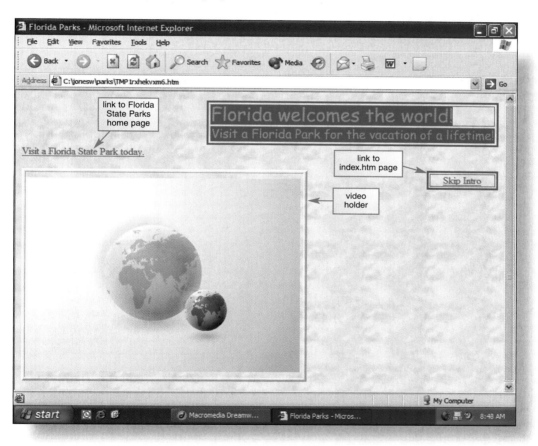

(a) Splash Page

FIGURE 9-1

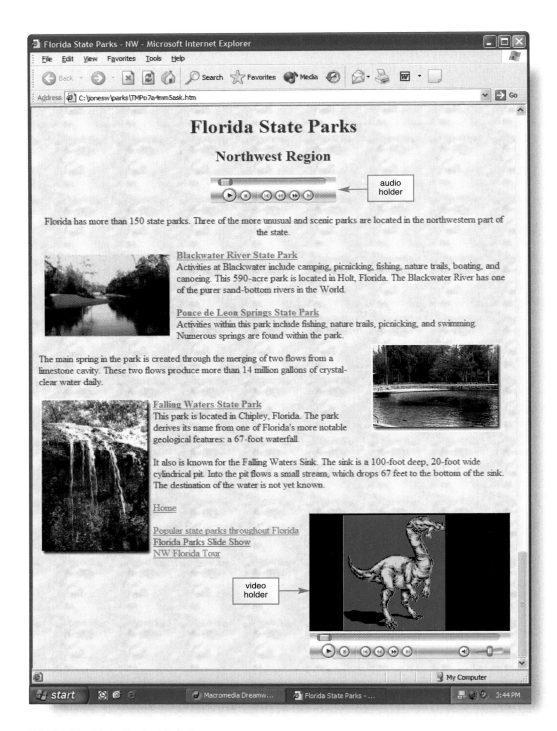

(b) Florida State Parks Web Page

FIGURE 9-1 (continued)

Workspace Organization

Organization and preparation lead to a more productive work setting. Successful Web site developers prepare their Dreamweaver workspace to provide an efficient work environment. As you learn to use additional Dreamweaver tools, including multimedia elements, you will become even more proficient working in the Dreamweaver environment.

Starting Dreamweaver and Closing Open Panels

When you start Dreamweaver, generally most or all of the panels are displayed by default. Closing unused panels provides uncluttered workspace in the Document window. To organize your workspace, you close the unused open panels. This gives you the maximum window space in the Dreamweaver Document window. Start Dreamweaver and close open panels using the following steps.

TO START DREAMWEAVER AND CLOSE OPEN PANELS

1 Start Dreamweaver. If necessary, maximize the Document window. Press the F4 key to close all open panels.

2 Press the F8 key to display the Site panel. Select the Florida Parks Web site.

3 If necessary, use the View menu to display the Standard toolbar. If necessary, turn off the rulers.

4 Use the Window menu to display the Property inspector and the Insert bar (Figure 9-2).

The Site panel, Standard toolbar, Insert bar, and Property inspector are displayed (Figure 9-2).

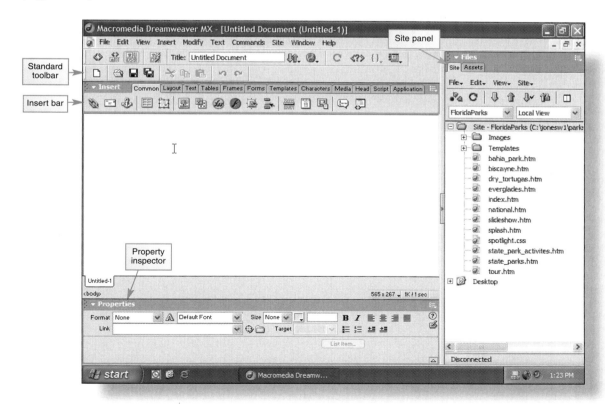

FIGURE 9-2

Copying Data Files to the Local Web Site

Your Data Disk contains a Media folder and a data file for Project 9. The Media folder and data file are located in the Proj09 folder. You use Dreamweaver's integrated file browser to copy the Project 9 Media folder and the data file to the Florida Parks folder.

The Data Files folder for this project is stored on Local Disk (C:). The location on your computer may be different. If necessary, verify with your instructor the location of the Data Files folder. Complete the following steps to copy the files and folder to the C:\jonesw\parks local root folder using the same procedure as in previous projects.

TO COPY DATA FILES TO THE FLORIDA PARKS WEB SITE

1 Click the plus sign (+) to the left of the Desktop icon in the Site panel. Click the plus sign to the left of the My Computer icon and then navigate through the file hierarchy to the Data Files folder as you did in Project 2 on pages DW 2.09–14.

2 Click the plus sign to the left of the Proj09 folder and then click the plus sign to the left of the parks folder.

3 Right-click the Media folder and then copy the Media folder to the jonesw/parks folder using the Copy and Paste commands on the context menus.

4 Copy the data file to the jonesw/parks/ folder using the Copy and Paste commands on the context menus.

5 Click the minus sign to the left of the Desktop icon to collapse the file list.

After completing Step 4, the Project 9 Media folder and the data file are copied into the jonesw/parks folder.

Media Objects

Dreamweaver provides two methods to insert media objects: the Media tab of the Insert bar and the Insert menu. The Media tab in the Insert bar contains buttons for inserting these special configurable objects (Figure 9-3). You use the Insert bar to complete the steps in this project. Table 9-1 describes the buttons on the Media tab in the Insert bar.

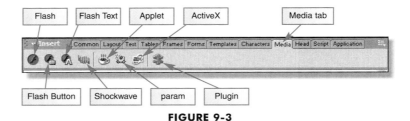

FIGURE 9-3

Table 9-1 Buttons on the Media Tab	
BUTTON NAME	DESCRIPTION
Flash	Places a Flash movie at the insertion point using the <OBJECT> and <EMBED> tags. A dialog box is displayed in which you can browse to an SWF file. An SWF file is a compressed version of the Flash (.fla) file, optimized for viewing on the Web.
Flash Button	Places a Flash button at the insertion point; a Flash button allows the insertion of a Flash movie into the Web page.
Flash Text	Places a Flash Text button at the insertion point; a Flash Text button lets you create and insert a Flash movie that contains just text.
Shockwave	Places a Macromedia Shockwave movie at the insertion point using the <OBJECT> and <EMBED> tags.
Applet	Places a Java applet at the insertion point. A dialog box is displayed in which you can specify the file that contains the applet's code, or click Cancel to leave the source unspecified. The Java applet is displayed only when the document is viewed in a browser.
Param	Inserts a tag that allows you to pass parameters to an applet or object.
ActiveX	Places an ActiveX control at the insertion point. Use the Property inspector to specify a source file and other properties for the ActiveX control.
Plugin	Inserts a file at the insertion point using an <EMBED> tag that requires a Netscape Navigator plug-in for playback. A dialog box is displayed in which you can specify the source file.

Macromedia Flash

Macromedia's Flash program is an excellent way to create and add animation and interactivity to a Web page. It is a collection of tools for animating and drawing graphics, adding sound, creating interactive elements, and playing movies. It quickly is becoming a standard for Web animation. Objects within Flash are created using vector graphics. Recall from Project 2 that mathematical formulas are used to describe vector images and produce relatively small file sizes. By contrast, GIF and JPEG graphics use **bitmap technology**, which includes data for every pixel within the object. The bitmap technology produces a large file size. Thus, vector images are a more efficient method of delivering this type of technology over the Internet because they are displayed faster on a downloading Web site.

Creating **Flash files** (also called Flash movies) requires that the developer use the Flash program. Learning to use this program and developing Flash movies can be time-consuming. A search of the Internet, however, produces many Web sites with free Flash and/or nominally priced Flash animations that can be downloaded and added to your Dreamweaver Web page.

Most media objects require a helper program or plug-in before they can be displayed in the browser. For instance, the **Flash player** is required to view Flash files. Plug-ins are discussed in more detail later in this project. The Flash player is available as both a Netscape Navigator plug-in and an ActiveX control for Microsoft Internet Explorer, and it is incorporated in the latest versions of Netscape Navigator, Microsoft Internet Explorer, and America Online. Macromedia also provides this player as a free download at the Macromedia Web site.

More About

External Editors

You can associate each file type that Dreamweaver does not handle directly with one or more external editors found on your system. The editor that launches when you double-click the file in the Site panel is called the primary editor. You can set which editor is associated with a file type in File Types/Editors preferences.

Flash Text

Recall that Dreamweaver comes with two Flash objects you can use without having the Flash program. These two objects are Flash buttons and Flash text. In Project 4, you created a framed Web site and added Flash buttons to the navigation

Flash Movies

When you insert a Flash movie into a document, Dreamweaver uses both the <OBJECT> tag (defined by Internet Explorer for ActiveX controls) and the <EMBED> tag (defined by Netscape Navigator) to get the best results in all browsers.

frame. In this project, you add Flash text. Also recall from Project 4 that an object created with the Flash program can generate three different files, as follows:

1. **Flash file (.fla)**   This is the source file for any project and is created in the Flash program. To open a .fla file requires the Flash program. Using Flash, you then can export it as a SWF or SWT file that can be viewed in a browser.
2. **Flash movie file (.swf)**   This is a compressed version of the Flash (.fla) file, optimized for viewing on the Web. This file can be played back in browsers and previewed in Dreamweaver but cannot be edited in Flash. This is the type of file you create when using the Flash button and text objects in Dreamweaver.
3. **Flash template file (.swt)**   These file types enable you to modify and replace information in a Flash movie file. These files are used in the Flash button object.

Flash text is self-contained. Therefore, when creating Flash text, you can use fonts that are not necessarily installed on the Web site visitor's computer. In this project, the Comic Sans MS font is used to create the Flash text file. If this font is not available on your computer, use another one of your own choosing or as directed by your instructor.

Adding Flash Text

To begin creating your splash page, you open the splash.htm data file and then you add Flash text. Tables are included on the page to facilitate page layout and to add borders to the text Flash object and other objects. The splash page contains three tables. Each table is identified with a table ID: table01, table02, and table03. The first table, table01, contains two rows, or two cells. You insert the Flash text into the table cells of table01. Complete the following steps to open the splash.htm page and add the the Flash text.

 To Add Flash Text

1 **Close the Untitled-1 page that opened when you started Dreamweaver and then open the splash.htm file. Click the Media tab on the Insert bar.**

The splash.htm file contains three tables: table01, table02, and table03. The Insert bar with the Media tab selected is displayed (Figure 9-4). The alignment for the first cell in table01 is left-aligned and the alignment for the second cell is right-aligned.

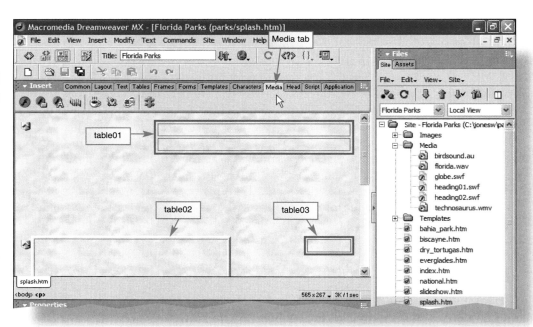

FIGURE 9-4

2 **Click the first cell in table01 and then point to the Flash Text button on the Media tab.**

The insertion point is blinking in cell 1 of table01 (Figure 9-5).

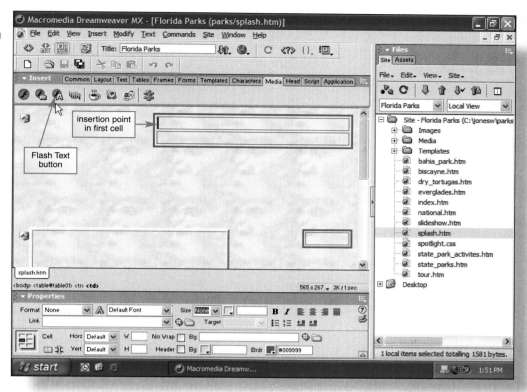

FIGURE 9-5

3 **Click the Flash Text button. Point to the Font box arrow.**

The Insert Flash Text dialog box is displayed (Figure 9-6).

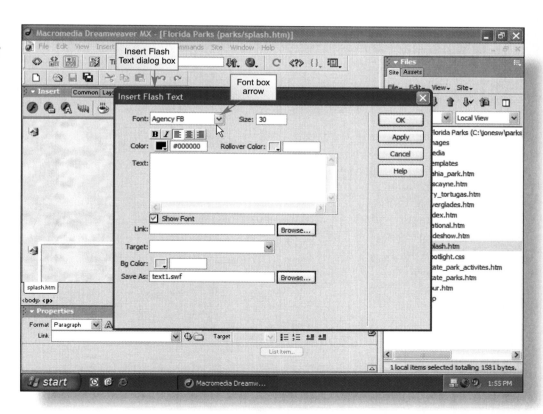

FIGURE 9-6

4 Click the Font box arrow, scroll down, and then click Comic Sans MS from the Font list. If the Comic Sans MS font is not available on your computer, select another one of your own choosing or as directed by your instructor. Point to the Color hexadecimal text box.

The Comic Sans MS font is displayed in the Font box (Figure 9-7).

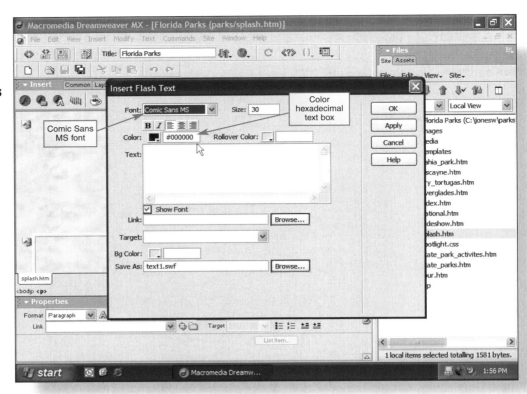

FIGURE 9-7

5 Double-click the Color hexadecimal text box, type #00FFFF and then press the TAB key. In the Rollover Color text box, type #0000CC and then press the TAB key. Type Florida welcomes the world! in the Text text box. Click the Bg Color hexadecimal text box. Type #009999 and then press the TAB key. Type Media/heading01.swf in the Save As text box and then point to the OK button.

The attributes are added for the Flash text (Figure 9-8).

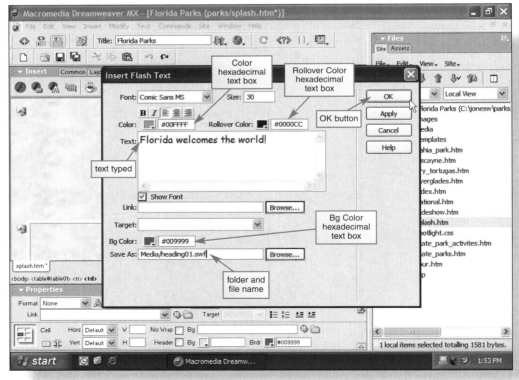

FIGURE 9-8

6 Click the OK button. Click cell 2 in table01 and then click the Flash Text button on the Media tab.

The Insert Text Flash dialog box is displayed (Figure 9-9).

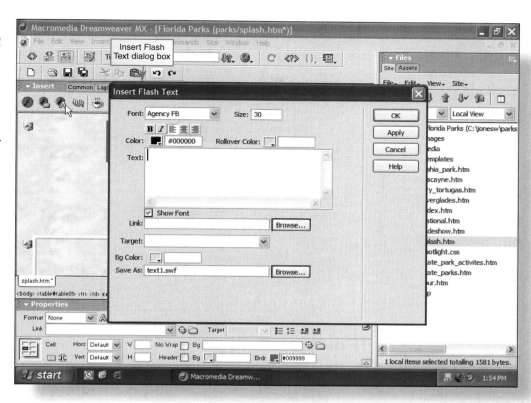

FIGURE 9-9

7 Add the following attributes to the Insert Flash Text dialog box. Font: Comic Sans MS, Size: 20, Color: #00FFFF, Rollover Color: #0000CC, Text: Visit a Florida park for a vacation of a lifetime!, Bg Color: #009999, and Media/heading02.swf in the Save As text box. Point to the OK button.

The attributes are added to the Insert Flash Text dialog box (Figure 9-10).

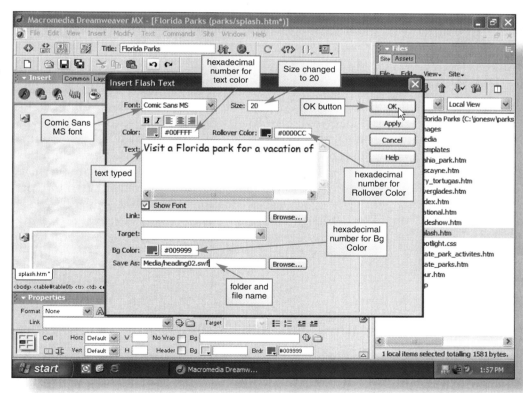

FIGURE 9-10

8 **Click the OK button.**

The Flash text is displayed (Figure 9-11).

FIGURE 9-11

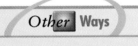

Other Ways

1. On Insert menu point to Interactive Images, click Flash Text

Flash Movies

The earliest Web pages were plain, consisting of mostly text with links on a gray or white background. Eventually, typefaces changed, and colors and static images were added. In 1997, Macromedia purchased a software program known as FutureSplash and changed the name to Flash. **Flash** is a multimedia program developed especially for the Internet and World Wide Web and changed the look of and added interactivity to Web pages. Today, it is a popular program for creating movies, Web graphics, and other multimedia elements.

Adding a Flash Movie

Dreamweaver makes it easy to insert a Flash movie into a Web page. Simply position the insertion point in the Document window at the location where you would like the movie to display. Then click the Flash button on the Media tab and select the file name. Flash movies end with a .swf extension. When you insert a movie, Dreamweaver adds the code for the movie. After the movie is inserted into the Document window, a gray rectangle is displayed on the page. This rectangle represents the width and height of the movie. The width and height are determined when the developer creates the movie. The Flash logo is displayed in the center of the gray rectangle.

When a Flash movie is inserted and selected, Dreamweaver displays the Flash Property inspector. The following section describes the Flash Property inspector (Figure 9-12).

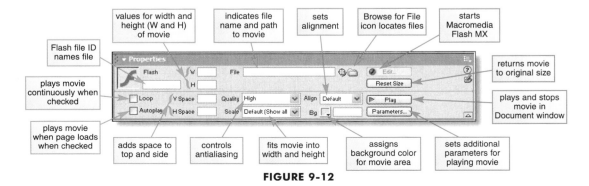

FIGURE 9-12

NAME **Name** is an identifier used to identify the movie for scripting.

W AND H The **W** and **H** boxes indicate the width and height of the movie in pixels. You can specify the movie size in the following units: pc (picas), pt (points), in (inches), mm (millimeters), cm (centimeters), or % (percentage of the parent object's value). The abbreviations must follow the value without a space (for example, 3mm).

FILE The **File** text box allows you to include a file name that specifies the path to the Flash or Shockwave movie file. Click the Browse for File icon to browse to a file, or type a path name.

EDIT The **Edit** button starts Macromedia Flash MX. If Flash is not installed on your computer, this button is disabled.

RESET SIZE The **Reset Size** button returns the selected movie to its original size.

LOOP When the **Loop** check box is checked, the movie plays continuously; when unchecked, the movie plays once and stops.

AUTOPLAY When the **Autoplay** check box is checked, the movie automatically plays when the page loads.

V SPACE AND H SPACE The values entered into the **V Space** and **H Space** boxes add space, in pixels, along the sides of the movie. V Space adds space along the top and bottom of the movie. H Space adds space along the left and right of the movie.

QUALITY **Quality** controls antialiasing during playback of the movie. A movie looks better with a high setting, but it requires a faster processor to render correctly on the screen. Low emphasizes speed over appearance, whereas High favors appearance over speed. Auto Low emphasizes speed at first, but improves appearance when possible. Auto High emphasizes both qualities at first, but sacrifices appearance for speed if necessary. **Antialiasing** is a technique for smoothing the jagged appearance caused by poor resolution.

SCALE **Scale** determines how the movie fits into the dimensions set in the width and height fields. The Default setting displays the entire movie. The other options are No border and Exact fit. No border fits the movie into the set dimensions so that no borders show and maintains the original aspect ratio. Exact fit scales the movie to the set dimensions, regardless of the aspect ratio.

ALIGN **Align** sets the alignment of the movie in relation to other elements on the page.

BG **Bg** specifies a background color for the movie area. This color also appears while the movie is not playing (while loading and after playing).

PARAMETERS The **Parameters** button opens a dialog box for entering additional parameters to pass to the movie. The movie must have been designed to receive these additional parameters.

PLAY/STOP The **Play** button plays the Flash movie in the Document window. Click the **Stop** button to stop the movie from playing.

FLASH FILE ID The **Flash File ID** is the ID number for the Flash file.

Steps **To Add a Flash Movie**

1 If necessary, scroll down and then click in table02.

The insertion point is blinking in table02 (Figure 9-13).

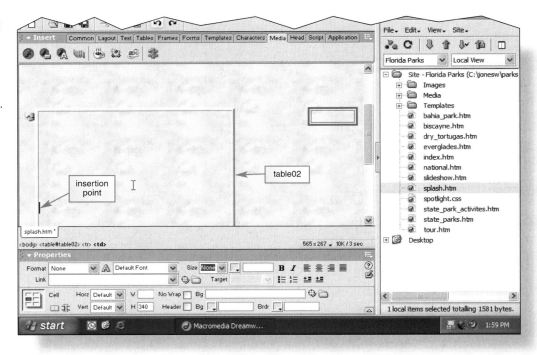

FIGURE 9-13

2 Click the plus sign to the left of the Media folder and then drag globe.swf to table02.

The Flash movie is inserted into the table and the Flash Property inspector is displayed (Figure 9-14).

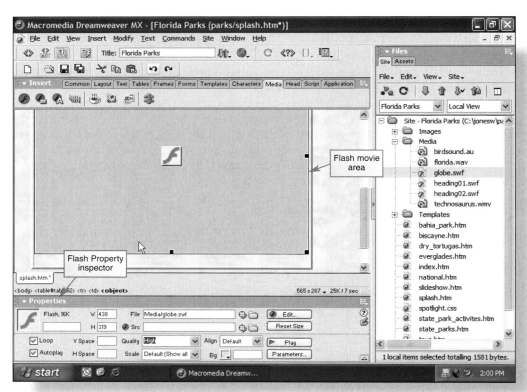

FIGURE 9-14

3 Click the Flash text box in the Property inspector and then type globe **as the movie name. Point to the Play button.**

The movie name, globe, appears in the text box in the Property inspector (Figure 9-15).

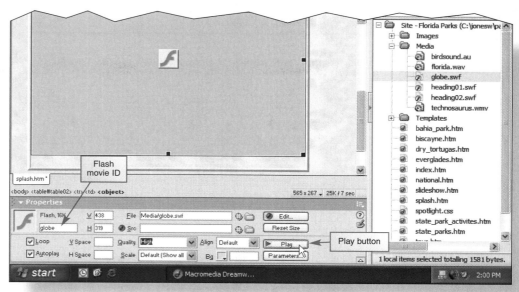

FIGURE 9-15

4 Click the Play button in the Property inspector.

The movie plays in the Document window (Figure 9-16). Notice that the Play button is a toggle button, and as soon as you clicked it, it was labeled Stop.

5 Click the Stop button in the Property inspector.

FIGURE 9-16

Adding a Link to Go to the Index Page

A splash page adds interest to a Web site, but may annoy frequent visitors. It is always best, therefore, to provide a link for the visitor to go directly to the index and/or home page. The steps on the next page add a link to table03. The steps on the next page add a link in table03 to the index page.

Other Ways

1. On Insert menu point to Media, click Flash

To Add a Link to Go to the Index Page

1 **Scroll up in the Document window and then click in table03.**

The centered insertion point is blinking in table03 (Figure 9-17).

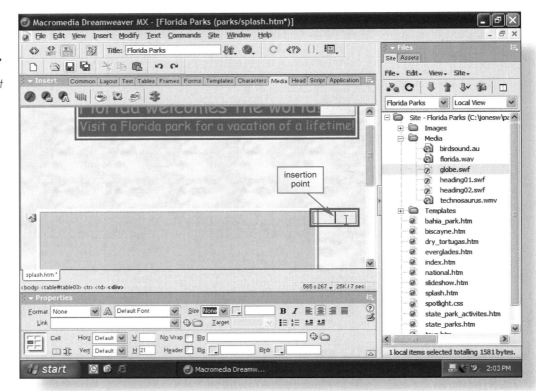

FIGURE 9-17

2 **Type** Skip Intro **and then select the text.**

The text Skip Intro is displayed and selected in table03 (Figure 9-18).

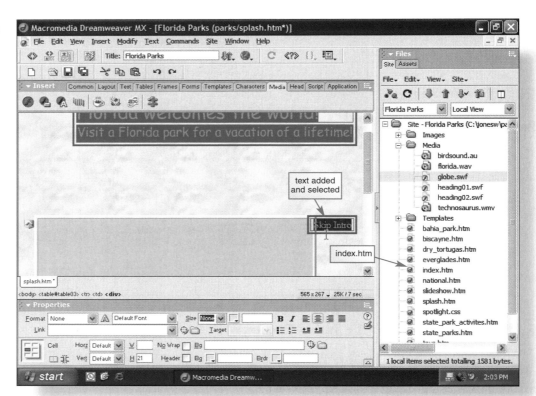

FIGURE 9-18

3 If necessary, scroll down in the Site panel and then drag index.htm to the Link box in the Property inspector. Press the ENTER key.

The link to the index.htm Web page is added (Figure 9-19).

4 Click the Save button on the Standard toolbar and then press the F12 key to view the page in your browser. Move the mouse pointer over the text in table01 to view the text color change. Click the link to verify that it works. Close the browser and return to Dreamweaver.

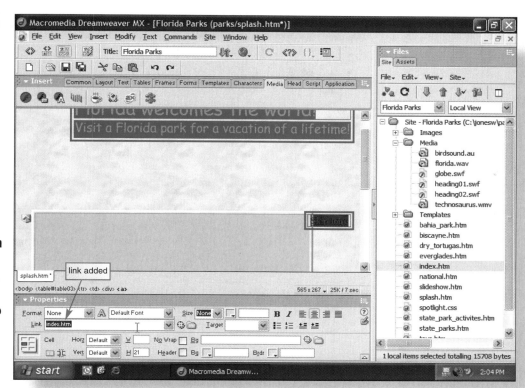

FIGURE 9-19

Audio on the Web Page

Adding sound to your Web page can add interest and set a mood. Background music can enhance your theme. Attaching sounds to objects, such as the sound of clicking buttons, can provide valuable feedback to the Web site visitor. Sound, however, can be expensive in terms of the file site size and download time, particularly for those visitors with baseband access. Another consideration is that adding sound to a Web page can be a challenging and confusing task. Most computers today have some type of sound card and some type of sound-capable plug-in that works with the browser. The difficult part, though, is generating the desirable sounds. The Web supports several popular sound file formats, along with their supporting plug-ins. The quest is to find the one most widely used. Table 9-2 on the next page contains a list and description of the commonly used sound file formats.

More About

Adding Sound

Some factors to consider before deciding on a format and method for adding sound are its purpose, your audience, the file size, the sound quality you want, and differences in browsers. For more information about Dreamweaver and adding sound, visit the Dreamweaver MX More About Web page (scsite .com/dreamweavermx/ more.htm) and then click Adding Sound.

More About

Linking to Sound

Linking to sound files lets visitors choose to listen to the file and makes the file available to the widest audience.

Table 9-2 Sound File Formats	
FILE NAME EXTENSION	*DESCRIPTION*
.aif (Audio Interchange File Format, or AIFF)	The AIFF format can be played by most browsers and does not require a plug-in; you also can record AIFF files from a CD, tape, microphone, and so on. The large file size, however, limits the length of sound clips that you can use on your Web pages.
.midi or .mid (Musical Instrument Digital Interface, or MIDI)	The MIDI format is for instrumental music. MIDI files are supported by many browsers and do not require a plug-in. The sound quality is good, but it can vary depending on a visitor's sound card. A small MIDI file can provide a long sound clip. MIDI files cannot be recorded and must be synthesized on a computer with special hardware and software.
.mp3 (Motion Picture Experts Group Audio, or MPEG-Audio Layer-3, or MP3)	The MP3 format is a compressed format that allows for substantially smaller sound files. The sound quality is very good; you can stream the file so that a visitor does not have to wait for the entire file to download before hearing it. To play MP3 files, visitors must download and install a helper application or plug-in such as QuickTime, Windows Media Player, or RealPlayer.
.ra, .ram, .rpm (RealAudio)	The RealAudio format has a very high degree of compression with smaller file sizes than MP3. Whole song files can be downloaded in a reasonable amount of time. The files can be streamed, so visitors can begin listening to the sound before the file has been downloaded completely. The sound quality is poorer than that of MP3 files. Visitors must download and install the RealPlayer helper application or plug-in to play these files.
.wav (Waveform Extension, or WAV)	WAV-formatted files have good sound quality, are supported by many browsers, and do not require a plug-in. The large file size, however, severely limits the length of sound clips that you can use on your Web pages.

ActiveX versus Plug-ins

ActiveX Controls

ActiveX is a set of rules for how applications should share information. ActiveX controls have full access to the Windows operating system. For more information about AxtiveX controls, visit the Dreamweaver MX More About Web page (scsite.com/dreamweavermx/more.htm) and then click ActiveX.

A Web browser basically is an HTML decoder. Recall that a plug-in is a program that is used to view plug-in applications through the Web browser. A plug-in adds functionality to the browser — it is not a stand-alone program and cannot start and run on its own. To work correctly, plug-in programs must be present in the browser's Plugins folder. Both Internet Explorer and Netscape include Plugins folders within their own application folder. When the browser encounters a file with an extension of .swf, for example, it looks for and attempts to start the Flash player plug-in.

Several years ago, Netscape developed the capability of incorporating plug-ins within the browser by creating the nonstandard HTML tag, <EMBED>. This tag never was made part of the W3C's official HTML specifications, but it became widely used.

Some of the more popular plug-ins are Adobe's Acrobat Reader, RealAudio and RealVideo, Apple's QuickTime, Macromedia's Flash and Shockwave, and VRML (Virtual Reality Modeling Language). Using these plug-ins, the Web site visitor can use the browser to view specialized content, such as animation, virtual reality, streaming audio and video, and formatted content. These plug-in programs and information are available for download at their related Web sites.

In contrast, **ActiveX** is a set of technologies developed by Microsoft and is an outgrowth of OLE (object linking and embedding). An **ActiveX control** is a control using ActiveX technologies and currently is limited to Windows environments. ActiveX objects use the <OBJECT> tag instead of the <EMBED> tag. When you insert media using ActiveX, you must specify a classID or ActiveX control and, in many instances, add parameters. Parameters are discussed in more detail later in this project.

As a result, two ways exist to insert media content into browsers: as plug-ins using the <EMBED> tag and as ActiveX objects using the <OBJECT> tag. Until recently, both Internet Explorer and Netscape supported Netscape-style plug-ins, but newer versions of Internet Explorer support only ActiveX controls, although Internet Explorer supports the <EMBED> tag for ActiveX content.

When adding media to a Web page, the Web page developer must try to predict how Web site visitors will have their browsers configured. One of the more common problems is that a particular plug-in may not be available on a visitor's computer. Fortunately, Dreamweaver helps by offering support for both plug-ins and ActiveX controls.

Windows Media Player is one of the more popular platforms for playing audio and video. This player is Internet Explorer's default multimedia player. This player plays the standard audio formats, including AIFF, AU, MIDI, and MP3.

Adding Sound to the Splash Page

Web site developers primarily use two methods to add sound to a Web page: linking to an audio file or embedding an audio file. Embedding a sound file integrates the audio into the Web page. The sound player is inserted directly into the Web page. This process lets Web site visitors choose whether they want to listen to the audio and the number of times they want to hear it.

The simplest and most effective way to add sound to a Web page is through linking. The link can be any object, such as text, an image, a table, and so on. The object is linked to a sound file. The WAV format (.wav), for example, is one of the more popular sound formats on the Internet, and it is supported by all the popular browsers.

In the next steps, you add text to the splash page and then add a link from the text to the florida.wav sound file. When the Web site visitor clicks the link, the browser will start the Windows Media Player to play the .wav file.

More About

Embed a Sound

When you embed a sound in a Web page, you can set the volume, the way the player looks on the page, and the beginning and ending points of the sound file. For more information about Dreamweaver and embedding sound, visit the Dreamweaver MX More About Web page (scsite .com/dreamweavermx/ more.htm) and then click Embedding Sound.

Steps To Link to a Sound File

1 **Click below table01, type** Visit a Florida State Park today. **and then select the text you just typed.**

The text is entered and selected (Figure 9-20).

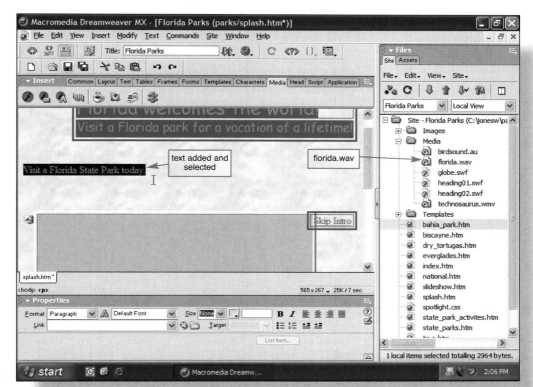

FIGURE 9-20

2 Drag the florida.wav file from the Site panel Media folder to the Link box in the Property inspector. Press the ENTER key.

The link is created to the florida.wav audio file (Figure 9-21).

3 Press the F12 key to open the browser and then click the link to verify that the audio works. A speaker or headphones must be attached to the computer to hear the audio. Close the browser. Click the Save button on the Standard toolbar and then close the splash.htm page.

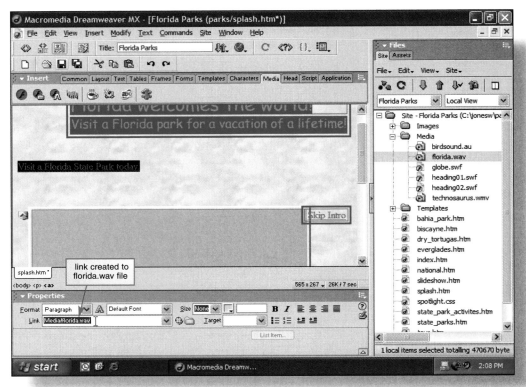

FIGURE 9-21

Embedding an Audio File

Embedding a sound in a Web page provides the Web site visitor with control over the audio player. The content developer determines the amount of control through parameters. In this project, you embed an audio player into the state_parks.htm page. When the user clicks the control, a bird sound is heard through the Windows Media Player. An ActiveX control is used, thereby requiring specific parameters. A **parameter** means defining the characteristics of something. For example, AutoRewind, AutoStart, and font specifications are considered parameters. Table 9-3 contains a list of frequently used parameters. This list is an example only and several other parameters also are available. You can find a list at the Microsoft Web site at http://msdn.microsoft.com/library/default.asp?url=/library/en-us/wmplay/mmp_sdk/paramtags.asp.

Table 9-3 ActiveX Parameters

PARAMETER	DEFAULT	DESCRIPTION
AutoStart	True	Defines whether the player should start automatically
AnimationAtStart	True	Defines whether an animation should show while the file loads
AutoRewind	False	Defines whether the player should rewind automatically
ClickToPlay	True	Defines whether the player should start when the user clicks the play area
DisplayBackColor	False	Shows a background color
EnablePositionControls	True	Provides the user with position controls
EnableFullScreenControls	False	Provides the user with screen controls
Filename	N/A	Indicates the URL of the file to play
InvokeURLs	True	Links to a URL
Mute	False	Mutes the sound
ShowControls	True	Defines if the player controls should show
ShowAudioControls	True	Defines whether the audio controls should show
ShowDisplay	False	Defines whether the display should show
Volume	-200	Specifies the volume

ActiveX controls also require a classID. Dreamweaver uses the classID to define the object when generating the code for the ActiveX control. This ID hexadecimal is added through the ActiveX Property inspector. Once added, it will become an option within the ClassID pop-up menu. The following section describes the ActiveX Property inspector (Figure 9-22).

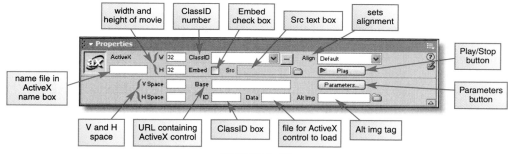

FIGURE 9-22

ACTIVEX NAME BOX The **name** in the ActiveX name box identifies the ActiveX object for scripting.

W AND H **W** and **H** are the width and height of the image, in pixels. Dreamweaver automatically inserts the dimensions when a image is inserted into the page. You can specify the image size in the following units: pc (picas), pt (points), in (inches), mm (millimeters), cm (centimeters), and combinations, such as 2in+5mm. Dreamweaver converts the values to pixels in the HTML source code.

CLASSID The **classID** identifies the ActiveX control to the browser. Enter a value or choose one on the pop-up menu. When the page is loaded, the browser uses the classID to locate the ActiveX control required for the ActiveX object associated with the page. For all versions of Windows Media Player beginning with version 7 and later, use the following classID: CLSID:22d6f312-b0f6-11d0-94ab-0080c74c7e95. This is assigned through the ActiveX Property inspector.

EMBED Checking the **Embed** check box adds an <EMBED> tag within the <OBJECT> tag for the ActiveX control. If the ActiveX control has a Netscape Navigator plug-in equivalent, the <EMBED> tag activates the plug-in. Dreamweaver assigns the values you entered as ActiveX properties to their Netscape Navigator plug-in equivalents.

ALIGN **Align** sets the alignment of an object on the page.

PARAMETERS The **Parameters** button opens a dialog box for entering additional parameters to pass to the ActiveX object.

SRC The **Src** value defines the data file to be used for a Netscape Navigator plug-in if the Embed check box is selected. If a value is not entered, Dreamweaver attempts to determine the value from the ActiveX properties entered already.

V SPACE AND H SPACE The **V Space** and **H Space** values add space, in pixels, along the sides of the object. V Space adds space along the top and bottom of an object. H Space adds space along the left and right of an object.

BASE The **Base** specifies the URL containing the ActiveX control. Internet Explorer downloads the ActiveX control from this location if it has not been installed in the visitor's system. If the Base parameter is not specified and if the Web site visitor does not have the relevant ActiveX control installed, the browser cannot display the ActiveX object.

ALT IMG The **Alt Img** indicates an image to be displayed if the browser does not support the <OBJECT> tag. This option is available only when the Embed check box is not selected.

DATA **Data** specifies a data file for the ActiveX control to load. Many ActiveX controls, such as Shockwave and RealPlayer, do not use this parameter.

ID Specifies the data file **ID**.

PLAY/STOP The Play/Stop button plays and stops the movie in the Document window.

To Embed an Audio File

Complete the following steps to embed an audio file in the state_parks.htm Web page and to view the HTML code. A speaker and/or headphones are required to hear the sound.

Steps **To Embed an Audio File**

1 **Open the state_parks.htm page, click to the right of the heading text, Northwest Region, and then press the ENTER key. Point to the ActiveX button on the Media tab.**

The insertion point is centered and below the heading text (Figure 9-23).

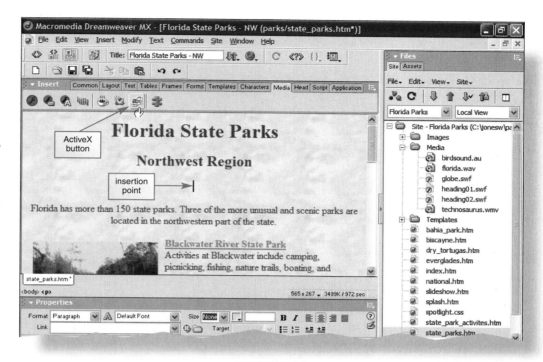

FIGURE 9-23

2 **Click the ActiveX button.**

An icon marks the location where the ActiveX control will appear on the page in Internet Explorer, and the ActiveX Property inspector is displayed (Figure 9-24).

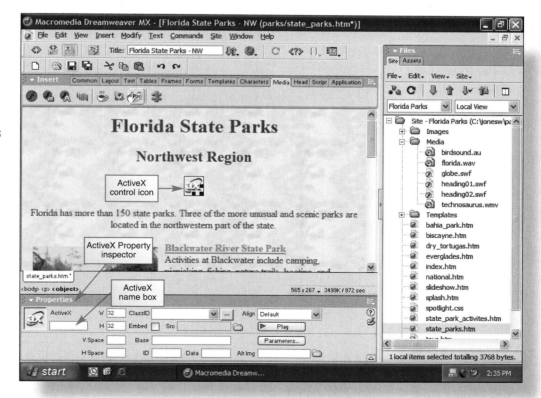

FIGURE 9-24

3 Click the ActiveX name box in the Property inspector and name the ActiveX control **birdsound**. Change the W value to 200 and the H value to 45. Type CLSID:22d6f312-b0f6-11d0-94ab-0080c74c7e95 **in the ClassID text box.**

The ActiveX name, W and H values, and classID attributes are added to the ActiveX Property inspector (Figure 9-25). Once you type in the classID number, it becomes part of the pop-up menu. It will not be necessary to add it again.

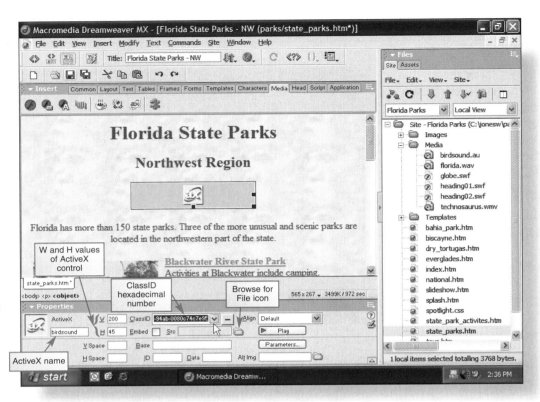

FIGURE 9-25

4 Click the Embed check box and then click the Browse for File icon to the right of the Src box. If necessary, when Dreamweaver displays the Select Netscape Plug-In File dialog box, double-click the Media folder. Point to the Files of type box arrow.

The Select Netscape Plug-In dialog box is displayed (Figure 9-26).

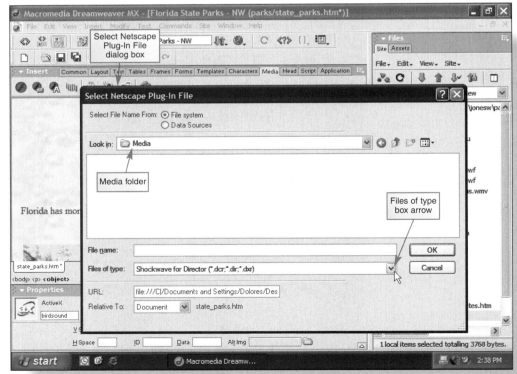

FIGURE 9-26

5 Click the Files of type box arrow and then click All Files. Click the birdsound.au file. Point to the OK button.

The birdsound.au file is highlighted (Figure 9-27).

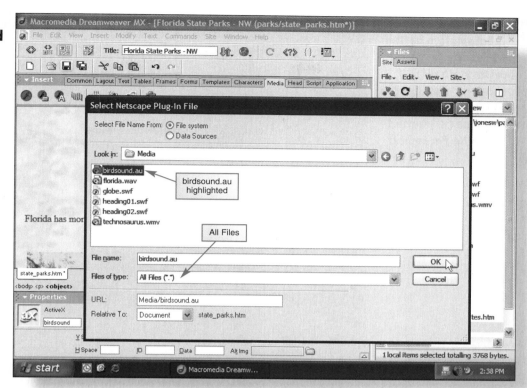

FIGURE 9-27

6 Click the OK button.

The link is created to the source text (Figure 9-28). The icon now has a large selected rectangle, which provides a holder for the audio controls. When viewed in a browser, this rectangle will contain the audio controls.

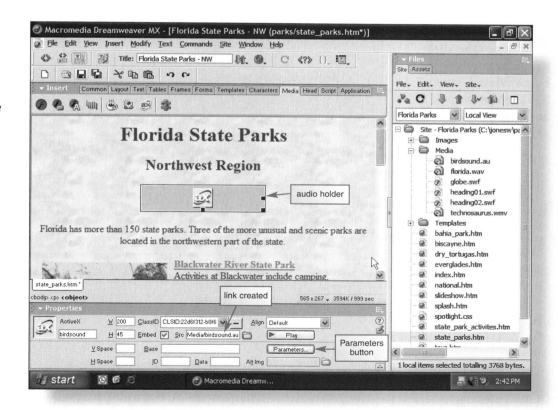

FIGURE 9-28

7 Click the Parameters button in the Property inspector. If necessary, when Dreamweaver displays the Parameters dialog box, click the plus (+) button to display the Parameter text box.

The Parameters dialog box is displayed and the insertion point is in the Parameter text box (Figure 9-29).

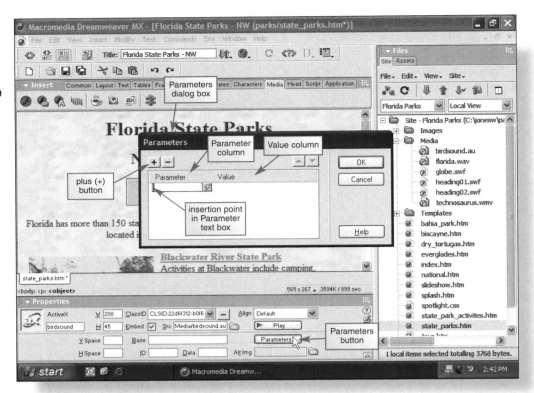

FIGURE 9-29

8 Type FileName and then click the parameter's Value column. Type Media/birdsound.au and then point to the plus (+) button.

The first parameter and value are added to the Parameters dialog box (Figure 9-30).

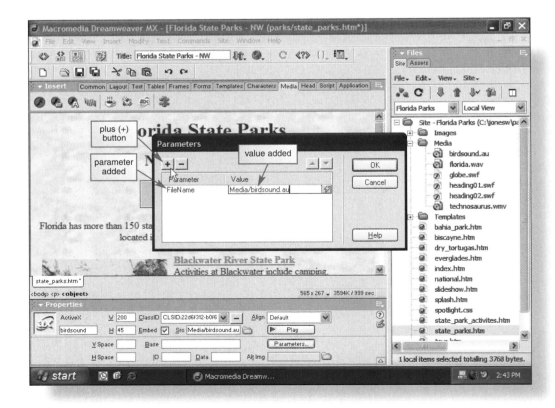

FIGURE 9-30

9 Click the plus (+) button. Use Table 9-4 to add the other parameters and values to the Parameters dialog box. After adding the last value, point to the OK button.

The parameters are added to the Parameters dialog box (Figure 9-31).

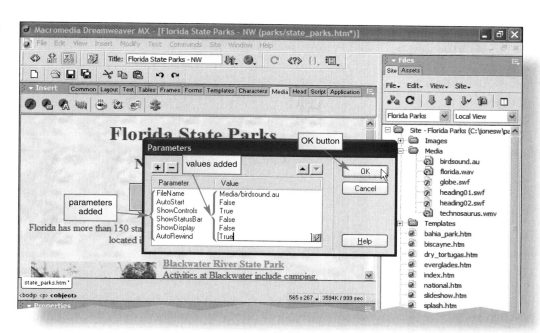

FIGURE 9-31

Table 9-4 Parameters and Values	
PARAMETER	**VALUE**
AutoStart	False
ShowControls	True
ShowStatusBar	False
ShowDisplay	False
AutoRewind	True

10 Click the OK button. Click the Files panel group expander arrow to collapse the panel group. Point to the Show Code View button on the Document toolbar.

The Site panel is collapsed. No parameter changes are evident in the Document window (Figure 9-32).

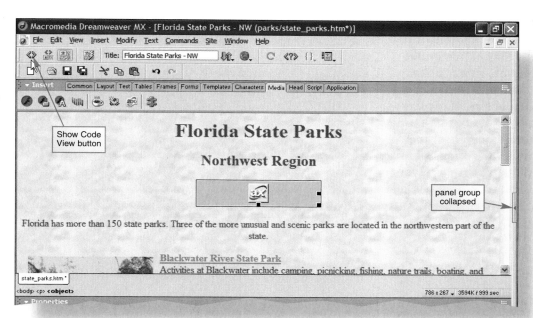

FIGURE 9-32

11 **Click the Show Code View button. Scroll the Code view window and review the code. Point to the Show Design View button.**

The parameters are added to the HTML code and are displayed highlighted (Figure 9-33).

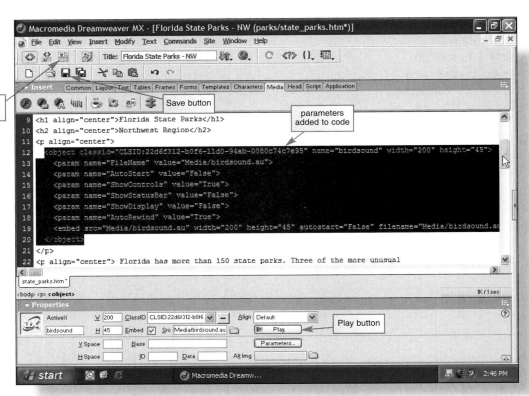

FIGURE 9-33

12 **Click the Show Design View button on the Document toolbar and then click the Save button on the Standard toolbar. Click the Play button in the Property inspector and then click the Play button on the control. Listen to the sound and then click the Stop button. A speaker and/or headphones are necessary to hear the sound. If a Dreamweaver dialog box is displayed, read the information and then click the OK button.**

The Media player is displayed and plays in the Document window (Figure 9-34). If a dialog box displays indicating that Dreamweaver is unable to find the plug-ins, try previewing in the browser. If the sound control bar does not display in the browser, see your instructor.

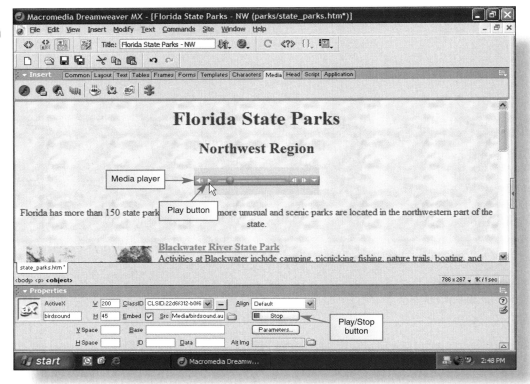

FIGURE 9-34

13 Press the F12 key to view the Web page in your browser. Click the Play button to listen to the audio.

The Windows Media Player audio control is displayed (Figure 9-35).

14 Close the browser.

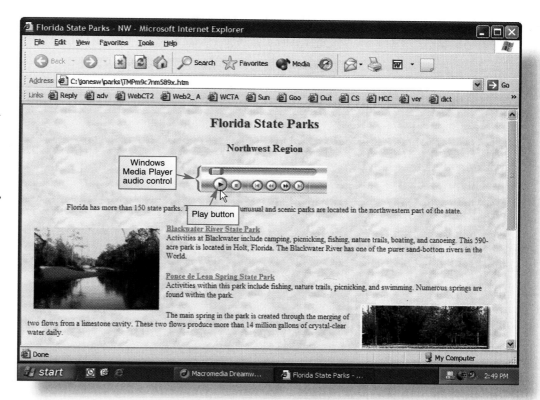

FIGURE 9-35

Video

Earlier in this project, you inserted a Flash movie into the splash page. Inserting the Flash movie was a fairly simple process because Flash also is a Macromedia product. Therefore, Dreamweaver comes with built-in controls to display a Flash movie. Movies, however, come in several other formats, and most likely occasions will arise in which you will want to insert a movie in another format. Table 9-5 contains a description of video file formats. All formats display in both Internet Explorer and Netscape.

Other Ways

1. On Insert menu point to Media, click ActiveX

More About

Adding Video

When adding video, you can let the user download it or it can be streamed so that it plays while downloading. For more information about Dreamweaver and video, visit the Dreamweaver MX More About Web page (scsite .com/dreamweavermx/ more.htm) and then click Streaming Video.

Table 9-5 Video File Formats	
FILE NAME EXTENSION	**DESCRIPTION**
.avi (Audio Video Interleave, or AVI)	The AVI format is supported by all computers running Windows.
.mpg or .mpeg (Moving Pictures Expert Group, or MPEG)	The MPEG format is one of the more popular formats on the Internet. It is cross-platform, running on Windows and Macintosh computers.
.mov (QuickTime — developed by Apple)	QuickTime is a common format on the Internet for both Windows and Macintosh computers. To play QuickTime movies on a Windows computer requires the QuickTime Player.
.rm or .ram (RealVideo)	The RealVideo format allows streaming of video, thus reducing downloading time; developed by Real Media.
.swf (Flash SWF)	The SWF format requires the Macromedia Flash player.
.wmv, .wvx (Windows Media Format, WMV)	The WMF format allows streaming of video, uses Windows Media Player, and plays on both Windows and Macintosh computers.

Dreamweaver MX

Adding Video to a Web Page

Complete the following steps to add a video file to the state_parks.htm Web page.

Steps **To Add Video to a Web Page**

1 **Click the Site panel expander arrow. Scroll to the bottom of the Web page and then click to the right of the Home link. Point to the ActiveX button on the Media tab in the Insert bar.**

The insertion point is blinking to the right of the Home link (Figure 9-36).

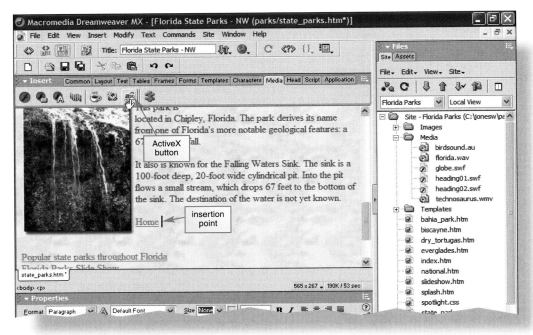

FIGURE 9-36

2 **Click the ActiveX button.**

The ActiveX control is displayed and selected in the Document window (Figure 9-37).

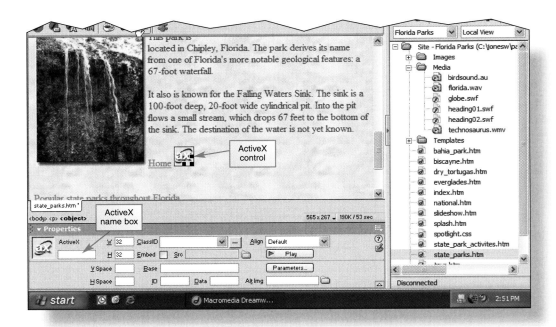

FIGURE 9-37

3 Click the ActiveX name box in the Property inspector and then type techno for the name. Press the TAB key and change the W value to 320 and the H value to 240. Click the ClassID box arrow and select the ClassID value you entered earlier in this project. Click the Align box arrow and align to the right.

The name, W and H, ClassID, and Align properties are added to the Property inspector (Figure 9-38).

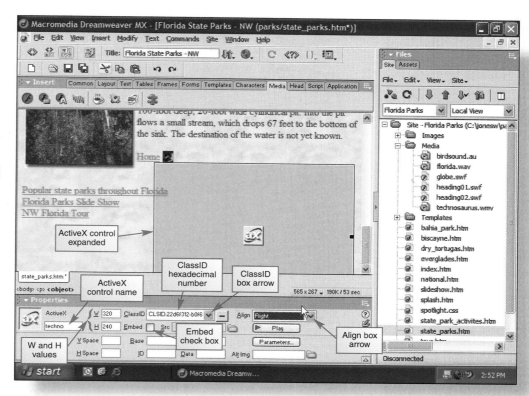

FIGURE 9-38

4 Click the Embed check box in the Property inspector. Click the Browse for File icon. If necessary, click the Media folder, click the Files of type box arrow, and then select All Files. Click the technosaurus.wmv file and then point to the OK button.

The Select Netscape Plug-In File dialog box is displayed (Figure 9-39).

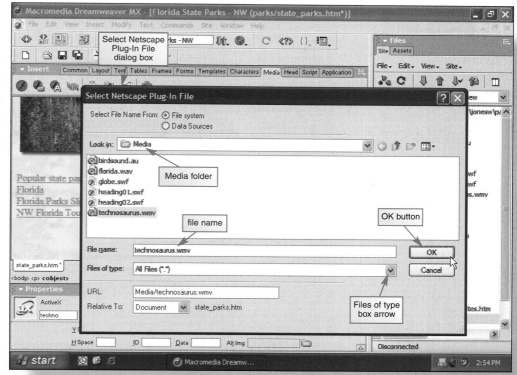

FIGURE 9-39

Dreamweaver MX

5   Click the OK button. Point to the Parameters button in the Property inspector.

The file name and path are added to the Src text box (Figure 9-40).

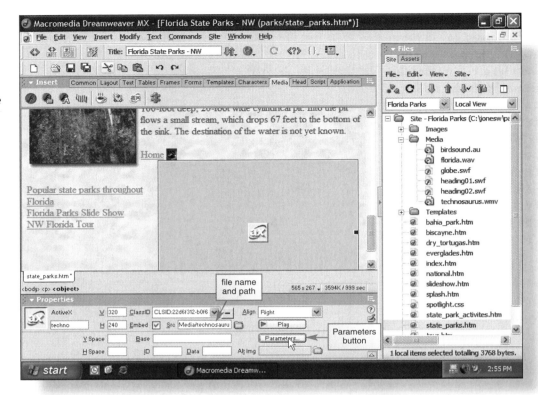

FIGURE 9-40

6   Click the Parameters button.

The Parameters dialog box is displayed and the insertion point is blinking in the Parameter text box (Figure 9-41).

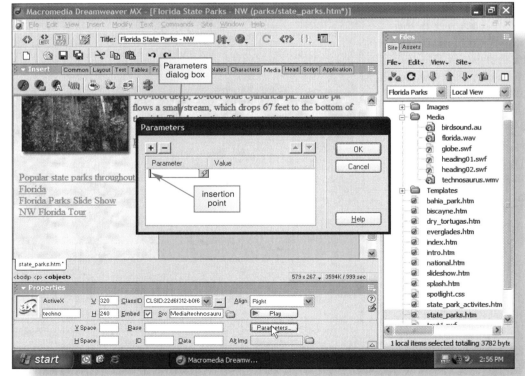

FIGURE 9-41

7 Use Table 9-6 and the steps you used on pages DW 9.26–27 to add the parameters and values to the Parameters dialog box and then point to the OK button.

The parameters and values are added to the Parameters dialog box (Figure 9-42).

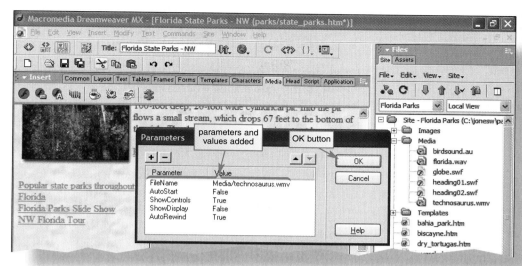

FIGURE 9-42

Table 9-6	Parameters and Values
PARAMETER	**VALUE**
FileName	Media/technosaurus.wmv
AutoStart	False
ShowControls	True
ShowDisplay	False
AutoRewind	True

8 Click the OK button. Press the F12 key to display the browser. Scroll down to display the video file. Click the Play button.

The video show holder is displayed and the video begins to play (Figure 9-43).

9 Close the browser to return to Dreamweaver. Click the Save button on the Standard toolbar and then close the file.

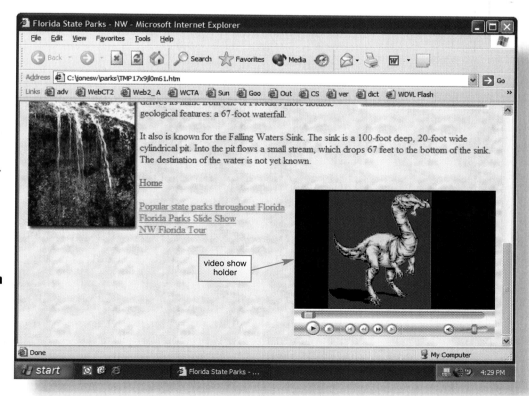

FIGURE 9-43

Checking for Plug-ins

If a visitor accesses a Web page and does not have the appropriate plug-in, it is helpful to provide a link where the visitor can download the plug-in. This is done through the Check Plugin behavior. This is particularly helpful for RealMedia, RealAudio, and other media applications that are not part of the Windows program (such as the Windows Media Player). The following steps provide information on how to add the Check Plugin behavior.

1. Select an object in the Document window and open the Behaviors panel.
2. Click the Action (+) button in the Behaviors panel and then click Check Plugin on the Actions pop-up menu.
3. Select a plug-in in the Plugin list in the Check Plugin dialog box or click the Enter option button and then type the exact name of the plug-in in the adjacent text box.
4. In the If Found, Go To URL text box, specify a URL for visitors who have the plug-in.
5. In the Otherwise, Go to URL text box, specify an alternative URL for visitors who do not have the plug-in.
6. Click the Always go to first URL if detection is not possible check box to select it. Click the OK button.

Shockwave

Another popular media type is **Shockwave**. Macromedia's Director program is used to create Shockwave files. Director often is referred to as an authoring tool or development platform. The developer uses a combination of graphics, video, sound, text, animation, and other elements to create interactive multimedia. After a developer creates the multimedia, it can be compressed into a Shockwave file and then added to a Web page. To play Shockwave content within your browser, the Shockwave player must be installed on your computer. You can download the latest version of the player from the Macromedia Web site. Information on Macromedia's Web site indicates that more than 280 million users have the Shockwave player installed.

Several file formats associated with Director and Shockwave are described below.

▶ **.dcr (Shockwave)** The .dcr file is a compressed file that can be previewed in Dreamweaver and viewed in your browser.
▶ **.dir** The .dir file is the source file created by Director. These files usually are exported through Director as .dcr files.
▶ **.dxr** The .dxr file is a locked Director file.
▶ **.cst** The .cst file contains additional information used in a .dxr or .dir file.
▶ **.cxt** The .cxt file is a file locked for distribution purposes.

The software that plays Shockwave movies is available both as a Netscape Navigator plug-in and as an ActiveX control. When you insert a Shockwave movie, Dreamweaver uses both the <OBJECT> tag (for the ActiveX control) and the <EMBED> tag (for the plug-in) to get the best results in all browsers. When you make changes in the Property inspector for the movie, Dreamweaver maps your entries to the appropriate parameters for both the <OBJECT> and <EMBED> tags.

Inserting a Shockwave file is similar to inserting a Flash movie. The following steps explain how to insert a Shockwave file into the Dreamweaver Document window.

1. Click in the Document window where you want to insert the movie.
2. Click the Shockwave button on the Media tab in the Insert bar.
3. Select a movie file in the Select File dialog box.
4. Enter the W and H values of the movie in the W and H text boxes in the Property inspector.
5. Add any necessary parameters.

Java Applets

An **applet** is a small program written in **Java**, which is a programming language for the Web. It can be downloaded by any computer. The applet also runs in HTML and usually is embedded in an HTML page on a Web site. Thus, it can be executed from within a browser. Hundreds, or even thousands, of applets are available on the Internet — many of them free. Some general categories of applets include text effects, audio effects, visual effects, navigation, games, utilities, and so on. Inserting a Java applet is similar to inserting a Flash or Shockwave movie. The following steps explain how to insert a Java applet into the Dreamweaver Document window.

1. Click in the Document window where you want to insert the applet.
2. Click the Applet button on the Media tab in the Insert bar.
3. Select an applet file in the Select File dialog box.
4. Set all necessary properties in the Property inspector.
5. Add any necessary parameters.

Quitting Dreamweaver

After you have added the Flash text, Flash movie, audio, and video, and verified that the media objects work, Project 9 is complete. To close the Web site, quit Dreamweaver MX, and return control to Windows, perform the following step.

TO CLOSE THE WEB SITE AND QUIT DREAMWEAVER

1 Click the Close button on the upper-right corner of the Dreamweaver title bar.

The Dreamweaver window, the Document window, and the Parks Web site are all closed. If you have unsaved changes, Dreamweaver will prompt you to save the changes. Clicking the Yes button in the Dreamweaver MX dialog box saves the changes.

Project Summary

Project 9 introduced you to Dreamweaver's media objects. You added a splash page with Flash text, a Flash movie, and a link to an audio file. Then you added a link to the index page from the splash page. Next, you opened the state_parks.htm page and embedded an audio file with controls. Then you added a video to the page. You learned the general procedure for adding Shockwave and Java applets.

What You Should Know

Having completed this project, you now should be able to perform the tasks in Table 9-7.

Table 9-7	Project 9 What You Should Know	
TASK NUMBER	TASK	PAGE NUMBER
1	Start Dreamweaver and Close Open Panels	DW 9.05
2	Copy Data Files to the Florida Parks Web Site	DW 9.06
3	Add Flash Text	DW 9.08
4	Add a Flash Movie	DW 9.14
5	Add a Link to Go to the Index Page	DW 9.16
6	Link to a Sound File	DW 9.19
7	Embed an Audio File	DW 9.23
8	Add Video to a Web Page	DW 9.30
9	Close the Web Site and Quit Dreamweaver	DW 9.35

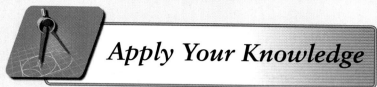

Apply Your Knowledge

1 Creating a Splash Page for B & B Lawn Service

Problem: B & B Lawn Service would like to add a splash page to its Web site. The management prefers something attractive and interesting, but somewhat conservative. You decide to copy a data file that contains five layers and images and then add Flash text for the page title. Next, you will add a Flash movie, a link to the index.htm page, and a theme song link. The splash page is shown in Figure 9-44. Appendix D contains instructions for uploading your local site to a remote server. For a selection of images and backgrounds, visit the Dreamweaver MX Media Web page (scsite.com/dreamweavermx/media) and then click Media below Project 9.

Instructions: Start Dreamweaver. If the panels display, press the F4 key to close all panels. See the inside back cover of this book for instructions for downloading the Data Disk or see your instructor for information on accessing the files in this book.

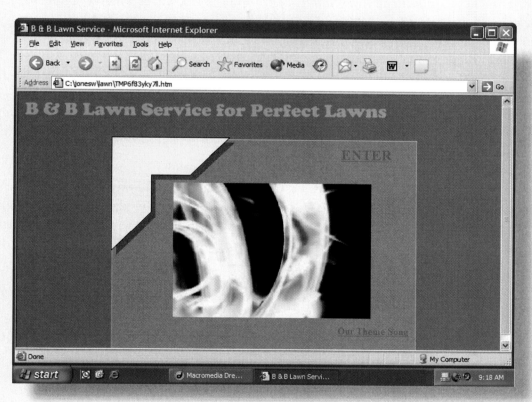

FIGURE 9-44

(continued)

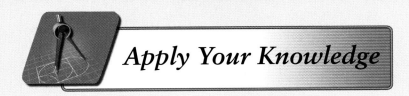

Apply Your Knowledge

Creating a Splash Page for B & B Lawn Service *(continued)*

1. Display the Property inspector, Standard toolbar, Site panel, Layers panel, and Insert bar. Select Lawn Service from the Site pop-up menu in the Site panel. Close the Untitled window.
2. Use Dreamweaver's integrated file browser to copy the Media folder, the images from the Images folder, and the data file to your lawn folder. Open the lawn_splash.htm file.
3. The lawn_splash.htm Web page contains five layers. Click to the right of the layer-code markers in the upper-left corner of the page.
4. Click the Flash Text button on the Insert bar Media tab. Change the font to Cooper Black or one of your choice, the Color to #CCCC00, the Rollover Color to #CCFF99, and the Bg Color to #669966. Type B & B Lawn Service for Perfect Lawns in the Text text box. Save the Flash text as Media/lawn01.swf.
5. Click Layer4 in the Layers panel and then click in Layer 4 in the Document window. Type ENTER and then create a link to the index.htm page.
6. Click Layer5 in the Layers panel and then, if necessary, scroll down and click in Layer 5 in the Document window. Type Our Theme Song and then create a link to the lawn.wav file in the Media folder.
7. Click Layer3 in the Layers panel, click inside Layer 3, and then click the Flash button on the Media tab to insert the Flash movie Media/lawns.swf into Layer 3.
8. In the Flash Property inspector, change the W to 315 and the H to 220. If necessary, click the Loop and AutoPlay check boxes to select them. Click the Scale box arrow and then click Exact fit. Adjust the size of Layer 3 to fit the Flash movie.
9. Click the Save button on the Standard toolbar.
10. Press the F12 key to view the page in your browser. Click the index link and then click the browser Back button. Click the Our Theme Song link. A speaker or headphones are required to hear the audio.
11. Print a copy of the lawn_splash page if instructed to do so. Upload the page to the lawn Web site on a remote server if instructed to do so.

In the Lab

1 The CandleDust Web Site

Problem: Mary would like a splash page for the CandleDust Web site. She is receiving orders from all over the world and wants to emphasize that her Web site is now an international site. Mary wants to use the same background, but wants a two-row table at the top of the page containing Flash text. She has found a Flash movie that she would like to add to the site. She also wants to add a link to the index page. The splash page is shown in Figure 9-45. For a selection of images and backgrounds, visit the Dreamweaver MX Media Web page (scsite.com/dreamweavermx/media) and then click Media below Project 9.

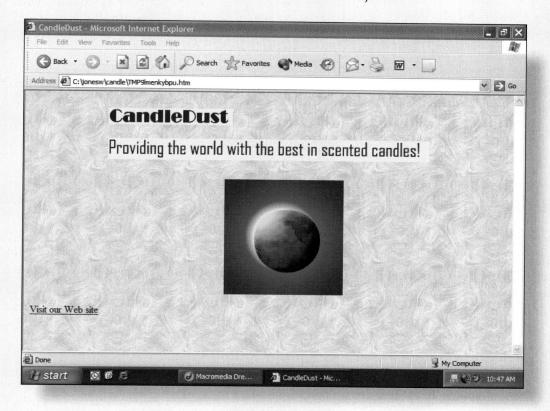

FIGURE 9-45

Instructions: Perform the following tasks:

1. Start Dreamweaver. If necessary, press F4 to close the open panels. Display the Property inspector, Standard toolbar, Site panel, and Insert bar. Select CandleDust from the Site pop-up menu in the Site panel. Copy the Media folder and the data file to the candles folder. Close the Untitled window. Open candle_splash.htm.
2. If necessary, click at the top of the page and then insert a two-row table with the following attributes in the Insert Table dialog box and Property inspector: 1 column, width of 60 percent, and cell padding of 10. Center-align the table.
3. Click in the first cell (row) in the table and then click the Flash Text button on the Media tab of the Insert bar.
4. Add the following attributes to the Insert Flash Text dialog box: Font: Broadway, Bold; Color: #660000; Rollover Color: #FF9966; Bg Color: #FFFFCC. Type the following in the Text text box: CandleDust and then save the Flash text as Media/heading01.swf.

(continued)

In the Lab

The CandleDust Web Site *(continued)*

5. Click in the second cell (row) in the table and then click the Flash Text button on the Media tab.
6. Add the following attributes to the Insert Flash Text dialog box: Font: Agency FB, Bold; Color: #660000; Rollover Color: #FF9966; Bg Color: #FFCCCC. Type `Providing the world with the best in scented candles!` in the Text text box. Save the file as Media/heading02.swf and then click the OK button. Click to the right of the table (outside the table) and then press the ENTER key.
7. Insert a layer and add the following properties: Layer ID — world; L — 320; T — 145; W — 200px; and H — 115px. Click inside the layer.
8. Click the Flash button on the Media tab and then insert the candle.swf file located in the CandleDust Media folder.
9. Scroll down and then select the text, Visit our Web site. Create a link to the index.htm page.
10. Save the splash page and then press the F12 key to view the page in the browser. Move the mouse pointer over the text heading to view the Flash text animation. Check your link to verify that it works.
11. Print a copy of the Web page if instructed to do so. Upload the page to the candle Web site on a remote server if instructed to do so. Close the browser. Quit Dreamweaver.

2 Adding Video and Sound to the Credit Web Site

Problem: Marcy is interested in what other countries are doing to help their citizens with identity theft. She has located a video file detailing some of the safeguards being proposed in Britain. She would like to create a dramatic splash page for her Web site and add this movie to the site. The splash page contains a title, the movie, and a link to the credit index.htm page. The splash page is shown in Figure 9-46. Appendix D contains instructions for uploading your local site to a remote server. For a selection of images and backgrounds, visit the Dreamweaver MX Media Web page (scsite.com/dreamweavermx/media) and then click Media below Project 9.

Instructions: Perform the following tasks:

1. Start Dreamweaver. Display the Property inspector, Standard toolbar, Site panel, and Insert bar.
2. Select Credit from the Site pop-up menu in the Site panel. Save the Untitled page as credit_splash in the Credit Web site. Use Dreamweaver's integrated file browser to copy the Media folder to the credit Web site and the images to the credit Web site Images folder.
3. Insert and center a one-column, one-row table with a width of 60 percent at the top of the page. Save the current document as credit_splash.
4. Click in the table cell and then click the Flash Text button. Add the following attributes to the Flash Text dialog box: Font: Lucida Calligraphy; Size: 45; Color: #FF3300; Rollover Color: #CC00FF; and Bg Color: #000000.
5. Type `What is Identity Theft?` in the Text text box. Save the Flash text as Media/heading1.swf.
6. Click to the right of the table (outside the table) and then press the ENTER key.
7. Insert a layer and then select the layer. Add the following properties: Layer ID — identity; L — 280; T — 130; W — 200px; and H — 115px. Click inside the layer.

In the Lab

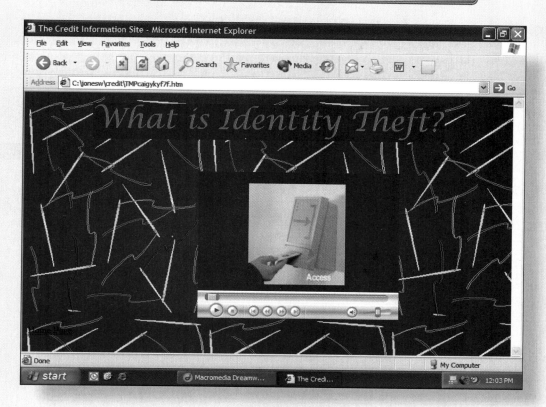

FIGURE 9-46

8. Click the ActiveX button on the Media tab. Add the following properties in the ActiveX Property inspector: ActiveX name box — identity_movie; W — 320 and H — 240; and align to the right. Click the ClassID box arrow and then click the hexadecimal number you entered earlier in this project.

9. Click the Embed check box and then click the Browse for File icon located to the right of the Src text box. If necessary, select the Media folder. Click the Files of type arrow and click All Files. Select the idcards.wmv from the Media folder within the credit site and then click the OK button.

10. Click the Parameters button and add the parameters listed in Table 9-8.

11. Click outside the layer. Press the ENTER key or scroll down to move to the end of the document. Type Home Page and then create a link to the credit index page.

12. Click Modify on the menu bar and then click Page Properties. Add the title The Credit Information Site.

13. Click the Browse button for the background image and select the bkg.gif file from the Images folder. Click the OK button.

14. Save the document. Press the F12 key to view the page in your browser. Click the Play button to view the movie. Print a copy of the Web pages if instructed to do so. Upload the page to the credit Web site on a remote server if instructed to do so. Close the browser. Quit Dreamweaver.

Table 9-8 Parameters for Credit Web site	
PARAMETER	**VALUE**
FileName	Media/idcards.wmv
AutoStart	False
ShowControls	True
ShowDisplay	False
AutoRewind	True

Dreamweaver MX

In the Lab

3 Creating a Splash Page for the Plant City Web Site

Problem: Juan wants to add some excitement to the Plant City Web site by adding a splash page. You explain to Juan that a splash page can be simple, but effective. You suggest adding some rollover text and a Flash movie. The page also will contain a link to the home page. The splash page is shown in Figure 9-47.

Instructions: Perform the following tasks:

1. Start Dreamweaver. Display the Property inspector, Standard toolbar, Site panel, Insert bar, and Layers panel. Close the Untitled page and select Plant City in the Site panel.

2. Use Dreamweaver's integrated file browser to copy the data file and the Media folder from the Data Files folder to your city folder. Open the city_splash.htm page. The page contains a two-column centered table and a layer.

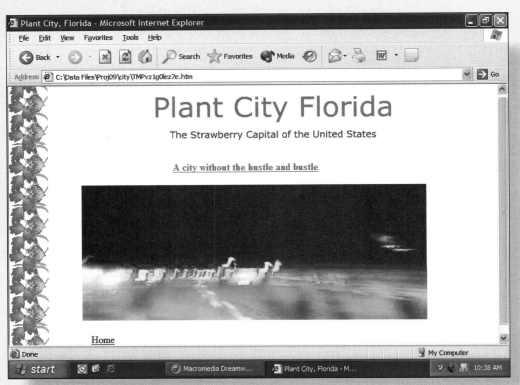

FIGURE 9-47

3. Click the first cell (row 1) in the table and then click the Flash Text button on the Media tab. Apply the following attributes: Font: Verdana, Size: 45, Color: FF0000, and Rollover Color: #000000. Type Plant City, Florida in the Text text box. Save as Media/heading01.swf.

4. Click the second cell (row 2) in the table and then click the Flash Text button on the Media tab. Apply the following attributes: Font: Verdana, Bold; Size: 15; Color: #000000; and Rollover Color: #FF0000. Type The Strawberry Capital of the United States in the Text text box. Save as Media/heading02.swf.

5. Select the layer and name it movie. Click in the layer and align to the right. Then type the following in Bold Red text: A city without the hustle and bustle and then press the ENTER key.

6. Click the Flash button on the Media tab and then open the Media folder. Click the city.swf file and then click the OK button to insert the Flash movie into the layer. Save the Web page.

7. Press the F12 key to view the page in your browser. Print a copy of the Web page if instructed to do so. Upload the page to the city Web site on a remote server if instructed to do so. Close the browser. Quit Dreamweaver.

Cases and Places

The difficulty of these case studies varies:
▶ are the least difficult; ▶▶ are more difficult; and ▶▶▶ are the most difficult.

1 ▶ You would like to add some pizzazz to your sports Web site. You decide to add a splash page. Add a background image to the page and add a title to the page. Add some Flash text and create a link to an audio file. Create a link to the home page. Save the page in your sports Web site.

2 ▶ You hobby Web site is receiving more and more hits each day. You would like to add some interactivity to your hobby Web site. You decide to do this by adding a splash page. First, you add a background image to the page and then add an appropriate title. Next, you insert Flash text and Flash buttons. Then you insert a Flash movie. Create a link to your home page. Upload to a remote site if instructed to do so.

3 ▶▶ Add a new page to your music hobby Web site and then add a background to the page. Add relevant content and then add Flash text. Add a Flash movie and embed an audio file. Create a link to and from your home page. Upload the page to a remote site.

4 ▶▶ Your campaign for political office is doing terrific and you want to enhance it by adding a splash page. Create a new Web page and add an appropriate background and title. Add Flash text and Flash buttons. Embed an audio file and then add a video file. Create a link to and from your index page. Upload the revised Web site to a remote server.

5 ▶▶▶ The Student Government Web site has become even more popular. You would like to add a splash page and then add videos to the page that includes various locations available for the student trips. On the splash page, add a Flash movie, Flash text, and a link to an audio file. On the page that includes vacation locations, add two or three videos illustrating some of the activities available at the different sites. Create a link to and from the index page. Upload the new pages to a remote server.

APPENDIX A
Dreamweaver Help

Dreamweaver Help

This appendix shows you how to use the many components of Dreamweaver Help. At anytime while you are using Dreamweaver, you can interact with its Help system and display information on any Dreamweaver topic. It is a complete reference manual at your fingertips.

The Using Dreamweaver MX Help system is viewed through your browser. Comprehensive HTML-based information about all Dreamweaver features is included. The Using Dreamweaver MX Help system contains the following:

- A table of contents in which the information is organized by subject.
- An alphabetical index that points to important terms and links to related topics.
- A search tool that allows you to find any character string in all topic text.
- A Favorites list in which you can create a Favorites folder and store named groups of assets within a given category.

Other Help features include tutorial lessons, Guided Tour movies, context-sensitive help, Extending Dreamweaver Help, Using Cold Fusion Help, and eight online reference manuals, including an HTML reference manual.

The Dreamweaver Help Menu

You access Dreamweaver's Help features through the **Help menu** and function keys. Dreamweaver's Help menu provides an easy method to access the available Help options (Figure A-1).

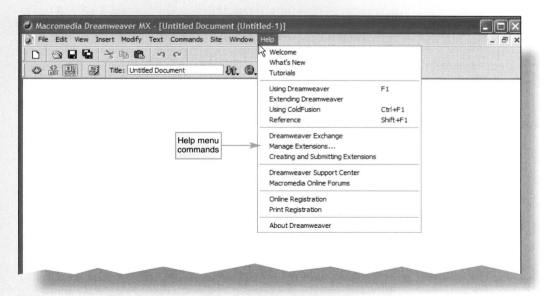

FIGURE A-1

The Help menu commands access the following components:

WELCOME AND WHAT'S NEW   The Welcome and What's New commands display buttons for an introduction to Design, Code, Develop, and What's New (Figure A-2). The What's New? button in the Welcome window and the What's New command both access the new features for returning Dreamweaver users.

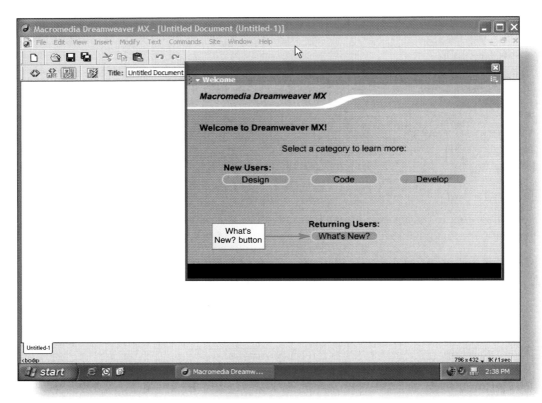

FIGURE A-2

TUTORIALS   The Tutorials command accesses the Using Dreamweaver MX window. This window provides links to six tutorials. Each tutorial takes 30 to 45 minutes to complete. Tutorials include:

- Using Tables to Design a Page Layout Tutorial
- Image Alignment and Image Maps Tutorial
- Working with Dreamweaver Design Files Tutorial
- Designing with Cascading Style Sheets Tutorial
- Building a Master-Detail Page Set Tutorial
- Building an Insert Record Page Tutorial

USING DREAMWEAVER   The Using Dreamweaver command displays the Using the Dreamweaver MX window. This feature is the most commonly used for locating information. Using Dreamweaver is covered in more detail later in this appendix.

EXTENDING DREAMWEAVER   The Extending Dreamweaver MX Help system contains descriptions of the tools that are available for developers to extend Dreamweaver using Dreamweaver application programming interfaces.

USING COLDFUSION   ColdFusion is an add-on Macromedia program used to build dynamic Web sites. ColdFusion Help in Dreamweaver MX is a subset of the documentation in ColdFusion MX. It includes all the topics that ColdFusion developers might find useful, including a full language reference.

REFERENCE   When you click the Reference command, the Reference manual is displayed on the Reference tab in the Code panel in the Dreamweaver workspace. The Reference manual contains the complete text from several Web reference manuals, including references on HTML, cascading style sheets, JavaScript, and other Web-related features.

DREAMWEAVER EXCHANGE   The Dreamweaver Exchange command allows access to the online Macromedia Exchange for Dreamweaver. This Web site contains resources for accessing extensions, learning about the extensions, and learning how to create extensions. Examples of extensions include a sales cart and a pop-up calendar. Some extensions are free and others are commercially developed and require payment.

MANAGE EXTENSIONS   An **extension** is an add-on piece of software or plug-in that enhances Dreamweaver's capabilities. Extensions provide the Dreamweaver developer with the capability to customize how Dreamweaver looks and works. Clicking the Manage Extensions command displays the Manage Extension dialog box. Through this dialog box, the developer can install, manage, and import extensions.

CREATING AND SUBMITTING EXTENSIONS   The Creating and Submitting Extensions command displays the Using the Extension Manager Help. This Help file is set up with the same configuration as Using Dreamweaver Help, which is covered in detail later in this appendix.

DREAMWEAVER SUPPORT CENTER   The Dreamweaver Support Center command provides access to the online Macromedia Dreamweaver Support Center. This Web site offers technical notes, tutorials, an online forum, and other support information.

MACROMEDIA ONLINE FORUMS   The Macromedia Online Forums command allows access to the Macromedia Online Forums Web page. The forums provide a place for developers of all experience levels to share ideas and techniques.

Using Dreamweaver MX Help

The Using Dreamweaver command accesses Dreamweaver's primary Help system and provides comprehensive information about all Dreamweaver features. Four options are available: Contents, Index, Search, and Favorites.

Using the Contents Sheet

The **Contents sheet** is useful for displaying Help when you know the general category of the topic in question, but not the specifics. Each topic in the Contents list is preceded by a book icon or question mark icon. A **book icon** indicates subtopics are available. Clicking the book icon (or associated link) displays the list of subtopics below that particular book. A **question mark icon** means information on the topic will display if you click the icon or the associated linked text. The steps on the next two pages show how to use the Contents sheet to obtain information on changing text color.

Steps | To Obtain Help Using the Contents Sheet

Click Help on the menu bar and then click Using Dreamweaver. Dreamweaver displays the Using Dreamweaver MX window. If necessary, double-click the title bar to maximize the window and click the Contents tab. If necessary, adjust the width of the left pane by moving the mouse pointer over the border separating the two panes. When the mouse pointer changes to a double-headed arrow, drag to the right to expand the left pane. Point to the Adding Content book.

The Using Dreamweaver MX Help window displays (Figure A-3). Four options are available: Contents, Index, Search, and Favorites.

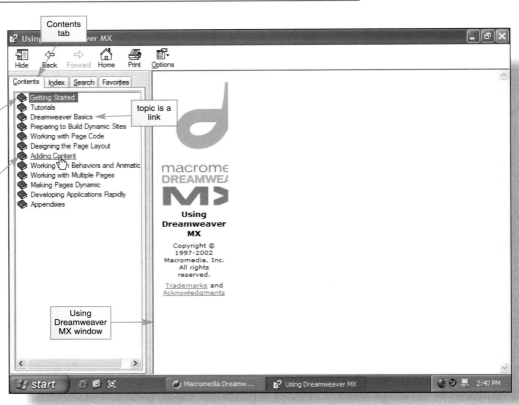

FIGURE A-3

2 | **Click the Adding Content book link.**

The Adding Content book is opened, and the help information is displayed in the right pane (Figure A-4). Additional books are displayed below the topic. Links to these books also are displayed in the right pane.

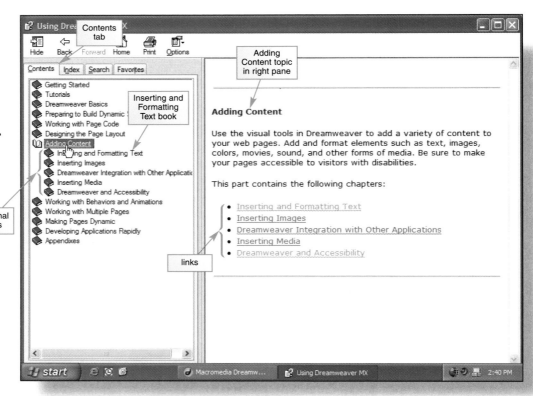

FIGURE A-4

3 **Click the Inserting and Formatting Text book, and then click the Formatting text book. Point to the Changing the text color link.**

The Formatting text book is opened and the linked topics are displayed in the left pane (Figure A-5). Related topics also are displayed in the right pane.

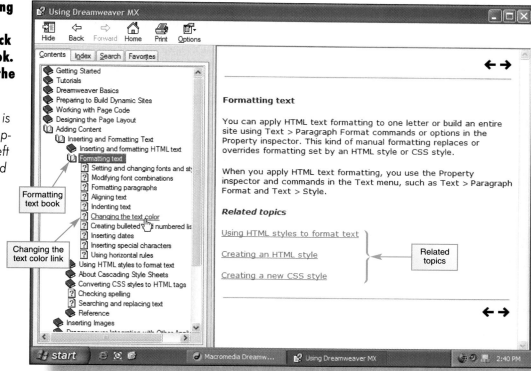

FIGURE A-5

4 **Click the Changing the text color link.**

The information on the subtopic is displayed in the right pane (Figure A-6).

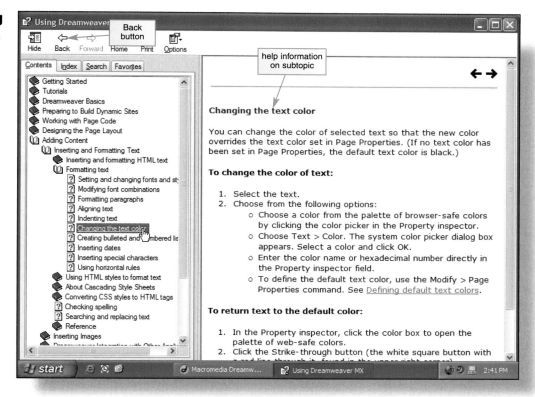

FIGURE A-6

Once the information on the subtopic is displayed, you can scroll through and read it or you can click the Print button to obtain a printed copy. If you decide to click another subtopic on the left or a link on the right, you can return to the original Help page by clicking the Back button.

Using the Index Sheet

The second sheet in the Using Dreamweaver MX window is the Index sheet. Use the **Index sheet** to display Help when you know the keyword or the first few letters of the keyword you want to look up. The following steps show how to use Index to obtain help on inserting images.

 To Use the Index Sheet

 Click the Index tab.

The Index sheet is displayed (Figure A-7). The insertion point is blinking in the Type in the keyword to find text box.

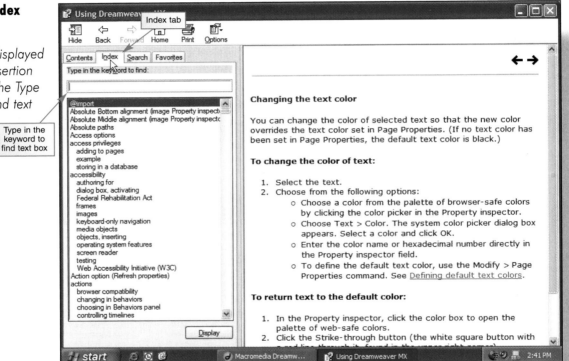

FIGURE A-7

2 **Type** images **in the text box. Click** inserting **and then point to the Display button.**

Dreamweaver scrolls through the list of topics. The topic, images, and subtopics below images are displayed in the left pane (Figure A-8). The subtopic, inserting, is highlighted.

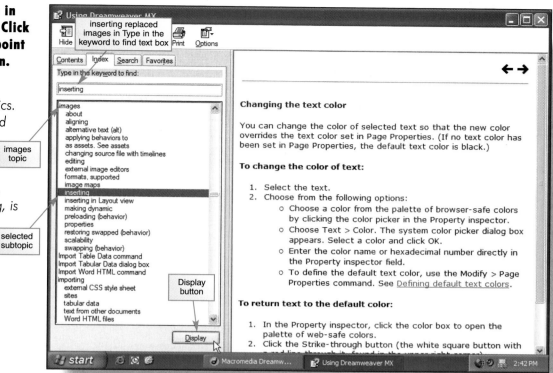

FIGURE A-8

3 **Click the Display button.**

Information about inserting an image is displayed in the right pane (Figure A-9).

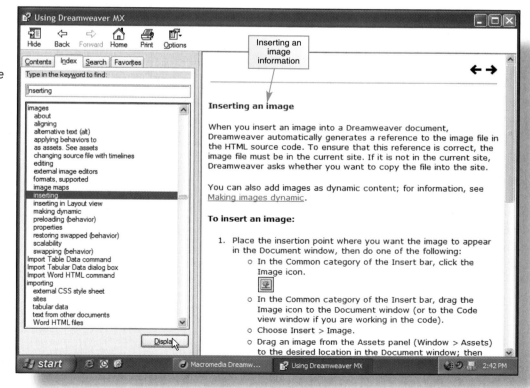

FIGURE A-9

Using the Search Sheet

Using the **Search** feature allows you to find any character string, anywhere in the text of the Help system. The following steps show how to use Search to obtain help about using bold text.

 To Use the Search Sheet

 Click the Search tab.

The Search sheet is displayed (Figure A-10). The insertion point is blinking in the Type in the keyword to find text box.

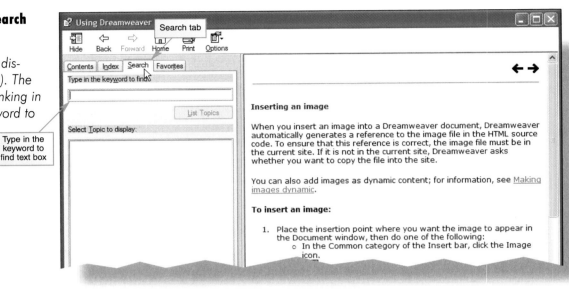

FIGURE A-10

2 **Type** Bold text **and then click the List Topics button. Click Setting Text property options and then point to the Display button.**

A list of topics containing references to bold and text is displayed in the left pane (Figure A-11). All of these topics contain the words bold and text somewhere within the document.

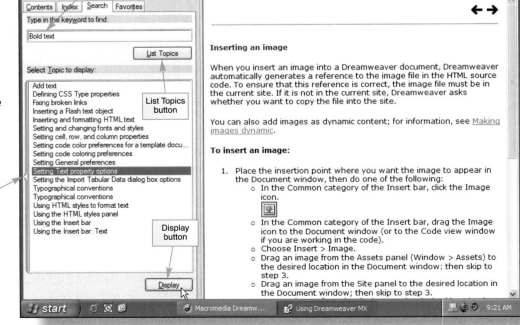

FIGURE A-11

3 Click the Display button.

The help screen for Setting Text property options is displayed in the right pane. All incidents of the words bold and text are highlighted in the document in the right pane (Figure A-12).

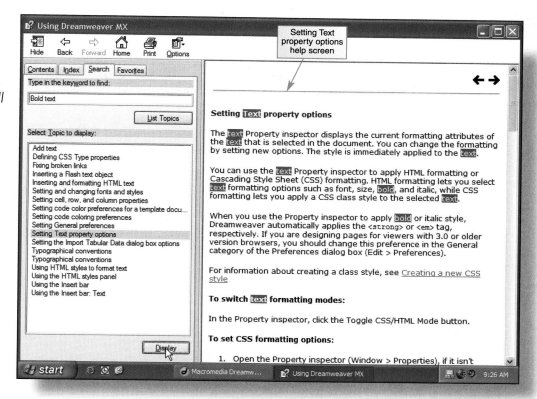

FIGURE A-12

Using the Favorites Sheet

If you find that you search or reference certain topics frequently, you can save these in the Favorites sheet. The steps on the next page show how to add the information about the bold text topic to the Favorites sheet.

Steps To Add a Topic to the Favorites Sheet

1 **Click the Favorites tab. Point to the Add button.**

The Favorites sheet is displayed in the left pane. The title of the information (Setting Text property options) is displayed in the Current topic text box in the left pane. The information on bold text that displayed as a result of your previous search is displayed in the right pane (Figure A-13).

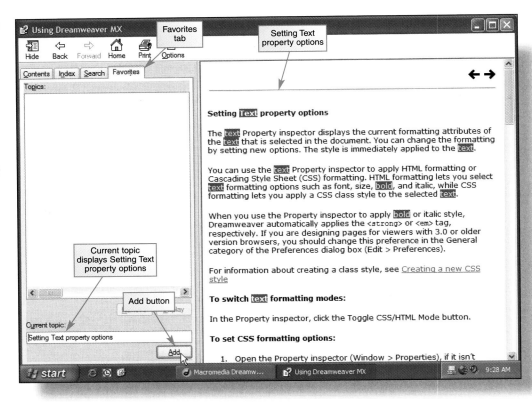

FIGURE A-13

2 **Click the Add button.**

The Setting Text property options topic is added to the Favorites sheet (Figure A-14).

3 **Close the Using Dreamweaver MX window and return to Dreamweaver.**

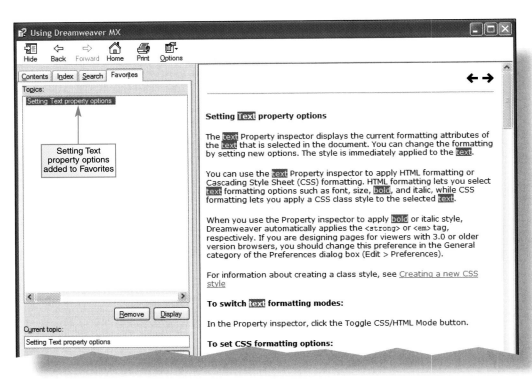

FIGURE A-14

You can add as many additional topics as you choose to the Favorites sheet. Then, when you need to reference the information, click Help on the menu bar, click Dreamweaver Help, and then click the Favorites tab. Another popular and easy-to-use Dreamweaver Help feature is context-sensitive help.

Context-Sensitive Help

Using **context-sensitive help,** you can open a relevant Help topic in each dialog box, panel, and inspector. To view these help features, click a Help button in a dialog box, choose Help on the Options pop-up menu in a panel group, or click the question mark icon in an inspector or other kind of window.

Using the Question Mark Icon to Display Help

Many of the windows and inspectors within Dreamweaver contain a question mark icon. Clicking this icon displays context-sensitive help. The following steps show how to use the question mark icon to view context-sensitive help about tables. In this example, a table is displayed and selected in the Document window and the Property inspector displays table properties.

 To Display Context-Sensitive Help on Tables

 Point to the question mark icon in the Property inspector (Figure A-15).

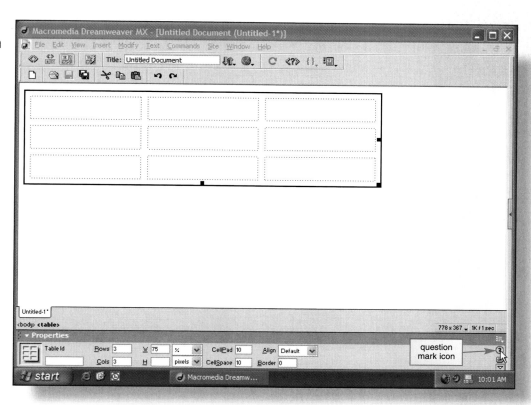

FIGURE A-15

2 **Click the question mark icon.**

The Using Dreamweaver MX window is displayed, and information pertaining to table properties is displayed in the right pane (Figure A-16). The Favorites tab is selected in the left pane because this was the last tab previously selected.

3 **Close the Using Dreamweaver MX window and return to Dreamweaver.**

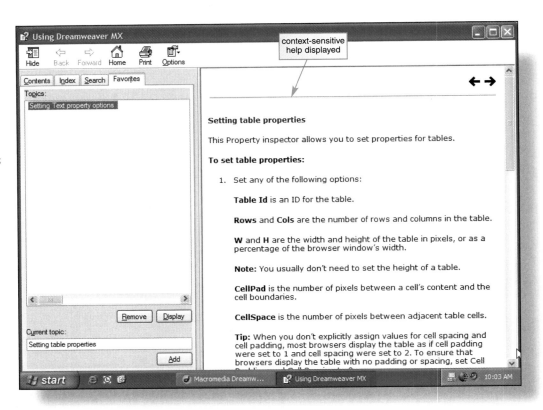

FIGURE A-16

Using the Options Menu to Display Help

All panels and dialog boxes also contain context-sensitive help. The following steps show how to display context-sensitive help for the Site panel. In this example, the Site panel is open and displayed within the Dreamweaver window.

To Use the Options Menu to Display Context-Sensitive Help for the Site Panel

1 **Click the Options button on the panel title bar and then point to Help on the Options pop-up menu.**

The Options pop-up menu is displayed (Figure A-17).

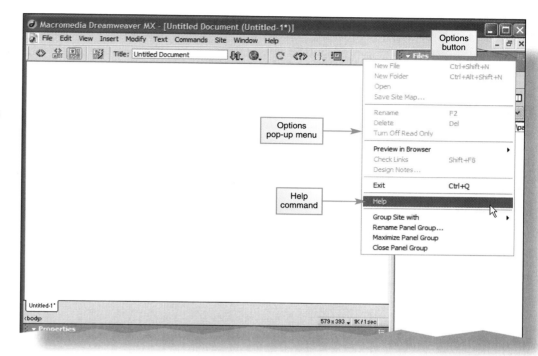

FIGURE A-17

2 **Click the Help command.**

The Using Dreamweaver MX window is displayed, and information pertaining to Using the Site panel is displayed in the right pane (Figure A-18). The Favorites tab is selected in the left pane because this was the last tab previously selected.

3 **Close the Using Dreamweaver MX window and return to Dreamweaver.**

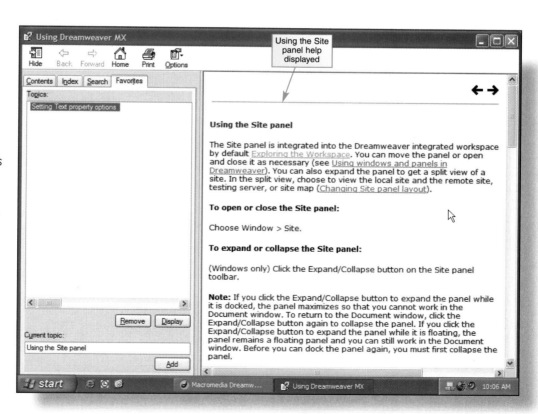

FIGURE A-18

Using the Reference Panel

The Reference panel in the Code panel group is another valuable Dreamweaver resource. The **Reference panel** provides you with a quick reference tool for HTML tags, JavaScript objects, cascading style sheets, and other Dreamweaver features. The following steps show how to access the Reference panel, review the various options, and select and display information on the <BODY> tag.

 To Use the Reference Panel

1 **Click Window on the menu bar and then point to Reference (Figure A-19).**

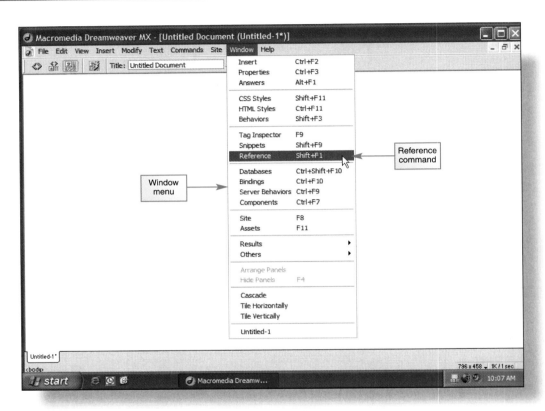

FIGURE A-19

2 Click Reference.

The Reference panel in the Code panel group is displayed (Figure A-20). The <A>...</A> tag is selected. Your screen may display a different tag.

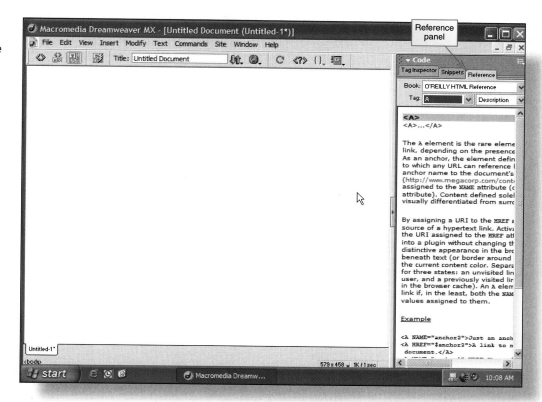

FIGURE A-20

3 Click the Tag box arrow and then point to BODY in the tag list.

BODY is highlighted in the tag list (Figure A-21).

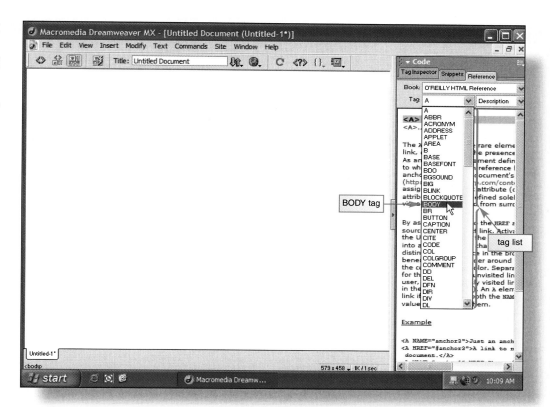

FIGURE A-21

4   **Click BODY.**

Information for the
<BODY> tag is displayed
(Figure A-22).

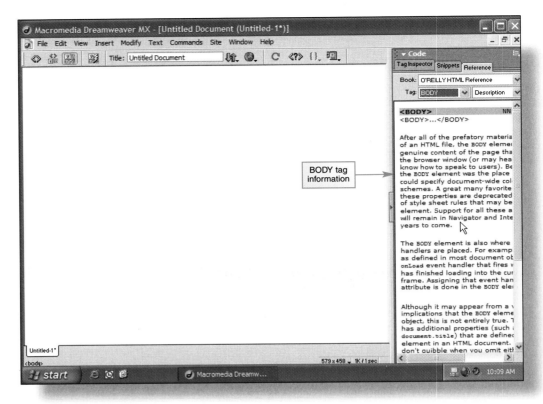

FIGURE A-22

5   **Click the Book box**
        arrow and review
the list of available
reference books.

A list of eight reference
books is displayed
(Figure A-23). These are
complete books and can be
accessed in the same way
the HTML reference book
was accessed.

6   **Close**
        Dreamweaver.
If the Macromedia
Dreamweaver dialog
box to save changes is
displayed, click the No
button.

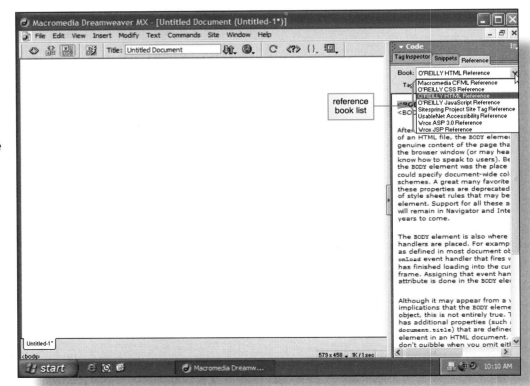

FIGURE A-23

Online Help Support

Dreamweaver provides several support Web sites, including online forums and links to third-party online forums. Examples of these online forums and discussion groups are as follows:

- ▶ Dreamweaver — For Dreamweaver users developing Web sites.
- ▶ Dreamweaver Application Development — For Dreamweaver users creating dynamic Web sites.
- ▶ Dreamweaver Extensibility — For Dreamweaver users interested in extending the functionality of Dreamweaver.
- ▶ Dynamic HTML — This group discusses questions and issues regarding Dynamic HTML.
- ▶ General Information — This group discusses general information regarding Macromedia products that does not pertain to the other online forums.

For a selection of Help links, visit the Dreamweaver MX Web page (scsite.com/dreamweavermx) and then click Appendix Help.

Use Help

1 Viewing the Dreamweaver What's New Features

Instructions: Start Dreamweaver. Perform the following tasks using the Dreamweaver What's New movie feature.

1. Click Help on the menu bar and then click What's New.
2. Select a movie in the What's New dialog box. The movie is a series of screens with forward and back buttons.
3. Click the buttons and view the movie by clicking the forward buttons.
4. Use a word processing program and write a short overview of what you learned.
5. Print a copy and hand in the printout to your instructor.

2 Using the Index Sheet

Instructions: Start Dreamweaver. Perform the following tasks using the Index sheet in the Using Dreamweaver MX Help system.

1. Click Help on the menu bar and then click Using Dreamweaver or press the F1 key to display the Using Dreamweaver MX window.
2. Click the Index tab and then type links in the Type in the keyword to find text box.
3. Click the subtopic, checking, and then click the Display button.
4. Read the information. Print a copy and hand in the printout to your instructor.

3 Using Context-Sensitive Help

Instructions: Start Dreamweaver. Perform the following tasks using context-sensitive help in the Assets panel.

1. Click Window on the menu bar and then click Assets to display the Assets panel.
2. Click the Assets panel Options button and then click Help on the Options pop-up menu.
3. Read each of the topics about the Assets panel.
4. Use your word processing program and prepare a report on how to set up a favorite list of assets.
5. Print a copy of your report and hand in the printout to your instructor.

APPENDIX B
Dreamweaver and Accessibility

Dreamweaver and Accessibility

Tim Berners-Lee, World Wide Web Consortium (W3C) founder, and inventor of the World Wide Web, indicates that the power of the Web is in its universality. He says that access by everyone regardless of disability is an essential aspect. In 1997, the World Wide Web Consortium launched the **Web Accessibility Initiative** and made a commitment to lead the Web to its full potential. The initiative includes promoting a high degree of usability for people with disabilities. The United States government established a second initiative addressing accessibility and the Web through Section 508 of the Federal Rehabilitation Act.

Dreamweaver includes features that assist you in creating accessible content. To design accessible content requires that you understand accessibility requirements and make subjective decisions as you create a Web site. Dreamweaver supports three accessibility options: screen readers, keyboard navigation, and operating system accessibility features.

Using Screen Readers with Dreamweaver

Screen readers assist the blind and vision impaired by reading text that is displayed on the screen through a speaker or headphones. The reader starts at the top-left corner of the page and reads the page content. If the Web site developer uses accessibility tags or attributes during the creation of the Web site, the screen reader also recites this information and reads non-textual information such as button labels and image descriptions. Dreamweaver makes it easy to add text equivalents for graphical elements and to add HTML tags to tables and forms through the accessibility dialog boxes. Dreamweaver supports two screen readers: JAWS and Window Eyes.

Activating the Accessibility Dialog Boxes

To create accessible pages in Dreamweaver, you associate information, such as labels and descriptions, with your page objects. After you have created this association, the screen reader recites the labels and descriptions information. You create the association by activating and attaching the accessibility dialog boxes to objects on your page. These dialog boxes appear when you insert an object for which you have activated the corresponding Accessibility dialog box. You activate the Accessibility dialog boxes through the Preferences dialog box. You can activate Accessibility dialog boxes for form objects, frames, images, media objects, and tables. The steps on the next two pages use the Florida Parks index page to show how to display the Preferences dialog box and activate the Image Accessibility dialog box.

Steps **To Activate the Images Accessibility Dialog Box**

1 **Start Dreamweaver and close all open panels. Click Edit on the menu bar and then point to Preferences (Figure B-1).**

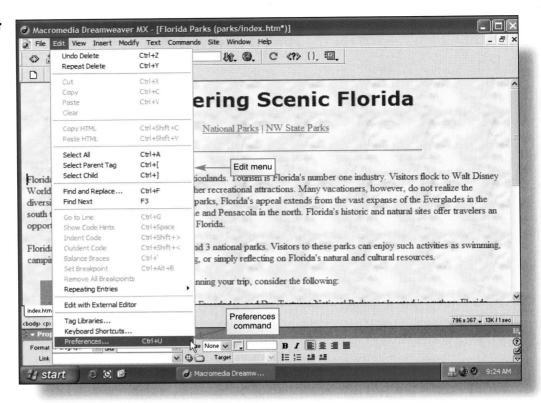

FIGURE B-1

2 **Click Preferences.**

The Preferences dialog box is displayed (Figure B-2).

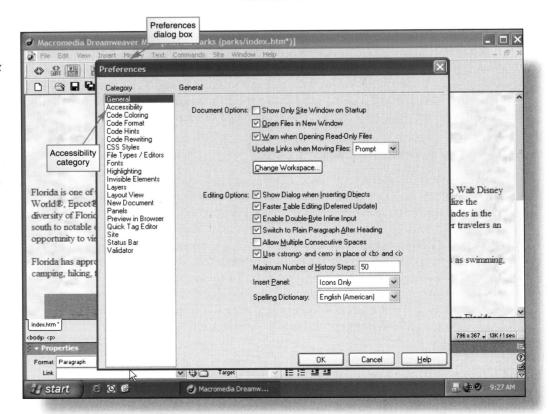

FIGURE B-2

3 Click Accessibility in the Category list, click Images in the Accessibility area, and then point to the OK button.

The Accessibility category is highlighted and the Images check box is selected (Figure B-3). The Accessibility area includes five different options for which you can activate Accessibility dialog boxes: Form Objects, Frames, Media, Images, and Tables.

4 Click the OK button.

The Preferences dialog box closes and the Dreamweaver Document window is displayed. No change is apparent in the Document window, but the Image Tag Accessibility Attributes dialog box is activated.

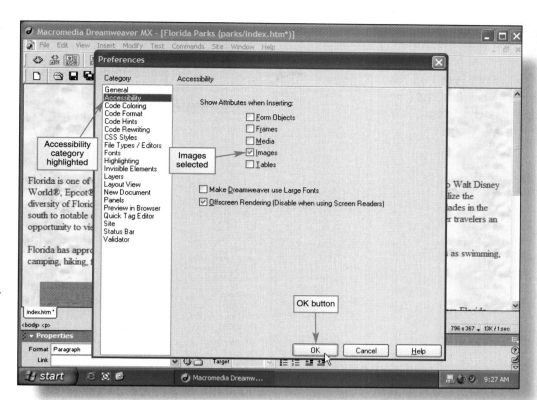

FIGURE B-3

Inserting Accessible Images

Selecting Images in the Accessibility area activates the Image Tag Accessibility Attributes dialog box. Thus, anytime you insert an image into a Web page, the dialog box will display. This dialog box contains two text boxes — Alternate Text and Long Description. The screen reader reads the information you enter in both text boxes. You should limit your Alternate Text entry to about 50 characters. For longer descriptions, provide a link in the Long Description text box to a file that gives more information about the image. It is not required that you enter data into both text boxes. The steps on the next three pages show how to use the Image Tag Accessibility Attributes dialog box when inserting an image.

Steps | **To Insert Accessible Images**

1 **Click Insert on the menu bar and then point to Image (Figure B-4).**

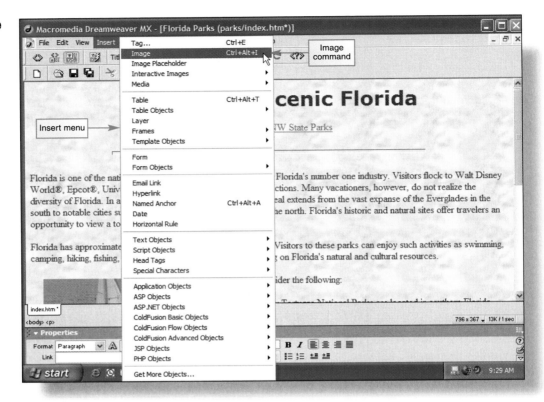

FIGURE B-4

2 **Click Image. If necessary, open the Images folder and then click a file name. Point to the OK button.**

The Select Image Source dialog box is displayed (Figure B-5).

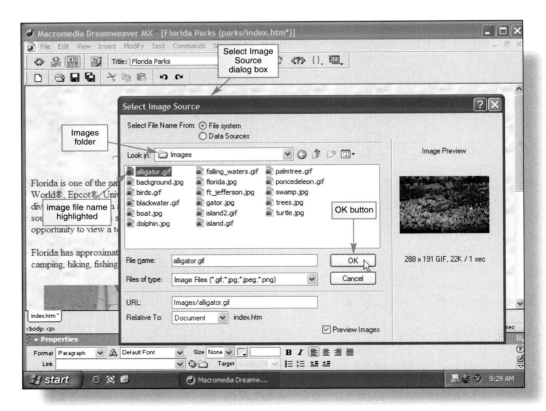

FIGURE B-5

3 **Click the OK button.**

The Image Tag Accessibility Attributes dialog box is displayed. The insertion point is blinking in the Alternate Text text box (Figure B-6). To display the Image Tag Accessibility Attributes dialog box requires that the image be inserted by using the Insert menu or by clicking the Image button on the Common tab of the Insert bar. Dragging an image from the Site panel to the Document window does not display the Image Tag Accessibility Attributes dialog box.

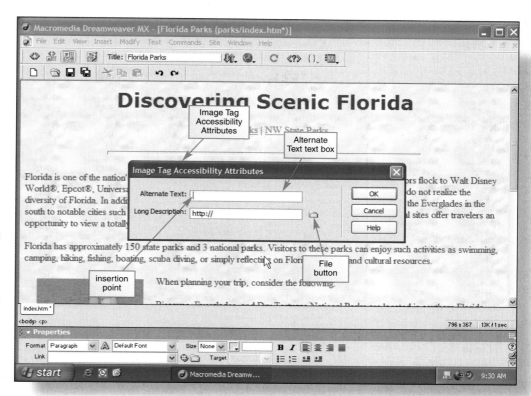

FIGURE B-6

4 **Type a description of the image. Click the File button to display the Select File dialog box. If necessary, open the Images folder and then locate and click the image file. Point to the OK button.**

The image description is displayed in the Alternate Text box and the long description file location is displayed in the Long Description text box (Figure B-7).

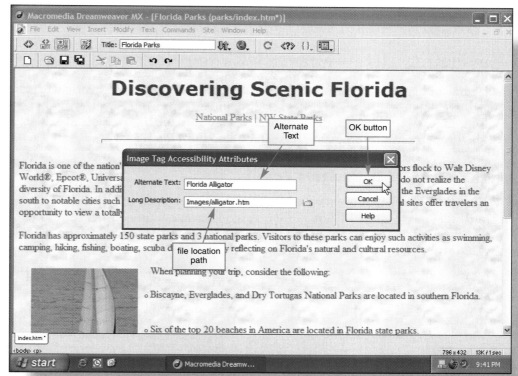

FIGURE B-7

Dreamweaver MX

5 **Click the OK button.**

The image is inserted into the Document window (Figure B-8). When the page is displayed in the browser, the screen reader recites the information you entered in the Image Tag Accessibility Attributes Alternate Text box. If you included a link to a file with additional information in the Long Description text box, the screen reader accesses the file and recites the text contained within the file.

6 **Close Dreamweaver. Do not save the changes to the Web page.**

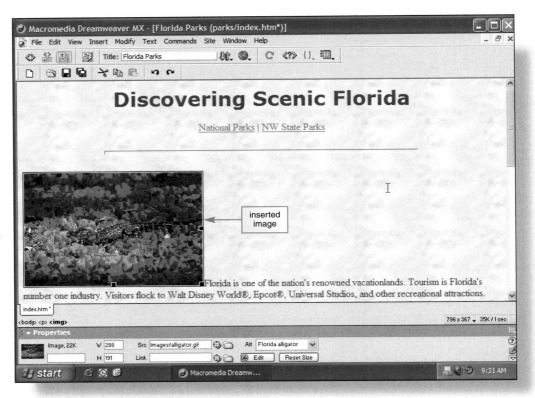

FIGURE B-8

Navigating Dreamweaver with the Keyboard

Keyboard navigation is a core aspect of accessibility. This feature also is of particular importance to users who have repetitive strain injuries (RSI) or other disabilities, or for those who would prefer to use the keyboard instead of a mouse. You can use the keyboard to navigate the following elements in Dreamweaver: floating panels, the Property inspector, dialog boxes, frames, and tables.

Using the Keyboard to Navigate Panels

When working in Dreamweaver, several panels may be open at one time. To move from panel to panel, press CTRL+ALT+TAB. A dotted white outline around the panel title bar indicates the panel is selected (Figure B-9). Press CTRL+ALT+SHIFT+TAB to move to the previous panel. If necessary, expand the selected panel by pressing the SPACEBAR. Pressing the SPACEBAR again collapses the panel.

FIGURE B-9

Using the Keyboard to Navigate the Property Inspector

The following steps use the Florida Parks index page to show how to use the keyboard to navigate the Property inspector.

 Steps **To Use the Keyboard to Navigate the Property Inspector**

1 **Start Dreamweaver and close all panels. Open a Web page. If necessary, press CTRL+F3 to display the Property inspector and then press CTRL+ALT+TAB until the Property inspector is selected.**

The dotted white outline around Properties indicates that the focus is on the Property inspector (Figure B-10).

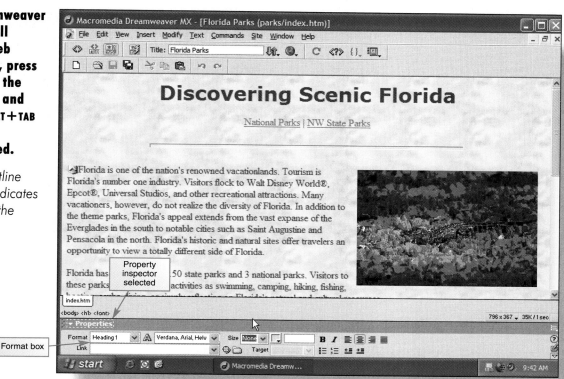

FIGURE B-10

2 **Press the TAB key to move to the Format box.**

Heading 1 is highlighted in the Format box (Figure B-11).

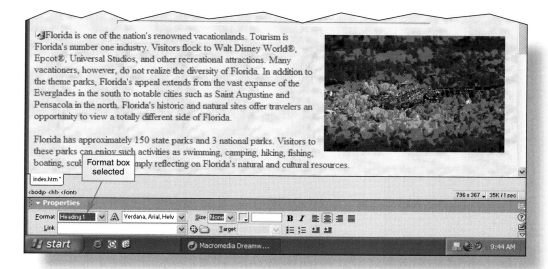

FIGURE B-11

3   **Use the keyboard DOWN ARROW key to select Heading 3 and then press the ENTER key.**

A dotted outline is displayed around the Heading 3 selection (Figure B-12). Heading 3 is applied to the text.

4   **Close Dreamweaver. Do not save any of the changes.**

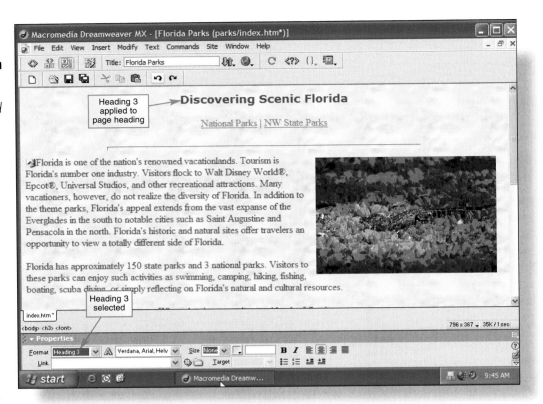

FIGURE B-12

Operating System Accessibility Features

The third method of accessibility support through Dreamweaver is through the Windows operating system high contrast setting. **High contrast** changes the desktop color themes for individuals who have vision impairment. The color schemes make the screen easier to view by heightening screen contrast with alternative color combinations. Some of the schemes also change font sizes.

You activate this option through the Windows Control Panel. The high contrast setting affects Dreamweaver in two ways:

- The dialog boxes and panels use system color settings.
- Code view syntax color is turned off.

Design view, however, continues to use the background and text colors you set in the Page Properties dialog box. The pages you design, therefore, continue to render colors as they will display in a browser. The following steps show how to turn on high contrast and how to change the current high contrast settings.

Steps **To Turn on High Contrast**

In Windows XP, click the Start button on the taskbar and then click Control Panel on the Start menu. If necessary, switch to Classic View and then double-click the Accessibility Options icon. Point to the Display tab.

The Accessibility Options dialog box is displayed (Figure B-13).

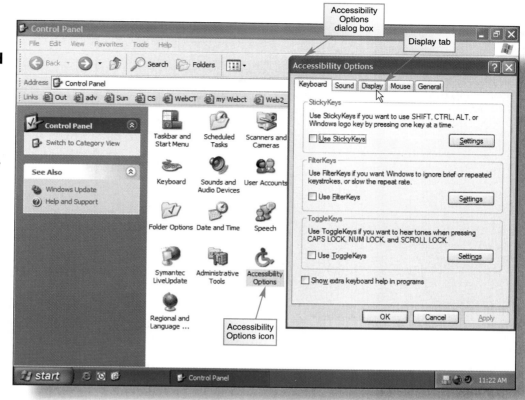

FIGURE B-13

2 **Click the Display tab and then click Use High Contrast. Point to the Settings button.**

The Display sheet is displayed. A check mark is in the Use High Contrast check box (Figure B-14).

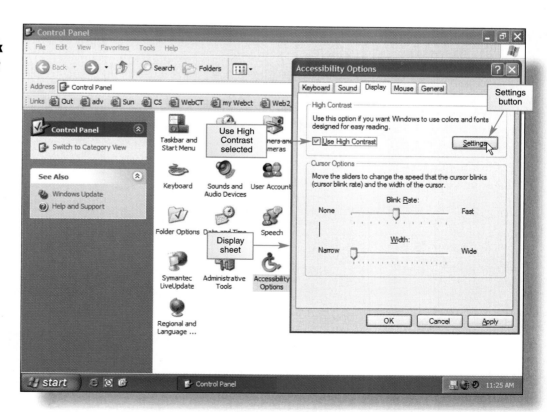

FIGURE B-14

3 **Click the Settings button. Point to the Your current high contrast scheme is box arrow.**

The Settings for High Contrast dialog box is displayed (Figure B-15).

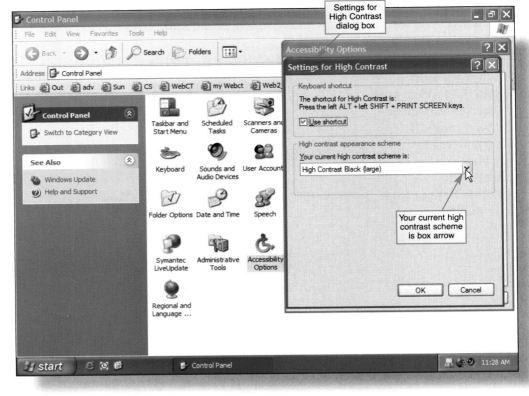

FIGURE B-15

4 **Click the Your current high contrast scheme is box arrow.**

A list of available high contrast options is displayed (Figure B-16). High Contrast Black (large) is selected. The Web designer, however, would select the option to meet the needs of the project for which he or she is designing.

5 **Click the Cancel button.**

The settings return to their original settings. To retain these settings on your computer would require that you click the OK button.

6 **Click the Control Panel Close button.**

The Control Panel closes and the Windows XP desktop displays.

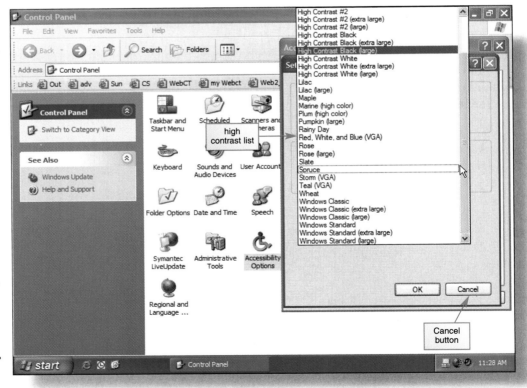

FIGURE B-16

APPENDIX C
Dreamweaver and Fireworks

Dreamweaver and Fireworks

Macromedia Fireworks MX is a graphics application and companion tool to Dreamweaver. Fireworks comes with a complete graphics toolset and includes workflow options that promote easy integration with Dreamweaver and other programs. Firework images are saved with a .png extension. The Fireworks interface is consistent with other applications in the Macromedia MX Studio suite, including Dreamweaver. Fireworks and Dreamweaver share many commonalities, including changes to links, image maps, table slices, and other elements. If set up properly, the two applications provide a streamlined workflow for editing, optimizing, and placing Web image files in HTML pages.

To create the integrated work environment, a local site must be defined in Dreamweaver and Design Notes enabled for the site. Design Notes are a default setting in Dreamweaver. The name of the original source file is saved in the Design Notes folder. Fireworks also must be set as the primary external image editor for Dreamweaver.

Setting Fireworks as the External Image Editor

One of Dreamweaver's more valuable features is the capability to open a selected image in an external image editor. You can edit the image, save the changes, and then return to Dreamweaver. Changes you make to the image are visible in the Document window. The steps on the next three pages use an image from the Florida Parks index page to show how to select Fireworks as the external image editor.

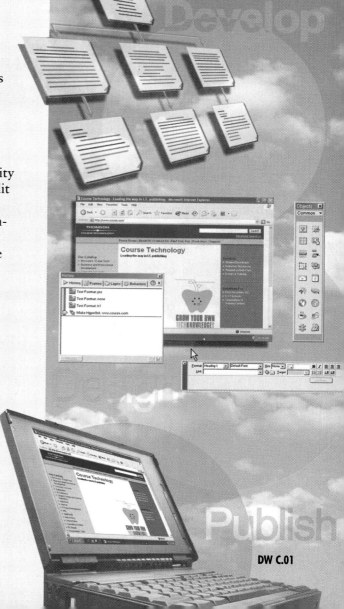

To Select Fireworks as the External Image Editor

1 **Start Dreamweaver and close all open panels. If necessary, insert an image in the Document window and then click the image to select it. Click Edit on the menu bar and then point to Preferences (Figure C-1).**

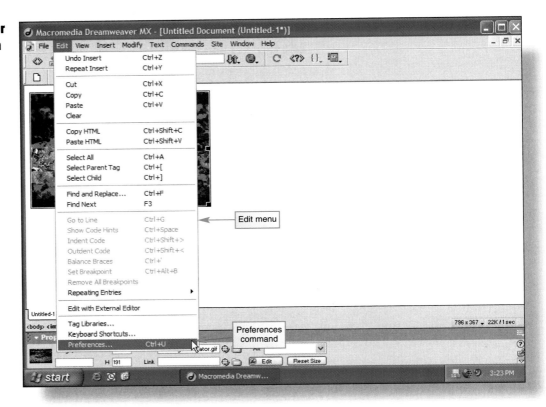

FIGURE C-1

2 **Click Preferences, click the File Types/Editors category, and then point to the plus sign (+) button (Figure C-2).**

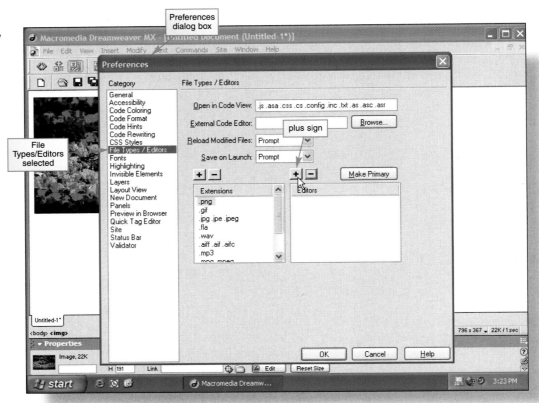

FIGURE C-2

3   Click the Plus sign.

The Select External Editor dialog box is displayed (Figure C-3). Most likely, the Look in text box displays Program Files and Macromedia is one of the choices in the Program Files folder. Your screen will display different files and folders.

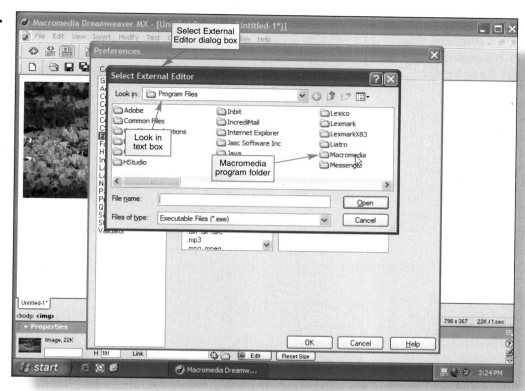

FIGURE C-3

4   Double-click Macromedia (or navigate to the Macromedia folder) and then click Fireworks MX. Point to the Open button.

Fireworks MX is selected in the Select External Editor dialog box (Figure C-4).

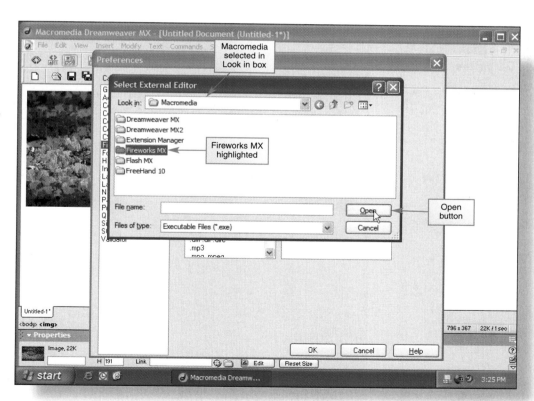

FIGURE C-4

5 **Click the Open button and then click Fireworks.exe. Point to the Open button.**

The file Fireworks.exe is selected (Figure C-5).

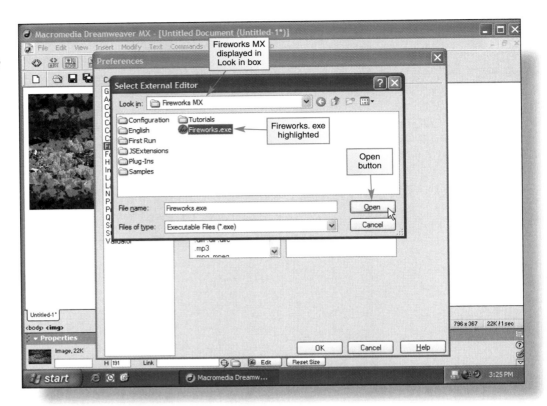

FIGURE C-5

6 **Click the Open button. Point to the OK button.**

Fireworks is selected as the primary editor for image, sound, and other file types (Figure C-6).

7 **Click the OK button.**

The Preferences dialog box closes.

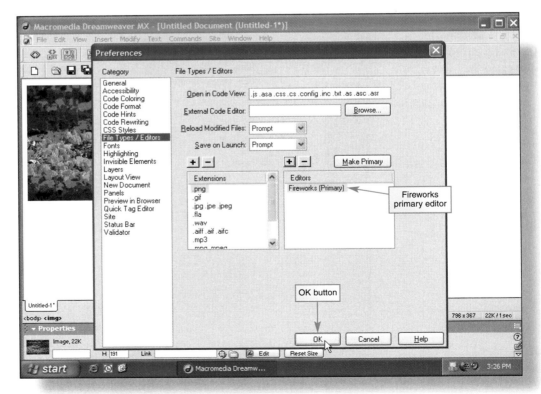

FIGURE C-6

Adding Text to an Image

You can launch Fireworks from within Dreamweaver to edit an image, add text to an image, resize an image, recolor an image, and so on. The following steps show how to launch Fireworks and add text to an image placed in a Dreamweaver document.

 Steps To Launch Fireworks and Add Text to an Image

1 **If necessary, insert an image into a Dreamweaver Document window and then select the image. If necessary, display the Property inspector. Point to the Edit button in the Property inspector.**

The image is selected and the image properties are displayed in the Property inspector (Figure C-7). The Edit button displays the Fireworks logo.

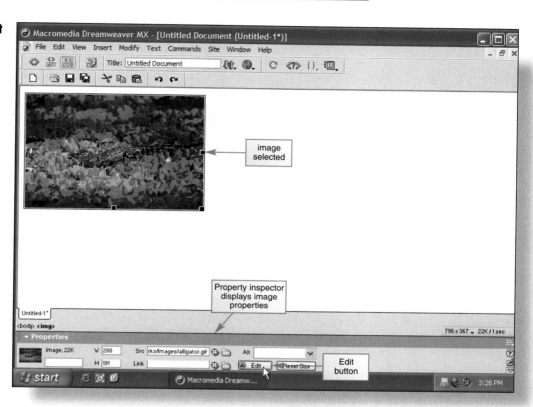

FIGURE C-7

<table>
<tr><td>2</td><td>Click the Edit button in the Property inspector. Point to the No button.</td></tr>
</table>

Fireworks Program opens

The Find Source dialog box is displayed (Figure C-8). The message indicates that the alligator.gif image (or the image you selected) is not an existing Fireworks document.

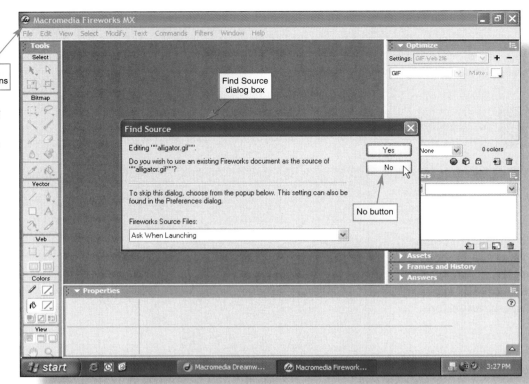

FIGURE C-8

<table>
<tr><td>3</td><td>Click the No button.</td></tr>
</table>

The image is displayed in the Fireworks window (Figure C-9).

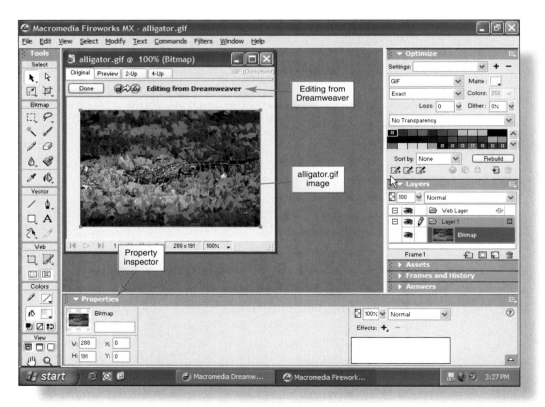

FIGURE C-9

4 **Click the Text tool and then click the image.**

The entry point for the text block displays (Figure C-10). The Property inspector changes to reflect that text is selected.

FIGURE C-10

5 **Use the Property inspector properties to change the font, font size, color, and other text features. Point to the Done button.**

In Figure C-11, the font is changed to Comic Sans MS, the font size to 26, the font color to red, and bold is applied. If you applied different properties, your screen will look different.

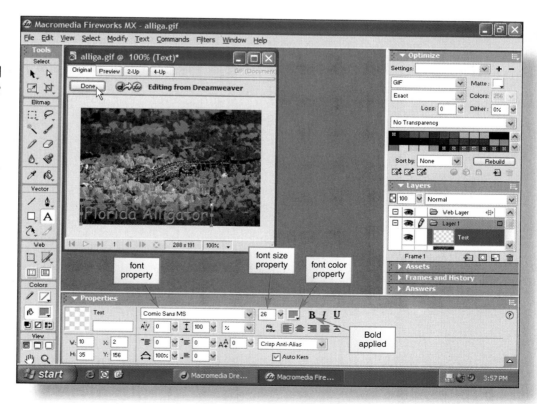

FIGURE C-11

6 **Click the Done button.**

The focus returns to Dreamweaver. The revised image is displayed in the Dreamweaver Document window (Figure C-12).

7 **Save the file and close Dreamweaver. Close Fireworks.**

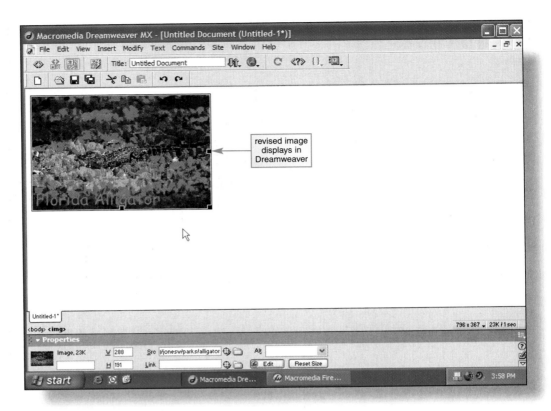

revised image displays in Dreamweaver

FIGURE C-12

Inserting a Fireworks Image in the Dreamweaver Document

In addition to editing a Dreamweaver image in Fireworks, several methods are available to insert Fireworks files into a Dreamweaver document. These methods are as follows:

▶ Insert Firework files the same way in which you insert other images — the Image command on the Insert menu, drag and drop from the Site panel or Library panel, and the Insert bar using the Image button on the Common tab.

▶ Copy and paste Fireworks HTML code into Dreamweaver code view.

▶ Insert Fireworks-generated HTML code, including the associated image(s), into the HTML document using the Interactive Images command on the Insert menu and then selecting the Fireworks HTML command on the Interactive Images submenu.

▶ Export a Fireworks file as a library item using the Export command on the Fireworks File menu and then selecting Save as type in the Dreamweaver Library. A library folder must exist in the Web site local root folder.

APPENDIX D
Publishing to a Web Server

Publishing to a Remote Site

With Dreamweaver, Web designers usually define a local site and then do the majority of their site designing using the local site. In Project 1 you defined a local site. In creating the projects in this book, you have added Web pages to the local site, which resides on your computer's hard disk, a network drive, or possibly a Zip disk. To prepare a Web site and make it available for others to view requires that you publish your site by putting it on a Web server for public access. A Web server is an Internet- or intranet-connected computer that delivers the Web pages to visitors online. Dreamweaver includes built-in support that enables you to connect and transfer your local site to a Web server. To complete the steps and exercises in this appendix to publish to a Web server requires that you have access to a Web server. Your instructor will provide you with the location, user name, and password information for the Web server on which you will publish your Web site.

After you establish access to a Web server, you will need a remote root folder. The remote folder is the folder that will reside on the Web server and will contain your Web site files. Generally, the remote folder is defined by the Web server administrator or your instructor. Your local root folder is your last name and first initial. Most likely, your remote folder also will be your last name and first initial. You upload your local site to the remote folder on the Web server. The remote site connection information must be defined in Dreamweaver through the Site Definition Wizard. You display the Site Definition Wizard and then enter the remote site information. Dreamweaver provides five different protocols for connecting to a remote site. These methods are as follows:

- **FTP** (File Transfer Protocol) is the protocol used on the Internet for sending and receiving files. It is the most widely used method for uploading and downloading pages to and from a Web server.
- **Local/Network** This option is used when the Web server is located on a local area network (LAN) or a company or school intranet. Files on LANs generally are available for internal viewing only.
- **SourceSafe Database, RDS (Remote Development Services), and WebDAV** These three protocols are versioning systems that permit users to edit and manage files collaboratively on remote Web servers.

Most likely, you will use the FTP option to upload your Web site to a remote server.

Defining a Remote Site

You define the remote site by changing some of the settings in the Site Definition Wizard. To create a remote site using FTP, your instructor will supply you with the following information:

- **FTP host** is the Web address for the remote host of your Web server.
- **Host directory** is the directory name and path on the server where your remote site will be located.
- **Login** is your user name.
- **Password** is the FTP password to authenticate and access your account.

Perform the following steps to define the remote site.

 Steps **To Define a Remote Site**

1 **Close the Property inspector. Click Site on the menu bar and then click Edit Sites to display the Edit Sites dialog box. If necessary, click Florida Parks in the Edit Sites dialog box. Point to the Edit button.**

The Edit Sites dialog box is displayed and Florida Parks is selected (Figure D-1).

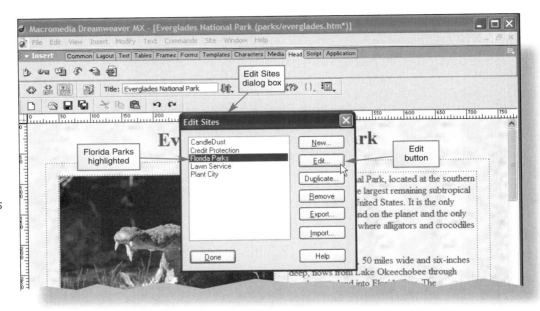

FIGURE D-1

2 **Click the Edit button. If necessary, click the Basic tab. Point to the Next button.**

The Site Definition dialog box is displayed (Figure D-2).

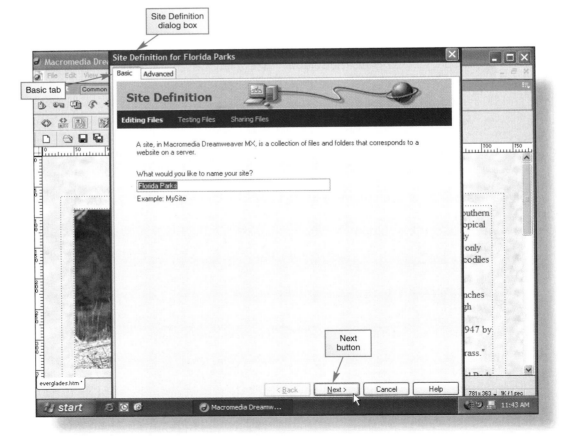

FIGURE D-2

3 **Click the Next button in the next three options of the Site Definition dialog box. Click the How do you connect to your remote server? box arrow and then click FTP.**

The Site Definition dialog box displays the Sharing Files options. FTP is selected in the How do you connect to your remote server? box (Figure D-3).

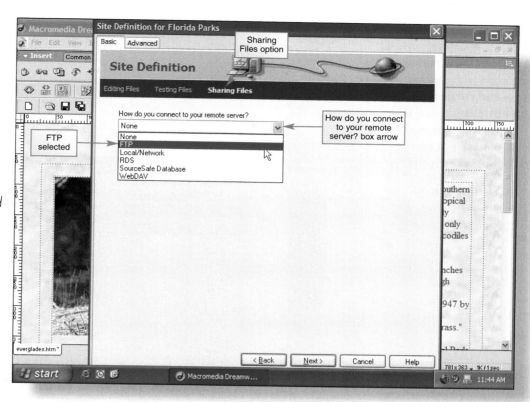

FIGURE D-3

4 **Click each of the other boxes on the page and fill in the information as provided by your instructor. Click Save. Point to the Test Connection button.**

Information for Will Jones is displayed in Figure D-4. Your screen will contain the information provided by your instructor.

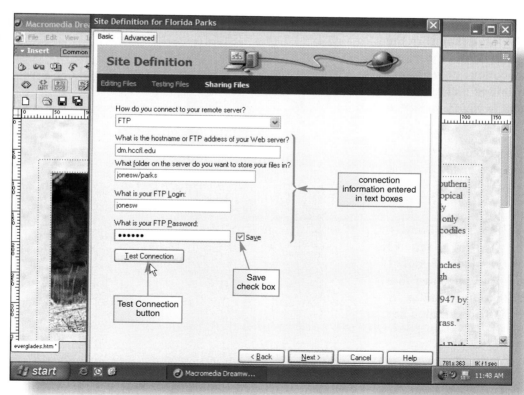

FIGURE D-4

5 **Click the Test Connection button. Point to the OK button. If your connection is not successful, review your text box entries and make any necessary corrections. If all entries are correct, check with your instructor.**

Dreamweaver tests the connection and responds with a Macromedia Dreamweaver MX dialog box (Figure D-5).

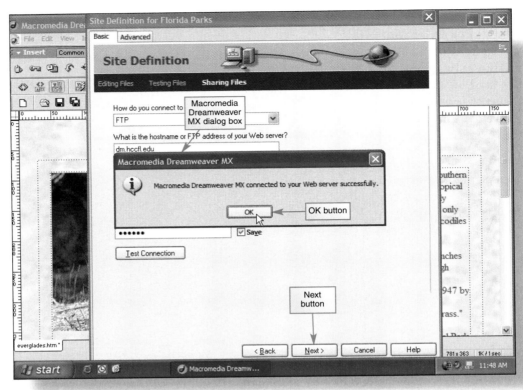

FIGURE D-5

6 **Click the OK button and then click the Next button in the next two options of the Site Definition dialog box. Point to the Done button.**

The Summary options are displayed and include both Local Info and Remote Info (Figure D-6).

7 **Click the Done button to return to the Everglades National Park Web page and then click the Done button in the Edit Sites dialog box. The Site panel displays.**

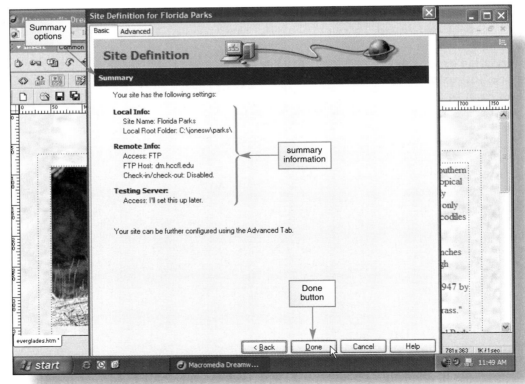

FIGURE D-6

Connecting to a Remote Site

Now that you completed the remote site information and tested your connection, you can interact with the remote server. The remote site folder on the Web server for your Web site must be established before a connection can be made. This folder, called the **remote site root**, generally is created by the Web server administrator or your instructor. This book uses the last name and the first initial (jonesw) for the remote site folder. Naming conventions other than your last name and first initial may be used on the Web server to which you are connecting. Your instructor will supply you with this information. If all information is correct, connecting to the remote site is done easily through the Site panel. Complete the following steps to connect to the remote site and your remote root folder.

Steps **To Connect to a Remote Site**

1 **Point to the Site panel Expand/ Collapse button (Figure D-7).**

FIGURE D-7

2 **Click the Expand/Collapse button. Point to the Connects to remote host button.**

The Site panel expands to show both a right and left pane (Figure D-8). The right pane contains the local site. The left pane contains information for accessing your remote files by clicking the Connects to remote host button.

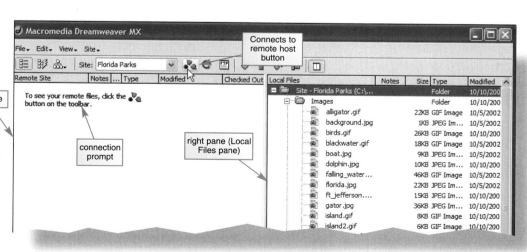

FIGURE D-8

3 **Click the Connects to remote host button. Point to the Put file(s) button.**

A brief message flashes on the screen, indicating Dreamweaver is connecting to the remote site and retrieving remote information. The jonesw/parks root folder is displayed (Figure D-9). The Connects to remote host/Disconnects from remote host button is a toggle button and changes to indicate that the connection has been made. The root folder on the remote site must be created by your instructor or Web server administrator before a connection can be made.

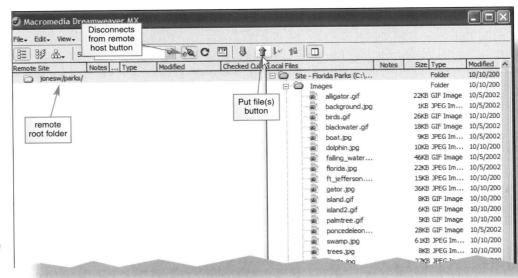

FIGURE D-9

Uploading Files to a Remote Server

Your next step will be to upload your files to the remote server. **Uploading** is the process of transferring your files from your computer to the remote server. **Downloading** is the process of transferring files from the remote server to your computer. Dreamweaver uses the term **put** for uploading and **get** for downloading.

 To Upload Files to a Remote Server

1 **Click the Put File(s) button. Point to the OK button.**

The Macromedia Dreamweaver MX dialog box is displayed to verify that you want to upload the entire site (Figure D-10).

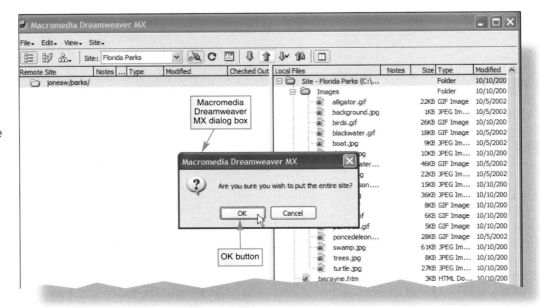

FIGURE D-10

2 **Click the OK button.**

As the files begin to upload, a Status dialog box displays the progress information. The files are uploaded to the server (Figure D-11). The files may display in a different order from that on the local site. The display order on the server is determined by the settings on that computer.

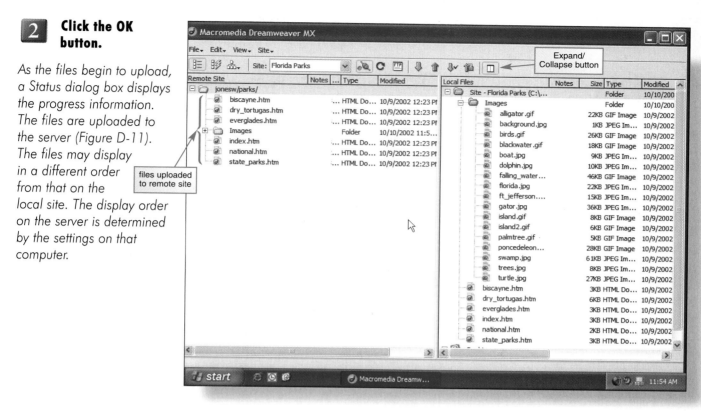

FIGURE D-11

Remote Site Maintenance and Site Synchronization

Now that your Web site is on a Web server, you will want to continue to maintain the site. When you are connected to the remote site, you can apply many of the same commands to a folder or file on the remote site as you do on the local site. You can create and delete folders; cut, copy, delete, duplicate, paste, and rename files; and so on. These commands are available through the context menu.

To mirror the local site with the remote site, Dreamweaver provides a synchronization feature. **Synchronizing** is the process of transferring files between the local and remote sites so that both sites have an identical set of the most recent files. You can select to synchronize the entire Web site or select only specific files. You also can specify Direction. Within **Direction**, you have three options: upload the newer files from the local site to the remote site (put); download newer files from the remote site to the local site (get); or, upload and download files to and from the remote and local sites. Once you specify a direction, Dreamweaver automatically synchronizes files. If the files are already in sync, Dreamweaver lets you know you that no synchronization is necessary.

To illustrate how synchronization works, a change will be made to the local site. You will make a change to the Everglades National Park Web page, and then resave the page. This will give the Everglades National Park Web page a different save date and time and will make it appear to the system as though a change was made in the page. Perform the steps on the next three pages to make the change and to synchronize your files.

Steps | To Synchronize the Local and Remote Sites

1 Click the Expand/Collapse button on the Site panel menu bar to display the Everglades National Park page. Click at the end of the heading and add an s to park and then backspace to delete the s. Click the Save button on the Standard toolbar and then click the Expand/ Collapse button to display the remote site pane.

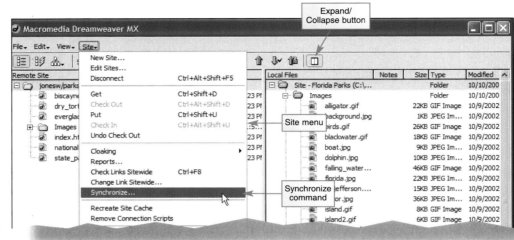

FIGURE D-12

2 Click the Site menu on the Site panel menu bar and then point to Synchronize (Figure D-12).

3 Click Synchronize and then click the Synchronize box arrow.

The Synchronize Files dialog box is displayed (Figure D-13). You can select the entire Florida Parks site or you can choose just the files you want to synchronize from the Synchronize pop-up menu.

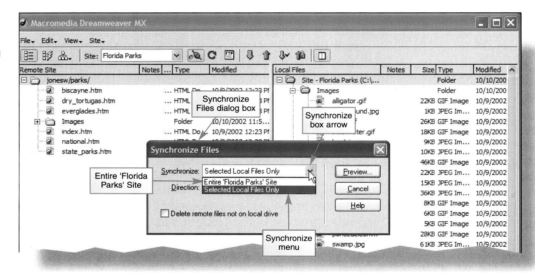

FIGURE D-13

4 Click the Entire 'Florida Parks' Site in the Synchronize pop-up menu and then click the Direction box arrow.

The Direction list is displayed and contains three options (Figure D-14).

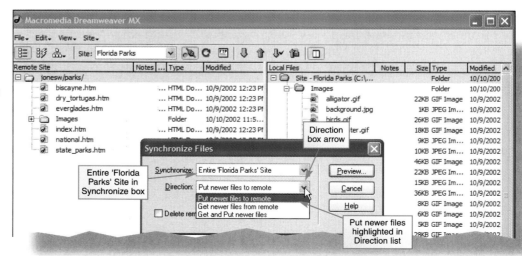

FIGURE D-14

5 **Select Get and Put newer files in the Direction list and then point to the Preview button (Figure D-15).**

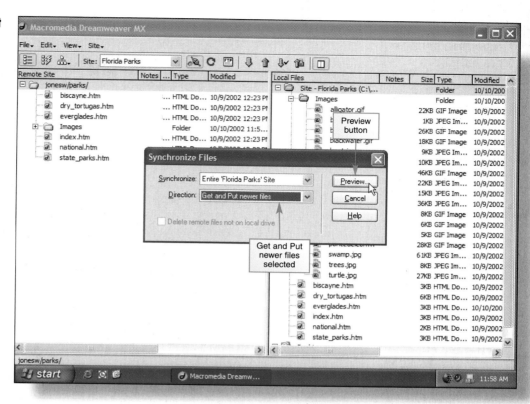

FIGURE D-15

6 **Click the Preview button. Point to the OK button.**

A list of files that need to be updated is displayed (Figure D-16). Unchecked files will not be uploaded.

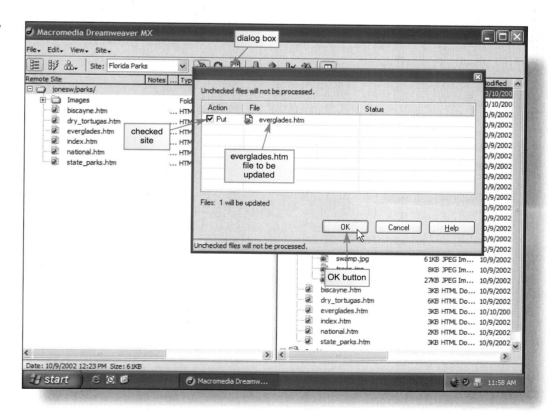

FIGURE D-16

7 **Click the OK button and then point to the Close button.**

The file is updated and the synchronization is complete (Figure D-17). Dreamweaver automatically transfers, and then updates the dialog box with the status.

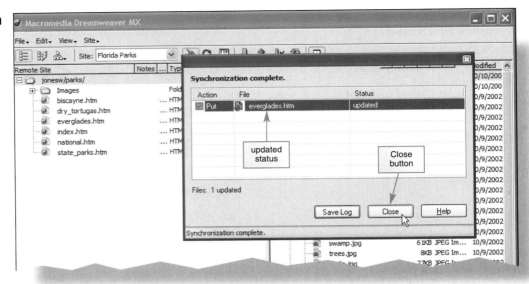

FIGURE D-17

8 **Click the Close button, click the Disconnects from remote host button, and then click the Expand/Collapse button to redisplay the Everglades National Park Web page.**

Dreamweaver displays the updated Everglades Web page (Figure D-18).

9 **Close Dreamweaver.**

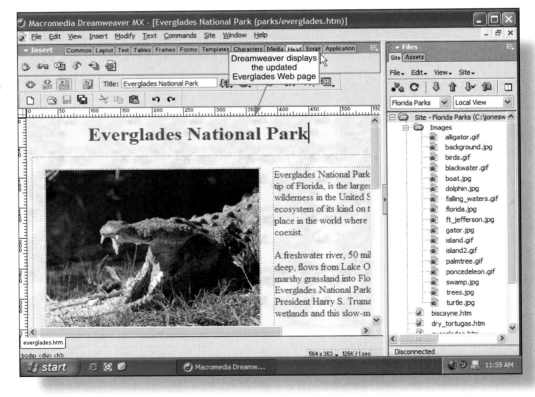

FIGURE D-18

To save the verification information to a local file, click the Save Log button at the completion of the synchronization process. Another feature within Dreamweaver is to verify which files are newer on the local site or the remote. These options are available through the Site panel Edit menu by selecting Select Newer Local or Select Newer Remote.

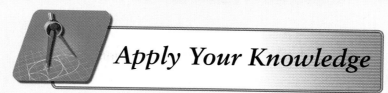

Apply Your Knowledge

1 Defining and Uploading the B & B Lawn Service Web to a Remote Server

Instructions: Perform the following steps to define and upload the B & B Lawn Service Web site to a remote server.

1. Click Site on the Document window menu bar and then click Edit Sites. Click Lawn Service and then click the Edit button. When the Site Definition dialog box is displayed, click the Next button in the next three options and then select FTP in the How do you connect to your remote server? list. Click each of the other boxes on the page, fill in the information as provided by your instructor, and then test the connection. Click the OK button, click the Next button in the next two options, and then click the Done button.
2. Click the Expand/Collapse button in the Site panel toolbar and then click the Connects to remote host button. Click the local file root folder and then click the Put File(s) button on the Site panel toolbar to upload your Web site. Click the OK button in response to the Are you sure you wish to put the entire site? dialog box. Review your files to verify that they were uploaded. The files on the remote server may be displayed in a different order from that on the local site.
3. Click the Disconnects from remote host button on the Site panel toolbar. Click the Expand/Collapse button on the Site panel toolbar to display the local site and the Document window.
4. Close Dreamweaver.

2 Defining and Uploading the CandleDust Web Site to a Remote Server

Instructions: Perform the following steps to define and upload the CandleDust Web site to a remote server.

1. Click Site on the Document window menu and then click Edit Sites. Click CandleDust and then click the Edit button. When the Site Definition dialog box displays, click the Next button three times and then select FTP in the How do you connect to your remote server? list. Click each of the other options boxes, fill in the information as provided by your instructor, and then test the connection. Click the OK button, click the Next button two times, and then click the Done button.
2. Click the Expand/Collapse button on the Site panel toolbar and then click the Connects to remote host button. Click the local file root folder and then click the Put File(s) button on the Site panel toolbar to upload your Web site. Click the OK button in response to the Are you sure you wish to put the entire site? box. Review your files to verify that they were uploaded. The files on the remote server may display in a different order from that on the local site.
3. Click the Disconnects from remote host button. Click the Expand/Collapse button to display the local site and the Document window. Close Dreamweaver.

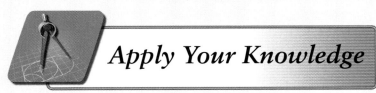

Apply Your Knowledge

3 Defining and Uploading the Credit Protection Web Site to a Remote Server

Instructions: Perform the following steps to define and upload the Credit Protection Web site to a remote server.

1. Click Site on the Document window menu and then click Edit Sites. Click Credit Protection and then click the Edit button. When the Site Definition dialog box displays, select FTP from the How do you connect to your remote server? list. Click each of the other boxes in the dialog box, fill in the information as provided by your instructor and then test the connection. Click the OK button, click the Next button two times, and then click the Done button.
2. Click the Expand/Collapse button on the Site panel toolbar and then click the Connects to remote site button. Click the local file root folder and then click the Put File(s) button on the Site panel menu bar to upload your Web site. Upload your files to the remote site. Review your files to verify that they were uploaded. The files on the remote server may display in a different order from that on the local site.
3. Disconnect from the site. Click the Expand/Collapse button to display the local site and the Document window. Close Dreamweaver.

4 Defining and Uploading the Plant City Web Site to a Remote Server

Instructions: Perform the following steps to define and upload the Plant City Web site to a remote server.

1. Click Site on the Document window menu bar and then click Edit Sites. Click Plant City and then click the Edit button. When the Site Definition dialog box displays, select FTP in the How do you connect to your remove server? list. Click each of the other option boxes, fill in the information as provided by your instructor, and then test the connection. Click the OK button, click the Next button two times, and then click the Done button.
2. Connect to the remote site and then click the local file root folder. Upload your files to the remote site. Disconnect from the site. Click the Expand/Collapse button to display the local site and the Document window. Close Dreamweaver.

MANAGING FILES

Action	Shortcut
New document	Control+N
Open an HTML file	Control+O
Open in frame	Control+Shift+O
Close	Control+W
Save	Control+S
Save as	Control+Shift+S
Exit/Quit	Alt+F4 or Control+Q

GENERAL EDITING

Action	Shortcut
Undo	Control+Z
Redo	Control+Y or Control+Shift+Z
Cut	Control+X or Shift+Delete
Copy	Control+C
Paste	Control+V or Shift+Insert
Clear	Delete
Bold	Control+B
Italic	Control+I
Select All	Control+A
Move to page up	Page Up
Move to page down	Page Down
Select to page up	Shift+Page Up
Select to page down	Shift+Page Down
Select line up/down	Shift+Up/Down
Move to start of line	Home
Move to end of line	End
Select to start of line	Shift+Home
Select to end of line	Shift+End
Go to previous/next paragraph	Control+Up/Down
Go to next/previous word	Control+Right/Left
Delete word left	Control+Backspace
Delete word right	Control+Delete
Select character left/right	Shift+Left/Right
Find and Replace	Control+F
Find next/find again	F3
Replace	Control+H
Copy HTML (in Design view)	Control+Shift+C
Paste HTML (in Design view)	Control+Shift+V
Preferences	Control+U

PAGE VIEWS

To toggle the display of	Shortcut
Standard view	Control+Shift+F6
Layout view	Control+F6
Live Data mode	Control+R
Live Data	Control+Shift+R
Switch to next document	Control+Tab
Switch to previous document	Control+Shift+Tab
Switch between Design and Code views	Control+`
Server debug	Control+Shift+G
Refresh Design view	F5

VIEWING PAGE ELEMENTS

To toggle the display of	Shortcut
Visual Aids	Control+Shift+I
Show Rulers	Control+Alt+R
Show Grid	Control+Alt+G
Snap to Grid	Control+Alt+Shift+G
Head content	Control+Shift+W
Page properties	Control+J
Selection properties	Control+Shift+J

CODE EDITING

Action	Shortcut
Switch to Design view	Control+`
Print Code	Control+P
Validate markup	Shift+F6
Open Quick Tag Editor	Control+T
Open Snippets panel	Shift+F9
Show Code Hints	Control+Spacebar
Indent Code	Control+Shift+›
Outdent Code	Control+Shift+‹
Insert tag	Control+E
Edit tag (in Design view)	Control+F5
Select parent tag	Control+[
Select child	Control+]
Balance Braces	Control+`
Toggle breakpoint	Control+Alt+B
Go to line	Control+G
Move to top of code	Control+Home
Move to end of code	Control+End
Select to top of code	Control+Shift+Home
Select to end of code	Control+Shift+End

TEXT EDITING

Action	Shortcut
Create a new paragraph	Enter
Insert a line break 	Shift+Enter
Insert a nonbreaking space	Control+Shift+ Spacebar
Move text or object to another place in the page	Drag selected item to new location
Copy text or object to another place in the page	Control-drag selected item to new location
Select a word	Double-click
Add selected items to library	Control+Shift+B
Open and close the Property inspector	Control+Shift+J
Check spelling	Shift+F7

FORMATTING TEXT

Action	Shortcut
Indent	Control+Alt+]
Outdent	Control+Alt+[
Format > None	Control+0 (zero)
Paragraph Format	Control+Shift+P
Apply Headings 1 through 6 to a paragraph	Control+1 through 6
Align > Left/Center/ Right/Justify	Control+Alt+Shift+L/C/ R/J
Edit Style Sheet	Control+Shift+E

WORKING IN TABLES

Action	Shortcut
Select table (with cursor inside the table)	Control+A
Move to the next cell	Tab
Move to the previous cell	Shift+Tab
Insert a row (before current)	Control+M
Add a row at end of table	Tab in the last cell
Delete the current row	Control+Shift+M
Insert a column	Control+Shift+A
Delete a column	Control+Shift+ - (hyphen)
Merge selected table cells	Control+Alt+M
Split table cell	Control+Alt+S
Defer table update	Control+Spacebar
Increase column span	Control+Shift+]
Decrease column span	Control+Shift+[

WORKING WITH IMAGES

Action	Shortcut
Change image source attribute	Double-click image
Edit image in external editor	Control–double-click image

WORKING IN FRAMES

Action	Shortcut
Select a frame	Alt-click in frame
Select next frame or frameset	Alt+Right Arrow
Select previous frame or frameset	Alt+Left Arrow
Select parent frameset	Alt+Up Arrow
Select first child frame or frameset	Alt+Down Arrow
Add a new frame to frameset	Select frame, then Alt-drag frame border
Add a new frame to frameset using push method	Select frame, then Alt+Control-drag frame border

WORKING WITH LAYERS

Action	Shortcut
Select a layer	Control+Shift-click
Select and move layer	Shift+Control-drag
Add or remove layer from selection	Shift-click layer
Move selected layer by pixels	Arrow keys
Move selected layer by snapping increment	Shift+arrow keys
Resize selected layer by pixels	Control+Arrow keys
Resize selected layer by snapping increment	Control+Shift+arrow keys
Toggle the display of the grid	Control+Alt+G
Snap To grid	Control+Shift+Alt+G
Align layers left	Control+Shift+1
Align layers right	Control+Shift+3
Align layers top	Control+Shift+4
Align layers bottom	Control+Shift+6
Make same width	Control+Shift+7
Make same height	Control+Shift+9

GETTING HELP

Action	Shortcut
Using Dreamweaver Help Topics	F1
Using ColdFusion Help Topics	Control+F1
Reference	Shift+F1

INSERTING OBJECTS

Action	Shortcut
Any object (image, Shockwave movie, and so on)	Drag file from the Explorer or Site panel to the Document window
Image	Control+Alt+I
Table	Control+Alt+T
Named anchor	Control+Alt+A

MANAGING HYPERLINKS

Action	Shortcut
Check links sitewide	Control+F8
Check selected links	Shift+F8
Create hyperlink (select text, image, or object)	Control+L
Remove hyperlink	Control+Shift+L
Drag and drop to create a hyperlink from a document	Select the text, image, or object, then Shift-drag the selection to a file in the Site panel
Drag and drop to create a hyperlink using the Property inspector	Select the text, image, or object, then drag the point-to-file icon in Property inspector to a file in the Site panel
Open the linked-to document in Dreamweaver	Control–double-click link

PREVIEWING AND DEBUGGING IN BROWSERS

Action	Shortcut
Preview in primary browser	F12
Preview in secondary browser	Shift+F12
Debug in primary browser	Alt+F12
Debug in secondary browser	Control+Alt+F12

SITE MANAGEMENT AND FTP

Action	Shortcut
Connect/Disconnect	Control+Alt+Shift+F5
Refresh	F5
Create new file	Control+Shift+N
Create new folder	Control+Alt+Shift+N
Open selection	Control+Shift+Alt+O
Delete file	Control+X
Copy file	Control+C
Paste file	Control+V
Duplicate file	Control+D
Rename file	F2
Get selected files or folders from remote site	Control+Shift+D
Put selected files or folders to remote site	Control+Shift+U
Check out	Control+Alt+Shift+D
Check in	Control+Alt+Shift+U
View site map	Alt+F8
Refresh Local pane	Shift+F5
Refresh Remote pane	Alt+F5

SITE MAP

Action	Shortcut
View site files	F8
Refresh Local pane	Shift+F5
View as root	Control+Shift+R
Link to new file	Control+Shift+N
Link to existing file	Control+Shift+K
Change link	Control+L
Remove link	Control+Shift+L
Show/Hide link	Control+Shift+Y
Show page titles	Control+Shift+T
Zoom in site map	Control+ + (plus)
Zoom out site map	Control+ - (hyphen)

OPENING AND CLOSING PANELS

Action	Shortcut
Insert bar	Control+F2
Properties	Control+F3
Answers	Alt+F1
CSS Styles	Shift+F11
HTML Styles	Control+F11
Behaviors	Shift+F3
Tag Inspector	F9
Snippets	Shift+F9
Reference	Shift+F1
Databases	Control+Shift+F10
Bindings	Control+F10
Server Behaviors	Control+F9
Components	Control+F7
Site	F8
Assets	F11
Results > Search	Control+Shift+F
Results > Validation	Control+Shift+F7
Results > Target Browser Check	Control+Shift+F8
Results > Link Checker	Control+Shift+F9
Results > Site Reports	Control+Shift+F11
Results > FTP Log	Control+Shift+F12
Results > Server Debug	Control+Shift+F5
Others > Code inspector	F10
Others > Frames	Shift+F2
Others > History	Shift+F10
Others > Layers	F2
Others > Sitespring	F7
Others > Timelines	Alt+F9
Show/Hide panels	F4

Index